CW01064607

CORE STATUTES ON EMPLOYMENT LAW

Dominique Lauterburg

This selection © Dominique Lauterburg 2008

All rights reserved. No reproduction, copy or transmission of this publication may be made without written permission.

Crown Copyright material is reproduced with the permission of the Controller of HMSO and the Queen's Printer for Scotland.

No paragraph of this publication may be reproduced, copied or transmitted save with written permission or in accordance with the provisions of the Copyright, Designs and Patents Act 1988, or under the terms of any licence permitting limited copying issued by the Copyright Licensing Agency, 90 Tottenham Court Road, London W1T 4LP.

Any person who does any unauthorized act in relation to this publication may be liable to criminal prosecution and civil claims for damages.

The author has asserted her right to be identified as the author of this work in accordance with the Copyright, Designs and Patents Act 1988.

Published 2007, 2008 by
PALGRAVE MACMILLAN
Houndmills, Basingstoke, Hampshire RG21 6XS and
175 Fifth Avenue, New York, N.Y. 10010
Companies and representatives throughout the world

PALGRAVE MACMILLAN is the global academic imprint of the Palgrave Macmillan division of St. Martin's Press, LLC and of Palgrave Macmillan Ltd. Macmillan® is a registered trademark in the United States, United Kingdom and other countries. Palgrave is a registered trademark in the European Union and other countries.

ISBN–13: 978–0–230–21843–7 paperback
ISBN–10:   0–230–21843–1 paperback

This book is printed on paper suitable for recycling and made from fully managed and sustained forest sources. Logging, pulping and manufacturing processes are expected to conform to the environmental regulations of the country of origin.

A catalogue record for this book is available from the British Library.

A catalog record for this book is available from the Library of Congress.

10   9   8   7   6   5   4   3   2   1
17 16 15 14 13 12 11 10 09 08

Typeset by L K Murdoch, Tonbridge, Kent
Printed and bound in Great Britain by
Cromwell Press Ltd, Trowbridge, Wiltshire

PREFACE

In compiling this collection I have selected the 'core' primary and secondary employment legislation. This book is intended to be used by students of employment law, labour law and industrial relations law at both undergraduate and postgraduate level. As an unannotated collection of legislation it will be appropriate for students who are permitted to take statutes into their exams. In addition, this book is also intended to be an accessible reference source for anyone who needs quick and easy access to up-to-date employment legislation.

Employment law is a very fast moving and exciting area of law, and the employment relationship and contract of employment are increasingly subject to new legislative provisions, many of them emanating from the European Union. Over the last few years there have been many new and amended pieces of employment legislation, and I hope that this selection is a timely and comprehensive collection of the key primary and secondary employment legislation. In this edition, the law is generally stated as at June 2008.

One of the most important legislative developments has been the introduction of the Employment Bill. If enacted the Employment Act will repeal the statutory dispute resolution procedures and implement new measures intended to encourage informal dispute resolution. Section 98A of the Employment Rights Act 1996 will also be repealed. The Bill also contains provisions to strengthen the National Minimum Wage enforcement procedures and provisions that amend trade union membership laws to allow trade unions to expel members on the basis of their membership of a particular political party.

It is anticipated that the Bill will receive Royal Assent later this year and come into force in April 2009. It will therefore be included in the next edition of this publication, together with the new ACAS Code of Practice on disciplinary and grievance procedures.

Dominique Lauterburg
Manchester
June 2008

CONTENTS

ALPHABETICAL LIST OF CONTENTS

STATUTES

EQUAL PAY ACT 1970
(1970, c. 41)

1   **Requirement of equal treatment for men and women in same employment**

(1)   If the terms of a contract under which a woman is employed at an establishment in Great Britain do not include (directly or by reference to a collective agreement or otherwise) an equality clause they shall be deemed to include one.

(2)   An equality clause is a provision which relates to terms (whether concerned with pay or not) of a contract under which a woman is employed (the 'woman's contract'), and has the effect that—

(a)   where the woman is employed on like work with a man in the same employment—

(i)   if (apart from the equality clause) any term of the woman's contract is or becomes less favourable to the woman than a term of a similar kind in the contract under which that man is employed, that term of the woman's contract shall be treated as so modified as not to be less favourable, and

(ii)   if (apart from the equality clause) at any time the woman's contract does not include a term corresponding to a term benefiting that man included in the contract under which he is employed, the woman's contract shall be treated as including such a term;

(b)   where the woman is employed on work rated as equivalent with that of a man in the same employment—

(i)   if (apart from the equality clause) any term of the woman's contract determined by the rating of the work is or becomes less favourable to the woman than a term of a similar kind in the contract under which that man is employed, that term of the woman's contract shall be treated as so modified as not to be less favourable, and

(ii)   if (apart from the equality clause) at any time the woman's contract does not include a term corresponding to a term benefiting that man included in the contract under which he is employed and determined by the rating of the work, the woman's contract shall be treated as including such a term.

(c)   where a woman is employed on work which, not being work in relation to which paragraph (a) or (b) above applies, is, in terms of the demands made on her (for instance under such headings as effort, skill and decision), of equal value to that of a man in the same employment—

(i)   if (apart from the equality clause) any term of the woman's contract is or becomes less favourable to the woman than a term of a similar kind in the contract under which that man is employed, that term of the woman's contract shall be treated as so modified as not to be less favourable, and

(ii)   if (apart from the equality clause) at any time the woman's contract does not include a term corresponding to a term benefiting that man included in the contract under which he is employed, the woman's contract shall be treated as including such a term.

(d)   where—

(i)   any term of the woman's contract regulating maternity-related pay provides for any of her maternity-related pay to be calculated by reference to her pay at a particular time,

(ii)   after that time (but before the end of the statutory maternity leave period) her pay is increased, or would have increased had she not been on statutory maternity leave, and

(iii)   the maternity-related pay is neither what her pay would have been had she not been on statutory maternity leave nor the difference between what her pay would have been had she not been on statutory maternity leave and any statutory maternity pay to which she is entitled, if (apart from the equality clause) the terms of the woman's contract do not provide for the increase to be taken into account for the purpose of calculating the maternity-related pay, the term mentioned in sub-paragraph (i) above shall be treated as so modified as to provide for the increase to be taken into account for that purpose;

(e)   if (apart from the equality clause) the terms of the woman's contract as to—

    (i)   pay (including pay by way of bonus) in respect of times before she begins to be on statutory maternity leave,

    (ii) pay by way of bonus in respect of times when she is absent from work in consequence of the prohibition in section 72(1) of the Employment Rights Act 1996 (compulsory maternity leave), or

    (iii) pay by way of bonus in respect of times after she returns to work following her having been on statutory maternity leave,

do not provide for such pay to be paid when it would be paid but for her having time off on statutory maternity leave, the woman's contract shall be treated as including a term providing for such pay to be paid when ordinarily it would be paid;

(f)   if (apart from the equality clause) the terms of the woman's contract regulating her pay after returning to work following her having been on statutory maternity leave provide for any of that pay to be calculated without taking into account any amount by which her pay would have increased had she not been on statutory maternity leave, the woman's contract shall be treated as including a term providing for the increase to be taken into account in calculating that pay.

(3)   An equality clause falling within subsection (2)(a), (b) or (c) above shall not operate in relation to a variation between the woman's contract and the man's contract if the employer proves that the variation is genuinely due to a material factor which is not the difference of sex and that factor—

(a)   in the case of an equality clause falling within subsection (2)(a) or (b) above, must be a material difference between the woman's case and the man's; and

(b)   in the case of an equality clause falling within subsection (2)(c) above, may be such a material difference.

(4)   A woman is to be regarded as employed on like work with men if, but only if, her work and theirs is of the same or a broadly similar nature, and the differences (if any) between the things she does and the things they do are not of practical importance in relation to terms and conditions of employment; and accordingly in comparing her work with theirs regard shall be had to the frequency or otherwise with which any such differences occur in practice as well as to the nature and extent of the differences.

(5)   A woman is to be regarded as employed on work rated as equivalent with that of any men if, but only if, her job and their job have been given an equal value, in terms of the demand made on a worker under various headings (for instance effort, skill, decision), on a study undertaken with a view to evaluating in those terms the jobs to be done by all or any of the employees in an undertaking or group of undertakings, or would have been given an equal value but for the evaluation being made on a system setting different values for men and women on the same demand under any heading.

(5A) For the purposes of subsection (2)(d) to (f) above—

(a)   'maternity-related pay', in relation to a woman, means pay (including pay by way of bonus) to which she is entitled as a result of being pregnant or in respect of times when she is on statutory maternity leave, except that it does not include any statutory maternity pay to which she is entitled;

(b)   'statutory maternity leave period', in relation to a woman, means the period during which she is on statutory maternity leave;

(c)   an increase in an amount is taken into account in a calculation if in the calculation the amount as increased is substituted for the unincreased amount.

(5B) For the purposes of subsections (2)(d) to (f) and (5A) above, 'on statutory maternity leave' means absent from work—

(a)   in exercise of the right conferred by section 71(1) or 73(1) of the Employment Rights Act 1996 (ordinary or additional maternity leave), or

(b)   in consequence of the prohibition in section 72(1) of that Act (compulsory maternity leave).

(6)   Subject to the following subsections, for purposes of this section—

(a)   'employed' means employed under a contract of service or of apprenticeship or a contract personally to execute any work or labour, and related expressions shall be construed accordingly;

(b)   …

(c)   Two employers are to be treated as associated if one is a company of which the other (directly or indirectly) has control or if both are companies of which a third person (directly or indirectly) has control,

and men shall be treated as in the same employment with a woman if they are men employed by her employer or any associated employer at the same establishment or at establishments in Great Britain which include that one and at which common terms and conditions of employment are observed either generally or for employees of the relevant classes.

(6A) This section applies to—

(a)   the holding of an office or post to which persons are appointed to discharge functions personally under the direction of another person, and in respect of which they are entitled to remuneration, or

(b)   any office or post to which appointments are made by (or on the recommendation of or subject to the approval of) a Minister of the Crown, a government department, the National Assembly of Wales or any part of the Scottish Administration,

as it applies to employment by a private person, and shall so apply as if references to a contract of employment included references to the terms of appointment, and as if references to the employer included references to the person responsible for paying any remuneration that a holder of the office or post is entitled to in respect of the office or post.

(6B) For the purposes of subsection (6A) the holder of an office or post—

(a)   is to regarded as discharging her functions under the direction of another person if that other person is entitled to direct her as to when and where she discharges those functions;

(b)   is not to be regarded as entitled to remuneration merely because she is entitled to payments—

(i)   in respect of expenses incurred by her in carrying out the functions of the office or post, or

(ii)   by way of compensation for the loss of income or benefits she would or might have received from any person had she not been carrying out the functions of the office or post.

(6C) For the purposes of subsection (6A)—

(a)   'office or post' does not include a political office (see section 1A), and

(b)   appointment to an office or post does not include election to an office or post.

(7)   …

(8)   This section shall apply to—

(a)   service for purposes of a Minister of the Crown or government department, other than service of a person holding a statutory office, or

(b)   service on behalf of the Crown for purposes of a person holding a statutory office or purposes of a statutory body,

as it applies to employment by a private person, and shall so apply as if references to a contract of employment included references to the terms of service.

(9)   …

(10) In this section 'statutory body' means a body set up by or in pursuance of an enactment (including an enactment comprised in, or an instrument made under, an Act of the Scottish Parliament), and 'statutory office' means an office so set up; and service 'for purposes of' a Minister of the Crown or government department does not include service in any office in

Schedule 2 (Ministerial offices) to the House of Commons Disqualification Act 1975 as for the time being in force.

...

(11) For the purposes of this Act it is immaterial whether the law which (apart from this subsection) in the law applicable to a contract is the law of any part of the United Kingdom or not.

...

(13) Provisions of this section and sections 2 to 2A below framed with reference to women and their treatment relative to men are to be read as applying equally in a converse case to men and their treatment relative to women.

1A   Meaning of 'political office' in section 1(6C)(a)

The following are political offices for the purposes of section 1(6C)(a)—

(a)   any office of the House of Commons held by a member of it,

(b)   a life peerage within the meaning of the Life Peerages Act 1958, or any office of the House of Lords held by a member of it,

(c)   any office mentioned in Schedule 2 (Ministerial offices) to the House of Commons Disqualification Act 1975,

(d)   the offices of Leader of the Opposition, Chief Opposition Whip or Assistant Opposition Whip within the meaning of the Ministerial and other Salaries Act 1975,

(e)   any office of the Scottish Parliament held by a member of it,

(f)   a member of the Scottish Executive within the meaning of section 44 of the Scotland Act 1998, or a junior Scottish Minister within the meaning of section 49 of that Act,

(g)   any office of the National Assembly for Wales held by a member of it,

(h)   in England, any office of a county council, a London borough council, a district council or a parish council held by a member of it,

(i)   in Wales, any office of a county council, a county borough council or a community council held by a member it,

(j)   in relation to a council constituted under section 2 of the Local Government etc. (Scotland) Act 1994 or a community council established under section 51 of the Local Government (Scotland) Act 1973, any office of such a council held by a member of it,

(k)   any office of the Greater London Authority held by a member of it,

(l)   any office of the Common Council of the City of London held by a member of it,

(m)   any office of the Council of the Isles of Scilly held by a member of it, and

(n)   any office of a political party.

...

2   Disputes as to, and enforcement of, requirement of equal treatment

(1)   Any claim in respect of the contravention of a term modified or included by virtue of an equality clause, including a claim for arrears of remuneration or damages in respect of the contravention, may be presented by way of a complaint to an employment tribunal.

(1A) Where a dispute arises in relation to the effect of an equality clause the employer may apply to an employment tribunal for an order declaring the rights of the employer and the employee in relation to the matter in question.

(2)   Where it appears to the Minister that there may be a question whether the employer of any women is or has been contravening a term modified or included by virtue of their equality clauses, but that it is not reasonable to expect them to take steps to have the question determined, the question may be referred by him as respects all or any of them to an employment tribunal and shall be dealt with as if the reference were of a claim by the women or woman against the employer.

(3)   Where it appears to the court in which any proceedings are pending that a claim or counterclaim in respect of the operation of an equality clause could more conveniently be disposed of separately by an employment tribunal, the court may direct that the claim or counterclaim shall be struck out; and (without prejudice to the foregoing) where in proceedings before any court a question arises as to the operation of an equality clause, the court may on the application of any party to the proceedings or otherwise refer that question,

or direct it to be referred by a party to the proceedings, to an employment tribunal for determination by the tribunal, and may stay or sist the proceedings in the meantime.

(4) No determination may be made by an employment tribunal in the following proceedings—

  (a) on a complaint under subsection (1) above,

  (b) on an application under subsection (1A) above, or

  (c) on a reference under subsection (2) above,

  unless the proceedings are instituted on or before the qualifying date (determined in accordance with section 2ZA below).

(5) A woman shall not be entitled, in proceedings brought in respect of a contravention of a term modified or included by virtue of an equality clause (including proceedings before an employment tribunal), to be awarded any payment by way of arrears of remuneration or damages—

  (a) in proceedings in England and Wales, in respect of a time earlier than the arrears date (determined in accordance with section 2ZB below), and

  (b) in proceedings in Scotland, in respect of a time before the period determined in accordance with section 2ZC below.

(5A) In this section 'employer', in relation to the holder of an office or post to which section 1 above applies by virtue of subsection (6A) of that section, shall be construed in accordance with that subsection.

(6), (7) ...

2A Procedure before tribunal in certain cases

(1) Where on a complaint or reference made to an employment tribunal under section 2 above, a dispute arises as to whether any work is of equal value as mentioned in section 1(2)(c) above the tribunal may either—

  (a) proceed to determine that question; or

  (b) require a member of the panel of independent experts to prepare a report with respect to that question;

  ...

(1A) Subsections (1B) and (1C) below apply in a case where the tribunal has required a member of the panel of independent experts to prepare a report under paragraph (b) of subsection (1) above.

(1B) The tribunal may—

  (a) withdraw the requirement, and

  (b) request the member of the panel of independent experts to provide it with any documentation specified by it or make any other request to him connected with the withdrawal of the requirement.

(1C) If the requirement has not been withdrawn under paragraph (a) of subsection (1B) above, the tribunal shall not make any determination under paragraph (a) of subsection (1) above unless it has received the report.

(2) Subsection (2A) below applies in a case where—

  (a) a tribunal is required to determine whether any work is of equal value as mentioned in section 1(2)(c) above, and

  (b) the work of the woman and that of the man in question have been given different values on a study such as is mentioned in section 1(5) above.

(2A) The tribunal shall determine that the work of the woman and that of the man are not of equal value unless the tribunal has reasonable grounds for suspecting that the evaluation contained in the study—

  (a) was (within the meaning of subsection (3) below) made on a system which discriminates on grounds of sex, or

  (b) is otherwise unsuitable to be relied upon.

(3) An evaluation contained in a study such as is mentioned in section 1(5) above is made on a system which discriminates on grounds of sex where a difference, or coincidence, between values set by that system on different demands under the same or different headings is not justifiable irrespective of the sex of the person on whom those demands are made.

(4)   In this section a reference to a member of the panel of independent experts is a reference to a person who is for the time being designated by the Advisory, Conciliation and Arbitration Service for the purposes of that paragraph as such a member, being neither a member of the Council of that Service nor one of its officers or servants.

6   Exclusion from ss 1 to 5 of pensions etc.

(1)   An equality clause shall not operate in relation to terms—

   (a)   affected by compliance with the laws regulating the employment of women, or

   (b)   affording special treatment to women in connection with pregnancy or childbirth.

(1AA) Subsection (1)(b) does not affect the operation of an equality clause falling within section 1(2)(d), (e) or (f).

(1A) ...

(1B) An equality clause shall not operate in relation to terms relating to a person's membership of, or rights under, an occupational pension scheme, being terms in relation to which, by reason only of any provision made by or under sections 62 to 64 of the Pensions Act 1995 (equal treatment), an equal treatment rule would not operate if the terms were included in the scheme.

(1C) In subsection (1B), 'occupational pension scheme' has the same meaning as in the Pension Schemes Act 1993 and 'equal treatment rule' has the meaning given by section 62 of the Pensions Act 1995.

(2)   ...

7B   Questioning of employer

(1)   For the purposes of this section—

   (a)   a person who considers that she may have a claim under section 1 above is referred to as 'the complainant', and

   (b)   a person against whom the complainant may decide to make, or has made, a complaint under section 2(1) or 7A(3) above is referred to as 'the respondent'.

(2)   With a view to helping a complainant to decide whether to institute proceedings and, if she does so, to formulate and present her case in the most effective manner, the Minister shall by order prescribe—

   (a)   forms by which the complainant may question the respondent on any matter which is or may be relevant, and

   (b)   forms by which the respondent may if he so wishes reply to any questions.

(3)   Where the complainant questions the respondent (whether in accordance with an order under subsection (2) above or not), the question and any reply by the respondent (whether in accordance with such an order or not) shall, subject to the following provisions of this section, be admissible as evidence in any proceedings under section 2(1) or 7A(3) above.

(4)   If in any proceedings under section 2(1) or 7A(3) above it appears to the employment tribunal that the complainant has questioned the respondent (whether in accordance with an order under subsection (2) above or not) and that—

   (a)   the respondent deliberately and without reasonable excuse omitted to reply within such period as the Minister may by order prescribe, or

   (b)   the respondent's reply is evasive or equivocal,

   it may draw any inference which it considers it just and equitable to draw, including an inference that the respondent has contravened a term modified or included by virtue of the complainant's equality clause or corresponding term of service.

(5)   Where the Minister questions an employer in relation to whom he may decide to make, or has made, a reference under section 2(2) above, the question and any reply by the employer shall, subject to the following provisions of this section, be admissible as evidence in any proceedings under that provision.

(6)   If in any proceedings on a reference under section 2(2) above it appears to the employment tribunal that the Minister has questioned the employer to whom the reference relates and that—

   (a)   the employer deliberately and without reasonable excuse omitted to reply within such period as the Minister may by order prescribe, or

(b)   the employer's reply is evasive or equivocal,

it may draw any inference which it considers it just and equitable to draw, including an inference that the employer has contravened a term modified or included by virtue of the equality clause of the woman, or women, as respects whom the reference is made.

(7) The Minister may by order—

    (a)   prescribe the period within which questions must be duly served in order to be admissible under subsection (3) or (5) above, and

    (b)   prescribe the manner in which a question, and any reply, may be duly served.

(8) This section is without prejudice to any other enactment or rule of law regulating interlocutory and preliminary matters in proceedings before an employment tribunal, and has effect subject to any enactment or rule of law regulating the admissibility of evidence in such proceedings.

(9) Power to make orders under this section is exercisable by statutory instrument subject to annulment in pursuance of a resolution of either House of Parliament.

(10) An order under this section may make different provision for different cases.

SEX DISCRIMINATION ACT 1975
(1975, c. 65)

PART I
DISCRIMINATION TO WHICH ACT APPLIES

1   Direct and indirect discrimination against women

(1) In any circumstances relevant for the purposes of any provision of this Act, other than a provision to which subsection (2) applies, a person discriminates against a woman if—

    (a)   on the ground of her sex he treats her less favourably than he treats or would treat a man, or

    (b)   he applies to her a requirement or condition which he applies or would apply equally to a man but—

         (i)   which is such that the proportion of women who can comply with it is considerably smaller than the proportion of men who can comply with it, and

         (ii)   which he cannot show to be justifiable irrespective of the sex of the person to whom it is applied, and

         (iii)   which is to her detriment because she cannot comply with it.

(2) In any circumstances relevant for the purposes of a provision to which this subsection applies, a person discriminates against a woman if—

    (a)   on the ground of her sex, he treats her less favourably than he treats or would treat a man, or

    (b)   he applies to her a provision, criterion or practice which he applies or would apply equally to a man, but—

         (i)   which puts or would put women at a particular disadvantage when compared with men,

         (ii)   which puts her at that disadvantage, and

         (iii)   which he cannot show to be a proportionate means of achieving a legitimate aim.

(3) Subsection (2) applies to—

    (a)   any provision of Part 2,

    (b)   sections 35A and 35B, and

    (c)   any other provision of Part 3, so far as it applies to vocational training.

(4) ...

2   Sex discrimination against men

(1) Section 1, and the provisions of Parts II and III relating to sex discrimination against women, are to be read as applying equally to the treatment of men, and for that purpose shall have effect with such modifications as are requisite.

(2)   In the application of subsection (1) no account shall be taken of special treatment afforded to women in connection with pregnancy or childbirth.

2A   **Discrimination on the grounds of gender reassignment**

(1)   A person ('A') discriminates against another person ('B') in any circumstances relevant for the purposes of—

     (a)   any provision of Part II,

     (b)   section 35A or 35B, or

     (c)   any other provision of Part III, so far as it applies to vocational training,

if he treats B less favourably than he treats or would treat other persons, and does so on the grounds that B intends to undergo, is undergoing or has undergone gender reassignment.

(2)   Subsection (3) applies to arrangements made by any person in relation to another's absence from work or from vocational training.

(3)   For the purposes of subsection (1), B is treated less favourably than others under such arrangements if, in the application of the arrangements to any absence due to B undergoing gender reassignment—

     (a)   he is treated less favourably than he would be if the absence was due to sickness or injury, or

     (b)   he is treated less favourably than he would be if the absence was due to some other cause and, having regard to the circumstances of the case, it is reasonable for him to be treated no less favourably.

(4)   In subsections (2) and (3) 'arrangements' includes terms, conditions or arrangements on which employment, a pupillage or tenancy or vocational training is offered.

(5)   For the purposes of subsection (1), a provision mentioned in that subsection framed with reference to discrimination against women shall be treated as applying equally to the treatment of men with such modifications as are requisite.

3   **Discrimination against married persons and civil partners in employment field**

(1)   In any circumstances relevant for the purposes of any provision of Part 2, a person discriminates against a person ('A') who fulfils the condition in subsection (2) if—

     (a)   on the ground of the fulfilment of the condition, he treats A less favourably than he treats or would treat a person who does not fulfil the condition, or

     (b)   he applies to A a provision, criterion or practice which he applies or would apply equally to a person who does not fulfil the condition, but—

         (i)   which puts or would put persons fulfilling the condition at a particular disadvantage when compared with persons not fulfilling the condition, and

         (ii)   which puts A at that disadvantage, and

         (iii)   which he cannot show to be a proportionate means of achieving a legitimate aim.

(2)   The condition is that the person is—

     (a)   married, or

     (b)   a civil partner.

(3)   For the purposes of subsection (1), a provision of Part 2 framed with reference to discrimination against women is to be treated as applying equally to the treatment of men, and for that purpose has effect with such modification as are requisite.

3A   **Discrimination on the ground of pregnancy or maternity leave**

(1)   In any circumstances relevant for the purposes of a provision to which this subsection applies, a person discriminates against a woman if—

     (a)   at a time in a protected period, and on the ground of the woman's pregnancy, the person treats her less favourably; or

     (b)   on the ground that the woman is exercising or seeking to exercise, or has exercised or sought to exercise, a statutory right to maternity leave, the person treats her less favourably.

(2)   In any circumstances relevant for the purposes of a provision to which this subsection applies, a person discriminates against a woman if, on the ground that section 72(1) of the

Employment Rights Act 1996 (compulsory maternity leave) has to be complied with in respect of the woman, he treats her less favourably.

(3) For the purposes of subsection (1)—

    (a) in relation to a woman, a protected period begins each time she becomes pregnant, and the protected period associated with any particular pregnancy of hers ends in accordance with the following rules—

        (i) if she is entitled to ordinary but not additional maternity leave in connection with the pregnancy, the protected period ends at the end of her period of ordinary maternity leave connected with the pregnancy or, if earlier, when she returns to work after the end of her pregnancy;

        (ii) if she is entitled to ordinary and additional maternity leave in connection with the pregnancy, the protected period ends at the end of her period of additional maternity leave connected with the pregnancy or, if earlier, when she returns to work after the end of her pregnancy;

        (iii) if she is not entitled to ordinary maternity leave in respect of the pregnancy, the protected period ends at the end of the 2 weeks beginning with the end of the pregnancy;

    (b) where a person's treatment of a woman is on grounds of illness suffered by the woman as a consequence of a pregnancy of hers, that treatment is to be taken to be on the ground of the pregnancy;

    (c) a 'statutory right to maternity leave' means a right conferred by section 71(1) or 73(1) of the Employment Rights Act 1996 (ordinary and additional maternity leave).

(4) In subsection (3) 'ordinary maternity leave' and 'additional maternity leave' shall be construed in accordance with sections 71 and 73 of the Employment Rights Act 1996.

(5) Subsections (1) and (2) apply to—

    (a) any provision of Part 2,

    (b) sections 35A and 35B, and

    (c) any other provision of Part 3, so far as it applies to vocational training.

4   Discrimination by way of victimisation

(1) A person ('the discriminator') discriminates against another person ('the person victimised') in any circumstances relevant for the purposes of any provision of this Act if he treats the person victimised less favourably than in those circumstances he treats or would treat other persons, and does so by reason that the person victimised has—

    (a) brought proceedings against the discriminator or any other person under this Act or the Equal Pay Act 1970 or sections 62 to 65 of the Pensions Act 1995, or

    (b) given evidence or information in connection with proceedings brought by any person against the discriminator or any other person under this Act or the Equal Pay Act 1970 or sections 62 to 65 of the Pensions Act 1995, or

    (c) otherwise done anything under or by reference to this Act or the Equal Pay Act 1970 or sections 62 to 65 of the Pensions Act 1995 in relation to the discriminator or any other person, or

    (d) alleged that the discriminator or any other person has committed an act which (whether or not the allegation so states) would amount to a contravention of this Act or give rise to a claim under the Equal Pay Act 1970 or under sections 62 to 65 of the Pensions Act 1995,

or by reason that the discriminator knows the person victimised intends to do any of those things, or suspects the person victimised has done, or intends to do, any of them.

(2) Subsection (1) does not apply to treatment of a person by reason of any allegation made by him if the allegation was false and not made in good faith.

(3) For the purposes of subsection (1), a provision of Part II or III framed with reference to discrimination against women shall be treated as applying equally to the treatment of men and for that purpose shall have effect with such modifications as are requisite.

4A   Harassment, including sexual harassment

(1) For the purposes of this Act, a person subjects a woman to harassment if—

    (a) he engages in unwanted contact that is related to her sex or that of another person and has the purpose or effect—

       (i) of violating her dignity, or

       (ii) of creating an intimidating, hostile, degrading, humiliating or offensive environment for her,

    (b) he engages in any form of unwanted verbal, non-verbal or physical conduct of a sexual nature that has the purpose or effect—

       (i) of violating her dignity, or

       (ii) of creating an intimidating, hostile, degrading, humiliating or offensive environment for her, or

    (c) on the ground of her rejection of or submission to unwanted conduct of a kind mentioned in paragraph (a) or (b), he treats her less favourably than he would treat her had she not rejected, or submitted to, the conduct.

(2) Conduct shall be regarded as having the effect mentioned in sub-paragraph (i) or (ii) of subsection (1)(a) or (b) only if, having regard to all the circumstances, including in particular the perception of the woman, it should reasonably be considered as having that effect.

(3) For the purposes of this Act, a person ('A') subjects another person ('B') to harassment if—

    (a) A, on the ground that B intents to undergo, is undergoing or has undergone gender reassignment, engages in unwanted conduct that has the purpose or effect—

       (i) of violating B's dignity, or

       (ii) of creating an intimidating, hostile, degrading, humiliating or offensive environment for B, or

    (b) A, on the ground of B's rejection of or submission to unwanted conduct of a kind mentioned in paragraph (a), treats B less favourably than A would treat B had B not rejected, or submitted to, the conduct.

(4) Conduct shall be regarded as having the effect mentioned in sub-paragraph (i) or (ii) of subsection (3)(a) only if, having regard to all the circumstances, including in particular the perception of B, it should reasonably be considered as having that effect.

(5) Subsection (1) is to be read as applying equally to the harassment of men, and for that purpose shall have effect with such modifications as are requisite.

(6) For the purposes of subsections (1) and (3), a provision of Part 2 or 3 framed with reference to harassment of women shall be treated as applying equally to the harassment of men and for that purpose will have effect with such modifications as are requisite.

5   Interpretation

(1) In this Act—

    (a) references to discrimination refer to any discrimination falling within sections 1 to 4; and

    (b) references to sex discrimination refer to any discrimination falling within section 1, 2 or 3A,

and related expressions shall be construed accordingly.

(2) In this Act—

'woman' includes a female of any age, and

'man' includes a male of any age.

(3) Each of the following comparisons, that is—

    (a) a comparison of the cases of persons of different sex under section 1(1) or (2),

    (b) a comparison of the cases of persons required for the purposes of section 2A, and

    (c) a comparison of the cases of persons who do and who do not fulfil the condition in section 3(2),

must be such that the relevant circumstances in the one case are the same, or not materially different, in the other.

PART II
EMPLOYMENT FIELD

Discrimination by employers

6   **Applicants and employees**

(1)   It is unlawful for a person, in relation to employment by him at an establishment in Great
      Britain, to discriminate against a woman—
      (a)   in the arrangements he makes for the purpose of determining who should be offered that
             employment, or
      (b)   in the terms on which he offers her that employment, or
      (c)   by refusing or deliberately omitting to offer her that employment.

(2)   It is unlawful for a person, in the case of a woman employed by him at an establishment in
      Great Britain, to discriminate against her—
      (a)   in the way he affords her access to opportunities for promotion, transfer or training, or
             to any other benefits, facilities or services, or by refusing or deliberately omitting to
             afford her access to them, or
      (b)   by dismissing her, or subjecting her to any other detriment.

(2A) It is unlawful for an employer, in relation to employment by him at an establishment in Great
      Britain, to subject to harassment—
      (a)   a woman whom he employs, or
      (b)   a woman who has applied to him for employment.

(2B) For the purposes of subsection (2A), the circumstances in which an employer is to be treated
      as subjecting a woman to harassment shall include those where—
      (a)   a third party subjects the woman to harassment in the course of her employment, and
      (b)   the employer has failed to take such steps as would have been reasonably practicable to
             prevent the third party from doing so.

(2C) Subsection (2B) does not apply unless the employer knows that the woman has been subject
      to harassment in the course of her employment on at least two other occasions by a third party.

(2D) In subsections (2B) and (2C), 'third party' means a person other than—
      (a)   the employer, or
      (b)   a person whom the employer employs,
      and for the purposes of those subsections it is immaterial whether the third party is the same
      or a different person on each occasion.

(3)   ...

(4)   Subsections (1)(b) and (2) do not render it unlawful for a person to discriminate against a
      woman in relation to her membership of, or rights under, an occupational pension scheme
      in such a way that, were any term of the scheme to provide for discrimination in that way,
      then, by reason only of any provision made by or under sections 62 to 64 of the Pensions
      Act 1995 (equal treatment), an equal treatment rule would not operate in relation to that
      term.

(4A) In subsection (4), 'occupational pension scheme' has the same meaning as in the Pension
      Schemes Act 1993 and 'equal treatment rule' has the meaning given by section 62 of the
      Pensions Act 1995.

(5)   Subject to section 8(3), subsection (1)(b) does not apply to any provision for the payment of
      money which, if the woman in question were given the employment, would be included
      (directly or otherwise) in the contract under which she was employed.

(6)   Subsection (2) does not apply to benefits consisting of the payment of money when the
      provision of those benefits is regulated by the woman's contract of employment.

(7)   Subsection (2) does not apply to benefits, facilities or services of any description if the
      employer is concerned with the provision (for payment or not) of benefits, facilities or services
      of that description to the public, or to a section of the public comprising the woman in
      question, unless—
      (a)   that provision differs in a material respect from the provision of the benefits, facilities
             or services by the employer to his employees, or

(b)   the provision of the benefits, facilities or services to the woman in question is regulated by her contract of employment, or

(c)   the benefits, facilities or services relate to training.

(8)   In its application to any discrimination falling within section 2A, this section shall have effect with the omission of subsections (4) to (6).

6A   **Exception relating to terms and conditions during maternity leave**

(1)   Subject to subsections (2) and (5), section 6(1)(b) and (2) does not make it unlawful to deprive a woman who is on ordinary maternity leave of any benefit from the terms and conditions of her employment relating to remuneration.

(2)   Subsection (1) does not apply to benefit by way of maternity-related remuneration.

(3)   Subject to subsections (4) and (5), section 6(1)(b) and (2) does not make it unlawful to deprive a woman who is on additional maternity leave of any benefit from the terms and conditions of her employment.

(4)   Subsection (3) does not apply to—

     (a)   benefit by way of maternity-related remuneration,

     (b)   the benefit of her employer's implied obligation to her of trust and confidence, or

     (c)   any benefit of terms and conditions in respect of—

         (i)   notice of the termination by her employer of her contract of employment,

         (ii)   compensation in the event of redundancy,

         (iii)   disciplinary or grievance procedures, or

         (iv)   membership of a pension scheme.

(5)   Neither of subsections (1) and (3) applies to—

     (a)   benefit by way of remuneration in respect of times when the woman is neither on ordinary maternity leave nor on additional maternity leave, including increase-related remuneration in respect of such times; or

     (b)   benefit by way of maternity-related remuneration that is increase-related.

(6)   For the purposes of subsection (5), remuneration is increase-related so far as it falls to be calculated by reference to increases in remuneration that the woman would have received had she not been on ordinary or additional maternity leave.

(7)   In this section—

'maternity-related remuneration', in relation to a woman, means remuneration to which she is entitled as a result of being pregnant or being on ordinary or additional maternity leave;

'on additional maternity leave' means absent from work in exercise of the right conferred by section 73(1) of the Employment Rights Act 1996;

'on ordinary maternity leave' means absent from work in exercise of the right conferred by section 71(1) of that Act (ordinary maternity leave) or in consequence of the prohibition in section 72(1) of that Act (compulsory maternity leave);

'remuneration' means benefits—

     (a)   that consist of the payment of money to an employee by way of wages or salary, and

     (b)   that are not benefits whose provision is regulated by the employee's contract of employment.

[*(1)   Subject to subsection (2), section 6(1)(b) and (2) does not make it unlawful to deprive a woman who is on maternity leave of any benefit from the terms and conditions of her employment relating to remuneration.*

(2)   The reference in subsection (1) to benefit from the terms and conditions of a woman's employment relating remuneration does not include a reference to—

     (a)   maternity-related remuneration (including maternity-related remuneration that is increase-related),

     (b)   remuneration (including increase-related remuneration) in respect of times when the woman is not on maternity leave, or

     (c)   remuneration by way of bonus in respect of times when a woman is on compulsory maternity leave.

(3) For the purposes of subsection (2), remuneration is increase-related so far as it falls to be calculated by reference to increases in remuneration that the woman would have received had she not been on maternity leave.

(4) In this section—

'maternity-related remuneration', in relation to a woman, means remuneration to which she is entitled as a result of being pregnant or being on maternity leave;

'on compulsory maternity leave' means absent from work in consequence of the prohibition in section 72(1) of the Employment Rights Act 1996;

'on maternity leave' means—

(a) on compulsory maternity leave.

(b) absent from work in exercise of the right conferred by section 71(1) of the Employment Rights Act 1996 (ordinary maternity leave), or

(c) absent from work in exercise of the right conferred by section 73(1) of that Act (additional matenrity leave); and

'remuneration' means benefits—

(a) that consist of the payment of money to an employee by way of wages or salary, and

(b) that are not benefits whose provision is regulated by the employee's contract of employment.]

Note: This amendment has effect in relation to a case where a woman's expected week of childbirth begins on or after 5 October 2008.

7 Exception where sex is a genuine occupational qualification

(1) In relation to sex discrimination—

(a) section 6(1)(a) or (c) does not apply to any employment where being a man is a genuine occupational qualification for the job, and

(b) section 6(2)(a) does not apply to opportunities for promotion or transfer to, or training for, such employment.

(2) Being a man is a genuine occupational qualification for a job only where—

(a) the essential nature of the job calls for a man for reasons of physiology (excluding physical strength or stamina) or, in dramatic performances or other entertainment, for reasons of authenticity, so that the essential nature or the job would be materially different if carried out by a woman; or

(b) the job needs to be held by a man to preserve decency or privacy because—

(i) it is likely to involve physical contact with men in circumstances where they might reasonably object to its being carried out by a woman, or

(ii) the holder of the job is likely to do his work in circumstances where men might reasonably object to the presence of a woman because they are in a state of undress or are using sanitary facilities; or

(ba) the job is likely to involve the holder of the job doing his work, or living, in a private home and needs to be held by a man because objection might reasonably be taken to allowing to a woman—

(i) the degree of physical or social contact with a person living in the home, or

(ii) the knowledge of intimate details of such a person's life,

which is likely, because of the nature or circumstances of the job or of the home, to be allowed to, or available to, the holder of the job; or

(c) the nature or location of the establishment makes it impracticable for the holder of the job to live elsewhere than in premises provided by the employer, and—

(i) the only such premises which are available for persons holding that kind of job are lived in, or normally lived in, by men and are not equipped with separate sleeping accommodation for women and sanitary facilities which could be used by women in privacy from men, and

(ii) it is not reasonable to expect the employer either to equip those premises with such accommodation and facilities or to provide other premises for women; or

(d) the nature of the establishment, or of the part of it within which the work is done, requires the job to be held by a man because—

        (i)   it is, or is part of, a hospital, prison or other establishment for persons requiring special care, supervision or attention, and

        (ii)   those persons are all men (disregarding any woman whose presence is exceptional), and

        (iii)   it is reasonable, having regard to the essential character of the establishment or that part, that the job should not be held by a woman; or

   (e)   the holder of the job provides individuals with personal services promoting their welfare or education, or similar personal services, and those services can most effectively be provided by a man, or

   (f)   ...

   (g)   the job needs to be held by a man because it is likely to involve the performance of duties outside the United Kingdom in a country whose laws or customs are such that the duties could not, effectively, be performed by a woman, or

   (h)   the job is one of two to be held by a married couple.

(3)   Subsection (2) applies where some only of the duties of the job fall within paragraphs (a) to (g) as well as where all of them do.

(4)   Paragraph (a), (b), (c), (d), (e) or (g) of subsection (2) does not apply in relation to the filling of a vacancy at a time when the employer already has male employees—

   (a)   who are capable of carrying out the duties falling within that paragraph, and

   (b)   whom it would be reasonable to employ on those duties, and

   (c)   whose numbers are sufficient to meet the employer's likely requirements in respect of those duties without undue inconvenience.

7A   Corresponding exception relating to gender reassignment

(1)   In their application to discrimination falling within section 2A, subsections (1) and (2) of section 6 do not make unlawful an employer's treatment of another person if—

   (a)   in relation to the employment in question—

        (i)   being a man is a genuine occupational qualification for the job, or

        (ii)   being a woman is a genuine occupational qualification for the job, and

   (b)   the employer can show that the treatment is reasonable in view of the circumstances described in the relevant paragraph of section 7(2) and any other relevant circumstances.

(2)   In subsection (1) the reference to the employment in question is a reference—

   (a)   in relation to any paragraph of section 6(1), to the employment mentioned in that paragraph;

   (b)   in relation to section 6(2)—

        (i)   in its application to opportunities for promotion or transfer to any employment or for training for any employment, to that employment;

        (ii)   otherwise, to the employment in which the person discriminated against is employed or from which that person is dismissed.

(3)   In determining for the purposes of subsection (1) whether being a man or being a woman is a genuine occupational qualification for a job, section 7(4) applies in relation to dismissal from employment as it applies in relation to the filling of a vacancy.

7B   Supplementary exceptions relating to gender reassignment

(1)   In relation to discrimination falling within section 2A—

   (a)   section 6(1)(a) or (c) does not apply to any employment where there is a supplementary genuine occupational qualification for the job,

   (b)   section 6(2)(a) does not apply to a refusal or deliberate omission to afford access to opportunities for promotion or transfer to or training for such employment, and

   (c)   section 6(2)(b) does not apply to dismissing an employee from, or otherwise not allowing him to continue in, such employment.

(2)   Subject to subsection (3), there is a supplementary genuine occupational qualification for a job only if—

   (a)   the job involves the holder of the job being liable to be called upon to perform intimate physical searches pursuant to statutory powers;

(b)   the job is likely to involve the holder of the job doing his work, or living, in a private home and needs to be held otherwise than by a person who is undergoing or has undergone gender reassignment, because objection might reasonably be taken to allowing to such a person—

    (i)   the degree of physical or social contact with a person living in the home, or

    (ii)   the knowledge of intimate details of such a person's life, which is likely, because of the nature or circumstances of the job or of the home, to be allowed to, or available to, the holder of the job;

(c)   the nature of location of the establishment makes it impracticable for the holder of the job to live elsewhere than in premises provided by the employer, and—

    (i)   the only such premises which are available for persons holding that kind of job are such that reasonable objection could be taken, for the purpose of preserving decency and privacy, to the holder of the job sharing accommodation and facilities with either sex whilst undergoing gender reassignment, and

    (ii)   it is not reasonable to except the employer either to equip those premises with suitable accommodation or to make alternative arrangements; or

(d)   the holder of the job provides vulnerable individuals with personal services promoting their welfare, or similar personal services, and in the reasonable view of the employer those services cannot be effectively provided by a person whilst that person is undergoing gender reassignment.

(2A) Paragraph (a) of subsection (2) does not apply in relation to the filling of a vacancy at a time when the employer already has employees falling within subsection (2B)—

(a)   who are capable of carrying out the duties falling within the paragraph, and

(b)   whom it would be reasonable to employ on those duties, and

(c)   whose numbers are sufficient to meet the employer's likely requirements in respect of those duties without undue inconvenience.

(2B) An employee falls within this subsection if the employee has not undergone and is not undergoing gender reassignment.

(3)   Subsection (2) does not apply in relation to discrimination against a person whose gender has become the acquired gender under the Gender Recognition Act 2004.

8   Equal Pay Act 1970

...

(2)   Section 1(1) of the Equal Pay Act 1970 does not apply in determining for the purposes of section 6(1)(b) of this Act the terms on which employment is offered.

(3)   Where a person offers a woman employment on certain terms, and if she accepted the offer then, by virtue of an equality clause, any of those terms would fall to be modified, or any additional term would fall to be included, the offer shall be taken to contravene section 6(1)(b).

(4)   Where a person offers a woman employment on certain terms, and subsection (3) would apply but for the fact that, on her acceptance of the offer, section 1(3) of the Equal Pay Act 1970 (as set out in subsection (1) above) would prevent the equality clause from operating, the offer shall be taken not to contravene section 6(1)(b).

(5)   An act does not contravene section 6(2) if—

(a)   it contravenes a term modified or included by virtue of an equality clause, or

(b)   it would contravene such a term but for the fact that the equality clause is prevented from operating by section 1(3) of the Equal Pay Act 1970.

...

(7)   In its application to any discrimination falling within section 2A, this section shall have effect with the omission of subsections (3), (4) and (5)(b).

9   Contract workers

(1)   This section applies to any work at an establishment in Great Britain for a person ('the principal') which is available for doing by individuals ('contract workers') who are employed not by the principal himself but by another person, who supplies them under a contract made with the principal.

(2)   It is unlawful for the principal, in relation to work to which this section applies, to discriminate against a woman who is a contract worker—
    (a)   in the terms on which he allows her to do that work, or
    (b)   by not allowing her to do it or continue to do it, or
    (c)   in the way he affords her access to any benefits, facilities or services or by refusing or deliberately omitting to afford her access to them, or
    (d)   by subjecting her to any other detriment.
(2A) It is unlawful for a principal, in relation to contract work at an establishment in Great Britain, to subject a contract worker to harassment.
(3)   Subject to section (3A), the principal does not contravene subsection (2)(b) by doing any act in relation to a woman at a time when if the work were to be done by a person taken into his employment being a man would be a genuine occupational qualification for the job.
(3A) Subsection (3) does not apply in relation to discrimination falling within section 2A.
(3B) In relation to discrimination falling within section 2A, the principal does not contravene subsection (2)(a), (b), (c) or (d) by doing any act in relation to a woman if—
    (a)   he does it at a time when, if the work were to be done by a person taken into his employment—
        (i)   being a man would be a genuine occupational qualification for the job, or
        (ii)   being a woman would be a genuine occupational qualification for the job, and
    (b)   he can show that the act is reasonable in view of the circumstances relevant for the purposes of paragraph (a) and any other relevant circumstances.
(3C) In relation to discrimination falling within section 2A, the principal does not contravene subsection (2)(b) by doing any act in relation to a woman at a time when, if the work were to be done by a person taken into his employment, there would be a supplementary genuine occupational qualification for the job.
(3D) Subsections (3B) and (3C) do not apply in relation to discrimination against a person whose gender has become the acquired gender under the Gender Recognition Act 2004.
(4)   Subsection (2)(c) does not apply to benefits, facilities or services of any description if the principal is concerned with the provision (for payment or not) of benefits, facilities or services of that description to the public, or to a section of the public to which the woman belongs, unless that provision differs in a material respect from the provision of the benefits, facilities or services by the principal to his contract workers.

10   Meaning of employment at establishment in Great Britain

(1)   For the purposes of this Part and section 1 of the Equal Pay Act 1970 ('the relevant purposes'), employment is to be regarded as being at an establishment in Great Britain if—
    (a)   the employee does his work wholly or partly in Great Britain, or
    (b)   the employee does his work wholly outside Great Britain and subsection (1A) applies.
(1A) This subsection applies if—
    (a)   the employer has a place of business at an establishment in Great Britain;
    (b)   the work is for the purposes of the business carried on at the establishment; and
    (c)   the employee is ordinarily resident in Great Britain—
        (i)   at the time when he applies for or is offered the employment, or
        (ii)   at any time during the course of the employment.
    …
(4)   Where work is not done at an establishment it shall be treated for the relevant purposes as done at the establishment from which it is done or (where it is not done from any establishment) at the establishment with which it has the closest connection.
    …

Discrimination by other bodies

12 Trade unions etc.

(1) This section applies to an organisation of workers, an organisation of employers, or any other organisation whose members carry on a particular profession or trade for the purposes of which the organisation exists.

(2) It is unlawful for an organisation to which this section applies, in the case of a woman who is not a member of the organisation, to discriminate against her—

   (a) in the terms on which it is prepared to admit her to membership, or

   (b) by refusing, or deliberately omitting to accept, her application for membership.

(3) It is unlawful for an organisation to which this section applies, in the case of a woman who is a member of the organisation, to discriminate against her—

   (a) in the way it affords her access to any benefits, facilities or services, or by refusing or deliberately omitting to afford her access to them, or

   (b) by depriving her of membership, or varying the terms on which she is a member, or

   (c) by subjecting her to any other detriment.

(3A) It is unlawful for an organisation to which this section applies, in relation to membership of that organisation, to subject to harassment a woman who—

   (a) is a member of the organisation, or

   (b) has applied for membership of the organisation.

(4) ...

20A Relationships which have come to an end

(1) This section applies where—

   (a) there has been a relevant relationship between a woman and another person ('the relevant person'), and

   (b) the relationship has come to an end (whether before or after the commencement of this section).

(2) In this section, a 'relevant relationship' is a relationship during the course of which an act of discrimination by one party to the relationship against the other party to it is unlawful under any preceding provision of this Part.

(3) It is unlawful for the relevant person to discriminate against the woman by subjecting her to a detriment where the discrimination arises out of and is closely connected to the relevant relationship.

(4) It is unlawful for the relevant person to subject a woman to harassment where that treatment arises out of or is closely connected to the relevant relationship.

PART IV
OTHER UNLAWFUL ACTS

37 Discriminatory practices

(1) In this section 'discriminatory practice' means—

   (a) the application of a provision, criterion or practice which results in an act of discrimination which is unlawful by virtue of any provision of Part 2 or 3 taken with section 1(2)(b) or 3(1)(b) or which would be likely to result in such an act of discrimination if the persons to whom it is applied were not all of one sex, or

   (b) the application of a requirement or condition which results in an act of discrimination which is unlawful by virtue of any provision of Part 3 taken with section 1(1)(b) or which would be likely to result in such an act of discrimination if the persons to whom it is applied were not all of one sex.

(2) A person acts in contravention of this section if and so long as—

   (a) he applies a discriminatory practice, or

   (b) he operates practices or other arrangements which in any circumstances would call for the application by him of a discriminatory practice.

(3) Proceedings in respect of a contravention of this section shall be brought only by the Commission in accordance with sections 20 to 24 of the Equality Act 2006.

38   Discriminatory advertisements

(1)   It is unlawful to publish or cause to be published an advertisement which indicates, or might reasonably be understood as indicating, an intention by a person to do any act which is or might be unlawful by virtue of Part II or III.

(2)   Subsection (1) does not apply to an advertisement if the intended act would not in fact be unlawful.

(3)   For the purposes of subsection (1), use of a job description with a sexual connotation (such as 'waiter', 'salesgirl', 'postman' or 'stewardess') shall be taken to indicate an intention to discriminate, unless the advertisement contains an indication to the contrary.

(4)   The publisher of an advertisement made unlawful by subsection (1) shall not be subject to any liability under that subsection in respect of the publication of the advertisement if he proves—

(a)   that the advertisement was published in reliance on a statement made to him by the person who caused it to be published to the effect that, by reason of the operation of subsection (2), the publication would not be unlawful, and

(b)   that it was reasonable for him to rely on the statement.

(5)   A person who knowingly or recklessly makes a statement such as is referred to in subsection (4) which in a material respect is false or misleading commits an offence, and shall be liable on summary conviction to a fine not exceeding level 5 on the standard scale.

(6)   Proceedings in respect of a contravention of subsection (1) may be brought only—

(a)   by the Commission, and

(b)   in accordance with section 25 of the Equality Act 2006.

39   Instructions to discriminate

(1)   It is unlawful for a person—

(a)   who has authority over another person, or

(b)   in accordance with whose wishes that other person is accustomed to act,

to instruct him to do any act which is unlawful by virtue of Part II or III, or procure or attempt to procure the doing by him of any such act.

(2)   Proceedings in respect of a contravention of subsection (1) may be brought only—

(a)   by the Commission, and

(b)   in accordance with section 25 of the Equality Act 2006.

40   Pressure to discriminate

(1)   It is unlawful to induce, or attempt to induce, a person to do any act which contravenes Part II or III by—

(a)   providing or offering to provide him with any benefit, or

(b)   subjecting or threatening to subject him to any detriment.

(2)   An offer or threat is not prevented from falling within subsection (1) because it is not made directly to the person in question, if it is made in such a way that he is likely to hear of it.

(3)   Proceedings in respect of a contravention of subsection (1) may be brought only—

(a)   by the Commission, and

(b)   in accordance with section 25 of the Equality Act 2006.

41   Liability of employers and principals

(1)   Anything done by a person in the course of his employment shall be treated for the purposes of this Act as done by his employer as well as by him, whether or not it was done with the employer's knowledge or approval.

(2)   Anything done by a person as agent for another person with the authority (whether express or implied, and whether precedent or subsequent) of that other person shall be treated for the purposes of this Act as done by that other person as well as by him.

(3)   In proceedings brought under this Act against any person in respect of an act alleged to have been done by an employee of his it shall be a defence for that person to prove that he took such steps as were reasonably practicable to prevent the employee from doing that act, or from doing in the course of his employment acts of that description.

42   Aiding unlawful acts

(1)   A person who knowingly aids another person to do an act made unlawful by this Act shall be treated for the purposes of this Act as himself doing an unlawful act of the like description.

(2)   For the purposes of subsection (1) an employee or agent for whose act the employer or principal is liable under section 41 (or would be so liable but for section 41(3)) shall be deemed to aid the doing of the act by the employer or principal.

(3)   A person does not under this section knowingly aid another to do an unlawful act if—

(a)   he acts in reliance on a statement made to him by that other person that, by reason of any provision of this Act, the act which he aids would not be unlawful, and

(b)   it is reasonable for him to rely on the statement.

(4)   A person who knowingly or recklessly makes a statement such as is referred to in subsection (3)(a) which in a material respect is false or misleading commits an offence, and shall be liable on summary conviction to a fine not exceeding level 5 on the standard scale.

PART V

GENERAL EXCEPTIONS FROM PARTS II TO IV

47   Discriminatory training by certain bodies

(1)   Nothing in Parts II to IV shall render unlawful any act done in relation to particular work by any person in, or in connection with—

(a)   affording women only, or men only, access to facilities for training which would help to fit them for that work, or

(b)   encouraging women only, or men only, to take advantage of opportunities for doing that work,

where it reasonably appears to that person that at any time within the 12 months immediately preceding the doing of the act there were no persons of the sex in question doing that work in Great Britain, or the number of persons of that sex doing the work in Great Britain was comparatively small.

(2)   Where in relation to particular work it reasonably appears to any person that although the condition for the operation of subsection (1) is not met for the whole of Great Britain it is met for an area within Great Britain, nothing in Parts II to IV shall render unlawful any act done by the training body in, or in connection with—

(a)   affording persons who are of the sex in question, and who appear likely to take up that work in that area, access to facilities for training which would help to fit them for that work, or

(b)   encouraging persons of that sex to take advantage of opportunities in the area for doing that work.

(3)   Nothing in Parts II to IV shall render unlawful any act done by a training body in, or in connection with, affording persons access to facilities for training which would help to fit them for employment, where it reasonably appears to that person that those persons are in special need of training by reason of the period for which they have been discharging domestic or family responsibilities to the exclusion of regular full time employment.

The discrimination in relation to which this subsection applies may result from confining the training to persons who have been discharging domestic or family responsibilities, or from the way persons are selected for training, or both.

(4)   The preceding provisions of this section shall not apply in relation to any discrimination which is rendered unlawful by section 6.

48   Other discriminatory training etc.

(1)   Nothing in Parts II to IV shall render unlawful any act done by an employer in relation to particular work in his employment, being an act done in, or in connection with,—

(a)   affording his female employees only, or his male employees only, access to facilities for training which would help to fit them for that work, or

(b)   encouraging women only, or men only, to take advantage of opportunities for doing that work, where at any time within the twelve months immediately preceding the doing of the act there were no persons of the sex in question among those doing that work or the number of persons of that sex doing the work was comparatively small.

(2)   Nothing in section 12 shall render unlawful any act done by an organisation to which that section applies in, or in connection with,—

(a)   affording female members of the organisation only, or male members of the organisation only, access to facilities for training which would help to fit them for holding a post of any kind in the organisation, or

(b)   encouraging female members only, or male members only, to take advantage of opportunities for holding such posts in the organisation, where at any time within the twelve months immediately preceding the doing of the act there were no persons of the sex in question among persons holding such posts in the organisation or the number of persons of that sex holding such posts was comparatively small.

(3)   Nothing in Parts II to IV shall render unlawful any act done by an organisation to which section 12 applies in, or in connection with, encouraging women only, or men only, to become members of the organisation where at any time within the twelve months immediately preceding the doing of the act there were no persons of the sex in question among those members or the number of persons of that sex among the members was comparatively small.

49   Trade unions etc.: elective bodies

(1)   If an organisation to which section 12 applies comprises a body the membership of which is wholly or mainly elected, nothing in section 12 shall render unlawful provision which ensures that a minimum number of persons of one sex are members of the body—

(a)   by reserving seats on the body for persons of that sex, or

(b)   by making extra seats on the body available (by election or co-option or otherwise) for persons of that sex on occasions when the number of persons of that sex in the other seats is below the minimum,

where in the opinion of the organisation the provision is in the circumstances needed to secure a reasonable lower limit to the number of members of that sex serving on the body; and nothing in Parts II to IV shall render unlawful any act done in order to give effect to such a provision.

(2)   This section shall not be taken as making lawful—

(a)   discrimination in the arrangements for determining the persons entitled to vote in an election of members of the body, or otherwise to choose the persons to serve on the body, or

(b)   discrimination in any arrangements concerning membership of the organisation itself.

50   Indirect access to benefits etc.

(1)   References in this Act to the affording by any person of access to benefits, facilities or services are not limited to benefits, facilities or services provided by that person himself, but include any means by which it is in that person's power to facilitate access to benefits, facilities or services provided by any other person (the 'actual provider').

(2)   Where by any provision of this Act the affording by any person of access to benefits, facilities or services in a discriminatory way is in certain circumstances prevented from being unlawful, the effect of the provision shall extend also to the liability under this Act of any actual provider.

51   Acts done for purposes of protection of women

(1)   Nothing in the following provisions, namely—

(a)   Part II,

(b)   Part III so far as it applies to vocational training, or

(c)   Part IV so far as it has effect in relation to the provisions mentioned in paragraphs (a) and (b),

shall render unlawful any act done by a person in relation to a woman if—

(i)   it was necessary for that person to do it in order to comply with a requirement of an existing statutory provision concerning the protection of women, or

(ii)   it was necessary for that person to do it in order to comply with a requirement of a relevant statutory provision (within the meaning of Part I of the Health and

Safety at Work etc. Act 1974) and it was done by that person for the purpose of the protection of the woman in question (or of any class of women that included that woman).

(2) In subsection (1)—

    (a) the reference in paragraph (i) of that subsection to an existing statutory provision concerning the protection of women is a reference to any such provision having effect for the purpose of protecting women as regards—

        (i) pregnancy or maternity, or

        (ii) other circumstances giving rise to risks specifically affecting women,

        whether the provision relates only to such protection or to the protection of any other class of persons as well; and

    (b) the reference in paragraph (ii) of that subsection to the protection of a particular woman or class of women is a reference to the protection of that woman or those women as regards any circumstances falling within paragraph (a)(i) or (ii) above.

(3) In this section 'existing statutory provision' means (subject to subsection (4)) any provision of—

    (a) an Act passed before this Act, or

    (b) an instrument approved or made by or under such an Act (including one approved or made after the passing of this Act).

(4) Where an Act passed after this Act re-enacts (with or without modification) a provision of an Act passed before this Act, that provision as re-enacted shall be treated for the purposes of subsection (3) as if it continued to be contained in an Act passed before this Act.

51A Acts done under statutory authority to be exempt from certain provisions of Part III

(1) Nothing in—

    (a) the relevant provisions of Part III, or

    (b) Part IV so far as it has effect in relation to those provisions,

shall render unlawful any act done by a person if it was necessary for that person to do it in order to comply with a requirement of an existing statutory provision within the meaning of section 51.

(2) In subsection (1) 'the relevant provisions of Part III' means the provisions of that Part except so far as they apply to vocational training.

PART VII

ENFORCEMENT

General

62 Restriction of proceedings for breach of Act

(1) Except as provided by this Act no proceedings, whether civil or criminal, shall lie against any person in respect of an act by reason that the act is unlawful by virtue of a provision of this Act.

(2) Subsection (1) does not preclude the making of an order of certiorari, mandamus or prohibition.

    ...

63 Jurisdiction of employment tribunals

(1) A complaint by any person ('the complainant') that another person ('the respondent')—

    (a) has committed an act of discrimination or harassment against the complainant which is unlawful by virtue of Part II, or section 35A or 35B, or

    (b) is by virtue of section 41 or 42 to be treated as having committed such an act of discrimination or harassment against the complainant,

may be presented to an employment tribunal.

(2) Subsection (1) does not apply to a complaint under section 13(1) of an act in respect of which an appeal, or proceedings in the nature of an appeal, may be brought under any enactment.

63A Burden of proof: employment tribunals

(1) This section applies to any complaint presented under section 63 to an employment tribunal.

(2) Where, on the hearing of the complaint, the complainant proves facts from which the tribunal could, apart from this section, conclude in the absence of an adequate explanation that the respondent—

    (a)   has committed an act of discrimination or harassment against the complainant which is unlawful by virtue of Part 2, or section 35A or 35B, or

    (b)   is by virtue of section 41 or 42 to be treated as having committed such an act of discrimination or harassment against the complainant,

the tribunal shall uphold the complaint unless the respondent proves that he did not commit, or, as the case may be, is not to be treated as having committed, that act.

65   Remedies on complaint under section 63

(1)   Where an employment tribunal finds that a complaint presented to it under section 63 is well-founded the tribunal shall make such of the following as it considers just and equitable—

    (a)   an order declaring the rights of the complainant and the respondent in relation to the act to which the complaint relates;

    (b)   an order requiring the respondent to pay to the complainant compensation of an amount corresponding to any damages he could have been ordered by a county court or by a sheriff court to pay to the complainant if the complaint had fallen to be dealt with under section 66;

    (c)   a recommendation that the respondent take within a specified period action appearing to the tribunal to be practicable for the purpose of obviating or reducing the adverse effect on the complainant of any act of discrimination to which the complaint relates.

(1A) In applying section 66 for the purposes of subsection (1)(b), no account shall be taken of subsection (3) of that section.

(1B) As respects an unlawful act of discrimination falling within section 1(2)(b) or section 3(1)(b), if the respondent proves that the requirement or condition in question was not applied with the intention of treating the complainant unfavourably on the ground of his sex or (as the case may be) fulfillment of the condition in section 3(2), an order may be made under subsection (1)(b) only if the employment tribunal—

    (a)   makes such order under subsection (1)(a) and such recommendation under subsection (1)(c) (if any) as it would have made if it had no power to make an order under subsection (1)(b); and

    (b)   (where it makes an order under subsection (1)(a) or a recommendation under subsection (1)(c) or both) considers that it is just and equitable to make an order under subsection (1)(b) as well.

(2)   ...

(3)   If without reasonable justification the respondent to a complaint fails to comply with a recommendation made by an employment tribunal under subsection (1)(c), then, if they think it just and equitable to do so—

    (a)   the tribunal may increase the amount of compensation required to be paid to the complainant in respect of the complaint by an order made under subsection (1)(b), or

    (b)   if an order under subsection (1)(b) was not made, the tribunal may make such an order.

66   Claims under Part III

(1)   A claim by any person ('the claimant') that another person ('the respondent')—

    (a)   has committed an act of discrimination or harassment against the claimant which is unlawful by virtue of Part III, other than section 35A or 35B, or

    (b)   is by virtue of section 41 or 42 to be treated as having committed such an act of discrimination or harassment against the claimant,

may be made the subject of civil proceedings in like manner as any other claim in tort or (in Scotland) in reparation for breach of statutory duty.

(2)   Proceedings under subsection (1)—

    (a)   shall be brought in England and Wales only in a county court, and

    (b)   shall be brought in Scotland only in a sheriff court,

but all such remedies shall be obtainable in such proceedings as, apart from this subsection and section 62(1), would be obtainable in the High Court or the Court of Session, as the case may be.

(3)   As respects an unlawful act of discrimination falling within section 1(1)(b) no award of damages shall be made if the respondent proves that the requirement or condition in question was not applied with the intention of treating the claimant unfavourably on the ground of his sex.

(3A) Subsection 3 does not affect the award of damages in respect of an unlawful act of discrimination falling within section 1(2)(b).

(4) For the avoidance of doubt it is hereby declared that damages in respect of an unlawful act of discrimination or harassment may include compensation for injury to feelings whether or not they include compensation under any other head.

...

66A   Burden of proof: county and sheriff courts

(1) This section applies to any claim brought under section 66(1) in a county court in England and Wales or a sheriff court in Scotland.

(2) Where, on the hearing of the claim, the claimant proves facts from which the court could, apart from this section, conclude in the absence of an adequate explanation that the respondent—

   (a)   has committed an act of discrimination or harassment against the claimant which is unlawful by virtue of any provision of Part 3 so far as it applies to vocational training, or

   (b)   is by virtue of section 41 or 42 to be treated as having committed such an act of discrimination or harassment against the claimant,

   the court shall uphold the claim unless the respondent proves that he did not commit, or, as the case may be, is not to be treated as having committed, that act.

(2A) Where in England and Wales—

   (a)   proceedings or prospective proceedings under section 66 relate to the act or omission of a qualifying institution, and

   (b)   the dispute concerned is referred as a complaint under the student complaints scheme before the end of the period of six months mentioned in subsection (2)(a),

   the period allowed by subsection (2)(a) shall be extended by two months.

(2B) In subsection (2A)—

   'qualifying institution' has the meaning given by section 11 of the Higher Education Act 2004; 'the student complaints scheme' means a scheme for the review of qualifying complaints, as defined by section 12 of that Act, that is provided by the designated operator, as defined by section 13(5)(b) of that Act.

74   Help for aggrieved persons in obtaining information etc.

(1) With a view to helping a person ('the person aggrieved') who considers he may have been discriminated against or subjected to harassment in contravention of this Act to decide whether to institute proceedings and, if he does so, to formulate and present his case in the most effective manner, the Minister shall by order prescribe—

   (a)   forms by which the person aggrieved may question the respondent on his reasons for doing any relevant act, or on any other matter which is or may be relevant;

   (b)   forms by which the respondent may if he so wishes reply to any questions.

(2) Where the person aggrieved questions the respondent (whether in accordance with an order under subsection (1) or not)—

   (a)   the question, and any reply by the respondent (whether in accordance with such an order or not) shall, subject to the following provisions of this section, be admissible as evidence in the proceedings;

   (b)   if it appears to the court or tribunal that the respondent deliberately, and without reasonable excuse, omitted to reply within the period applicable under subsection (2A) or that his reply is evasive or equivocal, the court or tribunal may draw any inference from that fact that it considers it just and equitable to draw, including an inference that he committed an unlawful act.

(2A) The period applicable for the purposes of subsection (2)(b)is—

   (a)   eight weeks beginning with the day when the question was served on the respondent, if the question related to discrimination under—

      (i)   any provision of Part 2

      (ii)   section 35A or 35B, or

      (iii)   any other provision of Part 3, so far as it applies to vocational training:

   (b)   a reasonable period as regards any other question.

Period within which proceedings to be brought

76 Period within which proceedings to be brought

(1) An employment tribunal shall not consider a complaint under section 63 unless it is presented to the tribunal before the end of

    (a) the period of three months beginning when the act complained of was done; or

    (b) in a case to which section 85(9A) applies, the period of six months so beginning.

(2) A county court or a sheriff court shall not consider a claim under section 66 unless proceedings in respect of the claim are instituted before the end of

    (a) the period of six months beginning when the act complained of was done; or

    (b) in a case to which section 66(5) applies, the period of eight months so beginning.

(2A) Where in England and Wales—

    (a) proceedings or prospective proceedings under section 66 relate to the act or omission of a qualifying institution, and

    (b) the dispute concerned is referred as a complaint under the student complaints scheme before the end of the period of six months mentioned in subsection (2)(a), the period allowed by subsection (2)(a) shall be extended by three months.

(2B) In subsection (2A)—

'qualifying institution' has the meaning given by section 11 of the Higher Education Act 2004;

'the student complaints scheme' means a scheme for the review of qualifying complaints, as defined by section 12 of that Act, that is provided by the designated operator, as defined by section 13(5)(b) of that Act.

(2C) The period allowed by subsection (2)(a) or (b) shall be extended by three months in the case of a dispute which is referred for conciliation in pursuance of arrangements under section 27 of the Equality Act 2006 (unless the period is extended under subsection (2A)).

(3), (4) …

(5) A court or tribunal may nevertheless consider any such complaint or claim which is out of time if, in all the circumstances of the case, it considers that it is just and equitable to do so.

(6) For the purposes of this section—

    (a) where the inclusion or any term in a contract renders the making of the contract an unlawful act that act shall be treated as extending throughout the duration of the contract, and

    (b) any act extending over a period shall be treated as done at the end of that period, and

    (c) a deliberate omission shall be treated as done when the person in question decided upon it,

and in the absence of evidence establishing the contrary a person shall be taken for the purposes of this section to decide upon an omission when he does an act inconsistent with doing the omitted act or, if he has done no such inconsistent act, when the period expires within which he might reasonably have been expected to do the omitted act if it was to be done.

RACE RELATIONS ACT 1976
(1976, c. 74)

PART I
DISCRIMINATION TO WHICH ACT APPLIES

1 Racial discrimination

(1) A person discriminates against another in any circumstances relevant for the purposes of any provision of this Act if—

    (a) on racial grounds he treats that other less favourably than he treats or would treat other persons; or

    (b) he applies to that other a requirement or condition which he applies or would apply equally to persons not of the same racial group as that other but—

(i)   which is such that the proportion of persons of the same racial group as that other who can comply with it is considerably smaller than the proportion of persons not of that racial group who can comply with it; and

(ii)   which he cannot show to be justifiable irrespective of the colour, race, nationality or ethnic or national origins of the person to whom it is applied; and

(iii) which is to the detriment of that other because he cannot comply with it.

(1A) A person also discriminates against another if, in any circumstances relevant for the purposes of any provision referred to in subsection (1B), he applies to that other a provision, criterion or practice which he applies or would apply equally to persons not of the same race or ethnic or national origins as that other, but—

(a)   which puts or would put persons of the same race or ethnic or national origins as that other at a particular disadvantage when compared with other persons,

(b)   which puts that other at that disadvantage, and

(c)   which he cannot show to be a proportionate means of achieving a legitimate aim.

(1B) The provisions mentioned in subsection (1A) are—

(a)   Part II;

(b)   sections 17 to 18D;

(c)   section 19B, so far as relating to—

(i)   any form of social security;

(ii)   health care;

(iii) any other form of social protection; and

(iv)   any form of social advantage;

which does not fall within section 20;

(d)   sections 20 to 24;

(e)   sections 26A and 26B;

(f)   sections 76 and 76ZA; and

(g)   Part IV, in its application to the provisions referred to in paragraphs (a) to (f).

(1C) Where, by virtue of subsection (1A), a person discriminates against another, subsection (1)(b) does not apply to him.

(2)   It is hereby declared that, for the purposes of this Act, segregating a person from other persons on racial grounds is treating him less favourably than they are treated.

2   Discrimination by way of victimisation

(1)   A person ('the discriminator') discriminates against another person ('the person victimised') in any circumstances relevant for the purposes of any provision of this Act if he treats the person victimised less favourably than in those circumstances he treats or would treat other persons, and does so by reason that the person victimised has—

(a)   brought proceedings against the discriminator or any other person under this Act; or

(b)   given evidence or information in connection with proceedings brought by any person against the discriminator or any other person under this Act; or

(c)   otherwise done anything under or by reference to this Act in relation to the discriminator or any other person; or

(d)   alleged that the discriminator or any other person has committed an act which (whether or not the allegation so states) would amount to a contravention of this Act,

or by reason that the discriminator knows that the person victimised intends to do any of those things, or suspects that the person victimised has done, or intends to do, any of them.

(2)   Subsection (1) does not apply to treatment of a person by reason of any allegation made by him if the allegation was false and not made in good faith.

3   Meaning of 'racial grounds', 'racial group' etc.

(1)   In this Act, unless the context otherwise requires—

'racial grounds' means any of the following grounds, namely colour, race, nationality or ethnic or national origins;

'racial group' means a group of persons defined by reference to colour, race, nationality or ethnic or national origins, and references to a person's racial group refer to any racial group into which he falls.

(2) The fact that a racial group comprises two or more distinct racial groups does not prevent it from constituting a particular racial group for the purposes of this Act.

(3) In this Act—

(a) references to discrimination refer to any discrimination falling within section 1 or 2; and

(b) references to racial discrimination refer to any discrimination falling within section 1,

and related expressions shall be construed accordingly.

(4) A comparison of the case of a person of a particular racial group with that of a person not of that group under section 1(1) or (1A) must be such that the relevant circumstances in the one case are the same, or not materially different, in the other.

3A   Harassment

(1) A person subjects another to harassment in any circumstances relevant for the purposes of any provision referred to in section 1(1B) where, on grounds of race or ethnic or national origins, he engages in unwanted conduct which has the purpose or effect of—

(a) violating that other person's dignity, or

(b) creating an intimidating, hostile, degrading, humiliating or offensive environment for him.

(2) Conduct shall be regarded as having the effect specified in paragraph (a) or (b) of subsection (1) only if, having regard to all the circumstances, including in particular the perception of that other person, it should reasonably be considered as having that effect.

PART II
DISCRIMINATION IN THE EMPLOYMENT FIELD

Discrimination by employers

4   Applicants and employees

(1) It is unlawful for a person, in relation to employment by him at an establishment in Great Britain, to discriminate against another—

(a) in the arrangements he makes for the purpose of determining who should be offered that employment; or

(b) in the terms on which he offers him that employment; or

(c) by refusing or deliberately omitting to offer him that employment.

(2) It is unlawful for a person, in the case of a person employed by him at an establishment in Great Britain, to discriminate against that employee—

(a) in the terms of employment which he affords him; or

(b) in the way he affords him access to opportunities for promotion, transfer or training, or to any other benefits, facilities or services, or by refusing or deliberately omitting to afford him access to them; or

(c) by dismissing him, or subjecting him to any other detriment.

(2A) It is unlawful for an employer, in relation to employment by him at an establishment in Great Britain, to subject to harassment a person whom he employs or who has applied to him for employment.

(3) Except in relation to discrimination falling within section 2 or discrimination on grounds of race or ethnic or national origins, subsections (1) and (2) do not apply to employment for the purposes of a private household.

(4) Subsection (2) does not apply to benefits, facilities or services of any description if the employer is concerned with the provision (for payment or not) of benefits, facilities or services of that description to the public, or to a section of the public comprising the employee in question, unless—

(a) that provision differs in a material respect from the provision of the benefits, facilities or services by the employer to his employees; or

(b) the provision of the benefits, facilities or services to the employee in question is regulated by his contract of employment; or

(c) the benefits, facilities or services relate to training.

(4A) In subsection (2)(c) reference to the dismissal of a person from employment includes, where the discrimination is on grounds of race or ethnic or national origins, reference—

(a) to the termination of that person's employment by the expiration of any period (including a period expiring by reference to an event or circumstance), not being a termination immediately after which the employment is renewed on the same terms; and

(b) to the termination of that person's employment by any act of his (including the giving of notice) in circumstances such that he is entitled to terminate it without notice by reason of the conduct of the employer.

4A Exception for genuine occupational requirement

(1) In relation to discrimination on grounds of race or ethnic or national origins—

(a) section 4(1)(a) or (c) does not apply to any employment; and

(b) section 4(2)(b) does not apply to promotion or transfer to, or training for, any employment; and

(c) section 4(2)(c) does not apply to dismissal from any employment;

where subsection (2) applies.

(2) This subsection applies where, having regard to the nature of the employment or the context in which it is carried out—

(a) being of a particular race or of particular ethnic or national origins is a genuine and determining occupational requirement;

(b) it is proportionate to apply that requirement in the particular case; and

(c) either—

(i) the person to whom that requirement is applied does not meet it, or

(ii) the employer is not satisfied, and in all the circumstances it is reasonable for him not to be satisfied, that that person meets it.

5 Exceptions for genuine occupational qualifications

(1) In relation to racial discrimination in cases where section 4A does not apply—

(a) section 4(1)(a) or (c) does not apply to any employment where being of a particular racial group is a genuine occupational qualification for the job; and

(b) section 4(2)(b) does not apply to opportunities for promotion or transfer to, or training for, such employment.

(2) Being of a particular racial group is a genuine occupational qualification for a job only where—

(a) the job involves participation in a dramatic performance or other entertainment in a capacity for which a person of that racial group is required for reasons of authenticity; or

(b) the job involves participation as an artist's or photographic model in the production of a work of art, visual image or sequence of visual images for which a person of that racial group is required for reasons of authenticity; or

(c) the job involves working in a place where food or drink is (for payment or not) provided to and consumed by members of the public or a section of the public in a particular setting for which, in that job, a person of that racial group is required for reasons of authenticity; or

(d) the holder of the job provides persons of that racial group with personal services promoting their welfare, and those services can most effectively be provided by a person of that racial group.

(3) Subsection (2) applies where some only of the duties of the job fall within paragraph (a), (b), (c) or (d) as well as where all of them do.

(4) Paragraph (a), (b), (c) or (d) of subsection (2) does not apply in relation to the filling of a vacancy at a time when the employer already has employees of the racial group in question—

(a) who are capable of carrying out the duties falling within that paragraph; and

(b) whom it would be reasonable to employ on those duties; and

(c) whose numbers are sufficient to meet the employer's likely requirements in respect of those duties without undue inconvenience.

7   Contract workers

(1)   This section applies to any work for a person ('the principal') which is available for doing by individuals ('contract workers') who are employed not by the principal himself but by another person, who supplies them under a contract made with the principal.

(2)   It is unlawful for the principal, in relation to work to which this section applies, to discriminate against a contract worker—

(a)   in the terms on which he allows him to do that work; or

(b)   by not allowing him to do it or continue to do it; or

(c)   in the way he affords him access to any benefits, facilities or services or by refusing or deliberately omitting to afford him access to them; or

(d)   by subjecting him to any other detriment.

(3)   The principal does not contravene subsection (2)(b) by doing any act in relation to a person not of a particular racial group, or not of a particular race or particular ethnic or national origins, at a time when, if the work were to be done by a person taken into the principal's employment, being of that racial group or of that race or those origins would be a genuine occupational qualification or, as the case may be, that act would be lawful by virtue of section 4A for the job.

(3A) It is unlawful for the principal, in relation to work to which this section applies, to subject a contract worker to harassment.

(4)   Nothing in this section shall render unlawful any act done by the principal [on grounds other than those of race or ethnic or national origins, for the benefit of a contract worker not ordinarily resident in Great Britain in or in connection with allowing him to do work to which this section applies, where the purpose of his being allowed to do that work is to provide him with training skills which he appears to the principal to intend to exercise wholly outside Great Britain.

(5)   Subsection (2)(c) does not apply to benefits, facilities or services of any description if the principal is concerned with the provision (for payment or not) of benefits, facilities or services of that description to the public, or to a section of the public to which the contract worker in question belongs, unless that provision differs in a material respect from the provision of the benefits, facilities or services by the principal to his contract workers.

PART IV

OTHER UNLAWFUL ACTS

27A   Relationships which have come to an end

(1)   In this section a 'relevant relationship' is a relationship during the course of which, by virtue of any provision referred to in section 1(1B), taken with section 1(1) or (1A), or (as the case may be) by virtue of section 3A—

(a)   an act of discrimination by one party to the relationship ('the relevant party') against another party to the relationship, on grounds of race or ethnic or national origins, or

(b)   harassment of another party to the relationship by the relevant party,

is unlawful.

(2)   Where a relevant relationship has come to an end it is unlawful for the relevant party—

(a)   to discriminate against another party, on grounds of race or ethnic or national origins, by subjecting him to a detriment, or

(b)   to subject another party to harassment,

where the discrimination or harassment arises out of and is closely connected to that relationship.

(3)   In subsection (1) reference to an act of discrimination or harassment which is unlawful includes, in the case of a relationship which has come to an end before 19th July 2003, reference to such an act which would, after that date, be unlawful.

(4)   For the purposes of any proceedings in respect of an unlawful act under subsection (2), that act shall be treated as falling within circumstances relevant for the purposes of such of the provisions, or Parts, referred to in subsection (1) as determine most closely the nature of the relevant relationship.

28   Discriminatory practices

(1)   In this section 'discriminatory practice' means—

    (a)   the application of a requirement or condition which results in an act of discrimination which is unlawful by virtue of any provision of Part II or III taken with section 1(1)(b), or which would be likely to result in such an act of discrimination if the persons to whom it is applied included persons of any particular racial group as regards which there has been no occasion for applying it; or

    (b)   the application of a provision, criterion or practice which results in an act of discrimination which is unlawful by virtue of any provision referred to in section 1(1B), taken with section 1(1A), or which would be likely to result in such an act of discrimination, if the persons to whom it is applied included persons of any particular race or of any particular ethnic or national origins, as regards which there has been no occasion for applying it.

(2)   A person acts in contravention of this section if and so long as—

    (a)   he applies a discriminatory practice; or

    (b)   he operates practices or other arrangements which in any circumstances would call for the application by him of a discriminatory practice.

(3)   Proceedings in respect of a contravention of this section shall be brought only by the Commission in accordance with sections 20 to 24 of the Equality Act 2006.

29   Discriminatory advertisements

(1)   It is unlawful to publish or to cause to be published an advertisement which indicates, or might reasonably be understood as indicating, an intention by a person to do an act of discrimination, whether the doing of that act by him would be lawful or, by virtue of Part II or III, unlawful.

(2)   Subsection (1) does not apply to an advertisement—

    (a)   if the intended act would be lawful by virtue of any of sections 5, 6, 7(3) and (4), 10(3), 26, 34(2)(b), 35 to 39 and 41; or

    (b)   if the advertisement relates to the services of an employment agency (within the meaning of section 14(1)) and the intended act only concerns employment which the employer could by virtue of section 5, 6 or 7(3) or (4) lawfully refuse to offer to persons against whom the advertisement indicates an intention to discriminate.

(3)   Subsection (1) does not apply to an advertisement which indicates that persons of any class defined otherwise than by reference to colour, race or ethnic or national origins are required for employment outside Great Britain.

(4)   The publisher of an advertisement made unlawful by subsection (1) shall not be subject to any liability under that subsection in respect of the publication of the advertisement if he proves—

    (a)   that the advertisement was published in reliance on a statement made to him by the person who caused it to be published to the effect that, by reason of the operation of subsection (2) or (3), the publication would not be unlawful; and

    (b)   that it was reasonable for him to rely on the statement.

(5)   A person who knowingly or recklessly makes a statement such as is mentioned in subsection (4)(a) which in a material respect is false or misleading commits an offence, and shall be liable on summary conviction to a fine not exceeding level 5 on the standard scale.

(6)   Proceedings in respect of a contravention of subsection (1) may be brought only—

    (a)   by the Commission, and

    (b)   in accordance with section 25 of the Equality Act 2006.

30   Instructions to commit unlawful acts

(1)   It is unlawful for a person—

    (a)   who has authority over another person; or

    (b)   in accordance with whose wishes that other person is accustomed to act,

    to instruct him to do any act which is unlawful by virtue of Part II or III, section 76ZA or, where it renders an act unlawful on grounds of race or ethnic or national origins, section 76, or procure or attempt to procure the doing by him of any such act.

(2)   Proceedings in respect of a contravention of subsection (1) may be brought only—

(a)   by the Commission, and

(b)   in accordance with section 25 of the Equality Act 2006.

31   Pressure to commit unlawful acts

(1)   It is unlawful to induce, or attempt to induce, a person to do any act which contravenes Part II or III, section 76ZA or, where it renders an act unlawful on grounds of race or ethnic or national origins, section 76.

(2)   An attempted inducement is not prevented from falling within subsection (1) because it is not made directly to the person in question, if it is made in such a way that he is likely to hear of it.

(3)   Proceedings in respect of a contravention of subsection (1) may be brought only—

(a)   by the Commission, and

(b)   in accordance with section 25 of the Equality Act 2006.

32   Liability of employers and principals

(1)   Anything done by a person in the course of his employment shall be treated for the purposes of this Act (except as regards offences thereunder) as done by his employer as well as by him, whether or not it was done with the employer's knowledge or approval.

(2)   Anything done by a person as agent for another person with the authority (whether express or implied, and whether precedent or subsequent) of that other person shall be treated for the purposes of this Act (except as regards offences thereunder) as done by that other person as well as by him.

(3)   In proceedings brought under this Act against any person in respect of an act alleged to have been done by an employee of his it shall be a defence for that person to prove that he took such steps as were reasonably practicable to prevent the employee from doing that act, or from doing in the course of his employment acts of that description.

33   Aiding unlawful acts

(1)   A person who knowingly aids another person to do an act made unlawful by this Act shall be treated for the purposes of this Act as himself doing an unlawful act of the like description.

(2)   For the purposes of subsection (1) an employee or agent for whose act the employer or principal is liable under section 32 (or would be so liable but for section 32(3)) shall be deemed to aid the doing of the act by the employer or principal.

(3)   A person does not under this section knowingly aid another to do an unlawful act if—

(a)   he acts in reliance on a statement made to him by that other person that, by reason of any provision of this Act, the act which he aids would not be unlawful; and

(b)   it is reasonable for him to rely on the statement.

(5)   A person who knowingly or recklessly makes a statement such as is mentioned in subsection (3)(a) which in a material respect is false or misleading commits an offence, and shall be liable on summary conviction to a fine not exceeding level 5 on the standard scale.

54A   Burden of proof: employment tribunals

(1)   This section applies where a complaint is presented under section 54 and the complaint is that the respondent—

(a)   has committed an act of discrimination, on grounds of race or ethnic or national origins, which is unlawful by virtue of any provision referred to in section 1(1B)(a), (e) or (f), or Part IV in its application to those provisions, or

(b)   has committed an act of harassment.

(2)   Where, on the hearing of the complaint, the complainant proves facts from which the tribunal could, apart from this section, conclude in the absence of an adequate explanation that the respondent—

(a)   has committed such an act of discrimination or harassment against the complainant, or

(b)   is by virtue of section 32 or 33 to be treated as having committed such an act of discrimination or harassment against the complainant,

the tribunal shall uphold the complaint unless the respondent proves that he did not commit or, as the case may be, is not to be treated as having committed, that act.

SEX DISCRIMINATION ACT 1986
(1986, c. 59)

6   Collective agreements and rules of undertakings

(1)   Without prejudice to the generality of section 77 of the 1975 Act (which makes provision with respect to the validity and revision of contracts), that section shall apply, as it applies in relation to the term of a contract, to the following, namely—

    (a)   any term of a collective agreement, including an agreement which was not intended, or is presumed not to have been intended, to be a legally enforceable contract;

    (b)   any rule made by an employer for application to all or any of the persons who are employed by him or who apply to be, or are, considered by him for employment;

    (c)   any rule made by an organisation, authority or body to which subsection (2) below applies for application to all or any of its members or prospective members or to all or any of the persons on whom it has conferred authorisations or qualifications or who are seeking the authorisations or qualifications which it has power to confer;

and that section shall so apply whether the agreement was entered into, or the rule made, before or after the coming into force of this section.

(2)   This subsection applies to—

    (a)   any organisation of workers;

    (b)   any organisation of employers;

    (c)   any organisation whose members carry on a particular profession or trade for the purposes of which the organisation exists;

    (d)   any authority or body which can confer an authorisation or qualification which is needed for, or facilitates, engagement in a particular profession or trade.

(3)   For the purposes of the said section 77 a term or rule shall be deemed to provide for the doing of an act which would be rendered unlawful by the 1975 Act if—

    (a)   it provides for the inclusion in any contract of employment of any term which by virtue of an equality clause would fall either to be modified or to be supplemented by an additional term; and

    (b)   that clause would not be prevented from operating in relation to the contract by section 1(3) of the Equal Pay Act 1970 (material factors justifying discrimination).

(4)   Nothing in the said section 77 shall affect the operation of any term or rule in so far as it provides for the doing of a particular act in circumstances where the doing of that act would not be, or be deemed by virtue of subsection (3) above to be, rendered unlawful by the 1975 Act.

(4A) A person to whom this subsection applies may present a complaint to an employment tribunal that a term or rule is void by virtue of subsection (1) of the said section 77 if he has reason to believe—

    (a)   that the term or rule may at some future time have effect in relation to him, and

    (b)   where he alleges that it is void by virtue of paragraph (c) of that subsection, that—

        (i)   an act for the doing of which it provides may at some such time be done in relation to him, and

        (ii)   the act would be, or be deemed by virtue of subsection (3) above to be, rendered unlawful by the 1975 Act if done in relation to him in present circumstances.

(4B) In the case of a complaint about—

    (a)   a term of a collective agreement made by or on behalf of—

        (i)   an employer,

        (ii)   an organisation of employers of which an employer is a member, or

        (iii) an association of such organisations of one of which an employer is a member, or

    (b)   a rule made by an employer, subsection (4A) applies to any person who is, or is genuinely and actively seeking to become, one of his employees.

(4C) In the case of a complaint about a rule made by an organisation, authority or body to which subsection (2) above applies, subsection (4A) applies to any person—

    (a)   who is, or is genuinely and actively seeking to become, a member of the organisation, authority or body,

(b)   on whom the organisation, authority or body has conferred an authorisation or qualification, or

(c)   who is genuinely and actively seeking an authorisation or qualification which the organisation, authority or body has power to confer.

(4D) When an employment tribunal finds that a complaint presented to it under subsection (4A) above is well-founded the tribunal shall make an order declaring that the term or rule is void.

(5)   The avoidance by virtue of the said section 77 of any term or rule which provides for any person to be discriminated against shall be without prejudice to the following rights except in so far as they enable any person to require another person to be treated less favourably than himself, namely—

(a)   such of the rights of the person to be discriminated against; and

(b)   such of the rights of any person who will be treated more favourably in direct or indirect consequence of the discrimination,

as are conferred by or in respect of a contract made or modified wholly or partly in pursuance of, or by reference to, that term or rule.

(6)   In this section 'collective agreement' means any agreement relating to one or more of the matters mentioned in section 178(2) of the Trade Union and Labour Relations (Consolidation) Act 1992 (meaning of trade dispute), being an agreement made by or on behalf of one or more employers or one or more organisations of employers or associations of such organisations with one or more organisations of workers or associations of such organisations.

(7)   Any expression used in this section and in the 1975 Act has the same meaning in this section as in that Act, and this section shall have effect as if the terms of any service to which Parts II and IV of that Act apply by virtue of subsection (2) of section 85 of that Act (Crown application) were terms of a contract of employment and, in relation to the terms of any such service, as if service for the purposes of any person mentioned in that subsection were employment by that person.

EMPLOYMENT ACT 1989
(1989, c. 38)

1   **Overriding of statutory requirements which conflict with certain provisions of 1975 Act**

(1)   Any provision of—

(a)   an Act passed before the Sex Discrimination Act 1975, or

(b)   an instrument approved or made by or under such an Act (including one approved or made after the passing of the 1975 Act),

shall be of no effect in so far as it imposes a requirement to do an act which would be rendered unlawful by any of the provisions of that Act referred to in subsection (2).

(2)   Those provisions are—

(a)   Part II (discrimination as respects employment);

(b)   Part III (discrimination as respects education etc.) so far as it applies to vocational training; and

(c)   Part IV (other unlawful acts) so far as it has effect in relation to the provisions mentioned in paragraphs (a) and (b) above.

(3)   Where in any legal proceedings (of whatever nature) there falls to be determined the question whether subsection (1) operates to negative the effect of any provision in so far as it requires the application by any person of a provision, criterion or practice falling within section 1(2)(b)(i) or 3(1)(b)(i) of the 1975 Act (indirect discrimination on grounds of sex or marital status)—

(a)   it shall be for any party to the proceedings who claims that subsection (1) does not so operate in relation to that provision to show the provision, criterion or practice in question to be justifiable as mentioned in section 1(2)(b)(ii) or 3(1)(b)(ii) of that Act; and

(b)   the said section 1(2)(b)(ii) or 3(1)(b)(ii) shall accordingly have effect in relation to the provision, criterion or practice as if the reference to the person applying it were a reference to any such party to the proceedings.

(4) Where an Act passed after the 1975 Act, whether before or after the passing of this Act, re-enacts (with or without modification) a provision of an Act passed before the 1975 Act, the provision as re-enacted shall be treated for the purposes of subsection (1) as if it continued to be contained in an Act passed before the 1975 Act.

4   Exemption for discrimination under certain provisions concerned with the protection of women at work

(1) Without prejudice to the operation of section 51 of the 1975 Act nothing in—

    (a)   Part II of that Act,

    (b)   Part III of that Act so far as it applies to vocational training, or

    (c)   Part IV of that Act so far as it has effect in relation to the provisions mentioned in paragraphs (a) and (b) above,

shall render unlawful any act done by a person in relation to a woman if it was necessary for that person to do that act in order to comply with any requirement of any of the provisions specified in Schedule 1 to this Act (which are concerned with the protection of women at work).

(3) In this section 'woman' means a female person of any age.

TRADE UNION AND LABOUR RELATIONS (CONSOLIDATION) ACT 1992
(1992, c. 52)

PART I
TRADE UNIONS

CHAPTER I
INTRODUCTORY

Meaning of 'trade union'

1   Meaning of 'trade union'

In this Act a 'trade union' means an organisation (whether temporary or permanent)—

    (a)   which consists wholly or mainly of workers of one or more descriptions and whose principal purposes include the regulation of relations between workers of that description or those descriptions and employers or employers' associations; or

    (b)   which consists wholly or mainly of—

        (i)   constituent or affiliated organisations which fulfil the conditions in paragraph (a) (or themselves consist wholly or mainly of constituent or affiliated organisations which fulfil those conditions), or

        (ii)   representatives of such constituent or affiliated organisations,

and whose principal purposes include the regulation of relations between workers and employers or between workers and employers' associations, or the regulation of relations between its constituent or affiliated organisations.

The list of trade unions

2   The list of trade unions

(1) The Certification Officer shall keep a list of trade unions containing the names of—

    (a)   the organisations whose names were, immediately before the commencement of this Act, duly entered in the list of trade unions kept by him under section 8 of the Trade Union and Labour Relations Act 1974, and

    (b)   the names of the organisations entitled to have their names entered in the list in accordance with this Part.

(2) The Certification Officer shall keep copies of the list of trade unions, as for the time being in force, available for public inspection at all reasonable hours free of charge.

(3) A copy of the list shall be included in his annual report.

(4) The fact that the name of an organisation is included in the list of trade unions is evidence (in Scotland, sufficient evidence) that the organisation is a trade union.

(5)   On the application of an organisation whose name is included in the list, the Certification Officer shall issue it with a certificate to that effect.

(6)   A document purporting to be such a certificate is evidence (in Scotland, sufficient evidence) that the name of the organisation is entered in the list.

3   Application to have name entered in the list

(1)   An organisation of workers, whenever formed, whose name is not entered in the list of trade unions may apply to the Certification Officer to have its name entered in the list.

(2)   The application shall be made in such form and manner as the Certification Officer may require and shall be accompanied by—
   (a)   a copy of the rules of the organisation,
   (b)   a list of its officers,
   (c)   the address of its head or main office, and
   (d)   the name under which it is or is to be known,
   and by the prescribed fee.

(3)   If the Certification Officer is satisfied—
   (a)   that the organisation is a trade union,
   (b)   that subsection (2) has been complied with, and
   (c)   that entry of the name in the list is not prohibited by subsection (4),
   he shall enter the name of the organisation in the list of trade unions.

(4)   The Certification Officer shall not enter the name of an organisation in the list of trade unions if the name is the same as that under which another organisation—
   (a)   was on 30 September 1971 registered as a trade union under the Trade Union Acts 1871 to 1964,
   (b)   was at any time registered as a trade union or employers' association under the Industrial Relations Act 1971, or
   (c)   is for the time being entered in the list of trade unions or in the list of employers' associations kept under Part II of this Act,
   or if the name is one so nearly resembling any such name as to be likely to deceive the public.

4   Removal of name from the list

(1)   If it appears to the Certification Officer, on application made to him or otherwise, that an organisation whose name is entered in the list of trade unions is not a trade union, he may remove its name from the list.

(2)   He shall not do so without giving the organisation notice of his intention and considering any representations made to him by the organisation within such period (of not less than 28 days beginning with the date of the notice) as may be specified in the notice.

(3)   The Certification Officer shall remove the name of an organisation from the list of trade unions if—
   (a)   he is requested by the organisation to do so, or
   (b)   he is satisfied that the organisation has ceased to exist.

Certification as independent trade union

5   Meaning of 'independent trade union'

In this Act an 'independent trade union' means a trade union which—
   (a)   is not under the domination or control of an employer or group of employers or of one or more employers' associations, and
   (b)   is not liable to interference by an employer or any such group or association (arising out of the provision of financial or material support or by any other means whatsoever) tending towards such control;
and references to 'independence', in relation to a trade union, shall be construed accordingly.

6   Application for certificate of independence

(1)   A trade union whose name is entered on the list of trade unions may apply to the Certification Officer for a certificate that it is independent.

The application shall be made in such form and manner as the Certification Officer may require and shall be accompanied by the prescribed fee.

(2) The Certification Officer shall maintain a record showing details of all applications made to him under this section and shall keep it available for public inspection (free of charge) at all reasonable hours.

(3) If an application is made by a trade union whose name is not entered on the list of trade unions, the Certification Officer shall refuse a certificate of independence and shall enter that refusal on the record.

(4) In any other case, he shall not come to a decision on the application before the end of the period of one month after it has been entered on the record; and before coming to his decision he shall make such enquiries as he thinks fit and shall take into account any relevant information submitted to him by any person.

(5) He shall then decide whether the applicant trade union is independent and shall enter his decision and the date of his decision on the record.

(6) If he decides that the trade union is independent he shall issue a certificate accordingly; and if he decides that it is not, he shall give reasons for his decision.

7 Withdrawal or cancellation of certificate

(1) The Certification Officer may withdraw a trade union's certificate of independence if he is of the opinion that the union is no longer independent.

(2) Where he proposes to do so he shall notify the trade union and enter notice of the proposal in the record.

(3) He shall not come to a decision on the proposal before the end of the period of one month after notice of it was entered on the record; and before coming to his decision he shall make such enquiries as he thinks fit and shall take into account any relevant information submitted to him by any person.

(4) He shall then decide whether the trade union is independent and shall enter his decision and the date of his decision on the record.

(5) He shall confirm or withdraw the certificate accordingly; and if he decides to withdraw it, he shall give reasons for his decision.

(6) Where the name of an organisation is removed from the list of trade unions, the Certification Officer shall cancel any certificate of independence in force in respect of that organisation by entering on the record the fact that the organisation's name has been removed from that list and that the certificate is accordingly cancelled.

8 Conclusive effect of Certification Officer's decision

(1) A certificate of independence which is in force is conclusive evidence for all purposes that a trade union is independent; and a refusal, withdrawal or cancellation of a certificate of independence, entered on the record, is conclusive evidence for all purposes that a trade union is not independent.

(2) A document purporting to be a certificate of independence and to be signed by the Certification Officer, or by a person authorised to act on his behalf, shall be taken to be such a certificate unless the contrary is proved.

(3) A document purporting to be a certified copy of an entry on the record and to be signed by the Certification Officer, or by a person authorised to act on his behalf, shall be taken to be a true copy of such an entry unless the contrary is proved.

(4) If in any proceedings before a court, the Employment Appeal Tribunal, the Central Arbitration Committee, ACAS or an employment tribunal a question arises whether a trade union is independent and there is no certificate of independence in force and no refusal, withdrawal or cancellation of a certificate recorded in relation to that trade union—

(a) that question shall not be decided in those proceedings, and

(b) the proceedings shall instead be stayed or sisted until a certificate of independence has been issued or refused by the Certification Officer.

(5) The body before whom the proceedings are stayed or sisted may refer the question of the independence of the trade union to the Certification Officer who shall proceed in accordance with section 6 as on an application by that trade union.

Supplementary

9   Appeal against decision of Certification Officer

(1)   An organisation aggrieved by the refusal of the Certification Officer to enter its name in the list of trade unions, or by a decision of his to remove its name from the list, may appeal to the Employment Appeal Tribunal.

(2)   A trade union aggrieved by the refusal of the Certification Officer to issue it with a certificate of independence, or by a decision of his to withdraw its certificate, may appeal to the Employment Appeal Tribunal.

(3)   If on appeal the Tribunal is satisfied that the organisation's name should be or remain entered in the list or, as the case may be, that the certificate should be issued or should not be withdrawn, it shall declare that fact and give directions to the Certification Officer accordingly.

(4)   The rights of appeal conferred by this section extend to any question of fact or law arising in the proceedings before, or arising from the decision of, the Certification Officer.

CHAPTER II
STATUS AND PROPERTY OF TRADE UNIONS

General

10   Quasi-corporate status of trade unions

(1)   A trade union is not a body corporate but—
   (a)   it is capable of making contracts;
   (b)   it is capable of suing and being sued in its own name, whether in proceedings relating to property or founded on contract or tort or any other cause of action; and
   (c)   proceedings for an offence alleged to have been committed by it or on its behalf may be brought against it in its own name.

(2)   A trade union shall not be treated as if it were a body corporate except to the extent authorised by the provisions of this Part.

(3)   A trade union shall not be registered—
   (a)   as a company under the Companies Act 1985; or
   (b)   under the Friendly Societies Act 1974 or the Industrial and Provident Societies Act 1965;
   and any such registration of a trade union (whenever effected) is void.

11   Exclusion of common law rules as to restraint of trade

(1)   The purposes of a trade union are not, by reason only that they are in restraint of trade, unlawful so as—
   (a)   to make any member of the trade union liable to criminal proceedings for conspiracy or otherwise, or
   (b)   to make any agreement or trust void or voidable.

(2)   No rule of a trade union is unlawful or unenforceable by reason only that it is in restraint of trade.

Property of trade union

12   Property to be vested in trustees

(1)   All property belonging to a trade union shall be vested in trustees in trust for it.

(2)   A judgment, order or award made in proceedings of any description brought against a trade union is enforceable, by way of execution, diligence, punishment for contempt or otherwise, against any property held in trust for it to the same extent and in the same manner as if it were a body corporate.

(3)   Subsection (2) has effect subject to section 23 (restriction on enforcement of awards against certain property).

13   Vesting of property in new trustees

(1)   The provisions of this section apply in relation to the appointment or discharge of trustees in whom any property is vested in trust for a trade union whose name is entered in the list of trade unions.

(2)   In the following sections as they apply to such trustees references to a deed shall be construed as references to an instrument in writing—

    (a)   section 39 of the Trustee Act 1925 and section 38 of the Trustee Act (Northern Ireland) 1958 (retirement of trustee without a new appointment), and

    (b)   section 40 of the Trustee Act 1925 and section 39 of the Trustee Act (Northern Ireland) 1958 (vesting of trust property in new or continuing trustees).

(3)   Where such a trustee is appointed or discharged by a resolution taken by or on behalf of the union, the written record of the resolution shall be treated for the purposes of those sections as an instrument in writing appointing or discharging the trustee.

(4)   In section 40 of the Trustee Act 1925 and section 39 of the Trustee Act (Northern Ireland) 1958 as they apply to such trustees, paragraphs (a) and (c) of subsection (4) (which exclude certain property from the section) shall be omitted.

15   Prohibition on use of funds to indemnify unlawful conduct

(1)   It is unlawful for property of a trade union to be applied in or towards—

    (a)   the payment for an individual of a penalty which has been or may be imposed on him for an offence or for contempt of court,

    (b)   the securing of any such payment, or

    (c)   the provision of anything for indemnifying an individual in respect of such a penalty.

(2)   Where any property of a trade union is so applied for the benefit of an individual on whom a penalty has been or may be imposed, then—

    (a)   in the case of a payment, an amount equal to the payment is recoverable by the union from him, and

    (b)   in any other case, he is liable to account to the union for the value of the property applied.

(3)   If a trade union fails to bring or continue proceedings which it is entitled to bring by virtue of subsection (2), a member of the union who claims that the failure is unreasonable may apply to the court on that ground for an order authorising him to bring or continue the proceedings on the union's behalf and at the union's expense.

(4)   In this section 'penalty', in relation to an offence, includes an order to pay compensation and an order for the forfeiture of any property; and references to the imposition of a penalty for an offence shall be construed accordingly.

(5)   The Secretary of State may by order designate offences in relation to which the provisions of this section do not apply.

Any such order shall be made by statutory instrument which shall be subject to annulment in pursuance of a resolution of either House of Parliament.

(6)   This section does not affect—

    (a)   any other enactment, any rule of law or any provision of the rules of a trade union which makes it unlawful for the property of a trade union to be applied in a particular way; or

    (b)   any other remedy available to a trade union, the trustees of its property or any of its members in respect of an unlawful application of the union's property.

(7)   In this section 'member', in relation to a trade union consisting wholly or partly of, or of representatives of, constituent or affiliated organisations, includes a member of any of the constituent or affiliated organisations.

16   Remedy against trustees for unlawful use of union property

(1)   A member of a trade union who claims that the trustees of the union's property—

    (a)   have so carried out their functions, or are proposing so to carry out their functions, as to cause or permit an unlawful application of the union's property, or

    (b)   have complied, or are proposing to comply, with an unlawful direction which has been or may be given, or purportedly given, to them under the rules of the union,

may apply to the court for an order under this section.

(2)   In a case relating to property which has already been unlawfully applied, or to an unlawful direction that has already been complied with, an application under this section may be made only by a person who was a member of the union at the time when the property was applied or, as the case may be, the direction complied with.

(3)   Where the court is satisfied that the claim is well-founded, it shall make such order as it considers appropriate.

The court may in particular—

    (a)   require the trustees (if necessary, on behalf of the union) to take all such steps as may be specified in the order for protecting or recovering the property of the union;

    (b)   appoint a receiver of, or in Scotland a judicial factor on, the property of the union;

    (c)   remove one or more of the trustees.

(4)   Where the court makes an order under this section in a case in which—

    (a)   property of the union has been applied in contravention of an order of any court, or in compliance with a direction given in contravention of such an order, or

    (b)   the trustees were proposing to apply property in contravention of such an order or to comply with any such direction,

the court shall by its order remove all the trustees except any trustee who satisfies the court that there is a good reason for allowing him to remain a trustee.

(5)   Without prejudice to any other power of the court, the court may on an application for an order under this section grant such interlocutory relief (in Scotland, such interim order) as it considers appropriate.

(6)   This section does not affect any other remedy available in respect of a breach of trust by the trustees of a trade union's property.

(7)   In this section 'member', in relation to a trade union consisting wholly or partly of, or of representatives of, constituent or affiliated organisations, includes a member of any of the constituent or affiliated organisations.

Liability of trade unions in proceedings in tort

20   Liability of trade union in certain proceedings in tort

(1)   Where proceedings in tort are brought against a trade union—

    (a)   on the ground that an act—

        (i)   induces another person to break a contract or interferes or induces another person to interfere with its performance, or

        (ii)   consists in threatening that a contract (whether one to which the union is a party or not) will be broken or its performance interfered with, or that the union will induce another person to break a contract or interfere with its performance, or

    (b)   in respect of an agreement or combination by two or more persons to do or to procure the doing of an act which, if it were done without any such agreement or combination, would be actionable in tort on such a ground,

then, for the purpose of determining in those proceedings whether the union is liable in respect of the act in question, that act shall be taken to have been done by the union if, but only if, it is to be taken to have been authorised or endorsed by the trade union in accordance with the following provisions.

(2)   An act shall be taken to have been authorised or endorsed by a trade union if it was done, or was authorised or endorsed—

    (a)   by any person empowered by the rules to do, authorise or endorse acts of the kind in question, or

    (b)   by the principal executive committee or the president or general secretary, or

    (c)   by any other committee of the union or any other official of the union (whether employed by it or not).

(3)   For the purposes of paragraph (c) of subsection (2)—

    (a)   any group of persons constituted in accordance with the rules of the union is a committee of the union; and

    (b)   an act shall be taken to have been done, authorised or endorsed by an official if it was done, authorised or endorsed by, or by any member of, any group of persons of which he was at the material time a member, the purposes of which included organising or co-ordinating industrial action.

(4) The provisions of paragraphs (b) and (c) of subsection (2) apply notwithstanding anything in the rules of the union, or in any contract or rule of law, but subject to the provisions of section 21 (repudiation by union of certain acts).

(5) Where for the purposes of any proceedings an act is by virtue of this section taken to have been done by a trade union, nothing in this section shall affect the liability of any other person, in those or any other proceedings, in respect of that act.

(6) In proceedings arising out of an act which is by virtue of this section taken to have been done by a trade union, the power of the court to grant an injunction or interdict includes power to require the union to take such steps as the court considers appropriate for ensuring—

    (a) that there is no, or no further, inducement of persons to take part or to continue to take part in industrial action, and

    (b) that no person engages in any conduct after the granting of the injunction or interdict by virtue of having been induced before it was granted to take part or to continue to take part in industrial action.

The provisions of subsections (2) to (4) above apply in relation to proceedings for failure to comply with any such injunction or interdict as they apply in relation to the original proceedings.

(7) In this section 'rules', in relation to a trade union, means the written rules of the union and any other written provision forming part of the contract between a member and the other members.

21   Repudiation by union of certain acts

(1) An act shall not be taken to have been authorised or endorsed by a trade union by virtue only of paragraph (c) of section 20(2) if it was repudiated by the executive, president or general secretary as soon as reasonably practicable after coming to the knowledge of any of them.

(2) Where an act is repudiated—

    (a) written notice of the repudiation must be given to the committee or official in question, without delay, and

    (b) the union must do its best to give individual written notice of the fact and date of repudiation, without delay—

        (i) to every member of the union who the union has reason to believe is taking part, or might otherwise take part, in industrial action as a result of the act, and

        (ii) to the employer of every such member.

(3) The notice given to members in accordance with paragraph (b)(i) of subsection (2) must contain the following statement—

'Your union has repudiated the call (or calls) for industrial action to which this notice relates and will give no support to unofficial industrial action taken in response to it (or them). If you are dismissed while taking unofficial industrial action, you will have no right to complain of unfair dismissal.'

(4) If subsection (2) or (3) is not complied with, the repudiation shall be treated as ineffective.

(5) An act shall not be treated as repudiated if at any time after the union concerned purported to repudiate it the executive, president or general secretary has behaved in a manner which is inconsistent with the purported repudiation.

(6) The executive, president or general secretary shall be treated as so behaving if, on a request made to any of them within three months of the purported repudiation by a person who—

    (a) is a party to a commercial contract whose performance has been or may be interfered with as a result of the act in question, and

    (b) has not been given written notice by the union of the repudiation,

it is not forthwith confirmed in writing that the act has been repudiated.

(7) In this section 'commercial contract' means any contract other than—

    (a) a contract of employment, or

    (b) any other contract under which a person agrees personally to do work or perform services for another.

22   Limit on damages awarded against trade unions in actions in tort

(1) This section applies to any proceedings in tort brought against a trade union, except—

(a)   proceedings for personal injury as a result of negligence, nuisance or breach of duty;
(b)   proceedings for breach of duty in connection with the ownership, occupation, possession, control or use of property;
(c)   proceedings brought by virtue of Part I of the Consumer Protection Act 1987 (product liability).

(2)   In any proceedings in tort to which this section applies the amount which may be awarded against the union by way of damages shall not exceed the following limit—

Number of members of union	Maximum award of damages
Less than 5,000	£10,000
5,000 or more but less than 25,000	£50,000
25,000 or more but less than 100,000	£125,000
100,000 or more	£250,000

...

(5)   In this section—
'breach of duty' means breach of a duty imposed by any rule of law or by or under any enactment;
'personal injury' includes any disease and any impairment of a person's physical or mental condition; and
'property' means any property, whether real or personal (or in Scotland, heritable or moveable).

Restriction on enforcement against certain property

23   Restriction on enforcement of awards against certain property

(1)   Where in any proceedings an amount is awarded by way of damages, costs or expenses—
(a)   against a trade union,
(b)   against trustees in whom property is vested in trust for a trade union, in their capacity as such (and otherwise than in respect of a breach of trust on their part), or
(c)   against members or officials of a trade union on behalf of themselves and all of the members of the union,
no part of that amount is recoverable by enforcement against any protected property.

(2)   The following is protected property—
(a)   property belonging to the trustees otherwise than in their capacity as such;
(b)   property belonging to any member of the union otherwise than jointly or in common with the other members;
(c)   property belonging to an official of the union who is neither a member nor a trustee;
(d)   property comprised in the union's political fund where that fund—
(i)   is subject to rules of the union which prevent property which is or has been comprised in the fund from being used for financing strikes or other industrial action, and
(ii)   was so subject at the time when the act in respect of which the proceedings are brought was done;
(e)   property comprised in a separate fund maintained in accordance with the rules of the union for the purpose only of providing provident benefits.

(3)   For this purpose 'provident benefits' includes—
(a)   any payment expressly authorised by the rules of the union which is made—
(i)   to a member during sickness or incapacity from personal injury or while out of work, or
(ii)   to an aged member by way of superannuation, or
(iii)   to a member who has met with an accident or has lost his tools by fire or theft;
(b)   a payment in discharge or aid of funeral expenses on the death of a member or the wife of a member or as provision for the children of a deceased member.

CHAPTER III
TRADE UNION ADMINISTRATION

Register of members' names and addresses

24   Duty to maintain register of members' names and addresses

(1)   A trade union shall compile and maintain a register of the names and addresses of its members, and shall secure, so far as is reasonably practicable, that the entries in the register are accurate and are kept up-to-date.

(2)   The register may be kept by means of a computer.

(3)   A trade union shall—

(a)   allow any member, upon reasonable notice, to ascertain from the register, free of charge and at any reasonable time, whether there is an entry on it relating to him; and

(b)   if requested to do so by any member, supply him as soon as reasonably practicable, either free of charge or on payment of a reasonable fee, with a copy of any entry on the register relating to him.

(4)   ...

(5)   For the purposes of this section a member's address means either his home address or another address which he has requested the union in writing to treat as his postal address.

(6)   The remedy for failure to comply with the requirements of this section is by way of application under section 25 (to the Certification Officer) or section 26 (to the court).

24A   Securing confidentiality of register during ballots

(1)   This section applies in relation to a ballot of the members of a trade union on—

(a)   an election under Chapter IV for a position to which that Chapter applies,

(b)   a political resolution under Chapter VI, and

(c)   a resolution to approve an instrument of amalgamation or transfer under Chapter VII.

(2)   Where this section applies in relation to a ballot the trade union shall impose the duty of confidentiality in relation to the register of members' names and addresses on the scrutineer appointed by the union for the purposes of the ballot and on any person appointed by the union as the independent person for the purposes of the ballot.

(3)   The duty of confidentiality in relation to the register of members' names and addresses is, when imposed on a scrutineer or on an independent person, a duty—

(a)   not to disclose any name or address in the register except in permitted circumstances; and

(b)   to take all reasonable steps to secure that there is no disclosure of any such name or address by any other person except in permitted circumstances;

and any reference in this Act to 'the duty of confidentiality' is a reference to the duty prescribed in this subsection.

(4)   The circumstances in which disclosure of a member's name and address is permitted are—

(a)   where the member consents;

(b)   where it is requested by the Certification Officer for the purposes of the discharge of any of his functions or it is required for the purposes of the discharge of any of the functions of an inspector appointed by him;

(c)   where it is required for the purposes of the discharge of any of the functions of the scrutineer or independent person, as the case may be, under the terms of his appointment;

(d)   where it is required for the purposes of the investigation of crime or of criminal proceedings.

(5)   Any provision of this Part which incorporates the duty of confidentiality as respects the register into the appointment of a scrutineer or an independent person has the effect of imposing that duty on the scrutineer or independent person as a duty owed by him to the trade union.

(6)   The remedy for failure to comply with the requirements of this section is by way of application under section 25 (to the Certification Officer) or section 26 (to the court).

25   Remedy for failure: application to Certification Officer

(1)   A member of a trade union who claims that the union has failed to comply with any of the requirements of section 24 or 24A (duties with respect to register of members' names and addresses) may apply to the Certification Officer for a declaration to that effect.

(2)   On an application being made to him, the Certification Officer shall—

    (a)   make such enquiries as he thinks fit, and

    (b)   give the applicant and the trade union an opportunity to be heard,

and may make or refuse the declaration asked for.

(3)   If he makes a declaration he shall specify in it the provisions with which the trade union has failed to comply.

(4)   Where he makes a declaration and is satisfied that steps have been taken by the union with a view to remedying the declared failure, or securing that a failure of the same or any similar kind does not occur in future, or that the union has agreed to take such steps, he shall specify those steps in the declaration.

(5)   Whether he makes or refuses a declaration, he shall give reasons for his decision in writing; and the reasons may be accompanied by written observations on any matter arising from, or connected with, the proceedings.

(5A) Where the Certification Officer makes a declaration he shall also, unless he considers that to do so would be inappropriate, make an enforcement order, that is, an order imposing on the union one or both of the following requirements—

    (a)   to take such steps to remedy the declared failure, within such period, as may be specified in the order;

    (b)   to abstain from such acts as may be so specified with a view to securing that a failure of the same or a similar kind does not occur in future.

(5B) Where an enforcement order has been made, any person who is a member of the union and was a member at the time it was made is entitled to enforce obedience to the order as if he had made the application on which the order was made.

(6)   In exercising his functions under this section the Certification Officer shall ensure that, so far as is reasonably practicable, an application made to him is determined within six months of being made.

(7)   Where he requests a person to furnish information to him in connection with enquiries made by him under this section, he shall specify the date by which that information is to be furnished and, unless he considers that it would be inappropriate to do so, shall proceed with his determination of the application notwithstanding that the information has not been furnished to him by the specified date.

(8)   The Certification Officer shall not entertain an application for a declaration as respects an alleged failure to comply with the requirements of section 24A in relation to a ballot to which that section applies unless the application is made before the end of the period of one year beginning with the last day on which votes could be cast in the ballot.

(9)   A declaration made by the Certification Officer under this section may be relied on as if it were a declaration made by the court.

(10) An enforcement order made by the Certification Officer under this section may be enforced in the same way as an order of the court.

(11) the following paragraphs have effect in a person applies under section 26 in relation to an alleged failure—

    (a)   that person may not apply under this section in relation to that failure;

    (b)   on an application by a different person under this section in relation to that failure, the Certification Officer shall have due regard to any declaration, order, observations or reasons made or given by the court regarding that failure and brought to the Certification Officer's notice.

26   Remedy for failure: application to court

(1)   A member of a trade union who claims that the union has failed to comply with any of the requirements of section 24 or 24A (duties with respect to register of members' names and addresses) may apply to the court for a declaration to that effect.

(2) ...

(3) If the court makes a declaration it shall specify in it the provisions with which the trade union has failed to comply.

(4) Where the court makes a declaration it shall also, unless it considers that to do so would be inappropriate, make an enforcement order, that is, an order imposing on the union one or both of the following requirements—

(a) to take such steps to remedy the declared failure, within such period, as may be specified in the order;

(b) to abstain from such acts as may be so specified with a view to securing that a failure of the same or a similar kind does not occur in future.

(5) Where an enforcement order has been made, any person who is a member of the union and was a member at the time it was made, is entitled to enforce obedience to the order as if he had made the application on which the order was made.

(6) Without prejudice to any other power of the court, the court may on an application under this section grant such interlocutory relief (in Scotland, such interim order) as it considers appropriate.

(7) The court shall not entertain an application for a declaration as respects an alleged failure to comply with the requirements of section 24A in relation to a ballot to which that section applies unless the application is made before the end of the period of one year beginning with the last day on which votes could be cast in the ballot.

(8) The following paragraphs have effect if a person applies under section 25 in relation to an alleged failure—

(a) that person may not apply under this section in relation to that failure;

(b) on an application by a different person under this section in relation to that failure, the court shall have due regard to any declaration, order, observations or reasons made or given by the Certification Officer regarding that failure and brought to the court's notice.

Duty to supply copy of rules

27   Duty to supply copy of rules

A trade union shall at the request of any person supply him with a copy of its rules either free of charge or on payment of a reasonable charge.

CHAPTER IV
ELECTIONS FOR CERTAIN POSITIONS

Duty to hold elections

46   Duty to hold elections for certain positions

(1) A trade union shall secure—

(a) that every person who holds a position in the union to which this Chapter applies does so by virtue of having been elected to it at an election satisfying the requirements of this Chapter, and

(b) that no person continues to hold such a position for more than five years without being re-elected at such an election.

(2) The positions to which this Chapter applies (subject as mentioned below) are—

(a) member of the executive,

(b) any position by virtue of which a person is a member of the executive,

(c) president, and

(d) general secretary;

and the requirements referred to above are those set out in sections 47 to 52 below.

(3) In this Chapter 'member of the executive' includes any person who, under the rules or practice of the union, may attend and speak at some or all of the meetings of the executive, otherwise than for the purpose of providing the committee with factual information or with technical or professional advice with respect to matters taken into account by the executive in carrying out its functions.

(4) This Chapter does not apply to the position of president or general secretary if the holder of that position—
   (a) is not, in respect of that position, either a voting member of the executive or an employee of the union,
   (b) holds that position for a period which under the rules of the union cannot end more than 13 months after he took it up, and
   (c) has not held either position at any time in the period of twelve months ending with the day before he took up that position.

(5) A 'voting member of the executive' means a person entitled in his own right to attend meetings of the executive and to vote on matters on which votes are taken by the executive (whether or not he is entitled to attend all such meetings or to vote on all such matters or in all circumstances).

(6) The provisions of this Chapter apply notwithstanding anything in the rules or practice of the union; and the terms and conditions on which a person is employed by the union shall be disregarded in so far as they would prevent the union from complying with the provisions of this Chapter.

Requirements to be satisfied with respect to elections

47   Candidates

(1) No member of the trade union shall be unreasonably excluded from standing as a candidate.

(2) No candidate shall be required, directly or indirectly, to be a member of a political party.

(3) A member of a trade union shall not be taken to be unreasonably excluded from standing as a candidate if he is excluded on the ground that he belongs to a class of which all the members are excluded by the rules of the union.
   But a rule which provides for such a class to be determined by reference to whom the union chooses to exclude shall be disregarded.

48   Election addresses

(1) The trade union shall—
   (a) provide every candidate with an opportunity of preparing an election address in his own words and of submitting it to the union to be distributed to the persons accorded entitlement to vote in the election; and
   (b) secure that, so far as reasonably practicable, copies of every election address submitted to it in time are distributed to each of those persons by post along with the voting papers for the election.

(2) The trade union may determine the time by which an election address must be submitted to it for distribution; but the time so determined must not be earlier than the latest time at which a person may become a candidate in the election.

(3) The trade union may provide that election addresses submitted to it for distribution—
   (a) must not exceed such length, not being less than one hundred words, as may be determined by the union, and
   (b) may, as regards photographs and other matter not in words, incorporate only such matter as the union may determine.

(4) The trade union shall secure that no modification of an election address submitted to it is made by any person in any copy of the address to be distributed except—
   (a) at the request or with the consent of the candidate, or
   (b) where the modification is necessarily incidental to the method adopted for producing that copy.

(5) The trade union shall secure that the same method of producing copies is applied in the same way to every election address submitted and, so far as reasonably practicable, that no such facility or information as would enable a candidate to gain any benefit from—
   (a) the method by which copies of the election addresses are produced, or
   (b) the modifications which are necessarily incidental to that method,
   is provided to any candidate without being provided equally to all the others.

(6) The trade union shall, so far as reasonably practicable, secure that the same facilities and restrictions with respect to the preparation, submission, length or modification of an election

address, and with respect to the incorporation of photographs or other matter not in words, are provided or applied equally to each of the candidates.

(7) The arrangements made by the trade union for the production of the copies to be so distributed must be such as to secure that none of the candidates is required to bear any of the expense of producing the copies.

(8) No-one other than the candidate himself shall incur any civil or criminal liability in respect of the publication of a candidate's election address or of any copy required to be made for the purposes of this section.

49 Appointment of independent scrutineer

(1) The trade union shall, before the election is held, appoint a qualified independent person ('the scrutineer') to carry out—

    (a) the functions in relation to the election which are required under this section to be contained in his appointment; and

    (b) such additional functions in relation to the election as may be specified in his appointment.

(2) A person is a qualified independent person in relation to an election if—

    (a) he satisfies such conditions as may be specified for the purposes of this section by order of the Secretary of State or is himself so specified; and

    (b) the trade union has no grounds for believing either that he will carry out any functions conferred on him in relation to the election otherwise than competently or that his independence in relation to the union, or in relation to the election, might reasonably be called into question.

An order under paragraph (a) shall be made by statutory instrument which shall be subject to annulment in pursuance of a resolution of either House of Parliament.

(3) The scrutineer's appointment shall require him—

    (a) to be the person who supervises the production of the voting papers and (unless he is appointed under section 51A to undertake the distribution of the voting papers) their distribution and to whom the voting papers are returned by those voting;

    (aa) to—

        (i) inspect the register of names and addresses of the members of the trade union, or

        (ii) examine the copy of the register as at the relevant date which is supplied to him in accordance with subsection (5A)(a),

    whenever it appears to him appropriate to do so and, in particular, when the conditions specified in subsection (3A) are satisfied;

    (b) to take such steps as appear to him to be appropriate for the purpose of enabling him to make his report (see section 52);

    (c) to make his report to the trade union as soon as reasonably practicable after the last date for the return of voting papers; and

    (d) to retain custody of all voting papers returned for the purposes of the election and the copy of the register supplied to him in accordance with subsection (5A)(a)—

        (i) until the end of the period of one year beginning with the announcement by the union of the result of the election; and

        (ii) if within that period an application is made under section 54 (complaint of failure to comply with election requirements), until the Certification Officer or the court authorises him to dispose of the papers or copy.

...

50 Entitlement to vote

(1) Subject to the provisions of this section, entitlement to vote shall be accorded equally to all members of the trade union.

(2) The rules of the union may exclude entitlement to vote in the case of all members belonging to one of the following classes, or to a class falling within one of the following—

    (a) members who are not in employment;

    (b) members who are in arrears in respect of any subscription or contribution due to the union;

    (c)   members who are apprentices, trainees or students or new members of the union.

(3)   The rules of the union may restrict entitlement to vote to members who fall within—

    (a)   a class determined by reference to a trade or occupation,

    (b)   a class determined by reference to a geographical area, or

    (c)   a class which is by virtue of the rules of the union treated as a separate section within the union,

or to members who fall within a class determined by reference to any combination of the factors mentioned in paragraphs (a), (b) and (c).

The reference in paragraph (c) to a section of a trade union includes a part of the union which is itself a trade union.

(4)   Entitlement may not be restricted in accordance with subsection (3) if the effect is that any member of the union is denied entitlement to vote at all elections held for the purposes of this Chapter otherwise than by virtue of belonging to a class excluded in accordance with subsection (2).

51   Voting

(1)   The method of voting must be by the marking of a voting paper by the person voting.

(2)   Each voting paper must—

    (a)   state the name of the independent scrutineer and clearly specify the address to which, and the date by which, it is to be returned,

    (b)   be given one of a series of consecutive whole numbers every one of which is used in giving a different number in that series to each voting paper printed or otherwise produced for the purposes of the election, and

    (c)   be marked with its number.

(3)   Every person who is entitled to vote at the election must—

    (a)   be allowed to vote without interference from, or constraint imposed by, the union or any of its members, officials or employees, and

    (b)   so far as is reasonably practicable, be enabled to do so without incurring any direct cost to himself.

(4)   So far as is reasonably practicable, every person who is entitled to vote at the election must—

    (a)   have sent to him by post, at his home address or another address which he has requested the trade union in writing to treat as his postal address, a voting paper which either lists the candidates at the election or is accompanied by a separate list of those candidates; and

    (b)   be given a convenient opportunity to vote by post.

(5)   The ballot shall be conducted so as to secure that—

    (a)   so far as is reasonably practicable, those voting do so in secret, and

    (b)   the votes given at the election are fairly and accurately counted.

For the purposes of paragraph (b) an inaccuracy in counting shall be disregarded if it is accidental and on a scale which could not affect the result of the election.

(6)   The ballot shall be so conducted as to secure that the result of the election is determined solely by counting the number of votes cast directly for each candidate.

(7)   Nothing in subsection (6) shall be taken to prevent the system of voting used for the election being the single transferable vote, that is, a vote capable of being given so as to indicate the voter's order of preference for the candidates and of being transferred to the next choice—

    (a)   when it is not required to give a prior choice the necessary quota of votes, or

    (b)   when, owing to the deficiency in the number of votes given for a prior choice, that choice is eliminated from the list of candidates.

51A   Counting of votes etc. by independent person

(1)   The trade union shall ensure that—

    (a)   the storage and distribution of the voting papers for the purposes of the election, and

    (b)   the counting of the votes cast in the election,

are undertaken by one or more independent persons appointed by the union.

(2) A person is an independent person in relation to an election if—

    (a) he is the scrutineer, or

    (b) he is a person other than the scrutineer and the trade union has no grounds for believing either that he will carry out any functions conferred on him in relation to the election otherwise than competently or that his independence in relation to the union, or in relation to the election, might reasonably be called into question.

(3) An appointment under this section shall require the person appointed to carry out his functions so as to minimise the risk of any contravention of requirements imposed by or under any enactment or the occurrence of any unfairness or malpractice.

(4) The duty of confidentiality as respects the register is incorporated in an appointment under this section.

(5) Where the person appointed to undertake the counting of votes is not the scrutineer, his appointment shall require him to send the voting papers back to the scrutineer as soon as reasonably practicable after the counting has been completed.

(6) The trade union—

    (a) shall ensure that nothing in the terms of an appointment under this section is such as to make it reasonable for any person to call into question the independence of the person appointed in relation to the union,

    (b) shall ensure that a person appointed under this section duly carries out his functions and that there is no interference with his carrying out of those functions which would make it reasonable for any person to call into question the independence of the person appointed in relation to the union, and

    (c) shall comply with all reasonable requests made by a person appointed under this section for the purposes of, or in connection with, the carrying out of his functions.

52　Scrutineer's report

(1) The scrutineer's report on the election shall state—

    (a) the number of voting papers distributed for the purposes of the election,

    (b) the number of voting papers returned to the scrutineer,

    (c) the number of valid votes cast in the election for each candidate,

    (d) the number of spoiled or otherwise invalid voting papers returned, and

    (e) the name of the person (or of each of the persons) appointed under section 51A or, if no person was so appointed, that fact.

(2) The report shall also state whether the scrutineer is satisfied—

    (a) that there are no reasonable grounds for believing that there was any contravention of a requirement imposed by or under any enactment in relation to the election,

    (b) that the arrangements made (whether by him or any other person) with respect to the production, storage, distribution, return or other handling of the voting papers used in the election, and the arrangements for the counting of the votes, included all such security arrangements as were reasonably practicable for the purpose of minimising the risk that any unfairness or malpractice might occur, and

    (c) that he has been able to carry out his functions without such interference as would make it reasonable for any person to call his independence in relation to the union into question;

and if he is not satisfied as to any of those matters, the report shall give particulars of his reasons for not being satisfied as to that matter.

...

53　Uncontested elections

Nothing in this Chapter shall be taken to require a ballot to be held at an uncontested election.

Remedy for failure to comply with requirements

54　Remedy for failure to comply with requirements: general

(1) The remedy for a failure on the part of a trade union to comply with the requirements of this Chapter is by way of application under section 55 (to the Certification Officer) or section 56 (to the court).

(2) An application under those sections may be made—

    (a)   by a person who is a member of the trade union (provided, where the election has been held, he was also a member at the time when it was held), or

    (b)   by a person who is or was a candidate at the election; and the references in those sections to a person having a sufficient interest are to such a person.

(3) No such application may be made after the end of the period of one year beginning with the day on which the union announced the result of the election.

55   Application to Certification Officer

(1) A person having a sufficient interest (see section 54(2)) who claims that a trade union has failed to comply with any of the requirements of this Chapter may apply to the Certification Officer for a declaration to that effect.

(2) On an application being made to him, the Certification Officer shall—

    (a)   make such enquiries as he thinks fit, and

    (b)   give the applicant and the trade union an opportunity to be heard,

and may make or refuse the declaration asked for.

(3) If he makes a declaration he shall specify in it the provisions with which the trade union has failed to comply.

(4) Where he makes a declaration and is satisfied that steps have been taken by the union with a view to remedying the declared failure, or securing that a failure of the same or any similar kind does not occur in future, or that the union has agreed to take such steps, he shall specify those steps in the declaration.

(5) Whether he makes or refuses a declaration, he shall give reasons for his decision in writing; and the reasons may be accompanied by written observations on any matter arising from, or connected with, the proceedings.

(5A) Where the Certification Officer makes a declaration he shall also, unless he considers that to do so would be inappropriate, make an enforcement order, that is, an order imposing on the union one or more of the following requirements—

    (a)   to secure the holding of an election in accordance with the order;

    (b)   to take such other steps to remedy the declared failure as may be specified in the order;

    (c)   to abstain from such acts as may be so specified with a view to securing that a failure of the same or a similar kind does not occur in future.

The Certification Officer shall in an order imposing any such requirement as is mentioned in paragraph (a) or (b) specify the period within which the union is to comply with the requirements of the order.

(5B) Where the Certification Officer makes an order requiring the union to hold a fresh election, he shall (unless he considers that it would be inappropriate to do so in the particular circumstances of the case) require the election to be conducted in accordance with the requirements of this Chapter and such other provisions as may be made by the order.

(5C) Where an enforcement order has been made—

    (a)   any person who is a member of the union and was a member at the time the order was made, or

    (b)   any person who is or was a candidate in the election in question,

is entitled to enforce obedience to the order as if he had made the application on which the order was made.

(6) In exercising his functions under this section the Certification Officer shall ensure that, so far as is reasonably practicable, an application made to him is determined within six months of being made.

(7) Where he requests a person to furnish information to him in connection with enquiries made by him under this section, he shall specify the date by which that information is to be furnished and, unless he considers that it would be inappropriate to do so, shall proceed with his determination of the application notwithstanding that the information has not been furnished to him by the specified date.

(8) A declaration made by the Certification Officer under this section may be relied on as if it were a declaration made by the court.

(9)   An enforcement order made by the Certification Officer under this section may be enforced in the same way as an order of the court.

(10) the following paragraphs have effect if a person applies under section 56 in relation to an alleged failure—

(a)   that person may not apply under this section in relation to that failure;

(b)   on an application by a different person under this section in relation to that failure, the Certification Officer shall have due regard to any declaration, order, observations or reasons made or given by the court regarding that failure and brought to the Certification Officer's notice.

56   Application to court

(1)   A person having a sufficient interest (see section 54(2)) who claims that a trade union has failed to comply with any of the requirements of this Chapter may apply to the court for a declaration to that effect.

(2)   ...

(3)   If the court makes the declaration asked for, it shall specify in the declaration the provisions with which the trade union has failed to comply.

(4)   Where the court makes a declaration it shall also, unless it considers that to do so would be inappropriate, make an enforcement order, that is, an order imposing on the union one or more of the following requirements—

(a)   to secure the holding of an election in accordance with the order;

(b)   to take such other steps to remedy the declared failure as may be specified in the order;

(c)   to abstain from such acts as may be so specified with a view to securing that a failure of the same or a similar kind does not occur in future.

The court shall in an order imposing any such requirement as is mentioned in paragraph (a) or (b) specify the period within which the union is to comply with the requirements of the order.

(5)   Where the court makes an order requiring the union to hold a fresh election, the court shall (unless it considers that it would be inappropriate to do so in the particular circumstances of the case) require the election to be conducted in accordance with the requirements of this Chapter and such other provisions as may be made by the order.

(6)   Where an enforcement order has been made—

(a)   any person who is a member of the union and was a member at the time the order was made, or

(b)   any person who is or was a candidate in the election in question,

is entitled to enforce obedience to the order as if he had made the application on which the order was made.

(7)   Without prejudice to any other power of the court, the court may on an application under this section grant such interlocutory relief (in Scotland, such interim order) as it considers appropriate.

(8)   The following paragraphs have effect if a person applies under section 55 in relation to an alleged failure—

(a)   that person may not apply under this section in relation to that failure;

(b)   on an application by a different person under this section in relation to that failure, the court shall have due regard to any declaration, order, observations or reasons made or given by the Certification Officer regarding that failure and brought to the court's notice.

56A   Appeals from Certification Officer

An appeal lies to the Employment Appeal Tribunal on any question of law arising in proceedings before or arising from any decision of the Certification Officer under section 55.

CHAPTER V
RIGHTS OF TRADE UNION MEMBERS

Right to a ballot before industrial action

62   Right to a ballot before industrial action

(1)   A member of a trade union who claims that members of the union, including himself, are likely to be or have been induced by the union to take part or to continue to take part in industrial action which does not have the support of a ballot may apply to the court for an order under this section.

In this section 'the relevant time' means the time when the application is made.

(2)   For this purpose industrial action shall be regarded as having the support of a ballot only if—

    (a)   the union has held a ballot in respect of the action—

        (i)   in relation to which the requirements of section 226B so far as applicable before and during the holding of the ballot were satisfied,

        (ii)   in relation to which the requirements of sections 227 to 231 were satisfied, and

        (iii)   in which the majority voting in the ballot answered 'Yes' to the question applicable in accordance with section 229(2) to industrial action of the kind which the applicant has been or is likely to be induced to take part in;

    (b)   such of the requirements of the following sections as have fallen to be satisfied at the relevant time have been satisfied, namely—

        (i)   section 226B so far as applicable after the holding of the ballot, and

        (ii)   section 231B; and

    (c)   the requirements of section 233 (calling of industrial action with support of ballot) are satisfied.

Any reference in this subsection to a requirement of a provision which is disapplied or modified by section 232 has effect subject to that section.

(3)   Where on an application under this section the court is satisfied that the claim is well-founded, it shall make such order as it considers appropriate for requiring the union to take steps for ensuring—

    (a)   that there is no, or no further, inducement of members of the union to take part or to continue to take part in the industrial action to which the application relates, and

    (b)   that no member engages in conduct after the making of the order by virtue of having been induced before the making of the order to take part or continue to take part in the action.

(4)   Without prejudice to any other power of the court, the court may on an application under this section grant such interlocutory relief (in Scotland, such interim order) as it considers appropriate.

(5)   For the purposes of this section an act shall be taken to be done by a trade union if it is authorised or endorsed by the union; and the provisions of section 20(2) to (4) apply for the purpose of determining whether an act is to be taken to be so authorised or endorsed.

Those provisions also apply in relation to proceedings for failure to comply with an order under this section as they apply in relation to the original proceedings.

(6)   In this section—

'inducement' includes an inducement which is or would be ineffective, whether because of the member's unwillingness to be influenced by it or for any other reason; and

'industrial action' means a strike or other industrial action by persons employed under contracts of employment.

(7)   Where a person holds any office or employment under the Crown on terms which do not constitute a contract of employment between that person and the Crown, those terms shall nevertheless be deemed to constitute such a contract for the purposes of this section.

(8)   References in this section to a contract of employment include any contract under which one person personally does work or performs services for another; and related expressions shall be construed accordingly.

(9)   Nothing in this section shall be construed as requiring a trade union to hold separate ballots for the purposes of this section and sections 226 to 234 (requirement of ballot before action by trade union).

Right not to be denied access to the courts

63   Right not to be denied access to the courts

(1)   This section applies where a matter is under the rules of a trade union required or allowed to be submitted for determination or conciliation in accordance with the rules of the union, but a provision of the rules purporting to provide for that to be a person's only remedy has no effect (or would have no effect if there were one).

(2)   Notwithstanding anything in the rules of the union or in the practice of any court, if a member or former member of the union begins proceedings in a court with respect to a matter to which this section applies, then if—

(a)   he has previously made a valid application to the union for the matter to be submitted for determination or conciliation in accordance with the union's rules, and

(b)   the court proceedings are begun after the end of the period of six months beginning with the day on which the union received the application,

the rules requiring or allowing the matter to be so submitted, and the fact that any relevant steps remain to be taken under the rules, shall be regarded for all purposes as irrelevant to any question whether the court proceedings should be dismissed, stayed or sisted, or adjourned.

(3)   An application shall be deemed to be valid for the purposes of subsection (2)(a) unless the union informed the applicant, before the end of the period of 28 days beginning with the date on which the union received the application, of the respects in which the application contravened the requirements of the rules.

(4)   If the court is satisfied that any delay in the taking of relevant steps under the rules is attributable to unreasonable conduct of the person who commenced the proceedings, it may treat the period specified in subsection (2)(b) as extended by such further period as it considers appropriate.

(5)   In this section—

(a)   references to the rules of a trade union include any arbitration or other agreement entered into in pursuance of a requirement imposed by or under the rules; and

(b)   references to the relevant steps under the rules, in relation to any matter, include any steps falling to be taken in accordance with the rules for the purposes of or in connection with the determination or conciliation of the matter, or any appeal, review or reconsideration of any determination or award.

(6)   This section does not affect any enactment or rule of law by virtue of which a court would apart from this section disregard any such rules of a trade union or any such fact as is mentioned in subsection (2).

Right not to be unjustifiably disciplined

64   Right not to be unjustifiably disciplined

(1)   An individual who is or has been a member of a trade union has the right not to be unjustifiably disciplined by the union.

(2)   For this purpose an individual is 'disciplined' by a trade union if a determination is made, or purportedly made, under the rules of the union or by an official of the union or a number of persons including an official that—

(a)   he should be expelled from the union or a branch or section of the union,

(b)   he should pay a sum to the union, to a branch or section of the union or to any other person;

(c)   sums tendered by him in respect of an obligation to pay subscriptions or other sums to the union, or to a branch or section of the union, should be treated as unpaid or paid for a different purpose,

(d)   he should be deprived to any extent of, or of access to, any benefits, services or facilities which would otherwise be provided or made available to him by virtue of his membership of the union, or a branch or section of the union,

> (e)   another trade union, or a branch or section of it, should be encouraged or advised not to accept him as a member, or
>
> (f)   he should be subjected to some other detriment;
>
> and whether an individual is 'unjustifiably disciplined' shall be determined in accordance with section 65.

(3)   Where a determination made in infringement of an individual's right under this section requires the payment of a sum or the performance of an obligation, no person is entitled in any proceedings to rely on that determination for the purpose of recovering the sum or enforcing the obligation.

(4)   Subject to that, the remedies for infringement of the right conferred by this section are as provided by sections 66 and 67, and not otherwise.

(5)   The right not to be unjustifiably disciplined is in addition to (and not in substitution for) any right which exists apart from this section; and, subject to section 66(4), nothing in this section or sections 65 to 67 affects any remedy for infringement of any such right.

65   Meaning of 'unjustifiably disciplined'

(1)   An individual is unjustifiably disciplined by a trade union if the actual or supposed conduct which constitutes the reason, or one of the reasons, for disciplining him is—

> (a)   conduct to which this section applies, or
>
> (b)   something which is believed by the union to amount to such conduct;
>
> but subject to subsection (6) (cases of bad faith in relation to assertion of wrongdoing).

(2)   This section applies to conduct which consists in—

> (a)   failing to participate in or support a strike or other industrial action (whether by members of the union or by others), or indicating opposition to or a lack of support for such action;
>
> (b)   failing to contravene, for a purpose connected with such a strike or other industrial action, a requirement imposed on him by or under a contract of employment;
>
> (c)   asserting (whether by bringing proceedings or otherwise) that the union, any official or representative of it or a trustee of its property has contravened, or is proposing to contravene, a requirement which is, or is thought to be, imposed by or under the rules of the union or any other agreement or by or under any enactment (whenever passed) or any rule of law;
>
> (d)   encouraging or assisting a person—
>
>> (i)   to perform an obligation imposed on him by a contract of employment, or
>>
>> (ii)   to make or attempt to vindicate any such assertion as is mentioned in paragraph (c);
>
> (e)   contravening a requirement imposed by or in consequence of a determination which infringes the individual's or another individual's right not to be unjustifiably disciplined;
>
> (f)   failing to agree, or withdrawing agreement, to the making from his wages (in accordance with arrangements between his employer and the union) of deductions representing payments to the union in respect of his membership,
>
> (g)   resigning or proposing to resign from the union or from another union, becoming or proposing to become a member of another union, refusing to become a member of another union, or being a member of another union,
>
> (h)   working with, or proposing to work with, individuals who are not members of the union or who are or are not members of another union,
>
> (i)   working for, or proposing to work for, an employer who employs or who has employed individuals who are not members of the union or who are or are not members of another union, or
>
> (j)   requiring the union to do an act which the union is, by any provision of this Act, required to do on the requisition of a member.

(3)   This section applies to conduct which involves the Certification Officer being consulted or asked to provide advice or assistance with respect to any matter whatever, or which involves any person being consulted or asked to provide advice or assistance with respect to a matter

which forms, or might form, the subject-matter of any such assertion as is mentioned in subsection (2)(c) above.

(4) This section also applies to conduct which consists in proposing to engage in, or doing anything preparatory or incidental to, conduct falling within subsection (2) or (3).

(5) This section does not apply to an act, omission or statement comprised in conduct falling within subsection (2), (3) or (4) above if it is shown that the act, omission or statement is one in respect of which individuals would be disciplined by the union irrespective of whether their acts, omissions or statements were in connection with conduct within subsection (2) or (3) above.

(6) An individual is not unjustifiably disciplined if it is shown—

    (a) that the reason for disciplining him, or one of them, is that he made such an assertion as is mentioned in subsection (2)(c), or encouraged or assisted another person to make or attempt to vindicate such an assertion,

    (b) that the assertion was false, and

    (c) that he made the assertion, or encouraged or assisted another person to make or attempt to vindicate it, in the belief that it was false or otherwise in bad faith,

and that there was no other reason for disciplining him or that the only other reasons were reasons in respect of which he does not fall to be treated as unjustifiably disciplined.

(7) In this section—

'conduct' includes statements, acts and omissions;

'contract of employment', in relation to an individual, includes any agreement between that individual and a person for whom he works or normally works,

'employer' includes such a person and related expressions shall be construed accordingly;

'representative', in relation to a union, means a person acting or purporting to act—

    (a) in his capacity as a member of the union, or

    (b) on the instructions or advice of a person acting or purporting to act in that capacity or in the capacity of an official of the union.

'require' (on the part of an individual) includes request or apply for, and 'requisition' shall be construed accordingly; and

'wages' shall be construed in accordance with the definitions of 'contract of employment', 'employer' and related expressions.

(8) Where a person holds any office or employment under the Crown on terms which do not constitute a contract of employment between him and the Crown, those terms shall nevertheless be deemed to constitute such a contract for the purposes of this section.

66 Complaint of infringement of right

(1) An individual who claims that he has been unjustifiably disciplined by a trade union may present a complaint against the union to an employment tribunal.

(2) The tribunal shall not entertain such a complaint unless it is presented—

    (a) before the end of the period of three months beginning with the date of the making of the determination claimed to infringe the right, or

    (b) where the tribunal is satisfied—

        (i) that it was not reasonably practicable for the complaint to be presented before the end of that period, or

        (ii) that any delay in making the complaint is wholly or partly attributable to a reasonable attempt to appeal against the determination or to have it reconsidered or reviewed,

    within such further period as the tribunal considers reasonable.

(3) Where the tribunal finds the complaint well-founded, it shall make a declaration to that effect.

(4) Where a complaint relating to an expulsion which is presented under this section is declared to be well-founded, no complaint in respect of the expulsion shall be presented or proceeded with under section 174 (right not to be excluded or expelled from trade union).

67 Further remedies for infringement of right

(1) An individual whose complaint under section 66 has been declared to be well-founded may make an application to an employment tribunal for one or both of the following—

(a)   an award of compensation to be paid to him by the union;

(b)   an order that the union pay him an amount equal to any sum which he has paid in pursuance of any such determination as is mentioned in section 64(2)(b).

(2)   ...

(3)   An application under this section shall not be entertained if made before the end of the period of four weeks beginning with the date of the declaration or after the end of the period of six months beginning with that date.

(4)   ...

(5)   The amount of compensation awarded shall, subject to the following provisions, be such as the employment tribunal considers just and equitable in all the circumstances.

(6)   In determining the amount of compensation to be awarded, the same rule shall be applied concerning the duty of a person to mitigate his loss as applies to damages recoverable under the common law in England and Wales or Scotland.

(7)   Where the employment tribunal finds that the infringement complained of was to any extent caused or contributed to by the action of the applicant, it shall reduce the amount of the compensation by such proportion as it considers just and equitable having regard to that finding.

(8)   The amount of compensation calculated in accordance with subsections (5) to (7) shall not exceed the aggregate of—

(a)   an amount equal to 30 times the limit for the time being imposed by section 227(1)(a) of the Employment Rights Act 1996 (maximum amount of a week's pay for basic award in unfair dismissal cases), and

(b)   an amount equal to the limit for the time being imposed by section 124(1) of that Act (maximum compensatory award in such cases) ...

(8A) If on the date on which the application was made—

(a)   the determination infringing the applicant's right not to be unjustifiably disciplined has not been revoked, or

(b)   the union has failed to take all the steps necessary for securing the reversal of anything done for the purpose of giving effect to the determination,

the amount of compensation shall be not less than the amount for the time being specified in section 176(6A).

(9)   ...

Right not to suffer deduction of unauthorised union subscriptions

68   Right not to suffer deduction of unauthorised union subscriptions

(1)   Where arrangements ('subscription deduction arrangements') exist between the employer of a worker and a trade union relating to the making from workers' wages of deductions representing payments to the union in respect of the workers' membership of the union ('subscription deductions'), the employer shall ensure that no subscription deduction is made from wages payable to the worker on any day unless—

(a)   the worker has authorised in writing the making from his wages of subscription deductions; and

(b)   the worker has not withdrawn the authorisation.

(2)   A worker withdraws an authorisation given for the purposes of subsection (1), in relation to a subscription deduction which falls to be made from wages payable to him on any day, if a written notice withdrawing the authorisation has been received by the employer in time for it to be reasonably practicable for the employer to secure that no such deduction is made.

(3)   A worker's authorisation of the making of subscription deductions from his wages shall not give rise to any obligation on the part of the employer to the worker to maintain or continue to maintain subscription deduction arrangements.

(4)   In this section and section 68A, 'employer', 'wages' and 'worker' have the same meanings as in the Employment Rights Act 1996.

68A Complaint of infringement of rights

(1) A worker may present a complaint to an employment tribunal that his employer has made a deduction from his wages in contravention of section 68—

    (a) within the period of three months beginning with the date of the payment of the wages from which the deduction, or (if the complaint relates to more than one deduction) the last of the deductions, was made, or

    (b) where the tribunal is satisfied that it was not reasonably practicable for the complaint to be presented within that period, within such further period as the tribunal considers reasonable.

(2) Where a tribunal finds that a complaint under this section is well-founded, it shall make a declaration to that effect and shall order the employer to pay to the worker the whole amount of the deduction, less any such part of the amount as has already been paid to the worker by the employer.

(3) Where the making of a deduction from the wages of a worker both contravenes section 68(1) and involves one or more of the contraventions specified in subsection (4) of this section, the aggregate amount which may be ordered by an employment tribunal or court (whether on the same occasion or on different occasions) to be paid in respect of the contraventions shall not exceed the amount, or (where different amounts may be ordered to be paid in respect of different contraventions) the greatest amount, which may be ordered to be paid in respect of any one of them.

(4) The contraventions referred to in subsection (3) are—

    (a) a contravention of the requirement not to make a deduction without having given the particulars required by section 8 (itemised pay statements) or 9(1) (standing statements of fixed deductions) of the Employment Rights Act 1996,

    (b) a contravention of section 13 of that Act (requirement not to make unauthorised deductions), and

    (c) a contravention of section 86(1) or 90(1) of this Act (requirements not to make deductions of political fund contributions in certain circumstances).

Right to terminate membership of union

69 Right to terminate membership of union

In every contract of membership of a trade union, whether made before or after the passing of this Act, a term conferring a right on the member, on giving reasonable notice and complying with any reasonable conditions, to terminate his membership of the union shall be implied.

Supplementary

70 Membership of constituent or affiliated organisation

In this Chapter 'member', in relation to a trade union consisting wholly or partly of, or of representatives of, constituent or affiliated organisations, includes a member of any of the constituent or affiliated organisations.

CHAPTER VIIA
BREACH OF RULES

108A Right to apply to Certification Officer

(1) A person who claims that there has been a breach or threatened breach of the rules of a trade union relating to any of the matters mentioned in subsection (2) may apply to the Certification Officer for a declaration to that effect, subject to subsections (3) to (7).

(2) The matters are—

    (a) the appointment or election of a person to, or the removal of a person from, any office;

    (b) disciplinary proceedings by the union (including expulsion);

    (c) the balloting of members on any issue other than industrial action;

    (d) the constitution or proceedings of any executive committee or of any decision-making meeting;

    (e) such other matters as may be specified in an order made by the Secretary of State.

(3) The applicant must be a member of the union, or have been one at the time of the alleged breach or threatened breach.

(4) A person may not apply under subsection (1) in relation to a claim if he is entitled to apply under section 80 in relation to the claim.

(5) No application may be made regarding—
    (a)   the dismissal of an employee of the union;
    (b)   disciplinary proceedings against an employee of the union.

(6) An application must be made—
    (a)   within the period of six months starting with the day on which the breach or threatened breach is alleged to have taken place, or
    (b)   if within that period any internal complaints procedure of the union is invoked to resolve the claim, within the period of six months starting with the earlier of the days specified in subsection (7).

(7) Those days are—
    (a)   the day on which the procedure is concluded, and
    (b)   the last day of the period of one year beginning with the day on which the procedure is invoked.

(8) The reference in subsection (1) to the rules of a union includes references to the rules of any branch or section of the union.

(9) In subsection (2)(c) 'industrial action' means a strike or other industrial action by persons employed under contracts of employment.

(10) For the purposes of subsection (2)(d) a committee is an executive committee if—
    (a)   it is a committee of the union concerned and has power to make executive decisions on behalf of the union or on behalf of a constituent body,
    (b)   it is a committee of a major constituent body and has power to make executive decisions on behalf of that body, or
    (c)   it is a sub-committee of a committee falling within paragraph (a) or (b).

(11) For the purposes of subsection (2)(d) a decision-making meeting is—
    (a)   a meeting of members of the union concerned (or the representatives of such members) which has power to make a decision on any matter which, under the rules of the union, is final as regards the union or which, under the rules of the union or a constituent body, is final as regards that body, or
    (b)   a meeting of members of a major constituent body (or the representatives of such members) which has power to make a decision on any matter which, under the rules of the union or the body, is final as regards that body.

(12) For the purposes of subsections (10) and (11), in relation to the trade union concerned—
    (a)   a constituent body is any body which forms part of the union, including a branch, group, section or region;
    (b)   a major constituent body is such a body which has more than 1,000 members.

(13) Any order under subsection (2)(e) shall be made by statutory instrument; and no such order shall be made unless a draft of it has been laid before and approved by resolution of each House of Parliament.

(14) If a person applies to the Certification Officer under this section in relation to an alleged breach or threatened breach he may not apply to the court in relation to the breach or threatened breach; but nothing in this subsection shall prevent such a person from exercising any right to appeal against or challenge the Certification Officer's decision on the application to him.

(15) If—
    (a)   a person applies to the court in relation to an alleged breach or threatened breach, and
    (b)   the breach or threatened breach is one in relation to which he could have made an application to the Certification Officer under this section,
    he may not apply to the Certification Officer under this section in relation to the breach or threatened breach.

108B Declarations and orders

  (1) The Certification Officer may refuse to accept an application under section 108A unless he is satisfied that the applicant has taken all reasonable steps to resolve the claim by the use of any internal complaints procedure of the union.

  (2) If he accepts an application under section 108A the Certification Officer—
    (a) shall make such enquiries as he thinks fit,
    (b) shall give the applicant and the union an opportunity to be heard,
    (c) shall ensure that, so far as is reasonably practicable, the application is determined within six months of being made,
    (d) may make or refuse the declaration asked for, and
    (e) shall, whether he makes or refuses the declaration, give reasons for his decision in writing.

  (3) Where the Certification Officer makes a declaration he shall also, unless he considers that to do so would be inappropriate, make an enforcement order, that is, an order imposing on the union one or both of the following requirements—
    (a) to take such steps to remedy the breach, or withdraw the threat of a breach, as may be specified in the order;
    (b) to abstain from such acts as may be so specified with a view to securing that a breach or threat of the same or a similar kind does not occur in future.

  (4) The Certification Officer shall in an order imposing any such requirement as is mentioned in subsection (3)(a) specify the period within which the union is to comply with the requirement.

  (5) Where the Certification Officer requests a person to furnish information to him in connection with enquiries made by him under this section, he shall specify the date by which that information is to be furnished and, unless he considers that it would be inappropriate to do so, shall proceed with his determination of the application notwithstanding that the information has not been furnished to him by the specified date.

  (6) A declaration made by the Certification Officer under this section may be relied on as if it were a declaration made by the court.

  (7) Where an enforcement order has been made, any person who is a member of the union and was a member at the time it was made is entitled to enforce obedience to the order as if he had made the application on which the order was made.

  (8) An enforcement order made by the Certification Officer under this section may be enforced in the same way as an order of the court.

  (9) An order under section 108A(2)(e) may provide that, in relation to an application under section 108A with regard to a prescribed matter, the preceding provisions of this section shall apply with such omissions or modifications as may be specified in the order; and a prescribed matter is such matter specified under section 108A(2)(e) as is prescribed under this subsection.

108C Appeals from Certification Officer

An appeal lies to the Employment Appeal Tribunal on any question of law arising in proceedings before or arising from any decision of the Certification Officer under this Chapter.

CHAPTER IX
MISCELLANEOUS AND GENERAL PROVISIONS

Exceptions and adaptations for certain bodies

117 Special register bodies

  (1) In this section a 'special register body' means an organisation whose name appeared in the special register maintained under section 84 of the Industrial Relations Act 1971 immediately before 16 September 1974, and which is a company registered under the Companies Act 1985 or is incorporated by charter or letters patent.

  (2) The provisions of this Part apply to special register bodies as to other trade unions, subject to the following exceptions and adaptations.

  (3) In Chapter II (status and property of trade unions)—
    (a) in section 10 (quasi-corporate status of trade unions)—

             (i)   subsections (1) and (2) (prohibition on trade union being incorporated) do not apply, and

             (ii)   subsection (3) (prohibition on registration under certain Acts) does not apply so far as it relates to registration as a company under the Companies Act 1985;

     (b)   section 11 (exclusion of common law rules as to restraint of trade) applies to the purposes or rules of a special register body only so far as they relate to the regulation of relations between employers or employers' associations and workers;

     (c)   sections 12 to 14 (vesting of property in trustees; transfer of securities) do not apply; and

     (d)   in section 20 (liability of trade union in certain proceedings in tort) in subsection (7) the reference to the contract between a member and the other members shall be construed as a reference to the contract between a member and the body.

(4)   Sections 33 to 35 (appointment and removal of auditors) do not apply to a special register body which is registered as a company under the Companies Act 1985; and sections 36 and 37 (rights and duties of auditors) apply to the auditors appointed by such a body under Chapter V of Part XI of that Act or Chapter 2 of Part 16 of the Companies Act 2006.

(5)   Sections 45B and 45C (disqualification) and Chapter IV (elections) apply only to—

     (a)   the position of voting member of the executive, and

     (b)   any position by virtue of which a person is a voting member of the executive. In this subsection 'voting member of the executive' has the meaning given by section 46(5).

118   Federated trade unions

(1)   In this section a 'federated trade union' means a trade union which consists wholly or mainly of constituent or affiliated organisations, or representatives of such organisations, as described in paragraph (b) of the definition of 'trade union' in section 1.

(2)   The provisions of this Part apply to federated trade unions subject to the following exceptions and adaptations.

(3)   For the purposes of section 22 (limit on amount of damages) as it applies to a federated trade union, the members of such of its constituent or affiliated organisations as have their head or main office in Great Britain shall be treated as members of the union.

(4)   The following provisions of Chapter III (trade union administration) do not apply to a federated trade union which consists wholly or mainly of representatives of constituent or affiliated organisations—

     (a)   section 27 (duty to supply copy of rules),

     (b)   section 28 (duty to keep accounting records),

     (c)   sections 32 to 37 (annual return, statement for members, accounts and audit),

     (ca)   sections 37A to 37E (investigation of financial affairs), and

     (d)   sections 38 to 42 (members' superannuation schemes).

(5)   Sections 29 to 31 (right of member to access to accounting records) do not apply to a federated trade union which has no members other than constituent or affiliated organisations or representatives of such organisations.

(6)   Sections 24 to 26 (register of members' names and addresses) and Chapter IV (elections for certain trade union positions) do not apply to a federated trade union—

     (a)   if it has no individual members other than representatives of constituent or affiliated organisations, or

     (b)   if its individual members (other than such representatives) are all merchant seamen and a majority of them are ordinarily resident outside the United Kingdom. For this purpose 'merchant seaman' means a person whose employment, or the greater part of it, is carried out on board sea-going ships.

(7)   The provisions of Chapter VI (application of funds for political objects) apply to a trade union which is in whole or part an association or combination of other unions as if the individual members of the component unions were members of that union and not of the component unions.

But nothing in that Chapter prevents a component union from collecting contributions on behalf of the association or combination from such of its members as are not exempt from the obligation to contribute to the political fund of the association or combination.

Interpretation

119   Expressions relating to trade unions

In this Act, in relation to a trade union—

'agent' means a banker or solicitor of, or any person employed as an auditor by, the union or any branch or section of the union;

'branch or section', except where the context otherwise requires, includes a branch or section which is itself a trade union;

'executive' means the principal committee of the union exercising executive functions, by whatever name it is called;

'financial affairs' means affairs of the union relating to any fund which is applicable for the purposes of the union (including any fund of a branch or section of the union which is so applicable);

'general secretary' means the official of the union who holds the office of general secretary or, where there is no such office, holds an office which is equivalent, or (except in section 14(4)) the nearest equivalent, to that of general secretary;

'officer' includes—

(a)   any member of the governing body of the union, and

(b)   any trustee of any fund applicable for the purposes of the union;

'official' means—

(a)   an officer of the union or of a branch or section of the union, or

(b)   a person elected or appointed in accordance with the rules of the union to be a representative of its members or of some of them,

and includes a person so elected or appointed who is an employee of the same employer as the members or one or more of the members whom he is to represent;

'president' means the official of the union who holds the office of president or, where there is no such office, who holds an office which is equivalent, or (except in section 14(4) or Chapter IV) the nearest equivalent, to that of president; and

'rules', except where the context otherwise requires, includes the rules of any branch or section of the union.

120   Northern Ireland unions

In this Part a 'Northern Ireland union' means a trade union whose principal office is situated in Northern Ireland.

121   Meaning of 'the court'

In this Part 'the court' (except where the reference is expressed to be to the county court or sheriff court) means the High Court or the Court of Session.

PART II

EMPLOYERS' ASSOCIATIONS

Introductory

122   Meaning of 'employers' association'

(1)   In this Act an 'employers' association' means an organisation (whether temporary or permanent)—

(a)   which consists wholly or mainly of employers or individual owners of undertakings of one or more descriptions and whose principal purposes include the regulation of relations between employers of that description or those descriptions and workers or trade unions; or

(b)   which consists wholly or mainly of—

(i)   constituent or affiliated organisations which fulfil the conditions in paragraph (a) (or themselves consist wholly or mainly of constituent or affiliated organisations which fulfil those conditions), or

(ii)   representatives of such constituent or affiliated organisations, and whose principal purposes include the regulation of relations between employers and workers or between employers and trade unions, or the regulation of relations between its constituent or affiliated organisations.

(2) References in this Act to employers' associations include combinations of employers and employers' associations.

PART III
RIGHTS IN RELATION TO UNION MEMBERSHIP AND ACTIVITIES

Access to employment

137 Refusal of employment on grounds related to union membership

(1) It is unlawful to refuse a person employment—
  (a) because he is, or is not, a member of a trade union, or
  (b) because he is unwilling to accept a requirement—
    (i) to take steps to become or cease to be, or to remain or not to become, a member of a trade union, or
    (ii) to make payments or suffer deductions in the event of his not being a member of a trade union.

(2) A person who is thus unlawfully refused employment has a right of complaint to an employment tribunal.

(3) Where an advertisement is published which indicates, or might reasonably be understood as indicating—
  (a) that employment to which the advertisement relates is open only to a person who is, or is not, a member of a trade union, or
  (b) that any such requirement as is mentioned in subsection (1)(b) will be imposed in relation to employment to which the advertisement relates,
  a person who does not satisfy that condition or, as the case may be, is unwilling to accept that requirement, and who seeks and is refused employment to which the advertisement relates, shall be conclusively presumed to have been refused employment for that reason.

(4) Where there is an arrangement or practice under which employment is offered only to persons put forward or approved by a trade union, and the trade union puts forward or approves only persons who are members of the union, a person who is not a member of the union and who is refused employment in pursuance of the arrangement or practice shall be taken to have been refused employment because he is not a member of the trade union.

(5) A person shall be taken to be refused employment if he seeks employment of any description with a person and that person—
  (a) refuses or deliberately omits to entertain and process his application or enquiry, or
  (b) causes him to withdraw or cease to pursue his application or enquiry, or
  (c) refuses or deliberately omits to offer him employment of that description, or
  (d) makes him an offer of such employment the terms of which are such as no reasonable employer who wished to fill the post would offer and which is not accepted, or
  (e) makes him an offer of such employment but withdraws it or causes him not to accept it.

(6) Where a person is offered employment on terms which include a requirement that he is, or is not, a member of a trade union, or any such requirement as is mentioned in subsection (1)(b), and he does not accept the offer because he does not satisfy or, as the case may be, is unwilling to accept the requirement, he shall be treated as having been refused employment for that reason.

(7) Where a person may not be considered for appointment or election to an office in a trade union unless he is a member of the union, or of a particular branch or section of the union or of one of a number of particular branches or sections of the union, nothing in this section applies to anything done for the purpose of securing compliance with that condition although as holder of the office he would be employed by the union.
  For this purpose an 'office' means any position—
  (a) by virtue of which the holder is an official of the union, or
  (b) to which Chapter IV of Part I applies (duty to hold elections).

(8)   The provisions of this section apply in relation to an employment agency acting, or purporting to act, on behalf of an employer as in relation to an employer.

138   Refusal of service of employment agency on grounds related to union membership

(1)   It is unlawful for an employment agency to refuse a person any of its services—

    (a)   because he is, or is not, a member of a trade union, or

    (b)   because he is unwilling to accept a requirement to take steps to become or cease to be, or to remain or not to become, a member of a trade union.

(2)   A person who is thus unlawfully refused any service of an employment agency has a right of complaint to an employment tribunal.

(3)   Where an advertisement is published which indicates, or might reasonably be understood as indicating—

    (a)   that any service of an employment agency is available only to a person who is, or is not, a member of a trade union, or

    (b)   that any such requirement as is mentioned in subsection (1)(b) will be imposed in relation to a service to which the advertisement relates,

a person who does not satisfy that condition or, as the case may be, is unwilling to accept that requirement, and who seeks to avail himself of and is refused that service, shall be conclusively presumed to have been refused it for that reason.

(4)   A person shall be taken to be refused a service if he seeks to avail himself of it and the agency—

    (a)   refuses or deliberately omits to make the service available to him, or

    (b)   causes him not to avail himself of the service or to cease to avail himself of it, or

    (c)   does not provide the same service, on the same terms, as is provided to others.

(5)   Where a person is offered a service on terms which include a requirement that he is, or is not, a member of a trade union, or any such requirement as is mentioned in subsection (1)(b), and he does not accept the offer because he does not satisfy or, as the case may be, is unwilling to accept that requirement, he shall be treated as having been refused the service for that reason.

139   Time limit for proceedings

(1)   An employment tribunal shall not consider a complaint under section 137 or 138 unless it is presented to the tribunal—

    (a)   before the end of the period of three months beginning with the date of the conduct to which the complaint relates, or

    (b)   where the tribunal is satisfied that it was not reasonably practicable for the complaint to be presented before the end of that period, within such further period as the tribunal considers reasonable.

(2)   The date of the conduct to which a complaint under section 137 relates shall be taken to be—

    (a)   in the case of an actual refusal, the date of the refusal;

    (b)   in the case of a deliberate omission—

        (i)   to entertain and process the complainant's application or enquiry, or

        (ii)   to offer employment,

the end of the period within which it was reasonable to except the employer to act;

    (c)   in the case of conduct causing the complainant to withdraw or cease to pursue his application or enquiry, the date of that conduct;

    (d)   in a case where an offer was made but withdrawn, the date when it was withdrawn;

    (e)   in any other case where an offer was made but not accepted, the date on which it was made.

(3)   The date of the conduct to which a complaint under section 138 relates shall be taken to be—

    (a)   in the case of an actual refusal, the date of the refusal;

    (b)   in the case of a deliberate omission to make a service available, the end of the period within which it was reasonable to expect the employment agency to act;

    (c)   in the case of conduct causing the complainant not to avail himself of a service or to cease to avail himself of it, the date of that conduct;

    (d)   in the case of failure to provide the same service, on the same terms, as is provided to others, the date or last date on which the service in fact provided was provided.

140   Remedies

(1)   Where the employment tribunal finds that a complaint under section 137 or 138 is well-founded, it shall make a declaration to that effect and may make such of the following as it considers just and equitable—

   (a)   an order requiring the respondent to pay compensation to the complainant of such amount as the tribunal may determine;

   (b)   a recommendation that the respondent take within a specified period action appearing to the tribunal to be practicable for the purpose of obviating or reducing the adverse effect on the complainant of any conduct to which the complaint relates.

(2)   Compensation shall be assessed on the same basis as damages for breach of statutory duty and may include compensation for injury to feelings.

(3)   If the respondent fails without reasonable justification to comply with a recommendation to take action, the tribunal may increase its award of compensation or, if it has not made such an award, make one.

(4)   The total amount of compensation shall not exceed the limit for the time being imposed by section 124(1) of the Employment Rights Act 1996 (limit on compensation for unfair dismissal).

141   Complaint against employer and employment agency

(1)   Where a person has a right of complaint against a prospective employer and against an employment agency arising out of the same facts, he may present a complaint against either of them or against them jointly.

(2)   If a complaint is brought against one only, he or the complainant may request the tribunal to join or sist the other as a party to the proceedings.

The request shall be granted if it is made before the hearing of the complaint begins, but may be refused if it is made after that time; and no such request may be made after the tribunal has made its decision as to whether the complaint is well-founded.

(3)   Where a complaint is brought against an employer and an employment agency jointly, or where it is brought against one and the other is joined or sisted as a party to the proceedings, and the tribunal—

   (a)   finds that the complaint is well-founded as against the employer and the agency, and

   (b)   makes an award of compensation,

it may order that the compensation shall be paid by the one or the other, or partly by one and partly by the other, as the tribunal may consider just and equitable in the circumstances.

142   Awards against third parties

(1)   If in proceedings on a complaint under section 137 or 138 either the complainant or the respondent claims that the respondent was induced to act in the manner complained of by pressure which a trade union or other person exercised on him by calling, organising, procuring or financing a strike or other industrial action, or by threatening to do so, the complainant or the respondent may request the employment tribunal to direct that the person who he claims exercised the pressure be joined or sisted as a party to the proceedings.

(2)   The request shall be granted if it is made before the hearing of the complaint begins, but may be refused if it is made after that time; and no such request may be made after the tribunal has made its decision as to whether the complaint is well-founded.

(3)   Where a person has been so joined or sisted as a party to the proceedings and the tribunal—

   (a)   finds that the complaint is well-founded,

   (b)   makes an award of compensation, and

   (c)   also finds that the claim in subsection (1) above is well-founded,

it may order that the compensation shall be paid by the person joined instead of by the respondent, or partly by that person and partly by the respondent, as the tribunal may consider just and equitable in the circumstances.

(4)   Where by virtue of section 141 (complaint against employer and employment agency) there is more than one respondent, the above provisions apply to either or both of them.

143   Interpretation and other supplementary provisions

(1)   In sections 137 to 143—

'advertisement' includes every form of advertisement or notice, whether to the public or not, and references to publishing an advertisement shall be construed accordingly;

'employment' means employment under a contract of employment, and related expressions shall be construed accordingly; and

'employment agency' means a person who, for profit or not, provides services for the purpose of finding employment for workers or supplying employers with workers, but subject to subsection (2) below.

(2)   For the purposes of sections 137 to 143 as they apply to employment agencies—

(a)   services other than those mentioned in the definition of 'employment agency' above shall be disregarded, and

(b)   a trade union shall not be regarded as an employment agency by reason of services provided by it only for, or in relation to, its members.

(3)   References in sections 137 to 143 to being or not being a member of a trade union are to being or not being a member of any trade union, of a particular trade union or of one of a number of particular trade unions.

Any such reference includes a reference to being or not being a member of a particular branch or section of a trade union or of one of a number of particular branches or sections of a trade union.

(4)   The remedy of a person for conduct which is unlawful by virtue of section 137 or 138 is by way of a complaint to an employment tribunal in accordance with this Part, and not otherwise. No other legal liability arises by reason that conduct is unlawful by virtue of either of those sections.

Detriment

146   Detriment on grounds related to union membership or activities

(1)   A worker has the right not to be subjected to any detriment as an individual by any act, or any deliberate failure to act, by his employer if the act or failure takes place for the sole or main purpose of—

(a)   preventing or deterring him from being or seeking to become a member of an independent trade union, or penalising him for doing so,

(b)   preventing or deterring him from taking part in the activities of an independent trade union at an appropriate time, or penalising him for doing so,

(ba)   preventing or deterring him from making use of trade union services at an appropriate time, or penalising him for doing so, or

(c)   compelling him to be or become a member of any trade union or of a particular trade union or of one of a number of particular trade unions.

(2)   In subsection (1) 'an appropriate time' means—

(a)   a time outside the worker's working hours, or

(b)   a time within his working hours at which, in accordance with arrangements agreed with or consent given by his employer, it is permissible for him to take part in the activities of a trade union or (as the case may be) make use of trade union services;

and for this purpose 'working hours', in relation to a worker, means any time when, in accordance with his contract of employment (or other contract personally to do work or perform services), he is required to be at work.

(2A) In this section—

(a)   'trade union services' means services made available to the worker by an independent trade union by virtue of his membership of the union, and

(b)   references to a worker's 'making use' of trade union services include his consenting to the raising of a matter on his behalf by an independent trade union of which he is a member.

(2B) If an independent trade union of which a worker is a member raises a matter on his behalf (with or without his consent), penalising the worker for that is to be treated as penalising him as mentioned in subsection (1)(ba).

(2C) A worker also has the right not to be subjected to any detriment as an individual by any act, or any deliberate failure to act, by his employer if the act or failure takes place because of the worker's failure to accept an offer made in contravention of section 145A or 145B.

(2D) For the purposes of subsection (2C), not conferring a benefit that, if the offer had been accepted by the worker, would have been conferred on him under the resulting agreement shall be taken to be subjecting him to a detriment as an individual (and to be a deliberate failure to act).

(3) A worker also has the right not to be subjected to any detriment as an individual by any act, or any deliberate failure to act, by his employer if the act or failure takes place for the sole or main purpose of enforcing a requirement (whether or not imposed by a contract of employment or in writing) that, in the event of his not being a member of any trade union or of a particular trade union or of one of a number of particular trade unions, he must make one or more payments.

(4) For the purposes of subsection (3) any deduction made by an employer from the remuneration payable to a worker in respect of his employment shall, if it is attributable to his not being a member of any trade union or of a particular trade union or of one of a number of particular trade unions, be treated as a detriment to which he has been subjected as an individual by an act of his employer taking place for the sole or main purpose of enforcing a requirement of a kind mentioned in that subsection.

(5) A worker or former worker may present a complaint to an employment tribunal on the ground that he has been subjected to a detriment by his employer in contravention of this section.

(5A) This section does not apply where—
(a)   the worker is an employee; and
(b)   the detriment in question amounts to dismissal.

147   Time limit for proceedings

(1) An employment tribunal shall not consider a complaint under section 146 unless it is presented—
(a)   before the end of the period of three months beginning with the date of the act or failure to which the complaint relates or, where that act or failure is part of a series of similar acts or failures (or both) the last of them, or
(b)   where the tribunal is satisfied that it was not reasonably practicable for the complaint to be presented before the end of that period, within such further period as it considers reasonable.

(2) For the purposes of subsection (1)—
(a)   where an act extends over a period, the reference to the date of the act is a reference to the last day of that period;
(b)   a failure to act shall be treated as done when it was decided on.

(3) For the purposes of subsection (2), in the absence of evidence establishing the contrary an employer shall be taken to decide on a failure to act—
(a)   when he does an act inconsistent with doing the failed act, or
(b)   if he has done no such inconsistent act, when the period expires within which he might reasonably have been expected to do the failed act if it was to be done.

148   Consideration of complaint

(1) On a complaint under section 146 it shall be for the employer to show the purpose for which he acted or failed to act.

(2) In determining any question whether the employer acted or failed to act, or the purpose for which he did so, no account shall be taken of any pressure which was exercised on him by calling, organising, procuring or financing a strike or other industrial action, or by threatening to do so; and that question shall be determined as if no such pressure had been exercised.

(3) In determining what was the purpose for which the employer acted or failed to act in a case where—
(a)   there is evidence that the employer's purpose was to further a change in his relationship with all or any class of his employees, and
(b)   there is also evidence that his purpose was one falling within section 146,

the tribunal shall regard the purpose mentioned in paragraph (a) (and not the purpose mentioned in paragraph (b)) as the purpose for which the employer acted or failed to act, unless it considers that no reasonable employer would act or fail to act in the way concerned having regard to the purpose mentioned in paragraph (a).

(4) Where the tribunal determines that—

    (a) the complainant has been subjected to a detriment by an act or deliberate failure to act by his employer, and

    (b) the act or failure took place in consequence of a previous act or deliberate failure to act by the employer,

paragraph (a) of subsection (3) is satisfied if the purpose mentioned in that paragraph was the purpose of the previous act or failure.

(5) In subsection (3) 'class', in relation to an employer and his employees, means those employed at a particular place of work, those employees of a particular grade, category or description or those of a particular grade, category or description employed at a particular place of work.

149   Remedies

(1) Where the employment tribunal finds that a complaint under section 146 is well-founded, it shall make a declaration to that effect and may make an award of compensation to be paid by the employer to the complainant in respect of the act or failure complained of.

(2) The amount of the compensation awarded shall be such as the tribunal considers just and equitable in all the circumstances having regard to the infringement complained of and to any loss sustained by the complainant which is attributable to the act or failure which infringed his right.

(3) The loss shall be taken to include—

    (a) any expenses reasonably incurred by the complainant in consequence of the act or failure complained of, and

    (b) loss of any benefit which he might reasonably be expected to have had but for that act or failure.

(4) In ascertaining the loss, the tribunal shall apply the same rule concerning the duty of a person to mitigate his loss as applies to damages recoverable under the common law of England and Wales or Scotland.

(5) In determining the amount of compensation to be awarded no account shall be taken of any pressure which was exercised on the employer by calling, organising, procuring or financing a strike or other industrial action, or by threatening to do so; and that question shall be determined as if no such pressure had been exercised.

(6) Where the tribunal finds that the act or failure complained of was to any extent caused or contributed to by action of the complainant, it shall reduce the amount of the compensation by such proportion as it considers just and equitable having regard to that finding.

150   Awards against third parties

(1) If in proceedings on a complaint under section 146—

    (a) the complaint is made on the ground that the complainant has been subjected to detriment by an act or failure by his employer taking place for the purpose of compelling him to be or become a member of any trade union or of a particular trade union or of one of a number of particular trade unions, and

    (b) either the complainant or the employer claims in proceedings before the tribunal that the employer was induced to act or fail to act in the way complained of by pressure which a trade union or other person exercised on him by calling, organising, procuring or financing a strike or other industrial action, or by threatening to do so,

the complainant or the employer may request the tribunal to direct that the person who he claims exercised the pressure be joined or sisted as a party to the proceedings.

(2) The request shall be granted if it is made before the hearing of the complaint begins, but may be refused if it is made after that time; and no such request may be made after the tribunal has made a declaration that the complaint is well-founded.

(3) Where a person has been so joined or sisted as a party to proceedings and the tribunal—

    (a)   makes an award of compensation, and

    (b)   finds that the claim mentioned in subsection (1)(b) is well-founded,

it may order that the compensation shall be paid by the person joined instead of by the employer, or partly by that person and partly by the employer, as the tribunal may consider just and equitable in the circumstances.

151   Interpretation and other supplementary provisions

(1) References in sections 146 to 150 to being, becoming or ceasing to remain a member of a trade union include references to being, becoming or ceasing to remain a member of a particular branch or section of that union and to being, becoming or ceasing to remain a member of one of a number of particular branches or sections of that union; and references to taking part in the activities of a trade union shall be similarly construed.

(2) The remedy of an employee for infringement of the right conferred on him by section 146 is by way of a complaint to an employment tribunal in accordance with this Part, and not otherwise.

Dismissal

152   Dismissal of employee on grounds related to union membership or activities

(1) For purposes of Part X of the Employment Rights Act 1996 (unfair dismissal) the dismissal of an employee shall be regarded as unfair if the reason for it (or, if more than one, the principal reason) was that the employee—

    (a)   was, or proposed to become, a member of an independent trade union,

    (b)   had taken part, or proposed to take part, in the activities of an independent trade union at an appropriate time,

    (ba)   had made use, or proposed to make use, of trade union services at an appropriate time,

    (bb)   had failed to accept an offer made in contravention of section 145A or 145B, or

    (c)   was not a member of any trade union, or of a particular trade union, or of one of a number of particular trade unions, or had refused, or proposed to refuse, to become or remain a member.

(2) In subsection (1) 'an appropriate time' means—

    (a)   a time outside the employee's working hours, or

    (b)   a time within his working hours at which, in accordance with arrangements agreed with or consent given by his employer, it is permissible for him to take part in the activities of a trade union or (as the case may be) make use of trade union services;

and for this purpose 'working hours', in relation to an employee, means any time when, in accordance with his contract of employment, he is required to be at work.

(2A) In this section—

    (a)   'trade union services' means services made available to the employee by an independent trade union by virtue of his membership of the union, and

    (b)   references to an employee's 'making use' of trade union services include his consenting to the raising of a matter on his behalf by an independent trade union of which he is a member.

(2B) Where the reason or one of the reasons for the dismissal was that an independent trade union (with or without the employee's consent) raised a matter on behalf of the employee as one of its members, the reason shall be treated as falling within subsection (1)(ba).

(3) Where the reason, or one of the reasons, for the dismissal was—

    (a)   the employee's refusal, or proposed refusal, to comply with a requirement (whether or not imposed by his contract of employment or in writing) that, in the event of his not being a member of any trade union, or of a particular trade union, or of one of a number of particular trade unions, he must make one or more payments, or

    (b)   his objection, or proposed objection, (however expressed) to the operation of a provision (whether or not forming part of his contract of employment or in writing) under which, in the event mentioned in paragraph (a), his employer is entitled to deduct one or more sums from the remuneration payable to him in respect of his employment, the reason shall be treated as falling within subsection (1)(c).

(4) References in this section to being, becoming or ceasing to remain a member of a trade union include references to being, becoming or ceasing to remain a member of a particular branch or section of that union or of one of a number of particular branches or sections of that trade union...

(5) References in this section—

    (a)   to taking part in the activities of a trade union, and

    (b)   to services made available by a trade union by virtue of membership of the union,

    shall be construed in accordance with subsection (4).

153 Selection for redundancy on grounds related to union membership or activities

Where the reason or principal reason for the dismissal of an employee was that he was redundant, but it is shown—

    (a)   that the circumstances constituting the redundancy applied equally to one or more other employees in the same undertaking who held positions similar to that held by him and who have not been dismissed by the employer, and

    (b)   that the reason (or, if more than one, the principal reason) why he was selected for dismissal was one of those specified in section 152(1),

the dismissal shall be regarded as unfair for the purposes of Part X of the Employment Rights Act 1996 (unfair dismissal).

154 Disapplication of qualifying period and upper age limit for unfair dismissal

Sections 108(1) and 109(1) of the Employment Rights Act 1996 (qualifying period and upper age limit for unfair dismissal protection) do not apply to a dismissal which by virtue of section 152 or 153 is regarded as unfair for the purposes of Part 10 of that Act.

155 Matters to be disregarded in assessing contributory fault

(1) Where an employment tribunal makes an award of compensation for unfair dismissal in a case where the dismissal is unfair by virtue of section 152 or 153, the tribunal shall disregard, in considering whether it would be just and equitable to reduce, or further reduce, the amount of any part of the award, any such conduct or action of the complainant as is specified below.

(2) Conduct or action of the complainant shall be disregarded in so far as it constitutes a breach or proposed breach of a requirement—

    (a)   to be or become a member of any trade union or of a particular trade union or of one of a number of particular trade unions,

    (b)   to cease to be, or refrain from becoming, a member of any trade union or of a particular trade union or of one of a number of particular trade unions, or

    (c)   not to take part in the activities of any trade union or of a particular trade union or of one of a number of particular trade unions.

For the purposes of this subsection a requirement means a requirement imposed on the complainant by or under an arrangement or contract of employment or other agreement.

(3) Conduct or action of the complainant shall be disregarded in so far as it constitutes a refusal, or proposed refusal, to comply with a requirement of a kind mentioned in section 152(3)(a) (payments in lieu of membership) or an objection, or proposed objection, (however expressed) to the operation of a provision of a kind mentioned in section 152(3)(b) (deductions in lieu of membership).

156 Minimum basic award

(1) Where a dismissal is unfair by virtue of section 152(1) or 153, the amount of the basic award of compensation, before any reduction is made under section 122 of the Employment Rights Act 1996 shall be not less than £4,400.

(2) But where the dismissal is unfair by virtue of section 153, subsection (2) of that section (reduction for contributory fault) applies in relation to so much of the basic award as is payable because of subsection (1) above.

160   Awards against third parties

(1)   If in proceedings before an employment tribunal on a complaint of unfair dismissal either the employer or the complainant claims—

  (a)   that the employer was induced to dismiss the complainant by pressure which a trade union or other person exercised on the employer by calling, organising, procuring or financing a strike or other industrial action, or by threatening to do so, and

  (b)   that the pressure was exercised because the complainant was not a member of any trade union or of a particular trade union or of one of a number of particular trade unions,

  the employer or the complainant may request the tribunal to direct that the person who he claims exercised the pressure be joined or sisted as a party to the proceedings.

(2)   The request shall be granted if it is made before the hearing of the complaint begins, but may be refused after that time; and no such request may be made after the tribunal has made an award of compensation for unfair dismissal or an order for reinstatement or re-engagement.

(3)   Where a person has been so joined or sisted as a party to the proceedings and the tribunal—

  (a)   makes an award of compensation for unfair dismissal, and

  (b)   finds that the claim mentioned in subsection (1) is well-founded,

  the tribunal may order that the compensation shall be paid by that person instead of the employer, or partly by that person and partly by the employer, as the tribunal may consider just and equitable.

161   Application for interim relief

(1)   An employee who presents a complaint of unfair dismissal alleging that the dismissal is unfair by virtue of section 152 may apply to the tribunal for interim relief.

(2)   The tribunal shall not entertain an application for interim relief unless it is presented to the tribunal before the end of the period of seven days immediately following the effective date of termination (whether before, on or after that date).

(3)   In a case where the employee relies on section 152(1)(a) or (b) the tribunal shall not entertain an application for interim relief unless before the end of that period there is also so presented a certificate in writing signed by an authorised official of the independent trade union of which the employee was or proposed to become a member stating—

  (a)   that on the date of the dismissal the employee was or proposed to become a member of the union, and

  (b)   that there appear to be reasonable grounds for supposing that the reason for his dismissal (or, if more than one, the principal reason) was one alleged in the complaint.

(4)   An 'authorised official' means an official of the trade union authorised by it to act for the purposes of this section.

(5)   A document purporting to be an authorisation of an official by a trade union to act for the purposes of this section and to be signed on behalf of the union shall be taken to be such an authorisation unless the contrary is proved; and a document purporting to be a certificate signed by such an official shall be taken to be signed by him unless the contrary is proved.

(6)   For the purposes of subsection (3) the date of dismissal shall be taken to be—

  (a)   where the employee's contract of employment was terminated by notice (whether given by his employer or by him), the date on which the employer's notice was given, and

  (b)   in any other case, the effective date of termination.

162   Application to be promptly determined

(1)   An employment tribunal shall determine an application for interim relief as soon as practicable after receiving the application and, where appropriate, the requisite certificate.

(2)   The tribunal shall give to the employer, not later than seven days before the hearing, a copy of the application and of any certificate, together with notice of the date, time and place of the hearing.

(3)   If a request under section 160 (awards against third parties) is made three days or more before the date of the hearing, the tribunal shall also give to the person to whom the request relates, as soon as reasonably practicable, a copy of the application and of any certificate, together with notice of the date, time and place of the hearing.

(4)   The tribunal shall not exercise any power it has of postponing the hearing of an application for interim relief except where it is satisfied that special circumstances exist which justify it in doing so.

163   Procedure on hearing of application and making of order

(1)   If on hearing an application for interim relief it appears to the tribunal that it is likely that on determining the complaint to which the application relates that it will find that, by virtue of section 152, the complainant has been unfairly dismissed, the following provisions apply.

(2)   The tribunal shall announce its findings and explain to both parties (if present) what powers the tribunal may exercise on the application and in what circumstances it will exercise them, and shall ask the employer (if present) whether he is willing, pending the determination or settlement of the complaint—

(a)   to reinstate the employee, that is to say, to treat him in all respects as if he had not been dismissed, or

(b)   if not, to re-engage him in another job on terms and conditions not less favourable than those which would have been applicable to him if he had not been dismissed.

(3)   For this purpose 'terms and conditions not less favourable than those which would have been applicable to him if he had not been dismissed' means as regards seniority, pension rights and other similar rights that the period prior to the dismissal shall be regarded as continuous with his employment following the dismissal.

(4)   If the employer states that he is willing to reinstate the employee, the tribunal shall make an order to that effect.

(5)   If the employer states that he is willing to re-engage the employee in another job, and specifies the terms and conditions on which he is willing to do so, the tribunal shall ask the employee whether he is willing to accept the job on those terms and conditions; and—

(a)   if the employee is willing to accept the job on those terms and conditions, the tribunal shall make an order to that effect, and

(b)   if he is not, then, if the tribunal is of the opinion that the refusal is reasonable, the tribunal shall make an order for the continuation of his contract of employment, and otherwise the tribunal shall make no order.

(6)   If on the hearing of an application for interim relief the employer fails to attend before the tribunal, or states that he is unwilling either to reinstate the employee or re-engage him as mentioned in subsection (2), the tribunal shall make an order for the continuation of the employee's contract of employment.

164   Order for continuation of contract of employment

(1)   An order under section 163 for the continuation of a contract of employment is an order that the contract of employment continue in force—

(a)   for the purposes of pay or any other benefit derived from the employment, seniority, pension rights and other similar matters, and

(b)   for the purpose of determining for any purpose the period for which the employee has been continuously employed,

from the date of its termination (whether before or after the making of the order) until the determination or settlement of the complaint.

(2)   Where the tribunal makes such an order it shall specify in the order the amount which is to be paid by the employer to the employee by way of pay in respect of each normal pay period, or part of any such period, falling between the date of dismissal and the determination or settlement of the complaint.

(3)   Subject as follows, the amount so specified shall be that which the employee could reasonably have been expected to earn during that period, or part, and shall be paid—

(a)   in the case of payment for any such period falling wholly or partly after the making of the order, on the normal pay day for that period, and

(b)   in the case of a payment for any past period, within such time as may be specified in the order.

(4) If an amount is payable in respect only of part of a normal pay period, the amount shall be calculated by reference to the whole period and reduced proportionately.

(5) Any payment made to an employee by an employer under his contract of employment, or by way of damages for breach of that contract, in respect of a normal pay period or part of any such period shall go towards discharging the employer's liability in respect of that period under subsection (2); and conversely any payment under that subsection in respect of a period shall go towards discharging any liability of the employer under, or in respect of the breach of, the contract of employment in respect of that period.

(6) If an employee, on or after being dismissed by his employer, receives a lump sum which, or part of which, is in lieu of wages but is not referable to any normal pay period, the tribunal shall take the payment into account in determining the amount of pay to be payable in pursuance of any such order.

(7) For the purposes of this section the amount which an employee could reasonably have been expected to earn, his normal pay period and the normal pay day for each such period shall be determined as if he had not been dismissed.

165   Application for variation or revocation of order

(1) At any time between the making of an order under section 163 and the determination or settlement of the complaint, the employer or the employee may apply to an employment tribunal for the revocation or variation of the order on the ground of a relevant change of circumstances since the making of the order.

(2) Sections 161 to 163 apply in relation to such an application as in relation to an original application for interim relief, except that—

(a) no certificate need be presented to the tribunal under section 161(3), and

(b) in the case of an application by the employer, section 162(2) (service of copy of application and notice of hearing) has effect with the substitution of a reference to the employee for the reference to the employer.

166   Consequences of failure to comply with order

(1) If on the application of an employee an employment tribunal is satisfied that the employer has not complied with the terms of an order for the reinstatement or re-engagement of the employee under section 163(4) or (5), the tribunal shall—

(a) make an order for the continuation of the employee's contract of employment, and

(b) order the employer to pay the employee such compensation as the tribunal considers just and equitable in all the circumstances having regard—

(i)   to the infringement of the employee's right to be reinstated or re-engaged in pursuance of the order, and

(ii) to any loss suffered by the employee in consequence of the noncompliance.

(2) Section 164 applies to an order under subsection (1)(a) as in relation to an order under section 163.

(3) If on the application of an employee an employment tribunal is satisfied that the employer has not complied with the terms of an order for the continuation of a contract of employment, the following provisions apply.

(4) If the non-compliance consists of a failure to pay an amount by way of pay specified in the order, the tribunal shall determine the amount owed by the employer on the date of the determination.

If on that date the tribunal also determines the employee's complaint that he has been unfairly dismissed, it shall specify that amount separately from any other sum awarded to the employee.

(5) In any other case, the tribunal shall order the employer to pay the employee such compensation as the tribunal considers just and equitable in all the circumstances having regard to any loss suffered by the employee in consequence of the noncompliance.

167   Interpretation and other supplementary provisions

(1) Part X of the Employment Rights Act 1996 (unfair dismissal) has effect subject to the provisions of sections 152 to 166 above.

(2) Those sections shall be construed as one with that Part; and in those sections—
'complaint of unfair dismissal' means a complaint under section 111 of the Employment Rights Act 1996;
'award of compensation for unfair dismissal' means an award of compensation for unfair dismissal under section 112(4) or 117(3)(a) of that Act; and
'order for reinstatement or re-engagement' means an order for reinstatement or re-engagement under section 113 of that Act.

(3) Nothing in those sections shall be construed as conferring a right to complain of unfair dismissal from employment of a description to which that Part does not otherwise apply.

Time off for trade union duties and activities

168 Time off for carrying out trade union duties

(1) An employer shall permit an employee of his who is an official of an independent trade union recognised by the employer to take time off during his working hours for the purpose of carrying out any duties of his, as such an official, concerned with—

(a) negotiations with the employer related to or connected with matters falling within section 178(2) (collective bargaining) in relation to which the trade union is recognised by the employer, or

(b) the performance on behalf of employees of the employer of functions related to or connected with matters falling within that provision which the employer has agreed may be so performed by the trade union, or

(c) receipt of information from the employer and consultation by the employer under section 188 (redundancies) or under the Transfer of Undertakings (Protection of Employment) Regulations 2006, or

(d) negotiations with a view to entering into an agreement under regulation 9 of the Transfer of Undertakings (Protection of Employment) Regulations 2006 that applies to employees of the employer, or

(e) the performance on behalf of employees of the employer of functions related to or connected with the making of an agreement under that regulation.

(2) He shall also permit such an employee to take time off during his working hours for the purpose of undergoing training in aspects of industrial relations—

(a) relevant to the carrying out of such duties as are mentioned in subsection (1), and

(b) approved by the Trades Union Congress or by the independent trade union of which he is an official.

(3) The amount of time off which an employee is to be permitted to take under this section and the purposes for which, the occasions on which and any conditions subject to which time off may be so taken are those that are reasonable in all the circumstances having regard to any relevant provisions of a Code of Practice issued by ACAS.

(4) An employee may present a complaint to an employment tribunal that his employer has failed to permit him to take time off as required by this section.

168A Time off for union learning representatives

(1) An employer shall permit an employee of his who is—

(a) a member of an independent trade union recognised by the employer, and

(b) a learning representative of the trade union,

to take time off during his working hours for any of the following purposes.

(2) The purposes are—

(a) carrying on any of the following activities in relation to qualifying members of the trade union—

(i) analysing learning or training needs,

(ii) providing information and advice about learning or training matters,

(iii) arranging learning or training, and

(iv) promoting the value of learning or training,

(b) consulting the employer about carrying on any such activities in relation to such members of the trade union,

(c)   preparing for any of the things mentioned in paragraphs (a) and (b).
(3)   Subsection (1) only applies if—
    (a)   the trade union has given the employer notice in writing that the employee is a learning representative of the trade union, and
    (b)   the training condition is met in relation to him.
(4)   The training condition is met if—
    (a)   the employee has undergone sufficient training to enable him to carry on the activities mentioned in subsection (2), and the trade union has given the employer notice in writing of that fact,
    (b)   the trade union has in the last six months given the employer notice in writing that the employee will be undergoing such training, or
    (c)   within six months of the trade union giving the employer notice in writing that the employee will be undergoing such training, the employee has done so, and the trade union has given the employer notice of that fact.
(5)   Only one notice under subsection (4)(b) may be given in respect of any one employee.
(6)   References in subsection (4) to sufficient training to carry out the activities mentioned in subsection (2) are to training that is sufficient for those purposes having regard to any relevant provision of a Code of Practice issued by ACAS or the Secretary of State.
(7)   If an employer is required to permit an employee to take time off under subsection (1), he shall also permit the employee to take time off during his working hours for the following purposes—
    (a)   undergoing training which is relevant to his functions as a learning representative, and
    (b)   where the trade union has in the last six months given the employer notice under subsection (4)(b) in relation to the employee, undergoing such training as is mentioned in subsection (4)(a).
(8)   The amount of time off which an employee is to be permitted to take under this section and the purposes for which, the occasions on which and any conditions subject to which time off may be so taken are those that are reasonable in all the circumstances having regard to any relevant provision of a Code of Practice issued by ACAS or the Secretary of State.
(9)   An employee may present a complaint to an employment tribunal that his employer has failed to permit him to take time off as required by this section.
(10) In subsection (2)(a), the reference to qualifying members of the trade union is to members of the trade union—
    (a)   who are employees of the employer of a description in respect of which the union is recognised by the employer, and
    (b)   in relation to whom it is the function of the union learning representative to act as such.
(11) For the purposes of this section, a person is a learning representative of a trade union if he is appointed or elected as such in accordance with its rules.

169   Payment for time off under section 168

(1)   An employer who permits an employee to take time off under section 168 or 168A shall pay him for the time taken off pursuant to the permission.
(2)   Where the employee's remuneration for the work he would ordinarily have been doing during that time does not vary with the amount of work done, he shall be paid as if he had worked at that work for the whole of that time.
(3)   Where the employee's remuneration for the work he would ordinarily have been doing during that time varies with the amount of work done, he shall be paid an amount calculated by reference to the average hourly earnings for that work.
The average hourly earnings shall be those of the employee concerned or, if no fair estimate can be made of those earnings, the average hourly earnings for work of that description of persons in comparable employment with the same employer or, if there are no such persons, a figure of average hourly earnings which is reasonable in the circumstances.
(4)   A right to be paid an amount under this section does not affect any right of an employee in relation to remuneration under his contract of employment, but—

(a)   any contractual remuneration paid to an employee in respect of a period of time off to which this section applies shall go towards discharging any liability of the employer under this section in respect of that period, and

(b)   any payment under this section in respect of a period shall go towards discharging any liability of the employer to pay contractual remuneration in respect of that period.

(5)   An employee may present a complaint to an employment tribunal that his employer has failed to pay him in accordance with this section.

170   Time off for trade union activities

(1)   An employer shall permit an employee of his who is a member of an independent trade union recognised by the employer in respect of that description of employee to take time off during his working hours for the purpose of taking part in—

(a)   any activities of the union, and

(b)   any activities in relation to which the employee is acting as a representative of the union.

(2)   The right conferred by subsection (1) does not extend to activities which themselves consist of industrial action, whether or not in contemplation or furtherance of a trade dispute.

(2A) The right conferred by subsection (1) does not extend to time off for the purpose of acting as, or having access to services provided by, a learning representative of a trade union.

(2B) An employer shall permit an employee of his who is a member of an independent trade union recognised by the employer in respect of that description of employee to take time off during his working hours for the purpose of having access to services provided by a person in his capacity as a learning representative of the trade union.

(2C) Subsection (2B) only applies if the learning representative would be entitled to time off under subsection (1) of section 168A for the purpose of carrying on in relation to the employee activities of the kind mentioned in subsection (2) of that section.

(3)   The amount of time off which an employee is to be permitted to take under this section and the purposes for which, the occasions on which and any conditions subject to which time off may be so taken are those that are reasonable in all the circumstances having regard to any relevant provisions of a Code of Practice issued by ACAS.

(4)   An employee may present a complaint to an employment tribunal that his employer has failed to permit him to take time off as required by this section.

(5)   For the purposes of this section—

(a)   a person is a learning representative of a trade union if he is appointed or elected as such in accordance with its rules, and

(b)   a person who is a learning representative of a trade union acts as such if he carries on the activities mentioned in section 168A(2) in that capacity.

171   Time limit for proceedings

An employment tribunal shall not consider a complaint under section 168, 168A, 169 or 170 unless it is presented to the tribunal—

(a)   within three months of the date when the failure occurred, or

(b)   where the tribunal is satisfied that it was not reasonably practicable for the complaint to be presented within that period, within such further period as the tribunal considers reasonable.

172   Remedies

(1)   Where the tribunal finds a complaint under section 168, 168A or 170 is well-founded, it shall make a declaration to that effect and may make an award of compensation to be paid by the employer to the employee.

(2)   The amount of the compensation shall be such as the tribunal considers just and equitable in all the circumstances having regard to the employer's default in failing to permit time off to be taken by the employee and to any loss sustained by the employee which is attributable to the matters complained of.

(3)   Where on a complaint under section 169 the tribunal finds that the employer has failed to pay the employee in accordance with that section, it shall order him to pay the amount which it finds to be due.

173   Interpretation and other supplementary provisions

(1) For the purposes of sections 168, 168A and 170 the working hours of an employee shall be taken to be any time when in accordance with his contract of employment he is required to be at work.

(2) The remedy of an employee for infringement of the rights conferred on him by section 168, 168A, 169 or 170 is by way of complaint to an employment tribunal in accordance with this Part, and not otherwise.

(3) The Secretary of State may by order made by statutory instrument amend section 168A for the purpose of changing the purposes for which an employee may take time off under that section.

(4) No order may be made under subsection (3) unless a draft of the order has been laid before and approved by resolution of each House of Parliament.

Right to membership of trade union

174   Right not to be excluded or expelled from union

(1) An individual shall not be excluded or expelled from a trade union unless the exclusion or expulsion is permitted by this section.

(2) The exclusion or expulsion of an individual from a trade union is permitted by this section if (and only if)—

(a)   he does not satisfy, or no longer satisfies, an enforceable membership requirement contained in the rules of the union,

(b)   he does not qualify, or no longer qualifies, for membership of the union by reason of the union operating only in a particular part or particular parts of Great Britain,

(c)   in the case of a union whose purpose is the regulation of relations between its members and one particular employer or a number of particular employers who are associated, he is not, or is no longer, employed by that employer or one of those employers, or

(d)   the exclusion or expulsion is entirely attributable to conduct of his (other than excluded conduct) and the conduct to which it is wholly or mainly attributable is not protected conduct.

(3) A requirement in relation to membership of a union is 'enforceable' for the purposes of subsection (2)(a) if it restricts membership solely by reference to one or more of the following criteria—

(a)   employment in a specified trade, industry or profession,

(b)   occupational description (including grade, level or category of appointment), and

(c)   possession of specified trade, industrial or professional qualifications or work experience.

(4) For the purposes of subsection (2)(d) 'excluded conduct', in relation to an individual, means—

(a)   conduct which consists in his being or ceasing to be, or having been or ceased to be, a member of another trade union,

(b)   conduct which consists in his being or ceasing to be, or having been or ceased to be, employed by a particular employer or at a particular place, or

(c)   conduct to which section 65 (conduct for which an individual may not be disciplined by a union) applies or would apply if the references in that section to the trade union which is relevant for the purposes of that section were references to any trade union.

(4A) For the purposes of subsection (2)(d) 'protected conduct' is conduct which consists in the individual's being or ceasing to be, or having been or ceased to be, a member of a political party.

(4B) Conduct which consists of activities undertaken by an individual as a member of a political party is not conduct falling within subsection (4A).

(5) An individual who claims that he has been excluded or expelled from a trade union in contravention of this section may present a complaint to an employment tribunal

175   Time limit for proceedings

An employment tribunal shall not entertain a complaint under section 174 unless it is presented—

(a)   before the end of the period of six months beginning with the date of the exclusion or expulsion, or

(b)   where the tribunal is satisfied that it was not reasonably practicable for the complaint to be presented before the end of that period, within such further period as the tribunal considers reasonable.

176   Remedies

(1)   Where the employment tribunal finds a complaint under section 174 is well-founded, it shall make a declaration to that effect.

(1A) If a tribunal makes a declaration under subsection (1) and it appears to the tribunal that the exclusion or expulsion was mainly attributable to conduct falling within section 174(4A) it shall make a declaration to that effect.

(1B) If a tribunal makes a declaration under subsection (1A) and it appears to the tribunal that the other conduct to which the exclusion or expulsion was attributable consisted wholly or mainly of conduct of the complainant which was contrary to—

(a)   a rule of the union, or

(b)   an objective of the union,

it shall make a declaration to that effect.

(1C) For the purposes of subsection (1B), it is immaterial whether the complainant was a member of the union at the time of the conduct contrary to the rule or objective.

(1D) A declaration by virtue of subsection (1B)(b) shall not be made unless the union shows that, at the time of the conduct of the complainant which was contrary to the objective in question, it was reasonably practicable for that objective to be ascertained—

(a)   if the complainant was not at that time a member of the union, by a member of the general public, and

(b)   if he was at that time a member of the union, by a member of the union.

(2)   An individual whose complaint has been declared to be well-founded may make an application to an employment tribunal for an award of compensation to be paid to him by the union.

...

(3)   The application shall not be entertained if made—

(a)   before the end of the period of four weeks beginning with the date of the declaration under subsection (1), or

(b)   after the end of the period of six months beginning with that date.

(4)   The amount of compensation awarded shall, subject to the following provisions, be such as the employment tribunal considers just and equitable in all the circumstances.

(5)   Where the employment tribunal finds that the exclusion or expulsion complained of was to any extent caused or contributed to by the action of the applicant, it shall reduce the amount of the compensation by such proportion as it considers just and equitable having regard to that finding.

(6)   The amount of compensation calculated in accordance with subsections (4) and (5) shall not exceed the aggregate of—

(a)   an amount equal to thirty times the limit for the time being imposed by section 227(1)(a) of the Employment Rights Act 1996 (maximum amount of a week's pay for basic award in unfair dismissal cases), and

(b)   an amount equal to the limit for the time being imposed by section 124(1) of that Act (maximum compensatory award in such cases);

...

(6A) If on the date on which the application was made the applicant had not been admitted or re-admitted to the union, the award shall not be less than £6,900.

(6B) Subsection (6A) does not apply in a case where the tribunal which made the declaration under subsection (1) also made declarations under subsections (1A) and (1B).

(7), (8) ...

177   Interpretation and other supplementary provisions

(1)   For the purposes of section 174—

(a)   'trade union' does not include an organisation falling within paragraph (b) of section 1,

(b)   'conduct' includes statements, acts and omissions, and

    (c)   'employment' includes any relationship whereby an individual personally does work or performs services for another person (related expressions being construed accordingly).

(2)   For the purposes of sections 174 to 176—

    (a)   if an individual's application for membership of a trade union is neither granted nor rejected before the end of the period within which it might reasonably have been expected to be granted if it was to be granted, he shall be treated as having been excluded from the union on the last day of that period, and

    (b)   an individual who under the rules of a trade union ceases to be a member of the union on the happening of an event specified in the rules shall be treated as having been expelled from the union.

(3)   The remedy of an individual for infringement of the rights conferred by section 174 is by way of a complaint to an employment tribunal in accordance with that section, sections 175 and 176 and this section, and not otherwise.

(4)   Where a complaint relating to an expulsion which is presented under section 174 is declared to be well-founded, no complaint in respect of the expulsion shall be presented or proceeded with under section 66 (complaint of infringement of right not to be unjustifiably disciplined).

(5)   The rights conferred by section 174 are in addition to, and not in substitution for, any right which exists apart from that section; and, subject to subsection (4), nothing in that section, section 175 or 176 or this section affects any remedy for infringement of any such right.

PART IV
INDUSTRIAL RELATIONS

CHAPTER I
COLLECTIVE BARGAINING

Introductory

178   Collective agreements and collective bargaining

(1)   In this Act 'collective agreement' means any agreement or arrangement made by or on behalf of one or more trade unions and one or more employers or employers' associations and relating to one or more of the matters specified below; and 'collective bargaining' means negotiations relating to or connected with one or more of those matters.

(2)   The matters referred to above are—

    (a)   terms and conditions of employment, or the physical conditions in which any workers are required to work;

    (b)   engagement or non-engagement, or termination or suspension of employment or the duties of employment, of one or more workers;

    (c)   allocation of work or the duties of employment between workers or groups of workers;

    (d)   matters of discipline;

    (e)   a worker's membership or non-membership of a trade union;

    (f)   facilities for officials of trade unions; and

    (g)   machinery for negotiation or consultation, and other procedures, relating to any of the above matters, including the recognition by employers or employers' associations of the right of a trade union to represent workers in such negotiation or consultation or in the carrying out of such procedures.

(3)   In this Act 'recognition', in relation to a trade union, means the recognition of the union by an employer, or two or more associated employers, to any extent, for the purpose of collective bargaining; and 'recognised' and other related expressions shall be construed accordingly.

Enforceability of collective agreements

179   Whether agreement intended to be a legally enforceable contract

(1)   A collective agreement shall be conclusively presumed not to have been intended by the parties to be a legally enforceable contract unless the agreement—

    (a)   is in writing, and

(b) contains a provision which (however expressed) states that the parties intend that the agreement shall be a legally enforceable contract.

(2) A collective agreement which does satisfy those conditions shall be conclusively presumed to have been intended by the parties to be a legally enforceable contract.

(3) If a collective agreement is in writing and contains a provision which (however expressed) states that the parties intend that one or more parts of the agreement specified in that provision, but not the whole of the agreement, shall be a legally enforceable contract, then—

(a) the specified part or parts shall be conclusively presumed to have been intended by the parties to be a legally enforceable contract, and

(b) the remainder of the agreement shall be conclusively presumed not to have been intended by the parties to be such a contract.

(4) A part of a collective agreement which by virtue of subsection (3)(b) is not a legally enforceable contract may be referred to for the purpose of interpreting a part of the agreement which is such a contract.

180 Effect of provisions restricting right to take industrial action

(1) Any terms of a collective agreement which prohibit or restrict the right of workers to engage in a strike or other industrial action, or have the effect of prohibiting or restricting that right, shall not form part of any contract between a worker and the person for whom he works unless the following conditions are met.

(2) The conditions are that the collective agreement—

(a) is in writing,

(b) contains a provision expressly stating that those terms shall or may be incorporated in such a contract,

(c) is reasonably accessible at his place of work to the worker to whom it applies and is available for him to consult during working hours, and

(d) is one where each trade union which is a party to the agreement is an independent trade union;

and that the contract with the worker expressly or impliedly incorporates those terms in the contract.

(3) The above provisions have effect notwithstanding anything in section 179 and notwithstanding any provision to the contrary in any agreement (including a collective agreement or a contract with any worker).

Disclosure of information for purposes of collective bargaining

181 General duty of employers to disclose information

(1) An employer who recognises an independent trade union shall, for the purposes of all stages of collective bargaining about matters, and in relation to descriptions of workers, in respect of which the union is recognised by him, disclose to representatives of the union, on request, the information required by this section.

In this section and sections 182 to 185 'representative', in relation to a trade union, means an official or other person authorised by the union to carry on such collective bargaining.

(2) The information to be disclosed is all information relating to the employer's undertaking which is in his possession, or that of an associated employer, and is information—

(a) without which the trade union representatives would be to a material extent impeded in carrying on collective bargaining with him, and

(b) which it would be in accordance with good industrial relations practice that he should disclose to them for the purposes of collective bargaining.

(3) A request by trade union representatives for information under this section shall, if the employer so requests, be in writing or be confirmed in writing.

(4) In determining what would be in accordance with good industrial relations practice, regard shall be had to the relevant provisions of any Code of Practice issued by ACAS, but not so as to exclude any other evidence of what that practice is.

(5) Information which an employer is required by virtue of this section to disclose to trade union representatives shall, if they so request, be disclosed or confirmed in writing.

182　Restrictions on general duty

(1)　An employer is not required by section 181 to disclose information—

(a)　the disclosure of which would be against the interests of national security, or

(b)　which he could not disclose without contravening a prohibition imposed by or under an enactment, or

(c)　which has been communicated to him in confidence, or which he has otherwise obtained in consequence of the confidence reposed in him by another person, or

(d)　which relates specifically to an individual (unless that individual has consented to its being disclosed), or

(e)　the disclosure of which would cause substantial injury to his undertaking for reasons other than its effect on collective bargaining, or

(f)　obtained by him for the purpose of bringing, prosecuting or defending any legal proceedings.

In formulating the provisions of any Code of Practice relating to the disclosure of information, ACAS shall have regard to the provisions of this subsection.

(2)　In the performance of his duty under section 181 an employer is not required—

(a)　to produce, or allow inspection of, any document (other than a document prepared for the purpose of conveying or confirming the information) or to make a copy of or extracts from any document, or

(b)　to compile or assemble any information where the compilation or assembly would involve an amount of work or expenditure out of reasonable proportion to the value of the information in the conduct of collective bargaining.

183　Complaint of failure to disclose information

(1)　A trade union may present a complaint to the Central Arbitration Committee that an employer has failed—

(a)　to disclose to representatives of the union information which he was required to disclose to them by section 181, or

(b)　to confirm such information in writing in accordance with that section.

The complaint must be in writing and in such form as the Committee may require.

(2)　If on receipt of a complaint the Committee is of the opinion that it is reasonably likely to be settled by conciliation, it shall refer the complaint to ACAS and shall notify the trade union and employer accordingly, whereupon ACAS shall seek to promote a settlement of the matter. If a complaint so referred is not settled or withdrawn and ACAS is of the opinion that further attempts at conciliation are unlikely to result in a settlement, it shall inform the Committee of its opinion.

(3)　If the complaint is not referred to ACAS or, if it is so referred, on ACAS informing the Committee of its opinion that further attempts at conciliation are unlikely to result in a settlement, the Committee shall proceed to hear and determine the complaint and shall make a declaration stating whether it finds the complaint well-founded, wholly or in part, and stating the reasons for its findings.

(4)　On the hearing of a complaint any person who the Committee considers has a proper interest in the complaint is entitled to be heard by the Committee, but a failure to accord a hearing to a person other than the trade union and employer directly concerned does not affect the validity of any decision of the Committee in those proceedings.

(5)　If the Committee finds the complaint wholly or partly well-founded, the declaration shall specify—

(a)　the information in respect of which the Committee finds that the complaint is well-founded,

(b)　the date (or, if more than one, the earliest date) on which the employer refused or failed to disclose or, as the case may be, to confirm in writing, any of the information in question, and

(c)　a period (not being less than one week from the date of the declaration) within which the employer ought to disclose that information, or, as the case may be, to confirm it in writing.

(6)   On a hearing of a complaint under this section a certificate signed by or on behalf of a Minister of the Crown and certifying that a particular request for information could not be complied with except by disclosing information the disclosure of which would have been against the interests of national security shall be conclusive evidence of that fact.
A document which purports to be such a certificate shall be taken to be such a certificate unless the contrary is proved.

184   Further complaint of failure to comply with declaration

(1)   After the expiration of the period specified in a declaration under section 183(5)(c) the trade union may present a further complaint to the Central Arbitration Committee that the employer has failed to disclose or, as the case may be, to confirm in writing to representatives of the union information specified in the declaration. The complaint must be in writing and in such form as the Committee may require.

(2)   On receipt of a further complaint the Committee shall proceed to hear and determine the complaint and shall make a declaration stating whether they find the complaint well-founded, wholly or in part, and stating the reasons for their finding.

(3)   On the hearing of a further complaint any person who the Committee consider has a proper interest in that complaint shall be entitled to be heard by the Committee, but a failure to accord a hearing to a person other than the trade union and employer directly concerned shall not affect the validity of any decision of the Committee in those proceedings.

(4)   If the Committee find the further complaint wholly or partly well-founded the declaration shall specify the information in respect of which the Committee find that that complaint is well-founded.

185   Determination of claim and award

(1)   On or after presenting a further complaint under section 184 the trade union may present to the Central Arbitration Committee a claim, in writing, in respect of one or more descriptions of employees (but not workers who are not employees) specified in the claim that their contracts should include the terms and conditions specified in the claim.

(2)   The right to present a claim expires if the employer discloses or, as the case may be, confirms in writing, to representatives of the trade union the information specified in the declaration under section 183(5) or 184(4); and a claim presented shall be treated as withdrawn if the employer does so before the Committee make an award on the claim.

(3)   If the Committee find, or have found, the further complaint wholly or partly well-founded, they may, after hearing the parties, make an award that in respect of any description of employees specified in the claim the employer shall, from a specified date, observe either—
    (a)   the terms and conditions specified in the claim; or
    (b)   other terms and conditions which the Committee consider appropriate.
The date specified may be earlier than that on which the award is made but not earlier than the date specified in accordance with section 183(5)(b) in the declaration made by the Committee on the original complaint.

(4)   An award shall be made only in respect of a description of employees, and shall comprise only terms and conditions relating to matters in respect of which the trade union making the claim is recognised by the employer.

(5)   Terms and conditions which by an award under this section an employer is required to observe in respect of an employee have effect as part of the employee's contract of employment as from the date specified in the award, except in so far as they are superseded or varied—
    (a)   by a subsequent award under this section,
    (b)   by a collective agreement between the employer and the union for the time being representing that employee, or
    (c)   by express or implied agreement between the employee and the employer so far as that agreement effects an improvement in terms and conditions having effect by virtue of the award.

(6)   Where—

    (a)   by virtue of any enactment, other than one contained in this section, providing for minimum remuneration or terms and conditions, a contract of employment is to have effect as modified by an award, order or other instrument under that enactment, and

    (b)   by virtue of an award under this section any terms and conditions are to have effect as part of that contract,

that contract shall have effect in accordance with that award, order or other instrument or in accordance with the award under this section, whichever is the more favourable, in respect of any terms and conditions of that contract, to the employee.

(7)   No award may be made under this section in respect of terms and conditions of employment which are fixed by virtue of any enactment.

Prohibition of union recognition requirements

186 Recognition requirement in contract for goods or services void

A term or condition of a contract for the supply of goods or services is void in so far as it purports to require a party to the contract—

    (a)   to recognise one or more trade unions (whether or not named in the contract) for the purpose of negotiating on behalf of workers, or any class of worker, employed by him, or

    (b)   to negotiate or consult with, or with an official of, one or more trade unions (whether or not so named).

187 Refusal to deal on grounds of union exclusion prohibited

(1)   A person shall not refuse to deal with a supplier or prospective supplier of goods or services if the ground or one of the grounds for his action is that the person against whom it is taken does not, or is not likely to—

    (a)   recognise one or more trade unions for the purpose of negotiating on behalf of workers, or any class of worker, employed by him, or

    (b)   negotiate or consult with, or with an official of, one or more trade unions.

(2)   A person refuses to deal with a person if—

    (a)   where he maintains (in whatever form) a list of approved suppliers of goods or services, or of persons from whom tenders for the supply of goods or services may be invited, he fails to include the name of that person in that list; or

    (b)   in relation to a proposed contract for the supply of goods or services—

       (i)   he excludes that person from the group of persons from whom tenders for the supply of the goods or services are invited, or

       (ii)   he fails to permit that person to submit such a tender, or

       (iii)   he otherwise determines not to enter into a contract with that person for the supply of the goods or services; or

    (c)   he terminates a contract with that person for the supply of goods or services.

(3)   The obligation to comply with this section is a duty owed to the person with whom there is a refusal to deal and to any other person who may be adversely affected by its contravention; and a breach of the duty is actionable accordingly (subject to the defences and other incidents applying to actions for breach of statutory duty).

CHAPTER II
PROCEDURE FOR HANDLING REDUNDANCIES

Duty of employer to consult representatives

188 Duty of employer to consult representatives

(1)   Where an employer is proposing to dismiss as redundant 20 or more employees at one establishment within a period of 90 days or less, the employer shall consult about the dismissals all the persons who are appropriate representatives of any of the employees who may be affected by the proposed dismissals or may be affected by measures taken in connection with those dismissals.

(1A)The consultation shall begin in good time and in any event—

  (a)   where the employer is proposing to dismiss 100 or more employees as mentioned in subsection (1), at least 90 days, and

  (b)   otherwise, at least 30 days,

before the first of the dismissals takes effect.

(1B) For the purposes of this section the appropriate representatives of any affected employees are—

  (a)   if the employees are of a description in respect of which an independent trade union is recognised by their employer, representatives of the trade union, or

  (b)   in any other case, whichever of the following employee representatives the employer chooses—

    (i)   employee representatives appointed or elected by the affected employees otherwise than for the purposes of this section, who (having regard to the purposes for and the method by which they were appointed or elected) have authority from those employees to receive information and to be consulted about the proposed dismissals on their behalf;

    (ii)   employee representatives elected by the affected employees, for the purposes of this section, in an election satisfying the requirements of section 188A(1).

(2)   The consultation shall include consultation about ways of—

  (a)   avoiding the dismissals,

  (b)   reducing the numbers of employees to be dismissed, and

  (c)   mitigating the consequences of the dismissals,

and shall be undertaken by the employer with a view to reaching agreement with the appropriate representatives.

(3)   In determining how many employees an employer is proposing to dismiss as redundant no account shall be taken of employees in respect of whose proposed dismissals consultation has already begun.

(4)   For the purposes of the consultation the employer shall disclose in writing to the appropriate representatives—

  (a)   the reasons for his proposals,

  (b)   the numbers and descriptions of employees whom it is proposed to dismiss as redundant,

  (c)   the total number of employees of any such description employed by the employer at the establishment in question,

  (d)   the proposed method of selecting the employees who may be dismissed,

  (e)   the proposed method of carrying out the dismissals, with due regard to any agreed procedure, including the period over which the dismissals are to take effect.

  (f)   the proposed method of calculating the amount of any redundancy payments to be made (otherwise than in compliance with an obligation imposed by or by virtue of any enactment) to employees who may be dismissed.

(5)   That information shall be given to each of the appropriate representatives by being delivered to them or sent by post to an address notified by them to the employer, or (in the case of representatives of a trade union) sent by post to the union at the address of its head or main office.

(5A) The employer shall allow the appropriate representatives access to the affected employees and shall afford to those representatives such accommodation and other facilities as may be appropriate.

(6)   ...

(7)   If in any case there are special circumstances which render it not reasonably practicable for the employer to comply with a requirement of subsection (1A), (2) or (4), the employer shall take all such steps towards compliance with that requirement as are reasonably practicable in those circumstances.

Where the decision leading to the proposed dismissals is that of a person controlling the employer (directly or indirectly), a failure on the part of that person to provide information to the employer shall not constitute special circumstances rendering it not reasonably practicable for the employer to comply with such a requirement.

(7A) Where—
    (a)   the employer has invited any of the affected employees to elect employee representatives, and
    (b)   the invitation was issued long enough before the time when the consultation is required by subsection (1A)(a) or (b) to begin to allow them to elect representatives by that time,
    the employer shall be treated as complying with the requirements of this section in relation to those employees if he complies with those requirements as soon as is reasonably practicable after the election of the representatives.

(7B) If, after the employer has invited affected employees to elect representatives, the affected employees fail to do so within a reasonable time, he shall give to each affected employee the information set out in subsection (4).

(8)   This section does not confer any rights on a trade union, a representative or an employee except as provided by sections 189 to 192 below.

188A Election of employee representatives

(1)   The requirements for the election of employee representatives under section 188(1B)(b)(ii) are that—
    (a)   the employer shall make such arrangements as are reasonably practical to ensure that the election is fair;
    (b)   the employer shall determine the number of representatives to be elected so that there are sufficient representatives to represent the interests of all the affected employees having regard to the number and classes of those employees;
    (c)   the employer shall determine whether the affected employees should be represented either by representatives of all the affected employees or by representatives of particular classes of those employees;
    (d)   before the election the employer shall determine the term of office as employee representatives so that it is of sufficient length to enable information to be given and consultations under section 188 to be completed;
    (e)   the candidates for election as employee representatives are affected employees on the date of the election;
    (f)   no affected employee is unreasonably excluded from standing for election;
    (g)   all affected employees on the date of the election are entitled to vote for employee representatives;
    (h)   the employees entitled to vote may vote for as many candidates as there are representatives to be elected to represent them or, if there are to be representatives for particular classes of employees, may vote for as many candidates as there are representatives to be elected to represent their particular class of employee;
    (i)   the election is conducted so as to secure that—
        (i)   so far as is reasonably practicable, those voting do so in secret, and
        (ii)   the votes given at the election are accurately counted.

(2)   Where, after an election of employee representatives satisfying the requirements of subsection (1) has been held, one of those elected ceases to act as an employee representative and any of those employees are no longer represented, they shall elect another representative by an election satisfying the requirements of subsection (1)(a), (e), (f) and (i).

189 Complaint and protective award

(1)   Where an employer has failed to comply with a requirement of section 188 or section 188A, a complaint may be presented to an employment tribunal on that ground—
    (a)   in the case of a failure relating to the election of employee representatives, by any of the affected employees or by any of the employees who have been dismissed as redundant;
    (b)   in the case of any other failure relating to employee representatives, by any of the employee representatives to whom the failure related,
    (c)   in the case of failure relating to representatives of a trade union, by the trade union, and
    (d)   in any other case, by any of the affected employees or by any of the employees who have been dismissed as redundant.

(1A) If on a complaint under subsection (1) a question arises as to whether or not any employee representative was an appropriate representative for the purposes of section 188, it shall be for the employer to show that the employee representative had the authority to represent the affected employees.

(1B) On a complaint under subsection (1)(a) it shall be for the employer to show that the requirements in section 188A have been satisfied.

(2) If the tribunal finds the complaint well-founded it shall make a declaration to that effect and may also make a protective award.

(3) A protective award is an award in respect of one or more descriptions of employees—

    (a) who has been dismissed as redundant, or whom it is proposed to dismiss as redundant, and

    (b) in respect of whose dismissal or proposed dismissal the employer has failed to comply with a requirement of section 188,

ordering the employer to pay remuneration for the protected period.

(4) The protected period—

    (a) begins with the date on which the first of the dismissals to which the complaint relates takes effect, or the date of the award, whichever is the earlier, and

    (b) is of such length as the tribunal determines to be just and equitable in all the circumstances having regard to the seriousness of the employer's default in complying with any requirement of section 188;

but shall not exceed 90 days.

(5) An employment tribunal shall not consider a complaint under this section unless it is presented to the tribunal—

    (a) before the date on which the last of the dismissals to which the complaint relates takes effect, or

    (b) during the period of three months beginning with that date, or

    (c) where the tribunal is satisfied that it was not reasonably practicable for the complaint to be presented within the period of three months, within such further period as it considers reasonable.

(6) If on a complaint under this section a question arises—

    (a) whether there were special circumstances which rendered it not reasonably practicable for the employer to comply with any requirement of section 188, or

    (b) whether he took all such steps towards compliance with that requirement as were reasonably practicable in those circumstances,

it is for the employer to show that there were and that he did.

190   **Entitlement under protective award**

(1) Where an employment tribunal has made a protective award, every employee of a description to which the award relates is entitled, subject to the following provisions and to section 191, to be paid remuneration by his employer for the protected period.

(2) The rate of remuneration payable is a week's pay for each week of the period; and remuneration in respect of a period less than one week shall be calculated by reducing proportionately the amount of a week's pay.

(3) ...

(4) An employee is not entitled to remuneration under a protective award in respect of a period during which he is employed by the employer unless he would be entitled to be paid by the employer in respect of that period—

    (a) by virtue of his contract of employment, or

    (b) by virtue of sections 87 to 91 of the Employment Rights Act 1996 (rights of employee in period of notice),

if that period fell within the period of notice required to be given by section 86(1) of that Act.

(5) Chapter II of Part XIV of the Employment Rights Act 1996 applies with respect to the calculation of a week's pay for the purposes of this section.

The calculation date for the purposes of that Chapter is the date on which the protective award was made or, in the case of an employee who was dismissed before the date on which the protective award was made, the date which by virtue of section 226(5) is the calculation date for the purpose of computing the amount of a redundancy payment in relation to that dismissal (whether or not the employee concerned is entitled to any such payment).

(6) If an employee of a description to which a protective award relates dies during the protected period, the award has effect in his case as if the protected period ended on his death.

191   Termination of employment during protected period

(1) Where the employee is employed by the employer during the protected period and—
   (a)   he is fairly dismissed by his employer otherwise than as redundant, or
   (b)   he unreasonably terminates the contract of employment,
   then, subject to the following provisions, he is not entitled to remuneration under the protective award in respect of any period during which but for that dismissal or termination he would have been employed.

(2) If an employer makes an employee an offer (whether in writing or not and whether before or after the ending of his employment under the previous contract) to renew his contract of employment, or to re-engage him under a new contract, so that the renewal or re-engagement would take effect before or during the protected period, and either—
   (a)   the provisions of the contract as renewed, or of the new contract, as to the capacity and place in which he would be employed, and as to the other terms and conditions of his employment, would not differ from the corresponding provisions of the previous contract, or
   (b)   the offer constitutes an offer of suitable employment in relation to the employee,
   the following subsections have effect.

(3) If the employee unreasonably refuses the offer, he is not entitled to remuneration under the protective award in respect of a period during which but for that refusal he would have been employed.

(4) If the employee's contract of employment is renewed, or he is re-engaged under a new contract of employment, in pursuance of such an offer as is referred to in subsection (2)(b), there shall be a trial period in relation to the contract as renewed, or the new contract (whether or not there has been a previous trial period under this section).

(5) The trial period begins with the ending of his employment under the previous contract and ends with the expiration of the period of four weeks beginning with the date on which he starts work under the contract as renewed, or the new contract, or such longer period as may be agreed in accordance with subsection (6) for the purpose of retraining the employee for employment under that contract.

(6) Any such agreement—
   (a)   shall be made between the employer and the employee or his representative before the employee starts work under the contract as renewed or, as the case may be, the new contract,
   (b)   shall be in writing,
   (c)   shall specify the date of the end of the trial period, and
   (d)   shall specify the terms and conditions of employment which will apply in the employee's case after the end of that period.

(7) If during the trial period—
   (a)   the employee, for whatever reason, terminates the contract, or gives notice to terminate it and the contract is thereafter, in consequence, terminated, or
   (b)   the employer, for a reason connected with or arising out of the change to the renewed, or new, employment, terminates the contract, or gives notice to terminate it and the contract is thereafter, in consequence, terminated,
   the employee remains entitled under the protective award unless, in a case falling within paragraph (a), he acted unreasonably in terminating or giving notice to terminate the contract.

192   Complaint by employee to employment tribunal

(1)   An employee may present a complaint to an employment tribunal on the ground that he is an employee of a description to which a protective award relates and that his employer has failed, wholly or in part, to pay him remuneration under the award.

(2)   An employment tribunal shall not entertain a complaint under this section unless it is presented to the tribunal—

(a)   before the end of the period of three months beginning with the day (or, if the complaint relates to more than one day, the last of the days) in respect of which the complaint is made of failure to pay remuneration, or

(b)   where the tribunal is satisfied that it was not reasonably practicable for the complaint to be presented within the period of three months, within such further period as it may consider reasonable.

(3)   Where the tribunal finds a complaint under this section well-founded it shall order the employer to pay the complainant the amount of remuneration which it finds is due to him.

(4)   The remedy of an employee for infringement of his right to remuneration under a protective award is by way of complaint under this section, and not otherwise.

Supplementary provisions

195   Construction of references to dismissal as redundant etc.

(1)   In this Chapter references to dismissal as redundant are references to dismissal for a reason not related to the individual concerned or for a number of reasons all of which are not so related.

(2)   For the purposes of any proceedings under this Chapter, where an employee is or is proposed to be dismissed it shall be presumed, unless the contrary is proved, that he is or is proposed to be dismissed as redundant.

196   Construction of references to representatives

(1)   For the purposes of this Chapter persons are employee representatives if—

(a)   they have been elected by employees for the specific purpose of being consulted by their employer about dismissals proposed by him, or

(b)   having been elected or appointed by employees (whether before or after dismissals have been proposed by their employer) otherwise than for that specific purpose, it is appropriate (having regard to the purposes for which they were elected) for the employer to consult them about dismissals proposed by him,

and (in either case) they are employed by the employer at the time when they are elected or appointed.

(2)   References in this Chapter to representatives of a trade union, in relation to an employer, are to officials or other persons authorised by the trade union to carry on collective bargaining with the employer.

(3)   References in this Chapter to affected employees are to employees who may be affected by the proposed dismissals or who may be affected by measures taken in connection with such dismissals.

198   Power to adapt provisions in case of collective agreement

(1)   This section applies where there is in force a collective agreement which establishes—

(a)   arrangements for providing alternative employment for employees to whom the agreement relates if they are dismissed as redundant by an employer to whom it relates, or

(b)   arrangements for handling the dismissal of employees as redundant.

(2)   On the application of all the parties to the agreement the Secretary of State may, if he is satisfied having regard to the provisions of the agreement that the arrangements are on the whole at least as favourable to those employees as the foregoing provisions of this Chapter, by order made by statutory instrument adapt, modify or exclude any of those provisions both in their application to all or any of those employees and in their application to any other employees of any such employer.

(3)   The Secretary of State shall not make such an order unless the agreement—

(a)   provides for procedures to be followed (whether by arbitration or otherwise) in cases where an employee to whom the agreement relates claims that any employer or other person to whom it relates has not complied with the provisions of the agreement, and

(b)   provides that those procedures include a right to arbitration or adjudication by an independent referee or body in cases where (by reason of an equality of votes or otherwise) a decision cannot otherwise be reached,

or indicates that any such employee may present a complaint to an employment tribunal that any such employer or other person has not complied with those provisions.

(4)   An order under this section may confer on an employment tribunal to whom a complaint is presented as mentioned in subsection (3) such powers and duties as the Secretary of State considers appropriate.

(5)   An order under this section may be varied or revoked by a subsequent order thereunder either in pursuance of an application made by all or any of the parties to the agreement in question or without any such application.

CHAPTER III
CODES OF PRACTICE

Codes of Practice issued by ACAS

199   Issue of Codes of Practice by ACAS

(1)   ACAS may issue Codes of Practice containing such practical guidance as it thinks fit for the purpose of promoting the improvement of industrial relations or for purposes connected with trade union learning representatives.

...

Codes of Practice issued by the Secretary of State

203   Issue of Codes of Practice by the Secretary of State

(1)   The Secretary of State may issue Codes of Practice containing such practical guidance as he thinks fit for the purpose or for purposes connected with trade union learning representatives—

(a)   of promoting the improvement of industrial relations, or

(b)   of promoting what appear to him to be desirable practices in relation to the conduct by trade unions of ballots and elections.

...

Supplementary provisions

207   Effect of failure to comply with Code

(1)   A failure on the part of any person to observe any provision of a Code of Practice issued under this Chapter shall not of itself render him liable to any proceedings.

(2)   In any proceedings before an employment tribunal or the Central Arbitration Committee any Code of Practice issued under this Chapter by ACAS shall be admissible in evidence, and any provision of the Code which appears to the tribunal or Committee to be relevant to any question arising in the proceedings shall be taken into account in determining that question.

(3)   In any proceedings before a court or employment tribunal or the Central Arbitration Committee any Code of Practice issued under this Chapter by the Secretary of State shall be admissible in evidence, and any provision of the Code which appears to the court, tribunal or Committee to be relevant to any question arising in the proceedings shall be taken into account in determining that question.

CHAPTER IV
GENERAL

Functions of ACAS

209   General duty to promote improvement of industrial relations

It is the general duty of ACAS to promote the improvement of industrial relations.

210   Conciliation

(1) Where a trade dispute exists or is apprehended ACAS may, at the request of one or more parties to the dispute or otherwise, offer the parties to the dispute its assistance with a view to bringing about a settlement.

(2) The assistance may be by way of conciliation or by other means, and may include the appointment of a person other than an officer or servant of ACAS to offer assistance to the parties to the dispute with a view to bringing about a settlement.

(3) In exercising its functions under this section ACAS shall have regard to the desirability of encouraging the parties to a dispute to use any appropriate agreed procedures for negotiation or the settlement of disputes.

210A   Information required by ACAS for purposes of settling recognition disputes

(1) This section applies where ACAS is exercising its functions under section 210 with a view to bringing about a settlement of a recognition dispute.

(2) The parties to the recognition dispute may jointly request ACAS or a person nominated by ACAS to do either or both of the following—
   (a)   hold a ballot of the workers involved in the dispute;
   (b)   ascertain the union membership of the workers involved in the dispute.

(3) In the following provisions of this section references to ACAS include references to a person nominated by ACAS; and anything done by such a person under this section shall be regarded as done in the exercise of the functions of ACAS mentioned in subsection (1).

(4) At any time after ACAS has received a request under subsection (2), it may require any party to the recognition dispute—
   (a)   to supply ACAS with specified information concerning the workers involved in the dispute, and
   (b)   to do so within such period as it may specify.

(5) ACAS may impose a requirement under subsection (4) only if it considers that it is necessary to do so—
   (a)   for the exercise of the functions mentioned in subsection (1); and
   (b)   in order to enable or assist it to comply with the request.

(6) The recipient of a requirement under this section must, within the specified period, supply ACAS with such of the specified information as is in the recipient's possession.

(7) A request under subsection (2) may be withdrawn by any party to the recognition dispute at any time and, if it is withdrawn, ACAS shall take no further steps to hold the ballot or to ascertain the union membership of the workers involved in the dispute.

(8) If a party to a recognition dispute fails to comply with subsection (6), ACAS shall take no further steps to hold the ballot or to ascertain the union membership of the workers involved in the dispute.

(9) Nothing in this section requires ACAS to comply with a request under subsection (2).

(10) In this section—

'party', in relation to a recognition dispute, means each of the employers, employers' associations and trade unions involved in the dispute;

'a recognition dispute' means a trade dispute between employers and workers which is connected wholly or partly with the recognition by employers or employers' associations of the right of a trade union to represent workers in negotiations, consultations or other procedures relating to any of the matters mentioned in paragraphs (a) to (f) of section 218(1);

'specified' means specified in a requirement under this section; and

'workers' has the meaning given in section 218(5).

211   Conciliation officers

(1) ACAS shall designate some of its officers to perform the functions of conciliation officers under any enactment (whenever passed) relating to matters which are or could be the subject to proceedings before an employment tribunal.

(2) References in any such enactment to a conciliation officer are to an officer designated under this section.

212   Arbitration

(1) Where a trade dispute exists or is apprehended ACAS may, at the request of one or more of the parties to the dispute and with the consent of all the parties to the dispute, refer all or any of the matters to which the dispute relates for settlement to the arbitration of—

    (a)   one or more persons appointed by ACAS for that purpose (not being officers or employees of ACAS), or

    (b)   the Central Arbitration Committee.

(2) In exercising its functions under this section ACAS shall consider the likelihood of the dispute being settled by conciliation.

(3) Where there exist appropriate agreed procedures for negotiation or the settlement of disputes, ACAS shall not refer a matter for settlement to arbitration under this section unless—

    (a)   those procedures have been used and have failed to result in a settlement, or

    (b)   there is, in ACAS's opinion a special reason which justifies arbitration under this section as an alternative to those procedures.

(4) Where a matter is referred to arbitration under subsection (1)(a)—

    (a)   if more than one arbitrator or arbiter is appointed, ACAS shall appoint one of them to act as chairman; and

    (b)   the award may be published if ACAS so decides and all the parties consent.

(5) Part I of the Arbitration Act 1996 (general provisions as to arbitration) does not apply to an arbitration under this section.

212B   Dismissal procedures agreements

ACAS may, in accordance with any dismissal procedures agreement (within the meaning of the Employment Rights Act 1996), refer any matter to the arbitration of a person appointed by ACAS for the purpose (not being an officer or employee of ACAS).

213   Advice

(1) ACAS may, on request or otherwise, give employers, employers' associations, workers and trade unions such advice as it thinks appropriate on matters concerned with or affecting or likely to affect industrial relations.

(2) ACAS may also publish general advice on matters concerned with or affecting or likely to affect industrial relations.

214   Inquiry

(1) ACAS may, if it thinks fit, inquire into any question relating to industrial relations generally or to industrial relations in any particular industry or in any particular undertaking or part of an undertaking.

(2) The findings of an inquiry under this section, together with any advice given by ACAS in connection with those findings, may be published by ACAS if—

    (a)   it appears to ACAS that publication is desirable for the improvement of industrial relations, either generally or in relation to the specific question inquired into, and

    (b)   after sending a draft of the findings to all parties appearing to be concerned and taking account of their views, it thinks fit.

Courts of inquiry

215   Inquiry and report by court of inquiry

(1) Where a trade dispute exists or is apprehended, the Secretary of State may inquire into the causes and circumstances of the dispute, and, if he thinks fit, appoint a court of inquiry and refer to it any matters appearing to him to be connected with or relevant to the dispute.

(2) The court shall inquire into the matters referred to it and report on them to the Secretary of State; and it may make interim reports if it thinks fit.

(3) Any report of the court, and any minority report, shall be laid before both Houses of Parliament as soon as possible.

(4) The Secretary of State may, before or after the report has been laid before Parliament, publish or cause to be published from time to time, in such manner as he thinks fit, any information obtained or conclusions arrived at by the court as the result or in the course of its inquiry.

(5) No report or publication made or authorised by the court or the Secretary of State shall include any information obtained by the court of inquiry in the course of its inquiry—

   (a) as to any trade union, or

   (b) as to any individual business (whether carried on by a person, firm, or company),

which is not available otherwise than through evidence given at the inquiry, except with the consent of the secretary of the trade union or of the person, firm, or company in question.

Nor shall any individual member of the court or any person concerned in the inquiry disclose such information without such consent.

(6) The Secretary of State shall from time to time present to Parliament a report of his proceedings under this section.

Supplementary provisions

218 Meaning of 'trade dispute' in Part IV

(1) In this Part 'trade dispute' means a dispute between employers and workers, or between workers and workers, which is connected with one or more of the following matters—

   (a) terms and conditions of employment, or the physical conditions in which any workers are required to work;

   (b) engagement or non-engagement, or termination or suspension of employment or the duties of employment, of one or more workers;

   (c) allocation of work or the duties of employment as between workers or groups of workers;

   (d) matters of discipline;

   (e) the membership or non-membership of a trade union on the part of a worker;

   (f) facilities for officials of trade unions; and

   (g) machinery for negotiation or consultation, and other procedures, relating to any of the foregoing matters, including the recognition by employers or employers' associations of the right of a trade union to represent workers in any such negotiation or consultation or in the carrying out of such procedures.

(2) A dispute between a Minister of the Crown and any workers shall, notwithstanding that he is not the employer of those workers, be treated for the purposes of this Part as a dispute between an employer and those workers if the dispute relates—

   (a) to matters which have been referred for consideration by a joint body on which, by virtue of any provision made by or under any enactment, that minister is represented, or

   (b) to matters which cannot be settled without that Minister exercising a power conferred on him by or under an enactment.

(3) There is a trade dispute for the purpose of this Part even though it relates to matters occurring outside Great Britain.

(4) A dispute to which a trade union or employer's association is a party shall be treated for the purposes of this Part as a dispute to which workers or, as the case may be, employers are parties.

(5) In this section—

'employment' includes any relationship whereby one person personally does work or performs services for another; and

'worker', in relation to a dispute to which an employer is a party, includes any worker even if not employed by that employer.

PART V

INDUSTRIAL ACTION

Protection of acts in contemplation or furtherance of trade dispute

219 Protection from certain tort liabilities

(1) An act done by a person in contemplation or furtherance of a trade dispute is not actionable in tort on the ground only—

      (a)   that it induces another person to break a contract or interferes or induces another person to interfere with its performance, or

      (b)   that it consists in his threatening that a contract (whether one to which he is a party or not) will be broken or its performance interfered with, or that he will induce another person to break a contract or interfere with its performance.

(2)   An agreement or combination by two or more persons to do or procure the doing of an act in contemplation or furtherance of a trade dispute is not actionable in tort if the act is one which if done without any such agreement or combination would not be actionable in tort.

(3)   Nothing in subsections (1) and (2) prevents an act done in the course of picketing from being actionable in tort unless it is done in the course of attendance declared lawful by section 220 (peaceful picketing).

(4)   Subsections (1) and (2) have effect subject to sections 222 to 225 (action excluded from protection) and to sections 226 (requirement of ballot before action by trade union) and 234A (requirement of notice to employer of industrial action); and in those sections 'not protected' means excluded from the protection afforded by this section or, where the expression is used with reference to a particular person, excluded from that protection as respects that person.

220   Peaceful picketing

(1)   It is lawful for a person in contemplation or furtherance of a trade dispute to attend—

      (a)   at or near his own place of work, or

      (b)   if he is an official of a trade union, at or near the place of work of a member of the union whom he is accompanying and whom he represents,

for the purpose only of peacefully obtaining or communicating information, or peacefully persuading any person to work or abstain from working.

(2)   If a person works or normally works—

      (a)   otherwise than at any one place, or

      (b)   at a place the location of which is such that attendance there for a purpose mentioned in subsection (1) is impracticable,

his place of work for the purposes of that subsection shall be any premises of his employer from which he works or from which his work is administered.

(3)   In the case of a worker not in employment where—

      (a)   his last employment was terminated in connection with a trade dispute, or

      (b)   the termination of his employment was one of the circumstances giving rise to a trade dispute,

in relation to that dispute his former place of work shall be treated for the purposes of subsection (1) as being his place of work.

(4)   A person who is an official of a trade union by virtue only of having been elected or appointed to be a representative of some of the members of the union shall be regarded for the purposes of subsection (1) as representing only those members; but otherwise an official of a union shall be regarded for those purposes as representing all its members.

221   Restrictions on grant of injunctions and interdicts

(1)   Where—

      (a)   an application for an injunction or interdict is made to a court in the absence of the party against whom it is sought or any representative of his, and

      (b)   he claims, or in the opinion of the court would be likely to claim, that he acted in contemplation or furtherance of a trade dispute,

the court shall not grant the injunction or interdict unless satisfied that all steps which in the circumstances were reasonable have been taken with a view to securing that notice of the application and an opportunity of being heard with respect to the application have been given to him.

(2)   Where—

(a)   an application for an interlocutory injunction is made to a court pending the trial of an action, and

(b)   the party against whom it is sought claims that he acted in contemplation or furtherance of a trade dispute,

the court shall, in exercising its discretion whether or not to grant the injunction, have regard to the likelihood of that party's succeeding at the trial of the action in establishing any matter which would afford a defence to the action under section 219 (protection from certain tort liabilities) or section 220 (peaceful picketing).

This subsection does not extend to Scotland.

Action excluded from protection

222   Action to enforce trade union membership

(1)   An act is not protected if the reason, or one of the reasons, for which it is done is the fact or belief that a particular employer—

(a)   is employing, has employed or might employ a person who is not a member of a trade union, or

(b)   is failing, has failed or might fail to discriminate against such a person.

(2)   For the purposes of subsection (1)(b) an employer discriminates against a person if, but only if, he ensures that his conduct in relation to—

(a)   persons, or persons of any description, employed by him, or who apply to be, or are, considered by him for employment, or

(b)   the provision of employment for such persons,

is different, in some or all cases, according to whether or not they are members of a trade union, and is more favourable to those who are.

(3)   An act is not protected if it constitutes, or is one of a number of acts which together constitute, an inducement or attempted inducement of a person—

(a)   to incorporate in a contract to which that person is a party, or a proposed contract to which he intends to be a party, a term or condition which is or would be void by virtue of section 144 (union membership requirement in contract for goods or services), or

(b)   to contravene section 145 (refusal to deal with person on grounds relating to union membership).

(4)   References in this section to an employer employing a person are to a person acting in the capacity of the person for whom a worker works or normally works.

(5)   References in this section to not being a member of a trade union are to not being a member of any trade union, of a particular trade union or of one of a number of particular trade unions.

Any such reference includes a reference to not being a member of a particular branch or section of a trade union or of one of a number of particular branches or sections of a trade union.

223   Action taken because of dismissal for taking unofficial action

An act is not protected if the reason, or one of the reasons, for doing it is the fact or belief that an employer has dismissed one or more employees in circumstances such that by virtue of section 237 (dismissal in connection with unofficial action) they have no right to complain of unfair dismissal.

224   Secondary action

(1)   An act is not protected if one of the facts relied on for the purpose of establishing liability is that there has been secondary action which is not lawful picketing.

(2)   There is secondary action in relation to a trade dispute when, and only when, a person—

(a)   induces another to break a contract of employment or interferes or induces another to interfere with its performance, or

(b)   threatens that a contract of employment under which he or another is employed will be broken or its performance interfered with, or that he will induce another to break a contract of employment or to interfere with its performance,

and the employer under the contract of employment is not the employer party to the dispute.

(3) Lawful picketing means acts done in the course of such attendance as is declared lawful by section 220 (peaceful picketing)—

    (a)   by a worker employed (or, in the case of a worker not in employment, last employed) by the employer party to the dispute, or

    (b)   by a trade union official whose attendance is lawful by virtue of subsection (1)(b) of that section.

(4) For the purposes of this section an employer shall not be treated as party to a dispute between another employer and workers of that employer; and where more than one employer is in dispute with his workers, the dispute between each employer and his workers shall be treated as a separate dispute.

In this subsection 'worker' has the same meaning as in section 244 (meaning of 'trade dispute').

(5) An act in contemplation or furtherance of a trade dispute which is primary action in relation to that dispute may not be relied on as secondary action in relation to another trade dispute.

Primary action means such action as is mentioned in paragraph (a) or (b) of subsection (2) where the employer under the contract of employment is the employer party to the dispute.

(6) In this section 'contract of employment' includes any contract under which one person personally does work or performs services for another, and related expressions shall be construed accordingly.

225   Pressure to impose union recognition requirement

(1) An act is not protected if it constitutes, or is one of a number of acts which together constitute, an inducement or attempted inducement of a person—

    (a)   to incorporate in a contract to which that person is a party, or a proposed contract to which he intends to be a party, a term or condition which is or would be void by virtue of section 186 (recognition requirement in contract for goods or services), or

    (b)   to contravene section 187 (refusal to deal with person on grounds of union exclusion).

(2) An act is not protected if—

    (a)   it interferes with the supply (whether or not under a contract) of goods or services, or can reasonably be expected to have that effect, and

    (b)   one of the facts relied upon for the purpose of establishing liability is that a person has—

        (i)   induced another to break a contract of employment or interfered or induced another to interfere with its performance, or

        (ii)   threatened that a contract of employment under which he or another is employed will be broken or its performance interfered with, or that he will induce another to break a contract of employment or to interfere with its performance, and

    (c)   the reason, or one of the reasons, for doing the act is the fact or belief that the supplier (not being the employer under the contract of employment mentioned in paragraph (b)) does not, or might not—

        (i)   recognise one or more trade unions for the purpose of negotiating on behalf of workers, or any class of worker, employed by him, or

        (ii)   negotiate or consult with, or with an official of, one or more trade unions.

Requirement of ballot before action by trade union

226   Requirement of ballot before action by trade union

(1) An act done by a trade union to induce a person to take part, or continue to take part, in industrial action

    (a)   is not protected unless the industrial action has the support of a ballot, and

    (b)   where section 226A falls to be complied with in relation to the person's employer, is not protected as respects the employer unless the trade union has complied with section 226A in relation to him.

In this section 'the relevant time', in relation to an act by a trade union to induce a person to take part, or continue to take part, in industrial action, means the time at which proceedings are commenced in respect of the act.

(2) Industrial action shall be regarded as having the support of a ballot only if—
    (a) the union has held a ballot in respect of the action—
        (i) in relation to which the requirements of section 226B so far as applicable before and during the holding of the ballot were satisfied,
        (ii) in relation to which the requirements of sections 227 to 231 were satisfied, and
        (iii) in which the majority voting in the ballot answered 'Yes' to the question applicable in accordance with section 229(2) to industrial action of the kind to which the act of inducement relates;
    (b) such of the requirements of the following sections as have fallen to be satisfied at the relevant time have been satisfied, namely—
        (i) section 226B so far as applicable after the holding of the ballot, and
        (ii) section 231B;
    (bb) section 232A does not prevent the industrial action from being regarded as having the support of the ballot; and
    (c) the requirements of section 233 (calling of industrial action with support of ballot) are satisfied.

Any reference in this subsection to a requirement of a provision which is disapplied or modified by section 232 has effect subject to that section.

(3) Where separate workplace ballots are held by virtue of section 228(1)—
    (a) industrial action shall be regarded as having the support of a ballot if the conditions specified in subsection (2) are satisfied, and
    (b) the trade union shall be taken to have complied with the requirements relating to a ballot imposed by section 226A if those requirements are complied with,

in relation to the ballot for the place of work of the person induced to take part, or continue to take part, in the industrial action.

(3A) If the requirements of section 231A fall to be satisfied in relation to an employer, as respects that employer industrial action shall not be regarded as having the support of a ballot unless those requirements are satisfied in relation to that employer.

(4) For the purposes of this section an inducement, in relation to a person, includes an inducement which is or would be ineffective, whether because of his unwillingness to be influenced by it or for any other reason.

226A Notice of ballot and sample voting paper for employers

(1) The trade union must take such steps as are reasonably necessary to ensure that—
    (a) not later than the seventh day before the opening day of the ballot, the notice specified in subsection (2), and
    (b) not later than the third day before the opening day of the ballot, the sample voting paper specified in subsection (2F),

is received by every person who it is reasonable for the union to believe (at the latest time when steps could be taken to comply with paragraph (a)) will be the employer of persons who will be entitled to vote in the ballot.

(2) The notice referred to in paragraph (a) of subsection (1) is a notice in writing—
    (a) stating that the union intends to hold the ballot,
    (b) specifying the date which the union reasonably believes will be the opening day of the ballot, and
    (c) containing—
        (i) the lists mentioned in subsection (2A) and the figures mentioned in subsection (2B), together with an explanation of how those figures were arrived at, or
        (ii) where some or all of the employees concerned are employees from whose wages the employer makes deductions representing payments to the union, either those lists and figures and that explanation or the information mentioned in subsection (2C)

(2A) The lists are—
    (a) a list of the categories of employee to which the employees concerned belong, and

    (b)   a list of the workplaces at which the employees concerned work.

(2B) The figures are—

    (a)   the total number of employees concerned,

    (b)   the number of the employees concerned in each of the categories in the list mentioned in subsection (2A)(a), and

    (c)   the number of the employees concerned who work at each workplace in the list mentioned in subsection (2A)(b).

(2C) The information referred to in subsection (2)(c)(ii) is such information as will enable the employer readily to deduce—

    (a)   the total number of employees concerned,

    (b)   the categories of employee to which the employees concerned belong and the number of the employees concerned in each of those categories, and

    (c)   the workplaces at which the employees concerned work and the number of them who work at each of those workplaces.

(2D) The lists and figures supplied under this section, or the information mentioned in subsection (2C) that is so supplied, must be as accurate as is reasonably practicable in the light of the information in the possession of the union at the time when it complies with subsection (1)(a).

(2E) For the purposes of subsection (2D) information is in the possession of the union if it is held, for union purposes—

    (a)   in a document, whether in electronic form or any other form, and

    (b)   in the possession or under the control of an officer or employee of the union.

(2F) The sample voting paper referred to in paragraph (b) of subsection (1) is—

    (a)   a sample of the form of voting paper which is to be sent to the employees concerned, or

    (b)   where the employees concerned are not all to be sent the same form of voting paper, a sample of each form of voting paper which is to be sent to any of them.

(2G) Nothing in this section requires a union to supply an employer with the names of the employees concerned.

(2H) In this section references to the "employees concerned" are references to those employees of the employer in question who the union reasonably believes will be entitled to vote in the ballot.

(2I) For the purposes of this section, the workplace at which an employee works is—

    (a)   in relation to an employee who works at or from a single set of premises, those premises, and

    (b)   in relation to any other employee, the premises with which his employment has the closest connection.

(3)–(3B) ...

(4)   In this section references to the opening day of the ballot are references to the first day when a voting paper is sent to any person entitled to vote in the ballot.

(5)   This section, in its application to a ballot in which merchant seamen to whom section 230(2A) applies are entitled to vote, shall have effect with the substitution in subsection (2F), for references to the voting paper which is to be sent to the employees, of references to the voting paper which is to be sent or otherwise provided to them.

226B Appointment of scrutineer

(1)   The trade union shall, before the ballot in respect of the industrial action is held, appoint a qualified person ('the scrutineer') whose terms of appointment shall require him to carry out in relation to the ballot the functions of—

    (a)   taking such steps as appear to him to be appropriate for the purpose of enabling him to make a report to the trade union (see section 231B); and

    (b)   making the report as soon as reasonably practicable after the date of the ballot and, in any event, not later than the end of the period of four weeks beginning with that date.

(2)   A person is a qualified person in relation to a ballot if—

    (a)   he satisfies such conditions as may be specified for the purposes of this section by order of the Secretary of State or is himself so specified; and

      (b)   the trade union has no grounds for believing either that he will carry out the functions conferred on him under subsection (1) otherwise than competently or that his independence in relation to the union, or in relation to the ballot, might reasonably be called into question.

      An order under paragraph (a) shall be made by statutory instrument which shall be subject to annulment in pursuance of a resolution of either House of Parliament.

  (3)   The trade union shall ensure that the scrutineer duly carries out the functions conferred on him under subsection (1) and that there is no interference with the carrying out of those functions from the union or any of its members, officials or employees.

  (4)   The trade union shall comply with all reasonable requests made by the scrutineer for the purposes of, or in connection with, the carrying out of those functions.

226C Exclusion for small ballots

Nothing in section 226B, section 229(1A)(a) or section 231B shall impose a requirement on a trade union unless—

      (a)   the number of members entitled to vote in the ballot, or

      (b)   where separate workplace ballots are held in accordance with section 228(1), the aggregate of the number of members entitled to vote in each of them,

exceeds 50.

227 Entitlement to vote in ballot

  (1)   Entitlement to vote in the ballot must be accorded equally to all the members of the trade union who it is reasonable at the time of the ballot for the union to believe will be induced by the union to take part or, as the case may be, to continue to take part in the industrial action in question, and to no others.

  (2)   ...

228 Separate workplace ballots

  (1)   Subject to subsection (2), this section applies if the members entitled to vote in a ballot by virtue of section 227 do not all have the same workplace.

  (2)   This section does not apply if the union reasonably believes that all those members have the same workplace.

  (3)   Subject to section 228A, a separate ballot shall be held for each workplace; and entitlement to vote in each ballot shall be accorded equally to, and restricted to, members of the union who—

      (a)   are entitled to vote by virtue of section 227, and

      (b)   have that workplace.

  (4)   In this section and section 228A 'workplace' in relation to a person who is employed means—

      (a)   if the person works at or from a single set of premises, those premises, and

      (b)   in any other case, the premises with which the person's employment has the closest connection.

228A Separate workplaces: single and aggregate ballots

  (1)   Where section 228(3) would require separate ballots to be held for each workplace, a ballot may be held in place of some or all of the separate ballots if one of subsections (2) to (4) is satisfied in relation to it.

  (2)   This subsection is satisfied in relation to a ballot if the workplace of each member entitled to vote in the ballot is the workplace of at least one member of the union who is affected by the dispute.

  (3)   This subsection is satisfied in relation to a ballot if entitlement to vote is accorded to, and limited to, all the members of the union who—

      (a)   according to the union's reasonable belief have an occupation of a particular kind or have any of a number of particular kinds of occupation, and

      (b)   are employed by a particular employer, or by any of a number of particular employers, with whom the union is in dispute.

  (4)   This subsection is satisfied in relation to a ballot if entitlement to vote is accorded to, and limited to, all the members of the union who are employed by a particular employer, or by any of a number of particular employers, with whom the union is in dispute.

(5)   For the purposes of subsection (2) the following are members of the union affected by a dispute—

    (a)   if the dispute relates (wholly or partly) to a decision which the union reasonably believes the employer has made or will make concerning a matter specified in subsection (1)(a), (b) or (c) of section 244 (meaning of 'trade dispute'), members whom the decision directly affects,

    (b)   if the dispute relates (wholly or partly) to a matter specified in subsection (1)(d) of that section, members whom the matter directly affects,

    (c)   if the dispute relates (wholly or partly) to a matter specified in subsection (2)(e) of that section, persons whose membership or non-membership is in dispute,

    (d)   if the dispute relates (wholly or partly) to a matter specified in subsection (1)(f) of that section, officials of the union who have used or would use the facilities concerned in the dispute.

229   Voting paper

(1)   The method of voting in a ballot must be by the marking of a voting paper by the person voting.

(1A) Each voting paper must—

    (a)   state the name of the independent scrutineer,

    (b)   clearly specify the address to which, and the date by which, it is to be returned,

    (c)   be given one of a series of consecutive whole numbers every one of which is used in giving a different number in that series to each voting paper printed or otherwise produced for the purposes of the ballot, and

    (d)   be marked with its number.

This subsection, in its application to a ballot in which merchant seamen to whom section 230(2A) applies are entitled to vote, shall have effect with the substitution, for the reference to the address to which the voting paper is to be returned, of a reference to the ship to which the seamen belong.

(2)   The voting paper must contain at least one of the following questions—

    (a)   a question (however framed) which requires the person answering it to say, by answering 'Yes' or 'No', whether he is prepared to take part or, as the case may be, to continue to take part in a strike;

    (b)   a question (however framed) which requires the person answering it to say, by answering 'Yes' or 'No', whether he is prepared to take part or, as the case may be, to continue to take part in industrial action short of a strike.

(2A) For the purposes of subsection (2) an overtime ban and a call-out ban constitute industrial action short of a strike.

(3)   The voting paper must specify who, in the event of a vote in favour of industrial action, is authorised for the purposes of section 233 to call upon members to take part or continue to take part in the industrial action.

The person or description of persons so specified need not be authorised under the rules of the union but must be within section 20(2) (persons for whose acts the union is taken to be responsible).

(4)   The following statement must (without being qualified or commented upon by anything else on the voting paper) appear on every voting paper—

'If you take part in a strike or other industrial action, you may be in breach of your contract of employment. However, if you are dismissed for taking part in strike or other industrial action which is called officially and is otherwise lawful, the dismissal will be unfair if it takes place fewer than twelve weeks after you started taking part in the action, and depending on the circumstances may be unfair if it takes place later.'

230   Conduct of ballot

(1)   Every person who is entitled to vote in the ballot must—

    (a)   be allowed to vote without interference from, or constraint imposed by, the union or any of its members, officials or employees, and

      (b)   so far as is reasonably practicable, be enabled to do so without incurring any direct cost to himself.

(2)   Except as regards persons falling within subsection (2A), so far as is reasonably practicable, every person who is entitled to vote in the ballot must—

      (a)   have a young paper sent to him by post at his home address or any other address which he has requested the trade union in writing to treat as his postal address; and

      (b)   be given a convenient opportunity to vote by post.

(2A) Subsection (2B) applies to a merchant seaman if the trade union reasonably believes that—

      (a)   he will be employed in a ship either at sea or at a place outside Great Britain at some time in the period during which votes may be cast, and

      (b)   it will be convenient for him to receive a voting paper and to vote while on the ship or while at a place where the ship is rather than in accordance with subsection (2).

(2B) Where this subsection applies to a merchant seaman he shall, if it is reasonably practicable—

      (a)   have a voting paper made available to him while on the ship or while at a place where the ship is, and

      (b)   be given an opportunity to vote while on the ship or while at a place where the ship is.

(2C) In subsections (2A) and (2B) 'merchant seaman' means a person whose employment, or the greater part of it, is carried out on board sea-going ships.

(3)   ...

(4)   A ballot shall be conducted so as to secure that—

      (a)   so far as is reasonably practicable, those voting do so in secret, and

      (b)   the votes given in the ballot are fairly and accurately counted.

For the purposes of paragraph (b) an inaccuracy in counting shall be disregarded if it is accidental and on a scale which could not affect the result of the ballot.

231   Information as to result of ballot

As soon as is reasonably practicable after the holding of the ballot, the trade union shall take such steps as are reasonably necessary to ensure that all persons entitled to vote in the ballot are informed of the number of—

      (a)   votes cast in the ballot,

      (b)   individuals answering 'Yes' to the question, or as the case may be, to each question,

      (c)   individuals answering 'No' to the question, or, as the case may be, to each question, and

      (d)   spoiled voting papers.

231A Employers to be informed of ballot result

(1)   As soon as reasonably practicable after the holding of the ballot, the trade union shall take such steps as are reasonably necessary to ensure that every relevant employer is informed of the matters mentioned in section 231.

(2)   In subsection (1) 'relevant employer' means a person who it is reasonable for the trade union to believe (at the time when the steps are taken) was at the time of the ballot the employer of any persons entitled to vote.

231B Scrutineer's report

(1)   The scrutineer's report on the ballot shall state whether the scrutineer is satisfied—

      (a)   that there are no reasonable grounds for believing that there was any contravention of a requirement imposed by or under any enactment in relation to the ballot,

      (b)   that the arrangements made with respect to the production, storage, distribution, return or other handling of the voting papers used in the ballot, and the arrangements for the counting of the votes, included all such security arrangements as were reasonably practicable for the purpose of minimising the risk that any unfairness or malpractice might occur, and

      (c)   that he has been able to carry out the functions conferred on him under section 226B(1) without any interference from the trade union or any of its members, officials or employees;

and if he is not satisfied as to any of those matters, the report shall give particulars of his reason for not being satisfied as to that matter.

(2)   If at any time within six months from the date of the ballot—
    (a)   any person entitled to vote in the ballot, or
    (b)   the employer of any such person,
requests a copy of the scrutineer's report, the trade union must, as soon as practicable, provide him with one either free of charge or on payment of such reasonable fee as may be specified by the trade union.

232A   Inducement of member denied entitlement to vote

Industrial action shall not be regarded as having the support of a ballot if the following conditions apply in the case of any person—
    (a)   he was a member of the trade union at the time when the ballot was held,
    (b)   it was reasonable at that time for the trade union to believe he would be induced to take part or, as the case may be, to continue to take part in the industrial action,
    (c)   he was not accorded entitlement to vote in the ballot, and
    (d)   he was induced by the trade union to take part or, as the case may be, to continue to take part in the industrial action.

232B   Small accidental failures to be disregarded

(1)   If—
    (a)   in relation to a ballot there is a failure (or there are failures) to comply with a provision mentioned in subsection (2) or with more than one of those provisions, and
    (b)   the failure is accidental and on a scale which is unlikely to affect the result of the ballot or, as the case may be, the failures are accidental and taken together are on a scale which is unlikely to affect the result of the ballot,
the failure (or failures) shall be disregarded for all purposes (including, in particular, those of section 232A(c)).
(2)   The provisions are section 227(1), section 230(2) and section 230(2B).

233   Calling of industrial action with support of ballot

(1)   Industrial action shall not be regarded as having the support of a ballot unless it is called by a specified person and the conditions specified below are satisfied.
(2)   A 'specified person' means a person specified or of a description specified in the voting paper for the ballot in accordance with section 229(3).
(3)   The conditions are that—
    (a)   there must have been no call by the trade union to take part or continue to take part in industrial action to which the ballot relates, or any authorisation or endorsement by the union of any such industrial action, before the date of the ballot;
    (b)   there must be a call for industrial action by a specified person, and industrial action to which it relates must begin, before the ballot ceases to be effective in accordance with section 234.
(4)   For the purposes of this section a call shall be taken to have been made by a trade union if it was authorised or endorsed by the union; and the provisions of section 20(2) to (4) apply for the purpose of determining whether a call, or industrial action, is to be taken to have been so authorised or endorsed.

234   Period after which ballot ceases to be effective

(1)   Subject to the following provisions, a ballot ceases to be effective for the purposes of section 233(3)(b) in relation to industrial action by members of a trade union at the end of the period, beginning with the date of the ballot—
    (a)   of four weeks, or
    (b)   of such longer duration not exceeding eight weeks as is agreed between the union and the members' employer.
(2)   Where for the whole or part of that period the calling or organising of industrial action is prohibited—
    (a)   by virtue of a court order which subsequently lapses or is discharged, recalled or set aside, or

(b)   by virtue of an undertaking given to a court by any person from which he is subsequently released or by which he ceases to be bound,

the trade union may apply to the court for an order that the period during which the prohibition had effect shall not count towards the period referred to in subsection (1).

(3)   The application must be made forthwith upon the prohibition ceasing to have effect—
   (a)   to the court by virtue of whose decision it ceases to have effect, or
   (b)   where an order lapses or an undertaking ceases to bind without any such decision, to the court by which the order was made or to which the undertaking was given;

and no application may be made after the end of the period of eight weeks beginning with the date of the ballot.

(4)   The court shall not make an order if it appears to the court—
   (a)   that the result of the ballot no longer represents the views of the union members concerned, or
   (b)   that an event is likely to occur as a result of which those members would vote against industrial action if another ballot were to be held.

(5)   No appeal lies from the decision of the court to make or refuse an order under this section.

(6)   The period between the making of an application under this section and its determination does not count towards the period referred to in subsection (1).

But a ballot shall not by virtue of this subsection (together with any order of the court) be regarded as effective for the purposes of section 233(3)(b) after the end of the period of twelve weeks beginning with the date of the ballot.

Requirement on trade union to give notice of industrial action

234A   Notice to employers of industrial action

(1)   An act done by a trade union to induce a person to take part, or continue to take part, in industrial action is not protected as respects his employer unless the union has taken or takes such steps as are reasonably necessary to ensure that the employer receives within the appropriate period a relevant notice covering the act.

(2)   Subsection (1) imposes a requirement in the case of an employer only if it is reasonable for the union to believe, at the latest time when steps could be taken to ensure that he receives such a notice, that he is the employer of persons who will be or have been induced to take part, or continue to take part, in the industrial action.

(3)   For the purposes of this section a relevant notice is a notice in writing which—
   (a)   contains—
      (i)   the lists mentioned in subsection (3A) and the figures mentioned in subsection (3B), together with an explanation of how those figures were arrived at, or
      (ii)   where some or all of the affected employees are employees from whose wages the employer makes deductions representing payments to the union, either those lists and figures and that explanation or the information mentioned in subsection (3C), and
   (b)   states whether industrial action is intended to be continuous or discontinuous and specifies—
      (i)   where it is to be continuous, the intended date for any of the affected employees to begin to take part in the action,
      (ii)   where it is to be discontinuous, the intended dates for any of the affected employees to take part in the action.

(3A) The lists referred to in subsection (3)(a) are—
   (a)   a list of the categories of employee to which the affected employees belong, an
   (b)   a list of the workplaces at which the affected employees work.

(3B) The figures referred to in subsection (3)(a) are—
   (a)   the total number of the affected employees,
   (b)   the number of the affected employees in each of the categories in the list mentioned in subsection (3A)(a), and

    (c)   the number of the affected employees who work at each workplace in the list mentioned in subsection (3A)(b).

(3C) The information referred to in subsection (3)(a)(ii) is such information as will enable the employer readily to deduce—

    (a)   the total number of the affected employees,

    (b)   the categories of employee to which the affected employees belong and the number of the affected employees in each of those categories, and

    (c)   the workplaces at which the affected employees work and the number of them who work at each of those workplaces.

(3D) The lists and figures supplied under this section, or the information mentioned in subsection (3C) that is so supplied, must be as accurate as is reasonably practicable in the light of the information in the possession of the union at the time when it complies with subsection (1).

(3E) For the purposes of subsection (3D) information is in the possession of the union if it is held, for union purposes—

    (a)   in a document, whether in electronic form or any other form, and

    (b)   in the possession or under the control of an officer or employee of the union.

(3F) Nothing in this section requires a union to supply an employer with the names of the affected employees.

(4)   For the purposes of subsection (1) the appropriate period is the period—

    (a)   beginning with the day when the union satisfies the requirement of section 231A in relation to the ballot in respect of the industrial action, and

    (b)   ending with the seventh day before the day, or before the first of the days, specified in the relevant notice.

(5)   For the purposes of subsection (1) a relevant notice covers an act done by the union if the person induced falls within a notified category of employee and the workplace at which he works is a notified workplace and—

    (a)   where he is induced to take part or continue to take part in industrial action which the union intends to be continuous, if—

        (i)   the notice states that the union intends the industrial action to be continuous, and

        (ii)   there is no participation by him in the industrial action before the date specified in the notice in consequence of any inducement by the union not covered by a relevant notice; and

    (b)   where he is induced to take part or continue to take part in industrial action which the union intends to be discontinuous, if there is no participation by him in the industrial action on a day not so specified in consequence of any inducement by the union not covered by a relevant notice.

(5B) In subsection (5)—

    (a)   a 'notified category of employee' means—

        (i)   a category of employee that is listed in the notice, or

        (ii)   where the notice contains the information mentioned in subsection (3C), a category of employee that the employer (at the time he receives the notice) can readily deduce from the notice is a category of employee to which some or all of the affected employees belong, and

    (b)   a 'notified workplace' means—

        (i)   a workplace that is listed in the notice, or

        (ii)   where the notice contains the information mentioned in subsection (3C), a workplace that the employer (at the time he receives the notice) can readily deduce from the notice is the workplace at which some or all of the affected employees work.

(5C) In this section references to the 'affected employees' are references to those employees of the employer who the union reasonably believes will be induced by the union, or have been so induced, to take part or continue to take part in the industrial action.

(5D) For the purposes of this section, the workplace at which an employee works is—

(a) in relation to an employee who works at or from a single set of premises, those premises, and

(b) in relation to any other employee, the premises with which his employment has the closest connection.

(6) For the purposes of this section—

(a) a union intends industrial action to be discontinuous if it intends it to take place only on some days on which there is an opportunity to take the action, and

(b) a union intends industrial action to be continuous if it intends it to be not so restricted.

(7) Subject to subsections (7A) and (7B), where—

(a) continuous industrial action which has been authorised or endorsed by a union ceases to be so authorised or endorsed, and

(b) the industrial action has at a later date again been authorised or endorsed by the union (whether as continuous or discontinuous action),

no relevant notice covering acts done to induce persons to take part in the earlier action shall operate to cover acts done to induce persons to take part in the action authorised or endorsed at the later date and this section shall apply in relation to an act to induce a person to take part, or continue to take part, in the industrial action after that date as if the references in subsection (3)(b)(i) to the industrial action were to the industrial action taking place after that date.

(7A) Subsection (7) shall not apply where industrial action ceases to be authorised or endorsed in order to enable the union to comply with a court order or an undertaking given to a court.

(7B) Subsection (7) shall not apply where—

(a) a union agrees with an employer, before industrial action ceases to be authorised or endorsed, that it will cease to be authorised or endorsed with effect from a date specified in the agreement ('the suspension date') and that it may again be authorised or endorsed with effect from a date not earlier than a date specified in the agreement ('the resumption date'),

(b) the action ceases to be authorised or endorsed with effect from the suspension date, and

(c) the action is again authorised or endorsed with effect from a date which is not earlier than the resumption date or such later date as may be agreed between the union and the employer.

(8) The requirement imposed on a trade union by subsection (1) shall be treated as having been complied with if the steps were taken by other relevant persons or committees whose acts were authorised or endorsed by the union and references to the belief or intention of the union in subsection (2) or, as the case may be, subsections (3), (5), (5C) and (6) shall be construed as references to the belief or the intention of the person or committee taking the steps.

(9) The provisions of section 20(2) to (4) apply for the purpose of determining for the purposes of subsection (1) who are relevant persons or committees and whether the trade union is to be taken to have authorised or endorsed the steps the person or committee took and for the purposes of subsections (7) to (7B) whether the trade union is to be taken to have authorised or endorsed the industrial action.

235 Construction of references to contract of employment

In sections 226 to 234A (requirement of ballot before action by trade union) references to a contract of employment include any contract under which one person personally does work or performs services for another; and 'employer' and other related expressions shall be construed accordingly.

Industrial action affecting supply of goods or services to an individual

235A Industrial action affecting supply of goods or services to an individual

(1) Where an individual claims that—

(a) any trade union or other person has done, or is likely to do, an unlawful act to induce any person to take part, or to continue to take part, in industrial action, and

(b) an effect, or a likely effect, of the industrial action is or will be to—

(i) prevent or delay the supply of goods or services, or

(ii) reduce the quality of goods or services supplied,

to the individual making the claim,

he may apply to the High Court or the Court of Session for an order under this section.

(2) For the purposes of this section an act to induce any person to take part, or to continue to take part, in industrial action is unlawful—

    (a)   if it is actionable in tort by any one or more persons, or

    (b)   (where it is or would be the act of a trade union) if it could form the basis of an application by a member under section 62.

(3) In determining whether an individual may make an application under this section it is immaterial whether or not the individual is entitled to be supplied with the goods or services in question.

(4) Where on an application under this section the court is satisfied that the claim is well-founded, it shall make such order as it considers appropriate for requiring the person by whom the act of inducement has been, or is likely to be, done to take steps for ensuring—

    (a)   that no, or no further, act is done by him to induce any persons to take part or to continue to take part in the industrial action, and

    (b)   that no person engages in conduct after the making of the order by virtue of having been induced by him before the making of the order to take part or continue to take part in the industrial action.

(5) Without prejudice to any other power of the court, the court may on an application under this section grant such interlocutory relief (in Scotland, such interim order) as it considers appropriate.

(6) For the purposes of this section an act of inducement shall be taken to be done by a trade union if it is authorised or endorsed by the union; and the provisions of section 20(2) to (4) apply for the purposes of determining whether such an act is to be taken to be so authorised or endorsed. Those provisions also apply in relation to proceedings for failure to comply with an order under this section as they apply in relation to the original proceedings.

No compulsion to work

236   No compulsion to work

No court shall, whether by way of—

    (a)   an order for specific performance or specific implement of a contract of employment, or

    (b)   an injunction or interdict restraining a breach or threatened breach of such a contract,

compel an employee to do any work or attend at any place for the doing of any work.

Loss of unfair dismissal protection

237   Dismissal of those taking part in unofficial industrial action

(1) An employee has no right to complain of unfair dismissal if at the time of dismissal he was taking part in an unofficial strike or other unofficial industrial action.

(1A) Subsection (1) does not apply to the dismissal of the employee if it is shown that the reason (or, if more than one, the principal reason) for the dismissal or, in a redundancy case, for selecting the employee for dismissal was one of those specified in or under—

    (a)   section 98B, 99, 100, 101A(d), 103, 103A or 104C of the Employment Rights Act 1996 (dismissal in jury service, family, health and safety, working time, employee representative, protected disclosure and flexible working cases),

    (b)   section 104 of that Act in its application in relation to time off under section 57A of that Act (dependants);

In this subsection 'redundancy case' has the meaning given in section 105(9) of that Act; and a reference to a specified reason for dismissal includes a reference to specified circumstances of dismissal.

(2) A strike or other industrial action is unofficial in relation to an employee unless—

    (a)   he is a member of a trade union and the action is authorised or endorsed by that union, or

    (b)   he is not a member of a trade union but there are among those taking part in the industrial action members of a trade union by which the action has been authorised or endorsed.

Provided that, a strike or other industrial action shall not be regarded as unofficial if none of those taking part in it are members of a trade union.

(3)　The provisions of section 20(2) apply for the purpose of determining whether industrial action is to be taken to have been authorised or endorsed by a trade union.

(4)　The question whether industrial action is to be so taken in any case shall be determined by reference to the facts as at the time of dismissal.

Provided that, where an act is repudiated as mentioned in section 21, industrial action shall not thereby be treated as unofficial before the end of the next working day after the day on which the repudiation takes place.

(5)　In this section the 'time of dismissal' means—

    (a)　where the employee's contract of employment is terminated by notice, when the notice is given,

    (b)　where the employee's contract of employment is terminated without notice, when the termination takes effect, and

    (c)　where the employee is employed under a contract for a fixed term which expires without being renewed under the same contract, when that term expires;

and a 'working day' means any day which is not a Saturday or Sunday, Christmas Day, Good Friday or a bank holiday under the Banking and Financial Dealings Act 1971.

(6)　For the purposes of this section membership of a trade union for purposes unconnected with the employment in question shall be disregarded; but an employee who was a member of a trade union when he began to take part in industrial action shall continue to be treated as a member for the purpose of determining whether that action is unofficial in relation to him or another notwithstanding that he may in fact have ceased to be a member.

238　Dismissals in connection with other industrial action

(1)　This section applies in relation to an employee who has a right to complain of unfair dismissal (the 'complainant') and who claims to have been unfairly dismissed, where at the date of the dismissal—

    (a)　the employer was conducting or instituting a lock-out, or

    (b)　the complainant was taking part in a strike or other industrial action.

(2)　In such a case an employment tribunal shall not determine whether the dismissal was fair or unfair unless it is shown—

    (a)　that one or more relevant employees of the same employer have not been dismissed, or

    (b)　that a relevant employee has before the expiry of the period of three months beginning with the date of his dismissal been offered re-engagement and that the complainant has not been offered re-engagement.

(2A) Subsection (2) does not apply to the dismissal of the employee if it is shown that the reason (or, if more than one, the principal reason) for the dismissal or, in a redundancy case, for selecting the employee for dismissal was one of those specified in or under—

    (a)　section 98B, 99, 100, 101A(d), 103 or 104C of the Employment Rights Act 1996 (dismissal in jury service, family, health and safety, working time, employee representative and flexible working cases),

    (b)　section 104 of that Act in its application in relation to time off under section 57A of that Act (dependants).

In this subsection 'redundancy case' has the meaning given in section 105(9) of that Act; and a reference to a specified reason for dismissal includes a reference to specified circumstances of dismissal.

(2B) Subsection (2) does not apply in relation to an employee who is regarded as unfairly dismissed by virtue of section 238A below.

(3)　For this purpose 'relevant employees' means—

    (a)　in relation to a lock-out, employees who were directly interested in the dispute in contemplation or furtherance of which the lock-out occurred, and

    (b)　in relation to a strike or other industrial action, those employees at the establishment of the employer at or from which the complainant works who at the date of his dismissal were taking part in the action.

Nothing in section 237 (dismissal of those taking part in unofficial industrial action) affects the question who are relevant employees for the purposes of this section.

(4) An offer of re-engagement means an offer (made either by the original employer or by a successor of that employer or an associated employer) to re-engage an employee, either in the job which he held immediately before the date of dismissal or in a different job which would be reasonably suitable in his case.

(5) In this section 'date of dismissal' means—

    (a) where the employee's contract of employment was terminated by notice, the date on which the employer's notice was given, and

    (b) in any other case, the effective date of termination.

238A   Participation in official industrial action

(1) For the purposes of this section an employee takes protected industrial action if he commits an act which, or a series of acts each of which, he is induced to commit by an act which by virtue of section 219 is not actionable in tort.

(2) An employee who is dismissed shall be regarded for the purposes of Part X of the Employment Rights Act 1996 (unfair dismissal) as unfairly dismissed if—

    (a) the reason (or, if more than one, the principal reason) for the dismissal is that the employee took protected industrial action, and

    (b) subsection (3), (4) or (5) applies to the dismissal.

(3) This subsection applies to a dismissal if the date of the dismissal is within the protected period.

(4) This subsection applies to a dismissal if—

    (a) the date of the dismissal is after the end of that period, and

    (b) the employee had stopped taking protected industrial action before the end of that period.

(5) This subsection applies to a dismissal if—

    (a) the date of the dismissal is after the end of that period,

    (b) the employee had not stopped taking protected industrial action before the end of that period, and

    (c) the employer had not taken such procedural steps as would have been reasonable for the purposes of resolving the dispute to which the protected industrial action relates.

(6) In determining whether an employer has taken those steps regard shall be had, in particular, to—

    (a) whether the employer or a union had complied with procedures established by any applicable collective or other agreement;

    (b) whether the employer or a union offered or agreed to commence or resume negotiations after the start of the protected industrial action;

    (c) whether the employer or a union unreasonably refused, after the start of the protected industrial action, a request that conciliation services be used;

    (d) whether the employer or a union unreasonably refused, after the start of the protected industrial action, a request that mediation services be used in relation to procedures to be adopted for the purposes of resolving the dispute;

    (e) where there was agreement to use either of the services mentioned in paragraphs (c) and (d), the matters specified in section 238B.

(7) In determining whether an employer has taken those steps no regard shall be had to the merits of the dispute.

(7A) For the purposes of this section 'the protected period', in relation to the dismissal of an employee, is the sum of the basic period and any extension period in relation to that employee.

(7B) The basic period is twelve weeks beginning with the first day of protected industrial action.

(7C) An extension period in relation to an employee is a period equal to the number of days falling on or after the first day of protected industrial action (but before the protected period ends) during the whole or any part of which the employee is locked out by his employer.

(7D) In subsections (7B) and (7C), the 'first day of protected industrial action' means the day on which the employee starts to take protected industrial action (even if on that day he is locked out by his employer).

(8)   For the purposes of this section no account shall be taken of the repudiation of any act by a trade union as mentioned in section 21 in relation to anything which occurs before the end of the next working day (within the meaning of section 237) after the day on which the repudiation takes place.

(9)   In this section 'date of dismissal' has the meaning given by section 238(5).

238B   Conciliation and mediation: supplementary provisions

(1)   The matters referred to in subsection (6)(e) of section 238A are those specified in subsections (2) to (5); and references in this section to 'the service provider' are to any person who provided a service mentioned in subsection (6)(c) or (d) of that section.

(2)   The first matter is: whether, at meetings arranged by the service provider, the employer or, as the case may be, a union was represented by an appropriate person.

(3)   The second matter is: whether the employer or a union, so far as requested to do so, co-operated in the making of arrangements for meetings to be held with the service provider.

(4)   The third matter is: whether the employer or a union fulfilled any commitment given by it during the provision of the service to take particular action.

(5)   The fourth matter is: whether, at meetings arranged by the service provider between the parties making use of the service, the representatives of the employer or a union answered any reasonable question put to them concerning the matter subject to conciliation or mediation.

(6)   For the purposes of subsection (2) an 'appropriate person' is—
    (a)   in relation to the employer—
        (i)   a person with the authority to settle the matter subject to conciliation or mediation on behalf of the employer, or
        (ii)   a person authorised by a person of that type to make recommendations to him with regard to the settlement of that matter, and
    (b)   in relation to a union, a person who is responsible for handling on the union's behalf the matter subject to conciliation or mediation.

(7)   For the purposes of subsection (4) regard may be had to any timetable which was agreed for the taking of the action in question or, if no timetable was agreed, to how long it was before the action was taken.

(8)   In any proceedings in which regard must be had to the matters referred to in section 238A(6)(e)—
    (a)   notes taken by or on behalf of the service provider shall not be admissible in evidence;
    (b)   the service provider must refuse to give evidence as to anything communicated to him in connection with the performance of his functions as a conciliator or mediator if, in his opinion, to give the evidence would involve his making a damaging disclosure; and
    (c)   the service provider may refuse to give evidence as to whether, for the purposes of subsection (5), a particular question was or was not a reasonable one.

(9)   For the purposes of subsection (8)(b) a 'damaging disclosure' is—
    (a)   a disclosure of information which is commercially sensitive, or
    (b)   a disclosure of information that has not previously been disclosed which relates to a position taken by a party using the conciliation or mediation service on the settlement of the matter subject to conciliation or mediation,
to which the person who communicated the information to the service provider has not consented.

239   Supplementary provisions relating to unfair dismissal

(1)   Sections 237 to 238A (loss of unfair dismissal protection in connection with industrial action) shall be construed as one with Part X of the Employment Rights Act 1996 (unfair dismissal); but sections 108 and 109 of that Act (qualifying period and age limit) shall not apply in relation to section 238A of this Act.

(2)   In relation to a complaint to which section 238 or 238A applies, section 111(2) of that Act (time limit for complaint) does not apply, but an employment tribunal shall not consider the complaint unless it is presented to the tribunal—

    (a)   before the end of the period of six months beginning with the date of the complainant's dismissal (as defined by section 238(5)), or

    (b)   where the tribunal is satisfied that it was not reasonably practicable for the complaint to be presented before the end of that period, within such further period as the tribunal considers reasonable.

(3)   Where it is shown that the condition referred to in section 238(2)(b) is fulfilled (discriminatory re-engagement), the references in—

    (a)   sections 98 to 106 of the Employment Rights Act 1996, and

    (b)   sections 152 and 153 of this Act,

to the reason or principal reason for which the complainant was dismissed shall be read as references to the reason or principal reason he has not been offered re-engagement.

(4)   In relation to a complaint under section 111 of the 1996 Act (unfair dismissal: complaint to employment tribunal) that a dismissal was unfair by virtue of section 238A of this Act—

    (a)   no order shall be made under section 113 of the 1996 Act (reinstatement or re-engagement) until after the conclusion of protected industrial action by any employee in relation to the relevant dispute,

    (b)   regulations under section 7 of the Employment Tribunals Act 1996 may make provision about the adjournment and renewal of applications (including provision requiring adjournment in specified circumstances), and

    (c)   regulations under section 9 of that Act may require a pre-hearing review to be carried out in specified circumstances.

Criminal offences

240   Breach of contract involving injury to persons or property

(1)   A person commits an offence who wilfully and maliciously breaks a contract of service or hiring, knowing or having reasonable cause to believe that the probable consequences of his so doing, either alone or in combination with others, will be—

    (a)   to endanger human life or cause serious bodily injury, or

    (b)   to expose valuable property, whether real or personal, to destruction or serious injury.

(2)   Subsection (1) applies equally whether the offence is committed from malice conceived against the person endangered or injured or, as the case may be, the owner of the property destroyed or injured, or otherwise.

(3)   A person guilty of an offence under this section is liable on summary conviction ... to a fine not exceeding level 2 on the standard scale.

(4)   This section does not apply to seamen.

241   Intimidation or annoyance by violence or otherwise

(1)   A person commits an offence who, with a view to compelling another person to abstain from doing or to do any act which that person has a legal right to do or abstain from doing, wrongfully and without legal authority—

    (a)   uses violence to or intimidates that person or his spouse or civil partner or children, or injures his property,

    (b)   persistently follows that person about from place to place,

    (c)   hides any tools, clothes or other property owned or used by that person, or deprives him of or hinders him in the use thereof,

    (d)   watches or besets the house or other place where that person resides, works, carries on business or happens to be, or the approach to any such house or place, or

    (e)   follows that person with two or more other persons in a disorderly manner in or through any street or road.

(2)   A person guilty of an offence under this section is liable on summary conviction to imprisonment for a term not exceeding six months or a fine not exceeding level 5 on the standard scale, or both.

(3)   ...

242 Restriction of offence of conspiracy: England and Wales

(1) Where in pursuance of any such agreement as is mentioned in section 1(1) of the Criminal Law Act 1977 (which provides for the offence of conspiracy) the acts in question in relation to an offence are to be done in contemplation or furtherance of a trade dispute, the offence shall be disregarded for the purposes of that subsection if it is a summary offence which is not punishable with imprisonment.

(2) This section extends to England and Wales only.

243 Restriction of offence of conspiracy: Scotland

(1) An agreement of combination by two or more persons to do or procure to be done an act in contemplation or furtherance of a trade dispute is not indictable as a conspiracy if that act committed by one person would not be punishable as a crime.

(2) A crime for this purpose means an offence punishable on indictment, or an offence punishable on summary conviction, and for the commission of which the offender is liable under the statute making the offence punishable to be imprisoned either absolutely or at the discretion of the court as an alternative for some other punishment.

(3) Where a person is convicted of any such agreement or combination as is mentioned above to do or procure to be done an act which is punishable only on summary conviction, and is sentenced to imprisonment, the imprisonment shall not exceed three months or such longer time as may be prescribed by the statute for the punishment of the act when committed by one person.

(4) Nothing in this section—

    (a) exempts from punishment a person guilty of a conspiracy for which a punishment is awarded by an Act of Parliament, or

    (b) affects the law relating to riot, unlawful assembly, breach of the peace, or sedition or any offence against the State or the Sovereign.

(5) This section extends to Scotland only.

Supplementary

244 Meaning of 'trade dispute' in Part V

(1) In this Part a 'trade dispute' means a dispute between workers and their employer which relates wholly or mainly to one or more of the following—

    (a) terms and conditions of employment, or the physical conditions in which any workers are required to work;

    (b) engagement or non-engagement, or termination or suspension of employment or the duties of employment, of one or more workers;

    (c) allocation of work or the duties of employment between workers or groups of workers;

    (d) matters of discipline;

    (e) a worker's membership or non-membership of a trade union;

    (f) facilities for officials of trade unions; and

    (g) machinery for negotiation or consultation, and other procedures, relating to any of the above matters, including the recognition by employers or employers' associations of the right of a trade union to represent workers in such negotiation or consultation or in the carrying out of such procedures.

(2) A dispute between a Minister of the Crown and any workers shall, notwithstanding that he is not the employer of those workers, be treated as a dispute between those workers and their employer if the dispute relates to matters which—

    (a) have been referred for consideration by a joint body on which, by virtue of provision made by or under any enactment, he is represented, or

    (b) cannot be settled without him exercising a power conferred on him by or under an enactment.

(3) There is a trade dispute even though it relates to matters occurring outside the United Kingdom, so long as the person or persons whose actions in the United Kingdom are said to be in contemplation or furtherance of a trade dispute relating to matters occurring outside the

United Kingdom are likely to be affected in respect of one or more of the matters specified in subsection (1) by the outcome of the dispute.

(4)   An act, threat or demand done or made by one person or organisation against another which, if restricted, would have led to a trade dispute with that other, shall be treated as being done or made in contemplation of a trade dispute with that other, notwithstanding that because that other submits to the act or threat or accedes to the demand no dispute arises.

(5)   In this section—

'employment' includes any relationship whereby one person personally does work or performs services for another; and

'worker', in relation to a dispute with an employer, means—

(a)   a worker employed by that employer; or

(b)   a person who has ceased to be so employed if his employment was terminated in connection with the dispute or if the termination of his employment was one of the circumstances giving rise to the dispute.

246   Minor definitions

In this Part—

'date of the ballot' means, in the case of a ballot in which votes may be cast on more than one day, the last of those days;

'strike' means any concerted stoppage of work;

'working hours', in relation to a person, means any time when under his contract of employment, or other contract personally to do work or perform services, he is required to be at work.

PART VI
ADMINISTRATIVE PROVISIONS
ACAS

247   ACAS

(1)   There shall continue to be a body called the Advisory, Conciliation and Arbitration Service (referred to in this Act as 'ACAS').

(2)   ACAS is a body corporate of which the corporators are the members of its Council.

(3)   Its functions, and those of its officers and servants, shall be performed on behalf of the Crown, but not so as to make it subject to directions of any kind from any Minister of the Crown as to the manner in which it is to exercise its functions under any enactment.

(4)   For the purposes of civil proceedings arising out of those functions the Crown Proceedings Act 1947 applies to ACAS as if it were a government department and the Crown Suits (Scotland) Act 1857 applies to it as if it were a public department.

...

The Certification Officer

254   The Certification Officer

(1)   There shall continue to be an officer called the Certification Officer.

(2)   The Certification Officer shall be appointed by the Secretary of State after consultation with ACAS.

(3)   The Certification Officer may appoint one or more assistant certification officers and shall appoint an assistant certification officer for Scotland.

(4)   The Certification Officer may delegate to an assistant certification officer such functions as he thinks appropriate, and in particular may delegate to the assistant certification officer for Scotland such functions as he thinks appropriate in relation to organisations whose principal office is in Scotland.

References to the Certification Officer in enactments relating to his functions shall be construed accordingly.

(5)   ACAS shall provide for the Certification Officer the requisite staff (from among the officers and servants of ACAS) and the requisite accommodation, equipment and other facilities.

(5A) Subject to subsection (6), ACAS shall pay to the Certification Officer such sums as he may require for the performance of any of his functions.

(6) The Secretary of State shall pay to the Certification Officer such sums as he may require for making payments under the scheme under section 115 (payments towards expenditure in connection with secret ballots).

256 Procedure before the Certification Officer

(1) Except in relation to matters as to which express provision is made by or under an enactment, the Certification Officer may regulate the procedure to be followed—
   (a)   on any application or complaint made to him, or
   (b)   where his approval is sought with respect to any matter.

(2) He shall in particular make provision about the disclosure, and restriction of the disclosure, of the identity of an individual who has made or is proposing to make any such application or complaint.

(2A) Provision under subsection (2) shall be such that if the application or complaint relates to a trade union—
   (a)   the individual's identity is disclosed to the union unless the Certification Officer thinks the circumstances are such that it should not be so disclosed;
   (b)   the individual's identity is disclosed to such other persons (if any) as the Certification Officer thinks fit.

...

Central Arbitration Committee

259 The Central Arbitration Committee

(1) There shall continue to be a body called the Central Arbitration Committee.

(2) The functions of the Committee shall be performed on behalf of the Crown, but not so as to make it subject to directions of any kind from any Minister of the Crown as to the manner in which it is to exercise its functions.

(3) ACAS shall provide for the Committee the requisite staff (from among the officers and servants of ACAS) and the requisite accommodation, equipment and other facilities.

PART VII
MISCELLANEOUS AND GENERAL

Interpretation

295 Meaning of 'employee' and related expressions

(1) In this Act—
'contract of employment' means a contract of service or of apprenticeship,
'employee' means an individual who has entered into or works under (or, where the employment has ceased, worked under) a contract of employment, and
'employer', in relation to an employee, means the person by whom the employee is (or, where the employment has ceased, was) employed.

(2) Subsection (1) has effect subject to section 235 and other provisions conferring a wider meaning on 'contract of employment', or related expressions.

296 Meaning of 'worker' and related expressions

(1) In this Act 'worker' means an individual who works, or normally works or seeks to work—
   (a)   under a contract of employment, or
   (b)   under any other contract whereby he undertakes to do or perform personally any work or services for another party to the contract who is not a professional client of his, or
   (c)   in employment under or for the purposes of a government department (otherwise than as a member of the naval, military or air forces of the Crown) in so far as such employment does not fall within paragraph (a) or (b) above.

(2) In this Act 'employer', in relation to a worker, means a person for whom one or more workers work, or have worked or normally work or seek to work.

(3) This section shall have effect subject to sections 68(4), 145F(3) and 151(1B).

297   **Associated employers**

For the purposes of this Act any two employers shall be treated as associated if—

    (a)   one is a company of which the other (directly or indirectly) has control, or

    (b)   both are companies of which a third person (directly or indirectly) has control;

and 'associated employer' shall be construed accordingly.

298   **Minor definitions: general**

In this Act, unless the context otherwise requires—

'act' and 'action' each includes omission, and references to doing an act or taking action shall be construed accordingly;

'contravention' includes a failure to comply, and cognate expressions shall be construed accordingly;

'dismiss', 'dismissal' and 'effective date of termination', in relation to an employee, shall be construed in accordance with Part X of the Employment Rights Act 1996;

'tort', as respects Scotland, means delict, and cognate expressions shall be construed accordingly.

DISABILITY DISCRIMINATION ACT 1995
(1995, c. 50)

PART I

DISABILITY

1   **Meaning of 'disability' and 'disabled person'**

(1)   Subject to the provisions of Schedule 1, a person has a disability for the purposes of this Act and Part III of the 2005 Order if he has a physical or mental impairment which has a substantial and long-term adverse effect on his ability to carry out normal day-to-day activities.

(2)   In this Act and Part III of the 2005 Order 'disabled person' means a person who has a disability.

2   **Past disabilities**

(1)   The provisions of this Part and Part 2 to 4 and 5A apply in relation to a person who has had a disability as they apply in relation to a person who has that disability.

(2)   Those provisions are subject to the modifications made by Schedule 2.

(3)   Any regulations or order made under this Act by the Secretary of State, the Scottish Ministers or the Welsh Minister may include provision with respect to persons who have had a disability.

(4)   In any proceedings under Part 2, 3, 4 or 5A of this Act, the question whether a person had a disability at a particular time ('the relevant time') shall be determined, for the purposes of this section, as if the provisions of, or made under, this Act in force when the act complained of was done had been in force at the relevant time.

(5)   The relevant time may be a time before the passing of this Act.

PART II

THE EMPLOYMENT FIELD

Meaning of 'discrimination' and 'harassment'

3A   **Meaning of 'discrimination'**

(1)   For the purposes of this Part, a person discriminates against a disabled person if—

    (a)   for a reason which relates to the disabled person's disability, he treats him less favourably than he treats or would treat others to whom that reason does not or would not apply, and

    (b)   he cannot show that the treatment in question is justified.

(2)   For the purposes of this Part, a person also discriminates against a disabled person if he fails to comply with a duty to make reasonable adjustments imposed on him in relation to the disabled person.

(3) Treatment is justified for the purposes of subsection (1)(b) if, but only if, the reason for it is both material to the circumstances of the particular case and substantial.

(4) But treatment of a disabled person cannot be justified under subsection (3) if it amounts to direct discrimination falling within subsection (5).

(5) A person directly discriminates against a disabled person if, on the ground of the disabled person's disability, he treats the disabled person less favourably than he treats or would treat a person not having that particular disability whose relevant circumstances, including his abilities, are the same as, or not materially different from, those of the disabled person.

(6) If, in a case falling within subsection (1), a person is under a duty to make reasonable adjustments in relation to a disabled person but fails to comply with that duty, his treatment of that person cannot be justified under subsection (3) unless it would have been justified even if he had complied with that duty.

3B   Meaning of 'harassment'

(1) For the purposes of this Part, a person subjects a disabled person to harassment where, for a reason which relates to the disabled person's disability, he engages in unwanted conduct which has the purpose or effect of—

(a)   violating the disabled person's dignity, or

(b)   creating an intimidating, hostile, degrading, humiliating or offensive environment for him.

(2) Conduct shall be regarded as having the effect referred to in paragraph (a) or (b) of subsection (1) only if, having regard to all the circumstances, including in particular the perception of the disabled person, it should reasonably be considered as having that effect.

Employment

4   Employers: discrimination and harassment

(1) It is unlawful for an employer to discriminate against a disabled person—

(a)   in the arrangements which he makes for the purpose of determining to whom he should offer employment;

(b)   in the terms on which he offers that person employment; or

(c)   by refusing to offer, or deliberately not offering, him employment.

(2) It is unlawful for an employer to discriminate against a disabled person whom he employs—

(a)   in the terms of employment which he affords him;

(b)   in the opportunities which he affords him for promotion, a transfer, training or receiving any other benefit;

(c)   by refusing to afford him, or deliberately not affording him, any such opportunity; or

(d)   by dismissing him, or subjecting him to any other detriment.

(3) It is also unlawful for an employer, in relation to employment by him, to subject to harassment—

(a)   a disabled person whom he employs; or

(b)   a disabled person who has applied to him for employment.

(4) Subsection (2) does not apply to benefits of any description if the employer is concerned with the provision (whether or not for payment) of benefits of that description to the public, or to a section of the public which includes the employee in question, unless—

(a)   that provision differs in a material respect from the provision of the benefits by the employer to his employees;

(b)   the provision of the benefits to the employee in question is regulated by his contract of employment; or

(c)   the benefits relate to training.

(5) The reference in subsection (2)(d) to the dismissal of a person includes a reference—

(a)   to the termination of that person's employment by the expiration of any period (including a period expiring by reference to an event or circumstance), not being a termination immediately after which the employment is renewed on the same terms; and

    (b)   to the termination of that person's employment by any act of his (including the giving of notice) in circumstances such that he is entitled to terminate it without notice by reason of the conduct of the employer.

(6)   This section applies only in relation to employment at an establishment in Great Britain.

4A   Employers: duty to make adjustments

(1)   Where—
    (a)   a provision, criterion or practice applied by or on behalf of an employer, or
    (b)   any physical feature of premises occupied by the employer,
places the disabled person concerned at a substantial disadvantage in comparison with persons who are not disabled, it is the duty of the employer to take such steps as it is reasonable, in all the circumstances of the case, for him to have to take in order to prevent the provision, criterion or practice, or feature, having that effect.

(2)   In subsection (1), 'the disabled person concerned' means—
    (a)   in the case of a provision, criterion or practice for determining to whom employment should be offered, any disabled person who is, or has notified the employer that he may be, an applicant for that employment;
    (b)   in any other case, a disabled person who is—
        (i)   an applicant for the employment concerned, or
        (ii)   an employee of the employer concerned.

(3)   Nothing in this section imposes any duty on an employer in relation to a disabled person if the employer does not know, and could not reasonably be expected to know—
    (a)   in the case of an applicant or potential applicant, that the disabled person concerned is, or may be, an applicant for the employment; or
    (b)   in any case, that that person has a disability and is likely to be affected in the way mentioned in subsection (1).

Contract workers

4B   Contract workers

(1)   It is unlawful for a principal, in relation to contract work, to discriminate against a disabled person who is a contract worker (a 'disabled contract worker')—
    (a)   in the terms on which he allows him to do that work;
    (b)   by not allowing him to do it or continue to do it;
    (c)   in the way he affords him access to any benefits or by refusing or deliberately omitting to afford him access to them; or
    (d)   by subjecting him to any other detriment.

(2)   It is also unlawful for a principal, in relation to contract work, to subject a disabled contract worker to harassment.

(3)   Subsection (1) does not apply to benefits of any description if the principal is concerned with the provision (whether or not for payment) of benefits of that description to the public, or to a section of the public which includes the contract worker in question, unless that provision differs in a material respect from the provision of the benefits by the principal to contract workers.

(4)   This subsection applies to a disabled contract worker where, by virtue of—
    (a)   a provision, criterion or practice applied by or on behalf of all or most of the principals to whom he is or might be supplied, or
    (b)   a physical feature of premises occupied by such persons,
he is likely, on each occasion when he is supplied to a principal to do contract work, to be placed at a substantial disadvantage in comparison with persons who are not disabled which is the same or similar in each case.

(5)   Where subsection (4) applies to a disabled contract worker, his employer must take such steps as he would have to take under section 4A if the provision, criterion or practice were applied by him or on his behalf or (as the case may be) if the premises were occupied by him.

(6)   Section 4A applies to any principal, in relation to contract work, as if he were, or would be, the employer of the disabled contract worker and as if any contract worker supplied to do work for him were an employee of his.

(7) However, for the purposes of section 4A as applied by subsection (6), a principal is not required to take a step in relation to a disabled contract worker if under that section the disabled contract worker's employer is required to take the step in relation to him.

(8) This section applies only in relation to contract work done at an establishment in Great Britain (the provisions of section 68 about the meaning of 'employment at an establishment in Great Britain' applying for the purposes of this subsection with the appropriate modifications).

(9) In this section—

'principal' means a person ('A') who makes work available for doing by individuals who are employed by another person who supplies them under a contract made with A;

'contract work' means work so made available; and

'contract worker' means any individual who is supplied to the principal under such a contract.

Other unlawful acts

16A Relationships which have come to an end

(1) This section applies where—
    (a) there has been a relevant relationship between a disabled person and another person ('the relevant person'), and
    (b) the relationship has come to an end.

(2) In this section a 'relevant relationship' is—
    (a) a relationship during the course of which an act of discrimination against, or harassment of, one party to the relationship by the other party to it is unlawful under any preceding provision of this Part, other than sections 15B and 15C; or
    (b) a relationship between a person providing employment services and a person receiving such services.

(3) It is unlawful for the relevant person—
    (a) to discriminate against the disabled person by subjecting him to a detriment, or
    (b) to subject the disabled person to harassment,
where the discrimination or harassment arises out of and is closely connected to the relevant relationship.

(4) This subsection applies where—
    (a) a provision, criterion or practice applied by the relevant person to the disabled person in relation to any matter arising out of the relevant relationship, or
    (b) a physical feature of premises which are occupied by the relevant person,
places the disabled person at a substantial disadvantage in comparison with persons who are not disabled, but are in the same position as the disabled person in relation to the relevant person.

(5) Where subsection (4) applies, it is the duty of the relevant person to take such steps as it is reasonable, in all the circumstances of the case, for him to have to take in order to prevent the provision, practice or criterion, or feature, having that effect.

(6) Nothing in subsection (5) imposes any duty on the relevant person if he does not know, and could not reasonably be expected to know, that the disabled person has a disability and is likely to be affected in the way mentioned in that subsection.

(7) In subsection (2), reference to an act of discrimination or harassment which is unlawful includes, in the case of a relationship which has come to an end before the commencement of this section, reference to such an act which would, after the commencement of this section, be unlawful.

16B Discriminatory advertisements

(1) It is unlawful for a person to publish or cause to be published an advertisement which—
    (a) invites applications for a relevant appointment or benefit; and
    (b) indicates, or might reasonably be understood to indicate, that an application will or may be determined to any extent by reference to—
        (i) the applicant not having any disability, or any particular disability,
        (ii) the applicant not having had any disability, or any particular disability, or

(iii) any reluctance of the person determining the application to comply with a duty to make reasonable adjustments or (in relation to employment services) with the duty imposed by section 21(1) as modified by section 21A(6).

(2) Subsection (1) does not apply where it would not in fact be unlawful under this Part or, to the extent that it relates to the provision of employment services, Part 3 for an application to be determined in the manner indicated (or understood to be indicated) in the advertisement.

(2A) A person who publishes an advertisement of the kind described in subsection (1) shall not be subject to any liability under subsection (1) in respect of the publication of the advertisement if he proves—

(a) that the advertisement was published in reliance on a statement made to him by the person who caused it to be published to the effect that, by reason of the operation of subsection (2), the publication would not be unlawful; and

(b) that it was reasonable for him to rely on the statement.

(2B) A person who knowingly or recklessly makes a statement such as is mentioned in subsection (2A)(a) which in a material respect is false or misleading commits an offence, and shall be liable on summary conviction to a fine not exceeding level 5 on the standard scale.

(2C) Subsection (1) does not apply in relation to an advertisement so far as it invites persons to apply, in their capacity as members of an authority to which sections 15B and 15C apply, for a relevant appointment or benefit which the authority is intending to make or confer.

(3) In this section, 'relevant appointment or benefit' means—

(a) any employment, promotion or transfer of employment;

(b) membership of, or a benefit under, an occupational pension scheme;

(c) an appointment to any office or post to which section 4D applies;

(d) any partnership in a firm (within the meaning of section 6A);

(e) any tenancy or pupillage (within the meaning of section 7A or 7C);

(f) any membership of a trade organisation (within the meaning of section 13);

(g) any professional or trade qualification (within the meaning of section 14A);

(h) any work placement (within the meaning of section 14C);

(i) any employment services.

(4) In this section, 'advertisement' includes every form of advertisement or notice, whether to the public or not.

(5) Proceedings in respect of a contravention of subsection (1) may be brought only—

(a) by the Commission for Equality and Human Rights, and

(b) in accordance with section 25 of the Equality Act 2006.

Enforcement etc

17A Enforcement, remedies and procedure

(1) A complaint by any person that another person—

(a) has discriminated against him, or subjected him to harassment, in a way which is unlawful under this Part, or

(b) is, by virtue of section 57 or 58, to be treated as having done so,

may be presented to an employment tribunal.

(1A) Subsection (1) does not apply to a complaint under section 14A(1) or (2) of an act in respect of which an appeal, or proceedings in the nature of an appeal, may be brought under any enactment.

(1B) ...

(1C) Where, on the hearing of a complaint under subsection (1), the complainant proves facts from which the tribunal could, apart from this subsection, conclude in the absence of an adequate explanation that the respondent has acted in a way which is unlawful under this Part, the tribunal shall uphold the complaint unless the respondent proves that he did not so act.

(2) Where an employment tribunal finds that a complaint presented to it under this section is well-founded, it shall take such of the following steps as it considers just and equitable—

(a) making a declaration as to the rights of the complainant and the respondent in relation to the matters to which the complaint relates;

(b)   ordering the respondent to pay compensation to the complainant;

(c)   recommending that the respondent take, within a specified period, action appearing to the tribunal to be reasonable, in all the circumstances of the case, for the purpose of obviating or reducing the adverse effect on the complainant of any matter to which the complaint relates.

(3)   Where a tribunal orders compensation under subsection (2)(b), the amount of the compensation shall be calculated by applying the principles applicable to the calculation of damages in claims in tort or (in Scotland) in reparation for breach of statutory duty.

(4)   For the avoidance of doubt it is hereby declared that compensation in respect of discrimination in a way which is unlawful under this Part may include compensation for injury to feelings whether or not it includes compensation under any other head.

(5)   If the respondent to a complaint fails, without reasonable justification, to comply with a recommendation made by an employment tribunal under subsection (2)(c) the tribunal may, if it thinks it just and equitable to do so—

(a)   increase the amount of compensation required to be paid to the complainant in respect of the complaint, where an order was made under subsection (2)(b); or

(b)   make an order under subsection (2)(b).

(6)   Regulations may make provision—

(a)   for enabling a tribunal, where an amount of compensation falls to be awarded under subsection (2)(b), to include in the award interest on that amount; and

(b)   specifying, for cases where a tribunal decides that an award is to include an amount in respect of interest, the manner in which and the periods and rate by reference to which the interest is to be determined.

(7)   Regulations may modify the operation of any order made under section 14 of the Employment Tribunals Act 1996 (power to make provision as to interest on sums payable in pursuance of employment tribunal decisions) to the extent that it relates to an award of compensation under subsection (2)(b).

(8)   Part I of Schedule 3 makes further provision about the enforcement of this Part and about procedure.

Supplementary and general

18B   Reasonable adjustments: supplementary

(1)   In determining whether it is reasonable for a person to have to take a particular step in order to comply with a duty to make reasonable adjustments, regard shall be had, in particular, to—

(a)   the extent to which taking the step would prevent the effect in relation to which the duty is imposed;

(b)   the extent to which it is practicable for him to take the step;

(c)   the financial and other costs which would be incurred by him in taking the step and the extent to which taking it would disrupt any of his activities;

(d)   the extent of his financial and other resources;

(e)   the availability to him of financial or other assistance with respect to taking the step;

(f)   the nature of his activities and the size of his undertaking;

(g)   where the step would be taken in relation to a private household, the extent to which taking it would—

(i)   disrupt that household, or

(ii)   disturb any person residing there.

(2)   The following are examples of steps which a person may need to take in relation to a disabled person in order to comply with a duty to make reasonable adjustments—

(a)   making adjustments to premises;

(b)   allocating some of the disabled person's duties to another person;

(c)   transferring him to fill an existing vacancy;

(d)   altering his hours of working or training;

(e)   assigning him to a different place of work or training;

     (f)   allowing him to be absent during working or training hours for rehabilitation, assessment or treatment;

     (g)   giving, or arranging for, training or mentoring (whether for the disabled person or any other person);

     (h)   acquiring or modifying equipment;

     (i)   modifying instructions or reference manuals;

     (j)   modifying procedures for testing or assessment;

     (k)   providing a reader or interpreter;

     (l)   providing supervision or other support.

(3) For the purposes of a duty to make reasonable adjustments, where under any binding obligation a person is required to obtain the consent of another person to any alteration of the premises occupied by him—

     (a)   it is always reasonable for him to have to take steps to obtain that consent; and

     (b)   it is never reasonable for him to have to make that alteration before that consent is obtained.

(4) The steps referred to in subsection (3)(a) shall not be taken to include an application to a court or tribunal.

(5) In subsection (3), 'binding obligation' means a legally binding obligation (not contained in a lease (within the meaning of section 18A(3)) in relation to the premises, whether arising from an agreement or otherwise.

(6) A provision of this Part imposing a duty to make reasonable adjustments applies only for the purpose of determining whether a person has discriminated against a disabled person; and accordingly a breach of any such duty is not actionable as such.

18D   Interpretation of Part 2

(1) Subject to any duty to make reasonable adjustments, nothing in this Part is to be taken to require a person to treat a disabled person more favourably than he treats or would treat others.

(2) In this Part—

'benefits', except in sections 4G to 4K, includes facilities and services;

'detriment', except in section 16C(2)(b), does not include conduct of the nature referred to in section 3B (harassment);

'discriminate', 'discrimination' and other related expressions are to be construed in accordance with section 3A;

'duty to make reasonable adjustments' means a duty imposed by or under section 4A, 4B(5) or (6), 4E, 4H, 6B, 7B, 7D, 14, 14B, 14D, 15C or 16A(5);

'employer' includes a person who has no employees but is seeking to employ another person;

'harassment' is to be construed in accordance with section 3B;

'physical feature', in relation to any premises, includes (subject to any provision under section 15C(4)(e)) any of the following (whether permanent or temporary)—

     (a)   any feature arising from the design or construction of a building on the premises,

     (b)   any feature on the premises of any approach to, exit from or access to such a building,

     (c)   any fixtures, fittings, furnishings, furniture, equipment or material in or on the premises,

     (d)   any other physical element or quality of any land comprised in the premises;

'provision, criterion or practice' includes any arrangements.

PART VII

SUPPLEMENTAL

55   Victimisation

(1) For the purposes of Part 2 or Part 4, or Part 3 other than sections 24A to 24L, a person ('A') discriminates against another person ('B') if—

     (a)   he treats B less favourably than he treats or would treat other persons whose circumstances are the same as B's; and

     (b)   he does so for a reason mentioned in subsection (2).

(2)   The reasons are that—

    (a)   B has—

        (i)   brought proceedings against A or any other person under this Act or Part III of the 2005 Order; or

        (ii)   given evidence or information in connection with such proceedings brought by any person; or

        (iii)   otherwise done anything under, or by reference to, this Act or Part III of the 2005 Order in relation to A or any other person; or

        (iv)   alleged that A or any other person has (whether or not the allegation so states) contravened this Act; or

    (b)   A believes or suspects that B has done or intends to do any of those things.

(3)   Where B is a disabled person, or a person who has had a disability, the disability in question shall be disregarded in comparing his circumstances with those of any other person for the purposes of subsection (1)(a).

(3A)   For the purposes of Chapter 1 of Part 4—

    (a)   references in subsection (2) to B include references to—

        (i)   a person who is, for the purposes of that Chapter, B's parent; and

        (ii)   a sibling of B; and

    (b)   references in that subsection to this Act are, as respects a person mentioned in sub-paragraph (i) or (ii) of paragraph (a), restricted to that Chapter.

(4)   Subsection (1) does not apply to treatment of a person because of an allegation made by him if the allegation was false and not made in good faith.

(5)   In the case of an act which constitutes discrimination by virtue of this section, sections 4, 4B, 4D, 4G, 6A, 7A, 7C, 13, 14A, 14C, 15B and 16A also apply to discrimination against a person who is not disabled.

(6)   ...

58   Liability of employers and principals

(1)   Anything done by a person in the course of his employment shall be treated for the purposes of this Act as also done by his employer, whether or not it was done with the employer's knowledge or approval.

(2)   Anything done by a person as agent for another person with the authority of that other person shall be treated for the purposes of this Act as also done by that other person.

(3)   Subsection (2) applies whether the authority was—

    (a)   express or implied; or

    (b)   given before or after the act in question was done.

(4)   Subsections (1) and (2) do not apply in relation to an offence under section 57(4).

(5)   In proceedings under this Act against any person in respect of an act alleged to have been done by an employee of his, it shall be a defence for that person to prove that he took such steps as were reasonably practicable to prevent the employee from—

    (a)   doing that act; or

    (b)   doing, in the course of his employment, acts of that description.

<h1 style="text-align:center">EMPLOYMENT RIGHTS ACT 1996
(1996, c. 18)</h1>

PART I
EMPLOYMENT PARTICULARS

Right to statements of employment particulars

1   Statement of initial employment particulars

(1)   Where an employee begins employment with an employer, the employer shall give to the employee a written statement of particulars of employment.

(2)   The statement may (subject to section 2(4)) be given in instalments and (whether or not given in instalments) shall be given not later than two months after the beginning of the employment.

   (3) The statement shall contain particulars of—
      (a) the names of the employer and employee,
      (b) the date when the employment began, and
      (c) the date on which the employee's period of continuous employment began (taking into account any employment with a previous employer which counts towards that period).
   (4) The statement shall also contain particulars, as at a specified date not more than seven days before the statement (or the instalment containing them) is given, of—
      (a) the scale or rate of remuneration or the method of calculating remuneration,
      (b) the intervals at which remuneration is paid (that is, weekly, monthly or other specified intervals),
      (c) any terms and conditions relating to hours of work (including any terms and conditions relating to normal working hours),
      (d) any terms and conditions relating to any of the following—
          (i) entitlement to holidays, including public holidays, and holiday pay (the particulars given being sufficient to enable the employee's entitlement, including any entitlement to accrued holiday pay on the termination of employment, to be precisely calculated),
          (ii) incapacity for work due to sickness or injury, including any provision for sick pay, and
          (iii) pensions and pension schemes,
      (e) the length of notice which the employee is obliged to give and entitled to receive to terminate his contract of employment,
      (f) the title of the job which the employee is employed to do or a brief description of the work for which he is employed,
      (g) where the employment is not intended to be permanent, the period for which it is expected to continue or, if it is for a fixed term, the date when it is to end,
      (h) either the place of work or, where the employee is required or permitted to work at various places, an indication of that and of the address of the employer,
      (j) any collective agreements which directly affect the terms and conditions of the employment including, where the employer is not a party, the persons by whom they were made, and
      (k) where the employee is required to work outside the United Kingdom for a period of more than one month—
          (i) the period for which he is to work outside the United Kingdom,
          (ii) the currency in which remuneration is to be paid while he is working outside the United Kingdom,
          (iii) any additional remuneration payable to him, and any benefits to be provided to or in respect of him, by reason of his being required to work outside the United Kingdom, and
          (iv) any terms and conditions relating to his return to the United Kingdom.
   (5) Subsection (4)(d)(iii) does not apply to an employee of a body or authority if—
      (a) the employee's pension rights depend on the terms of a pension scheme established under any provision contained in or having effect under any Act, and
      (b) any such provision requires the body or authority to give to a new employee information concerning the employee's pension rights or the determination of questions affecting those rights.

2 Statement of initial particulars: supplementary

   (1) If, in the case of a statement under section 1, there are no particulars to be entered under any of the heads of paragraph (d) or (k) of subsection (4) of that section, or under any of the other paragraphs of subsection (3) or (4) of that section, that fact shall be stated.
   (2) A statement under section 1 may refer the employee for particulars of any of the matters specified in subsection (4)(d)(ii) and (iii) of that section to the provisions of some other document which is reasonably accessible to the employee.

(3)   A statement under section 1 may refer the employee for particulars of either of the matters specified in subsection (4)(e) of that section to the law or to the provisions of any collective agreement directly affecting the terms and conditions of the employment which is reasonably accessible to the employee.

(4)   The particulars required by section 1(3) and (4)(a) to (c), (d)(i), (f) and (h) shall be included in a single document.

(5)   Where before the end of the period of two months after the beginning of an employee's employment the employee is to begin to work outside the United Kingdom for a period of more than one month, the statement under section 1 shall be given to him not later than the time when he leaves the United Kingdom in order to begin so to work.

(6)   A statement shall be given to a person under section 1 even if his employment ends before the end of the period within which the statement is required to be given.

3   Note about disciplinary procedures and pensions

(1)   A statement under section 1 shall include a note—

    (a)   specifying any disciplinary rules applicable to the employee or referring the employee to the provisions of a document specifying such rules which is reasonably accessible to the employee,

    (aa)   specifying any procedure applicable to the taking of disciplinary decisions relating to the employee, or to a decision to dismiss the employee, or referring the employee to the provisions of a document specifying such a procedure which is reasonably accessible to the employee,

    (b)   specifying (by description or otherwise)—

        (i)   a person to whom the employee can apply if dissatisfied with any disciplinary decision relating to him or any decision to dismiss him, and

        (ii)   a person to whom the employee can apply for the purpose of seeking redress of any grievance relating to his employment,

and the manner in which any such application should be made, and

    (c)   where there are further steps consequent on any such application, explaining those steps or referring to the provisions of a document explaining them which is reasonably accessible to the employee.

(2)   Subsection (1) does not apply to rules, disciplinary decisions, decisions to dismiss, grievances or procedures relating to health or safety at work.

(3), (4) …

(5)   The note shall also state whether there is in force a contracting-out certificate (issued in accordance with Chapter I of Part III of the Pension Schemes Act 1993) stating that the employment is contracted-out employment (for the purposes of that Part of that Act).

4   Statement of changes

(1)   If, after the material date, there is a change in any of the matters particulars of which are required by sections 1 to 3 to be included or referred to in a statement under section 1, the employer shall give to the employee a written statement containing particulars of the change.

(2)   For the purposes of subsection (1)—

    (a)   in relation to a matter particulars of which are included or referred to in a statement given under section 1 otherwise than in instalments, the material date is the date to which the statement relates,

    (b)   in relation to a matter particulars of which—

        (i)   are included or referred to in an instalment of a statement given under section 1, or

        (ii)   are required by section 2(4) to be included in a single document but are not included in an instalment of a statement given under section 1 which does include other particulars to which that provision applies,

the material date is the date to which the instalment relates, and

    (c)   in relation to any other matter, the material date is the date by which a statement under section 1 is required to be given.

(3) A statement under subsection (1) shall be given at the earliest opportunity and, in any event, not later than—

    (a) one month after the change in question, or

    (b) where that change results from the employee being required to work outside the United Kingdom for a period of more than one month, the time when he leaves the United Kingdom in order to begin so to work, if that is earlier.

(4) A statement under subsection (1) may refer the employee to the provisions of some other document which is reasonably accessible to the employee for a change in any of the matters specified in sections 1(4)(d)(ii) and (iii) and 3(1)(a) and (c).

(5) A statement under subsection (1) may refer the employee for a change in either of the matters specified in section 1(4)(e) to the law or to the provisions of any collective agreement directly affecting the terms and conditions of the employment which is reasonably accessible to the employee.

(6) Where, after an employer has given to an employee a statement under section 1, either—

    (a) the name of the employer (whether an individual or a body corporate or partnership) is changed without any change in the identity of the employer, or

    (b) the identity of the employer is changed in circumstances in which the continuity of the employee's period of employment is not broken,

and subsection (7) applies in relation to the change, the person who is the employer immediately after the change is not required to give to the employee a statement under section 1; but the change shall be treated as a change falling within subsection (1) of this section.

(7) This subsection applies in relation to a change if it does not involve any change in any of the matters (other than the names of the parties) particulars of which are required by sections 1 to 3 to be included or referred to in the statement under section 1.

(8) A statement under subsection (1) which informs an employee of a change such as is referred to in subsection (6)(b) shall specify the date on which the employee's period of continuous employment began.

5   Exclusion from rights to statements

(1) Sections 1 to 4 apply to an employee who at any time comes or ceases to come within the exceptions from those sections provided by section 199, and under section 209, as if his employment with his employer terminated or began at that time.

(2) The fact that section 1 is directed by subsection (1) to apply to an employee as if his employment began on his ceasing to come within the exceptions referred to in that subsection does not affect the obligation under section 1(3)(b) to specify the date on which his employment actually began.

6   Reasonably accessible document or collective agreement

In sections 2 to 4 references to a document or collective agreement which is reasonably accessible to an employee are references to a document or collective agreement which—

    (a) the employee has reasonable opportunities of reading in the course of his employment, or

    (b) is made reasonably accessible to the employee in some other way.

7   Power to require particulars of further matters

The Secretary of State may by order provide that section 1 shall have effect as if particulars of such further matters as may be specified in the order were included in the particulars required by that section; and, for that purpose, the order may include such provisions amending that section as appear to the Secretary of State to be expedient.

7A   Use of alternative documents to give particulars

(1) Subsections (2) and (3) apply where—

    (a) an employer gives an employee a document in writing in the form of a contract of employment or letter of engagement,

(b)   the document contains information which, were the document in the form of a statement under section 1, would meet the employer's obligation under that section in relation to the matters mentioned in subsections (3) and (4)(a) to (c), (d)(i), (f) and (h) of that section, and

(c)   the document is given after the beginning of the employment and before the end of the period for giving a statement under that section.

(2)   The employer's duty under section 1 in relation to any matter shall be treated as met if the document given to the employee contains information which, were the document in the form of a statement under that section, would meet the employer's obligation under that section in relation to that matter.

(3)   The employer's duty under section 3 shall be treated as met if the document given to the employee contains information which, were the document in the form of a statement under section 1 and the information included in the form of a note, would meet the employer's obligation under section 3.

(4)   For the purposes of this section a document to which subsection (1)(a) applies shall be treated, in relation to information in respect of any of the matters mentioned in section 1(4), as specifying the date on which the document is given to the employee as the date as at which the information applies.

(5)   Where subsection (2) applies in relation to any matter, the date on which the document by virtue of which that subsection applies is given to the employee shall be the material date in relation to that matter for the purposes of section 4(1).

(6)   Where subsection (3) applies, the date on which the document by virtue of which that subsection applies is given to the employee shall be the material date for the purposes of section 4(1) in relation to the matters of which particulars are required to be given under section 3.

(7)   The reference in section 4(6) to an employer having given a statement under section 1 shall be treated as including his having given a document by virtue of which his duty to give such a statement is treated as met.

7B   Giving of alternative documents before start of employment

A document in the form of a contract of employment or letter of engagement given by an employer to an employee before the beginning of the employee's employment with the employer shall, when the employment begins, be treated for the purposes of section 7A as having been given at that time.

Right to itemised pay statement

8   Itemised pay statement

(1)   An employee has the right to be given by his employer, at or before the time at which any payment of wages or salary is made to him, a written itemised pay statement.

(2)   The statement shall contain particulars of—

(a)   the gross amount of the wages or salary,

(b)   the amounts of any variable, and (subject to section 9) any fixed, deductions from that gross amount and the purposes for which they are made,

(c)   the net amount of wages or salary payable, and

(d)   where different parts of the net amount are paid in different ways, the amount and method of payment of each part-payment.

9   Standing statement of fixed deductions

(1)   A pay statement given in accordance with section 8 need not contain separate particulars of a fixed deduction if—

(a)   it contains instead an aggregate amount of fixed deductions, including that deduction, and

(b)   the employer has given to the employee, at or before the time at which the pay statement is given, a standing statement of fixed deductions which satisfies subsection (2).

(2)   A standing statement of fixed deductions satisfies this subsection if—

(a)   it is in writing,

(b)   it contains, in relation to each deduction comprised in the aggregate amount of deductions, particulars of—

      (i)   the amount of the deduction,

      (ii)   the intervals at which the deduction is to be made, and

      (iii)   the purpose for which it is made, and

(c)   it is (in accordance with subsection (5)) effective at the date on which the pay statement is given.

(3)   A standing statement of fixed deductions may be amended, whether by—

      (a)   addition of a new deduction,

      (b)   a change in the particulars, or

      (c)   cancellation of an existing deduction,

      by notice in writing, containing particulars of the amendment, given by the employer to the employee.

(4)   An employer who has given to an employee a standing statement of fixed deductions shall—

      (a)   within the period of twelve months beginning with the date on which the first standing statement was given, and

      (b)   at intervals of not more than twelve months afterwards,

      re-issue it in a consolidated form incorporating any amendments notified in accordance with subsection (3).

(5)   For the purposes of subsection (2)(c) a standing statement of fixed deductions—

      (a)   becomes effective on the date on which it is given to the employee, and

      (b)   ceases to be effective at the end of the period of twelve months beginning with that date or, where it is re-issued in accordance with subsection (4), with the end of the period of twelve months beginning with the date of the last re-issue.

Enforcement

11   References to employment tribunals

(1)   Where an employer does not give an employee a statement as required by section 1, 4 or 8 (either because he gives him no statement or because the statement he gives does not comply with what is required), the employee may require a reference to be made to an employment tribunal to determine what particulars ought to have been included or referred to in a statement so as to comply with the requirements of the section concerned.

(2)   Where—

      (a)   a statement purporting to be a statement under section 1 or 4, or a pay statement or a standing statement of fixed deductions purporting to comply with section 8 or 9, has been given to an employee, and

      (b)   a question arises as to the particulars which ought to have been included or referred to in the statement so as to comply with the requirements of this Part,

      either the employer or the employee may require the question to be referred to and determined by an employment tribunal.

(3)   For the purposes of this section—

      (a)   a question as to the particulars which ought to have been included in the note required by section 3 to be included in the statement under section 1 does not include any question whether the employment is, has been or will be contracted-out employment (for the purposes of Part III of the Pension Schemes Act 1993), and

      (b)   a question as to the particulars which ought to have been included in a pay statement or standing statement of fixed deductions does not include a question solely as to the accuracy of an amount stated in any such particulars.

(4)   An employment tribunal shall not consider a reference under this section in a case where the employment to which the reference relates has ceased unless an application requiring the reference to be made was made—

      (a)   before the end of the period of three months beginning with the date on which the employment ceased, or

(b)   within such further period as the tribunal considers reasonable in a case where it is satisfied that it was not reasonably practicable for the application to be made before the end of that period of three months.

12   Determination of references

(1)   Where, on a reference under section 11(1), an employment tribunal determines particulars as being those which ought to have been included or referred to in a statement given under section 1 or 4, the employer shall be deemed to have given to the employee a statement in which those particulars were included, or referred to, as specified in the decision of the tribunal.

(2)   On determining a reference under section 11(2) relating to a statement purporting to be a statement under section 1 or 4, an employment tribunal may—

(a)   confirm the particulars as included or referred to in the statement given by the employer,

(b)   amend those particulars, or

(c)   substitute other particulars for them,

as the tribunal may determine to be appropriate; and the statement shall be deemed to have been given by the employer to the employee in accordance with the decision of the tribunal.

(3)   Where on a reference under section 11 an employment tribunal finds—

(a)   that an employer has failed to give an employee any pay statement in accordance with section 8, or

(b)   that a pay statement or standing statement of fixed deductions does not, in relation to a deduction, contain the particulars required to be included in that statement by that section or section 9,

the tribunal shall make a declaration to that effect.

(4)   Where on a reference in the case of which subsection (3) applies the tribunal further finds that any unnotified deductions have been made from the pay of the employee during the period of thirteen weeks immediately preceding the date of the application for the reference (whether or not the deductions were made in breach of the contract of employment), the tribunal may order the employer to pay the employee a sum not exceeding the aggregate of the unnotified deductions so made.

(5)   For the purposes of subsection (4) a deduction is an unnotified deduction if it is made without the employer giving the employee, in any pay statement or standing statement of fixed deductions, the particulars of the deduction required by section 8 or 9.

PART II
PROTECTION OF WAGES

Deductions by employer

13   Right not to suffer unauthorised deductions

(1)   An employer shall not make a deduction from wages of a worker employed by him unless—

(a)   the deduction is required or authorised to be made by virtue of a statutory provision or a relevant provision of the worker's contract, or

(b)   the worker has previously signified in writing his agreement or consent to the making of the deduction.

(2)   In this section 'relevant provision', in relation to a worker's contract, means a provision of the contract comprised—

(a)   in one or more written terms of the contract of which the employer has given the worker a copy on an occasion prior to the employer making the deduction in question, or

(b)   in one or more terms of the contract (whether express or implied and, if express, whether oral or in writing) the existence and effect, or combined effect, of which in relation to the worker the employer has notified to the worker in writing on such an occasion.

(3)   Where the total amount of wages paid on any occasion by an employer to a worker employed by him is less than the total amount of the wages properly payable by him to the worker on that occasion (after deductions), the amount of the deficiency shall be treated for the purposes of this Part as a deduction made by the employer from the worker's wages on that occasion.

(4) Subsection (3) does not apply in so far as the deficiency is attributable to an error of any description on the part of the employer affecting the computation by him of the gross amount of the wages properly payable by him to the worker on that occasion.

(5) For the purposes of this section a relevant provision of a worker's contract having effect by virtue of a variation of the contract does not operate to authorise the making of a deduction on account of any conduct of the worker, or any other event occurring, before the variation took effect.

(6) For the purposes of this section an agreement or consent signified by a worker does not operate to authorise the making of a deduction on account of any conduct of the worker, or any other event occurring, before the agreement or consent was signified.

(7) This section does not affect any other statutory provision by virtue of which a sum payable to a worker by his employer but not constituting 'wages' within the meaning of this Part is not to be subject to a deduction at the instance of the employer.

14   Excepted deductions

(1) Section 13 does not apply to a deduction from a worker's wages made by his employer where the purpose of the deduction is the reimbursement of the employer in respect of—
    (a) an overpayment of wages, or
    (b) an overpayment in respect of expenses incurred by the worker in carrying out his employment,
made (for any reason) by the employer to the worker.

(2) Section 13 does not apply to a deduction from a worker's wages made by his employer in consequence of any disciplinary proceedings if those proceedings were held by virtue of a statutory provision.

(3) Section 13 does not apply to a deduction from a worker's wages made by his employer in pursuance of a requirement imposed on the employer by a statutory provision to deduct and pay over to a public authority amounts determined by that authority as being due to it from the worker if the deduction is made in accordance with the relevant determination of that authority.

(4) Section 13 does not apply to a deduction from a worker's wages made by his employer in pursuance of any arrangements which have been established—
    (a) in accordance with a relevant provision of his contract to the inclusion of which in the contract the worker has signified his agreement or consent in writing, or
    (b) otherwise with the prior agreement or consent of the worker signified in writing,
and under which the employer is to deduct and pay over to a third person amounts notified to the employer by that person as being due to him from the worker, if the deduction is made in accordance with the relevant notification by that person.

(5) Section 13 does not apply to a deduction from a worker's wages made by his employer where the worker has taken part in a strike or other industrial action and the deduction is made by the employer on account of the worker's having taken part in that strike or other action.

(6) Section 13 does not apply to a deduction from a worker's wages made by his employer with his prior agreement or consent signified in writing where the purpose of the deduction is the satisfaction (whether wholly or in part) of an order of a court or tribunal requiring the payment of an amount by the worker to the employer.

Payments to employer

15   Right not to have to make payments to employer

(1) An employer shall not receive a payment from a worker employed by him unless—
    (a) the payment is required or authorised to be made by virtue of a statutory provision or a relevant provision of the worker's contract, or
    (b) the worker has previously signified in writing his agreement or consent to the making of the payment.

(2) In this section 'relevant provision', in relation to a worker's contract, means a provision of the contract comprised—

(a)   in one or more written terms of the contract of which the employer has given the worker a copy on an occasion prior to the employer receiving the payment in question, or

(b)   in one or more terms of the contract (whether express or implied and, if express, whether oral or in writing) the existence and effect, or combined effect, of which in relation to the worker the employer has notified to the worker in writing on such an occasion.

(3)   For the purposes of this section a relevant provision of a worker's contract having effect by virtue of a variation of the contract does not operate to authorise the receipt of a payment on account of any conduct of the worker, or any other event occurring, before the variation took effect.

(4)   For the purposes of this section an agreement or consent signified by a worker does not operate to authorise the receipt of a payment on account of any conduct of the worker, or any other event occurring, before the agreement or consent was signified.

(5)   Any reference in this Part to an employer receiving a payment from a worker employed by him is a reference to his receiving such a payment in his capacity as the worker's employer.

16   Excepted payments

(1)   Section 15 does not apply to a payment received from a worker by his employer where the purpose of the payment is the reimbursement of the employer in respect of—

(a)   an overpayment of wages, or

(b)   an overpayment in respect of expenses incurred by the worker in carrying out his employment,

made (for any reason) by the employer to the worker.

(2)   Section 15 does not apply to a payment received from a worker by his employer in consequence of any disciplinary proceedings if those proceedings were held by virtue of a statutory provision.

(3)   Section 15 does not apply to a payment received from a worker by his employer where the worker has taken part in a strike or other industrial action and the payment has been required by the employer on account of the worker's having taken part in that strike or other action.

(4)   Section 15 does not apply to a payment received from a worker by his employer where the purpose of the payment is the satisfaction (whether wholly or in part) of an order of a court or tribunal requiring the payment of an amount by the worker to the employer.

Enforcement

23   Complaints to employment tribunals

(1)   A worker may present a complaint to an employment tribunal—

(a)   that his employer has made a deduction from his wages in contravention of section 13 (including a deduction made in contravention of that section as it applies by virtue of section 18(2)),

(b)   that his employer has received from him a payment in contravention of section 15 (including a payment received in contravention of that section as it applies by virtue of section 20(1)),

(c)   that his employer has recovered from his wages by means of one or more deductions falling within section 18(1) an amount or aggregate amount exceeding the limit applying to the deduction or deductions under that provision, or

(d)   that his employer has received from him in pursuance of one or more demands for payment made (in accordance with section 20) on a particular pay day, a payment or payments of an amount or aggregate amount exceeding the limit applying to the demand or demands under section 21(1).

(2)   Subject to subsection (4), an employment tribunal shall not consider a complaint under this section unless it is presented before the end of the period of three months beginning with—

(a)   in the case of a complaint relating to a deduction by the employer, the date of payment of the wages from which the deduction was made, or

(b)   in the case of a complaint relating to a payment received by the employer, the date when the payment was received.

(3)   Where a complaint is brought under this section in respect of—

      (a)   a series of deductions or payments, or

      (b)   a number of payments falling within subsection (1)(d) and made in pursuance of demands for payment subject to the same limit under section 21(1) but received by the employer on different dates,

the references in subsection (2) to the deduction or payment are to the last deduction or payment in the series or to the last of the payments so received.

(4)   Where the employment tribunal is satisfied that it was not reasonably practicable for a complaint under this section to be presented before the end of the relevant period of three months, the tribunal may consider the complaint if it is presented within such further period as the tribunal considers reasonable.

(5)   No complaint shall be presented under this section in respect of any deduction made in contravention of section 86 of the Trade Union and Labour Relations (Consolidation) Act 1992 (deduction of political fund contribution where certificate of exemption or objection has been given).

24   Determination of complaints

Where a tribunal finds a complaint under section 23 well-founded, it shall make a declaration to that effect and shall order the employer—

      (a)   in the case of a complaint under section 23(1)(a), to pay to the worker the amount of any deduction made in contravention of section 13,

      (b)   in the case of a complaint under section 23(1)(b), to repay to the worker the amount of any payment received in contravention of section 15,

      (c)   in the case of a complaint under section 23(1)(c), to pay to the worker any amount recovered from him in excess of the limit mentioned in that provision, and

      (d)   in the case of a complaint under section 23(1)(d), to repay to the worker any amount received from him in excess of the limit mentioned in that provision.

25   Determinations: supplementary

(1)   Where, in the case of any complaint under section 23(1)(a), a tribunal finds that, although neither of the conditions set out in section 13(1)(a) and (b) was satisfied with respect to the whole amount of the deduction, one of those conditions was satisfied with respect to any lesser amount, the amount of the deduction shall for the purposes of section 24(a) be treated as reduced by the amount with respect to which that condition was satisfied.

(2)   Where, in the case of any complaint under section 23(1)(b), a tribunal finds that, although neither of the conditions set out in section 15(1)(a) and (b) was satisfied with respect to the whole amount of the payment, one of those conditions was satisfied with respect to any lesser amount, the amount of the payment shall for the purposes of section 24(b) be treated as reduced by the amount with respect to which that condition was satisfied.

(3)   An employer shall not under section 24 be ordered by a tribunal to pay or repay to a worker any amount in respect of a deduction or payment, or in respect of any combination of deductions or payments, in so far as it appears to the tribunal that he has already paid or repaid any such amount to the worker.

(4)   Where a tribunal has under section 24 ordered an employer to pay or repay to a worker any amount in respect of a particular deduction or payment falling within section 23(1)(a) to (d), the amount which the employer is entitled to recover (by whatever means) in respect of the matter in relation to which the deduction or payment was originally made or received shall be treated as reduced by that amount.

(5)   Where a tribunal has under section 24 ordered an employer to pay or repay to a worker any amount in respect of any combination of deductions or payments falling within section 23(1)(c) or (d), the aggregate amount which the employer is entitled to recover (by whatever means) in respect of the cash shortages or stock deficiencies in relation to which the deductions or payments were originally made or required to be made shall be treated as reduced by that amount.

26   Complaints and other remedies

Section 23 does not affect the jurisdiction of an employment tribunal to consider a reference under section 11 in relation to any deduction from the wages of a worker; but the aggregate of any amounts ordered by an employment tribunal to be paid under section 12(4) and under section 24 (whether on the same or different occasions) in respect of a particular deduction shall not exceed the amount of the deduction.

Supplementary

27   Meaning of 'wages' etc.

(1)   In this Part 'wages', in relation to a worker, means any sums payable to the worker in connection with his employment, including—

(a)   any fee, bonus, commission, holiday pay or other emolument referable to his employment, whether payable under his contract or otherwise,

(b)   statutory sick pay under Part XI of the Social Security Contributions and Benefits Act 1992,

(c)   statutory maternity pay under Part XII of that Act,

(ca) ordinary statutory paternity pay or additional statutory paternity pay under Part 12ZA of that Act,

(cb) statutory adoption pay under Part 12ZB of that Act,

(d)   a guarantee payment (under section 28 of this Act),

(e)   any payment for time off under Part VI of this Act or section 169 of the Trade Union and Labour Relations (Consolidation) Act 1992 (payment for time off for carrying out trade union duties etc.),

(f)   remuneration on suspension on medical grounds under section 64 of this Act and remuneration on suspension on maternity grounds under section 68 of this Act,

(g)   any sum payable in pursuance of an order for reinstatement or re-engagement under section 113 of this Act,

(h)   any sum payable in pursuance of an order for the continuation of a contract of employment under section 130 of this Act or section 164 of the Trade Union and Labour Relations (Consolidation) Act 1992, and

(j)   remuneration under a protective award under section 189 of that Act,

but excluding any payments within subsection (2).

(2)   Those payments are—

(a)   any payment by way of an advance under an agreement for a loan or by way of an advance of wages (but without prejudice to the application of section 13 to any deduction made from the worker's wages in respect of any such advance),

(b)   any payment in respect of expenses incurred by the worker in carrying out his employment,

(c)   any payment by way of a pension, allowance or gratuity in connection with the worker's retirement or as compensation for loss of office,

(d)   any payment referable to the worker's redundancy, and

(e)   any payment to the worker otherwise than in his capacity as a worker.

(3)   Where any payment in the nature of a non-contractual bonus is (for any reason) made to a worker by his employer, the amount of the payment shall for the purposes of this Part—

(a)   be treated as wages of the worker, and

(b)   be treated as payable to him as such on the day on which the payment is made.

(4)   In this Part 'gross amount', in relation to any wages payable to a worker, means the total amount of those wages before deductions of whatever nature.

(5)   For the purposes of this Part any monetary value attaching to any payment or benefit in kind furnished to a worker by his employer shall not be treated as wages of the worker except in the case of any voucher, stamp or similar document which is—

(a)   of a fixed value expressed in monetary terms, and

(b)   capable of being exchanged (whether on its own or together with other vouchers, stamps or documents, and whether immediately or only after a time) for money, goods or services (or for any combination of two or more of those things).

PART III
GUARANTEE PAYMENTS

28   Right to guarantee payment

(1)   Where throughout a day during any part of which an employee would normally be required to work in accordance with his contract of employment the employee is not provided with work by his employer by reason of—

     (a)   a diminution in the requirements of the employer's business for work of the kind which the employee is employed to do, or

     (b)   any other occurrence affecting the normal working of the employer's business in relation to work of the kind which the employee is employed to do,

   the employee is entitled to be paid by his employer an amount in respect of that day.

(2)   In this Act a payment to which an employee is entitled under subsection (1) is referred to as a guarantee payment.

(3)   In this Part—

     (a)   a day falling within subsection (1) is referred to as a 'workless day', and

     (b)   'workless period' has a corresponding meaning.

(4)   In this Part 'day' means the period of twenty-four hours from midnight to midnight.

(5)   Where a period of employment begun on any day extends, or would normally extend, over midnight into the following day—

     (a)   if the employment before midnight is, or would normally be, of longer duration than that after midnight, the period of employment shall be treated as falling wholly on the first day, and

     (b)   in any other case, the period of employment shall be treated as falling wholly on the second day.

29   Exclusions from right to guarantee payment

(1)   An employee is not entitled to a guarantee payment unless he has been continuously employed for a period of not less than one month ending with the day before that in respect of which the guarantee payment is claimed.

(2)   ...

(3)   An employee is not entitled to a guarantee payment in respect of a workless day if the failure to provide him with work for that day occurs in consequence of a strike, lock-out or other industrial action involving any employee of his employer or of an associated employer.

(4)   An employee is not entitled to a guarantee payment in respect of a workless day if—

     (a)   his employer has offered to provide alternative work for that day which is suitable in all the circumstances (whether or not it is work which the employee is under his contract employed to perform), and

     (b)   the employee has unreasonably refused that offer.

(5)   An employee is not entitled to a guarantee payment if he does not comply with reasonable requirements imposed by his employer with a view to ensuring that his services are available.

30   Calculation of guarantee payment

(1)   Subject to section 31, the amount of a guarantee payment payable to an employee in respect of any day is the sum produced by multiplying the number of normal working hours on the day by the guaranteed hourly rate; and, accordingly, no guarantee payment is payable to an employee in whose case there are no normal working hours on the day in question.

(2)   The guaranteed hourly rate, in relation to an employee, is the amount of one week's pay divided by the number of normal working hours in a week for that employee when employed under the contract of employment in force on the day in respect of which the guarantee payment is payable.

(3)   But where the number of normal working hours differs from week to week or over a longer period, the amount of one week's pay shall be divided instead by—

     (a)   the average number of normal working hours calculated by dividing by twelve the total number of the employee's normal working hours during the period of twelve weeks ending with the last complete week before the day in respect of which the guarantee payment is payable, or

(b)   where the employee has not been employed for a sufficient period to enable the calculation to be made under paragraph (a), a number which fairly represents the number of normal working hours in a week having regard to such of the considerations specified in subsection (4) as are appropriate in the circumstances.

(4)   The considerations referred to in subsection (3)(b) are—

(a)   the average number of normal working hours in a week which the employee could expect in accordance with the terms of his contract, and

(b)   the average number of normal working hours of other employees engaged in relevant comparable employment with the same employer.

(5)   If in any case an employee's contract has been varied, or a new contract has been entered into, in connection with a period of short-time working, subsections (2) and (3) have effect as if for the references to the day in respect of which the guarantee payment is payable there were substituted references to the last day on which the original contract was in force.

31   Limits on amount of and entitlement to guarantee payment

(1)   The amount of a guarantee payment payable to an employee in respect of any day shall not exceed £20.40.

(2)   An employee is not entitled to guarantee payments in respect of more than the specified number of days in any period of three months.

(3)   The specified number of days for the purposes of subsection (2) is the number of days, not exceeding five, on which the employee normally works in a week under the contract of employment in force on the day in respect of which the guarantee payment is claimed.

(4)   But where that number of days varies from week to week or over a longer period, the specified number of days is instead—

(a)   the average number of such days, not exceeding five, calculated by dividing by twelve the total number of such days during the period of twelve weeks ending with the last complete week before the day in respect of which the guarantee payment is claimed, and rounding up the resulting figure to the next whole number, or

(b)   where the employee has not been employed for a sufficient period to enable the calculation to be made under paragraph (a), a number which fairly represents the number of the employee's normal working days in a week, not exceeding five, having regard to such of the considerations specified in subsection (5) as are appropriate in the circumstances.

(5)   The considerations referred to in subsection (4)(b) are—

(a)   the average number of normal working days in a week which the employee could expect in accordance with the terms of his contract, and

(b)   the average number of such days of other employees engaged in relevant comparable employment with the same employer.

(6)   If in any case an employee's contract has been varied, or a new contract has been entered into, in connection with a period of short-time working, subsections (3) and (4) have effect as if for the references to the day in respect of which the guarantee payment is claimed there were substituted references to the last day on which the original contract was in force.

(7)   The Secretary of State may by order vary—

(a)   the length of the period specified in subsection (2);

(b)   a limit specified in subsection (3) or (4).

32   Contractual remuneration

(1)   A right to a guarantee payment does not affect any right of an employee in relation to remuneration under his contract of employment ('contractual remuneration').

(2)   Any contractual remuneration paid to an employee in respect of a workless day goes towards discharging any liability of the employer to pay a guarantee payment in respect of that day; and, conversely, any guarantee payment paid in respect of a day goes towards discharging any liability of the employer to pay contractual remuneration in respect of that day.

(3)   For the purposes of subsection (2), contractual remuneration shall be treated as paid in respect of a workless day—

(a) where it is expressed to be calculated or payable by reference to that day or any part of that day, to the extent that it is so expressed, and

(b) in any other case, to the extent that it represents guaranteed remuneration, rather than remuneration for work actually done, and is referable to that day when apportioned rateably between that day and any other workless period falling within the period in respect of which the remuneration is paid.

34 Complaints to employment tribunals

(1) An employee may present a complaint to an employment tribunal that his employer has failed to pay the whole or any part of a guarantee payment to which the employee is entitled.

(2) An employment tribunal shall not consider a complaint relating to a guarantee payment in respect of any day unless the complaint is presented to the tribunal—

(a) before the end of the period of three months beginning with that day, or

(b) within such further period as the tribunal considers reasonable in a case where it is satisfied that it was not reasonably practicable for the complaint to be presented before the end of that period of three months.

(3) Where an employment tribunal finds a complaint under this section well-founded, the tribunal shall order the employer to pay to the employee the amount of guarantee payment which it finds is due to him.

PART IV
SUNDAY WORKING FOR SHOP AND BETTING WORKERS

Protected shop workers and betting workers

36 Protected shop workers and betting workers

(1) Subject to subsection (5), a shop worker or betting worker is to be regarded as 'protected' for the purposes of any provision of this Act if (and only if) subsection (2) or (3) applies to him.

(2) This subsection applies to a shop worker or betting worker if—

(a) on the day before the relevant commencement date he was employed as a shop worker or a betting worker but not to work only on Sunday,

(b) he has been continuously employed during the period beginning with that day and ending with the day which, in relation to the provision concerned, is the appropriate date, and

(c) throughout that period, or throughout every part of it during which his relations with his employer were governed by a contract of employment, he was a shop worker or a betting worker.

(3) This subsection applies to any shop worker or betting worker whose contract of employment is such that under it he—

(a) is not, and may not be, required to work on Sunday, and

(b) could not be so required even if the provisions of this Part were disregarded.

(4) Where on the day before the relevant commencement date an employee's relations with his employer had ceased to be governed by a contract of employment, he shall be regarded as satisfying subsection (2)(a) if—

(a) that day fell in a week which counts as a period of employment with that employer under section 212(2) or (3) or under regulations under section 219, and

(b) on the last day before the relevant commencement date on which his relations with his employer were governed by a contract of employment, the employee was employed as a shop worker or a betting worker but not to work only on Sunday.

(5) A shop worker is not a protected shop worker, and a betting worker is not a protected betting worker, if—

(a) he has given his employer an opting-in notice on or after the relevant commencement date, and

(b) after giving the notice, he has expressly agreed with his employer to do shop work, or betting work, on Sunday or on a particular Sunday.

(6) In this Act 'opting-in notice', in relation to a shop worker or a betting worker, means written notice, signed and dated by the shop worker or betting worker, in which the shop worker or betting worker expressly states that he wishes to work on Sunday or that he does not object to Sunday working.

(7) In this Act 'the relevant commencement date' means—

    (a) in relation to a shop worker, 26th August 1994, and

    (b) in relation to a betting worker, 3rd January 1995.

37 Contractual requirements relating to Sunday work

(1) Any contract of employment under which a shop worker or betting worker who satisfies section 36(2)(a) was employed on the day before the relevant commencement date is unenforceable to the extent that it—

    (a) requires the shop worker to do shop work, or the betting worker to do betting work, on Sunday on or after that date, or

    (b) requires the employer to provide the shop worker with shop work, or the betting worker with betting work, on Sunday on or after that date.

(2) Subject to subsection (3), any agreement entered into after the relevant commencement date between a protected shop worker, or a protected betting worker, and his employer is unenforceable to the extent that it—

    (a) requires the shop worker to do shop work, or the betting worker to do betting work, on Sunday, or

    (b) requires the employer to provide the shop worker with shop work, or the betting worker with betting work, on Sunday.

(3) Where, after giving an opting-in notice, a protected shop worker or a protected betting worker expressly agrees with his employer to do shop work or betting work on Sunday or on a particular Sunday (and so ceases to be protected), his contract of employment shall be taken to be varied to the extent necessary to give effect to the terms of the agreement.

(4) ...

(5) For the purposes of section 36(2)(b), the appropriate date—

    (a) in relation to subsections (2) and (3) of this section, is the day on which the agreement is entered into, and

    (b) ...

38 Contracts with guaranteed hours

(1) This section applies where—

    (a) under the contract of employment under which a shop worker or betting worker who satisfies section 36(2)(a) was employed on the day before the relevant commencement date, the employer is, or may be, required to provide him with shop work, or betting work, for a specified number of hours each week,

    (b) under the contract the shop worker or betting worker was, or might have been, required to work on Sunday before that date, and

    (c) the shop worker has done shop work, or the betting worker betting work, on Sunday in that employment (whether or not before that day) but has, on or after that date, ceased to do so.

(2) So long as the shop worker remains a protected shop worker, or the betting worker remains a protected betting worker, the contract shall not be regarded as requiring the employer to provide him with shop work, or betting work, on weekdays in excess of the hours normally worked by the shop worker or betting worker on weekdays before he ceased to do shop work, or betting work, on Sunday.

(3) For the purposes of section 36(2)(b), the appropriate date in relation to this section is any time in relation to which the contract is to be enforced.

39 Reduction of pay etc.

(1) This section applies where—

    (a) under the contract of employment under which a shop worker or betting worker who satisfies section 36(2)(a) was employed on the day before the relevant commencement date, the shop worker or betting worker was, or might have been, required to work on Sunday before the relevant commencement date,

  (b)   the shop worker has done shop work, or the betting worker has done betting work, on Sunday in that employment (whether or not before that date) but has, on or after that date, ceased to do so, and

  (c)   it is not apparent from the contract what part of the remuneration payable, or of any other benefit accruing, to the shop worker or betting worker was intended to be attributable to shop work, or betting work, on Sunday.

(2)   So long as the shop worker remains a protected shop worker, or the betting worker remains a protected betting worker, the contract shall be regarded as enabling the employer to reduce the amount of remuneration paid, or the extent of the other benefit provided, to the shop worker or betting worker in respect of any period by the relevant proportion.

(3)   In subsection (2) 'the relevant proportion' means the proportion which the hours of shop work, or betting work, which (apart from this Part) the shop worker, or betting worker, could have been required to do on Sunday in the period ('the contractual Sunday hours') bears to the aggregate of those hours and the hours of work actually done by the shop worker, or betting worker, in the period.

(4)   Where, under the contract of employment, the hours of work actually done on weekdays in any period would be taken into account in determining the contractual Sunday hours, they shall be taken into account in determining the contractual Sunday hours for the purposes of subsection (3).

(5)   For the purposes of section 36(2)(b), the appropriate date in relation to this section is the end of the period in respect of which the remuneration is paid or the benefit accrues.

Opting-out of Sunday work

40   Notice of objection to Sunday working

(1)   A shop worker or betting worker to whom this section applies may at any time give his employer written notice, signed and dated by the shop worker or betting worker, to the effect that he objects to Sunday working.

(2)   In this Act 'opting-out notice' means a notice given under subsection (1) by a shop worker or betting worker to whom this section applies.

(3)   This section applies to any shop worker or betting worker who under his contract of employment—

  (a)   is or may be required to work on Sunday (whether or not as a result of previously giving an opting-in notice), but

  (b)   is not employed to work only on Sunday.

41   Opted-out shop workers and betting workers

(1)   Subject to subsection (2), a shop worker or betting worker is to be regarded as 'opted-out' for the purposes of any provision of this Act if (and only if)—

  (a)   he has given his employer an opting-out notice,

  (b)   he has been continuously employed during the period beginning with the day on which the notice was given and ending with the day which, in relation to the provision concerned, is the appropriate date, and

  (c)   throughout that period, or throughout every part of it during which his relations with his employer were governed by a contract of employment, he was a shop worker or a betting worker.

(2)   A shop worker is not an opted-out shop worker, and a betting worker is not an opted-out betting worker, if—

  (a)   after giving the opting-out notice concerned, he has given his employer an opting-in notice, and

  (b)   after giving the opting-in notice, he has expressly agreed with his employer to do shop work, or betting work, on Sunday or on a particular Sunday.

(3)   In this Act 'notice period', in relation to an opted-out shop worker or an opted-out betting worker, means, subject to section 42(2), the period of three months beginning with the day on which the opting-out notice concerned was given.

42 Explanatory statement

(1) Where a person becomes a shop worker or betting worker to whom section 40 applies, his employer shall, before the end of the period of two months beginning with the day on which that person becomes such a worker, give him a written statement in the prescribed form.

(2) If—

    (a) an employer fails to comply with subsection (1) in relation to any shop worker or betting worker, and

    (b) the shop worker or betting worker, on giving the employer an opting-out notice, becomes an opted-out shop worker or an opted-out betting worker,

section 41(3) has effect in relation to the shop worker or betting worker with the substitution for 'three months' of 'one month'.

(3) An employer shall not be regarded as failing to comply with subsection (1) in any case where, before the end of the period referred to in that subsection, the shop worker or betting worker has given him an opting-out notice.

(4) Subject to subsection (6), the prescribed form in the case of a shop worker is as follows—

'STATUTORY RIGHTS IN RELATION TO SUNDAY SHOP WORK

You have become employed as a shop worker and are or can be required under your contract of employment to do the Sunday work your contract provides for.

However, if you wish, you can give a notice, as described in the next paragraph, to your employer and you will then have the right not to work in or about a shop on any Sunday on which the shop is open once three months have passed from the date on which you gave the notice.

Your notice must—

    be in writing;

    be signed and dated by you;

    say that you object to Sunday working.

For three months after you give the notice, your employer can still require you to do all the Sunday work your contract provides for. After the three month period has ended, you have the right to complain to an employment tribunal if, because of your refusal to work on Sundays on which the shop is open, your employer—

    dismisses you, or

    does something else detrimental to you, for example, failing to promote you.

Once you have the rights described, you can surrender them only by giving your employer a further notice, signed and dated by you, saying that you wish to work on Sunday or that you do not object to Sunday working and then agreeing with your employer to work on Sundays or on a particular Sunday.'

(5) Subject to subsection (6), the prescribed form in the case of a betting worker is as follows—

'STATUTORY RIGHTS IN RELATION TO SUNDAY BETTING WORK

You have become employed under a contract of employment under which you are or can be required to do Sunday betting work, that is to say, work—

    at a track on a Sunday on which your employer is taking bets at the track, or

    in a licensed betting office on a Sunday on which it is open for business.

However, if you wish, you can give a notice, as described in the next paragraph, to your employer and you will then have the right not to do Sunday betting work once three months have passed from the date on which you gave the notice.

Your notice must—

    be in writing;

    be signed and dated by you;

    say that you object to doing Sunday betting work.

For three months after you give the notice, your employer can still require you to do all the Sunday betting work your contract provides for. After the three month period has ended, you have the right to complain to an employment tribunal if, because of your refusal to do Sunday betting work, your employer—

dismisses you, or

does something else detrimental to you, for example, failing to promote you.

Once you have the rights described, you can surrender them only by giving your employer a further notice, signed and dated by you, saying that you wish to do Sunday betting work or that you do not object to doing Sunday betting work and then agreeing with your employer to do such work on Sundays or on a particular Sunday.'

(6) The Secretary of State may by order amend the prescribed forms set out in subsections (4) and (5).

43   Contractual requirements relating to Sunday work

(1) Where a shop worker or betting worker gives his employer an opting-out notice, the contract of employment under which he was employed immediately before he gave that notice becomes unenforceable to the extent that it—

    (a) requires the shop worker to do shop work, or the betting worker to do betting work, on Sunday after the end of the notice period, or

    (b) requires the employer to provide the shop worker with shop work, or the betting worker with betting work, on Sunday after the end of that period.

(2) Subject to subsection (3), any agreement entered into between an opted-out shop worker, or an opted-out betting worker, and his employer is unenforceable to the extent that it—

    (a) requires the shop worker to do shop work, or the betting worker to do betting work, on Sunday after the end of the notice period, or

    (b) requires the employer to provide the shop worker with shop work, or the betting worker with betting work, on Sunday after the end of that period.

(3) Where, after giving an opting-in notice, an opted-out shop worker or an opted-out betting worker expressly agrees with his employer to do shop work or betting work on Sunday or on a particular Sunday (and so ceases to be opted-out), his contract of employment shall be taken to be varied to the extent necessary to give effect to the terms of the agreement.

(4) ...

(5) For the purposes of section 41(1)(b), the appropriate date—

    (a) in relation to subsections (2) and (3) of this section, is the day on which the agreement is entered into,

    (b) ...

PART IVA
PROTECTED DISCLOSURES

43A   Meaning of 'protected disclosure'

In this Act a 'protected disclosure' means a qualifying disclosure (as defined by section 43B) which is made by a worker in accordance with any of sections 43C to 43H.

43B   Disclosures qualifying for protection

(1) In this Part a 'qualifying disclosure' means any disclosure of information which, in the reasonable belief of the worker making the disclosure, tends to show one or more of the following—

    (a) that a criminal offence has been committed, is being committed or is likely to be committed,

    (b) that a person has failed, is failing or is likely to fail to comply with any legal obligation to which he is subject,

    (c) that a miscarriage of justice has occurred, is occurring or is likely to occur,

    (d) that the health or safety of any individual has been, is being or is likely to be endangered,

    (e) that the environment has been, is being or is likely to be damaged, or

    (f) that information tending to show any matter falling within any one of the preceding paragraphs has been, is being or is likely to be deliberately concealed.

(2) For the purposes of subsection (1), it is immaterial whether the relevant failure occurred, occurs or would occur in the United Kingdom or elsewhere, and whether the law applying to it is that of the United Kingdom or of any other country or territory.

(3) A disclosure of information is not a qualifying disclosure if the person making the disclosure commits an offence by making it.

(4) A disclosure of information in respect of which a claim to legal professional privilege (or, in Scotland, to confidentiality as between client and professional legal adviser) could be maintained in legal proceedings is not a qualifying disclosure if it is made by a person to whom the information had been disclosed in the course of obtaining legal advice.

(5) In this Part 'the relevant failure', in relation to a qualifying disclosure, means the matter falling within paragraphs (a) to (f) of subsection (1).

43C Disclosure to employer or other responsible person

(1) A qualifying disclosure is made in accordance with this section if the worker makes the disclosure in good faith—

(a) to his employer, or

(b) where the worker reasonably believes that the relevant failure relates solely or mainly to—

(i) the conduct of a person other than his employer, or

(ii) any other matter for which a person other than his employer has legal responsibility,

to that other person.

(2) A worker who, in accordance with a procedure whose use by him is authorised by his employer, makes a qualifying disclosure to a person other than his employer, is to be treated for the purposes of this Part as making the qualifying disclosure to his employer.

43D Disclosure to legal adviser

A qualifying disclosure is made in accordance with this section if it is made in the course of obtaining legal advice.

43E Disclosure to Minister of the Crown

A qualifying disclosure is made in accordance with this section if—

(a) the worker's employer is—

(i) an individual appointed under any enactment (including any enactment comprised in, or in an instrument made under, an Act of the Scottish Parliament) by a Minister of the Crown or a member of the Scottish Executive, or

(ii) a body any of whose members are so appointed, and

(b) the disclosure is made in good faith to a Minister of the Crown or a member of the Scottish Executive.

43F Disclosure to prescribed person

(1) A qualifying disclosure is made in accordance with this section if the worker—

(a) makes the disclosure in good faith to a person prescribed by an order made by the Secretary of State for the purposes of this section, and

(b) reasonably believes—

(i) that the relevant failure falls within any description of matters in respect of which that person is so prescribed, and

(ii) that the information disclosed, and any allegation contained in it, are substantially true.

(2) An order prescribing persons for the purposes of this section may specify persons or descriptions of persons and shall specify the descriptions of matters in respect of which each person, or persons of each description, is or are prescribed.

43G Disclosure in other cases

(1) A qualifying disclosure is made in accordance with this section if—

(a) the worker makes the disclosure in good faith,

(b) he reasonably believes that the information disclosed, and any allegation contained in it, are substantially true,

(c) he does not make the disclosure for purposes of personal gain,

(d)   any of the conditions in subsection (2) is met, and

(e)   in all the circumstances of the case, it is reasonable for him to make the disclosure.

(2)   The conditions referred to in subsection (1)(d) are—

   (a)   that, at the time he makes the disclosure, the worker reasonably believes that he will be subjected to a detriment by his employer if he makes a disclosure to his employer or in accordance with section 43F,

   (b)   that, in a case where no person is prescribed for the purposes of section 43F in relation to the relevant failure, the worker reasonably believes that it is likely that evidence relating to the relevant failure will be concealed or destroyed if he makes a disclosure to his employer, or

   (c)   that the worker has previously made a disclosure of substantially the same information—

      (i)   to his employer, or

      (ii)   in accordance with section 43F.

(3)   In determining for the purposes of subsection (1)(e) whether it is reasonable for the worker to make the disclosure, regard shall be had, in particular, to—

   (a)   the identity of the person to whom the disclosure is made,

   (b)   the seriousness of the relevant failure,

   (c)   whether the relevant failure is continuing or is likely to occur in the future,

   (d)   whether the disclosure is made in breach of a duty of confidentiality owed by the employer to any other person,

   (e)   in a case falling within subsection (2)(c)(i) or (ii), any action which the employer or the person to whom the previous disclosure in accordance with section 43F was made has taken or might reasonably be expected to have taken as a result of the previous disclosure, and

   (f)   in a case falling within subsection (2)(c)(i), whether in making the disclosure to the employer the worker complied with any procedure whose use by him was authorised by the employer.

(4)   For the purposes of this section a subsequent disclosure may be regarded as a disclosure of substantially the same information as that disclosed by a previous disclosure as mentioned in subsection (2)(c) even though the subsequent disclosure extends to information about action taken or not taken by any person as a result of the previous disclosure.

43H   Disclosure of exceptionally serious failure

(1)   A qualifying disclosure is made in accordance with this section if—

   (a)   the worker makes the disclosure in good faith,

   (b)   he reasonably believes that the information disclosed, and any allegation contained in it, are substantially true,

   (c)   he does not make the disclosure for purposes of personal gain,

   (d)   the relevant failure is of an exceptionally serious nature, and

   (e)   in all the circumstances of the case, it is reasonable for him to make the disclosure.

(2)   In determining for the purposes of subsection (1)(e) whether it is reasonable for the worker to make the disclosure, regard shall be had, in particular, to the identity of the person to whom the disclosure is made.

43J   Contractual duties of confidentiality

(1)   Any provision in an agreement to which this section applies is void in so far as it purports to preclude the worker from making a protected disclosure.

(2)   This section applies to any agreement between a worker and his employer (whether a worker's contract or not), including an agreement to refrain from instituting or continuing any proceedings under this Act or any proceedings for breach of contract.

43K   Extension of meaning of 'worker' etc. for Part IVA

(1)   For the purposes of this Part 'worker' includes an individual who is not a worker as defined by section 230(3) but who—

     (a)   works or worked for a person in circumstances in which—
         (i)   he is or was introduced or supplied to do that work by a third person, and
         (ii)   the terms on which he is or was engaged to do the work are or were in practice substantially determined not by him but by the person for whom he works or worked, by the third person or by both of them,

     (b)   contracts or contracted with a person, for the purposes of that person's business, for the execution of work to be done in a place not under the control or management of that person and would fall within section 230(3)(b) if for 'personally' in that provision there were substituted '(whether personally or otherwise)',

    (ba) works or worked as a person performing services under a contract entered into by him with a Primary Care Trust under section 84 or 100 of the National Health Service Act 2006 or with a Local Health Board under section 42 or 57 of the National Health Service (Wales) Act 2006 or with a Primary Care Trust under section 117 of that Act,

    (bb) works or worked as a person performing services under a contract entered into by him with a Health Board under section 17J of the National Health Service (Scotland) Act 1978,

     (c)   works or worked as a person providing general medical services, general dental services, general ophthalmic services or pharmaceutical services in accordance with arrangements made—
         (i)   by a Primary Care Trust or Health Authority under section 126 of the National Health Service Act 2006, or Local Health Board under section 71 or 80 of the National Health Service (Wales) Act 2006, or
         (ii)   by a Health Board under section 25, 26 or 27 of the National Health Service (Scotland) Act 1978, or

    (ca) works or worked as a person performing services under a contract entered into by him with a Health Board under section 17Q of the National Health Service (Scotland) Act 1978,

     (d)   is or was provided with work experience provided pursuant to a training course or programme or with training for employment (or with both) otherwise than—
         (i)   under a contract of employment, or
         (ii)   by an educational establishment on a course run by that establishment;

and any reference to a worker's contract, to employment or to a worker being 'employed' shall be construed accordingly.

  (2) For the purposes of this Part 'employer' includes—
     (a)   in relation to a worker falling within paragraph (a) of subsection (1), the person who substantially determines or determined the terms on which he is or was engaged,
    (aa) in relation to a worker falling within paragraph (ba) of that subsection, the Primary Care Trust or Local Health Board referred to in that paragraph,
    (ab) in relation to a worker falling within paragraph (bb) of that subsection, the Health Board referred to in that paragraph,
     (b)   in relation to a worker falling within paragraph (c) of that subsection, the authority or board referred to in that paragraph, and
     (c)   in relation to a worker falling within paragraph (d) of that subsection, the person providing the work experience or training.

  (3) In this section 'educational establishment' includes any university, college, school or other educational establishment.

43L   Other interpretative provisions

  (1) In this Part—
'qualifying disclosure' has the meaning given by section 43B;
'the relevant failure', in relation to a qualifying disclosure, has the meaning given by section 43B(5).

  (2) In determining for the purposes of this Part whether a person makes a disclosure for purposes of personal gain, there shall be disregarded any reward payable by or under any enactment.

(3) Any reference in this Part to the disclosure of information shall have effect, in relation to any case where the person receiving the information is already aware of it, as a reference to bringing the information to his attention.

PART V

PROTECTION FROM SUFFERING DETRIMENT IN EMPLOYMENT

Rights not to suffer detriment

43M   Jury service

(1) An employee has the right not to be subjected to any detriment by any act, or any deliberate failure to act, by his employer on the ground that the employee—

    (a) has been summoned under the Juries Act 1974, the Coroners Act 1988, the Court of Session Act 1988 or the Criminal Procedure (Scotland) Act 1995 to attend for service as a juror, or

    (b) has been absent from work because he attended at any place in pursuance of being so summoned.

(2) This section does not apply where the detriment in question amounts to dismissal within the meaning of Part 10.

(3) For the purposes of this section, an employee is not to be regarded as having been subjected to a detriment by a failure to pay remuneration in respect of a relevant period unless under his contract of employment he is entitled to be paid that remuneration.

(4) In subsection (3) 'a relevant period' means any period during which the employee is absent from work because of his attendance at any place in pursuance of being summoned as mentioned in subsection (1)(a).

44   Health and safety cases

(1) An employee has the right not to be subjected to any detriment by any act, or any deliberate failure to act, by his employer done on the ground that—

    (a) having been designated by the employer to carry out activities in connection with preventing or reducing risks to health and safety at work, the employee carried out (or proposed to carry out) any such activities,

    (b) being a representative of workers on matters of health and safety at work or member of a safety committee—

        (i)   in accordance with arrangements established under or by virtue of any enactment, or

        (ii) by reason of being acknowledged as such by the employer,

the employee performed (or proposed to perform) any functions as such a representative or a member of such a committee,

    (ba) the employee took part (or proposed to take part) in consultation with the employer pursuant to the Health and Safety (Consultation with Employees) Regulations 1996 or in an election of representatives of employee safety within the meaning of those Regulations (whether as a candidate or otherwise),

    (c) being an employee at a place where—

        (i)   there was no such representative or safety committee, or

        (ii) there was such a representative or safety committee but it was not reasonably practicable for the employee to raise the matter by those means,

he brought to his employer's attention, by reasonable means, circumstances connected with his work which he reasonably believed were harmful or potentially harmful to health or safety,

    (d) in circumstances of danger which the employee reasonably believed to be serious and imminent and which he could not reasonably have been expected to avert, he left (or proposed to leave) or (while the danger persisted) refused to return to his place of work or any dangerous part of his place of work, or

    (e) in circumstances of danger which the employee reasonably believed to be serious and imminent, he took (or proposed to take) appropriate steps to protect himself or other persons from the danger.

(2) For the purposes of subsection (1)(e) whether steps which an employee took (or proposed to take) were appropriate is to be judged by reference to all the circumstances including, in particular, his knowledge and the facilities and advice available to him at the time.

(3) An employee is not to be regarded as having been subjected to any detriment on the ground specified in subsection (1)(e) if the employer shows that it was (or would have been) so negligent for the employee to take the steps which he took (or proposed to take) that a reasonable employer might have treated him as the employer did.

(4) This section does not apply where the detriment in question amounts to dismissal (within the meaning of Part X).

45   Sunday working for shop and betting workers

(1) An employee who is—
   (a)   a protected shop worker or an opted-out shop worker, or
   (b)   a protected betting worker or an opted-out betting worker,
   has the right not to be subjected to any detriment by any act, or any deliberate failure to act, by his employer done on the ground that the employee refused (or proposed to refuse) to do shop work, or betting work, on Sunday or on a particular Sunday.

(2) Subsection (1) does not apply to anything done in relation to an opted-out shop worker or an opted-out betting worker on the ground that he refused (or proposed to refuse) to do shop work, or betting work, on any Sunday or Sundays falling before the end of the notice period.

(3) An employee who is a shop worker or a betting worker has the right not to be subjected to any detriment by any act, or any deliberate failure to act, by his employer done on the ground that the employee gave (or proposed to give) an opting-out notice to his employer.

(4) Subsections (1) and (3) do not apply where the detriment in question amounts to dismissal (within the meaning of Part X).

(5) For the purposes of this section a shop worker or betting worker who does not work on Sunday or on a particular Sunday is not to be regarded as having been subjected to any detriment by—
   (a)   a failure to pay remuneration in respect of shop work, or betting work, on a Sunday which he has not done,
   (b)   a failure to provide him with any other benefit, where that failure results from the application (in relation to a Sunday on which the employee has not done shop work, or betting work) of a contractual term under which the extent of that benefit varies according to the number of hours worked by the employee or the remuneration of the employee, or
   (c)   a failure to provide him with any work, remuneration or other benefit which by virtue of section 38 or 39 the employer is not obliged to provide.

(6) Where an employer offers to pay a sum specified in the offer to any one or more employees—
   (a)   who are protected shop workers or opted-out shop workers or protected betting workers or opted-out betting workers, or
   (b)   who under their contracts of employment are not obliged to do shop work, or betting work, on Sunday,
   if they agree to do shop work, or betting work, on Sunday or on a particular Sunday subsections (7) and (8) apply.

(7) An employee to whom the offer is not made is not to be regarded for the purposes of this section as having been subjected to any detriment by any failure to make the offer to him or to pay him the sum specified in the offer.

(8) An employee who does not accept the offer is not to be regarded for the purposes of this section as having been subjected to any detriment by any failure to pay him the sum specified in the offer.

(9) For the purposes of section 36(2)(b) or 41(1)(b), the appropriate date in relation to this section is the date of the act or failure to act.

(10) For the purposes of subsection (9)—
   (a)   where an act extends over a period, the 'date of the act' means the first day of that period, and

(b) a deliberate failure to act shall be treated as done when it was decided on;

and, in the absence of evidence establishing the contrary, an employer shall be taken to decide on a failure to act when he does an act inconsistent with doing the failed act or, if he has done no such inconsistent act, when the period expires within which he might reasonably have been expected to do the failed act if it was to be done.

45A Working time cases

(1) A worker has the right not to be subjected to any detriment by any act, or any deliberate failure to act, by his employer done on the ground that the worker—

(a) refused (or proposed to refuse) to comply with a requirement which the employer imposed (or proposed to impose) in contravention of the Working Time Regulations 1998,

(b) refused (or proposed to refuse) to forgo a right conferred on him by those Regulations,

(c) failed to sign a workforce agreement for the purposes of those Regulations, or to enter into, or agree to vary or extend, any other agreement with his employer which is provided for in those Regulations,

(d) being—

(i) a representative of members of the workforce for the purposes of Schedule 1 to those Regulations, or

(ii) a candidate in an election in which any person elected will, on being elected, be such a representative,

performed (or proposed to perform) any functions or activities as such a representative or candidate,

(e) brought proceedings against the employer to enforce a right conferred on him by those Regulations, or

(f) alleged that the employer had infringed such a right.

(2) It is immaterial for the purposes of subsection (1)(e) or (f)—

(a) whether or not the worker has the right, or

(b) whether or not the right has been infringed,

but, for those provisions to apply, the claim to the right and that it has been infringed must be made in good faith.

(3) It is sufficient for subsection (1)(f) to apply that the worker, without specifying the right, made it reasonably clear to the employer what the right claimed to have been infringed was.

(4) This section does not apply where a worker is an employee and the detriment in question amounts to dismissal within the meaning of Part X.

(5) A reference in this section to the Working Time Regulations 1998 includes a reference to—

(a) the Merchant Shipping (Working Time: Inland Waterways) Regulations 2003;

(b) the Fishing Vessels (Working Time: Sea-fishermen) Regulations 2004.

46 Trustees of occupational pension schemes

(1) An employee has the right not to be subjected to any detriment by any act, or any deliberate failure to act, by his employer done on the ground that, being a trustee of a relevant occupational pension scheme which relates to his employment, the employee performed (or proposed to perform) any functions as such a trustee.

(2) This section does not apply where the detriment in question amounts to dismissal (within the meaning of Part X).

(2A) This section applies to an employee who is a director of a company which is a trustee of a relevant occupational pension scheme as it applies to an employee who is a trustee of such a scheme (references to such a trustee being read for this purpose as references to such a director).

(3) In this section 'relevant occupational pension scheme' means an occupational pension scheme (as defined in section 1 of the Pension Schemes Act 1993) established under a trust.

47 Employee representatives

(1) An employee has the right not to be subjected to any detriment by any act, or any deliberate failure to act, by his employer done on the ground that, being—

    (a)   an employee representative for the purposes of Chapter II of Part IV of the Trade Union and Labour Relations (Consolidation) Act 1992 (redundancies) or Regulations 9, 13 and 15 of the Transfer of Undertakings (Protection of Employment) Regulations 2006, or

    (b)   a candidate in an election in which any person elected will, on being elected, be such an employee representative,

he performed (or proposed to perform) any functions or activities as such an employee representative or candidate.

(1A) An employee has the right not to be subjected to any detriment by any act, or by any deliberate failure to act, by his employer done on the ground of his participation in an election of employee representatives for the purposes of Chapter II of Part IV of the Trade Union and Labour Relations (Consolidation) Act 1992 (redundancies) or Regulations 9, 13 and 15 of the Transfer of Undertakings (Protection of Employment) Regulations 2006.

(2)   This section does not apply where the detriment in question amounts to a dismissal (within the meaning of Part X).

47A   Employees exercising right to time off work for study or training

(1)   An employee has the right not to be subjected to any detriment by any act, or any deliberate failure to act, by his employer or the principal (within the meaning of section 63A(3)) done on the ground that, being a person entitled to—

    (a)   time off under section 63A(1) or (3), and

    (b)   remuneration under section 63B(1) in respect of that time taken off,

the employee exercised (or proposed to exercise) that right or received (or sought to receive) such remuneration.

(2)   This section does not apply where the detriment in question amounts to dismissal (within the meaning of Part X).

47B   Protected disclosures

(1)   A worker has the right not to be subjected to any detriment by any act, or any deliberate failure to act, by his employer done on the ground that the worker has made a protected disclosure.

(2)   This section does not apply where—

    (a)   the worker is an employee, and

    (b)   the detriment in question amounts to dismissal (within the meaning of Part X).

(3)   For the purposes of this section, and of sections 48 and 49 so far as relating to this section, 'worker', 'worker's contract', 'employment' and 'employer' have the extended meaning given by section 43K.

47C   Leave for family and domestic reasons

(1)   An employee has the right not to be subjected to any detriment by any act, or any deliberate failure to act, by his employer done for a prescribed reason.

(2)   A prescribed reason is one which is prescribed by regulations made by the Secretary of State and which relates to—

    (a)   pregnancy, childbirth or maternity,

    (b)   ordinary, compulsory or additional maternity leave,

    (ba)   ordinary or additional adoption leave,

    (c)   parental leave, or

    (ca)   paternity leave, or

    (d)   time off under section 57A.

(3)   A reason prescribed under this section in relation to parental leave may relate to action which an employee takes, agrees to take or refuses to take under or in respect of a collective or workforce agreement.

(4)   Regulations under this section may make different provision for different cases or circumstances.

47D   Tax credits

(1)   An employee has the right not to be subjected to any detriment by any act, or any deliberate failure to act, by his employer, done on the ground that—

    (a)   any action was taken, or was proposed to be taken, by or on behalf of the employee with a view to enforcing, or otherwise securing the benefit of, a right conferred on the employee by regulations under section 25 of the Tax Credits Act 2002,

    (b)   a penalty was imposed on the employer, or proceedings for a penalty were brought against him, under that Act, as a result of action taken by or on behalf of the employee for the purpose of enforcing, or otherwise securing the benefit of, such a right, or

    (c)   the employee is entitled, or will or may be entitled, to working tax credit.

(2)   It is immaterial for the purposes of subsection (1)(a) or (b)—

    (a)   whether or not the employee has the right, or

    (b)   whether or not the right has been infringed,

but, for those provisions to apply, the claim to the right and (if applicable) the claim that it has been infringed must be made in good faith.

(3)   Subsections (1) and (2) apply to a person who is not an employee within the meaning of this Act but who is an employee within the meaning of section 25 of the Tax Credits Act 2002, with references to his employer in those subsections (and sections 48(2) and (4) and 49(1)) being construed in accordance with that section.

(5)   Subsections (1) and (2) do not apply to an employee if the detriment in question amounts to dismissal (within the meaning of Part 10).

47E   Flexible working

(1)   An employee has the right not to be subjected to any detriment by any act, or any deliberate failure to act, by his employer done on the ground that the employee—

    (a)   made (or proposed to make) an application under section 80F,

    (b)   exercised (or proposed to exercise) a right conferred on him under section 80G,

    (c)   brought proceedings against the employer under section 80H, or

    (d)   alleged the existence of any circumstance which would constitute a ground for bringing such proceedings.

(2)   This section does not apply where the detriment in question amounts to dismissal within the meaning of Part 10.

Enforcement

48   Complaints to employment tribunals

(1)   An employee may present a complaint to an employment tribunal that he has been subjected to a detriment in contravention of section 43M, 44, 45, 46, 47, 47A, 47C or 47E.

(1ZA)   A worker may present a complaint to an employment tribunal that he has been subjected to a detriment in contravention of section 45A.

(1A)   A worker may present a complaint to an employment tribunal that he has been subjected to a detriment in contravention of section 47B.

(1B)   A person may present a complaint to an employment tribunal that he has been subjected to a detriment in contravention of section 47D.

(2)   On such a complaint it is for the employer to show the ground on which any act, or deliberate failure to act, was done.

(3)   An employment tribunal shall not consider a complaint under this section unless it is presented—

    (a)   before the end of the period of three months beginning with the date of the act or failure to act to which the complaint relates or, where that act or failure is part of a series of similar acts or failures, the last of them, or

    (b)   within such further period as the tribunal considers reasonable in a case where it is satisfied that it was not reasonably practicable for the complaint to be presented before the end of that period of three months.

(4)   For the purposes of subsection (3)—

    (a)   where an act extends over a period, the 'date of the act' means the last day of hat period, and

    (b)   a deliberate failure to act shall be treated as done when it was decided on;

and, in the absence of evidence establishing the contrary, an employer shall be taken to decide on a failure to act when he does an act inconsistent with doing the failed act or, if he has done no such inconsistent act, when the period expires within which he might reasonably have been expected to do the failed act if it was to be done.

(5)   In this section and section 49 any reference to the employer includes, where a person complains that he has been subjected to a detriment in contravention of section 47A, the principal (within the meaning of section 63A(3)).

49   Remedies

(1)   Where an employment tribunal finds a complaint under section 48 well-founded, the tribunal—
   (a)   shall make a declaration to that effect, and
   (b)   may make an award of compensation to be paid by the employer to the complainant in respect of the act or failure to act to which the complaint relates.

(2)   Subject to subsections (5A) and (6) the amount of the compensation awarded shall be such as the tribunal considers just and equitable in all the circumstances having regard to—
   (a)   the infringement to which the complaint relates, and
   (b)   any loss which is attributable to the act, or failure to act, which infringed the complainant's right.

(3)   The loss shall be taken to include—
   (a)   any expenses reasonably incurred by the complainant in consequence of the act, or failure to act, to which the complaint relates, and
   (b)   loss of any benefit which he might reasonably be expected to have had but for that act or failure to act.

(4)   In ascertaining the loss the tribunal shall apply the same rule concerning the duty of a person to mitigate his loss as applies to damages recoverable under the common law of England and Wales or (as the case may be) Scotland.

(5)   Where the tribunal finds that the act, or failure to act, to which the complaint relates was to any extent caused or contributed to by action of the complainant, it shall reduce the amount of the compensation by such proportion as it considers just and equitable having regard to that finding.

(5A) Where—
   (a)   the complaint is made under section 48(1ZA),
   (b)   the detriment to which the worker is subjected is the termination of his worker's contract, and
   (c)   that contract is not a contract of employment,
   any compensation must not exceed the compensation that would be payable under Chapter II of Part X if the worker had been an employee and had been dismissed for the reason specified in section 101A.

(6)   Where—
   (a)   the complaint is made under section 48(1A),
   (b)   the detriment to which the worker is subjected is the termination of his worker's contract, and
   (c)   that contract is not a contract of employment,
   any compensation must not exceed the compensation that would be payable under Chapter II of Part X if the worker had been an employee and had been dismissed for the reason specified in section 103A.

...

PART VI
TIME OFF WORK

Public duties

50   Rights to time off for public duties

(1)   An employer shall permit an employee of his who is a justice of the peace to take time off during the employee's working hours for the purpose of performing any of the duties of his office.

(2) An employer shall permit an employee of his who is a member of—
    (a)   a local authority,
    (b)   a statutory tribunal,
    (c)   a police authority established under section 3 of the Police Act 1996 or the Metropolitan Police Authority,
    (ca)   ...
    (d)   a board of prison visitors or a prison visiting committee,
    (e)   a relevant health body,
    (f)   a relevant education body,
    (g)   the Environment Agency or the Scottish Environment Protection Agency, or
    (h)   a water and sewerage authority under section 62(1) of the Local Government (Scotland) Act 1994 or a Water Industry Consultative Committee established under section 67A(2) of that Act,
to take time off during the employee's working hours for the purposes specified in subsection (3).

(3) The purposes referred to in subsection (2) are—
    (a)   attendance at a meeting of the body or any of its committees or subcommittees, and
    (b)   the doing of any other thing approved by the body, or anything of a class so approved, for the purpose of the discharge of the functions of the body or of any of its committees or sub-committees, and
    (c)   in the case of a local authority which are operating executive arrangements—
        (i)   attendance at a meeting of the executive of that local authority or committee of that executive; and
        (ii)   the doing of any other thing, by an individual member of that executive, for the purposes of the discharge of any function which is to any extent the responsibility of that executive.

(4) The amount of time off which an employee is to be permitted to take under this section, and the occasions on which and any conditions subject to which time off may be so taken, are those that are reasonable in all the circumstances having regard, in particular, to—
    (a)   how much time off is required for the performance of the duties of the office or as a member of the body in question, and how much time off is required for the performance of the particular duty,
    (b)   how much time off the employee has already been permitted under this section or sections 168 and 170 of the Trade Union and Labour Relations (Consolidation) Act 1992 (time off for trade union duties and activities), and
    (c)   the circumstances of the employer's business and the effect of the employee's absence on the running of that business.

...

51   Complaints to employment tribunals

(1) An employee may present a complaint to an employment tribunal that his employer has failed to permit him to take time off as required by section 50.

(2) An employment tribunal shall not consider a complaint under this section that an employer has failed to permit an employee to take time off unless it is presented—
    (a)   before the end of the period of three months beginning with the date on which the failure occurred, or
    (b)   within such further period as the tribunal considers reasonable in a case where it is satisfied that it was not reasonably practicable for the complaint to be presented before the end of that period of three months.

(3) Where an employment tribunal finds a complaint under this section well-founded, the tribunal—
    (a)   shall make a declaration to that effect, and
    (b)   may make an award of compensation to be paid by the employer to the employee.

(4) The amount of the compensation shall be such as the tribunal considers just and equitable in all the circumstances having regard to—

(a)   the employer's default in failing to permit time off to be taken by the employee, and

(b)   any loss sustained by the employee which is attributable to the matters to which the complaint relates.

Looking for work and making arrangements for training

52   Right to time off to look for work or arrange training

(1)   An employee who is given notice of dismissal by reason of redundancy is entitled to be permitted by his employer to take reasonable time off during the employee's working hours before the end of his notice in order to—

(a)   look for new employment, or

(b)   make arrangements for training for future employment.

(2)   An employee is not entitled to take time off under this section unless, on whichever is the later of—

(a)   the date on which the notice is due to expire, and

(b)   the date on which it would expire were it the notice required to be given by section 86(1),

he will have been (or would have been) continuously employed for a period of two years or more.

(3)   For the purposes of this section the working hours of an employee shall be taken to be any time when, in accordance with his contract of employment, the employee is required to be at work.

53   Right to remuneration for time off under section 52

(1)   An employee who is permitted to take time off under section 52 is entitled to be paid remuneration by his employer for the period of absence at the appropriate hourly rate.

(2)   The appropriate hourly rate, in relation to an employee, is the amount of one week's pay divided by the number of normal working hours in a week for that employee when employed under the contract of employment in force on the day when the notice of dismissal was given.

(3)   But where the number of normal working hours differs from week to week or over a longer period, the amount of one week's pay shall be divided instead by the average number of normal working hours calculated by dividing by twelve the total number of the employee's normal working hours during the period of twelve weeks ending with the last complete week before the day on which the notice was given.

(4)   If an employer unreasonably refuses to permit an employee to take time off from work as required by section 52, the employee is entitled to be paid an amount equal to the remuneration to which he would have been entitled under subsection (1) if he had been permitted to take the time off.

(5)   The amount of an employer's liability to pay remuneration under subsection (1) shall not exceed, in respect of the notice period of any employee, forty per cent. of a week's pay of that employee.

(6)   A right to any amount under subsection (1) or (4) does not affect any right of an employee in relation to remuneration under his contract of employment ('contractual remuneration').

(7)   Any contractual remuneration paid to an employee in respect of a period of time off under section 52 goes towards discharging any liability of the employer to pay remuneration under subsection (1) in respect of that period; and, conversely, any payment of remuneration under subsection (1) in respect of a period goes towards discharging any liability of the employer to pay contractual remuneration in respect of that period.

54   Complaints to employment tribunals

(1)   An employee may present a complaint to an employment tribunal that his employer—

(a)   has unreasonably refused to permit him to take time off as required by section 52, or

(b)   has failed to pay the whole or any part of any amount to which the employee is entitled under section 53(1) or (4).

(2)   An employment tribunal shall not consider a complaint under this section unless it is presented—

    (a)   before the end of the period of three months beginning with the date on which it is alleged that the time off should have been permitted, or

    (b)   within such further period as the tribunal considers reasonable in a case where it is satisfied that it was not reasonably practicable for the complaint to be presented before the end of that period of three months.

(3)   Where an employment tribunal finds a complaint under this section well-founded, the tribunal shall—

    (a)   make a declaration to that effect, and

    (b)   order the employer to pay to the employee the amount which it finds due to him.

(4)   The amount which may be ordered by a tribunal to be paid by an employer under subsection (3) (or, where the employer is liable to pay remuneration under section 53, the aggregate of that amount and the amount of that liability) shall not exceed, in respect of the notice period of any employee, forty per cent. of a week's pay of that employee.

Ante-natal care

55   Right to time off for ante-natal care

(1)   An employee who—

    (a)   is pregnant, and

    (b)   has, on the advice of a registered medical practitioner, registered midwife or registered nurse, made an appointment to attend at any place for the purpose of receiving ante-natal care,

is entitled to be permitted by her employer to take time off during the employee's working hours in order to enable her to keep the appointment.

(2)   An employee is not entitled to take time off under this section to keep an appointment unless, if her employer requests her to do so, she produces for his inspection—

    (a)   a certificate from a registered medical practitioner, registered midwife or registered nurse stating that the employee is pregnant, and

    (b)   an appointment card or some other document showing that the appointment has been made.

(3)   Subsection (2) does not apply where the employee's appointment is the first appointment during her pregnancy for which she seeks permission to take time off in accordance with subsection (1).

(4)   For the purposes of this section the working hours of an employee shall be taken to be any time when, in accordance with her contract of employment, the employee is required to be at work.

…

56   Right to remuneration for time off under section 55

(1)   An employee who is permitted to take time off under section 55 is entitled to be paid remuneration by her employer for the period of absence at the appropriate hourly rate.

(2)   The appropriate hourly rate, in relation to an employee, is the amount of one week's pay divided by the number of normal working hours in a week for that employee when employed under the contract of employment in force on the day when the time off is taken.

(3)   But where the number of normal working hours differs from week to week or over a longer period, the amount of one week's pay shall be divided instead by—

    (a)   the average number of normal working hours calculated by dividing by twelve the total number of the employee's normal working hours during the period of twelve weeks ending with the last complete week before the day on which the time off is taken, or

    (b)   where the employee has not been employed for a sufficient period to enable the calculation to be made under paragraph (a), a number which fairly represents the number of normal working hours in a week having regard to such of the considerations specified in subsection (4) as are appropriate in the circumstances.

(4)   The considerations referred to in subsection (3)(b) are—

    (a)   the average number of normal working hours in a week which the employee could expect in accordance with the terms of her contract, and (b)　the average number of normal working hours of other employees engaged in relevant comparable employment with the same employer.

(5)　A right to any amount under subsection (1) does not affect any right of an employee in relation to remuneration under her contract of employment ('contractual remuneration').

(6)　Any contractual remuneration paid to an employee in respect of a period of time off under section 55 goes towards discharging any liability of the employer to pay remuneration under subsection (1) in respect of that period; and, conversely, any payment of remuneration under subsection (1) in respect of a period goes towards discharging any liability of the employer to pay contractual remuneration in respect of that period.

57　　Complaints to employment tribunals

(1)　An employee may present a complaint to an employment tribunal that her employer—
　　(a)　has unreasonably refused to permit her to take time off as required by section 55, or
　　(b)　has failed to pay the whole or any part of any amount to which the employee is entitled under section 56.

(2)　An employment tribunal shall not consider a complaint under this section unless it is presented—
　　(a)　before the end of the period of three months beginning with the date of the appointment concerned, or
　　(b)　within such further period as the tribunal considers reasonable in a case where it is satisfied that it was not reasonably practicable for the complaint to be presented before the end of that period of three months.

(3)　Where an employment tribunal finds a complaint under this section well-founded, the tribunal shall make a declaration to that effect.

(4)　If the complaint is that the employer has unreasonably refused to permit the employee to take time off, the tribunal shall also order the employer to pay to the employee an amount equal to the remuneration to which she would have been entitled under section 56 if the employer had not refused.

(5)　If the complaint is that the employer has failed to pay the employee the whole or part of any amount to which she is entitled under section 56, the tribunal shall also order the employer to pay to the employee the amount which it finds due to her.

Dependants

57A　Time off for dependants

(1)　An employee is entitled to be permitted by his employer to take a reasonable amount of time off during the employee's working hours in order to take action which is necessary—
　　(a)　to provide assistance on an occasion when a dependant falls ill, gives birth or is injured or assaulted,
　　(b)　to make arrangements for the provision of care for a dependant who is ill or injured,
　　(c)　in consequence of the death of a dependant,
　　(d)　because of the unexpected disruption or termination of arrangements for the care of a dependant, or
　　(e)　to deal with an incident which involves a child of the employee and which occurs unexpectedly in a period during which an educational establishment which the child attends is responsible for him.

(2)　Subsection (1) does not apply unless the employee—
　　(a)　tells his employer the reason for his absence as soon as reasonably practicable, and
　　(b)　except where paragraph (a) cannot be complied with until after the employee has returned to work, tells his employer for how long he expects to be absent.

(3)　Subject to subsections (4) and (5), for the purposes of this section 'dependant' means, in relation to an employee—
　　(a)　a spouse or civil partner,
　　(b)　a child,
　　(c)　a parent,

(d)   a person who lives in the same household as the employee, otherwise than by reason of being his employee, tenant, lodger or boarder.

(4) For the purposes of subsection (1)(a) or (b) 'dependant' includes, in addition to the persons mentioned in subsection (3), any person who reasonably relies on the employee—

(a)   for assistance on an occasion when the person falls ill or is injured or assaulted, or

(b)   to make arrangements for the provision of care in the event of illness or injury.

(5) For the purposes of subsection (1)(d) 'dependant' includes, in addition to the persons mentioned in subsection (3), any person who reasonably relies on the employee to make arrangements for the provision of care.

(6) A reference in this section to illness or injury includes a reference to mental illness or injury.

57B   Complaint to employment tribunal

(1) An employee may present a complaint to an employment tribunal that his employer has unreasonably refused to permit him to take time off as required by section 57A.

(2) An employment tribunal shall not consider a complaint under this section unless it is presented—

(a)   before the end of the period of three months beginning with the date when the refusal occurred, or

(b)   within such further period as the tribunal considers reasonable in a case where it is satisfied that it was not reasonably practicable for the complaint to be presented before the end of that period of three months.

(3) Where an employment tribunal finds a complaint under subsection (1) well-founded, it—

(a)   shall make a declaration to that effect, and

(b)   may make an award of compensation to be paid by the employer to the employee.

(4) the amount of compensation shall be such as the tribunal considers just and equitable in all the circumstances having regard to—

(a)   the employer's default in refusing to permit time off to be taken by the employee, and

(b)   any loss sustained by the employee which is attributable to the matters complained of.

Occupational pension scheme trustees

58   Right to time off for pension scheme trustees

(1) The employer in relation to a relevant occupational pension scheme shall permit an employee of his who is a trustee of the scheme to take time off during the employee's working hours for the purpose of—

(a)   performing any of his duties as such a trustee, or

(b)   undergoing training relevant to the performance of those duties.

(2) The amount of time off which an employee is to be permitted to take under this section and the purposes for which, the occasions on which and any conditions subject to which time off may be so taken are those that are reasonable in all the circumstances having regard, in particular, to—

(a)   how much time off is required for the performance of the duties of a trustee of the scheme and the undergoing of relevant training, and how much time off is required for performing the particular duty or for undergoing the particular training, and

(b)   the circumstances of the employer's business and the effect of the employee's absence on the running of that business.

(2A) This section applies to an employee who is a director of a company which is a trustee of a relevant occupational pension scheme as it applies to an employee who is a trustee of such a scheme (references to such a trustee being read for this purpose as references to such a director).

(3) In this section—

(a)   'relevant occupational pension scheme' means an occupational pension scheme (as defined in section 1 of the Pension Schemes Act 1993) established under a trust, and

(b)   references to the employer, in relation to such a scheme, are to an employer of persons in the description of employment to which the scheme relates, and

(c)   reference to training are to training on the employer's premises or elsewhere.

(4) For the purposes of this section the working hours of an employee shall be taken to be any time when, in accordance with his contract of employment, the employee is required to be at work.

59 Right to payment for time off under section 58

(1) An employer who permits an employee to take time off under section 58 shall pay him for the time taken off pursuant to the permission.

(2) Where the employee's remuneration for the work he would ordinarily have been doing during that time does not vary with the amount of work done, he must be paid as if he had worked at that work for the whole of that time.

(3) Where the employee's remuneration for the work he would ordinarily have been doing during that time varies with the amount of work done, he must be paid an amount calculated by reference to the average hourly earnings for that work.

(4) The average hourly earnings mentioned in subsection (3) are—

    (a) those of the employee concerned, or

    (b) if no fair estimate can be made of those earnings, the average hourly earnings for work of that description of persons in comparable employment with the same employer or, if there are no such persons, a figure of average hourly earnings which is reasonable in the circumstances.

(5) A right to be paid an amount under subsection (1) does not affect any right of an employee in relation to remuneration under his contract of employment ('contractual remuneration').

(6) Any contractual remuneration paid to an employee in respect of a period of time off under section 58 goes towards discharging any liability of the employer under subsection (1) in respect of that period; and, conversely, any payment under subsection (1) in respect of a period goes towards discharging any liability of the employer to pay contractual remuneration in respect of that period.

60 Complaints to employment tribunals

(1) An employee may present a complaint to an employment tribunal that his employer—

    (a) has failed to permit him to take time off as required by section 58, or

    (b) has failed to pay him in accordance with section 59.

(2) An employment tribunal shall not consider a complaint under this section unless it is presented—

    (a) before the end of the period of three months beginning with the date when the failure occurred, or

    (b) within such further period as the tribunal considers reasonable in a case where it is satisfied that it was not reasonably practicable for the complaint to be presented before the end of that period of three months.

(3) Where an employment tribunal finds a complaint under subsection (1)(a) well-founded, the tribunal—

    (a) shall make a declaration to that effect, and

    (b) may make an award of compensation to be paid by the employer to the employee.

(4) The amount of the compensation shall be such as the tribunal considers just and equitable in all the circumstances having regard to—

    (a) the employer's default in failing to permit time off to be taken by the employee, and

    (b) any loss sustained by the employee which is attributable to the matters complained of.

(5) Where on a complaint under subsection (1)(b) an employment tribunal finds that an employer has failed to pay an employee in accordance with section 59, it shall order the employer to pay the amount which it finds to be due.

Employee representatives

61 Right to time off for employee representatives

(1) An employee who is—

    (a) an employee representative for the purposes of Chapter II of Part IV of the Trade Union and Labour Relations (Consolidation) Act 1992 (redundancies) or Regulations 9, 13 and 15 of the Transfer of Undertakings (Protection of Employment) Regulations 2006, or

(b)   a candidate in an election in which any person elected will, on being elected, be such an employee representative,

is entitled to be permitted by his employer to take reasonable time off during the employee's working hours in order to perform his functions as such an employee representative or candidate or in order to undergo training to perform such functions.

(2)   For the purposes of this section the working hours of an employee shall be taken to be any time when, in accordance with his contract of employment, the employee is required to be at work.

62   Right to remuneration for time off under section 61

(1)   An employee who is permitted to take time off under section 61 is entitled to be paid remuneration by his employer for the time taken off at the appropriate hourly rate.

(2)   The appropriate hourly rate, in relation to an employee, is the amount of one week's pay divided by the number of normal working hours in a week for that employee when employed under the contract of employment in force on the day when the time off is taken.

(3)   But where the number of normal working hours differs from week to week or over a longer period, the amount of one week's pay shall be divided instead by—

      (a)   the average number of normal working hours calculated by dividing by twelve the total number of the employee's normal working hours during the period of twelve weeks ending with the last complete week before the day on which the time off is taken, or

      (b)   where the employee has not been employed for a sufficient period to enable the calculation to be made under paragraph (a), a number which fairly represents the number of normal working hours in a week having regard to such of the considerations specified in subsection (4) as are appropriate in the circumstances.

(4)   The considerations referred to in subsection (3)(b) are—

      (a)   the average number of normal working hours in a week which the employee could expect in accordance with the terms of his contract, and

      (b)   the average number of normal working hours of other employees engaged in relevant comparable employment with the same employer.

(5)   A right to any amount under subsection (1) does not affect any right of an employee in relation to remuneration under his contract of employment ('contractual remuneration').

(6)   Any contractual remuneration paid to an employee in respect of a period of time off under section 61 goes towards discharging any liability of the employer to pay remuneration under subsection (1) in respect of that period; and, conversely, any payment of remuneration under subsection (1) in respect of a period goes towards discharging any liability of the employer to pay contractual remuneration in respect of that period.

63   Complaints to employment tribunals

(1)   An employee may present a complaint to an employment tribunal that his employer—

      (a)   has unreasonably refused to permit him to take time off as required by section 61, or

      (b)   has failed to pay the whole or any part of any amount to which the employee is entitled under section 62.

(2)   An employment tribunal shall not consider a complaint under this section unless it is presented—

      (a)   before the end of the period of three months beginning with the day on which the time off was taken or on which it is alleged the time off should have been permitted, or

      (b)   within such further period as the tribunal considers reasonable in a case where it is satisfied that it was not reasonably practicable for the complaint to be presented before the end of that period of three months.

(3)   Where an employment tribunal finds a complaint under this section well-founded, the tribunal shall make a declaration to that effect.

(4) If the complaint is that the employer has unreasonably refused to permit the employee to take time off, the tribunal shall also order the employer to pay to the employee an amount equal to the remuneration to which he would have been entitled under section 62 if the employer had not refused.

(5) If the complaint is that the employer has failed to pay the employee the whole or part of any amount to which he is entitled under section 62, the tribunal shall also order the employer to pay to the employee the amount which it finds due to him.

63A   Right to time off for young person for study or training

(1) An employee who—

    (a)   is aged 16 or 17,

    (b)   is not receiving full-time secondary or further education, and

    (c)   has not attained such standard of achievement as is prescribed by regulations made by the Secretary of State,

is entitled to be permitted by his employer to take time off during the employee's working hours in order to undertake study or training leading to a relevant qualification.

...

(3) An employee who—

    (a)   satisfies the requirements of paragraphs (a) to (c) of subsection (1), and

    (b)   is for the time being supplied by his employer to another person ('the principal') to perform work in accordance with a contract made between the employer and the principal,

is entitled to be permitted by the principal to take time off during the employee's working hours in order to undertake study or training leading to a relevant qualification.

(4) Where an employee—

    (a)   is aged 18,

    (b)   is undertaking study or training leading to a relevant qualification, and

    (c)   began such study or training before attaining that age,

subsections (1) and (3) shall apply to the employee, in relation to that study or training, as if 'or 18' were inserted at the end of subsection (1)(a).

(5) The amount of time off which an employee is to be permitted to take under this section, and the occasions on which and any conditions subject to which time off may be so taken, are those that are reasonable in all the circumstances having regard, in particular, to—

    (a)   the requirements of the employee's study or training, and

    (b)   the circumstances of the business of the employer or the principal and the effect of the employee's time off on the running of that business.

...

(7) References in this section to study or training are references to study or training on the premises of the employer or (as the case may be) principal or elsewhere.

(8) For the purposes of this section the working hours of an employee shall be taken to be any time when, in accordance with his contract of employment, the employee is required to be at work.

63B   Right to remuneration for time off under section 63A

(1) An employee who is permitted to take time off under section 63A is entitled to be paid remuneration by his employer for the time taken off at the appropriate hourly rate.

(2) The appropriate hourly rate, in relation to an employee, is the amount of one week's pay divided by the number of normal working hours in a week for that employee when employed under the contract of employment in force on the day when the time off is taken.

(3) But where the number of normal working hours differs from week to week or over a longer period, the amount of one week's pay shall be divided instead by—

    (a)   the average number of normal working hours calculated by dividing by twelve the total number of the employee's working hours during the period of twelve weeks ending with the last complete week before the day on which the time off is taken, or

    (b)   where the employee has not been employed for a sufficient period to enable the calculation to be made under paragraph (a), a number which fairly represents the number of normal working hours in a week having regard to such of the considerations specified in subsection (4) as are appropriate in the circumstances.

(4)   The considerations referred to in subsection (3)(b) are—

　　(a)   the average number of normal working hours in a week which the employee could expect in accordance with the terms of his contract, and

　　(b)   the average number of normal working hours of other employees engaged in relevant comparable employment with the same employer.

(5)   A right to any amount under subsection (1) does not affect any right of an employee in relation to remuneration under his contract of employment ('contractual remuneration').

(6)   Any contractual remuneration paid to an employee in respect of a period of time off under section 63A goes towards discharging any liability of the employer to pay remuneration under subsection (1) in respect of that period; and, conversely, any payment of remuneration under subsection (1) in respect of a period goes towards discharging any liability of the employer to pay contractual remuneration in respect of that period.

63C   Complaints to employment tribunals

(1)   An employee may present a complaint to an employment tribunal that—

　　(a)   his employer, or the principal referred to in subsection (3) of section 63A, has unreasonably refused to permit him to take time off as required by that section, or

　　(b)   his employer has failed to pay the whole or any part of any amount to which the employee is entitled under section 63B.

(2)   An employment tribunal shall not consider a complaint under this section unless it is presented—

　　(a)   before the end of the period of three months beginning with the day on which the time off was taken or on which it is alleged the time off should have been permitted, or

　　(b)   within such further period as the tribunal considers reasonable in a case where it is satisfied that it was not reasonably practicable for the complaint to be presented before the end of that period of three months.

(3)   Where an employment tribunal finds a complaint under this section well-founded, the tribunal shall make a declaration to that effect.

(4)   If the complaint is that the employer or the principal has unreasonably refused to permit the employee to take time off, the tribunal shall also order the employer or the principal, as the case may be, to pay to the employee an amount equal to the remuneration to which he would have been entitled under section 63B if the employer or the principal had not refused.

(5)   If the complaint is that the employer has failed to pay the employee the whole or part of any amount to which he is entitled under section 63B, the tribunal shall also order the employer to pay to the employee the amount which it finds due to him.

PART VII
SUSPENSION FROM WORK

Suspension on medical grounds

64   Right to remuneration on suspension on medical grounds

(1)   An employee who is suspended from work by his employer on medical grounds is entitled to be paid by his employer remuneration while he is so suspended for a period not exceeding twenty-six weeks.

(2)   For the purposes of this Part an employee is suspended from work on medical grounds if he is suspended from work in consequence of—

　　(a)   a requirement imposed by or under a provision of an enactment or of an instrument made under an enactment, or

　　(b)   a recommendation in a provision of a code of practice issued or approved under section 16 of the Health and Safety at Work etc. Act 1974,

and the provision is for the time being specified in subsection (3).

(3)   The provisions referred to in subsection (2) are—

Regulation 16 of the Control of Lead at Work Regulations 1980,

Regulation 24 of the Ionising Radiations Regulations 1999, and

Regulation 11 of the Control of Substances Hazardous to Health Regulations 1988.

(4) The Secretary of State may by order add provisions to or remove provisions from the list of provisions specified in subsection (3).

(5) For the purposes of this Part an employee shall be regarded as suspended from work on medical grounds only if and for so long as he—

    (a) continues to be employed by his employer, but

    (b) is not provided with work or does not perform the work he normally performed before the suspension.

65 Exclusions from right to remuneration

(1) An employee is not entitled to remuneration under section 64 unless he has been continuously employed for a period of not less than one month ending with the day before that on which the suspension begins.

(2) …

(3) An employee is not entitled to remuneration under section 64 in respect of any period during which he is incapable of work by reason of disease or bodily or mental disablement.

(4) An employee is not entitled to remuneration under section 64 in respect of any period if—

    (a) his employer has offered to provide him with suitable alternative work during the period (whether or not it is work which the employee is under his contract, or was under the contract in force before the suspension, employed to perform) and the employee has unreasonably refused to perform that work, or

    (b) he does not comply with reasonable requirements imposed by his employer with a view to ensuring that his services are available.

Suspension on maternity grounds

66 Meaning of suspension on maternity grounds

(1) For the purposes of this Part an employee is suspended from work on maternity grounds if, in consequence of any relevant requirement or relevant recommendation, she is suspended from work by her employer on the ground that she is pregnant, has recently given birth or is breastfeeding a child.

(2) In subsection (1)—

'relevant requirement' means a requirement imposed by or under a specified provision of an enactment or of an instrument made under an enactment, and

'relevant recommendation' means a recommendation in a specified provision of a code of practice issued or approved under section 16 of the Health and Safety at Work etc. Act 1974;

and in this subsection 'specified provision' means a provision for the time being specified in an order made by the Secretary of State under this subsection.

(3) For the purposes of this Part an employee shall be regarded as suspended from work on maternity grounds only if and for so long as she—

    (a) continues to be employed by her employer, but

    (b) is not provided with work or (disregarding alternative work for the purposes of section 67) does not perform the work she normally performed before the suspension.

67 Right to offer of alternative work

(1) Where an employer has available suitable alternative work for an employee, the employee has a right to be offered to be provided with the alternative work before being suspended from work on maternity grounds.

(2) For alternative work to be suitable for an employee for the purposes of this section—

    (a) the work must be of a kind which is both suitable in relation to her and appropriate for her to do in the circumstances, and

    (b) the terms and conditions applicable to her for performing the work, if they differ from the corresponding terms and conditions applicable to her for performing the work she normally performs under her contract of employment, must not be substantially less favourable to her than those corresponding terms and conditions.

68   Right to remuneration

(1)   An employee who is suspended from work on maternity grounds is entitled to be paid remuneration by her employer while she is so suspended.

(2)   An employee is not entitled to remuneration under this section in respect of any period if—

(a)   her employer has offered to provide her during the period with work which is suitable alternative work for her for the purposes of section 67, and

(b)   the employee has unreasonably refused to perform that work.

General

69   Calculation of remuneration

(1)   The amount of remuneration payable by an employer to an employee under section 64 or 68 is a week's pay in respect of each week of the period of suspension; and if in any week remuneration is payable in respect of only part of that week the amount of a week's pay shall be reduced proportionately.

(2)   A right to remuneration under section 64 or 68 does not affect any right of an employee in relation to remuneration under the employee's contract of employment ('contractual remuneration').

(3)   Any contractual remuneration paid by an employer to an employee in respect of any period goes towards discharging the employer's liability under section 64 or 68 in respect of that period; and, conversely, any payment of remuneration in discharge of an employer's liability under section 64 or 68 in respect of any period goes towards discharging any obligation of the employer to pay contractual remuneration in respect of that period.

70   Complaints to employment tribunals

(1)   An employee may present a complaint to an employment tribunal that his or her employer has failed to pay the whole or any part of remuneration to which the employee is entitled under section 64 or 68.

(2)   An employment tribunal shall not consider a complaint under subsection (1) relating to remuneration in respect of any day unless it is presented—

(a)   before the end of the period of three months beginning with that day, or

(b)   within such further period as the tribunal considers reasonable in a case where it is satisfied that it was not reasonably practicable for the complaint to be presented within that period of three months.

(3)   Where an employment tribunal finds a complaint under subsection (1) well-founded, the tribunal shall order the employer to pay the employee the amount of remuneration which it finds is due to him or her.

(4)   An employee may present a complaint to an employment tribunal that in contravention of section 67 her employer has failed to offer to provide her with work.

(5)   An employment tribunal shall not consider a complaint under subsection (4) unless it is presented—

(a)   before the end of the period of three months beginning with the first day of the suspension, or

(b)   within such further period as the tribunal considers reasonable in a case where it is satisfied that it was not reasonably practicable for the complaint to be presented within that period of three months.

(6)   Where an employment tribunal finds a complaint under subsection (4) well-founded, the tribunal may make an award of compensation to be paid by the employer to the employee.

(7)   The amount of the compensation shall be such as the tribunal considers just and equitable in all the circumstances having regard to—

(a)   the infringement of the employee's right under section 67 by the failure on the part of the employer to which the complaint relates, and

(b)   any loss sustained by the employee which is attributable to that failure.

PART VIII
GENERAL RIGHT TO MATERNITY LEAVE

CHAPTER I
MATERNITY LEAVE

71 Ordinary maternity leave

(1) An employee may, provided that she satisfies any conditions which may be prescribed, be absent from work at any time during an ordinary maternity leave period.

(2) An ordinary maternity leave period is a period calculated in accordance with regulations made by the Secretary of State.

(3) Regulations under subsection (2)—

(a) shall secure that no ordinary maternity leave period is less than 18 weeks;

(b) may allow an employee to choose, subject to any prescribed restrictions, the date on which an ordinary maternity leave period starts;

(c) may specify circumstances in which an employee may work for her employer during an ordinary maternity leave period without bringing that period to an end.

(4) Subject to section 74, an employee who exercises her right under subsection (1)—

(a) is entitled for such purposes and to such extent as may be prescribed to the benefit of the terms and conditions of employment which would have applied if she had not been absent,

(b) is bound for such purposes and to such extent as may be prescribed by any obligations arising under those terms and conditions (except in so far as they are inconsistent with subsection (1)), and

(c) is entitled to return from leave to the job of a prescribed kind.

(5) In subsection (4)(a) 'terms and conditions of employment'—

(a) includes matters connected with an employee's employment whether or not they arise under her contract of employment, but

(b) does not include terms and conditions about remuneration.

(6) The Secretary of State may make regulations specifying matters which are, or are not, to be treated as remuneration for the purposes of this section.

(7) The Secretary of State may make regulations making provision, in relation to the right to return under subsection (4)(c) above, about—

(a) seniority, pension rights and similar rights;

(b) terms and conditions of employment on return.

72 Compulsory maternity leave

(1) An employer shall not permit an employee who satisfies prescribed conditions to work during a compulsory maternity leave period.

(2) A compulsory maternity leave period is a period calculated in accordance with regulations made by the Secretary of State.

(3) Regulations under subsection (2) shall secure—

(a) that no compulsory leave period is less than two weeks, and

(b) that every compulsory maternity leave period falls within an ordinary maternity leave period.

(4) Subject to subsection (5), any provision of or made under the Health and Safety at Work etc. Act 1974 shall apply in relation to the prohibition under subsection (1) as if it were imposed by regulations under section 15 of that Act.

(5) Section 33(1)(c) of the 1974 Act shall not apply in relation to the prohibition under subsection (1); and an employer who contravenes that subsection shall be—

(a) guilty of an offence, and

(b) liable on summary conviction to a fine not exceeding level 2 on the standard scale.

73 Additional maternity leave

(1) An employee who satisfies prescribed conditions may be absent from work at any time during an additional maternity leave period.

(2)   An additional maternity leave period is a period calculated in accordance with regulations made by the Secretary of State.

(3)   Regulations under subsection (2) may allow an employee to choose, subject to prescribed restrictions, the date on which an additional maternity leave period ends.

(4)   Subject to section 74, an employee who exercises her right under subsection (1)—

    (a)   is entitled, for such purposes and to such extent as may be prescribed, to the benefit of the terms and conditions of employment which would have applied if she had not been absent,

    (b)   is bound, for such purposes and to such extent as may be prescribed, by obligations arising under those terms and conditions (except in so far as they are inconsistent with subsection (1), and

    (c)   is entitled to return from leave to a job of a prescribed kind.

(5)   In subsection (4)(a) 'terms and conditions of employment'—

    (a)   includes matters connected with an employee's employment whether or not they arise under her contract of employment, but

    (b)   does not include terms and conditions about remuneration.

(5A) In subsection (4)(c), the reference to return from leave includes, where appropriate, a reference to a continuous period of absence attributable partly to additional maternity leave and partly to ordinary maternity leave.

…

CHAPTER II
PARENTAL LEAVE

80   Complaint to employment tribunal

(1)   An employee may present a complaint to an employment tribunal that his employer—

    (a)   has unreasonably postponed a period of parental leave requested by the employee, or

    (b)   has prevented or attempted to prevent the employee from taking parental leave.

(2)   An employment tribunal shall not consider a complaint under this section unless it is presented—

    (a)   before the end of the period of three months beginning with the date (or last date) of the matters complained of, or

    (b)   within such further period as the tribunal considers reasonable in a case where it is satisfied that it was not reasonably practicable for the complaint to be presented before the end of that period of three months.

(3)   Where an employment tribunal finds a complaint under this section well-founded it—

    (a)   shall make a declaration to that effect, and

    (b)   may make an award of compensation to be paid by the employer to the employee.

(4)   The amount of compensation shall be such as the tribunal considers just and equitable in all the circumstances having regard to—

    (a)   the employer's behaviour, and

    (b)   any loss sustained by the employee which is attributable to the matters complained of.

CHAPTER III
PATERNITY LEAVE

80A   Entitlement to ordinary paternity leave: birth

(1)   The Secretary of State shall make regulations entitling an employee who satisfies specified conditions—

    (a)   as to duration of employment,

    (b)   as to relationship with a newborn, or expected, child, and

    (c)   as to relationship with the child's mother,

to be absent from work on leave under this section for the purpose of caring for the child or supporting the mother.

(2)   The regulations shall include provision for determining—

    (a)   the extent of an employee's entitlement to leave under this section in respect of a child;

    (b)   when leave under this section may be taken.

(3) Provision under subsection (2)(a) shall secure that where an employee is entitled to leave under this section in respect of a child he is entitled to at least two weeks' leave.

(4) Provision under subsection (2)(b) shall secure that leave under this section must be taken before the end of a period of at least 56 days beginning with the date of the child's birth.

(5) Regulations under subsection (1) may—

    (a) specify things which are, or are not, to be taken as done for the purpose of caring for a child or supporting the child's mother;

    (b) make provision excluding the right to be absent on leave under this section in respect of a child where more than one child is born as a result of the same pregnancy;

    (c) make provision about how leave under this section may be taken.

(6) Where more than one child is born as a result of the same pregnancy, the reference in subsection (4) to the date of the child's birth shall be read as a reference to the date of birth of the first child born as a result of the pregnancy.

(7) In this section—

'newborn child' includes a child stillborn after twenty-four weeks of pregnancy;

'week' means any period of seven days.

80AA Entitlement to additional paternity leave: birth

(1) The Secretary of State may make regulations entitling an employee who satisfies specified conditions—

    (a) as to duration of employment,

    (b) as to relationship with a child, and

    (c) as to relationship with the child's mother,

to be absent from work on leave under this section for the purpose of caring for the child, at a time when the child's mother satisfies any conditions prescribed under subsection (2).

(2) The conditions that may be prescribed under this subsection are conditions relating to any one or more of the following—

    (a) any employment or self-employment of the child's mother;

    (b) her entitlement (or lack of entitlement) to leave under this Part or to statutory maternity pay or maternity allowance;

    (c) whether, and to what extent, she is exercising or has exercised any such entitlement.

(3) Any regulations under this section shall include provision for determining—

    (a) the extent of an employee's entitlement to leave under this section in respect of a child;

    (b) when leave under this section may be taken.

(4) Provision under subsection (3)(a) shall secure that an employee is not entitled to more than 26 weeks' leave in respect of a child.

(5) Provision under subsection (3)(b) shall secure that leave under this section—

    (a) may not be taken before the end of a specified period beginning with the date of the child's birth, but

    (b) must be taken before the end of the period of twelve months beginning with that date.

(6) Subsections (4) and (5)(a) do not limit the provision that may be made under subsection (3) in relation to cases where the child's mother has died before the end of the period mentioned in subsection (5)(b).

(7) Regulations under subsection (1) may—

    (a) specify things which are, or are not, to be taken as done for the purpose of caring for a child;

    (b) make provision excluding the right to be absent on leave under this section in respect of a child where more than one child is born as a result of the same pregnancy;

    (c) specify a minimum period which may be taken as leave under this section;

    (d) make provision about how leave under this section may be taken;

    (e) specify circumstances in which an employee may work for his employer during a period of leave under this section without bringing the period of leave to an end.

(8) Where more than one child is born as a result of the same pregnancy, the reference in subsection (5) to the date of the child's birth shall be read as a reference to the date of birth of the first child born as a result of the pregnancy.

(9) In this section 'week' means any period of seven days.

80B   Entitlement to ordinary paternity leave: adoption

(1) The Secretary of State shall make regulations entitling an employee who satisfies specified conditions—

    (a)   as to duration of employment,

    (b)   as to relationship with a child placed, or expected to be placed, for adoption under the law of any part of the United Kingdom, and

    (c)   as to relationship with a person with whom the child is, or is expected to be, so placed for adoption,

to be absent from work on leave under this section for the purpose of caring for the child or supporting the person by reference to whom he satisfies the condition under paragraph (c).

(2) The regulations shall include provision for determining—

    (a)   the extent of an employee's entitlement to leave under this section in respect of a child;

    (b)   when leave under this section may be taken.

(3) Provision under subsection (2)(a) shall secure that where an employee is entitled to leave under this section in respect of a child he is entitled to at least two weeks' leave.

(4) Provision under subsection (2)(b) shall secure that leave under this section must be taken before the end of a period of at least 56 days beginning with the date of the child's placement for adoption.

(5) Regulations under subsection (1) may—

    (a)   specify things which are, or are not, to be taken as done for the purpose of caring for a child or supporting a person with whom a child is placed for adoption;

    (b)   make provision excluding the right to be absent on leave under this section in the case of an employee who exercises a right to be absent from work on adoption leave;

    (c)   make provision excluding the right to be absent on leave under this section in respect of a child where more than one child is placed for adoption as part of the same arrangement;

    (d)   make provision about how leave under this section may be taken.

(6) Where more than one child is placed for adoption as part of the same arrangement, the reference in subsection (4) to the date of the child's placement shall be read as a reference to the date of placement of the first child to be placed as part of the arrangement.

(7) In this section, 'week' means any period of seven days.

(8) The Secretary of State may by regulations provide for this section to have effect in relation to cases which involve adoption, but not the placement of a child for adoption under the law of any part of the United Kingdom, with such modifications as the regulations may prescribe.

80BB   Entitlement to additional paternity leave: adoption

(1) The Secretary of State may make regulations entitling an employee who satisfies specified conditions—

    (a)   as to duration of employment,

    (b)   as to relationship with a child placed for adoption under the law of any part of the United Kingdom, and

    (c)   as to relationship with a person with whom the child is so placed for adoption ('the adopter'),

to be absent from work on leave under this section for the purpose of caring for the child, at a time when the adopter satisfies any conditions prescribed under subsection (2).

(2) The conditions that may be prescribed under this subsection are conditions relating to any one or more of the following—

    (a)   any employment or self-employment of the adopter;

    (b)   the adopter's entitlement (or lack of entitlement) to leave under this Part or to statutory adoption pay;

    (c)   whether, and to what extent, the adopter is exercising or has exercised any such entitlement.

(3) Any regulations under this section shall include provision for determining—

    (a)   the extent of an employee's entitlement to leave under this section in respect of a child;

    (b)   when leave under this section may be taken.

(4) Provision under subsection (3)(a) shall secure that an employee is not entitled to more than 26 weeks' leave in respect of a child.

(5) Provision under subsection (3)(b) shall secure that leave under this section—

    (a) may not be taken before the end of a specified period beginning with the date of the child's placement for adoption, but

    (b) must be taken before the end of the period of twelve months beginning with that date.

(6) Subsections (4) and (5)(a) do not limit the provision that may be made under subsection (3) in relation to cases where the adopter has died before the end of the period mentioned in subsection (5)(b).

(7) Regulations under subsection (1) may—

    (a) specify things which are, or are not, to be taken as done for the purpose of caring for a child;

    (b) make provision excluding the right to be absent on leave under this section in the case of an employee who exercises a right to be absent from work on adoption leave;

    (c) make provision excluding the right to be absent on leave under this section in respect of a child where more than one child is placed for adoption as part of the same arrangement;

    (d) specify a minimum period which may be taken as leave under this section;

    (e) make provision about how leave under this section may be taken;

    (f) specify circumstances in which an employee may work for his employer during a period of leave under this section without bringing the period of leave to an end.

(8) Where more than one child is placed for adoption as part of the same arrangement, the reference in subsection (5) to the date of the child's placement shall be read as a reference to the date of placement of the first child to be placed as part of the arrangement.

(9) In this section 'week' means any period of seven days.

(10) The Secretary of State may by regulations provide for this section to have effect in relation to cases which involve adoption, but not the placement of a child for adoption under the law of any part of the United Kingdom, with such modifications as the regulations may prescribe.

80C Rights during and after paternity leave

(1) Regulations under section 80A or 80AA shall provide—

    (a) that an employee who is absent on leave under that section is entitled, for such purposes and to such extent as the regulations may prescribe, to the benefit of the terms and conditions of employment which would have applied if he had not been absent;

    (b) that an employee who is absent on leave under that section is bound, for such purposes and to such extent as the regulations may prescribe, by obligations arising under those terms and conditions (except in so far as they are inconsistent with subsection (1) of that section), and

    (c) that an employee who is absent on leave under that section is entitled to return from leave to a job of a kind prescribed by regulations, subject to section 80D(1).

(2) The reference in subsection (1)(c) to absence on leave under section 80A or 80AA includes, where appropriate, a reference to a continuous period of absence attributable partly to leave under that section and partly to any one or more of the following—

    (za) leave under the other section,

    (a) maternity leave,

    (b) adoption leave, and

    (c) parental leave.

(3) Subsection (1) shall apply to regulations under section 80B as it applies to regulations under section 80A or 80BB as it applies to regulations under section 80A or 80AA.

(4) In the application of subsection (1)(c) to regulations under section 80B or 80BB, the reference to absence on leave under that section includes, where appropriate, a reference to a continuous period of absence attributable partly to leave under that section and partly to any one or more of the following—

    (za) leave under the other section,

    (a) maternity leave,

       (b)   adoption leave,

       (c)   parental leave, and

       (d)   leave under section 80A or 80AA.

(5)   In subsection (1)(a), 'terms and conditions of employment'—

       (a)   includes matters connected with an employee's employment whether or not they arise under his contract of employment, but

       (b)   does not include terms and conditions about remuneration.

(6)   Regulations under any of sections 80A to 80BB may specify matters which are, or are not, to be treated as remuneration for the purposes of this section.

(7)   Regulations under any of sections 80A to 80BB may make provision, in relation to the right to return mentioned in subsection (1)(c), about—

       (a)   seniority, pension rights and similar rights;

       (b)   terms and conditions of employment on return.

PART 8A

FLEXIBLE WORKING

80F   **Statutory right to request contract variation**

(1)   A qualifying employee may apply to his employer for a change in his terms and conditions of employment if—

       (a)   the change relates to—

           (i)   the hours he is required to work,

           (ii)   the times when he is required to work,

           (iii)   where, as between his home and a place of business of his employer, he is required to work, or

           (iv)   such other aspect of his terms and conditions of employment as the Secretary of State may specify by regulations, and

       (b)   his purpose in applying for the change is to enable him to care for someone who, at the time of application, is—

           (i)   a child who has not reached the prescribed age or falls within a prescribed description and in respect of whom (in either case) the employee satisfies prescribed conditions as to relationship, or

           (ii)   a person aged 18 or over who falls within a prescribed description and in respect of whom the employee satisfies prescribed conditions as to relationship.

(2)   An application under this section must—

       (a)   state that it is such an application,

       (b)   specify the change applied for and the date on which it is proposed the change should become effective,

       (c)   explain what effect, if any, the employee thinks making the change applied for would have on his employer and how, in his opinion, any such effect might be dealt with, and

       (d)   explain how the employee meets, in respect of the child or other person to be cared for, the conditions as to relationship mentioned in subsection (1)(b)(i) or (ii).

(3)   ...

(4)   If an employee has made an application under this section, he may not make a further application under this section to the same employer before the end of the period of twelve months beginning with the date on which the previous application was made.

(5)   The Secretary of State may by regulations make provision about—

       (a)   the form of applications under this section, and

       (b)   when such an application is to be taken as made.

(6), (7) ...

(8)   For the purposes of this section, an employee is—

       (a)   a qualifying employee if he—

           (i)   satisfies such conditions as to duration of employment as the Secretary of State may specify by regulations, and

           (ii)   is not an agency worker;

(b)   an agency worker if he is supplied by a person ('the agent') to do work for another ('the principal') under a contract or other arrangement made between the agent and the principal.

(9)   Regulations under this section may make different provision for different cases.

(10) In this section—

'child' means a person aged under 18;

'prescribed' means prescribed by regulations made by the Secretary of State.

80G   Employer's duties in relation to application under section 80F

(1)   An employer to whom an application under section 80F is made—

    (a)   shall deal with the application in accordance with regulations made by the Secretary of State, and

    (b)   shall only refuse the application because he considers that one or more of the following grounds applies—

        (i)   the burden of additional costs,

        (ii)   detrimental effect on ability to meet customer demand,

        (iii) inability to re-organise work among existing staff,

        (iv) inability to recruit additional staff,

        (v)   detrimental impact on quality,

        (vi) detrimental impact on performance,

        (vii) insufficiency of work during the periods the employee proposes to work,

        (viii) planned structural changes, and

        (ix) such other grounds as the Secretary of State may specify by regulations.

(2)   Regulations under subsection (1)(a) shall include—

    (a)   provision for the holding of a meeting between the employer and the employee to discuss an application under section 80F within twenty eight days after the date the application is made;

    (b)   provision for the giving by the employer to the employee of notice of his decision on the application within fourteen days after the date of the meeting under paragraph (a);

    (c)   provision for notice under paragraph (b) of a decision to refuse the application to state the grounds for the decision;

    (d)   provision for the employee to have a right, if he is dissatisfied with the employer's decision, to appeal against it within fourteen days after the date on which notice under paragraph (b) is given;

    (e)   provision about the procedure for exercising the right of appeal under paragraph (d), including provision requiring the employee to set out the grounds of appeal;

    (f)   provision for notice under paragraph (b) to include such information as the regulations may specify relating to the right of appeal under paragraph (d);

    (g)   provision for the holding, within fourteen days after the date on which notice of appeal is given by the employee, of a meeting between the employer and the employee to discuss the appeal;

    (h)   provision for the employer to give the employee notice of his decision on any appeal within fourteen days after the date of the meeting under paragraph (g);

    (i)   provision for notice under paragraph (h) of a decision to dismiss an appeal to state the grounds for the decision;

    (j)   provision for a statement under paragraph (c) or (i) to contain a sufficient explanation of the grounds for the decision;

    (k)   provision for the employee to have a right to be accompanied at meetings under paragraph (a) or (g) by a person of such description as the regulations may specify;

    (l)   provision for postponement in relation to any meeting under paragraph (a) or (g) which a companion under paragraph (k) is not available to attend;

    (m)   provision in relation to companions under paragraph (k) corresponding to section 10(6) and (7) of the Employment Relations Act 1999 (c 26) (right to paid time off to act as companion, etc);

    (n)   provision, in relation to the rights under paragraphs (k) and (l), for the application (with or without modification) of sections 11 to 13 of the Employment Relations Act 1999 (provisions ancillary to right to be accompanied under section 10 of that Act).

  (3)   Regulations under subsection (1)(a) may include—

    (a)   provision for any requirement of the regulations not to apply where an application is disposed of by agreement or withdrawn;

    (b)   provision for extension of a time limit where the employer and employee agree, or in such other circumstances as the regulations may specify;

    (c)   provision for applications to be treated as withdrawn in specified circumstances;

    and may make different provision for different cases.

  (4)   The Secretary of State may by order amend subsection (2).

80H   Complaints to employment tribunals

  (1)   An employee who makes an application under section 80F may present a complaint to an employment tribunal—

    (a)   that his employer has failed in relation to the application to comply with section 80G(1), or

    (b)   that a decision by his employer to reject the application was based on incorrect facts.

  (2)   No complaint under this section may be made in respect of an application which has been disposed of by agreement or withdrawn.

  (3)   In the case of an application which has not been disposed of by agreement or withdrawn, no complaint under this section may be made until the employer—

    (a)   notifies the employee of a decision to reject the application on appeal, or

    (b)   commits a breach of regulations under section 80G(1)(a) of such description as the Secretary of State may specify by regulations.

  (4)   No complaint under this section may be made in respect of failure to comply with provision included in regulations under subsection (1)(a) of section 80G because of subsection (2)(k), (l) or (m) of that section.

  (5)   An employment tribunal shall not consider a complaint under this section unless it is presented—

    (a)   before the end of the period of three months beginning with the relevant date, or

    (b)   within such further period as the tribunal considers reasonable in a case where it is satisfied that it was not reasonably practicable for the complaint to be presented before the end of that period of three months.

  (6)   In subsection (5)(a), the reference to the relevant date is—

    (a)   in the case of a complaint permitted by subsection (3)(a), the date on which the employee is notified of the decision on the appeal, and

    (b)   in the case of a complaint permitted by subsection (3)(b), the date on which the breach concerned was committed.

80I   Remedies

  (1)   Where an employment tribunal finds a complaint under section 80H well-founded it shall make a declaration to that effect and may—

    (a)   make an order for reconsideration of the application, and

    (b)   make an award of compensation to be paid by the employer to the employee.

  (2)   The amount of compensation shall be such amount, not exceeding the permitted maximum, as the tribunal considers just and equitable in all the circumstances.

  (3)   For the purposes of subsection (2), the permitted maximum is such number of weeks' pay as the Secretary of State may specify by regulations.

  (4)   Where an employment tribunal makes an order under subsection (1)(a), section 80G, and the regulations under that section, shall apply as if the application had been made on the date of the order.

PART IX
TERMINATION OF EMPLOYMENT

Minimum period of notice

86   Rights of employer and employee to minimum notice

(1)   The notice required to be given by an employer to terminate the contract of employment of a person who has been continuously employed for one month or more—

(a)   is not less than one week's notice if his period of continuous employment is less than two years,

(b)   is not less than one week's notice for each year of continuous employment if his period of continuous employment is two years or more but less than twelve years, and

(c)   is not less than twelve weeks' notice if his period of continuous employment is twelve years or more.

(2)   The notice required to be given by an employee who has been continuously employed for one month or more to terminate his contract of employment is not less than one week.

(3)   Any provision for shorter notice in any contract of employment with a person who has been continuously employed for one month or more has effect subject to subsections (1) and (2); but this section does not prevent either party from waiving his right to notice on any occasion or from accepting a payment in lieu of notice.

(4)   Any contract of employment of a person who has been continuously employed for three months or more which is a contract for a term certain of one month or less shall have effect as if it were for an indefinite period; and, accordingly, subsections (1) and (2) apply to the contract.

(5)   ...

(6)   This section does not affect any right of either party to a contract of employment to treat the contract as terminable without notice by reason of the conduct of the other party.

87   Rights of employee in period of notice

(1)   If an employer gives notice to terminate the contract of employment of a person who has been continuously employed for one month or more, the provisions of sections 88 to 91 have effect as respects the liability of the employer for the period of notice required by section 86(1).

(2)   If an employee who has been continuously employed for one month or more gives notice to terminate his contract of employment, the provisions of sections 88 to 91 have effect as respects the liability of the employer for the period of notice required by section 86(2).

(3)   In sections 88 to 91 'period of notice' means—

(a)   where notice is given by an employer, the period of notice required by section 86(1), and

(b)   where notice is given by an employee, the period of notice required by section 86(2).

(4)   This section does not apply in relation to a notice given by the employer or the employee if the notice to be given by the employer to terminate the contract must be at least one week more than the notice required by section 86(1).

88   Employments with normal working hours

(1)   If an employee has normal working hours under the contract of employment in force during the period of notice and during any part of those normal working hours—

(a)   the employee is ready and willing to work but no work is provided for him by his employer,

(b)   the employee is incapable of work because of sickness or injury,

(c)   the employee is absent from work wholly or partly because of pregnancy or childbirth or on adoption leave, parental leave or ordinary or additional paternity leave, or

(d)   the employee is absent from work in accordance with the terms of his employment relating to holidays,

the employer is liable to pay the employee for the part of normal working hours covered by any of paragraphs (a), (b), (c) and (d) a sum not less than the amount of remuneration for that part of normal working hours calculated at the average hourly rate of remuneration produced by dividing a week's pay by the number of normal working hours.

(2) Any payments made to the employee by his employer in respect of the relevant part of the period of notice (whether by way of sick pay, statutory sick pay, maternity pay, statutory maternity pay, paternity pay, ordinary statutory paternity pay, additional statutory paternity pay, adoption pay, statutory adoption pay, holiday pay or otherwise) go towards meeting the employer's liability under this section.

(3) Where notice was given by the employee, the employer's liability under this section does not arise unless and until the employee leaves the service of the employer in pursuance of the notice.

89   Employments without normal working hours

(1) If an employee does not have normal working hours under the contract of employment in force in the period of notice, the employer is liable to pay the employee for each week of the period of notice a sum not less than a week's pay.

(2) The employer's liability under this section is conditional on the employee being ready and willing to do work of a reasonable nature and amount to earn a week's pay.

(3) Subsection (2) does not apply—

    (a) in respect of any period during which the employee is incapable of work because of sickness or injury,

    (b) in respect of any period during which the employee is absent from work wholly or partly because of pregnancy or childbirth or on adoption leave, parental leave or ordinary or additional paternity leave, or

    (c) in respect of any period during which the employee is absent from work in accordance with the terms of his employment relating to holidays.

(4) Any payment made to an employee by his employer in respect of a period within subsection (3) (whether by way of sick pay, statutory sick pay, maternity pay, statutory maternity pay, paternity pay, ordinary statutory paternity pay, additional statutory paternity pay, adoption pay, statutory adoption pay, holiday pay or otherwise) shall be taken into account for the purposes of this section as if it were remuneration paid by the employer in respect of that period.

(5) Where notice was given by the employee, the employer's liability under this section does not arise unless and until the employee leaves the service of the employer in pursuance of the notice.

90   Short-term incapacity benefit and industrial injury benefit

(1) This section has effect where the arrangements in force relating to the employment are such that—

    (a) payments by way of sick pay are made by the employer to employees to whom the arrangements apply, in cases where any such employees are incapable of work because of sickness or injury, and

    (b) in calculating any payment so made to any such employee an amount representing, or treated as representing, short-term incapacity benefit or industrial injury benefit is taken into account, whether by way of deduction or by way of calculating the payment as a supplement to that amount.

(2) If—

    (a) during any part of the period of notice the employee is incapable of work because of sickness or injury,

    (b) one or more payments by way of sick pay are made to him by the employer in respect of that part of the period of notice, and

    (c) in calculating any such payment such an amount as is referred to in paragraph (b) of subsection (1) is taken into account as mentioned in that paragraph,

for the purposes of section 88 or 89 the amount so taken into account shall be treated as having been paid by the employer to the employee by way of sick pay in respect of that part of that period, and shall go towards meeting the liability of the employer under that section accordingly.

91   Supplementary

(1)   An employer is not liable under section 88 or 89 to make any payment in respect of a period during which an employee is absent from work with the leave of the employer granted at the request of the employee, including any period of time off taken in accordance with—

(a)   Part VI of this Act, or

(b)   section 168 or 170 of the Trade Union and Labour Relations (Consolidation) Act 1992 (trade union duties and activities).

(2)   No payment is due under section 88 or 89 in consequence of a notice to terminate a contract given by an employee if, after the notice is given and on or before the termination of the contract, the employee takes part in a strike of employees of the employer.

(3)   If, during the period of notice, the employer breaks the contract of employment, payments received under section 88 or 89 in respect of the part of the period after the breach go towards mitigating the damages recoverable by the employee for loss of earnings in that part of the period of notice.

(4)   If, during the period of notice, the employee breaks the contract and the employer rightfully treats the breach as terminating the contract, no payment is due to the employee under section 88 or 89 in respect of the part of the period falling after the termination of the contract.

(5)   If an employer fails to give the notice required by section 86, the rights conferred by sections 87 to 90 and this section shall be taken into account in assessing his liability for breach of the contract.

(6)   Sections 86 to 90 and this section apply in relation to a contract all or any of the terms of which are terms which take effect by virtue of any provision contained in or having effect under an Act (whether public or local) as in relation to any other contract; and the reference in this subsection to an Act includes, subject to any express provision to the contrary, an Act passed after this Act.

Written statement of reasons for dismissal

92   Right to written statement of reasons for dismissal

(1)   An employee is entitled to be provided by his employer with a written statement giving particulars of the reasons for the employee's dismissal—

(a)   if the employee is given by the employer notice of termination of his contract of employment,

(b)   if the employee's contract of employment is terminated by the employer without notice, or

(c)   if the employee is employed under a limited-term contract and the contract terminates by virtue of the limiting event without being renewed under the same contract.

(2)   Subject to subsections (4) and (4A), an employee is entitled to a written statement under this section only if he makes a request for one; and a statement shall be provided within fourteen days of such a request.

(3)   Subject to subsections (4) and (4A), an employee is not entitled to a written statement under this section unless on the effective date of termination he has been, or will have been, continuously employed for a period of not less than one year ending with that date.

(4)   An employee is entitled to a written statement under this section without having to request it and irrespective of whether she has been continuously employed for any period if she is dismissed—

(a)   at any time while she is pregnant, or

(b)   after childbirth in circumstances in which her ordinary or additional maternity leave period ends by reason of the dismissal.

(4A) An employee who is dismissed while absent from work during an ordinary or additional adoption leave period is entitled to a written statement under this section without having to request it and irrespective of whether he has been continuously employed for any period if he is dismissed in circumstances in which that period ends by reason of the dismissal.

(5) A written statement under this section is admissible in evidence in any proceedings.

(6) Subject to subsection (7), in this section 'the effective date of termination'—

    (a) in relation to an employee whose contract of employment is terminated by notice, means the date on which the notice expires,

    (b) in relation to an employee whose contract of employment is terminated without notice, means the date on which the termination takes effect, and

    (c) in relation to an employee who is employed under a limited-term contract which terminates by virtue of the limiting event without being renewed under the same contract, means the date on which the termination takes effect.

(7) Where—

    (a) the contract of employment is terminated by the employer, and

    (b) the notice required by section 86 to be given by an employer would, if duly given on the material date, expire on a date later than the effective date of termination (as defined by subsection (6)),

the later date is the effective date of termination.

(8) In subsection (7)(b) 'the material date' means—

    (a) the date when notice of termination was given by the employer, or

    (b) where no notice was given, the date when the contract of employment was terminated by the employer.

93   Complaints to employment tribunal

(1) A complaint may be presented to an employment tribunal by an employee on the ground that—

    (a) the employer unreasonably failed to provide a written statement under section 92, or

    (b) the particulars of reasons given in purported compliance with that section are inadequate or untrue.

(2) Where an employment tribunal finds a complaint under this section well-founded, the tribunal—

    (a) may make a declaration as to what it finds the employer's reasons were for dismissing the employee, and

    (b) shall make an award that the employer pay to the employee a sum equal to the amount of two weeks' pay.

(3) An employment tribunal shall not consider a complaint under this section relating to the reasons for a dismissal unless it is presented to the tribunal at such a time that the tribunal would, in accordance with section 111, consider a complaint of unfair dismissal in respect of that dismissal presented at the same time.

PART X

UNFAIR DISMISSAL

CHAPTER I

RIGHT NOT TO BE UNFAIRLY DISMISSED

The right

94   The right

(1) An employee has the right not to be unfairly dismissed by his employer.

(2) Subsection (1) has effect subject to the following provisions of this Part (in particular sections 108 to 110) and to the provisions of the Trade Union and Labour Relations (Consolidation) Act 1992 (in particular sections 237 to 239).

Dismissal

95   Circumstances in which an employee is dismissed

(1) For the purposes of this Part an employee is dismissed by his employer if (and, subject to subsection (2) only if)—

    (a) the contract under which he is employed is terminated by the employer (whether with or without notice),

     (b)   he is employed under a limited term contract and that contract terminates by virtue of the limiting event without being renewed under the same contract, or

     (c)   the employee terminates the contract under which he is employed (with or without notice) in circumstances in which he is entitled to terminate it without notice by reason of the employer's conduct.

(2)   An employee shall be taken to be dismissed by his employer for the purposes of this Part if—

     (a)   the employer gives notice to the employee to terminate his contract of employment, and

     (b)   at a time within the period of that notice the employee gives notice to the employer to terminate the contract of employment on a date earlier than the date on which the employer's notice is due to expire;

and the reason for the dismissal is to be taken to be the reason for which the employer's notice is given.

97 Effective date of termination

(1)   Subject to the following provisions of this section, in this Part 'the effective date of termination'—

     (a)   in relation to an employee whose contract of employment is terminated by notice, whether given by his employer or by the employee, means the date on which the notice expires,

     (b)   in relation to an employee whose contract of employment is terminated without notice, means the date on which the termination takes effect, and

     (c)   in relation to an employee who is employed under a limited term contract which terminates by virtue of the limiting event without being renewed under the same contract, means the date on which the termination takes effect.

(2)   Where—

     (a)   the contract of employment is terminated by the employer, and

     (b)   the notice required by section 86 to be given by an employer would, if duly given on the material date, expire on a date later than the effective date of termination (as defined by subsection (1)),

for the purposes of sections 108(1), 119(1) and 227(3) the later date is the effective date of termination.

(3)   In subsection (2)(b) 'the material date' means—

     (a)   the date when notice of termination was given by the employer, or

     (b)   where no notice was given, the date when the contract of employment was terminated by the employer.

(4)   Where—

     (a)   the contract of employment is terminated by the employee,

     (b)   the material date does not fall during a period of notice given by the employer to terminate that contract, and

     (c)   had the contract been terminated not by the employee but by notice given on the material date by the employer, that notice would have been required by section 86 to expire on a date later than the effective date of termination (as defined by subsection (1)),

for the purposes of sections 108(1), 119(1) and 227(3) the later date is the effective date of termination.

(5)   In subsection (4) 'the material date' means—

     (a)   the date when notice of termination was given by the employee, or

     (b)   where no notice was given, the date when the contract of employment was terminated by the employee.

(6)   ...

Fairness

98 General

(1)   In determining for the purposes of this Part whether the dismissal of an employee is fair or unfair, it is for the employer to show—

(a)   the reason (or, if more than one, the principal reason) for the dismissal, and

(b)   that it is either a reason falling within subsection (2) or some other substantial reason of a kind such as to justify the dismissal of an employee holding the position which the employee held.

(2)   A reason falls within this subsection if it—

(a)   relates to the capability or qualifications of the employee for performing work of the kind which he was employed by the employer to do,

(b)   relates to the conduct of the employee,

(ba)   is retirement of the employee,

(c)   is that the employee was redundant, or

(d)   is that the employee could not continue to work in the position which he held without contravention (either on his part or on that of his employer) of a duty or restriction imposed by or under an enactment.

(2A)Subsections (1) and (2) are subject to sections 98ZA to 98ZF.

(3)   In subsection (2)(a)—

(a)   'capability', in relation to an employee, means his capability assessed by reference to skill, aptitude, health or any other physical or mental quality, and

(b)   'qualifications', in relation to an employee, means any degree, diploma or other academic, technical or professional qualification relevant to the position which he held.

(3A)In any case where the employer has fulfilled the requirements of subsection (1) by showing that the reason (or the principal reason) for the dismissal is retirement of the employee, the question whether the dismissal is fair or unfair shall be determined in accordance with section 98ZG.

(4)   In any other case where the employer has fulfilled the requirements of subsection (1), the determination of the question whether the dismissal is fair or unfair (having regard to the reason shown by the employer)—

(a)   depends on whether in the circumstances (including the size and administrative resources of the employer's undertaking) the employer acted reasonably or unreasonably in treating it as a sufficient reason for dismissing the employee, and

(b)   shall be determined in accordance with equity and the substantial merits of the case.

(5)   ...

(6)   Subsection (4) is subject to—

(a)   sections 98A to 107 of this Act, and

(b)   sections 152, 153, 238 and 238A of the Trade Union and Labour Relations (Consolidation) Act 1992 (dismissal on ground of trade union membership or activities or in connection with industrial action).

Retirement

98ZA No normal retirement age: dismissal before 65

(1)   This section applies to the dismissal of an employee if—

(a)   the employee has no normal retirement age, and

(b)   the operative date of termination falls before the date when the employee reaches the age of 65.

(2)   Retirement of the employee shall not be taken to be the reason (or a reason) for the dismissal.

98ZB No normal retirement age: dismissal at or after 65

(1)   This section applies to the dismissal of an employee if—

(a)   the employee has no normal retirement age, and

(b)   the operative date of termination falls on or after the date when the employee reaches the age of 65.

(2)   In a case where—

(a)   the employer has notified the employee in accordance with paragraph 2 of Schedule 6 to the 2006 Regulations, and

(b)   the contract of employment terminates on the intended date of retirement,

retirement of the employee shall be taken to be the only reason for the dismissal by the employer and any other reason shall be disregarded.

 (3) In a case where—

  (a) the employer has notified the employee in accordance with paragraph 2 of Schedule 6 to the 2006 Regulations, but

  (b) the contract of employment terminates before the intended date of retirement,

  retirement of the employee shall not be taken to be the reason (or a reason) for dismissal.

 (4) In a case where—

  (a) the employer has not notified the employee in accordance with paragraph 2 of Schedule 6 to the 2006 Regulations, and

  (b) there is an intended date of retirement in relation to the dismissal, but

  (c) the contract of employment terminates before the intended date of retirement,

  retirement of the employee shall not be taken to be the reason (or a reason) for dismissal.

 (5) In all other cases where the employer has not notified the employee in accordance with paragraph 2 of Schedule 6 to the 2006 Regulations, particular regard shall be had to the matters in section 98ZF when determining the reason (or principal reason) for dismissal.

98ZC Normal retirement age: dismissal before retirement age

 (1) This section applies to the dismissal of an employee if—

  (a) the employee has a normal retirement age, and

  (b) the operative date of termination falls before the date when the employee reaches the normal retirement age.

 (2) Retirement of the employee shall not be taken to be the reason (or a reason) for the dismissal.

98ZD Normal retirement age 65 or higher: dismissal at or after retirement age

 (1) This section applies to the dismissal of an employee if—

  (a) the employee has a normal retirement age,

  (b) the normal retirement age is 65 or higher, and

  (c) the operative date of termination falls on or after the date when the employee reaches the normal retirement age.

 (2) In a case where—

  (a) the employer has notified the employee in accordance with paragraph 2 of Schedule 6 to the 2006 Regulations, and

  (b) the contract of employment terminates on the intended date of retirement,

  retirement of the employee shall be taken to be the only reason for the dismissal by the employer and any other reason shall be disregarded.

 (3) In a case where—

  (a) the employer has notified the employee in accordance with paragraph 2 of Schedule 6 to the 2006 Regulations, but

  (b) the contract of employment terminates before the intended date of retirement,

  retirement of the employee shall not be taken to be the reason (or a reason) for dismissal.

 (4) In a case where—

  (a) the employer has not notified the employee in accordance with paragraph 2 of Schedule 6 to the 2006 Regulations, and

  (b) there is an intended date of retirement in relation to the dismissal, but

  (c) the contract of employment terminates before the intended date of retirement,

  retirement of the employee shall not be taken to be the reason (or a reason) for dismissal.

 (5) In all other cases where the employer has not notified the employee in accordance with paragraph 2 of Schedule 6 to the 2006 Regulations, particular regard shall be had to the matters in section 98ZF when determining the reason (or principal reason) for dismissal.

98ZE Normal retirement age below 65: dismissal at or after retirement age

 (1) This section applies to the dismissal of an employee if—

  (a) the employee has a normal retirement age,

  (b) the normal retirement age is below 65, and

  (c) the operative date of termination falls on or after the date when the employee reaches the normal retirement age.

(2) If it is unlawful discrimination under the 2006 Regulations for the employee to have that normal retirement age, retirement of the employee shall not be taken to be the reason (or a reason) for dismissal.

(3) Subsections (4) to (7) apply if it is not unlawful discrimination under the 2006 Regulations for the employee to have that normal retirement age.

(4) In a case where—
   (a) the employer has notified the employee in accordance with paragraph 2 of Schedule 6 to the 2006 Regulations, and
   (b) the contract of employment terminates on the intended date of retirement,
retirement of the employee shall be taken to be the only reason for dismissal by the employer and any other reason shall be disregarded.

(5) In a case where—
   (a) the employer has notified the employee in accordance with paragraph 2 of Schedule 6 to the 2006 Regulations, but
   (b) the contract of employment terminates before the intended date of retirement,
retirement of the employee shall not be taken to be the reason (or a reason) for dismissal.

(6) In a case where—
   (a) the employer has not notified the employee in accordance with paragraph 2 of Schedule 6 to the 2006 Regulations, and
   (b) there is an intended date of retirement in relation to the dismissal, but
   (c) the contract of employment terminates before the intended date of retirement,
retirement of the employee shall not be taken to be the reason (or a reason) for dismissal.

(7) In all other cases where the employer has not notified the employee in accordance with paragraph 2 of Schedule 6 to the 2006 Regulations, particular regard shall be had to the matters in section 98ZF when determining the reason (or principal reason) for dismissal.

98ZF Reason for dismissal: particular matters

(1) These are the matters to which particular regard is to be had in accordance with section 98ZB(5), 98ZD(5) or 98ZE(7)—
   (a) whether or not the employer has notified the employee in accordance with paragraph 4 of Schedule 6 to the 2006 Regulations;
   (b) if the employer has notified the employee in accordance with that paragraph, how long before the notified retirement date the notification was given;
   (c) whether or not the employer has followed, or sought to follow, the procedures in paragraph 7 of Schedule 6 to the 2006 Regulations.

(2) In subsection (1)(b) 'notified retirement date' means the date notified to the employee in accordance with paragraph 4 of Schedule 6 to the 2006 Regulations as the date on which the employer intends to retire the employee.

98ZG Retirement dismissals: fairness

(1) This section applies if the reason (or principal reason) for a dismissal is retirement of the employee.

(2) The employee shall be regarded as unfairly dismissed if, and only if, there has been a failure on the part of the employer to comply with an obligation imposed on him by any of the following provisions of Schedule 6 to the 2006 Regulations—
   (a) paragraph 4 (notification of retirement, if not already given under paragraph 2),
   (b) paragraphs 6 and 7 (duty to consider employee's request not to be retired),
   (c) paragraph 8 (duty to consider appeal against decision to refuse request not to be retired).

98ZH Interpretation

In sections 98ZA to 98ZG—
   '2006 Regulations' means the Employment Equality (Age) Regulations 2006;
   'intended date of retirement' means the date which, by virtue of paragraph 1(2) of Schedule 6 to the 2006 Regulations, is the intended date of retirement in relation to a particular dismissal;

'normal retirement age', in relation to an employee, means the age at which employees in the employer's undertaking who hold, or have held, the same kind of position as the employee are normally required to retire;

'operative date of termination' means—

(a)   where the employer terminates the employee's contract of employment by notice, the date on which the notice expires, or

(b)   where the employer terminates the contract of employment without notice, the date on which the termination takes effect.

Other dismissals

98A   Procedural fairness

(1)   An employee who is dismissed shall be regarded for the purposes of this Part as unfairly dismissed if—

(a)   one of the procedures set out in Part 1 of Schedule 2 to the Employment Act 2002 (dismissal and disciplinary procedures) applies in relation to the dismissal,

(b)   the procedure has not been completed, and

(c)   the non-completion of the procedure is wholly or mainly attributable to failure by the employer to comply with its requirements.

(2)   Subject to subsection (1), failure by an employer to follow a procedure in relation to the dismissal of an employee shall not be regarded for the purposes of section 98(4)(a) as by itself making the employer's action unreasonable if he shows that he would have decided to dismiss the employee if he had followed the procedure.

(3)   For the purposes of this section, any question as to the application of a procedure set out in Part 1 of Schedule 2 to the Employment Act 2002, completion of such a procedure or failure to comply with the requirements of such a procedure shall be determined by reference to regulations under section 31 of that Act.

99   Leave for family reasons

(1)   An employee who is dismissed shall be regarded for the purposes of this Part as unfairly dismissed if—

(a)   the reason or principal reason for the dismissal is of a prescribed kind, or

(b)   the dismissal takes place in prescribed circumstances.

(2)   In this section 'prescribed' means prescribed by regulations made by the Secretary of State.

(3)   A reason or set of circumstances prescribed under this section must relate to—

(a)   pregnancy, childbirth or maternity,

(b)   ordinary, compulsory or additional maternity leave,

(ba) ordinary or additional adoption leave,

(c)   parental leave,

(ca) ordinary or additional paternity leave, or

(d)   time off under section 57A;

and it may also relate to redundancy or other factors.

(4)   A reason or set of circumstances prescribed under subsection (1) satisfies subsection (3)(c) or (d) if it relates to action which an employee—

(a)   takes,

(b)   agrees to take, or

(c)   refuses to take, under or in respect of a collective or workforce agreement which deals with parental leave.

(5)   Regulations under this section may—

(a)   make different provision for different cases or circumstances;

(b)   apply any enactment, in such circumstances as may be specified, in relation to persons regarded as unfairly dismissed by reason of this section.

100   Health and safety cases

(1)   An employee who is dismissed shall be regarded for the purposes of this Part as unfairly dismissed if the reason (or, if more than one, the principal reason) for the dismissal is that—

     (a)   having been designated by the employer to carry out activities in connection with preventing or reducing risks to health and safety at work, the employee carried out (or proposed to carry out) any such activities,

     (b)   being a representative of workers on matters of health and safety at work or member of a safety committee—

          (i)   in accordance with arrangements established under or by virtue of any enactment, or

          (ii)   by reason of being acknowledged as such by the employer,

          the employee performed (or proposed to perform) any functions as such a representative or a member of such a committee,

    (ba)   the employee took part (or proposed to take part) in consultation with the employer pursuant to the Health and Safety (Consultation with Employees) Regulations 1996 or in an election of representatives of employee safety within the meaning of those Regulations (whether as a candidate or otherwise),

     (c)   being an employee at a place where—

          (i)   there was no such representative or safety committee, or

          (ii)   there was such a representative or safety committee but it was not reasonably practicable for the employee to raise the matter by those means,

          he brought to his employer's attention, by reasonable means, circumstances connected with his work which he reasonably believed were harmful or potentially harmful to health or safety,

     (d)   in circumstances of danger which the employee reasonably believed to be serious and imminent and which he could not reasonably have been expected to avert, he left (or proposed to leave) or (while the danger persisted) refused to return to his place of work or any dangerous part of his place of work, or

     (e)   in circumstances of danger which the employee reasonably believed to be serious and imminent, he took (or proposed to take) appropriate steps to protect himself or other persons from the danger.

(2)   For the purposes of subsection (1)(e) whether steps which an employee took (or proposed to take) were appropriate is to be judged by reference to all the circumstances including, in particular, his knowledge and the facilities and advice available to him at the time.

(3)   Where the reason (or, if more than one, the principal reason) for the dismissal of an employee is that specified in subsection (1)(e), he shall not be regarded as unfairly dismissed if the employer shows that it was (or would have been) so negligent for the employee to take the steps which he took (or proposed to take) that a reasonable employer might have dismissed him for taking (or proposing to take) them.

101   Shop workers and betting workers who refuse Sunday work

(1)   Where an employee who is—

     (a)   a protected shop worker or an opted-out shop worker, or

     (b)   a protected betting worker or an opted-out betting worker,

     is dismissed, he shall be regarded for the purposes of this Part as unfairly dismissed if the reason (or, if more than one, the principal reason) for the dismissal is that he refused (or proposed to refuse) to do shop work, or betting work, on Sunday or on a particular Sunday.

(2)   Subsection (1) does not apply in relation to an opted-out shop worker or an opted-out betting worker where the reason (or principal reason) for the dismissal is that he refused (or proposed to refuse) to do shop work, or betting work, on any Sunday or Sundays falling before the end of the notice period.

(3)   A shop worker or betting worker who is dismissed shall be regarded for the purposes of this Part as unfairly dismissed if the reason (or, if more than one, the principal reason) for the dismissal is that the shop worker or betting worker gave (or proposed to give) an opting-out notice to the employer.

(4)   For the purposes of section 36(2)(b) or 41(1)(b), the appropriate date in relation to this section is the effective date of termination.

101A Working time cases

(1) An employee who is dismissed shall be regarded for the purposes of this Part as unfairly dismissed if the reason (or, if more than one, the principal reason) for the dismissal is that the employee—

    (a) refused (or proposed to refuse) to comply with a requirement which the employer imposed (or proposed to impose) in contravention of the Working Time Regulations 1998,

    (b) refused (or proposed to refuse) to forgo a right conferred on him by those Regulations,

    (c) failed to sign a workforce agreement for the purposes of those Regulations, or to enter into, or agree to vary or extend, any other agreement with his employer which is provided for in those Regulations, or

    (d) being—

        (i) a representative of members of the workforce for the purposes of Schedule 1 to those Regulations, or

        (ii) a candidate in an election in which any person elected will, on being elected, be such a representative,

    performed (or proposed to perform) any functions or activities as such a representative or candidate.

...

102 Trustees of occupational pension schemes

(1) An employee who is dismissed shall be regarded for the purposes of this Part as unfairly dismissed if the reason (or, if more than one, the principal reason) for the dismissal is that, being a trustee of a relevant occupational pension scheme which relates to his employment, the employee performed (or proposed to perform) any functions as such a trustee.

(1A) This section applies to an employee who is a director of a company which is a trustee of a relevant occupational pension scheme as it applies to an employee who is a trustee of such a scheme (references to such a trustee being read for this purpose as references to such a director).

(2) In this section 'relevant occupational pension scheme' means an occupational pension scheme (as defined in section 1 of the Pension Schemes Act 1993) established under a trust.

103 Employee representatives

(1) An employee who is dismissed shall be regarded for the purposes of this Part as unfairly dismissed if the reason (or, if more than one, the principal reason) for the dismissal is that the employee, being—

    (a) an employee representative for the purposes of Chapter II of Part IV of the Trade Union and Labour Relations (Consolidation) Act 1992 (redundancies) or Regulations 9, 13 and 15 of the Transfer of Undertakings (Protection of Employment) Regulations 2006, or

    (b) a candidate in an election in which any person elected will, on being elected, be such an employee representative,

    performed (or proposed to perform) any functions or activities as such an employee representative or candidate.

(2) An employee who is dismissed shall be regarded for the purposes of this Part as unfairly dismissed if the reason (or, if more than one, the principal reason) for the dismissal is that the employee took part in an election of employee representatives for the purposes of Chapter II of Part IV of the Trade Union and Labour Relations (Consolidation) Act 1992 (redundancies) or Regulations 9, 13 and 15 of the Transfer of Undertakings (Protection of Employment) Regulations 2006.

103A Protected disclosure

An employee who is dismissed shall be regarded for the purposes of this Part as unfairly dismissed if the reason (or, if more than one, the principal reason) for the dismissal is that the employee made a protected disclosure.

104 Assertion of statutory right

(1) An employee who is dismissed shall be regarded for the purposes of this Part as unfairly dismissed if the reason (or, if more than one, the principal reason) for the dismissal is that the employee—

    (a) brought proceedings against the employer to enforce a right of his which is a relevant statutory right, or

    (b) alleged that the employer had infringed a right of his which is a relevant statutory right.

(2) It is immaterial for the purposes of subsection (1)—

    (a) whether or not the employee has the right, or

    (b) whether or not the right has been infringed;

but, for that subsection to apply, the claim to the right and that it has been infringed must be made in good faith.

(3) It is sufficient for subsection (1) to apply that the employee, without specifying the right, made it reasonably clear to the employer what the right claimed to have been infringed was.

(4) The following are relevant statutory rights for the purposes of this section—

    (a) any right conferred by this Act for which the remedy for its infringement is by way of a complaint or reference to an employment tribunal,

    (b) the right conferred by section 86 of this Act,

    (c) the rights conferred by sections 68, 86, 145A, 145B, 146, 168, 168A, 169 and 170 of the Trade Union and Labour Relations (Consolidation) Act 1992 (deductions from pay, union activities and time off),

    (d) the rights conferred by the Working Time Regulations 1998, the Merchant Shipping (Working Time: Inland Waterway) Regulations 2003, or the Fishing Vessels (Working Time: Sea Fishermen) Regulations 2004, and

    (e) the rights conferred by the Transfer of Undertakings (Protection of Employment) Regulations 2006.

(5) In this section any reference to an employer includes, where the right in question is conferred by section 63A, the principal (within the meaning of section 63A(3)).

104A The national minimum wage

(1) An employee who is dismissed shall be regarded for the purposes of this Part as unfairly dismissed if the reason (or, if more than one, the principal reason) for the dismissal is that—

    (a) any action was taken, or was proposed to be taken, by or on behalf of the employee with a view to enforcing, or otherwise securing the benefit of, a right of the employee's to which this section applies; or

    (b) the employer was prosecuted for an offence under section 31 of the National Minimum Wage Act 1998 as a result of action taken by or on behalf of the employee for the purpose of enforcing, or otherwise securing the benefit of, a right of the employee's to which this section applies; or

    (c) the employee qualifies, or will or might qualify, for the national minimum wage or for a particular rate of national minimum wage.

(2) It is immaterial for the purposes of paragraph (a) or (b) of subsection (1) above—

    (a) whether or not the employee has the right, or

    (b) whether or not the right has been infringed,

but, for that subsection to apply, the claim to the right and, if applicable, the claim that it has been infringed must be made in good faith.

(3) The following are the rights to which this section applies—

    (a) any right conferred by, or by virtue of, any provision of the National Minimum Wage Act 1998 for which the remedy for its infringement is by way of a complaint to an employment tribunal; and

    (b) any right conferred by section 17 of the National Minimum Wage Act 1998 (worker receiving less than national minimum wage entitled to additional remuneration).

104C   Flexible working

An employee who is dismissed shall be regarded for the purposes of this Part as unfairly dismissed if the reason (or, if more than one, the principal reason) for the dismissal is that the employee—

(a)   made (or proposed to make) an application under section 80F,

(b)   exercised (or proposed to exercise) a right conferred on him under section 80G,

(c)   brought proceedings against the employer under section 80H, or

(d)   alleged the existence of any circumstance which would constitute a ground for bringing such proceedings.

105   Redundancy

(1)   An employee who is dismissed shall be regarded for the purposes of this Part as unfairly dismissed if—

(a)   the reason (or, if more than one, the principal reason) for the dismissal is that the employee was redundant,

(b)   it is shown that the circumstances constituting the redundancy applied equally to one or more other employees in the same undertaking who held positions similar to that held by the employee and who have not been dismissed by the employer, and

(c)   it is shown that any of subsections (2A) to (7K) applies.

(2)   ...

(2A) This subsection applies if the reason (or, if more than one, the principal reason) for which the employee was selected for dismissal was one of those specified in subsection (1) of section 98B (unless the case is one to which subsection (2) of that section applies).

(3)   This subsection applies if the reason (or, if more than one, the principal reason) for which the employee was selected for dismissal was one of those specified in subsection (1) of section 100 (read with subsections (2) and (3) of that section).

(4)   This subsection applies if either—

(a)   the employee was a protected shop worker or an opted-out shop worker, or a protected betting worker or an opted-out betting worker, and the reason (or, if more than one, the principal reason) for which the employee was selected for dismissal was that specified in subsection (1) of section 101 (read with subsection (2) of that section), or

(b)   the employee was a shop worker or a betting worker and the reason (or, if more than one, the principal reason) for which the employee was selected for dismissal was that specified in subsection (3) of that section.

(4A) This subsection applies if the reason (or, if more than one, the principal reason) for which the employee was selected for dismissal was one of those specified in section 101A.

(5)   This subsection applies if the reason (or, if more than one, the principal reason) for which the employee was selected for dismissal was that specified in section 102(1).

(6)   This subsection applies if the reason (or, if more than one, the principal reason) for which the employee was selected for dismissal was that specified in section 103.

(6A) This subsection applies if the reason (or, if more than one, the principal reason) for which the employee was selected for dismissal was that specified in section 103A.

(7)   This subsection applies if the reason (or, if more than one, the principal reason) for which the employee was selected for dismissal was one of those specified in subsection (1) of section 104 (read with subsections (2) and (3) of that section).

(7A) his subsection applies if the reason (or, if more than one, the principal reason) for which the employee was selected for dismissal was one of those specified in subsection (1) of section 104A (read with subsection (2) of that section).

(7B) This subsection applies if the reason (or, if more than one, the principal reason) for which the employee was selected for dismissal was one of those specified in subsection (1) of section 104B (read with subsection (2) of that section).

(7BA) This subsection applies if the reason (or, if more than one, the principal reason) for which the employee was selected for dismissal was one of those specified in section 104C.

(7C) This subsection applies if—

     (a)   the reason (or, if more than one, the principal reason) for which the employee was selected for dismissal was the reason mentioned in section 238A(2) of the Trade Union and Labour Relations (Consolidation) Act 1992 (participation in official industrial action), and

     (b)   subsection (3), (4) or (5) of that section applies to the dismissal.

(7D) This subsection applies if the reason (or, if more than one, the principal reason) for which the employee was selected for dismissal was one specified in paragraph (3) or (6) of regulation 28 of the Transnational Information and Consultation of Employees Regulations 1999 (read with paragraphs (4) and (7) of that regulation).

(7E) This subsection applies if the reason (or, if more than one, the principal reason) for which the employee was selected for dismissal was one specified in paragraph (3) of regulation 7 of the Part-time Workers (Prevention of Less Favourable Treatment) Regulations 2000 (unless the case is one to which paragraph (4) of that regulation applies).

(7F) This subsection applies if the reason (or, if more than one, the principal reason) for which the employee was selected for dismissal was one specified in paragraph (3) of regulation 6 of the Fixed-term Employees (Prevention of Less Favourable Treatment) Regulations 2002 (unless the case is one to which paragraph (4) of that regulation applies).

(7G) This subsection applies if the reason (or, if more than one, the principal reason) for which the employee was selected for dismissal was one specified in paragraph (3) or (6) of regulation 42 of the European Public Limited-Liability Company Regulations 2004 (read with paragraphs (4) and (7) of that regulation).

(7H) This subsection applies if the reason (or, if more than one, the principal reason) for which the employee was selected for dismissal was one specified in paragraph (3) or (6) of regulation 30 of the Information and Consultation of Employees Regulations 2004 (read with paragraphs (4) and (7) of that regulation).

(7I) This subsection applies if the reason (or, if more than one, the principal reason) for which the employee was selected for dismissal was one specified in paragraph 5(3) or (5) of the Schedule to the Occupational and Personal Pension Schemes (Consultation by Employers and Miscellaneous Amendment) Regulations 2006 (read with paragraph 5(6) of that Schedule).

(7IA) This subsection applies if the reason (or, if more than one, the principal reason) for which the employee was selected for dismissal was that he—

     (a)   exercised or sought to exercise his right to be accompanied in accordance with paragraph 9 of Schedule 6 to the Employment Equality (Age) Regulations 2006, or

     (b)   accompanied or sought to accompany an employee pursuant to a request under that paragraph.

(7J) This subsection applies if the reason (or, if more than one, the principal reason) for which the employee was selected for dismissal was one specified in paragraph (3) or (6) of regulation 31 of the European Cooperative Society (Involvement of Employees) Regulations 2006 (read with paragraphs (4) and (7) of that regulation).

(8)   For the purposes of section 36(2)(b) or 41(1)(b), the appropriate date in relation to this section is the effective date of termination.

(9)   In this Part 'redundancy case' means a case where paragraphs (a) and (b) of subsection (1) of this section are satisfied.

106   Replacements

(1)   Where this section applies to an employee he shall be regarded for the purposes of section 98(1)(b) as having been dismissed for a substantial reason of a kind such as to justify the dismissal of an employee holding the position which the employee held.

(2)   This section applies to an employee where—

     (a)   on engaging him the employer informs him in writing that his employment will be terminated on the resumption of work by another employee who is, or will be, absent wholly or partly because of pregnancy or childbirth, or on adoption leave or leave under section 80AA or 80BB (additional paternity leave), and

     (b)   the employer dismisses him in order to make it possible to give work to the other employee.

(3) This section also applies to an employee where—

    (a) on engaging him the employer informs him in writing that his employment will be terminated on the end of a suspension of another employee from work on medical grounds or maternity grounds (within the meaning of Part VII), and

    (b) the employer dismisses him in order to make it possible to allow the resumption of work by the other employee.

(4) Subsection (1) does not affect the operation of section 98(4) in a case to which this section applies.

107 Pressure on employer to dismiss unfairly

(1) This section applies where there falls to be determined for the purposes of this Part a question—

    (a) as to the reason, or principal reason, for which an employee was dismissed,

    (b) whether the reason or principal reason for which an employee was dismissed was a reason fulfilling the requirement of section 98(1)(b), or

    (c) whether an employer acted reasonably in treating the reason or principal reason for which an employee was dismissed as a sufficient reason for dismissing him.

(2) In determining the question no account shall be taken of any pressure which by calling, organising, procuring or financing a strike or other industrial action, or threatening to do so, was exercised on the employer to dismiss the employee; and the question shall be determined as if no such pressure had been exercised.

Exclusion of right

108 Qualifying period of employment

(1) Section 94 does not apply to the dismissal of an employee unless he has been continuously employed for a period of not less than one year ending with the effective date of termination.

(2) If an employee is dismissed by reason of any such requirement or recommendation as is referred to in section 64(2), subsection (1) has effect in relation to that dismissal as if for the words 'one year' there were substituted the words 'one month'.

(3) Subsection (1) does not apply if—

    (a) ...

    (aa) subsection (1) of section 98B (read with subsection (2) of that section) applies,

    (b) subsection (1) of section 99 (read with any regulations made under that section) applies,

    (c) subsection (1) of section 100 (read with subsections (2) and (3) of that section) applies,

    (d) subsection (1) of section 101 (read with subsection (2) of that section) or subsection (3) of that section applies,

    (dd) section 101A applies,

    (e) section 102 applies,

    (f) section 103 applies,

    (ff) section 103A applies,

    (g) subsection (1) of section 104 (read with subsections (2) and (3) of that section) applies,

    (gg) subsection (1) of section 104A (read with subsection (2) of that section) applies,

    (gh) subsection (1) of section 104B (read with subsection (2) of that section) applies,

    (gi) section 104C applies,

    (h) section 105 applies,

    (hh) paragraph (3) or (6) of regulation 28 of the Transnational Information and Consultation of Employees Regulations 1999 (read with paragraphs (4) and (7) of that regulation) applies,

    (i) paragraph (1) of regulation 7 of the Part-time Workers (Prevention of Less Favourable Treatment) Regulations 2000 applies,

    (j) paragraph (1) of regulation 6 of the Fixed-term Employees (Prevention of Less Favourable Treatment) Regulations 2002 applies,

    (k) paragraph (3) or (6) of regulation 42 of the European Public Limited-Liability Company Regulations 2004 applies;

    (l)   paragraph (3) or (6) of regulation 30 of the Information and Consultation of Employees Regulations 2004 (read with paragraphs (4) and (7) of that regulation) applies; or

    (m) paragraph 5(3) or (5) of the Schedule to the Occupational and Personal Pension Schemes (Consultation by Employers and Miscellaneous Amendment) Regulations 2006 (read with paragraph 5(6) of that Schedule) applies.

110   Dismissal procedures agreements

(1) Where a dismissal procedures agreement is designated by an order under subsection (3) which is for the time being in force—

    (a)   the provisions of that agreement relating to dismissal shall have effect in substitution for any rights under section 94, and

    (b)   accordingly, section 94 does not apply to the dismissal of an employee from any employment if it is employment to which, and he is an employee to whom, those provisions of the agreement apply.

(2) But if the agreement includes provision that it does not apply to dismissals of particular descriptions, subsection (1) does not apply in relation to a dismissal of any such description.

(3) An order designating a dismissal procedures agreement may be made by the Secretary of State, on an application being made to him jointly by all the parties to the agreement, if he is satisfied that—

    (a)   every trade union which is a party to the agreement is an independent trade union,

    (b)   the agreement provides for procedures to be followed in cases where an employee claims that he has been, or is in the course of being, unfairly dismissed,

    (c)   those procedures are available without discrimination to all employees falling within any description to which the agreement applies,

    (d)   the remedies provided by the agreement in respect of unfair dismissal are on the whole as beneficial as (but not necessarily identical with) those provided in respect of unfair dismissal by this Part,

    (e)   the agreement includes provision either for arbitration in every case or for—

        (i)   arbitration where (by reason of equality of votes or for any other reason) a decision under the agreement cannot otherwise be reached, and

        (ii)   a right to submit to arbitration any question of law arising out of such a decision, and

    (f)   the provisions of the agreement are such that it can be determined with reasonable certainty whether or not a particular employee is one to whom the agreement applies.

(3A) The Secretary of State may by order amend subsection (3) so as to add to the conditions specified in that subsection such conditions as he may specify in the order.

(4) If at any time when an order under subsection (3) is in force in relation to a dismissal procedures agreement the Secretary of State is satisfied, whether on an application made to him by any of the parties to the agreement or otherwise, either—

    (a)   that it is the desire of all the parties to the agreement that the order should be revoked, or

    (b)   that the agreement no longer satisfies all the conditions specified in subsection (3), the Secretary of State shall revoke the order by an order under this subsection.

(5) The transitional provisions which may be made in an order under subsection (4) include, in particular, provisions directing—

    (a)   that an employee—

        (i)   shall not be excluded from his right under section 94 where the effective date of termination falls within a transitional period which ends with the date on which the order takes effect and which is specified in the order, and

        (ii)   shall have an extended time for presenting a complaint under section 111 in respect of a dismissal where the effective date of termination falls within that period, and

    (b)   that, where the effective date of termination falls within such a transitional period, an employment tribunal shall, in determining any complaint of unfair dismissal presented by an employee to whom the dismissal procedures agreement applies, have regard to such considerations as are specified in the order (in addition to those specified in this Part and section 10(4) and (5) of the Employment Tribunals Act 1996).

(6) Where an award is made under a designated dismissal procedures agreement—

    (a) in England and Wales it may be enforced, by leave of a county court, in the same manner as a judgment of the court to the same effect and, where leave is given, judgment may be entered in terms of the award, and

    (b) in Scotland it may be recorded for execution in the Books of Council and Session and shall be enforceable accordingly.

CHAPTER II
REMEDIES FOR UNFAIR DISMISSAL

Introductory

111   **Complaints to employment tribunal**

(1) A complaint may be presented to an employment tribunal against an employer by any person that he was unfairly dismissed by the employer.

(2) Subject to subsection (3), an employment tribunal shall not consider a complaint under this section unless it is presented to the tribunal—

    (a) before the end of the period of three months beginning with the effective date of termination, or

    (b) within such further period as the tribunal considers reasonable in a case where it is satisfied that it was not reasonably practicable for the complaint to be presented before the end of that period of three months.

(3) Where a dismissal is with notice, an employment tribunal shall consider a complaint under this section if it is presented after the notice is given but before the effective date of termination.

(4) In relation to a complaint which is presented as mentioned in subsection (3), the provisions of this Act, so far as they relate to unfair dismissal, have effect as if—

    (a) references to a complaint by a person that he was unfairly dismissed by his employer included references to a complaint by a person that his employer has given him notice in such circumstances that he will be unfairly dismissed when the notice expires,

    (b) references to reinstatement included references to the withdrawal of the notice by the employer,

    (c) references to the effective date of termination included references to the date which would be the effective date of termination on the expiry of the notice, and

    (d) references to an employee ceasing to be employed included references to an employee having been given notice of dismissal.

112   **The remedies: orders and compensation**

(1) This section applies where, on a complaint under section 111, an employment tribunal finds that the grounds of the complaint are well-founded.

(2) The tribunal shall—

    (a) explain to the complainant what orders may be made under section 113 and in what circumstances they may be made, and

    (b) ask him whether he wishes the tribunal to make such an order.

(3) If the complainant expresses such a wish, the tribunal may make an order under section 113.

(4) If no order is made under section 113, the tribunal shall make an award of compensation for unfair dismissal (calculated in accordance with sections 118 to 126) to be paid by the employer to the employee.

(5) Where—

    (a) an employee is regarded as unfairly dismissed by virtue of section 98ZG or 98A(1) (whether or not his dismissal is unfair or regarded as unfair for any other reason), and

    (b) an order is made in respect of the employee under section 113,

the employment tribunal shall, subject to subsection (6), also make an award of four weeks' pay to be paid by the employer to the employee.

(6) An employment tribunal shall not be required to make an award under subsection (5) if it considers that such an award would result in injustice to the employer.

Orders for reinstatement or re-engagement

113 The orders

An order under this section may be—

    (a) an order for reinstatement (in accordance with section 114), or

    (b) an order for re-engagement (in accordance with section 115),

as the tribunal may decide.

114 Order for reinstatement

(1) An order for reinstatement is an order that the employer shall treat the complainant in all respects as if he had not been dismissed.

(2) On making an order for reinstatement the tribunal shall specify—

    (a) any amount payable by the employer in respect of any benefit which the complainant might reasonably be expected to have had but for the dismissal (including arrears of pay) for the period between the date of termination of employment and the date of reinstatement,

    (b) any rights and privileges (including seniority and pension rights) which must be restored to the employee, and

    (c) the date by which the order must be complied with.

(3) If the complainant would have benefited from an improvement in his terms and conditions of employment had he not been dismissed, an order for reinstatement shall require him to be treated as if he had benefited from that improvement from the date on which he would have done so but for being dismissed.

(4) In calculating for the purposes of subsection (2)(a) any amount payable by the employer, the tribunal shall take into account, so as to reduce the employer's liability, any sums received by the complainant in respect of the period between the date of termination of employment and the date of reinstatement by way of—

    (a) wages in lieu of notice or ex gratia payments paid by the employer, or

    (b) remuneration paid in respect of employment with another employer,

and such other benefits as the tribunal thinks appropriate in the circumstances.

(5) …

115 Order for re-engagement

(1) An order for re-engagement is an order, on such terms as the tribunal may decide, that the complainant be engaged by the employer, or by a successor of the employer or by an associated employer, in employment comparable to that from which he was dismissed or other suitable employment.

(2) On making an order for re-engagement the tribunal shall specify the terms on which re-engagement is to take place, including—

    (a) the identity of the employer,

    (b) the nature of the employment,

    (c) the remuneration for the employment,

    (d) any amount payable by the employer in respect of any benefit which the complainant might reasonably be expected to have had but for the dismissal (including arrears of pay) for the period between the date of termination of employment and the date of re-engagement,

    (e) any rights and privileges (including seniority and pension rights) which must be restored to the employee, and

    (f) the date by which the order must be complied with.

(3) In calculating for the purposes of subsection (2)(d) any amount payable by the employer, the tribunal shall take into account, so as to reduce the employer's liability, any sums received by the complainant in respect of the period between the date of termination of employment and the date of re-engagement by way of—

  (a)   wages in lieu of notice or ex gratia payments paid by the employer, or
  (b)   remuneration paid in respect of employment with another employer,
  and such other benefits as the tribunal thinks appropriate in the circumstances.
  (4)   ...

116   Choice of order and its terms

  (1)   In exercising its discretion under section 113 the tribunal shall first consider whether to make
         an order for reinstatement and in so doing shall take into account—
         (a)   whether the complainant wishes to be reinstated,
         (b)   whether it is practicable for the employer to comply with an order for reinstatement, and
         (c)   where the complainant caused or contributed to some extent to the dismissal, whether it
                would be just to order his reinstatement.
  (2)   If the tribunal decides not to make an order for reinstatement it shall then consider whether to
         make an order for re-engagement and, if so, on what terms.
  (3)   In so doing the tribunal shall take into account—
         (a)   any wish expressed by the complainant as to the nature of the order to be made,
         (b)   whether it is practicable for the employer (or a successor or an associated employer) to
                comply with an order for re-engagement, and
         (c)   where the complainant caused or contributed to some extent to the dismissal, whether it
                would be just to order his re-engagement and (if so) on what terms.
  (4)   Except in a case where the tribunal takes into account contributory fault under subsection
         (3)(c) it shall, if it orders re-engagement, do so on terms which are, so far as is reasonably
         practicable, as favourable as an order for reinstatement.
  (5)   Where in any case an employer has engaged a permanent replacement for a dismissed
         employee, the tribunal shall not take that fact into account in determining, for the purposes of
         subsection (1)(b) or (3)(b), whether it is practicable to comply with an order for reinstatement
         or re-engagement.
  (6)   Subsection (5) does not apply where the employer shows—
         (a)   that it was not practicable for him to arrange for the dismissed employee's work to be
                done without engaging a permanent replacement, or
         (b)   that—
                (i)   he engaged the replacement after the lapse of a reasonable period, without having
                       heard from the dismissed employee that he wished to be reinstated or re-engaged,
                       and
                (ii)   when the employer engaged the replacement it was no longer reasonable for him
                       to arrange for the dismissed employee's work to be done except by a permanent
                       replacement.

117   Enforcement of order and compensation

  (1)   An employment tribunal shall make an award of compensation, to be paid by the employer to
         the employee, if—
         (a)   an order under section 113 is made and the complainant is reinstated or re-engaged, but
         (b)   the terms of the order are not fully complied with.
  (2)   Subject to section 124, the amount of the compensation shall be such as the tribunal thinks fit
         having regard to the loss sustained by the complainant in consequence of the failure to comply
         fully with the terms of the order.
  (2A)   There shall be deducted from any award under subsection (1) the amount of any award made
         under section 112(5) at the time of the order under section 113.
  (3)   Subject to subsections (1) and (2), if an order under section 113 is made but the complainant
         is not reinstated or re-engaged in accordance with the order, the tribunal shall make—
         (a)   an award of compensation for unfair dismissal (calculated in accordance with sections
                118 to 126), and
         (b)   except where this paragraph does not apply, an additional award of compensation of an
                amount not less than twenty-six nor more than fifty-two weeks' pay,
         to be paid by the employer to the employee.

(4)   Subsection (3)(b) does not apply where—
    (a)   the employer satisfies the tribunal that it was not practicable to comply with the order,
    (b)   ...
(5), (6) ...
(7)   Where in any case an employer has engaged a permanent replacement for a dismissed employee, the tribunal shall not take that fact into account in determining for the purposes of subsection (4)(a) whether it was practicable to comply with the order for reinstatement or re-engagement unless the employer shows that it was not practicable for him to arrange for the dismissed employee's work to be done without engaging a permanent replacement.
(8)   Where in any case an employment tribunal finds that the complainant has unreasonably prevented an order under section 113 from being complied with, in making an award of compensation for unfair dismissal it shall take that conduct into account as a failure on the part of the complainant to mitigate his loss.

Compensation

118   General
(1)   Where a tribunal makes an award of compensation for unfair dismissal under section 112(4) or 117(3)(a) the award shall consist of—
    (a)   a basic award (calculated in accordance with sections 119 to 122 and 126), and
    (b)   a compensatory award (calculated in accordance with sections 123, 124, 124A and 126).
(2)–(3)–(4) ...

119   Basic award
(1)   Subject to the provisions of this section, sections 120 to 122 and section 126, the amount of the basic award shall be calculated by—
    (a)   determining the period, ending with the effective date of termination, during which the employee has been continuously employed,
    (b)   reckoning backwards from the end of that period the number of years of employment falling within that period, and
    (c)   allowing the appropriate amount for each of those years of employment.
(2)   In subsection (1)(c) 'the appropriate amount' means—
    (a)   one and a half weeks' pay for a year of employment in which the employee was not below the age of forty-one,
    (b)   one week's pay for a year of employment (not within paragraph (a)) in which he was not below the age of twenty-two, and
    (c)   half a week's pay for a year of employment not within paragraph (a) or (b).
(3)   Where twenty years of employment have been reckoned under subsection (1), no account shall be taken under that subsection of any year of employment earlier than those twenty years.
(4)   Where the effective date of termination is after the sixty-fourth anniversary of the day of the employee's birth, the amount arrived at under subsections (1) to (3) shall be reduced by the appropriate fraction.
(5)   In subsection (4) 'the appropriate fraction' means the fraction of which—
    (a)   the numerator is the number of whole months reckoned from the sixty-fourth anniversary of the day of the employee's birth in the period beginning with that anniversary and ending with the effective date of termination, and
    (b)   the denominator is twelve.
(6)   ...

120   Basic award: minimum in certain cases
(1)   The amount of the basic award (before any reduction under section 122) shall not be less than £4,200 where the reason (or, if more than one, the principal reason)—
    (a)   in a redundancy case, for selecting the employee for dismissal, or

(b)   otherwise, for the dismissal,

is one of those specified in section 100(1)(a) and (b), 101A(d), 102(1) or 103.

(1A) Where—

    (a)   an employee is regarded as unfairly dismissed by virtue of section 98ZG or 98A(1) (whether or not his dismissal is unfair or regarded as unfair for any other reason),

    (b)   an award of compensation falls to be made under section 98ZG or 112(4), and

    (c)   the amount of the award under section 98ZG or 118(1)(a), before any reduction under section 122(3A) or (4), is less than the amount of four weeks' pay,

the employment tribunal shall, subject to subsection (1B), increase the award under section 118(1)(a) to the amount of four weeks' pay.

(1B) An employment tribunal shall not be required by subsection (1A) to increase the amount of an award if it considers that the increase would result in injustice to the employer.

(2)   ...

121   Basic award of two weeks' pay in certain cases

The amount of the basic award shall be two weeks' pay where the tribunal finds that the reason (or, where there is more than one, the principal reason) for the dismissal of the employee is that he was redundant and the employee—

    (a)   by virtue of section 138 is not regarded as dismissed for the purposes of Part XI, or

    (b)   by virtue of section 141 is not, or (if he were otherwise entitled) would not be, entitled to a redundancy payment.

122   Basic award: reductions

(1)   Where the tribunal finds that the complainant has unreasonably refused an offer by the employer which (if accepted) would have the effect of reinstating the complainant in his employment in all respects as if he had not been dismissed, the tribunal shall reduce or further reduce the amount of the basic award to such extent as it considers just and equitable having regard to that finding.

(2)   Where the tribunal considers that any conduct of the complainant before the dismissal (or, where the dismissal was with notice, before the notice was given) was such that it would be just and equitable to reduce or further reduce the amount of the basic award to any extent, the tribunal shall reduce or further reduce that amount accordingly.

(3)   Subsection (2) does not apply in a redundancy case unless the reason for selecting the employee for dismissal was one of those specified in section 100(1)(a) and (b), 101A(d), 102(1) or 103; and in such a case subsection (2) applies only to so much of the basic award as is payable because of section 120.

(3A) Where the complainant has been awarded any amount in respect of the dismissal under a designated dismissal procedures agreement, the tribunal shall reduce or further reduce the amount of the basic award to such extent as it considers just and equitable having regard to that award.

(4)   The amount of the basic award shall be reduced or further reduced by the amount of—

    (a)   any redundancy payment awarded by the tribunal under Part XI in respect of the same dismissal, or

    (b)   any payment made by the employer to the employee on the ground that the dismissal was by reason of redundancy (whether in pursuance of Part XI or otherwise).

123   Compensatory award

(1)   Subject to the provisions of this section and sections 124, 124A and 126, the amount of the compensatory award shall be such amount as the tribunal considers just and equitable in all the circumstances having regard to the loss sustained by the complainant in consequence of the dismissal in so far as that loss is attributable to action taken by the employer.

(2)   The loss referred to in subsection (1) shall be taken to include—

    (a)   any expenses reasonably incurred by the complainant in consequence of the dismissal, and

       (b)   subject to subsection (3), loss of any benefit which he might reasonably be expected to have had but for the dismissal.

(3)   The loss referred to in subsection (1) shall be taken to include in respect of any loss of—

       (a)   any entitlement or potential entitlement to a payment on account of dismissal by reason of redundancy (whether in pursuance of Part XI or otherwise), or

       (b)   any expectation of such a payment,

only the loss referable to the amount (if any) by which the amount of that payment would have exceeded the amount of a basic award (apart from any reduction under section 122) in respect of the same dismissal.

(4)   In ascertaining the loss referred to in subsection (1) the tribunal shall apply the same rule concerning the duty of a person to mitigate his loss as applies to damages recoverable under the common law of England and Wales or (as the case may be) Scotland.

(5)   In determining, for the purposes of subsection (1), how far any loss sustained by the complainant was attributable to action taken by the employer, no account shall be taken of any pressure which by—

       (a)   calling, organising, procuring or financing a strike or other industrial action, or

       (b)   threatening to do so,

was exercised on the employer to dismiss the employee; and that question shall be determined as if no such pressure had been exercised.

(6)   Where the tribunal finds that the dismissal was to any extent caused or contributed to by any action of the complainant, it shall reduce the amount of the compensatory award by such proportion as it considers just and equitable having regard to that finding.

(7)   If the amount of any payment made by the employer to the employee on the ground that the dismissal was by reason of redundancy (whether in pursuance of Part XI or otherwise) exceeds the amount of the basic award which would be payable but for section 122(4), that excess goes to reduce the amount of the compensatory award.

(8)   Where the amount of the compensatory award falls to be calculated for the purposes of an award under section 117(3)(a), there shall be deducted from the compensatory award any award made under section 112(5) at the time of the order under section 113.

124   Limit of compensatory award etc.

(1)   The amount of—

       (a)   any compensation awarded to a person under section 117(1) and (2), or

       (b)   a compensatory award to a person calculated in accordance with section 123, shall not exceed £83,000.

(1A) Subsection (1) shall not apply to compensation awarded, or a compensatory award made, to a person in a case where he is regarded as unfairly dismissed by virtue of section 100, 103A, 105(3) or 105(6A).

(2)   ...

(3)   In the case of compensation awarded to a person under section 117(1) and (2), the limit imposed by this section may be exceeded to the extent necessary to enable the award fully to reflect the amount specified as payable under section 114(2)(a) or section 115(2)(d).

(4)   Where—

       (a)   a compensatory award is an award under paragraph (a) of subsection (3) of section 117, and

       (b)   an additional award falls to be made under paragraph (b) of that subsection,

the limit imposed by this section on the compensatory award may be exceeded to the extent necessary to enable the aggregate of the compensatory and additional awards fully to reflect the amount specified as payable under section 114(2)(a) or section 115(2)(d).

(5)   The limit imposed by this section applies to the amount which the employment tribunal would, apart from this section, award in respect of the subject matter of the complaint after taking into account—

       (a)   any payment made by the respondent to the complainant in respect of that matter, and

       (b)   any reduction in the amount of the award required by any enactment or rule of law.

124A Adjustments under the Employment Act 2002

Where an award of compensation for unfair dismissal falls to be—

    (a)   reduced or increased under section 31 of the Employment Act 2002 (non-completion of statutory procedures), or

    (b)   increased under section 38 of that Act (failure to give statement of employment particulars),

the adjustment shall be in the amount awarded under section 118(1)(b) and shall be applied immediately before any reduction under section 123(6) or (7).

126 Acts which are both unfair dismissal and discrimination

    (1)   This section applies where compensation falls to be awarded in respect of any act both under—

        (a)   the provisions of this Act relating to unfair dismissal, and

        (b)   any one or more of the following—

            (i)   the Sex Discrimination Act 1975;

            (ii)   the Race Relations Act 1976;

            (iii)   the Disability Discrimination Act 1995;

            (iv)   the Employment Equality (Sexual Orientation) Regulations 2003;

            (v)   the Employment Equality (Religion or Belief) Regulations 2003;

            (vi)   the Employment Equality (Age) Regulations 2006.

    (2)   An employment tribunal shall not award compensation under any one of those Acts or Regulations in respect of any loss or other matter which is or has been taken into account under any other of them by the tribunal (or another employment tribunal) in awarding compensation on the same or another complaint in respect of that act.

Interim relief

128 Interim relief pending determination of complaint

    (1)   An employee who presents a complaint to an employment tribunal—

        (a)   that he has been unfairly dismissed by his employer, and

        (b)   that the reason (or, if more than one, the principal reason) for the dismissal is one of those specified in section 100(1)(a) and (b), 101A(d), 102(1), 103 or 103A, or in paragraph 161(2) Schedule A1 to the Trade Union and Labour Relations Consolidation Act 1992,

    may apply to the tribunal for interim relief.

    (2)   The tribunal shall not entertain an application for interim relief unless it is presented to the tribunal before the end of the period of seven days immediately following the effective date of termination (whether before, on or after that date).

    (3)   The tribunal shall determine the application for interim relief as soon as practicable after receiving the application.

    (4)   The tribunal shall give to the employer not later than seven days before the date of the hearing a copy of the application together with notice of the date, time and place of the hearing.

    (5)   The tribunal shall not exercise any power it has of postponing the hearing of an application for interim relief except where it is satisfied that special circumstances exist which justify it in doing so.

129 Procedure on hearing of application and making of order

    (1)   This section applies where, on hearing an employee's application for interim relief, it appears to the tribunal that it is likely that on determining the complaint to which the application relates the tribunal will find that the reason (or, if more than one, the principal reason) for his dismissal is one of those specified in section 100(1)(a) and (b), 101A(d), 102(1), 103 or 103A or in paragraph 161(2) Schedule A1 to the Trade Union and Labour Relations Consolidation Act 1992.

    (2)   The tribunal shall announce its findings and explain to both parties (if present)—

        (a)   what powers the tribunal may exercise on the application, and

        (b)   in what circumstances it will exercise them.

(3) The tribunal shall ask the employer (if present) whether he is willing, pending the determination or settlement of the complaint—

    (a)   to reinstate the employee (that is, to treat him in all respects as if he had not been dismissed), or

    (b)   if not, to re-engage him in another job on terms and conditions not less favourable than those which would have been applicable to him if he had not been dismissed.

(4) For the purposes of subsection (3)(b) 'terms and conditions not less favourable than those which would have been applicable to him if he had not been dismissed' means, as regards seniority, pension rights and other similar rights, that the period prior to the dismissal should be regarded as continuous with his employment following the dismissal.

(5) If the employer states that he is willing to reinstate the employee, the tribunal shall make an order to that effect.

(6) If the employer—

    (a)   states that he is willing to re-engage the employee in another job, and

    (b)   specifies the terms and conditions on which he is willing to do so,

the tribunal shall ask the employee whether he is willing to accept the job on those terms and conditions.

(7) If the employee is willing to accept the job on those terms and conditions, the tribunal shall make an order to that effect.

(8) If the employee is not willing to accept the job on those terms and conditions—

    (a)   where the tribunal is of the opinion that the refusal is reasonable, the tribunal shall make an order for the continuation of his contract of employment, and

    (b)   otherwise, the tribunal shall make no order.

(9) If on the hearing of an application for interim relief the employer—

    (a)   fails to attend before the tribunal, or

    (b)   states that he is unwilling either to reinstate or re-engage the employee as mentioned in subsection (3),

the tribunal shall make an order for the continuation of the employee's contract of employment.

130   Order for continuation of contract of employment

(1) An order under section 129 for the continuation of a contract of employment is an order that the contract of employment continue in force—

    (a)   for the purposes of pay or any other benefit derived from the employment, seniority, pension rights and other similar matters, and

    (b)   for the purposes of determining for any purpose the period for which the employee has been continuously employed,

from the date of its termination (whether before or after the making of the order) until the determination or settlement of the complaint.

(2) Where the tribunal makes such an order it shall specify in the order the amount which is to be paid by the employer to the employee by way of pay in respect of each normal pay period, or part of any such period, falling between the date of dismissal and the determination or settlement of the complaint.

(3) Subject to the following provisions, the amount so specified shall be that which the employee could reasonably have been expected to earn during that period, or part, and shall be paid—

    (a)   in the case of a payment for any such period falling wholly or partly after the making of the order, on the normal pay day for that period, and

    (b)   in the case of a payment for any past period, within such time as may be specified in the order.

(4) If an amount is payable in respect only of part of a normal pay period, the amount shall be calculated by reference to the whole period and reduced proportionately.

(5) Any payment made to an employee by an employer under his contract of employment, or by way of damages for breach of that contract, in respect of a normal pay period, or part of any

such period, goes towards discharging the employer's liability in respect of that period under subsection (2); and, conversely, any payment under that subsection in respect of a period goes towards discharging any liability of the employer under, or in respect of breach of, the contract of employment in respect of that period.

(6) If an employee, on or after being dismissed by his employer, receives a lump sum which, or part of which, is in lieu of wages but is not referable to any normal pay period, the tribunal shall take the payment into account in determining the amount of pay to be payable in pursuance of any such order.

(7) For the purposes of this section, the amount which an employee could reasonably have been expected to earn, his normal pay period and the normal pay day for each such period shall be determined as if he had not been dismissed.

131 Application for variation or revocation of order

(1) At any time between—

    (a) the making of an order under section 129, and

    (b) the determination or settlement of the complaint,

the employer or the employee may apply to an employment tribunal for the revocation or variation of the order on the ground of a relevant change of circumstances since the making of the order.

(2) Sections 128 and 129 apply in relation to such an application as in relation to an original application for interim relief except that, in the case of an application by the employer, section 128(4) has effect with the substitution of a reference to the employee for the reference to the employer.

132 Consequence of failure to comply with order

(1) If, on the application of an employee, an employment tribunal is satisfied that the employer has not complied with the terms of an order for the reinstatement or re-engagement of the employee under section 129(5) or (7), the tribunal shall—

    (a) make an order for the continuation of the employee's contract of employment, and

    (b) order the employer to pay compensation to the employee.

(2) Compensation under subsection (1)(b) shall be of such amount as the tribunal considers just and equitable in all the circumstances having regard—

    (a) to the infringement of the employee's right to be reinstated or re-engaged in pursuance of the order, and

    (b) to any loss suffered by the employee in consequence of the non-compliance.

(3) Section 130 applies to an order under subsection (1)(a) as in relation to an order under section 129.

(4) If on the application of an employee an employment tribunal is satisfied that the employer has not complied with the terms of an order for the continuation of a contract of employment subsection (5) or (6) applies.

(5) Where the non-compliance consists of a failure to pay an amount by way of pay specified in the order—

    (a) the tribunal shall determine the amount owed by the employer on the date of the determination, and

    (b) if on that date the tribunal also determines the employee's complaint that he has been unfairly dismissed, it shall specify that amount separately from any other sum awarded to the employee.

(6) In any other case, the tribunal shall order the employer to pay the employee such compensation as the tribunal considers just and equitable in all the circumstances having regard to any loss suffered by the employee in consequence of the noncompliance.

CHAPTER III

SUPPLEMENTARY

133 Death of employer or employee

(1) Where—

(a) an employer has given notice to an employee to terminate his contract of employment, and

(b) before that termination the employee or the employer dies,

this Part applies as if the contract had been duly terminated by the employer by notice expiring on the date of the death.

(2) Where—

(a) an employee's contract of employment has been terminated,

(b) by virtue of subsection (2) or (4) of section 97 a date later than the effective date of termination as defined in subsection (1) of that section is to be treated for certain purposes as the effective date of termination, and

(c) the employer or the employee dies before that date,

subsection (2) or (4) of section 97 applies as if the notice referred to in that subsection as required by section 86 expired on the date of the death.

(3) Where an employee has died, sections 113 to 116 do not apply; and, accordingly, if the employment tribunal finds that the grounds of the complaint are well-founded, the case shall be treated as falling within section 112(4) as a case in which no order is made under section 113.

(4) Subsection (3) does not prejudice an order for reinstatement or re-engagement made before the employee's death.

(5) Where an order for reinstatement or re-engagement has been made and the employee dies before the order is complied with—

(a) if the employer has before the death refused to reinstate or re-engage the employee in accordance with the order, subsections (3) to (6) of section 117 apply, and an award shall be made under subsection (3)(b) of that section, unless the employer satisfies the tribunal that it was not practicable at the time of the refusal to comply with the order, and

(b) if there has been no such refusal, subsections (1) and (2) of that section apply if the employer fails to comply with any ancillary terms of the order which remain capable of fulfilment after the employee's death as they would apply to such a failure to comply fully with the terms of an order where the employee had been reinstated or re-engaged.

PART XI
REDUNDANCY PAYMENTS ETC.

CHAPTER I
RIGHT TO REDUNDANCY PAYMENT

135 The right

(1) An employer shall pay a redundancy payment to any employee of his if the employee—

(a) is dismissed by the employer by reason of redundancy, or

(b) is eligible for a redundancy payment by reason of being laid off or kept on short-time.

(2) Subsection (1) has effect subject to the following provisions of this Part (including, in particular, sections 140 to 144, 149 to 152, 155 to 161 and 164).

CHAPTER II
RIGHT ON DISMISSAL BY REASON OF REDUNDANCY

Dismissal by reason of redundancy

136 Circumstances in which an employee is dismissed

(1) Subject to the provisions of this section and sections 137 and 138, for the purposes of this Part an employee is dismissed by his employer if (and only if)—

(a) the contract under which he is employed by the employer is terminated by the employer (whether with or without notice),

(b) he is employed under a limited term contract and that contract terminates by virtue of the limiting event without being renewed under the same contract, or

    (c)   the employee terminates the contract under which he is employed (with or without notice) in circumstances in which he is entitled to terminate it without notice by reason of the employer's conduct.

(2) Subsection (1)(c) does not apply if the employee terminates the contract without notice in circumstances in which he is entitled to do so by reason of a lock-out by the employer.

(3) An employee shall be taken to be dismissed by his employer for the purposes of this Part if—

    (a)   the employer gives notice to the employee to terminate his contract of employment, and

    (b)   at a time within the obligatory period of notice the employee gives notice in writing to the employer to terminate the contract of employment on a date earlier than the date on which the employer's notice is due to expire.

(4) In this Part the 'obligatory period of notice', in relation to notice given by an employer to terminate an employee's contract of employment, means—

    (a)   the actual period of the notice in a case where the period beginning at the time when the notice is given and ending at the time when it expires is equal to the minimum period which (by virtue of any enactment or otherwise) is required to be given by the employer to terminate the contract of employment, and

    (b)   the period which—

        (i)   is equal to the minimum period referred to in paragraph (a), and

        (ii)   ends at the time when the notice expires,

in any other case.

(5) Where in accordance with any enactment or rule of law—

    (a)   an act on the part of an employer, or

    (b)   an event affecting an employer (including, in the case of an individual, his death),

operates to terminate a contract under which an employee is employed by him, the act or event shall be taken for the purposes of this Part to be a termination of the contract by the employer.

138   No dismissal in cases of renewal of contract or re-engagement

(1) Where—

    (a)   an employee's contract of employment is renewed, or he is re-engaged under a new contract of employment in pursuance of an offer (whether in writing or not) made before the end of his employment under the previous contract, and

    (b)   the renewal or re-engagement takes effect either immediately on, or after an interval of not more than four weeks after, the end of that employment, the employee shall not be regarded for the purposes of this Part as dismissed by his employer by reason of the ending of his employment under the previous contract.

(2) Subsection (1) does not apply if—

    (a)   the provisions of the contract as renewed, or of the new contract, as to—

        (i)   the capacity and place in which the employee is employed, and

        (ii)   the other terms and conditions of his employment,

differ (wholly or in part) from the corresponding provisions of the previous contract, and

    (b)   during the period specified in subsection (3)—

        (i)   the employee (for whatever reason) terminates the renewed or new contract, or gives notice to terminate it and it is in consequence terminated, or

        (ii)   the employer, for a reason connected with or arising out of any difference between the renewed or new contract and the previous contract, terminates the renewed or new contract, or gives notice to terminate it and it is in consequence terminated.

(3) The period referred to in subsection (2)(b) is the period—

    (a)   beginning at the end of the employee's employment under the previous contract, and

    (b)   ending with—

        (i)   the period of four weeks beginning with the date on which the employee starts work under the renewed or new contract, or

        (ii)   such longer period as may be agreed in accordance with subsection (6) for the purpose of retraining the employee for employment under that contract;

and is in this Part referred to as the 'trial period'.

(4) Where subsection (2) applies, for the purposes of this Part—

    (a)   the employee shall be regarded as dismissed on the date on which his employment under the previous contract (or, if there has been more than one trial period, the original contract) ended, and

    (b)   the reason for the dismissal shall be taken to be the reason for which the employee was then dismissed, or would have been dismissed had the offer (or original offer) of renewed or new employment not been made, or the reason which resulted in that offer being made.

(5) Subsection (2) does not apply if the employee's contract of employment is again renewed, or he is again re-engaged under a new contract of employment, in circumstances such that subsection (1) again applies.

(6) For the purposes of subsection (3)(b)(ii) a period of retraining is agreed in accordance with this subsection only if the agreement—

    (a)   is made between the employer and the employee or his representative before the employee starts work under the contract as renewed, or the new contract,

    (b)   is in writing,

    (c)   specifies the date on which the period of retraining ends, and

    (d)   specifies the terms and conditions of employment which will apply in the employee's case after the end of that period.

139 Redundancy

(1) For the purposes of this Act an employee who is dismissed shall be taken to be dismissed by reason of redundancy if the dismissal is wholly or mainly attributable to—

    (a)   the fact that his employer has ceased or intends to cease—

        (i)   to carry on the business for the purposes of which the employee was employed by him, or

        (ii)   to carry on that business in the place where the employee was so employed, or

    (b)   the fact that the requirements of that business—

        (i)   for employees to carry out work of a particular kind, or

        (ii)   for employees to carry out work of a particular kind in the place where the employee was employed by the employer,

    have ceased or diminished or are expected to cease or diminish.

(2) For the purposes of subsection (1) the business of the employer together with the business or businesses of his associated employers shall be treated as one (unless either of the conditions specified in paragraphs (a) and (b) of that subsection would be satisfied without so treating them).

(3) For the purposes of subsection (1) the activities carried on by a local education authority with respect to the schools maintained by it, and the activities carried on by the governing bodies of those schools, shall be treated as one business (unless either of the conditions specified in paragraphs (a) and (b) of that subsection would be satisfied without so treating them).

(4) Where—

    (a)   the contract under which a person is employed is treated by section 136(5) as terminated by his employer by reason of an act or event, and

    (b)   the employee's contract is not renewed and he is not re-engaged under a new contract of employment,

    he shall be taken for the purposes of this Act to be dismissed by reason of redundancy if the circumstances in which his contract is not renewed, and he is not re-engaged, are wholly or mainly attributable to either of the facts stated in paragraphs (a) and (b) of subsection (1).

(5) In its application to a case within subsection (4), paragraph (a)(i) of subsection (1) has effect as if the reference in that subsection to the employer included a reference to any person to whom, in consequence of the act or event, power to dispose of the business has passed.

(6) In subsection (1) 'cease' and 'diminish' mean cease and diminish either permanently or temporarily and for whatever reason.

Exclusions

140   Summary dismissal

(1)   Subject to subsections (2) and (3), an employee is not entitled to a redundancy payment by reason of dismissal where his employer, being entitled to terminate his contract of employment without notice by reason of the employee's conduct, terminates it either—

(a)   without notice,

(b)   by giving shorter notice than that which, in the absence of conduct entitling the employer to terminate the contract without notice, the employer would be required to give to terminate the contract, or

(c)   by giving notice which includes, or is accompanied by, a statement in writing that the employer would, by reason of the employee's conduct, be entitled to terminate the contract without notice.

(2)   Where an employee who—

(a)   has been given notice by his employer to terminate his contract of employment, or

(b)   has given notice to his employer under section 148(1) indicating his intention to claim a redundancy payment in respect of lay-off or short-time,

takes part in a strike at any relevant time in circumstances which entitle the employer to treat the contract of employment as terminable without notice, subsection (1) does not apply if the employer terminates the contract by reason of his taking part in the strike.

(3)   Where the contract of employment of an employee who—

(a)   has been given notice by his employer to terminate his contract of employment, or

(b)   has given notice to his employer under section 148(1) indicating his intention to claim a redundancy payment in respect of lay-off or short-time,

is terminated as mentioned in subsection (1) at any relevant time otherwise than by reason of his taking part in a strike, an employment tribunal may determine that the employer is liable to make an appropriate payment to the employee if on a reference to the tribunal it appears to the tribunal, in the circumstances of the case, to be just and equitable that the employee should receive it.

(4)   In subsection (3) 'appropriate payment' means—

(a)   the whole of the redundancy payment to which the employee would have been entitled apart from subsection (1), or

(b)   such part of that redundancy payment as the tribunal thinks fit.

(5)   In this section 'relevant time'—

(a)   in the case of an employee who has been given notice by his employer to terminate his contract of employment, means any time within the obligatory period of notice, and

(b)   in the case of an employee who has given notice to his employer under section 148(1), means any time after the service of the notice.

141   Renewal of contract or re-engagement

(1)   This section applies where an offer (whether in writing or not) is made to an employee before the end of his employment—

(a)   to renew his contract of employment, or

(b)   to re-engage him under a new contract of employment,

with renewal or re-engagement to take effect either immediately on, or after an interval of not more than four weeks after, the end of his employment.

(2)   Where subsection (3) is satisfied, the employee is not entitled to a redundancy payment if he unreasonably refuses the offer.

(3)   This subsection is satisfied where—

(a)   the provisions of the contract as renewed, or of the new contract, as to—

(i)   the capacity and place in which the employee would be employed, and

(ii)   the other terms and conditions of his employment,

would not differ from the corresponding provisions of the previous contract, or

(b)   those provisions of the contract as renewed, or of the new contract, would differ from the corresponding provisions of the previous contract but the offer constitutes an offer of suitable employment in relation to the employee.

(4) The employee is not entitled to a redundancy payment if—
    (a)   his contract of employment is renewed, or he is re-engaged under a new contract of employment, in pursuance of the offer,
    (b)   the provisions of the contract as renewed or new contract as to the capacity or place in which he is employed or the other terms and conditions of his employment differ (wholly or in part) from the corresponding provisions of the previous contract,
    (c)   the employment is suitable in relation to him, and
    (d)   during the trial period he unreasonably terminates the contract, or unreasonably gives notice to terminate it and it is in consequence terminated.

142 Employee anticipating expiry of employer's notice

(1) Subject to subsection (3), an employee is not entitled to a redundancy payment where—
    (a)   he is taken to be dismissed by virtue of section 136(3) by reason of giving to his employer notice terminating his contract of employment on a date earlier than the date on which notice by the employer terminating the contract is due to expire,
    (b)   before the employee's notice is due to expire, the employer gives him a notice such as is specified in subsection (2), and
    (c)   the employee does not comply with the requirements of that notice.
(2) The employer's notice referred to in subsection (1)(b) is a notice in writing—
    (a)   requiring the employee to withdraw his notice terminating the contract of employment and to continue in employment until the date on which the employer's notice terminating the contract expires, and
    (b)   stating that, unless he does so, the employer will contest any liability to pay to him a redundancy payment in respect of the termination of his contract of employment.
(3) An employment tribunal may determine that the employer is liable to make an appropriate payment to the employee if on a reference to the tribunal it appears to the tribunal, having regard to—
    (a)   the reasons for which the employee seeks to leave the employment, and
    (b)   the reasons for which the employer requires him to continue in it,
to be just and equitable that the employee should receive the payment.
(4) In subsection (3) 'appropriate payment' means—
    (a)   the whole of the redundancy payment to which the employee would have been entitled apart from subsection (1), or
    (b)   such part of that redundancy payment as the tribunal thinks fit.

143 Strike during currency of employer's notice

(1) This section applies where—
    (a)   an employer has given notice to an employee to terminate his contract of employment ('notice of termination'),
    (b)   after the notice is given the employee begins to take part in a strike of employees of the employer, and
    (c)   the employer serves on the employee a notice of extension.
(2) A notice of extension is a notice in writing which—
    (a)   requests the employee to agree to extend the contract of employment beyond the time of expiry by a period comprising as many available days as the number of working days lost by striking ('the proposed period of extension'),
    (b)   indicates the reasons for which the employer makes that request, and
    (c)   states that the employer will contest any liability to pay the employee a redundancy payment in respect of the dismissal effected by the notice of termination unless either—
        (i)   the employee complies with the request, or
        (ii)   the employer is satisfied that, in consequence of sickness or injury or otherwise, the employee is unable to comply with it or that (even though he is able to comply with it) it is reasonable in the circumstances for him not to do so.

(3) Subject to subsections (4) and (5), if the employee does not comply with the request contained in the notice of extension, he is not entitled to a redundancy payment by reason of the dismissal effected by the notice of termination.

(4) Subsection (3) does not apply if the employer agrees to pay a redundancy payment to the employee in respect of the dismissal effected by the notice of termination even though he has not complied with the request contained in the notice of extension.

(5) An employment tribunal may determine that the employer is liable to make an appropriate payment to the employee if on a reference to the tribunal it appears to the tribunal that—

   (a)   the employee has not complied with the request contained in the notice of extension and the employer has not agreed to pay a redundancy payment in respect of the dismissal effected by the notice of termination, but

   (b)   either the employee was unable to comply with the request or it was reasonable in the circumstances for him not to comply with it.

(6) In subsection (5) 'appropriate payment' means—

   (a)   the whole of the redundancy payment to which the employee would have been entitled apart from subsection (3), or

   (b)   such part of that redundancy payment as the tribunal thinks fit.

(7) If the employee—

   (a)   complies with the request contained in the notice of extension, or

   (b)   does not comply with it but attends at his proper or usual place of work and is ready and willing to work on one or more (but not all) of the available days within the proposed period of extension,

   the notice of termination has effect, and shall be deemed at all material times to have had effect, as if the period specified in it had been appropriately extended; and sections 87 to 91 accordingly apply as if the period of notice required by section 86 were extended to a corresponding extent.

(8) In subsection (7) 'appropriately extended' means—

   (a)   in a case within paragraph (a) of that subsection, extended beyond the time of expiry by an additional period equal to the proposed period of extension, and

   (b)   in a case within paragraph (b) of that subsection, extended beyond the time of expiry up to the end of the day (or last of the days) on which he attends at his proper or usual place of work and is ready and willing to work.

144   Provisions supplementary to section 143

(1) For the purposes of section 143 an employee complies with the request contained in a notice of extension if, but only if, on each available day within the proposed period of extension, he—

   (a)   attends at his proper or usual place of work, and

   (b)   is ready and willing to work,

   whether or not he has signified his agreement to the request in any other way.

(2) The reference in section 143(2) to the number of working days lost by striking is a reference to the number of working days in the period—

   (a)   beginning with the date of service of the notice of termination, and

   (b)   ending with the time of expiry, which are days on which the employee in question takes part in a strike of employees of his employer.

(3) In section 143 and this section—

   'available day', in relation to an employee, means a working day beginning at or after the time of expiry which is a day on which he is not taking part in a strike of employees of the employer, 'available day within the proposed period of extension' means an available day which begins before the end of the proposed period of extension,

   'time of expiry', in relation to a notice of termination, means the time at which the notice would expire apart from section 143, and

   'working day', in relation to an employee, means a day on which, in accordance with his contract of employment, he is normally required to work.

(4) Neither the service of a notice of extension nor any extension by virtue of section 143(7) of the period specified in a notice of termination affects—

    (a)   any right either of the employer or of the employee to terminate the contract of employment (whether before, at or after the time of expiry) by a further notice or without notice, or

    (b)   the operation of this Part in relation to any such termination of the contract of employment.

Supplementary

145   The relevant date

(1)   For the purposes of the provisions of this Act relating to redundancy payments 'the relevant date' in relation to the dismissal of an employee has the meaning given by this section.

(2)   Subject to the following provisions of this section, 'the relevant date'—

    (a)   in relation to an employee whose contract of employment is terminated by notice, whether given by his employer or by the employee, means the date on which the notice expires,

    (b)   in relation to an employee whose contract of employment is terminated without notice, means the date on which the termination takes effect, and

    (c)   in relation to an employee who is employed under a limited term contract which terminates by virtue of the limiting event without being renewed under the same contract, means the date on which the termination takes effect.

(3)   Where the employee is taken to be dismissed by virtue of section 136(3) the 'relevant date' means the date on which the employee's notice to terminate his contract of employment expires.

(4)   Where the employee is regarded by virtue of section 138(4) as having been dismissed on the date on which his employment under an earlier contract ended, 'the relevant date' means—

    (a)   for the purposes of section 164(1), the date which is the relevant date as defined by subsection (2) in relation to the renewed or new contract or, where there has been more than one trial period, the last such contract, and

    (b)   for the purposes of any other provision, the date which is the relevant date as defined by subsection (2) in relation to the previous contract or, where there has been more than one such trial period, the original contract.

(5)   Where—

    (a)   the contract of employment is terminated by the employer, and

    (b)   the notice required by section 86 to be given by an employer would, if duly given on the material date, expire on a date later than the relevant date (as defined by the previous provisions of this section),

for the purposes of sections 155, 162(1) and 227(3) the later date is the relevant date.

(6)   In subsection (5)(b) 'the material date' means—

    (a)   the date when notice of termination was given by the employer, or

    (b)   where no notice was given, the date when the contract of employment was terminated by the employer.

(7)   ...

146   Provisions supplementing sections 138 and 141

(1)   In sections 138 and 141—

    (a)   references to re-engagement are to re-engagement by the employer or an associated employer, and

    (b)   references to an offer are to an offer made by the employer or an associated employer.

(2)   For the purposes of the application of section 138(1) or 141(1) to a contract under which the employment ends on a Friday, Saturday or Sunday—

    (a)   the renewal or re-engagement shall be treated as taking effect immediately on the ending of the employment under the previous contract if it takes effect on or before the next Monday after that Friday, Saturday or Sunday, and

    (b)   the interval of four weeks to which those provisions refer shall be calculated as if the employment had ended on that next Monday.

(3)   ...

CHAPTER III
RIGHT BY REASON OF LAY-OFF OR SHORT-TIME

Lay-off and short-time

147   Meaning of 'lay-off' and 'short-time'

(1)   For the purposes of this Part an employee shall be taken to be laid off for a week if—

(a)   he is employed under a contract on terms and conditions such that his remuneration under the contract depends on his being provided by the employer with work of the kind which he is employed to do, but

(b)   he is not entitled to any remuneration under the contract in respect of the week because the employer does not provide such work for him.

(2)   For the purposes of this Part an employee shall be taken to be kept on short-time for a week if by reason of a diminution in the work provided for the employee by his employer (being work of a kind which under his contract the employee is employed to do) the employee's remuneration for the week is less than half a week's pay.

148   Eligibility by reason of lay-off or short-time

(1)   Subject to the following provisions of this Part, for the purposes of this Part an employee is eligible for a redundancy payment by reason of being laid off or kept on short-time if—

(a)   he gives notice in writing to his employer indicating (in whatever terms) his intention to claim a redundancy payment in respect of lay-off or short-time (referred to in this Part as 'notice of intention to claim'), and

(b)   before the service of the notice he has been laid off or kept on short-time in circumstances in which subsection (2) applies.

(2)   This subsection applies if the employee has been laid off or kept on short-time—

(a)   for four or more consecutive weeks of which the last before the service of the notice ended on, or not more than four weeks before, the date of service of the notice, or

(b)   for a series of six or more weeks (of which not more than three were consecutive) within a period of thirteen weeks, where the last week of the series before the service of the notice ended on, or not more than four weeks before, the date of service of the notice.

Exclusions

149   Counter-notices

Where an employee gives to his employer notice of intention to claim but—

(a)   the employer gives to the employee, within seven days after the service of that notice, notice in writing (referred to in this Part as a 'counter-notice') that he will contest any liability to pay to the employee a redundancy payment in pursuance of the employee's notice, and

(b)   the employer does not withdraw the counter-notice by a subsequent notice in writing,

the employee is not entitled to a redundancy payment in pursuance of his notice of intention to claim except in accordance with a decision of an employment tribunal.

150   Resignation

(1)   An employee is not entitled to a redundancy payment by reason of being laid off or kept on short-time unless he terminates his contract of employment by giving such period of notice as is required for the purposes of this section before the end of the relevant period.

(2)   The period of notice required for the purposes of this section—

(a)   where the employee is required by his contract of employment to give more than one week's notice to terminate the contract, is the minimum period which he is required to give, and

(b)   otherwise, is one week.

(3)   In subsection (1) 'the relevant period'—

(a)   if the employer does not give a counter-notice within seven days after the service of the notice of intention to claim, is three weeks after the end of those seven days,

(b)   if the employer gives a counter-notice within that period of seven days but withdraws it by a subsequent notice in writing, is three weeks after the service of the notice of withdrawal, and

(c)   if—

(i)   the employer gives a counter-notice within that period of seven days, and does not so withdraw it, and

(ii)   a question as to the right of the employee to a redundancy payment in pursuance of the notice of intention to claim is referred to an employment tribunal,

is three weeks after the tribunal has notified to the employee its decision on that reference.

(4)   For the purposes of subsection (3)(c) no account shall be taken of—

(a)   any appeal against the decision of the tribunal, or

(b)   any proceedings or decision in consequence of any such appeal.

151   Dismissal

(1)   An employee is not entitled to a redundancy payment by reason of being laid off or kept on short-time if he is dismissed by his employer.

(2)   Subsection (1) does not prejudice any right of the employee to a redundancy payment in respect of the dismissal.

152   Likelihood of full employment

(1)   An employee is not entitled to a redundancy payment in pursuance of a notice of intention to claim if—

(a)   on the date of service of the notice it was reasonably to be expected that the employee (if he continued to be employed by the same employer) would, not later than four weeks after that date, enter on a period of employment of not less than thirteen weeks during which he would not be laid off or kept on short-time for any week, and

(b)   the employer gives a counter-notice to the employee within seven days after the service of the notice of intention to claim.

(2)   Subsection (1) does not apply where the employee—

(a)   continues or has continued, during the next four weeks after the date of service of the notice of intention to claim, to be employed by the same employer, and

(b)   is or has been laid off or kept on short-time for each of those weeks.

Supplementary

153   The relevant date

For the purposes of the provisions of this Act relating to redundancy payments 'the relevant date' in relation to a notice of intention to claim or a right to a redundancy payment in pursuance of such a notice—

(a)   in a case falling within paragraph (a) of subsection (2) of section 148, means the date on which the last of the four or more consecutive weeks before the service of the notice came to an end, and

(b)   in a case falling within paragraph (b) of that subsection, means the date on which the last of the series of six or more weeks before the service of the notice came to an end.

154   Provisions supplementing sections 148 and 152

For the purposes of sections 148(2) and 152(2)—

(a)   it is immaterial whether a series of weeks consists wholly of weeks for which the employee is laid off or wholly of weeks for which he is kept on short-time or partly of the one and partly of the other, and

(b)   no account shall be taken of any week for which an employee is laid off or kept on short-time where the lay-off or short-time is wholly or mainly attributable to a strike or a lock-out (whether or not in the trade or industry in which the employee is employed and whether in Great Britain or elsewhere).

CHAPTER IV
GENERAL EXCLUSIONS FROM RIGHT

155   Qualifying period of employment

An employee does not have any right to a redundancy payment unless he has been continuously employed for a period of not less than two years ending with the relevant date.

CHAPTER V
OTHER PROVISIONS ABOUT REDUNDANCY PAYMENTS

162   Amount of a redundancy payment

(1)   The amount of a redundancy payment shall be calculated by—

    (a)   determining the period, ending with the relevant date, during which the employee has been continuously employed,

    (b)   reckoning backwards from the end of that period the number of years of employment falling within that period, and

    (c)   allowing the appropriate amount for each of those years of employment.

(2)   In subsection (1)(c) 'the appropriate amount' means—

    (a)   one and a half weeks' pay for a year of employment in which the employee was not below the age of forty-one,

    (b)   one week's pay for a year of employment (not within paragraph (a)) in which he was not below the age of twenty-two, and

    (c)   half a week's pay for each year of employment not within paragraph (a) or (b).

(3)   Where twenty years of employment have been reckoned under subsection (1), no account shall be taken under that subsection of any year of employment earlier than those twenty years.

(4), (5) …

(6)   Subsections (1) to (3) apply for the purposes of any provision of this Part by virtue of which an employment tribunal may determine that an employer is liable to pay to an employee—

    (a)   the whole of the redundancy payment to which the employee would have had a right apart from some other provision, or

    (b)   such part of the redundancy payment to which the employee would have had a right apart from some other provision as the tribunal thinks fit,

as if any reference to the amount of a redundancy payment were to the amount of the redundancy payment to which the employee would have been entitled apart from that other provision.

(7), (8) …

163   References to employment tribunals

(1)   Any question arising under this Part as to—

    (a)   the right of an employee to a redundancy payment, or

    (b)   the amount of a redundancy payment,

shall be referred to and determined by an employment tribunal.

(2)   For the purposes of any such reference, an employee who has been dismissed by his employer shall, unless the contrary is proved, be presumed to have been so dismissed by reason of redundancy.

(3)   Any question whether an employee will become entitled to a redundancy payment if he is not dismissed by his employer and he terminates his contract of employment as mentioned in section 150(1) shall for the purposes of this Part be taken to be a question as to the right of the employee to a redundancy payment.

(4)   Where an order under section 157 is in force in respect of an agreement, this section has effect in relation to any question arising under the agreement as to the right of an employee to a payment on the termination of his employment, or as to the amount of such a payment, as if the payment were a redundancy payment and the question arose under this Part.

164   Claims for redundancy payment

(1)   An employee does not have any right to a redundancy payment unless, before the end of the period of six months beginning with the relevant date—

    (a)   the payment has been agreed and paid,

    (b)   the employee has made a claim for the payment by notice in writing given to the employer,

    (c)   a question as to the employee's right to, or the amount of, the payment has been referred to an employment tribunal, or

    (d)   a complaint relating to his dismissal has been presented by the employee under section 111.

(2)   An employee is not deprived of his right to a redundancy payment by subsection (1) if, during the period of six months immediately following the period mentioned in that subsection, the employee—

    (a)   makes a claim for the payment by notice in writing given to the employer,

    (b)   refers to an employment tribunal a question as to his right to, or the amount of, the payment, or

    (c)   presents a complaint relating to his dismissal under section 111,

and it appears to the tribunal to be just and equitable that the employee should receive a redundancy payment.

(3)   In determining under subsection (2) whether it is just and equitable that an employee should receive a redundancy payment an employment tribunal shall have regard to—

    (a)   the reason shown by the employee for his failure to take any such step as is referred to in subsection (2) within the period mentioned in subsection (1), and

    (b)   all the other relevant circumstances.

165   Written particulars of redundancy payment

(1)   On making any redundancy payment, otherwise than in pursuance of a decision of a tribunal which specifies the amount of the payment to be made, the employer shall give to the employee a written statement indicating how the amount of the payment has been calculated.

(2)   An employer who without reasonable excuse fails to comply with subsection (1) is guilty of an offence and liable on summary conviction to a fine not exceeding level 1 on the standard scale.

(3)   If an employer fails to comply with the requirements of subsection (1), the employee may by notice in writing to the employer require him to give to the employee a written statement complying with those requirements within such period (not being less than one week beginning with the day on which the notice is given) as may be specified in the notice.

(4)   An employer who without reasonable excuse fails to comply with a notice under subsection (3) is guilty of an offence and liable on summary conviction to a fine not exceeding level 3 on the standard scale.

CHAPTER VI
PAYMENTS BY SECRETARY OF STATE

166   Applications for payments

(1)   Where an employee claims that his employer is liable to pay to him an employer's payment and either—

    (a)   that the employee has taken all reasonable steps, other than legal proceedings, to recover the payment from the employer and the employer has refused or failed to pay it, or has paid part of it and has refused or failed to pay the balance, or

    (b)   that the employer is insolvent and the whole or part of the payment remains unpaid,

the employee may apply to the Secretary of State for a payment under this section.

(2)   In this Part 'employer's payment', in relation to an employee, means—

    (a)   a redundancy payment which his employer is liable to pay to him under this Part,

    (aa)   a payment which his employer is liable to make to him under an agreement to refrain from instituting or continuing proceedings for a contravention or alleged contravention of section 135 which has effect by virtue of section 203(2)(e) or (f), or

     (b)   a payment which his employer is, under an agreement in respect of which an order is in force under section 157, liable to make to him on the termination of his contract of employment.

(3)   In relation to any case where (in accordance with any provision of this Part) an employment tribunal determines that an employer is liable to pay part (but not the whole) of a redundancy payment the reference in subsection (2)(a) to a redundancy payment is to the part of the redundancy payment.

(4)   In subsection (1)(a) 'legal proceedings'—

     (a)   does not include any proceedings before an employment tribunal, but

     (b)   includes any proceedings to enforce a decision or award of an employment tribunal.

(5)   An employer is insolvent for the purposes of subsection (1)(b)—

     (a)   where the employer is an individual, if (but only if) subsection (6) is satisfied,

     (b)   where the employer is a company, if (but only if) subsection (7) is satisfied, and

     (c)   where the employer is a limited liability partnership, if (but only if) subsection (8) is satisfied.

(6)   This subsection is satisfied in the case of an employer who is an individual—

     (a)   in England and Wales if—

         (i)   he has been adjudged bankrupt or has made a composition or arrangement with his creditors, or

         (ii)   he has died and his estate falls to be administered in accordance with an order under section 421 of the Insolvency Act 1986, and

     (b)   in Scotland if—

         (i)   sequestration of his estate has been awarded or he has executed a trust deed for his creditors or has entered into a composition contract, or

         (ii)   he has died and a judicial factor appointed under section 11A of the Judicial Factors (Scotland) Act 1889 is required by that section to divide his insolvent estate among his creditors.

(7)   This subsection is satisfied in the case of an employer which is a company—

     (a)   if a winding up order has been made, or a resolution for voluntary winding up has been passed, with respect to the company,

     (aa)   if the company is in administration for the purposes of the Insolvency Act 1986,

     (b)   if a receiver or (in England and Wales only) a manager of the company's undertaking has been duly appointed, or (in England and Wales only) possession has been taken, by or on behalf of the holders of any debentures secured by a floating charge, of any property of the company comprised in or subject to the charge, or

     (c)   if a voluntary arrangement proposed in the case of the company for the purposes of Part I of the Insolvency Act 1986 has been approved under that Part of that Act.

(8)   This subsection is satisfied in the case of an employer which is a limited liability partnership—

     (a)   if a winding-up order, an administration order or a determination for a voluntary winding-up has been made with respect to the limited liability partnership,

     (b)   if a receiver or (in England and Wales only) a manager of the undertaking of the limited liability partnership has been duly appointed, or (in England and Wales only) possession has been taken, by or on behalf of the holders of any debentures secured by a floating charge, of any property of the limited liability partnership comprised in or subject to the charge, or

     (c)   if a voluntary arrangement proposed in the case of the limited liability partnership for the purpose of Part I of the Insolvency Act 1986 has been approved under that Part of that Act.

167   Making of payments

(1)   Where, on an application under section 166 by an employee in relation to an employer's payment, the Secretary of State is satisfied that the requirements specified in subsection (2) are met, he shall pay to the employee out of the National Insurance Fund a sum calculated in accordance with section 168 but reduced by so much (if any) of the employer's payment as has already been paid.

(2) The requirements referred to in subsection (1) are—

    (a) that the employee is entitled to the employer's payment, and

    (b) that one of the conditions specified in paragraphs (a) and (b) of subsection (1) of section 166 is fulfilled,

and, in a case where the employer's payment is a payment such as is mentioned in subsection (2)(b) of that section, that the employee's right to the payment arises by virtue of a period of continuous employment (computed in accordance with the provisions of the agreement in question) which is not less than two years.

(3) Where under this section the Secretary of State pays a sum to an employee in respect of an employer's payment—

    (a) all rights and remedies of the employee with respect to the employer's payment, or (if the Secretary of State has paid only part of it) all the rights and remedies of the employee with respect to that part of the employer's payment, are transferred to and vest in the Secretary of State, and

    (b) any decision of an employment tribunal requiring the employer's payment to be paid to the employee has effect as if it required that payment, or that part of it which the Secretary of State has paid, to be paid to the Secretary of State.

(4) Any money recovered by the Secretary of State by virtue of subsection (3) shall be paid into the National Insurance Fund.

168   Amount of payments

(1) The sum payable to an employee by the Secretary of State under section 167—

    (a) where the employer's payment to which the employee's application under section 166 relates is a redundancy payment or a part of a redundancy payment, is a sum equal to the amount of the redundancy payment or part,

    (aa) where the employer's payment to which the employee's application under section 166 relates is a payment which his employer is liable to make to him under an agreement having effect by virtue of section 203(2)(e) or (f), is a sum equal to the amount of the employer's payment or of any redundancy payment which the employer would have been liable to pay to the employee but for the agreement, whichever is less, and

    (b) where the employer's payment to which the employee's application under section 166 relates is a payment which the employer is liable to make under an agreement in respect of which an order is in force under section 157, is a sum equal to the amount of the employer's payment or of the relevant redundancy payment, whichever is less.

(2) The reference in subsection (1)(b) to the amount of the relevant redundancy payment is to the amount of the redundancy payment which the employer would have been liable to pay to the employee on the assumptions specified in subsection (3).

(3) The assumptions referred to in subsection (2) are that—

    (a) the order in force in respect of the agreement had not been made,

    (b) the circumstances in which the employer's payment is payable had been such that the employer was liable to pay a redundancy payment to the employee in those circumstances,

    (c) the relevant date, in relation to any such redundancy payment, had been the date on which the termination of the employee's contract of employment is treated as having taken effect for the purposes of the agreement, and

    (d) in so far as the provisions of the agreement relating to the circumstances in which the continuity of an employee's period of employment is to be treated as broken, and the weeks which are to count in computing a period of employment, are inconsistent with the provisions of Chapter I of Part XIV, the provisions of the agreement were substituted for those provisions.

169   Information relating to applications for payments

(1) Where an employee makes an application to the Secretary of State under section 166, the Secretary of State may, by notice in writing given to the employer, require the employer—

    (a) to provide the Secretary of State with such information, and

(b)   to produce for examination on behalf of the Secretary of State documents in his custody or under his control of such description,

as the Secretary of State may reasonably require for the purpose of determining whether the application is well-founded.

(2)   Where a person on whom a notice is served under subsection (1) fails without reasonable excuse to comply with a requirement imposed by the notice, he is guilty of an offence and liable on summary conviction to a fine not exceeding level 3 on the standard scale.

(3)   A person is guilty of an offence if—

(a)   in providing any information required by a notice under subsection (1), he makes a statement which he knows to be false in a material particular or recklessly makes a statement which is false in a material particular, or

(b)   he produces for examination in accordance with a notice under subsection (1) a document which to his knowledge has been wilfully falsified.

(4)   A person guilty of an offence under subsection (3) is liable—

(a)   on summary conviction, to a fine not exceeding the statutory maximum or to imprisonment for a term not exceeding three months, or to both, or

(b)   on conviction on indictment, to a fine or to imprisonment for a term not exceeding two years, or to both.

170   References to employment tribunals

(1)   Where on an application made to the Secretary of State for a payment under section 166 it is claimed that an employer is liable to pay an employer's payment, there shall be referred to an employment tribunal—

(a)   any question as to the liability of the employer to pay the employer's payment, and

(b)   any question as to the amount of the sum payable in accordance with section 168.

(2)   For the purposes of any reference under this section an employee who has been dismissed by his employer shall, unless the contrary is proved, be presumed to have been so dismissed by reason of redundancy.

CHAPTER VII
SUPPLEMENTARY

Death of employer or employee

174   Death of employer: dismissal

(1)   Where the contract of employment of an employee is taken for the purposes of this Part to be terminated by his employer by reason of the employer's death, this Part has effect in accordance with the following provisions of this section.

(2)   Section 138 applies as if—

(a)   in subsection (1)(a), for the words 'in pursuance' onwards there were substituted 'by a personal representative of the deceased employer',

(b)   in subsection (1)(b), for the words 'either immediately' onwards there were substituted 'not later than eight weeks after the death of the deceased employer', and

(c)   in subsections (2)(b) and (6)(a), for the word 'employer' there were substituted 'personal representative of the deceased employer'.

(3)   Section 141(1) applies as if—

(a)   for the words 'before the end of his employment' there were substituted 'by a personal representative of the deceased employer', and

(b)   for the words 'either immediately' onwards there were substituted 'not later than eight weeks after the death of the deceased employer.'

(4)   For the purposes of section 141—

(a)   provisions of the contract as renewed, or of the new contract, do not differ from the corresponding provisions of the contract in force immediately before the death of the deceased employer by reason only that the personal representative would be substituted for the deceased employer as the employer, and

     (b)   no account shall be taken of that substitution in determining whether refusal of the offer was unreasonable or whether the employee acted reasonably in terminating or giving notice to terminate the new or renewed employment.

  (5) Section 146 has effect as if—

     (a)   subsection (1) were omitted, and

     (b)   in subsection (2), paragraph (a) were omitted and, in paragraph (b), for the word 'four' there were substituted 'eight'.

  (6) For the purposes of the application of this Part (in accordance with section 161(2)) in relation to an employee who was employed as a domestic servant in a private household, references in this section and sections 175 and 218(4) and (5) to a personal representative include a person to whom the management of the household has passed, otherwise than in pursuance of a sale or other disposition for valuable consideration, in consequence of the death of the employer.

175   Death of employer: lay-off and short-time

  (1) Where an employee is laid off or kept on short-time and his employer dies, this Part has effect in accordance with the following provisions of this section.

  (2) Where the employee—

     (a)   has been laid off or kept on short-time for one or more weeks before the death of the employer,

     (b)   has not given the deceased employer notice of intention to claim before the employer's death,

     (c)   after the employer's death has his contract of employment renewed, or is re-engaged under a new contract, by a personal representative of the deceased employer, and

     (d)   after renewal or re-engagement is laid off or kept on short-time for one or more weeks by the personal representative,

the week in which the employer died and the first week of the employee's employment by the personal representative shall be treated for the purposes of Chapter III as consecutive weeks (and references to four weeks or thirteen weeks shall be construed accordingly).

  (3) The following provisions of this section apply where—

     (a)   the employee has given the deceased employer notice of intention to claim before the employer's death,

     (b)   the employer's death occurred before the end of the period of four weeks after the service of the notice, and

     (c)   the employee has not terminated his contract of employment by notice expiring before the employer's death.

  (4) If the contract of employment is not renewed, and the employee is not re-engaged under a new contract, by a personal representative of the deceased employer before the end of the period of four weeks after the service of the notice of intention to claim—

     (a)   sections 149 and 152 do not apply, but

     (b)   (subject to that) Chapter III applies as if the employer had not died and the employee had terminated the contract of employment by a week's notice, or by the minimum notice which he is required to give to terminate the contract (if longer than a week), expiring at the end of that period.

  (5) If—

     (a)   the contract of employment is renewed, or the employee is re-engaged under a new contract, by a personal representative of the deceased employer before the end of the period of four weeks after the service of the notice of intention to claim, and

     (b)   the employee was laid off or kept on short-time by the deceased employer for one or more of those weeks and is laid off or kept on short-time by the personal representative for the week, or for the next two or more weeks, following the renewal or re-engagement,

subsection (6) has effect.

  (6) Where this subsection has effect Chapter III applies as if—

     (a)   all the weeks mentioned in subsection (5) were consecutive weeks during which the employee was employed (but laid off or kept on short-time) by the same employer, and

      (b)   the periods specified by section 150(3)(a) and (b) as the relevant period were extended by any week or weeks any part of which was after the death of the employer and before the date on which the renewal or re-engagement took effect.

176 Death of employee

(1) Where an employee whose employer has given him notice to terminate his contract of employment dies before the notice expires, this Part applies as if the contract had been duly terminated by the employer by notice expiring on the date of the employee's death.

(2) Where—

      (a)   an employee's contract of employment has been terminated by the employer,

      (b)   (by virtue of subsection (5) of section 145) a date later than the relevant date as defined by the previous provisions of that section is the relevant date for the purposes of certain provisions of this Act, and

      (c)   the employee dies before that date,

that subsection applies as if the notice to which it refers would have expired on the employee's death.

(3) Where—

      (a)   an employer has given notice to an employee to terminate his contract of employment and has offered to renew his contract of employment or to re-engage him under a new contract, and

      (b)   the employee dies without having accepted or refused the offer and without the offer having been withdrawn,

section 141(2) applies as if for the words 'he unreasonably refuses' there were substituted 'it would have been unreasonable on his part to refuse'.

(4) Where an employee's contract of employment has been renewed or he has been re-engaged under a new contract—

      (a)   if he dies during the trial period without having terminated, or given notice to terminate, the contract, section 141(4) applies as if for paragraph (d) there were substituted—

            '(d)   it would have been unreasonable for the employee during the trial period to terminate or give notice to terminate the contract.', and

      (b)   if during that trial period he gives notice to terminate the contract but dies before the notice expires, sections 138(2) and 141(4) apply as if the notice had expired (and the contract had been terminated by its expiry) on the date of the employee's death.

(5) Where in the circumstances specified in paragraphs (a) and (b) of subsection (3) of section 136 the employee dies before the notice given by him under paragraph (b) of that subsection expires—

      (a)   if he dies before his employer has given him a notice such as is specified in subsection (2) of section 142, subsections (3) and (4) of that section apply as if the employer had given him such a notice and he had not complied with it, and

      (b)   if he dies after his employer has given him such a notice, that section applies as if the employee had not died but did not comply with the notice.

(6) Where an employee has given notice of intention to claim—

      (a)   if he dies before he has given notice to terminate his contract of employment and before the relevant period (as defined in subsection (3) of section 150) has expired, that section does not apply, and

      (b)   if he dies within the period of seven days after the service of the notice of intention to claim, and before the employer has given a counter-notice, Chapter III applies as if the employer had given a counter-notice within that period of seven days.

(7) Where a claim for a redundancy payment is made by a personal representative of a deceased employee—

      (a)   if the employee died before the end of the period of six months beginning with the relevant date, subsection (1) of section 164, and

      (b)   if the employee died after the end of the period of six months beginning with the relevant date but before the end of the following period of six months, subsection (2) of that section,

applies as if for the words 'six months' there were substituted 'one year'.

Other supplementary provisions

180   Offences

(1)   Where an offence under this Part committed by a body corporate is proved—

    (a)   to have been committed with the consent or connivance of, or

    (b)   to be attributable to any neglect on the part of,

any director, manager, secretary or other similar officer of the body corporate, or any person who was purporting to act in any such capacity, he (as well as the body corporate) is guilty of the offence and liable to be proceeded against and punished accordingly.

(2)   In this section 'director', in relation to a body corporate established by or under any enactment for the purpose of carrying on under national ownership any industry or part of an industry or undertaking, being a body corporate whose affairs are managed by its members, means a member of that body corporate.

181   Interpretation

(1)   In this Part—

'counter-notice' shall be construed in accordance with section 149(a),

'dismissal' and 'dismissed' shall be construed in accordance with sections 136 to 138,

'employer's payment' has the meaning given by section 166,

'notice of intention to claim' shall be construed in accordance with section 148(1),

'obligatory period of notice' has the meaning given by section 136(4), and

'trial period' shall be construed in accordance with section 138(3).

(2)   In this Part—

    (a)   references to an employee being laid off or being eligible for a redundancy payment by reason of being laid off, and

    (b)   references to an employee being kept on short-time or being eligible for a redundancy payment by reason of being kept on short-time, shall be construed in accordance with sections 147 and 148.

PART XII

INSOLVENCY OF EMPLOYERS

182   Employee's rights on insolvency of employer

If, on an application made to him in writing by an employee, the Secretary of State is satisfied that—

    (a)   the employee's employer has become insolvent,

    (b)   the employee's employment has been terminated, and

    (c)   on the appropriate date the employee was entitled to be paid the whole or part of any debt to which this Part applies,

the Secretary of State shall, subject to section 186, pay the employee out of the National Insurance Fund the amount to which, in the opinion of the Secretary of State, the employee is entitled in respect of the debt.

183   Insolvency

(1)   An employer has become insolvent for the purposes of this Part—

    (a)   where the employer is an individual, if (but only if) subsection (2) is satisfied,

    (b)   where the employer is a company, if (but only if) subsection (3) is satisfied, and

    (c)   where the employer is a limited liability partnership if (but only if) subsection (4) is satisfied.

(2)   This subsection is satisfied in the case of an employer who is an individual—

    (a)   in England and Wales if—

        (i)   he has been adjudged bankrupt or has made a composition or arrangement with his creditors, or

        (ii)   he has died and his estate falls to be administered in accordance with an order under section 421 of the Insolvency Act 1986, and

    (b)   in Scotland if—

    (i) sequestration of his estate has been awarded or he has executed a trust deed for his creditors or has entered into a composition contract, or

    (ii) he has died and a judicial factor appointed under section 11A of the Judicial Factors (Scotland) Act 1889 is required by that section to divide his insolvent estate among his creditors.

  (3) This subsection is satisfied in the case of an employer which is a company—

    (a) if a winding up order has been made, or a resolution for voluntary winding up has been passed, with respect to the company,

    (aa) if the company is in administration for the purposes of the Insolvency Act 1986,

    (b) if a receiver or (in England and Wales only) a manager of the company's undertaking has been duly appointed, or (in England and Wales only) possession has been taken, by or on behalf of the holders of any debentures secured by a floating charge, of any property of the company comprised in or subject to the charge, or

    (c) if a voluntary arrangement proposed in the case of the company for the purposes of Part I of the Insolvency Act 1986 has been approved under that Part of that Act.

  (4) This subsection is satisfied in the case of an employer which is a limited liability partnership—

    (a) if a winding-up order, an administration order or a determination for a voluntary winding-up has been made with respect to the limited liability partnership,

    (b) if a receiver or (in England and Wales only) a manager of the undertaking of the limited liability partnership has been duly appointed, or (in England and Wales only) possession has been taken, by or on behalf of the holders of any debentures secured by a floating charge, of any property of the limited liability partnership comprised in or subject to the charge, or

    (c) if a voluntary arrangement proposed in the case of the limited liability partnership for the purposes of Part I of the Insolvency Act 1986 has been approved under that Part of that Act.

184 Debts to which Part applies

  (1) This Part applies to the following debts—

    (a) any arrears of pay in respect of one or more (but not more than eight) weeks,

    (b) any amount which the employer is liable to pay the employee for the period of notice required by section 86(1) or (2) or for any failure of the employer to give the period of notice required by section 86(1),

    (c) any holiday pay—

      (i) in respect of a period or periods of holiday not exceeding six weeks in all, and

      (ii) to which the employee became entitled during the twelve months ending with the appropriate date,

    (d) any basic award of compensation for unfair dismissal or so much of an award under a designated dismissal procedures agreement as does not exceed any basic award of compensation for unfair dismissal to which the employee would be entitled but for the agreement, and

    (e) any reasonable sum by way of reimbursement of the whole or part of any fee or premium paid by an apprentice or articled clerk.

  (2) For the purposes of subsection (1)(a) the following amounts shall be treated as arrears of pay—

    (a) a guarantee payment,

    (b) any payment for time off under Part VI of this Act or section 169 of the Trade Union and Labour Relations (Consolidation) Act 1992 (payment for time off for carrying out trade union duties etc.),

    (c) remuneration on suspension on medical grounds under section 64 of this Act and remuneration on suspension on maternity grounds under section 68 of this Act, and

    (d) remuneration under a protective award under section 189 of the Trade Union and Labour Relations (Consolidation) Act 1992.

(3) In subsection (1)(c) 'holiday pay', in relation to an employee, means—
     (a) pay in respect of a holiday actually taken by the employee, or
     (b) any accrued holiday pay which, under the employee's contract of employment, would
          in the ordinary course have become payable to him in respect of the period of a holiday
          if his employment with the employer had continued until he became entitled to a
          holiday.
(4) A sum shall be taken to be reasonable for the purposes of subsection (1)(e) in a case where
     a trustee in bankruptcy, or (in Scotland) a permanent or interim trustee (within the meaning
     of the Bankruptcy (Scotland) Act 1985), or liquidator has been or is required to be
     appointed—
     (a) as respects England and Wales, if it is admitted to be reasonable by the trustee in
          bankruptcy or liquidator under section 348 of the Insolvency Act 1986 (effect of
          bankruptcy on apprenticeships etc.), whether as originally enacted or as applied to the
          winding up of a company by rules under section 411 of that Act, and
     (b) as respects Scotland, if it is accepted by the permanent or interim trustee or liquidator
          for the purposes of the sequestration or winding up.

185   The appropriate date
In this Part 'the appropriate date'—
     (a) in relation to arrears of pay (not being remuneration under a protective award made
          under section 189 of the Trade Union and Labour Relations (Consolidation) Act 1992
          and to holiday pay, means the date on which the employer became insolvent,
     (b) in relation to a basic award of compensation for unfair dismissal and to remuneration
          under a protective award so made, means whichever is the latest of—
          (i)   the date on which the employer became insolvent,
          (ii)   the date of the termination of the employee's employment, and
          (iii) the date on which the award was made, and
     (c) in relation to any other debt to which this Part applies, means whichever is the latter
          of—
          (i)   the date on which the employer became insolvent, and
          (ii)   the date of the termination of the employee's employment.

186   Limit on amount payable under section 182
(1) The total amount payable to an employee in respect of any debt to which this Part applies,
     where the amount of the debt is referable to a period of time, shall not exceed—
     (a) £330 in respect of any one week, or
     (b) in respect of a shorter period, an amount bearing the same proportion to £330 as that
          shorter period bears to a week.
(2) ...

188   Complaints to employment tribunals
(1) A person who has applied for a payment under section 182 may present a complaint to an
     employment tribunal—
     (a) that the Secretary of State has failed to make any such payment, or
     (b) that any such payment made by him is less than the amount which should have been
          paid.
(2) An employment tribunal shall not consider a complaint under subsection (1) unless it is
     presented—
     (a) before the end of the period of three months beginning with the date on which the
          decision of the Secretary of State on the application was communicated to the applicant,
          or
     (b) within such further period as the tribunal considers reasonable in a case where it is not
          reasonably practicable for the complaint to be presented before the end of that period of
          three months.
(3) Where an employment tribunal finds that the Secretary of State ought to make a payment
     under section 182, the tribunal shall—

(a)   make a declaration to that effect, and

(b)   declare the amount of any such payment which it finds the Secretary of State ought to make.

189   Transfer to Secretary of State of rights and remedies

(1)   Where, in pursuance of section 182, the Secretary of State makes a payment to an employee in respect of a debt to which this Part applies—

(a)   on the making of the payment any rights and remedies of the employee in respect of the debt (or, if the Secretary of State has paid only part of it, in respect of that part) become rights and remedies of the Secretary of State, and

(b)   any decision of an employment tribunal requiring an employer to pay that debt to the employee has the effect that the debt (or the part of it which the Secretary of State has paid) is to be paid to the Secretary of State.

(2)   Where a debt (or any part of a debt) in respect of which the Secretary of State has made a payment in pursuance of section 182 constitutes—

(a)   a preferential debt within the meaning of the Insolvency Act 1986 for the purposes of any provision of that Act (including any such provision as applied by any order made under that Act) or any provision of the Companies Act 2006, or

(b)   a preferred debt within the meaning of the Bankruptcy (Scotland) Act 1985 for the purposes of any provision of that Act (including any such provision as applied by section 11A of the Judicial Factors (Scotland) Act 1889),

the rights which become rights of the Secretary of State in accordance with subsection (1) include any right arising under any such provision by reason of the status of the debt (or that part of it) as a preferential or preferred debt.

(3)   In computing for the purposes of any provision mentioned in subsection (2)(a) or (b) the aggregate amount payable in priority to other creditors of the employer in respect of—

(a)   any claim of the Secretary of State to be paid in priority to other creditors of the employer by virtue of subsection (2), and

(b)   any claim by the employee to be so paid made in his own right, any claim of the Secretary of State to be so paid by virtue of subsection (2) shall be treated as if it were a claim of the employee.

(4)   ...

PART XIII
MISCELLANEOUS

CHAPTER I
PARTICULAR TYPES OF EMPLOYMENT

198   Short-term employment

Sections 1 to 7 do not apply to an employee if his employment continues for less than one month.

CHAPTER II
OTHER MISCELLANEOUS MATTERS

Contracting out etc. and remedies

203   Restrictions on contracting out

(1)   Any provision in an agreement (whether a contract of employment or not) is void in so far as it purports—

(a)   to exclude or limit the operation of any provision of this Act, or

(b)   to preclude a person from bringing any proceedings under this Act before an employment tribunal.

(2)   Subsection (1)—

(a)   does not apply to any provision in a collective agreement excluding rights under section 28 if an order under section 35 is for the time being in force in respect of it,

(b)   does not apply to any provision in a dismissal procedures agreement excluding the right under section 94 if that provision is not to have effect unless an order under section 110 is for the time being in force in respect of it,

    (c)   does not apply to any provision in an agreement if an order under section 157 is for the time being in force in respect of it,

    (d)   ...

    (e)   does not apply to any agreement to refrain from instituting or continuing proceedings where a conciliation officer has taken action under section 18 of the Employment Tribunals Act 1996, and

    (f)   does not apply to any agreement to refrain from instituting or continuing any proceedings within the following provisions of section 18(1) of the Employment Tribunals Act 1996 (cases where conciliation available)—

        (i)   paragraph (d) (proceedings under this Act),

        (ii)   paragraph (h) (proceedings arising out of the Part-time Workers (Prevention of Less Favourable Treatment) Regulations 2000),

        (iii)   paragraph (i) (proceedings arising out of the Fixed-term Employees (Prevention of Less Favourable Treatment) Regulations 2002),

        (iv)   paragraph (j) (proceedings under those Regulations),

        if the conditions regulating compromise agreements under this Act are satisfied in relation to the agreement.

(3)   For the purposes of subsection (2)(f) the conditions regulating compromise agreements under this Act are that—

    (a)   the agreement must be in writing,

    (b)   the agreement must relate to the particular proceedings,

    (c)   the employee or worker must have received advice from a relevant independent adviser as to the terms and effect of the proposed agreement and, in particular, its effect on his ability to pursue his rights before an employment tribunal,

    (d)   there must be in force, when the adviser gives the advice, a contract of insurance, or an indemnity provided for members of a profession or professional body covering the risk of a claim by the employee or worker in respect of loss arising in consequence of the advice,

    (e)   the agreement must identify the adviser, and

    (f)   the agreement must state that the conditions regulating compromise agreements under this Act are satisfied.

(3A) A person is a relevant independent adviser for the purposes of subsection (3)(c)—

    (a)   if he is a qualified lawyer,

    (b)   if he is an officer, official, employee or member of an independent trade union who has been certified in writing by the trade union as competent to give advice and as authorised to do so on behalf of the trade union,

    (c)   if he works at an advice centre (whether as an employee or a volunteer) and has been certified in writing by the centre as competent to give advice and as authorised to do so on behalf of the centre, or

    (d)   if he is a person of a description specified in an order made by the Secretary of State.

(3B) But a person is not a relevant independent adviser for the purposes of subsection (3)(c) in relation to the employee or worker—

    (a)   if he is, is employed by or is acting in the matter for the employer or an associated employer,

    (b)   in the case of a person within subsection (3A)(b) or (c), if the trade union or advice centre is the employer or an associated employer,

    (c)   in the case of a person within subsection (3A)(c), if the employee or worker makes a payment for the advice received from him, or

    (d)   in the case of a person of a description specified in an order under subsection (3A)(d), if any condition specified in the order in relation to the giving of advice by persons of that description is not satisfied.

(4)   In subsection (3A)(a) 'qualified lawyer' means—

    (a)   as respects England and Wales, a barrister (whether in practice as such or employed to give legal advice), a solicitor who holds a practising certificate, or a person other than a barrister or solicitor who is an authorised advocate or authorised litigator (within the meaning of the Courts and Legal Services Act 1990), and

    (b)   as respects Scotland, an advocate (whether in practice as such or employed to give legal advice), or a solicitor who holds a practising certificate.

(5)   An agreement under which the parties agree to submit a dispute to arbitration—

    (a)   shall be regarded for the purposes of subsection (2)(e) and (f) as being an agreement to refrain from instituting or continuing proceedings if—

        (i)   the dispute is covered by a scheme having effect by virtue of an order under section 212A of the Trade Union and Labour Relations (Consolidation) Act 1992, and

        (ii)   the agreement is to submit it to arbitration in accordance with the scheme, but

    (b)   shall be regarded as neither being nor including such an agreement in any other case.

204   Law governing employment

(1)   For the purposes of this Act it is immaterial whether the law which (apart from this Act) governs any person's employment is the law of the United Kingdom, or of a part of the United Kingdom, or not.

(2)   ...

205   Remedy for infringement of certain rights

(1)   The remedy of an employee for infringement of any of the rights conferred by section 8, Part III, Parts V to VIII, section 92, Part X and Part XII is, where provision is made for a complaint or the reference of a question to an employment tribunal, by way of such a complaint or reference and not otherwise.

(1ZA) In relation to the right conferred by section 45A, the reference in subsection (1) to an employee has effect as a reference to a worker.

(1A) In relation to the right conferred by section 47B, the reference in subsection (1) to an employee has effect as a reference to a worker.

(2)   The remedy of a worker in respect of any contravention of section 13, 15, 18(1) or 21(1) is by way of a complaint under section 23 and not otherwise.

PART XIV

INTERPRETATION

CHAPTER I

CONTINUOUS EMPLOYMENT

210   Introductory

(1)   References in any provision of this Act to a period of continuous employment are (unless provision is expressly made to the contrary) to a period computed in accordance with this Chapter.

(2)   In any provision of this Act which refers to a period of continuous employment expressed in months or years—

    (a)   a month means a calendar month, and

    (b)   a year means a year of twelve calendar months.

(3)   In computing an employee's period of continuous employment for the purposes of any provision of this Act, any question—

    (a)   whether the employee's employment is of a kind counting towards a period of continuous employment, or

    (b)   whether periods (consecutive or otherwise) are to be treated as forming a single period of continuous employment,

shall be determined week by week; but where it is necessary to compute the length of an employee's period of employment it shall be computed in months and years of twelve months in accordance with section 211.

(4)   Subject to sections 215 to 217, a week which does not count in computing the length of a period of continuous employment breaks continuity of employment.

(5) A person's employment during any period shall, unless the contrary is shown, be presumed to have been continuous.

211 Period of continuous employment

(1) An employee's period of continuous employment for the purposes of any provision of this Act—

  (a) (subject to subsections (2) and (3)) begins with the day on which the employee starts work, and

  (b) ends with the day by reference to which the length of the employee's period of continuous employment is to be ascertained for the purposes of the provision.

(2) ...

(3) If an employee's period of continuous employment includes one or more periods which (by virtue of section 215, 216 or 217) while not counting in computing the length of the period do not break continuity of employment, the beginning of the period shall be treated as postponed by the number of days falling within that intervening period, or the aggregate number of days falling within those periods, calculated in accordance with the section in question.

212 Weeks counting in computing period

(1) Any week during the whole or part of which an employee's relations with his employer are governed by a contract of employment counts in computing the employee's period of employment.

(2) ...

(3) Subject to subsection (4), any week (not within subsection (1)) during the whole or part of which an employee is—

  (a) incapable of work in consequence of sickness or injury,

  (b) absent from work on account of a temporary cessation of work, or

  (c) absent from work in circumstances such that, by arrangement or custom, he is regarded as continuing in the employment of his employer for any purpose,

  (d) ...

(4) Not more than twenty-six weeks count under subsection (3)(a) between any periods falling under subsection (1).

213 Intervals in employment

(1) Where in the case of an employee a date later than the date which would be the effective date of termination by virtue of subsection (1) of section 97 is treated for certain purposes as the effective date of termination by virtue of subsection (2) or (4) of that section, the period of the interval between the two dates counts as a period of employment in ascertaining for the purposes of section 108(1) or 119(1) the period for which the employee has been continuously employed.

(2) Where an employee is by virtue of section 138(1) regarded for the purposes of Part XI as not having been dismissed by reason of a renewal or re-engagement taking effect after an interval, the period of the interval counts as a period of employment in ascertaining for the purposes of section 155 or 162(1) the period for which the employee has been continuously employed (except so far as it is to be disregarded under section 214 or 215).

(3) Where in the case of an employee a date later than the date which would be the relevant date by virtue of subsections (2) to (4) of section 145 is treated for certain purposes as the relevant date by virtue of subsection (5) of that section, the period of the interval between the two dates counts as a period of employment in ascertaining for the purposes of section 155 or 162(1) the period for which the employee has been continuously employed (except so far as it is to be disregarded under section 214 or 215).

214 Special provisions for redundancy payments

(1) This section applies where a period of continuous employment has to be determined in relation to an employee for the purposes of the application of section 155 or 162(1).

(2) The continuity of a period of employment is broken where—

    (a)   a redundancy payment has previously been paid to the employee (whether in respect of dismissal or in respect of lay-off or short-time), and

    (b)   the contract of employment under which the employee was employed was renewed (whether by the same or another employer) or the employee was re-engaged under a new contract of employment (whether by the same or another employer).

(3)   The continuity of a period of employment is also broken where—

    (a)   a payment has been made to the employee (whether in respect of the termination of his employment or lay-off or short-time) in accordance with a scheme under section 1 of the Superannuation Act 1972 or arrangements falling within section 177(3), and

    (b)   he commenced new, or renewed, employment.

(4)   The date on which the person's continuity of employment is broken by virtue of this section—

    (a)   if the employment was under a contract of employment, is the date which was the relevant date in relation to the payment mentioned in subsection (2)(a) or (3)(a), and

    (b)   if the employment was otherwise than under a contract of employment, is the date which would have been the relevant date in relation to the payment mentioned in subsection (2)(a) or (3)(a) had the employment been under a contract of employment.

(5)   For the purposes of this section a redundancy payment shall be treated as having been paid if—

    (a)   the whole of the payment has been paid to the employee by the employer,

    (b)   a tribunal has determined liability and found that the employer must pay part (but not all) of the redundancy payment and the employer has paid that part, or

    (c)   the Secretary of State has paid a sum to the employee in respect of the redundancy payment under section 167.

215   Employment abroad etc.

(1)   This Chapter applies to a period of employment—

    (a)   (subject to the following provisions of this section) even where during the period the employee was engaged in work wholly or mainly outside Great Britain, and

    (b)   even where the employee was excluded by or under this Act from any right conferred by this Act.

(2)   For the purposes of sections 155 and 162(1) a week of employment does not count in computing a period of employment if the employee—

    (a)   was employed outside Great Britain during the whole or part of the week, and

    (b)   was not during that week an employed earner for the purposes of the Social Security Contributions and Benefits Act 1992 in respect of whom a secondary Class 1 contribution was payable under that Act (whether or not the contribution was in fact paid).

(3)   Where by virtue of subsection (2) a week of employment does not count in computing a period of employment, the continuity of the period is not broken by reason only that the week does not count in computing the period; and the number of days which, for the purposes of section 211(3), fall within the intervening period is seven for each week within this subsection.

(4)   Any question arising under subsection (2) whether—

    (a)   a person was an employed earner for the purposes of the Social Security Contributions and Benefits Act 1992, or

    (b)   if so, whether a secondary Class 1 contribution was payable in respect of him under that Act,

shall be determined by an officer of the Commissioners of the Inland Revenue.

(5)   Part II of the Social Security Contributions (Transfer of Functions, etc.) Act 1999 (decisions and appeals) shall apply in relation to the determination of any issue by the Inland Revenue under subsection (4) as if it were a decision falling within section 8(1) of that Act.

(6)   Subsection (2) does not apply in relation to a person who is—

    (a)   employed as a master or seaman in a British ship, and

    (b)   ordinarily resident in Great Britain.

216   Industrial disputes

(1)   A week does not count under section 212 if during the week, or any part of the week, the employee takes part in a strike.

(2)   The continuity of an employee's period of employment is not broken by a week which does not count under this Chapter (whether or not by virtue only of subsection (1)) if during the week, or any part of the week, the employee takes part in a strike; and the number of days which, for the purposes of section 211(3), fall within the intervening period is the number of days between the last working day before the strike and the day on which work was resumed.

(3)   The continuity of an employee's period of employment is not broken by a week if during the week, or any part of the week, the employee is absent from work because of a lock-out by the employer; and the number of days which, for the purposes of section 211(3), fall within the intervening period is the number of days between the last working day before the lock-out and the day on which work was resumed.

218   Change of employer

(1)   Subject to the provisions of this section, this Chapter relates only to employment by the one employer.

(2)   If a trade or business, or an undertaking (whether or not established by or under an Act), is transferred from one person to another—

(a)   the period of employment of an employee in the trade or business or undertaking at the time of the transfer counts as a period of employment with the transferee, and

(b)   the transfer does not break the continuity of the period of employment.

(3)   If by or under an Act (whether public or local and whether passed before or after this Act) a contract of employment between any body corporate and an employee is modified and some other body corporate is substituted as the employer—

(a)   the employee's period of employment at the time when the modification takes effect counts as a period of employment with the second body corporate, and

(b)   the change of employer does not break the continuity of the period of employment.

(4)   If on the death of an employer the employee is taken into the employment of the personal representatives or trustees of the deceased—

(a)   the employee's period of employment at the time of the death counts as a period of employment with the employer's personal representatives or trustees, and

(b)   the death does not break the continuity of the period of employment.

(5)   If there is a change in the partners, personal representatives or trustees who employ any person—

(a)   the employee's period of employment at the time of the change counts as a period of employment with the partners, personal representatives or trustees after the change, and

(b)   the change does not break the continuity of the period of employment.

(6)   If an employee of an employer is taken into the employment of another employer who, at the time when the employee enters the second employer's employment, is an associated employer of the first employer—

(a)   the employee's period of employment at that time counts as a period of employment with the second employer, and

(b)   the change of employer does not break the continuity of the period of employment.

...

CHAPTER III
OTHER INTERPRETATION PROVISIONS

230   Employees, workers etc.

(1)   In this Act 'employee' means an individual who has entered into or works under (or, where the employment has ceased, worked under) a contract of employment.

(2)   In this Act 'contract of employment' means a contract of service or apprenticeship, whether express or implied, and (if it is express) whether oral or in writing.

(3)　In this Act 'worker' (except in the phrases 'shop worker' and 'betting worker') means an individual who has entered into or works under (or, where the employment has ceased, worked under)—

    (a)　a contract of employment, or

    (b)　any other contract, whether express or implied and (if it is express) whether oral or in writing, whereby the individual undertakes to do or perform personally any work or services for another party to the contract whose status is not by virtue of the contract that of a client or customer of any profession or business undertaking carried on by the individual;

and any reference to a worker's contract shall be construed accordingly.

(4)　In this Act 'employer', in relation to an employee or a worker, means the person by whom the employee or worker is (or, where the employment has ceased, was) employed.

(5)　In this Act 'employment'—

    (a)　in relation to an employee, means (except for the purposes of section 171) employment under a contract of employment, and

    (b)　in relation to a worker, means employment under his contract;

and 'employed' shall be construed accordingly.

(6)　This section has effect subject to sections 43K and 47B(3); and for the purposes of Part XIII so far as relating to Part IVA or section 47B, 'worker', 'worker's contract' and, in relation to a worker, 'employer', 'employment' and 'employed' have the extended meaning given by section 43K.

231　Associated employer

For the purposes of this Act any two employers shall be treated as associated if—

    (a)　one is a company of which the other (directly or indirectly) has control, or

    (b)　both are companies of which a third person (directly or indirectly) has control;

and 'associated employer' shall be construed accordingly.

232　Shop workers

(1)　In this Act 'shop worker' means an employee who, under his contract of employment, is or may be required to do shop work.

(2)　In this Act 'shop work' means work in or about a shop on a day on which the shop is open for the serving of customers.

(3)　Subject to subsection (4), in this Act 'shop' includes any premises where any retail trade or business is carried on.

(4)　Where premises are used mainly for purposes other than those of retail trade or business and would not (apart from subsection (3)) be regarded as a shop, only such part of the premises as—

    (a)　is used wholly or mainly for the purposes of retail trade or business, or

    (b)　is used both for the purposes of retail trade or business and for the purposes of wholesale trade and is used wholly or mainly for those two purposes considered together,

is to be regarded as a shop for the purposes of this Act.

(5)　In subsection (4)(b) 'wholesale trade' means the sale of goods for use or resale in the course of a business or the hire of goods for use in the course of a business.

(6)　In this section 'retail trade or business' includes—

    (a)　the business of a barber or hairdresser,

    (b)　the business of hiring goods otherwise than for use in the course of a trade or business, and

    (c)　retail sales by auction,

but does not include catering business or the sale at theatres and places of amusement of programmes, catalogues and similar items.

(7)　In subsection (6) 'catering business' means—

    (a)　the sale of meals, refreshments or intoxicating liquor alcohol (in Scotland, alcoholic liquor) for consumption on the premises on which they are sold, or

(b)   the sale of meals or refreshments prepared to order for immediate consumption off the premises;

and in paragraph (a) 'intoxicating liquor' has the same meaning as in the Licensing Act 1964 'alcohol' has the same meaning as in the Licensing Act 2003 and 'alcoholic liquor' the same meaning as in the Licensing (Scotland) Act 1976.

(8)   In this Act—

'notice period', in relation to an opted-out shop worker, has the meaning given by section 41(3),

'opted-out', in relation to a shop worker, shall be construed in accordance with section 41(1) and (2),

'opting-in notice', in relation to a shop worker, has the meaning given by section 36(6),

'opting-out notice', in relation to a shop worker, has the meaning given by section 40(2), and

'protected', in relation to a shop worker, shall be construed in accordance with section 36(1) to (5).

235   Other definitions

(1)   In this Act, except in so far as the context otherwise requires—

'act' and 'action' each includes omission and references to doing an act or taking action shall be construed accordingly,

'basic award of compensation for unfair dismissal' shall be construed in accordance with section 118,

'business' includes a trade or profession and includes any activity carried on by a body of persons (whether corporate or unincorporated),

'childbirth' means the birth of a living child or the birth of a child whether living or dead after twenty-four weeks of pregnancy,

'collective agreement' has the meaning given by section 178(1) and (2) of the Trade Union and Labour Relations (Consolidation) Act 1992,

'conciliation officer' means an officer designated by the Advisory, Conciliation and Arbitration Service under section 211 of that Act,

'dismissal procedures agreement' means an agreement in writing with respect to procedures relating to dismissal made by or on behalf of one or more independent trade unions and one or more employers or employers' associations,

'employers' association' has the same meaning as in the Trade Union and Labour Relations (Consolidation) Act 1992,

'expected week of childbirth' means the week, beginning with midnight between Saturday and Sunday, in which it is expected that childbirth will occur,

'guarantee payment' has the meaning given by section 28,

'independent trade union' means a trade union which—

(a)   is not under the domination or control of an employer or a group of employers or of one or more employers' associations, and

(b)   is not liable to interference by an employer or any such group or association (arising out of the provision of financial or material support or by any other means whatever) tending towards such control,

'job', in relation to an employee, means the nature of the work which he is employed to do in accordance with his contract and the capacity and place in which he is so employed,

'ordinary or additional paternity leave' means leave under any of sections 80A to 80BB,

'position', in relation to an employee, means the following matters taken as a whole—

(a)   his status as an employee,

(b)   the nature of his work, and

(c)   his terms and conditions of employment,

'protected disclosure' has the meaning given by section 43A,

'redundancy payment' has the meaning given by Part XI,

'relevant date' has the meaning given by sections 145 and 153,

'renewal' includes extension, and any reference to renewing a contract or a fixed term shall be construed accordingly, 'statutory provision' means a provision, whether of a general or a special nature, contained in, or in any document made or issued under, any Act, whether of a general or special nature,

'successor', in relation to the employer of an employee, means (subject to subsection (2)) a person who in consequence of a change occurring (whether by virtue of a sale or other disposition or by operation of law) in the ownership of the undertaking, or of the part of the undertaking, for the purposes of which the employee was employed, has become the owner of the undertaking or part,

'trade union' has the meaning given by section 1 of the Trade Union and Labour Relations (Consolidation) Act 1992,

'week'—

    (a)   in Chapter I of this Part means a week ending with Saturday, and

    (b)   otherwise, except in sections 80A, 80B and 86, means, in relation to an employee whose remuneration is calculated weekly by a week ending with a day other than Saturday, a week ending with that other day and, in relation to any other employee, a week ending with Saturday.

(2)   The definition of 'successor' in subsection (1) has effect (subject to the necessary modifications) in relation to a case where—

    (a)   the person by whom an undertaking or part of an undertaking is owned immediately before a change is one of the persons by whom (whether as partners, trustees or otherwise) it is owned immediately after the change, or

    (b)   the persons by whom an undertaking or part of an undertaking is owned immediately before a change (whether as partners, trustees or otherwise) include the persons by whom, or include one or more of the persons by whom, it is owned immediately after the change,

as it has effect where the previous owner and the new owner are wholly different persons.

(2A) For the purposes of this Act a contract of employment is a 'limited-term contract' if—

    (a)   the employment under the contract is not intended to be permanent, and

    (b)   provision is accordingly made in the contract for it to terminate by virtue of a limiting event.

(2B) In this Act, 'limiting event', in relation to a contract of employment means—

    (a)   in the case of a contract for a fixed-term, the expiry of the term,

    (b)   in the case of a contract made in contemplation of the performance of a specific task, the performance of the task, and

    (c)   in the case of a contract which provides for its termination on the occurrence of an event (or the failure of an event to occur), the occurrence of the event (or the failure of the event to occur).

(3)   References in this Act to redundancy, dismissal by reason of redundancy and similar expressions shall be construed in accordance with section 139.

(4)   In sections 136(2), 154 and 216(3) and paragraph 14 of Schedule 2 'lock-out' means—

    (a)   the closing of a place of employment,

    (b)   the suspension of work, or

    (c)   the refusal by an employer to continue to employ any number of persons employed by him in consequence of a dispute,

done with a view to compelling persons employed by the employer, or to aid another employer in compelling persons employed by him, to accept terms or conditions of or affecting employment.

(5)   In sections 91(2), 140(2) and (3), 143(1), 144(2) and (3), 154 and 216(1) and (2) and paragraph 14 of Schedule 2 'strike' means—

    (a)   the cessation of work by a body of employed persons acting in combination, or

    (b)   a concerted refusal, or a refusal under a common understanding, of any number of employed persons to continue to work for an employer in consequence of a dispute,

done as a means of compelling their employer or any employed person or body of employed persons, or to aid other employees in compelling their employer or any employed person or body of employed persons, to accept or not to accept terms or conditions of or affecting employment.

NATIONAL MINIMUM WAGE ACT 1998
(1998, c. 39)

Entitlement to the national minimum wage

1 **Workers to be paid at least the national minimum wage**

(1) A person who qualifies for the national minimum wage shall be remunerated by his employer in respect of his work in any pay reference period at a rate which is not less than the national minimum wage.

(2) A person qualifies for the national minimum wage if he is an individual who—

    (a) is a worker;

    (b) is working, or ordinarily works, in the United Kingdom under his contract; and

    (c) has ceased to be of compulsory school age.

(3) The national minimum wage shall be such single hourly rate as the Secretary of State may from time to time prescribe.

(4) For the purposes of this Act a 'pay reference period' is such period as the Secretary of State may prescribe for the purpose.

(5) Subsections (1) to (4) above are subject to the following provisions of this Act.

Regulations relating to the national minimum wage

2 **Determination of hourly rate of remuneration**

(1) The Secretary of State may by regulations make provision for determining what is the hourly rate at which a person is to be regarded for the purposes of this Act as remunerated by his employer in respect of his work in any pay reference period.

(2) The regulations may make provision for determining the hourly rate in cases where—

    (a) the remuneration, to the extent that it is at a periodic rate, is at a single rate;

    (b) the remuneration is, in whole or in part, at different rates applicable at different times or in different circumstances;

    (c) the remuneration is, in whole or in part, otherwise than at a periodic rate or rates;

    (d) the remuneration consists, in whole or in part, of benefits in kind.

(3) The regulations may make provision with respect to—

    (a) circumstances in which, times at which, or the time for which, a person is to be treated as, or as not, working, and the extent to which a person is to be so treated;

    (b) the treatment of periods of paid or unpaid absence from, or lack of, work and of remuneration in respect of such periods.

(4) The provision that may be made by virtue of paragraph (a) of subsection (3) above includes provision for or in connection with—

    (a) treating a person as, or as not, working for a maximum or minimum time, or for a proportion of the time, in any period;

    (b) determining any matter to which that paragraph relates by reference to the terms of an agreement.

(5) The regulations may make provision with respect to—

    (a) what is to be treated as, or as not, forming part of a person's remuneration, and the extent to which it is to be so treated;

    (b) the valuation of benefits in kind;

    (c) the treatment of deductions from earnings;

    (d) the treatment of any charges or expenses which a person is required to bear.

(6) The regulations may make provision with respect to—

    (a) the attribution to a period, or the apportionment between two or more periods, of the whole or any part of any remuneration or work, whether or not the remuneration is received or the work is done within the period or periods in question;

    (b) the aggregation of the whole or any part of the remuneration for different periods;

    (c) the time at which remuneration is to be treated as received or accruing.

(7) Subsections (2) to (6) above are without prejudice to the generality of subsection (1) above.

(8) No provision shall be made under this section which treats the same circumstances differently in relation to—
  (a)   different areas;
  (b)   different sectors of employment;
  (c)   undertakings of different sizes;
  (d)   persons of different ages; or
  (c)   persons of different occupations.

3   Exclusion of, and modifications for, certain classes of person

(1)   This section applies to persons who have not attained the age of 26.

(1A) This section also applies to persons who have attained the age of 26 who are—
  (a)   within the first six months after the commencement of their employment with an employer by whom they have not previously been employed;
  (b)   participating in a scheme under which shelter is provided in return for work;
  (c)   participating in a scheme designed to provide training, work experience or temporary work;
  (d)   participating in a scheme to assist in the seeking or obtaining of work;
  (e)   undertaking a course of higher education requiring attendance for a period of work experience; or
  (f)   undertaking a course of further education requiring attendance for a period of work experience.

(2)   The Secretary of State may by regulations make provision in relation to any of the persons to whom this section applies—
  (a)   preventing them being persons who qualify for the national minimum wage; or
  (b)   prescribing an hourly rate for the national minimum wage other than the single hourly rate for the time being prescribed under section 1(3) above.

(3)   No provision shall be made under subsection (2) above which treats persons differently in relation to—
  (a)   different areas;
  (b)   different sectors of employment;
  (c)   undertakings of different sizes; or
  (d)   different occupations.

(4)   If any description of persons who have attained the age of 26 is added by regulations under section 4 below to the descriptions of person to whom this section applies, no provision shall be made under subsection (2) above which treats persons of that description differently in relation to different ages over 26.

4   Power to add to the persons to whom section 3 applies

(1)   The Secretary of State may by regulations amend section 3 above by adding descriptions of persons who have attained the age of 26 to the descriptions of person to whom that section applies.

(2)   No amendment shall be made under subsection (1) above which treats persons differently in relation to—
  (a)   different areas;
  (b)   different sectors of employment;
  (c)   undertakings of different sizes;
  (d)   different ages over 26; or
  (e)   different occupations.

The Low Pay Commission

5   The first regulations: referral to the Low Pay Commission

(1)   Before making the first regulations under section 1(3) or (4) or 2 above, the Secretary of State shall refer the matters specified in subsection (2) below to the Low Pay Commission for their consideration.

(2)   Those matters are—

(a)   what single hourly rate should be prescribed under section 1(3) above as the national minimum wage;

(b)   what period or periods should be prescribed under section 1(4) above;

(c)   what method or methods should be used for determining under section 2 above the hourly rate at which a person is to be regarded as remunerated for the purposes of this Act;

(d)   whether any, and if so what, provision should be made under section 3 above; and

(e)   whether any, and if so what, descriptions of person should be added to the descriptions of person to whom section 3 above applies and what provision should be made under that section in relation to persons of those descriptions.

(3) Where matters are referred to the Low Pay Commission under subsection (1) above, the Commission shall, after considering those matters, make a report to the Prime Minister and the Secretary of State which shall contain the Commission's recommendations about each of those matters.

(4) If, following the report of the Low Pay Commission under subsection (3) above, the Secretary of State decides—

(a)   not to make any regulations implementing the Commission's recommendations, or

(b)   to make regulations implementing only some of the Commission's recommendations, or

(c)   to prescribe under section 1(3) above a single hourly rate which is different from the rate recommended by the Commission, or

(d)   to make regulations which in some other respect differ from the recommendations of the Commission, or

(e)   to make regulations which do not relate to a recommendation of the Commission,

the Secretary of State shall lay a report before each House of Parliament containing a statement of the reasons for the decision.

(5) If the Low Pay Commission fail to make their report under subsection (3) above within the time allowed for doing so under section 7 below, any power of the Secretary of State to make regulations under this Act shall be exercisable as if subsection (1) above had not been enacted.

6   Referral of matters to the Low Pay Commission at any time

(1) The Secretary of State may at any time refer to the Low Pay Commission such matters relating to this Act as the Secretary of State thinks fit.

(2) Where matters are referred to the Low Pay Commission under subsection (1) above, the Commission shall, after considering those matters, make a report to the Prime Minister and the Secretary of State which shall contain the Commission's recommendations about each of those matters.

(3) If on a referral under this section—

(a)   the Secretary of State seeks the opinion of the Low Pay Commission on a matter falling within section 5(2) above,

(b)   the Commission's report under subsection (2) above contains recommendations in relation to that matter, and

(c)   implementation of any of those recommendations involves the exercise of any power to make regulations under sections 1 to 4 above,

subsection (4) of section 5 above shall apply in relation to the report, so far as relating to the recommendations falling within paragraph (c) above, as it applies in relation to a report under subsection (3) of that section.

(4) If on a referral under this section—

(a)   the Secretary of State seeks the opinion of the Low Pay Commission on any matter falling within section 5(2) above,but

(b)   the Commission fail to make their report under subsection (2) above within the time allowed under section 7 below,

the Secretary of State may make regulations under sections 1 to 4 above as if the opinion of the Commission had not been sought in relation to that matter.

7   Referrals to, and reports of, the Low Pay Commission: supplementary

(1)   This section applies where matters are referred to the Low Pay Commission under section 5 or 6 above.

(2)   The Secretary of State may by notice require the Low Pay Commission to make their report within such time as may be specified in the notice.

(3)   The time allowed to the Low Pay Commission for making their report may from time to time be extended by further notice given to them by the Secretary of State.

(4)   Before arriving at the recommendations to be included in their report, the Low Pay Commission shall consult—
   (a)   such organisations representative of employers as they think fit;
   (b)   such organisations representative of workers as they think fit; and
   (c)   if they think fit, any other body or person.

(5)   In considering what recommendations to include in their report, the Low Pay Commission—
   (a)   shall have regard to the effect of this Act on the economy of the United Kingdom as a whole and on competitiveness; and
   (b)   shall take into account any additional factors which the Secretary of State specifies in referring the matters to them.

(6)   The report of the Low Pay Commission must—
   (a)   identify the members of the Commission making the report;
   (b)   explain the procedures adopted in respect of consultation, the taking of evidence and the receiving of representations;
   (c)   set out the reasons for their recommendations; and
   (d)   if the Secretary of State has specified any additional factor to be taken into account under subsection (5)(b) above, state that they have taken that factor into account in making their recommendations.

(7)   The Secretary of State shall—
   (a)   lay a copy of any report of the Low Pay Commission before each House of Parliament; and
   (b)   arrange for the report to be published.

(8)   In this section—
   'recommendations' means the recommendations required to be contained in a report under section 5(3) or 6(2) above, as the case may be;
   'report' means the report which the Low Pay Commission are required to make under section 5(3) or 6(2) above, as the case may be, on the matters referred to them as mentioned in subsection (1) above.

Enforcement

17   Non-compliance: worker entitled to additional remuneration

(1)   If a worker who qualifies for the national minimum wage is remunerated for any pay reference period by his employer at a rate which is less than the national minimum wage, the worker shall be taken to be entitled under his contract to be paid, as additional remuneration in respect of that period, the amount described in subsection (2) below.

(2)   That amount is the difference between—
   (a)   the relevant remuneration received by the worker for the pay reference period; and
   (b)   the relevant remuneration which the worker would have received for that period had he been remunerated by the employer at a rate equal to the national minimum wage.

(3)   In subsection (2) above, 'relevant remuneration' means remuneration which falls to be brought into account for the purposes of regulations under section 2 above.

18   Enforcement in the case of special classes of worker

(1)   If the persons who are the worker and the employer for the purposes of section 17 above would not (apart from this section) fall to be regarded as the worker and the employer for the purposes of—
   (a)   Part II of the Employment Rights Act 1996 (protection of wages), or

(b)   in relation to Northern Ireland, Part IV of the Employment Rights (Northern Ireland) Order 1996,

they shall be so regarded for the purposes of the application of that Part in relation to the entitlement conferred by that section.

(2)   In the application by virtue of subsection (1) above of—

(a)   Part II of the Employment Rights Act 1996, or

(b)   Part IV of the Employment Rights (Northern Ireland) Order 1996,

in a case where there is or was, for the purposes of that Part, no worker's contract between the persons who are the worker and the employer for the purposes of section 17 above, it shall be assumed that there is or, as the case may be, was such a contract.

(3)   For the purpose of enabling the amount described as additional remuneration in subsection (1) of section 17 above to be recovered in civil proceedings on a claim in contract in a case where in fact there is or was no worker's contract between the persons who are the worker and the employer for the purposes of that section, it shall be assumed for the purpose of any civil proceedings, so far as relating to that amount, that there is or, as the case may be, was such a contract.

19   Power of officer to issue enforcement notice

(1)   If an officer acting for the purposes of this Act is of the opinion that a worker who qualifies for the national minimum wage has not been remunerated for any pay reference period by his employer at a rate at least equal to the national minimum wage, the officer may serve a notice (an 'enforcement notice') on the employer requiring the employer to remunerate the worker for pay reference periods ending on or after the date of the notice at a rate equal to the national minimum wage.

(2)   An enforcement notice may also require the employer to pay to the worker within such time as may be specified in the notice the sum due to the worker under section 17 above in respect of the employer's previous failure to remunerate the worker at a rate at least equal to the national minimum wage.

(2A) If an officer acting for the purposes of this Act is of the opinion that a worker who has at any time qualified for the national minimum wage has not been remunerated for any pay reference period (whether ending before or after the coming into force of this subsection) by his employer at a rate at least equal to the national minimum wage, the officer may serve on the employer an enforcement notice which imposes a requirement under subsection (2) above in relation to the worker, whether or not a requirement under subsection (1) above is, or may be, imposed in relation to that worker (or any other worker to whom the notice relates).

(2B) An enforcement notice may not impose a requirement under subsection (2) above in respect of any pay reference period ending more than 6 years before the date on which the notice is served.

(2C) Where an enforcement notice imposes a requirement under subsection (2) above, the amount specified in the notice as the sum due to the worker under section 17 above need not include any sum so due to him in respect of any very recent pay reference period (although the amount so specified may include any such sum).

(2D) In subsection (2C) above a 'very recent' pay reference period means a pay reference period ending less than 3 months before the date on which the notice is served.

(3)   An enforcement notice may relate to more than one worker (and, where it does so, may be so framed as to relate to workers specified in the notice or to workers of a description so specified).

(4)   A person on whom an enforcement notice is served may appeal against the notice before the end of the period of four weeks following the date of service of the notice.

(5)   An appeal under subsection (4) above lies to an employment tribunal.

(6)   On an appeal under subsection (4) above, the employment tribunal shall dismiss the appeal unless it is established—

(a)   that, in the case of the worker or workers to whom the enforcement notice relates, the facts are such that an officer who was aware of them would have had no reason to serve any enforcement notice on the appellant; or

(b)   where the enforcement notice relates to two or more workers, that the facts are such that an officer who was aware of them would have had no reason to include some of the workers in any enforcement notice served on the appellant; or

(c)   where the enforcement notice imposes a requirement under subsection (2) above in relation to a worker,—

    (i)   that no sum was due to the worker under section 17 above; or

    (ii)   that the amount specified in the notice as the sum due to the worker under that section is too great; or

    (iii)   that the notice contravenes subsection (2B) above;

and in this subsection any reference to a worker includes a reference to a person whom the enforcement notice purports to treat as a worker.

(7)   Where an appeal is allowed by virtue of paragraph (a) of subsection (6) above, the employment tribunal shall rescind the enforcement notice.

(8)   If, in a case where subsection (7) above does not apply, an appeal is allowed by virtue of paragraph (b) or (c) of subsection (6) above—

(a)   the employment tribunal shall rectify the enforcement notice; and

(b)   the enforcement notice shall have effect as if it had originally been served as so rectified.

(9)   The powers of an employment tribunal in allowing an appeal in a case where subsection (8) above applies shall include power to rectify, as the tribunal may consider appropriate in consequence of its decision on the appeal, any penalty notice which has been served under section 21 below in respect of the enforcement notice.

(10)   Where a penalty notice is rectified under subsection (9) above, it shall have effect as if it had originally been served as so rectified.

20   Non-compliance: power of officer to sue on behalf of worker

(1)   If an enforcement notice is not complied with in whole or in part, an officer acting for the purposes of this Act may, on behalf of any worker to whom the notice relates,—

(a)   present a complaint under section 23(1)(a) of the Employment Rights Act 1996 (deductions from worker's wages in contravention of section 13 of that Act) to an employment tribunal in respect of any sums due to the worker by virtue of section 17 above; or

(b)   in relation to Northern Ireland, present a complaint under Article 55(1)(a) of the Employment Rights (Northern Ireland) Order 1996 (deductions from worker's wages in contravention of Article 45 of that Order) to an industrial tribunal in respect of any sums due to the worker by virtue of section 17 above; or

(c)   commence other civil proceedings for the recovery, on a claim in contract, of any sums due to the worker by virtue of section 17 above.

(2)   The powers conferred by subsection (1) above for the recovery of sums due from an employer to a worker shall not be in derogation of any right which the worker may have to recover such sums by civil proceedings.

21   Financial penalty for non-compliance

(1)   If an officer acting for the purposes of this Act is satisfied that a person on whom an enforcement notice has been served has failed, in whole or in part, to comply with the notice, the officer may serve on that person a notice (a 'penalty notice') requiring the person to pay a financial penalty to the Secretary of State.

(2)   A penalty notice must state—

(a)   the amount of the financial penalty;

(b)   the time within which the financial penalty is to be paid (which must not be less than four weeks from the date of service of the notice);

(c)   the period to which the financial penalty relates;

(d)   the respects in which the officer is of the opinion that the enforcement notice has not been complied with; and

(e)   the calculation of the amount of the financial penalty.

(3) The amount of the financial penalty shall be calculated at a rate equal to twice the hourly amount of she national minimum wage (as in force at the date of the penalty notice) in respect of each worker to whom the failure to comply relates for each day worker.

(4) The Secretary of State may by regulations from time to time amend the multiplier for the time being specified in subsection (3) above in relation to the hourly amount of the national minimum wage.

(5) A financial penalty under this section—

    (a) in England and Wales, shall be recoverable, if a county court so orders, by execution issued from the county court or otherwise as if it were payable under an order of that court;

    (b) in Scotland, may be enforced in the same manner as an extract registered decree arbitral bearing a warrant for execution issued by the sheriff court of any sheriffdom in Scotland;

    (c) in Northern Ireland, shall be recoverable, if the county court so orders, as if it were payable under an order of that court.

(6) Where a person has appealed under subsection (4) of section 19 above against an enforcement notice and the appeal has not been withdrawn or finally determined, then, notwithstanding the appeal—

    (a) the enforcement notice shall have effect; and

    (b) an officer may serve a penalty notice in respect of the enforcement notice.

(7) If, in a case falling within subsection (6) above, an officer serves a penalty notice in respect of the enforcement notice, the penalty notice—

    (a) shall not be enforceable until the appeal has been withdrawn or finally determined; and

    (b) shall be of no effect if the enforcement notice is rescinded as a result of the appeal; but

    (c) subject to paragraph (b) above and section 22(4) and (6)(a) below, as from the withdrawal or final determination of the appeal shall be enforceable as if paragraph (a) above had not had effect.

(8) Any sums received by the Secretary of State by virtue of this section shall be paid into the Consolidated Fund.

22   Appeals against penalty notices

(1) A person on whom a penalty notice is served may appeal against the notice before the end of the period of four weeks following the date of service of the notice.

(2) An appeal under subsection (1) above lies to an employment tribunal.

(3) On an appeal under subsection (1) above, the employment tribunal shall dismiss the appeal unless it is shown—

    (a) that, in the case of each of the allegations of failure to comply with the enforcement notice, the facts are such that an officer who was aware of them would have had no reason to serve any penalty notice on the appellant; or

    (b) that the amount of the financial penalty is too great because the penalty notice is incorrect in some of the particulars which affect that amount; or

    (c) that the amount of the financial penalty is too great because its calculation is incorrect;

    and for the purposes of any appeal relating to a penalty notice, the enforcement notice in question shall (subject to rescission or rectification on any appeal brought under section 19 above) be taken to be correct.

(4) Where an appeal is allowed by virtue of paragraph (a) of subsection (3) above, the employment tribunal shall rescind the penalty notice.

(5) If, in a case where subsection (4) above does not apply, an appeal is allowed by virtue of paragraph (b) or (c) of subsection (3) above—

    (a) the employment tribunal shall rectify the penalty notice; and

    (b) the penalty notice shall have effect as if it had originally been served as so rectified.

(6) Where a person has appealed under subsection (1) above against a penalty notice and the appeal has not been withdrawn or finally determined, the penalty notice—

    (a) shall not be enforceable until the appeal has been withdrawn or finally determined; but

(b)   subject to subsection (4) above and section 21(7)(a) and (b) above, as from the withdrawal or final determination of the appeal shall be enforceable as if paragraph (a) above had not had effect.

Rights not to suffer unfair dismissal or other detriment

23   The right not to suffer detriment

(1)   A worker has the right not to be subjected to any detriment by any act. or any deliberate failure to act by his employer, cone on the ground that—

(a)   any action was taken, or was proposed to be taken, by or on behalf of the worker with a view to enforcing, or otherwise securing the benefit of, a right of the worker's to which this section applies; or

(b)   the employer was prosecuted for an offence under section 31 below as a result of action taken by or on behalf of the worker for the purpose of enforcing, or otherwise securing the benefit of, a right of the worker's to which this section applies; or

(c)   the worker qualifies, or will or might qualify, for the national minimum wage or for a particular rate of national minimum wage.

(2)   It is immaterial for the purposes of paragraph (a) or (b) of subsection (1) above—

(a)   whether or not the worker has the right, or

(b)   whether or not the right has been infringed,

but, for that subsection to apply, the claim to the right and, if applicable, the claim that it has been infringed must be made in good faith.

(3)   The following are the rights to which this section applies—

(a)   any right conferred by, or by virtue of, any provision of this Act for which the remedy for its infringement is by way of a complaint to an employment tribunal; and

(b)   any right conferred by section 17 above.

(4)   This section does not apply where the detriment in question amounts to dismissal within the meaning of—

(a)   Part X of the Employment Rights Act 1996 (unfair dismissal), or

(b)   Part XI of the Employment Rights (Northern Ireland) Order 1996 (corresponding provision for Northern Ireland),

except where in relation to Northern Ireland the person in question is dismissed in circumstances in which, by virtue of Article 240 of that Order (fixed term contracts), Part XI does not apply to the dismissal.

24   Enforcement of the right

(1)   A worker may present a complaint to an employment tribunal that he has been subjected to a detriment in contravention of section 23 above.

(2)   Subject to the following provisions of this section, the provisions of—

(a)   sections 48(2) to (4) and 49 of the Employment Rights Act 1996 (complaints to employment tribunals and remedies), or

(b)   in relation to Northern Ireland, Articles 71(2) to (4) and 72 of the Employment Rights (Northern Ireland) Order 1996 (complaints to industrial tribunals and remedies),

shall apply in relation to a complaint under this section as they apply in relation to a complaint under section 48 of that Act or Article 71 of that Order (as the case may be), but taking references in those provisions to the employer as references to the employer within the meaning of section 23(1) above.

(3)   Where—

(a)   the detriment to which the worker is subjected is the termination of his worker's contract, but

(b)   that contract is not a contract of employment,

any compensation awarded under section 49 of the Employment Rights Act 1996 or Article 72 of the Employment Rights (Northern Ireland) Order 1996 by virtue of subsection (2) above must not exceed the limit specified in subsection (4) below.

(4)   The limit mentioned in subsection (3) above is the total of—

    (a)   the sum which would he the basic award for unfair dismissal, calculated in accordance with section 119 of the Employment Rights Act 1996 or Article 153 of the Employment Rights (Northern Ireland) Order 1996 (as the case may be), if the worker had been an employee and the contract terminated had been a contract of employment; and

    (b)   the sum for the time being specified in section 124(1) of that Act or Article 158(1) of that Order (as the case may be) which is the limit for a compensatory award to a person calculated in accordance with section 123 of that Act or Article 157 of that Order (as the case may be).

(5)   Where the worker has been working under arrangements which do not fall to be regarded as a worker's contract for the purposes of—

    (a)   the Employment Rights Act 1996, or

    (b)   in relation to Northern Ireland, the Employment Rights (Northern Ireland) Order 1996,

he shall be treated for the purposes of subsections (3) and (4) above as if any arrangements under which he has been working constituted a worker's contract falling within section 230(3)(b) of that Act or Article 3(3)(b) of that Order (as the case may be).

28   Reversal of burden of proof

(1)   Where in any civil proceedings any question arises as to whether an individual qualifies or qualified at any time for the national minimum wage, it shall be presumed that the individual qualifies or, as the case may be, qualified at that time for the national minimum wage unless the contrary is established.

(2)   Where—

    (a)   a complaint is made—

        (i)   to an employment tribunal under section 23(1)(a) of the Employment Rights Act 1996 (unauthorised deductions from wages), or

        (ii)   to an industrial tribunal under Article 55(1)(a) of the Employment Rights (Northern Ireland) Order 1996, and

    (b)   the complaint relates in whole or in part to the deduction of the amount described as additional remuneration in section 17(1) above,

it shall be presumed for the purposes of the complaint, so far as relating to the deduction of that amount, that the worker in question was remunerated at a rate less than the national minimum wage unless the contrary is established.

(3)   Where in any civil proceedings a person seeks to recover on a claim in contract the amount described as additional remuneration in section 17(1) above, it shall be presumed for the purposes of the proceedings, so far as relating to that amount, that the worker in question was remunerated at a rate less than the national minimum wage unless the contrary is established.

Offences

31   Offences

(1)   If the employer of a worker who qualifies for the national minimum wage refuses or wilfully neglects to remunerate the worker for any pay reference period at a rate which is at least equal to the national minimum wage, that employer is guilty of an offence.

(2)   If a person who is required to keep or preserve any record in accordance with regulations under section 9 above fails to do so, that person is guilty of an offence.

(3)   If a person makes, or knowingly causes or allows to be made, in a record required to be kept in accordance with regulations under section 9 above any entry which he knows to be false in a material particular, that person is guilty of an offence.

(4)   If a person, for purposes connected with the provisions of this Act, produces or furnishes, or knowingly causes or allows to be produced or furnished, any record or information which he knows to be false in a material particular, that person is guilty of an offence.

(5)   If a person—

    (a)   intentionally delays or obstructs an officer acting for the purposes of this Act in the exercise of any power conferred by this Act, or

    (b)   refuses or neglects to answer any question, furnish any information or produce any document when required to do so under section 14(1) above, that person is guilty of an offence.

(6)   Where the commission by any person of an offence under subsection (1) or (2) above is due to the act or default of some other person, that other person is also guilty of the offence.

(7)   A person may be charged with and convicted of an offence by virtue of subsection (6) above whether or not proceedings are taken against any other person.

(8)   In any proceedings for an offence under subsection (1) or (2) above it shall be a defence for the person charged to prove that he exercised all due diligence and took all reasonable precautions to secure that the provisions of this Act, and of any relevant regulations made under it, were complied with by himself and by any person under his control.

(9)   A person guilty of an offence under this section shall be liable on summary conviction to a fine not exceeding level 5 on the standard scale.

32   Offences by bodies corporate etc.

(1)   This section applies to any offence under this Act.

(2)   If an offence committed by a body corporate is proved—

(a)   to have been committed with the consent or connivance of an officer of the body, or

(b)   to be attributable to any neglect on the part of such an officer,

the officer as well as the body corporate is guilty of the offence and liable to be proceeded against and punished accordingly.

(3)   In subsection (2) above 'officer', in relation to a body corporate, means a director, manager, secretary or other similar officer of the body, or a person purporting to act in any such capacity.

(4)   If the affairs of a body corporate are managed by its members, subsection (2) above applies in relation to the acts and defaults of a member in connection with his functions of management as if he were a director of the body corporate.

(5)   If an offence committed by a partnership in Scotland is proved—

(a)   to have been committed with the consent or connivance of a partner, or

(b)   to be attributable to any neglect on the part of a partner,

the partner as well as the partnership is guilty of the offence and liable to be proceeded against and punished accordingly.

(6)   In subsection (5) above, 'partner' includes a person purporting to act as a partner.

33   Proceedings for offences

(1)   The persons who may conduct proceedings for an offence under this Act—

(a)   in England and Wales, before a magistrates' court, or

(b)   in Northern Ireland, before a court of summary jurisdiction,

shall include any person authorised for the purpose by the Secretary of State even if that person is not a barrister or solicitor.

(2)   In England and Wales or Northern Ireland, proceedings for an offence under this Act may be begun at any time within whichever of the following periods expires the later, that is to say—

(a)   the period of 6 months from the date on which evidence, sufficient in the opinion of the Secretary of State to justify a prosecution for the offence, comes to the knowledge of the Secretary of State, or

(b)   the period of 12 months from the commission of the offence,

notwithstanding anything in any other enactment (including an enactment comprised in Northern Ireland legislation) or in any instrument made under an enactment.

(3)   For the purposes of subsection (2) above, a certificate purporting to be signed by or on behalf of the Secretary of State as to the date on which such evidence as is mentioned in paragraph (a) of that subsection came to the knowledge of the Secretary of State shall be conclusive evidence of that date.

(4)   In Scotland, proceedings for an offence under this Act may, notwithstanding anything in section 136 of the Criminal Procedure (Scotland) Act 1995, be commenced at any time within—

(a)   the period of 6 months from the date on which evidence, sufficient in the opinion of the procurator fiscal to justify proceedings, comes to the knowledge of the procurator fiscal, or

(b)   the period of 12 months from the commission of the offence,
whichever period expires the later.
(5)   For the purposes of subsection (4) above—
　　(a)   a certificate purporting to be signed by or on behalf of the procurator fiscal as to the date
　　　　on which such evidence as is mentioned above came to the knowledge of the procurator
　　　　fiscal shall be conclusive evidence of that date; and
　　(b)   subsection (3) of section 136 of the said Act of 1995 (date of commencement of
　　　　proceedings) shall have effect as it has effect for the purposes of that section.

Special classes of person

34   Agency workers who are not otherwise 'workers'
(1)   This section applies in any case where an individual ('the agency worker')—
　　(a)   is supplied by a person ('the agent') to do work for another ('the principal') under a
　　　　contract or other arrangements made between the agent and the principal; but
　　(b)   is not, as respects that work, a worker, because of the absence of a worker's contract
　　　　between the individual and the agent or the principal; and
　　(c)   is not a party to a contract under which he undertakes to do the work for another party
　　　　to the contract whose status is, by virtue of the contract, that of a client or customer of
　　　　any profession or business undertaking carried on by the individual.
(2)   In a case where this section applies, the other provisions of this Act shall have effect as if there
were a worker's contract for the doing of the work by the agency worker made between the
agency worker and—
　　(a)   whichever of the agent and the principal is responsible for paying the agency worker in
　　　　respect of the work; or
　　(b)   if neither the agent nor the principal is so responsible, whichever of them pays the
　　　　agency worker in respect of the work.

35   Home workers who are not otherwise 'workers'
(1)   In determining for the purposes of this Act whether a home worker is or is not a worker,
section 54(3)(b) below shall have effect as if for the word 'personally' there were substituted
'(whether personally or otherwise)'.
(2)   In this section 'home worker' means an individual who contracts with a person, for the
purposes of that person's business, for the execution of work to be done in a place not under
the control or management of that person.

Extensions

41   Power to apply Act to individuals who are not otherwise 'workers'
The Secretary of State may by regulations make provision for this Act to apply, with or without
modifications, as if—
(a)   any individual of a prescribed description who would not otherwise be a worker for the
purposes of this Act were a worker for those purposes;
(b)   there were in the case of any such individual a worker's contract of a prescribed description
under which the individual works; and
(c)   a person of a prescribed description were the employer under that contract.

Supplementary

54   Meaning of 'worker', 'employee' etc.
(1)   In this Act 'employee' means an individual who has entered into or works under (or, where the
employment has ceased, worked under) a contract of employment.
(2)   In this Act 'contract of employment' means a contract of service or apprenticeship, whether
express or implied, and (if it is express) whether oral or in writing.
(3)   In this Act 'worker' (except in the phrases 'agency worker' and 'home worker') means an
individual who has entered into or works under (or, where the employment has ceased, worked
under)—

(a)   a contract of employment; or

(b)   any other contract, whether express or implied and (if it is express) whether oral or in writing, whereby the individual undertakes to do or perform personally any work or services for another party to the contract whose status is not by virtue of the contract that of a client or customer of any profession or business undertaking carried on by the individual;

and any reference to a worker's contract shall be construed accordingly.

(4)   In this Act 'employer', in relation to an employee or a worker, means the person by whom the employee or worker is (or, where the employment has ceased, was) employed.

(5)   In this Act 'employment'—

(a)   in relation to an employee, means employment under a contract of employment; and

(b)   in relation to a worker, means employment under his contract;

and 'employed' shall be construed accordingly.

EMPLOYMENT RELATIONS ACT 1999
(1999, c. 26)

Disciplinary and grievance hearings

10   Right to be accompanied

(1)   This section applies where a worker—

(a)   is required or invited by his employer to attend a disciplinary or grievance hearing, and

(b)   reasonably requests to be accompanied at the hearing.

(2A) Where this section applies, the employer must permit the worker to be accompanied at the hearing by one companion who—

(a)   is chosen by the worker; and

(b)   is within subsection (3).

(2B) The employer must permit the worker's companion to—

(a)   address the hearing in order to do any or all of the following—

(i)   put the worker's case;

(ii)   sum up that case;

(iii)   respond on the worker's behalf to any view expressed at the hearing;

(b)   confer with the worker during the hearing.

(2C) Subsection (2B) does not require the employer to permit the worker's companion to—

(a)   answer questions on behalf of the worker;

(b)   address the hearing if the worker indicates at it that he does not wish his companion to do so; or

(c)   use the powers conferred by that subsection in a way that prevents the employer from explaining his case or prevents any other person at the hearing from making his contribution to it.

(3)   A person is within this subsection if he is—

(a)   employed by a trade union of which he is an official within the meaning of section 1 and 119 of the Trade Union and Labour Relations (Consolidation) Act 1992,

(b)   an official of a trade union (within that meaning) whom the union has reasonably certified in writing as having experience of, or as having received training in, acting as a worker's companion at disciplinary or grievance hearings, or

(c)   another of the employer's workers.

(4)   If—

(a)   a worker has a right under this section to be accompanied at a hearing,

(b)   his chosen companion will not be available at the time proposed for the hearing by the employer, and

(c)   the worker proposes an alternative time which satisfies subsection (5),

the employer must postpone the hearing to the time proposed by the worker.

(5)   An alternative time must—

(a)   be reasonable, and

(b) fall before the end of the period of five working days beginning with the first working day after the day proposed by the employer.

(6) An employer shall permit a worker to take time off during working hours for the purpose of accompanying another of the employer's workers in accordance with a request under subsection (1)(b).

(7) Sections 168(3) and (4), 169 and 171 to 173 of the Trade Union and Labour Relations (Consolidation) Act 1992 (time off for carrying out trade union duties) shall apply in relation to subsection (6) above as they apply in relation to section 168(1) of that Act.

11 Complaint to employment tribunal

(1) A worker may present a complaint to an employment tribunal that his employer has failed, or threatened to fail, to comply with section 10(2A), (2B) or (4).

(2) A tribunal shall not consider a complaint under this section in relation to a failure or threat unless the complaint is presented—

(a) before the end of the period of three months beginning with the date of the failure or threat, or

(b) within such further period as the tribunal considers reasonable in a case where it is satisfied that it was not reasonably practicable for the complaint to be presented before the end of that period of three months.

(3) Where a tribunal finds that a complaint under this section is well-founded it shall order the employer to pay compensation to the worker of an amount not exceeding two weeks' pay.

(4) Chapter II of Part XIV of the Employment Rights Act 1996 (calculation of a week's pay) shall apply for the purposes of subsection (3); and in applying that Chapter the calculation date shall be taken to be—

(a) in the case of a claim which is made in the course of a claim for unfair dismissal, the date on which the employer's notice of dismissal was given or, if there was no notice, the effective date of termination, and

(b) in any other case, the date on which the relevant hearing took place (or was to have taken place).

(5), (6) ...

12 Detriment and dismissal

(1) A worker has the right not to be subjected to any detriment by any act, or any deliberate failure to act, by his employer done on the ground that he—

(a) exercised or sought to exercise the right under section 10(2A), (2B) or (4), or

(b) accompanied or sought to accompany another worker (whether of the same employer or not) pursuant to a request under that section.

(2) Section 48 of the Employment Rights Act 1996 shall apply in relation to contraventions of subsection (1) above as it applies in relation to contraventions of certain sections of that Act.

(3) A worker who is dismissed shall be regarded for the purposes of Part X of the Employment Rights Act 1996 as unfairly dismissed if the reason (or, if more than one, the principal reason) for the dismissal is that he—

(a) exercised or sought to exercise the right under section 10(2) or (4), or

(b) accompanied or sought to accompany another worker (whether of the same employer or not) pursuant to a request under that section.

(4) Sections 108 and 109 of that Act (qualifying period of employment and upper age limit) shall not apply in relation to subsection (3) above.

(5) Sections 128 to 132 of that Act (interim relief) shall apply in relation to dismissal for the reason specified in subsection (3)(a) or (b) above as they apply in relation to dismissal for a reason specified in section 128(1)(b) of that Act.

(6) In the application of Chapter II of Part X of that Act in relation to subsection (3) above, a reference to an employee shall be taken as a reference to a worker.

(7) References in this section to a worker having accompanied or sought to accompany another worker include references to his having exercised or sought to exercise any of the powers conferred by section 10(2A) or (2B).

13   Interpretation

(1) In sections 10 to 12 and this section 'worker' means an individual who is—

    (a)   a worker within the meaning of section 230(3) of the Employment Rights Act 1996,

    (b)   an agency worker,

    (c)   a home worker,

    (d)   a person in Crown employment within the meaning of section 191 of that Act, other than a member of the naval, military, air or reserve forces of the Crown, or

    (e)   employed as a relevant member of the House of Lords staff or the House of Commons staff within the meaning of section 194(6) or 195(5) of that Act.

(2) In subsection (1) 'agency worker' means an individual who—

    (a)   is supplied by a person ('the agent') to do work for another ('the principal') by arrangement between the agent and the principal,

    (b)   is not a party to a worker's contract, within the meaning of section 230(3) of that Act, relating to that work, and

    (c)   is not a party to a contract relating to that work under which he undertakes to do the work for another party to the contract whose status is, by virtue of the contract, that of a client or customer of any professional or business undertaking carried on by the individual;

and, for the purposes of sections 10 to 12, both the agent and the principal are employers of an agency worker.

(3) In subsection (1) 'home worker' means an individual who—

    (a)   contracts with a person, for the purposes of the person's business, for the execution of work to be done in a place not under the person's control or management, and

    (b)   is not a party to a contract relating to that work under which the work is to be executed for another party to the contract whose status is, by virtue of the contract, that of a client or customer of any professional or business undertaking carried on by the individual;

and, for the purposes of sections 10 to 12, the person mentioned in paragraph (a) is the home worker's employer.

(4) For the purposes of section 10 a disciplinary hearing is a hearing which could result in—

    (a)   the administration of a formal warning to a worker by his employer,

    (b)   the taking of some other action in respect of a worker by his employer, or

    (c)   the confirmation of a warning issued or some other action taken.

(5) For the purposes of section 10 a grievance hearing is a hearing which concerns the performance of a duty by an employer in relation to a worker.

(6) For the purposes of section 10(5)(b) in its application to a part of Great Britain a working day is a day other than—

    (a)   a Saturday or a Sunday,

    (b)   Christmas Day or Good Friday, or

    (c)   a day which is a bank holiday under the Banking and Financial Dealings Act 1971 in that part of Great Britain.

14   Contracting out and conciliation

Sections 10 to 13 of this Act shall be treated as provisions of Part V of the Employment Rights Act 1996 for the purposes of—

    (a)   section 203(1), (2)(e) and (f), (3) and (4) of that Act (restrictions on contracting out), and

    (b)   section 18(1)(d) of the Employment Tribunals Act 1996 (conciliation).

15   National security employees

Sections 10 to 13 of this Act shall not apply in relation to a person employed for the purposes of—

     (a)   the Security Service,

     (b)   the Secret Intelligence Service, or

     (c)   the Government Communications Headquarters.

Other rights of individuals

23   **Power to confer rights on individuals**

(1)   This section applies to any right conferred on an individual against an employer (however defined) under or by virtue of any of the following—

     (a)   the Trade Union and Labour Relations (Consolidation) Act 1992;

     (b)   the Employment Rights Act 1996;

     (ba)   the Employment Act 2002;

     (c)   this Act;

     (d)   any instrument made under section 2(2) of the European Communities Act 1972.

(2)   The Secretary of State may by order make provision which has the effect of conferring any such right on individuals who are of a specified description.

(3)   the reference in subsection (2) to individuals includes a reference to individuals expressly excluded from exercising the right.

(4)   An order under this section may—

     (a)   provide that individuals are to be treated as parties to workers' contracts or contracts of employment;

     (b)   make provision as to who are to be regarded as the employers of individuals;

     (c)   make provision which has the effect of modifying the operation of any right as conferred on individuals by the order;

     (d)   include such consequential, incidental or supplementary provisions as the Secretary of State thinks fit.

...

EMPLOYMENT ACT 2002
(2002, c. 22)

30   **Contracts of employment**

(1)   Every contract of employment shall have effect to require the employer and employee to comply, in relation to any matter to which a statutory procedure applies, with the requirements of the procedure.

(2)   Subsection (1) shall have effect notwithstanding any agreement to the contrary, but does not affect so much of an agreement to follow a particular procedure as requires the employer or employee to comply with a requirement which is additional to, and not inconsistent with, the requirements of the statutory procedure.

(3)   The Secretary of State may for the purpose of this section by regulations make provision about the application of the statutory procedures.

(4)   In this section, 'contract of employment' has the same meaning as in the Employment Rights Act 1996.

31   **Non-completion of statutory procedure: adjustment of awards**

(1)   This section applies to proceedings before an employment tribunal relating to a claim under any of the jurisdictions listed in Schedule 3 by an employee.

(2)   If, in the case of proceedings to which this section applies, it appears to the employment tribunal that—

     (a)   the claim to which the proceedings relate concerns a matter to which one of the statutory procedures applies,

     (b)   the statutory procedure was not completed before the proceedings were begun, and

     (c)   the non-completion of the statutory procedure was wholly or mainly attributable to failure by the employee—

          (i)   to comply with a requirement of the procedure, or

        (ii)   to exercise a right of appeal under it,

it must, subject to subsection (4), reduce any award which it makes to the employee by 10 per cent, and may, if it considers it just and equitable in all the circumstances to do so, reduce it by a further amount, but not so as to make a total reduction of more than 50 per cent.

(3) If, in the case of proceedings to which this section applies, it appears to the employment tribunal that—

    (a)   the claim to which the proceedings relate concerns a matter to which one of the statutory procedures applies,

    (b)   the statutory procedure was not completed before the proceedings were begun, and

    (c)   the non-completion of the statutory procedure was wholly or mainly attributable to failure by the employer to comply with a requirement of the procedure,

it must, subject to subsection (4), increase any award which it makes to the employee by 10 per cent and may, if it considers it just and equitable in all the circumstances to do so, increase it by a further amount, but not so as to make a total increase of more than 50 per cent.

(4) The duty under subsection (2) or (3) to make a reduction or increase of 10 per cent does not apply if there are exceptional circumstances which would make a reduction or increase of that percentage unjust or inequitable, in which case the tribunal may make no reduction or increase or a reduction or increase of such lesser percentage as it considers just and equitable in all the circumstances.

(5) Where an award falls to be adjusted under this section and under section 38, the adjustment under this section shall be made before the adjustment under that section.

(6) The Secretary of State may for the purposes of this section by regulations—

    (a)   make provision about the application of the statutory procedures;

    (b)   make provision about when a statutory procedure is to be taken to be completed;

    (c)   make provision about what constitutes compliance with a requirement of a statutory procedure;

    (d)   make provision about circumstances in which a person is to be treated as not subject to, or as having complied with, such a requirement;

    (e)   make provision for a statutory procedure to have effect in such circumstances as may be specified by the regulations with such modifications as may be so specified;

    (f)   make provision about when an employee is required to exercise a right of appeal under a statutory procedure.

(7) The Secretary of State may by order—

    (a)   amend Schedule 3 for the purpose of—

        (i)   adding a jurisdiction to the list in that Schedule, or

        (ii)   removing a jurisdiction from that list;

    (b)   make provision, in relation to a jurisdiction listed in Schedule 3, for this section not to apply to proceedings relating to claims of a description specified in the order;

    (c)   make provision for this section to apply, with or without modifications, as if—

        (i)   any individual of a description specified in the order who would not otherwise be an employee for the purposes of this section were an employee for those purposes, and

        (ii)   a person of a description specified in the order were, in the case of any such individual, the individual's employer for those purposes.

32   Complaints about grievances

(1) This section applies to the jurisdictions listed in Schedule 4.

(2) An employee shall not present a complaint to an employment tribunal under a jurisdiction to which this section applies if—

    (a)   it concerns a matter in relation to which the requirement in paragraph 6 or 9 of Schedule 2 applies, and

    (b)   the requirement has not been complied with.

(3)   An employee shall not present a complaint to an employment tribunal under a jurisdiction to which this section applies if—

    (a)   it concerns a matter in relation to which the requirement in paragraph 6 or 9 of Schedule 2 has been complied with, and

    (b)   less than 28 days have passed since the day on which the requirement was complied with.

(4)   An employee shall not present a complaint to an employment tribunal under a jurisdiction to which this section applies if—

    (a)   it concerns a matter in relation to which the requirement in paragraph 6 or 9 of Schedule 2 has been complied with, and

    (b)   the day on which the requirement was complied with was more than one month after the end of the original time limit for making the complaint.

(5)   In such circumstances as the Secretary of State may specify by regulations, an employment tribunal may direct that subsection (4) shall not apply in relation to a particular matter.

(6)   An employment tribunal shall be prevented from considering a complaint presented in breach of subsections (2) to (4), but only if—

    (a)   the breach is apparent to the tribunal from the information supplied to it by the employee in connection with the bringing of the proceedings, or

    (b)   the tribunal is satisfied of the breach as a result of his employer raising the issue of compliance with those provisions in accordance with regulations under section 7 of the Employment Tribunals Act 1996 (employment tribunal procedure regulations).

(7)   The Secretary of State may for the purposes of this section by regulations—

    (a)   make provision about the application of the procedures set out in Part 2 of Schedule 2;

    (b)   make provision about what constitutes compliance with paragraph 6 or 9 of that Schedule;

    (c)   make provision about circumstances in which a person is to be treated as having complied with paragraph 6 or 9 of that Schedule;

    (d)   make provision for paragraph 6 or 9 of that Schedule to have effect in such circumstances as may be specified by the regulations with such modifications as may be so specified.

(8)   The Secretary of State may by order—

    (a)   amend, repeal or replace any of subsections (2) to (4);

    (b)   amend Schedule 4;

    (c)   make provision for this section to apply, with or without modifications, as if—

        (i)   any individual of a description specified in the order who would not otherwise be an employee for the purposes of this section were an employee for those purposes, and

        (ii)   a person of a description specified in the order were, in the case of any such individual, the individual's employer for those purposes.

(9)   Before making an order under subsection (8)(a), the Secretary of State must consult the Advisory, Conciliation and Arbitration Service.

(10) In its application to orders under subsection (8)(a), section 51(1)(b) includes power to amend this section.

38   Failure to give statement of employment particulars etc.

(1)   This section applies to proceedings before an employment tribunal relating to a claim by an employee under any of the jurisdictions listed in Schedule 5.

(2)   If in the case of proceedings to which this section applies—

    (a)   the employment tribunal finds in favour of the employee, but makes no award to him in respect of the claim to which the proceedings relate, and

    (b)   when the proceedings were begun the employer was in breach of his duty to the employee under section 1(1) or 4(1) of the Employment Rights Act 1996 (duty to give a written statement of initial employment particulars or of particulars of change), the tribunal must, subject to subsection (5), make an award of the minimum amount to be paid by the employer to the employee and may, if it considers it just and equitable in all the circumstances, award the higher amount instead.

(3) If in the case of proceedings to which this section applies—

(a) the employment tribunal makes an award to the employee in respect of the claim to which the proceedings relate, and

(b) when the proceedings were begun the employer was in breach of his duty to the employee under section 1(1) or 4(1) of the Employment Rights Act 1996,

the tribunal must, subject to subsection (5), increase the award by the minimum amount and may, if it considers it just and equitable in all the circumstances, increase the award by the higher amount instead.

(4) In subsections (2) and (3)—

(a) references to the minimum amount are to an amount equal to two weeks' pay, and

(b) references to the higher amount are to an amount equal to four weeks' pay.

(5) The duty under subsection (2) or (3) does not apply if there are exceptional circumstances which would make an award or increase under that subsection unjust or inequitable.

(6) The amount of a week's pay of an employee shall—

(a) be calculated for the purposes of this section in accordance with Chapter 2 of Part 14 of the Employment Rights Act 1996 (c 18), and

(b) not exceed the amount for the time being specified in section 227 of that Act (maximum amount of week's pay).

(7) For the purposes of Chapter 2 of Part 14 of the Employment Rights Act 1996 as applied by subsection (6), the calculation date shall be taken to be—

(a) if the employee was employed by the employer on the date the proceedings were begun, that date, and

(b) if he was not, the effective date of termination as defined by section 97 of that Act.

(8) The Secretary of State may by order—

(a) amend Schedule 5 for the purpose of—

(i) adding a jurisdiction to the list in that Schedule, or

(ii) removing a jurisdiction from that list;

(b) make provision, in relation to a jurisdiction listed in Schedule 5, for this section not to apply to proceedings relating to claims of a description specified in the order;

(c) make provision for this section to apply, with or without modifications, as if—

(i) any individual of a description specified in the order who would not otherwise be an employee for the purposes of this section were an employee for those purposes, and

(ii) a person of a description specified in the order were, in the case of any such individual, the individual's employer for those purposes.

SCHEDULE 2
STATUTORY DISPUTE RESOLUTION PROCEDURES

PART 1
DISMISSAL AND DISCIPLINARY PROCEDURES

CHAPTER 1
STANDARD PROCEDURE

Step 1: Statement of grounds for action and invitation to meeting

1.   (1) The employer must set out in writing the employee's alleged conduct or characteristics, or other circumstances, which lead him to contemplate dismissing or taking disciplinary action against the employee.

(2) The employer must send the statement or a copy of it to the employee and invite the employee to attend a meeting to discuss the matter.

Step 2: Meeting

2. (1) The meeting must take place before action is taken, except in the case where the disciplinary action consists of suspension.
   (2) The meeting must not take place unless—
       (a) the employer has informed the employee what the basis was for including in the statement under paragraph 1(1) the ground or grounds given in it, and
       (b) the employee has had a reasonable opportunity to consider his response to that information.
   (3) The employee must take all reasonable steps to attend the meeting.
   (4) After the meeting, the employer must inform the employee of his decision and notify him of the right to appeal against the decision if he is not satisfied with it.

Step 3: Appeal

3. (1) If the employee does wish to appeal, he must inform the employer.
   (2) If the employee informs the employer of his wish to appeal, the employer must invite him to attend a further meeting.
   (3) The employee must take all reasonable steps to attend the meeting.
   (4) The appeal meeting need not take place before the dismissal or disciplinary action takes effect.
   (5) After the appeal meeting, the employer must inform the employee of his final decision.

CHAPTER 2
MODIFIED PROCEDURE

Step 1: Statement of grounds for action

4. The employer must—
       (a) set out in writing—
           (i) the employee's alleged misconduct which has led to the dismissal,
           (ii) what the basis was for thinking at the time of the dismissal that the employee was guilty of the alleged misconduct, and
           (iii) the employee's right to appeal against dismissal, and
       (b) send the statement or a copy of it to the employee.

Step 2: Appeal

5. (1) If the employee does wish to appeal, he must inform the employer.
   (2) If the employee informs the employer of his wish to appeal, the employer must invite him to attend a meeting.
   (3) The employee must take all reasonable steps to attend the meeting.
   (4) After the appeal meeting, the employer must inform the employee of his final decision.

PART 2
GRIEVANCE PROCEDURES

CHAPTER 1
STANDARD PROCEDURE

Step 1: Statement of grievance

6. The employee must set out the grievance in writing and send the statement or a copy of it to the employer.

Step 2: Meeting

7. (1) The employer must invite the employee to attend a meeting to discuss the grievance.
   (2) The meeting must not take place unless—
       (a) the employee has informed the employer what the basis for the grievance was when he made the statement under paragraph 6, and

(b)   the employer has had a reasonable opportunity to consider his response to that information.

(3)   The employee must take all reasonable steps to attend the meeting.

(4)   After the meeting, the employer must inform the employee of his decision as to his response to the grievance and notify him of the right to appeal against the decision if he is not satisfied with it.

Step 3: Appeal

8.   (1)   If the employee does wish to appeal, he must inform the employer.

(2)   If the employee informs the employer of his wish to appeal, the employer must invite him to attend a further meeting.

(3)   The employee must take all reasonable steps to attend the meeting.

(4)   After the appeal meeting, the employer must inform the employee of his final decision.

CHAPTER 2
MODIFIED PROCEDURE

Step 1: Statement of grievance

9.   The employee must—

(a)   set out in writing—

(i)   the grievance, and

(ii)   the basis for it, and

(b)   send the statement or a copy of it to the employer.

Step 2: Response

10.   The employer must set out his response in writing and send the statement or a copy of it to the employee.

PART 3
GENERAL REQUIREMENTS

Introductory

11.   The following requirements apply to each of the procedures set out above (so far as applicable).

Timetable

12.   Each step and action under the procedure must be taken without unreasonable delay.

Meetings

13.   (1)   Timing and location of meetings must be reasonable.

(2)   Meetings must be conducted in a manner that enables both employer and employee to explain their cases.

(3)   In the case of appeal meetings which are not the first meeting, the employer should, as far as is reasonably practicable, be represented by a more senior manager than attended the first meeting (unless the most senior manager attended that meeting).

PART 4
SUPPLEMENTARY

Status of meetings

14.   A meeting held for the purposes of this Schedule is a hearing for the purposes of section 13(4) and (5) of the Employment Relations Act 1999 (definition of 'disciplinary hearing' and 'grievance hearing' in relation to the right to be accompanied under section 10 of that Act).

Scope of grievance procedures

15.   (1)   The procedures set out in Part 2 are only applicable to matters raised by an employee with his employer as a grievance.

(2)   Accordingly, those procedures are only applicable to the kind of disclosure dealt with in Part 4A of the Employment Rights Act 1996 (protected disclosures of information) if information is disclosed by an employee to his employer in circumstances where—

    (a)   the information relates to a matter which the employee could raise as a grievance with his employer, and

    (b)   it is the intention of the employee that the disclosure should constitute the raising of the matter with his employer as a grievance.

EQUALITY ACT 2006
(2006, c. 3)

PART 1
THE COMMISSION FOR EQUALITY AND HUMAN RIGHTS

The Commission

1   Establishment

There shall be a body corporate known as the Commission for Equality and Human Rights.

2   Constitution, &c

Schedule 1 (constitution of the Commission, proceedings, money, etc) shall have effect.

3   General duty

The Commission shall exercise its functions under this Part with a view to encouraging and supporting the development of a society in which—

    (a)   people's ability to achieve their potential is not limited by prejudice or discrimination,

    (b)   there is respect for and protection of each individual's human rights,

    (c)   there is respect for the dignity and worth of each individual,

    (d)   each individual has an equal opportunity to participate in society, and

    (e)   there is mutual respect between groups based on understanding and valuing of diversity and on shared respect for equality and human rights.

4   Strategic plan

(1)   The Commission shall prepare a plan showing—

    (a)   activities or classes of activity to be undertaken by the Commission in pursuance of its functions under this Act,

    (b)   an expected timetable for each activity or class, and

    (c)   priorities for different activities or classes, or principles to be applied in determining priorities.

(2)   The Commission shall review the plan—

    (a)   at least once during the period of three years beginning with its completion,

    (b)   at least once during each period of three years beginning with the completion of a review, and

    (c)   at such other times as the Commission thinks appropriate.

(3)   If the Commission thinks it appropriate as a result of a review, the Commission shall revise the plan.

(4)   The Commission shall send the plan and each revision to the Minister, who shall lay a copy before Parliament.

(5)   The Commission shall publish the plan and each revision.

5   Strategic plan: consultation

Before preparing or reviewing a plan in accordance with section 4 the Commission shall—

    (a)   consult such persons having knowledge or experience relevant to the Commission's functions as the Commission thinks appropriate,

    (b)   consult such other persons as the Commission thinks appropriate,

    (c)   issue a general invitation to make representations, in a manner likely in the Commission's opinion to bring the invitation to the attention of as large a class of persons who may wish to make representations as is reasonably practicable, and

(d)   take account of any representations made.

Duties

8   Equality and diversity

(1)   The Commission shall, by exercising the powers conferred by this Part—
    (a)   promote understanding of the importance of equality and diversity,
    (b)   encourage good practice in relation to equality and diversity,
    (c)   promote equality of opportunity,
    (d)   promote awareness and understanding of rights under the equality enactments,
    (e)   enforce the equality enactments,
    (f)   work towards the elimination of unlawful discrimination, and
    (g)   work towards the elimination of unlawful harassment.

(2)   In subsection (1)—
'diversity' means the fact that individuals are different,
'equality' means equality between individuals, and
'unlawful' is to be construed in accordance with section 34.

(3)   In promoting equality of opportunity between disabled persons and others, the Commission may, in particular, promote the favourable treatment of disabled persons.

(4)   In this Part 'disabled person' means a person who—
    (a)   is a disabled person within the meaning of the Disability Discrimination Act 1995, or
    (b)   has been a disabled person within that meaning (whether or not at a time when that Act had effect).

9   Human rights

(1)   The Commission shall, by exercising the powers conferred by this Part—
    (a)   promote understanding of the importance of human rights,
    (b)   encourage good practice in relation to human rights,
    (c)   promote awareness, understanding and protection of human rights, and
    (d)   encourage public authorities to comply with section 6 of the Human Rights Act 1998 (compliance with Convention rights).

(2)   In this Part 'human rights' means—
    (a)   the Convention rights within the meaning given by section 1 of the Human Rights Act 1998, and
    (b)   other human rights.

(3)   In determining what action to take in pursuance of this section the Commission shall have particular regard to the importance of exercising the powers conferred by this Part in relation to the Convention rights.

(4)   In fulfilling a duty under section 8 or 10 the Commission shall take account of any relevant human rights.

(5)   A reference in this Part (including this section) to human rights does not exclude any matter by reason only of its being a matter to which section 8 or 10 relates.

10   Groups

(1)   The Commission shall, by exercising the powers conferred by this Part—
    (a)   promote understanding of the importance of good relations—
        (i)   between members of different groups, and
        (ii)   between members of groups and others,
    (b)   encourage good practice in relation to relations—
        (i)   between members of different groups, and
        (ii)   between members of groups and others,
    (c)   work towards the elimination of prejudice against, hatred of and hostility towards members of groups, and
    (d)   work towards enabling members of groups to participate in society.

(2) In this Part 'group' means a group or class of persons who share a common attribute in respect of any of the following matters—

    (a)   age,

    (b)   disability,

    (c)   gender,

    (d)   proposed, commenced or completed reassignment of gender (within the meaning given by section 82(1) of the Sex Discrimination Act 1975),

    (e)   race,

    (f)   religion or belief, and

    (g)   sexual orientation.

(3) For the purposes of this Part a reference to a group (as defined in subsection (2)) includes a reference to a smaller group or smaller class, within a group, of persons who share a common attribute (in addition to the attribute by reference to which the group is defined) in respect of any of the matters specified in subsection (2)(a) to (g).

(4) In determining what action to take in pursuance of this section the Commission shall have particular regard to the importance of exercising the powers conferred by this Part in relation to groups defined by reference to race, religion or belief.

(5) The Commission may, in taking action in pursuance of subsection (1) in respect of groups defined by reference to disability and others, promote or encourage the favourable treatment of disabled persons.

(6) The Minister may by order amend the list in subsection (2) so as to—

    (a)   add an entry, or

    (b)   vary an entry.

(7) This section is without prejudice to the generality of section 8.

11   Monitoring the law

(1) The Commission shall monitor the effectiveness of the equality and human rights enactments.

(2) The Commission may—

    (a)   advise central government about the effectiveness of any of the equality and human rights enactments;

    (b)   recommend to central government the amendment, repeal, consolidation (with or without amendments) or replication (with or without amendments) of any of the equality and human rights enactments;

    (c)   advise central or devolved government about the effect of an enactment (including an enactment in or under an Act of the Scottish Parliament);

    (d)   advise central or devolved government about the likely effect of a proposed change of law.

(3) In this section—

    (a)   'central government' means Her Majesty's Government,

    (b)   'devolved government' means—

        (i)   the Scottish Ministers, and

        (ii)   the Welsh Ministers, the First Minister for Wales and the Counsel General to the Welsh Assembly Government, and

    (c)   a reference to the equality enactments shall be treated as including a reference to any provision of this Act.

12   Monitoring progress

(1) The Commission shall from time to time identify—

    (a)   changes in society that have occurred or are expected to occur and are relevant to the aim specified in section 3,

    (b)   results at which to aim for the purpose of encouraging and supporting the development of the society described in section 3 ('outcomes'), and

    (c)   factors by reference to which progress towards those results may be measured ('indicators').

(2) In identifying outcomes and indicators the Commission shall—

(a)   consult such persons having knowledge or experience relevant to the Commission's functions as the Commission thinks appropriate,

(b)   consult such other persons as the Commission thinks appropriate,

(c)   issue a general invitation to make representations, in a manner likely in the Commission's opinion to bring the invitation to the attention of as large a class of persons who may wish to make representations as is reasonably practicable, and

(d)   take account of any representations made.

(3) The Commission shall from time to time monitor progress towards each identified outcome by reference to any relevant identified indicator.

(4) The Commission shall publish a report on progress towards the identified outcomes by reference to the identified indicators—

(a)   within the period of three years beginning with the date on which this section comes into force, and

(b)   within each period of three years beginning with the date on which a report is published under this subsection.

(5) The Commission shall send each report to the Minister, who shall lay a copy before Parliament.

13   Information, advice, etc

(1) In pursuance of its duties under sections 8 to 10 the Commission may—

(a)   publish or otherwise disseminate ideas or information;

(b)   undertake research;

(c)   provide education or training;

(d)   give advice or guidance (whether about the effect or operation of an enactment or otherwise);

(e)   arrange for a person to do anything within paragraphs (a) to (d);

(f)   act jointly with, co-operate with or assist a person doing anything within paragraphs (a) to (d).

(2) The reference to giving advice in subsection (1)(d) does not include a reference to preparing, or assisting in the preparation of, a document to be used for the purpose of legal proceedings.

14   Codes of practice

(1) The Commission may issue a code of practice in connection with a matter addressed by any of the following—

(a)   the Equal Pay Act 1970,

(b)   Parts 2 to 4 and section 76A of the Sex Discrimination Act 1975 or an order under section 76B or 76C of that Act,

(c)   Parts 2 to 4 and section 71 of the Race Relations Act 1976,

(d)   Parts 2 to 4 and 5A of the Disability Discrimination Act 1995 except for sections 28D and 28E (accessibility in schools),

(e)   Part 2 of this Act,

(f)   regulations under Part 3 of this Act,

(g)   Parts 2 and 3 of the Employment Equality (Sexual Orientation) Regulations 2003,

(h)   Parts 2 and 3 of the Employment Equality (Religion or Belief) Regulations 2003, and

(i)   Parts 2 and 3 of the Employment Equality (Age) Regulations 2006.

(2) A code of practice under subsection (1) shall contain provision designed—

(a)   to ensure or facilitate compliance with a provision or enactment listed in subsection (1), or

(b)   to promote equality of opportunity.

(3) The Commission may issue a code of practice giving practical guidance to landlords and tenants in England or Wales about—

(a)   circumstances in which a tenant requires the consent of his landlord to make a relevant improvement, within the meaning of section 49G(7) of the Disability Discrimination Act 1995 (improvements), to a dwelling house,

(b)   reasonableness in relation to that consent, and

     (c)   the application in relation to relevant improvements (within that meaning) to dwelling houses of—

         (i)   section 19(2) of the Landlord and Tenant Act 1927 (consent to improvements),

         (ii)   sections 81 to 85 of the Housing Act 1980 (tenant's improvements),

         (iii)   sections 97 to 99 of the Housing Act 1985 (tenant's improvements), and

         (iv)   section 49G of the Disability Discrimination Act 1995.

(4)   The Commission may issue a code of practice giving practical guidance to landlords and tenants of houses (within the meaning of the Housing (Scotland) Act 2006) in Scotland about—

     (a)   circumstances in which the tenant requires the consent of the landlord to carry out work in relation to the house for the purpose of making the house suitable for the accommodation, welfare or employment of any disabled person who occupies, or intends to occupy, the house as a sole or main residence,

     (b)   circumstances in which it is unreasonable to withhold that consent,

     (c)   circumstances in which any condition imposed on the granting of that consent is unreasonable, and

     (d)   the application in relation to such work of—

         (i)   sections 28 to 31 and 34(6) of the Housing (Scotland) Act 2001, and

         (ii)   sections 52, 53 and 64(6) of the Housing (Scotland) Act 2006.

(5)   The Commission shall comply with a direction of the Minister to issue a code under this section in connection with a specified matter if—

     (a)   the matter is not listed in subsection (1), but

     (b)   the Minister expects to add it by order under section 15(6).

(6)   Before issuing a code under this section the Commission shall—

     (a)   publish proposals, and

     (b)   consult such persons as it thinks appropriate.

(7)   Before issuing a code under this section the Commission shall submit a draft to the Minister, who shall—

     (a)   if he approves the draft—

         (i)   notify the Commission, and

         (ii)   lay a copy before Parliament, or

     (b)   otherwise, give the Commission written reasons why he does not approve the draft.

(8)   Where a draft is laid before Parliament under subsection (7)(a)(ii), if neither House passes a resolution disapproving the draft within 40 days—

     (a)   the Commission may issue the code in the form of the draft, and

     (b)   it shall come into force in accordance with provision made by the Minister by order.

(9)   If, or in so far as, a code relates to a duty imposed by or under section 76A, 76B or 76C of the Sex Discrimination Act 1975, section 71 of the Race Relations Act 1976 or section 49A or 49D of the Disability Discrimination Act 1995 (public authorities: general anti-discrimination duties) the Minister shall consult the Scottish Ministers and the Welsh Ministers before—

     (a)   approving a draft under subsection (7)(a) above, or

     (b)   making an order under subsection (8)(b) above.

(10) In relation to a code of practice under subsection (4), the Minister shall consult the Scottish Ministers before—

     (a)   approving a draft under subsection (7)(a) above, or

     (b)   making an order under subsection (8)(b) above.

15   Codes of practice: supplemental

(1)   The Commission may revise a code issued under section 14; and a reference in this section or in that section to the issue of a code shall be treated as including a reference to the revision of a code.

(2)   The 40 day period specified in section 14(8)—

     (a)   shall begin with the date on which the draft is laid before both Houses (or, if laid before each House on a different date, with the later date), and

     (b)   shall be taken not to include a period during which—

         (i)   Parliament is prorogued or dissolved, or

(ii)   both Houses are adjourned for more than four days.

(3)   A code issued under section 14 may be revoked by the Minister, at the request of the Commission, by order.

(4)   A failure to comply with a provision of a code shall not of itself make a person liable to criminal or civil proceedings; but a code—

   (a)   shall be admissible in evidence in criminal or civil proceedings, and

   (b)   shall be taken into account by a court or tribunal in any case in which it appears to the court or tribunal to be relevant.

(5)   Subsection (4)(b) does not apply in relation to a code issued under section 14(4).

(6)   The Minister may by order amend section 14 so as to vary the range of matters that codes of practice under that section may address.

16   Inquiries

(1)   The Commission may conduct an inquiry into a matter relating to any of the Commission's duties under sections 8, 9 and 10.

(2)   If in the course of an inquiry the Commission begins to suspect that a person may have committed an unlawful act—

   (a)   in continuing the inquiry the Commission shall, so far as possible, avoid further consideration of whether or not the person has committed an unlawful act,

   (b)   the Commission may commence an investigation into that question under section 20,

   (c)   the Commission may use information or evidence acquired in the course of the inquiry for the purpose of the investigation, and

   (d)   the Commission shall so far as possible ensure (whether by aborting or suspending the inquiry or otherwise) that any aspects of the inquiry which concern the person investigated, or may require his involvement, are not pursued while the investigation is in progress.

(3)   The report of an inquiry—

   (a)   may not state (whether expressly or by necessary implication) that a specified or identifiable person has committed an unlawful act, and

   (b)   shall not otherwise refer to the activities of a specified or identifiable person unless the Commission thinks that the reference—

      (i)   will not harm the person, or

      (ii)   is necessary in order for the report adequately to reflect the results of the inquiry.

(4)   Subsections (2) and (3) shall not prevent an inquiry from considering or reporting a matter relating to human rights (whether or not a necessary implication arises in relation to the equality enactments).

(5)   Before settling a report of an inquiry which records findings which in the Commission's opinion are of an adverse nature and relate (whether expressly or by necessary implication) to a specified or identifiable person the Commission shall—

   (a)   send a draft of the report to the person,

   (b)   specify a period of at least 28 days during which he may make written representations about the draft, and

   (c)   consider any representations made.

(6)   Schedule 2 makes supplemental provision about inquiries

17   Grants

(1)   In pursuance of any of its duties under sections 8 to 10 the Commission may make grants to another person.

(2)   A grant under subsection (1) may be made subject to conditions (which may, in particular, include conditions as to repayment).

(3)   A power under this Part to co-operate with or assist a person may not be exercised by the provision of financial assistance otherwise than in accordance with this section.

18   Human rights

In pursuance of its duties under section 9 the Commission may (without prejudice to the generality of section 13) co-operate with persons interested in human rights within the United Kingdom or elsewhere.

19 Groups

(1) In pursuance of its duties under section 10 the Commission may do anything specified in this section (without prejudice to the generality of section 13).

(2) The Commission may make, co-operate with or assist in arrangements—

    (a) for the monitoring of kinds of crime affecting certain groups;

    (b) designed to prevent or reduce crime within or affecting certain groups;

    (c) for activities (whether social, recreational, sporting, civic, educational or otherwise) designed to involve members of groups.

20 Investigations

(1) The Commission may investigate whether or not a person—

    (a) has committed an unlawful act,

    (b) has complied with a requirement imposed by an unlawful act notice under section 21, or

    (c) has complied with an undertaking given under section 23.

(2) The Commission may conduct an investigation under subsection (1)(a) only if it suspects that the person concerned may have committed an unlawful act.

(3) A suspicion for the purposes of subsection (2) may (but need not) be based on the results of, or a matter arising during the course of, an inquiry under section 16.

(4) Before settling a report of an investigation recording a finding that a person has committed an unlawful act or has failed to comply with a requirement or undertaking the Commission shall—

    (a) send a draft of the report to the person,

    (b) specify a period of at least 28 days during which he may make written representations about the draft, and

    (c) consider any representations made.

(5) Schedule 2 makes supplemental provision about investigations.

21 Unlawful act notice

(1) The Commission may give a person a notice under this section (an 'unlawful act notice') if—

    (a) he is or has been the subject of an investigation under section 20(1)(a), and

    (b) the Commission is satisfied that he has committed an unlawful act.

(2) A notice must specify—

    (a) the unlawful act, and

    (b) the provision of the equality enactments by virtue of which the act is unlawful.

(3) A notice must inform the recipient of the effect of—

    (a) subsections (5) to (7),

    (b) section 20(1)(b), and

    (c) section 24(1).

(4) A notice may—

    (a) require the person to whom the notice is given to prepare an action plan for the purpose of avoiding repetition or continuation of the unlawful act;

    (b) recommend action to be taken by the person for that purpose.

(5) A person who is given a notice may, within the period of six weeks beginning with the day on which the notice is given, appeal to the appropriate court or tribunal on the grounds—

    (a) that he has not committed the unlawful act specified in the notice, or

    (b) that a requirement for the preparation of an action plan imposed under subsection (4)(a) is unreasonable.

(6) On an appeal under subsection (5) the court or tribunal may—

    (a) affirm a notice;

    (b) annul a notice;

    (c) vary a notice;

    (d) affirm a requirement;

    (e) annul a requirement;

    (f) vary a requirement;

    (g) make an order for costs or expenses.

(7) In subsection (5) 'the appropriate court or tribunal' means—

    (a) an employment tribunal, if a claim in respect of the alleged unlawful act could be made to it, or

    (b) a county court (in England and Wales) or the sheriff (in Scotland), if a claim in respect of the alleged unlawful act could be made to it or to him.

22 Action plans

(1) This section applies where a person has been given a notice under section 21 which requires him (under section 21(4)(a)) to prepare an action plan.

(2) The notice must specify a time by which the person must give the Commission a first draft plan.

(3) After receiving a first draft plan from a person the Commission shall—

    (a) approve it, or

    (b) give the person a notice which—

        (i) states that the draft is not adequate,

        (ii) requires the person to give the Commission a revised draft by a specified time, and

        (iii) may make recommendations about the content of the revised draft.

(4) Subsection (3) shall apply in relation to a revised draft plan as it applies in relation to a first draft plan.

(5) An action plan comes into force—

    (a) if the period of six weeks beginning with the date on which a first draft or revised draft is given to the Commission expires without the Commission—

        (i) giving a notice under subsection (3)(b), or

        (ii) applying for an order under subsection (6)(b), or

    (b) upon a court's declining to make an order under subsection (6)(b) in relation to a revised draft of the plan.

(6) The Commission may apply to a county court (in England and Wales) or to the sheriff (in Scotland)—

    (a) for an order requiring a person to give the Commission a first draft plan by a time specified in the order,

    (b) for an order requiring a person who has given the Commission a revised draft plan to prepare and give to the Commission a further revised draft plan—

        (i) by a time specified in the order, and

        (ii) in accordance with any directions about the plan's content specified in the order, or

    (c) during the period of five years beginning with the date on which an action plan prepared by a person comes into force, for an order requiring the person—

        (i) to act in accordance with the action plan, or

        (ii) to take specified action for a similar purpose.

(7) An action plan may be varied by agreement between the Commission and the person who prepared it.

(8) Paragraphs 10 to 14 of Schedule 2 apply (but omitting references to oral evidence) in relation to consideration by the Commission of the adequacy of a draft action plan as they apply in relation to the conduct of an inquiry.

(9) A person commits an offence if without reasonable excuse he fails to comply with an order under subsection (6); and a person guilty of an offence under this subsection shall be liable on summary conviction to a fine not exceeding level 5 on the standard scale.

23 Agreements

(1) The Commission may enter into an agreement with a person under which—

    (a) the person undertakes—

        (i) not to commit an unlawful act of a specified kind, and

        (ii) to take, or refrain from taking, other specified action (which may include the preparation of a plan for the purpose of avoiding an unlawful act), and

    (b) the Commission undertakes not to proceed against the person under section 20 or 21 in respect of any unlawful act of the kind specified under paragraph (a)(i).

(2)   The Commission may enter into an agreement with a person under this section only if it thinks that the person has committed an unlawful act.

(3)   But a person shall not be taken to admit to the commission of an unlawful act by reason only of entering into an agreement under this section.

(4)   An agreement under this section—

    (a)   may be entered into whether or not the person is or has been the subject of an investigation under section 20,

    (b)   may include incidental or supplemental provision (which may include provision for termination in specified circumstances), and

    (c)   may be varied or terminated by agreement of the parties.

(5)   This section shall apply in relation to the breach of a duty specified in section 34(2) as it applies in relation to the commission of an unlawful act; and for that purpose the reference in subsection (1)(b) above to section 20 or 21 shall be taken as a reference to section 32.

24   Applications to court

(1)   If the Commission thinks that a person is likely to commit an unlawful act, it may apply—

    (a)   in England and Wales, to a county court for an injunction restraining the person from committing the act, or

    (b)   in Scotland, to the sheriff for an interdict prohibiting the person from committing the act.

(2)   Subsection (3) applies if the Commission thinks that a party to an agreement under section 23 has failed to comply, or is likely not to comply, with an undertaking under the agreement.

(3)   The Commission may apply to a county court (in England and Wales) or to the sheriff (in Scotland) for an order requiring the person—

    (a)   to comply with his undertaking, and

    (b)   to take such other action as the court or the sheriff may specify

25   Application to restrain unlawful advertising, pressure, etc

(1)   This section applies to an act which is unlawful under any of the following—

    (a)   sections 38 to 40 of the Sex Discrimination Act 1975 (advertising; and instructions or pressure to discriminate),

    (b)   sections 29 to 31 of the Race Relations Act 1976 (advertising; and instructions or pressure to discriminate),

    (c)   sections 16B and 16C of the Disability Discrimination Act 1995 (advertising; and instructions or pressure to discriminate),

    (ca)   sections 28UB and 28UC of that Act (advertising; and instructions or pressure to discriminate), and

    (d)   sections 54 and 55 below (religious discrimination: advertising; and instructions or pressure to discriminate), and

    (e)   regulations 10 and 11 of the Equality Act (Sexual Orientation) Regulations 2007.

(2)   Legal proceedings in relation to action to which this section applies—

    (a)   may be brought by the Commission in accordance with this section, and

    (b)   may not be brought by anyone else.

(3)   Where the Commission thinks that a person has done an act to which this section applies the Commission may—

    (a)   present a complaint to an employment tribunal, where the act is alleged to be unlawful by reference to—

        (i)   Part 2 of the Sex Discrimination Act 1975,

        (ii)   Part 2 of the Race Relations Act 1976,

        (iii)   Part 2 of the Disability Discrimination Act 1995,

        (iv)   Part 3 of that Act in so far as it relates to employment services, or

        (v)   Part 2 of this Act, or

    (b)   in any other case, apply to a county court (in England and Wales) or the sheriff (in Scotland).

(4)   On a complaint or application under subsection (3) in respect of an alleged act to which this section applies, the tribunal, court or sheriff shall determine whether the allegation is correct.

(5)   The Commission may apply to a county court (in England and Wales) for an injunction restraining a person from doing an act to which this section applies where—

    (a)   either—

        (i)   a tribunal or court has determined under subsection (4) that the person has done an act to which this section applies, or

        (ii)   the Commission thinks that the person has done an act to which this section applies, and

    (b)   the Commission thinks that if unrestrained the person is likely to do another act to which this section applies.

(6)   The Commission may apply to the sheriff (in Scotland) for an interdict prohibiting a person from doing an act to which this section applies where—

    (a)   either—

        (i)   a tribunal or the sheriff has determined under subsection (4) that the person has done an act to which this section applies, or

        (ii)   the Commission thinks that the person has done an act to which this section applies, and

    (b)   the Commission thinks that without an interdict the person is likely to do another act to which this section applies.

(7)   Subsection (1) does not apply to an act which constitutes an offence.

26   Section 25: supplemental

(1)   A complaint or application under section 25(3) may be presented or made only—

    (a)   within the period of six months beginning with the date (or last date) on which the alleged unlawful act occurred, or

    (b)   with the permission of the tribunal, court or sheriff.

(2)   A determination under section 25(4) shall not be relied upon by a county court or the sheriff in proceedings under section 25(5) or (6) while an appeal against the determination—

    (a)   is pending, or

    (b)   may be brought (disregarding the possibility of an appeal out of time with permission).

(3)   An application under section 25(5) or (6) may be made only—

    (a)   within the period of five years beginning with the date (or last date) on which the unlawful act referred to in that subsection occurred, or

    (b)   with the permission of the court or sheriff.

27   Conciliation

(1)   The Commission may make arrangements for the provision of conciliation services for disputes in respect of which proceedings have been or could be brought under or by virtue of—

    (a)   section 66 of the Sex Discrimination Act 1975 (civil proceedings),

    (b)   section 57 of the Race Relations Act 1976 (civil proceedings),

    (c)   section 25, 28I, 28N, 28V, 31ADA or 31AE(1) of the Disability Discrimination Act 1995 (civil proceedings),

    (d)   section 66 below,

    (e)   a provision of regulations under Part 3 of this Act corresponding to section 66 below,

    (f)   regulation 31 of the Employment Equality (Religion or Belief) Regulations 2003 (civil proceedings),

    (g)   regulation 31 of the Employment Equality (Sexual Orientation) Regulations 2003 (civil proceedings), or

    (h)   regulation 39 of the Employment Equality (Age) Regulations 2006 (Jurisdiction of County and Sheriff Courts).

(1A) The Commission may make arrangements for the provision of conciliation services for disputes in respect of which proceedings have been or could be brought in England and Wales or Scotland under regulation 9 of the Civil Aviation (Access to Air Travel for Disabled Persons and Persons with Reduced Mobility) Regulations 2007 (civil proceedings).

(2)   The Commission may make arrangements for the provision of conciliation services for disputes about a landlord's reasonableness in relation to consent to the making of an

improvement to a dwelling in England or Wales where the improvement would be likely to facilitate the enjoyment of the premises by the tenant or another lawful occupier having regard to a disability.

(3) The Commission may make arrangements for the provision of conciliation services for disputes about whether—

    (a) it is unreasonable for a landlord of a house (within the meaning of the Housing (Scotland) Act 2006) in Scotland to withhold consent to the carrying out of work in relation to the house for the purpose of making the house suitable for the accommodation, welfare or employment of any disabled person who occupies, or intends to occupy, the house as a sole or main residence, or

    (b) any condition imposed by such a landlord on consenting to the carrying out of such work is unreasonable.

(4) The Commission shall aim to exercise the powers in subsections (1) to (3) so as to ensure that, so far as is reasonably practicable, conciliation services are available to parties who want them.

(5) Information communicated to a person providing conciliation services in accordance with arrangements under this section may not be adduced in legal proceedings without the consent of the person who communicated the information.

(6) None of the following shall participate in the provision of conciliation services for which arrangements are made under this section—

    (a) a Commissioner,

    (b) a member of the Commission's staff,

    (c) a member of a committee established by the Commission, and

    (d) an Investigating Commissioner.

(7) The Commission shall make administrative arrangements designed to secure that information in connection with conciliation services provided in accordance with arrangements made under this section is not disclosed to—

    (a) a Commissioner, or

    (b) a member of the Commission's staff.

(8) But subsection (7) shall not apply to a disclosure—

    (a) made with the consent of the parties to the dispute to which it relates,

    (b) which does not identify individuals or enable them to be identified, or

    (c) of information without which arrangements under this section cannot be made.

(9) In this section 'conciliation services' means a service which is provided—

    (a) by a person who is not party to a dispute,

    (b) to the parties to the dispute, and

    (c) with the aim of enabling the dispute to be settled by agreement and without legal proceedings.

(10) The Minister may by order amend this section so as to vary the range of disputes in respect of which the Commission may make arrangements for the provision of conciliation services.

28   Legal assistance

(1) The Commission may assist an individual who is or may become party to legal proceedings if—

    (a) the proceedings relate or may relate (wholly or partly) to a provision of the equality enactments, and

    (b) the individual alleges that he has been the victim of behaviour contrary to a provision of the equality enactments.

(2) The Commission may assist an individual who is or may become party to legal proceedings in England and Wales if and in so far as the proceedings concern or may concern the question of a landlord's reasonableness in relation to consent to the making of an improvement to a dwelling where the improvement would be likely to facilitate the enjoyment of the premises by the tenant or another lawful occupier having regard to a disability.

(3) The Commission may assist an individual who is or may become a party to legal proceedings in Scotland if and in so far as the proceedings concern or may concern the question whether—

    (a)   it is unreasonable for a landlord to withhold consent to the carrying out of work in relation to a house (within the meaning of the Housing (Scotland) Act 2006) for the purpose of making the house suitable for the accommodation, welfare or employment of any disabled person who occupies, or intends to occupy, the house as a sole or main residence, or

    (b)   any condition imposed by a landlord on consenting to the carrying out of such work is unreasonable.

(4) In giving assistance under this section the Commission may provide or arrange for the provision of—

    (a)   legal advice;

    (b)   legal representation;

    (c)   facilities for the settlement of a dispute;

    (d)   any other form of assistance.

(5) Assistance may not be given under subsection (1) in relation to alleged behaviour contrary to a provision of Part V of the Disability Discrimination Act 1995 (public transport).

(6) Where proceedings relate or may relate partly to a provision of the equality enactments and partly to other matters—

    (a)   assistance may be given under subsection (1) in respect of any aspect of the proceedings while they relate to a provision of the equality enactments, but

    (b)   if the proceedings cease to relate to a provision of the equality enactments, assistance may not be continued under subsection (1) in respect of the proceedings (except in so far as it is permitted by virtue of subsection (7) or (8)).

(7) The Lord Chancellor may by order disapply subsection (6)(b), and enable the Commission to give assistance under subsection (1), in respect of legal proceedings which—

    (a)   when instituted, related (wholly or partly) to a provision of the equality enactments,

    (b)   have ceased to relate to the provision of the equality enactments, and

    (c)   relate (wholly or partly) to any of the Convention rights within the meaning given by section 1 of the Human Rights Act 1998.

(8) The Minister may by order enable the Commission to give assistance under this section in respect of legal proceedings in the course of which an individual who is or has been a disabled person relies or proposes to rely on a matter relating to his disability; but an order under this subsection may not permit assistance in relation to alleged behaviour contrary to a provision of Part V of the Disability Discrimination Act 1995.

(9) An order under subsection (7) or (8) may make provision generally or only in relation to proceedings of a specified kind or description (which in the case of an order under subsection (7) may, in particular, refer to specified provisions of the equality enactments) or in relation to specified circumstances.

(10) This section is without prejudice to the effect of any restriction imposed, in respect of representation—

    (a)   by virtue of an enactment (including an enactment in or under an Act of the Scottish Parliament), or

    (b)   in accordance with the practice of a court.

(11) A legislative provision which requires insurance or an indemnity in respect of advice given in connection with a compromise contract or agreement shall not apply to advice provided by the Commission under this section.

(12) A reference in this section to a provision of the equality enactments includes a reference to a provision of Community law which—

    (a)   relates to discrimination on grounds of sex (including reassignment of gender), racial origin, ethnic origin, religion, belief, disability, age or sexual orientation, and

    (b)   confers rights on individuals.

(13) In its application by virtue of subsection (12), subsection (1)(b) shall have effect as if it referred to an allegation by an individual that he is disadvantaged by—

    (a)   an enactment (including an enactment in or under an Act of the Scottish Parliament) which is contrary to a provision of Community law, or

    (b)   a failure by the United Kingdom to implement a right as required by Community law.

29   Legal assistance: costs

(1)   This section applies where—

    (a)   the Commission has assisted an individual under section 28 in relation to proceedings, and

    (b)   the individual becomes entitled to some or all of his costs in the proceedings (whether by virtue of an award or by virtue of an agreement).

(2)   The Commission's expenses in providing the assistance—

    (a)   shall be charged on sums paid to the individual by way of costs, and

    (b)   may be enforced as a debt due to the Commission.

(3)   A requirement to pay money to the Commission under subsection (2) ranks, in England and Wales, after a requirement imposed by virtue of section 11(4)(f) of the Access to Justice Act 1999 (recovery of costs in funded cases).

(4)   Subsection (2), in its application to Scotland, shall not affect the operation of section 17(2A) of the Legal Aid (Scotland) Act 1986 (requirement in certain cases to pay to the Scottish Legal Aid Board sums recovered under awards of, or agreements as to, expenses).

(5)   For the purposes of subsection (2) the Commission's expenses shall be calculated in accordance with such provision (if any) as the Minister makes for the purpose by regulations; and regulations may, in particular, provide for the apportionment of expenditure incurred by the Commission—

    (a)   partly for one purpose and partly for another, or

    (b)   for general purposes.

(6)   In the application of this section to Scotland a reference to costs shall be taken as a reference to expenses.

30   Judicial review and other legal proceedings

(1)   The Commission shall have capacity to institute or intervene in legal proceedings, whether for judicial review or otherwise, if it appears to the Commission that the proceedings are relevant to a matter in connection with which the Commission has a function.

(2)   The Commission shall be taken to have title and interest in relation to the subject matter of any legal proceedings in Scotland which it has capacity to institute, or in which it has capacity to intervene, by virtue of subsection (1).

(3)   The Commission may, in the course of legal proceedings for judicial review which it institutes (or in which it intervenes), rely on section 7(1)(b) of the Human Rights Act 1998 (breach of Convention rights); and for that purpose—

    (a)   the Commission need not be a victim or potential victim of the unlawful act to which the proceedings relate,

    (b)   the Commission may act only if there is or would be one or more victims of the unlawful act,

    (c)   section 7(3) and (4) of that Act shall not apply, and

    (d)   no award of damages may be made to the Commission (whether or not the exception in section 8(3) of that Act applies);

and an expression used in this subsection and in section 7 of the Human Rights Act 1998 has the same meaning in this subsection as in that section.

(4)   Subsections (1) and (2)—

    (a)   do not create a cause of action, and

    (b)   are, except as provided by subsection (3), subject to any limitation or restriction imposed by virtue of an enactment (including an enactment in or under an Act of the Scottish Parliament) or in accordance with the practice of a court.

31   Public sector duties: assessment

(1)   The Commission may assess the extent to which or the manner in which a person has complied with a duty under or by virtue of—

    (a)   section 76A, 76B or 76C of the Sex Discrimination Act 1975 (public authorities: duty to eliminate discrimination, etc),

    (b)   section 71 of the Race Relations Act 1976 (public authorities: duty to eliminate discrimination, etc), or

(c)   section 49A or 49D of the Disability Discrimination Act 1995 (public authorities: duty to eliminate discrimination, etc).

(2)   Schedule 2 makes supplemental provision about assessments.

(3)   This section is without prejudice to the generality of sections 16 and 20.

32   Public sector duties: compliance notice

(1)   This section applies where the Commission thinks that a person has failed to comply with a duty under or by virtue of—

(a)   section 76A, 76B or 76C of the Sex Discrimination Act 1975 (public authorities: duty to eliminate discrimination, etc),

(b)   section 71 of the Race Relations Act 1976 (public authorities: duty to eliminate discrimination, etc), or

(c)   section 49A or 49D of the Disability Discrimination Act 1995 (public authorities: duty to eliminate discrimination, etc).

(2)   The Commission may give the person a notice requiring him—

(a)   to comply with the duty, and

(b)   to give the Commission, within the period of 28 days beginning with the date on which he receives the notice, written information of steps taken or proposed for the purpose of complying with the duty.

(3)   A notice under this section may require a person to give the Commission information required by the Commission for the purposes of assessing compliance with the duty; in which case the notice shall specify—

(a)   the period within which the information is to be given (which shall begin with the date on which the notice is received and shall not exceed three months), and

(b)   the manner and form in which the information is to be given.

(4)   The Commission may not give a notice under this section in respect of a duty under section 76A of the Sex Discrimination Act 1975, section 71(1) of the Race Relations Act 1976 or section 49A of the Disability Discrimination Act 1995 unless—

(a)   the Commission has carried out an assessment under section 31 above, and

(b)   the notice relates to the results of the assessment.

(5)   A person who receives a notice under this section shall comply with it.

(6)   But a notice under this section shall not oblige a person to give information—

(a)   that he is prohibited from disclosing by virtue of an enactment, or

(b)   that he could not be compelled to give in proceedings before the High Court or the Court of Session.

(7)   Paragraphs 11 and 14 of Schedule 2 shall have effect (with any necessary modifications) in relation to a requirement imposed by a notice under this section as they have effect in relation to a requirement imposed by a notice under paragraph 9 of that Schedule.

(8)   If the Commission thinks that a person, to whom a notice under this section has been given, has failed to comply with a requirement of the notice, the Commission may apply to the court for an order requiring the person to comply.

(9)   In subsection (8) 'the court' means—

(a)   where the notice related to a duty under section 76A of the Sex Discrimination Act 1975, section 71(1) of the Race Relations Act 1976 or section 49A of the Disability Discrimination Act 1995, the High Court (in England and Wales) or (in Scotland) the Court of Session, and

(b)   in any other case, a county court (in England and Wales) or the sheriff (in Scotland).

(10)   A notice under this section shall specify a time before which the Commission may not make an application under subsection (8) in respect of the notice.

(11)   Legal proceedings in relation to a duty by virtue of section 76B or 76C of the Sex Discrimination Act 1975, section 71(2) of the Race Relations Act 1976 or section 49D of the Disability Discrimination Act 1995—

(a)   may be brought by the Commission in accordance with subsection (8) above, and

(b)   may not be brought in any other way.

Interpretation

33   Equality and human rights enactments

(1) In this Part 'the equality enactments' means—

(a)   the Equal Pay Act 1970,

(b)   the Sex Discrimination Act 1975,

(c)   the Race Relations Act 1976,

(d)   the Disability Discrimination Act 1995,

(e)   Part 2 of this Act,

(f)   regulations under Part 3 of this Act,

(g)   the Employment Equality (Sexual Orientation) Regulations 2003,

(h)   the Employment Equality (Religion or Belief) Regulations 2003, and

(i)   the Employment Equality (Age) Regulations 2006.

(2) In this Part 'the equality and human rights enactments' means the equality enactments and the Human Rights Act 1998.

(3) The Minister may by order amend the list in subsection (1) so as to—

(a)   add an entry,

(b)   remove an entry, or

(c)   vary an entry.

34   Unlawful

(1) In this Part (except section 30(3)) 'unlawful' means contrary to a provision of the equality enactments.

(2) But action is not unlawful for the purposes of this Part by reason only of the fact that it contravenes a duty under or by virtue of—

(a)   section 76A, 76B or 76C of the Sex Discrimination Act 1975 (public authorities: duty to eliminate discrimination, etc),

(b)   section 71 of the Race Relations Act 1976 (public authorities: duty to eliminate discrimination, etc), or

(c)   any of the following provisions of the Disability Discrimination Act 1995—

(i)   Part 5 (public transport),

(ii)   sections 49A and 49D (public authorities), and

(iii)   section 49G (consent to tenant's improvements).

35   General

In this Part—

'act' includes deliberate omission,

'groups' has the meaning given by section 10,

'the Commission' means the Commission for Equality and Human Rights,

'disabled person' has the meaning given by section 8,

'human rights' has the meaning given by section 9,

'the Minister' means the Lord Privy Seal,

'race' includes colour, nationality, ethnic origin and national origin,

'religion or belief' has the same meaning as in Part 2 (as defined by section 44), and

'sexual orientation' means an individual's sexual orientation towards—

(a)   persons of the same sex as him or her,

(b)   persons of the opposite sex, or

(c)   both.

Corporate Manslaughter and Corporate Homicide Act 2007
(2007, c. 19)

Corporate manslaughter and corporate homicide

1   The offence

(1) An organisation to which this section applies is guilty of an offence if the way in which its activities are managed or organised—

      (a)   causes a person's death, and

      (b)   amounts to a gross breach of a relevant duty of care owed by the organisation to the deceased.

(2) The organisations to which this section applies are—

      (a)   a corporation;

      (b)   a department or other body listed in Schedule 1;

      (c)   a police force;

      (d)   a partnership, or a trade union or employers' association, that is an employer.

(3) An organisation is guilty of an offence under this section only if the way in which its activities are managed or organised by its senior management is a substantial element in the breach referred to in subsection (1).

(4) For the purposes of this Act—

      (a)   'relevant duty of care' has the meaning given by section 2, read with sections 3 to 7;

      (b)   a breach of a duty of care by an organisation is a 'gross' breach if the conduct alleged to amount to a breach of that duty falls far below what can reasonably be expected of the organisation in the circumstances;

      (c)   'senior management', in relation to an organisation, means the persons who play significant roles in—

           (i)   the making of decisions about how the whole or a substantial part of its activities are to be managed or organised, or

          (ii)   the actual managing or organising of the whole or a substantial part of those activities.

(5) The offence under this section is called—

      (a)   corporate manslaughter, in so far as it is an offence under the law of England and Wales or Northern Ireland;

      (b)   corporate homicide, in so far as it is an offence under the law of Scotland.

(6) An organisation that is guilty of corporate manslaughter or corporate homicide is liable on conviction on indictment to a fine.

(7) The offence of corporate homicide is indictable only in the High Court of Justiciary.

2   Meaning of 'relevant duty of care'

(1) A 'relevant duty of care', in relation to an organisation, means any of the following duties owed by it under the law of negligence—

      (a)   a duty owed to its employees or to other persons working for the organisation or performing services for it;

      (b)   a duty owed as occupier of premises;

      (c)   a duty owed in connection with—

           (i)   the supply by the organisation of goods or services (whether for consideration or not),

          (ii)   the carrying on by the organisation of any construction or maintenance operations,

         (iii)   the carrying on by the organisation of any other activity on a commercial basis, or

         (iv)   the use or keeping by the organisation of any plant, vehicle or other thing;

...

(4) A reference in subsection (1) to a duty owed under the law of negligence includes a reference to a duty that would be owed under the law of negligence but for any statutory provision under which liability is imposed in place of liability under that law.

(5) For the purposes of this Act, whether a particular organisation owes a duty of care to a particular individual is a question of law.

The judge must make any findings of fact necessary to decide that question.

(6) For the purposes of this Act there is to be disregarded—

      (a)   any rule of the common law that has the effect of preventing a duty of care from being owed by one person to another by reason of the fact that they are jointly engaged in unlawful conduct;

(b)   any such rule that has the effect of preventing a duty of care from being owed to a person by reason of his acceptance of a risk of harm.

...

8   Factors for jury

(1) This section applies where—

    (a)   it is established that an organisation owed a relevant duty of care to a person, and

    (b)   it falls to the jury to decide whether there was a gross breach of that duty.

(2) The jury must consider whether the evidence shows that the organisation failed to comply with any health and safety legislation that relates to the alleged breach, and if so—

    (a)   how serious that failure was;

    (b)   how much of a risk of death it posed.

(3) The jury may also—

    (a)   consider the extent to which the evidence shows that there were attitudes, policies, systems or accepted practices within the organisation that were likely to have encouraged any such failure as is mentioned in subsection (2), or to have produced tolerance of it;

    (b)   have regard to any health and safety guidance that relates to the alleged breach.

(4) This section does not prevent the jury from having regard to any other matters they consider relevant.

(5) In this section 'health and safety guidance' means any code, guidance, manual or similar publication that is concerned with health and safety matters and is made or issued (under a statutory provision or otherwise) by an authority responsible for the enforcement of any health and safety legislation.

9   Power to order breach etc to be remedied

(1) A court before which an organisation is convicted of corporate manslaughter or corporate homicide may make an order (a 'remedial order') requiring the organisation to take specified steps to remedy—

    (a)   the breach mentioned in section 1(1) ('the relevant breach');

    (b)   any matter that appears to the court to have resulted from the relevant breach and to have been a cause of the death;

    (c)   any deficiency, as regards health and safety matters, in the organisation's policies, systems or practices of which the relevant breach appears to the court to be an indication.

(2) A remedial order may be made only on an application by the prosecution specifying the terms of the proposed order.

Any such order must be on such terms (whether those proposed or others) as the court considers appropriate having regard to any representations made, and any evidence adduced, in relation to that matter by the prosecution or on behalf of the organisation.

(3) Before making an application for a remedial order the prosecution must consult such enforcement authority or authorities as it considers appropriate having regard to the nature of the relevant breach.

(4) A remedial order—

    (a)   must specify a period within which the steps referred to in subsection (1) are to be taken;

    (b)   may require the organisation to supply to an enforcement authority consulted under subsection (3), within a specified period, evidence that those steps have been taken.

A period specified under this subsection may be extended or further extended by order of the court on an application made before the end of that period or extended period.

(5) An organisation that fails to comply with a remedial order is guilty of an offence, and liable on conviction on indictment to a fine.

10   Power to order conviction etc to be publicised

(1) A court before which an organisation is convicted of corporate manslaughter or corporate homicide may make an order (a 'publicity order') requiring the organisation to publicise in a specified manner—

    (a)   the fact that it has been convicted of the offence;

    (b)   specified particulars of the offence;

    (c)   the amount of any fine imposed;

    (d)   the terms of any remedial order made.

(2) In deciding on the terms of a publicity order that it is proposing to make, the court must—

    (a)   ascertain the views of such enforcement authority or authorities (if any) as it considers appropriate, and

    (b)   have regard to any representations made by the prosecution or on behalf of the organisation.

(3) A publicity order—

    (a)   must specify a period within which the requirements referred to in subsection (1) are to be complied with;

    (b)   may require the organisation to supply to any enforcement authority whose views have been ascertained under subsection (2), within a specified period, evidence that those requirements have been complied with.

(4) An organisation that fails to comply with a publicity order is guilty of an offence, and liable on conviction on indictment to a fine.

17 DPP's consent required for proceedings

Proceedings for an offence of corporate manslaughter—

    (a)   may not be instituted in England and Wales without the consent of the Director of Public Prosecutions;

    (b)   may not be instituted in Northern Ireland without the consent of the Director of Public Prosecutions for Northern Ireland.

18 No individual liability

(1) An individual cannot be guilty of aiding, abetting, counselling or procuring the commission of an offence of corporate manslaughter.

(1A) An individual cannot be guilty of an offence under Part 2 of the Serious Crime Act 2007 (encouraging or assisting crime) by reference to an offence of corporate manslaughter.

(2) An individual cannot be guilty of aiding, abetting, counselling or procuring, or being art and part in, the commission of an offence of corporate homicide.

19 Convictions under this Act and under health and safety legislation

(1) Where in the same proceedings there is—

    (a)   a charge of corporate manslaughter or corporate homicide arising out of a particular set of circumstances, and

    (b)   a charge against the same defendant of a health and safety offence arising out of some or all of those circumstances,

the jury may, if the interests of justice so require, be invited to return a verdict on each charge.

(2) An organisation that has been convicted of corporate manslaughter or corporate homicide arising out of a particular set of circumstances may, if the interests of justice so require, be charged with a health and safety offence arising out of some or all of those circumstances.

(3) In this section 'health and safety offence' means an offence under any health and safety legislation.

20 Abolition of liability of corporations for manslaughter at common law

The common law offence of manslaughter by gross negligence is abolished in its application to corporations, and in any application it has to other organisations to which section 1 applies.

STATUTORY INSTRUMENTS

EMPLOYMENT PROTECTION (CONTINUITY OF EMPLOYMENT) REGULATIONS 1996
(SI 1996 No. 3147)

2   Application

These Regulations apply to any action taken in relation to the dismissal of an employee which consists of—

    (a)   his making a claim in accordance with a dismissal procedures agreement designated by an order under section 110 of the Employment Rights Act 1996,

    (b)   the presentation by him of a relevant complaint of dismissal,

    (c)   any action taken by a conciliation officer under section 18 of the Employment Tribunals Act 1996,

    (d)   the making of a relevant compromise contract,

    (e)   the making of an agreement to submit a dispute to arbitration in accordance with a scheme having effect by virtue of an order under section 212A of the Trade Union and Labour Relations (Consolidation) Act 1992,

    (f)   a decision taken arising out of the use of a statutory dispute resolution procedure contained in Schedule 2 to the Employment Act 2002 (Dispute Resolution) Regulations 2004, such a procedure applies, or

    (g)   a decision taken arising out of the use of the statutory duty to consider procedure contained in Schedule 6 of the Employment Equality (Age) Regulations 2006.

3   Continuity of employment where employee re-engaged

(1)   The provisions of this regulation shall have effect to preserve the continuity of a person's period of employment for the purposes of—

    (a)   Chapter I of Part XIV of the Employment Rights Act 1996 (continuous employment), and

    (b)   that Chapter as applied by subsection (2) of section 282 of the Trade Union and Labour Relations (Consolidation) Act 1992 for the purposes of that section.

(2)   If in consequence of any action to which these Regulations apply a dismissed employee is reinstated or re-employed by his employer or by a successor or associated employer of the employer—

    (a)   the continuity of that employee's period of employment shall be preserved, and

    (b)   the period beginning with the date on which the dismissal takes effect and ending with the date of reinstatement or re-engagement shall count in the computation of the employee's period of continuous employment.

4   Exclusion of operation of section 214 of the Employment Rights Act 1996 where redundancy or equivalent payment repaid

(1)   Section 214 of the Employment Rights Act 1996 (continuity broken where employee re-employed after the making of a redundancy payment or equivalent payment) shall not apply where—

    (a)   in consequence of any action to which these Regulations apply a dismissed employee is reinstated or re-employed by his employer or by a successor or associated employer of the employer,

    (b)   the terms upon which he is so reinstated or re-engaged include provision for him to repay the amount of a redundancy payment or an equivalent payment paid in respect of the relevant dismissal, and

    (c)   that provision is complied with.

(2)   For the purposes of this regulation the cases in which a redundancy payment shall be treated as having been paid are the cases mentioned in section 214(5) of the Employment Rights Act 1996.

WORKING TIME REGULATIONS 1998
(SI 1998 No. 1833)

PART II
RIGHTS AND OBLIGATIONS CONCERNING WORKING TIME

3   General

(1)   The provisions of this Part have effect subject to the exceptions provided for in Part III of these Regulations.

(2)   Where, in this Part, separate provision is made as respects the same matter in relation to workers generally and to young workers, the provision relating to workers generally applies only to adult workers and those young workers to whom, by virtue of any exception in Part 3, the provision relating to young workers does not apply.

4   Maximum weekly working time

(1)   Unless his employer has first obtained the worker's agreement in writing to perform such work a worker's working time, including overtime, in any reference period which is applicable in his case shall not exceed an average of 48 hours for each seven days.

(2)   An employer shall take all reasonable steps, in keeping with the need to protect the health and safety of workers, to ensure that the limit specified in paragraph (1) is complied with in the case of each worker employed by him in relation to whom it applies and shall keep up-to-date records of all workers who carry out work to which it does not apply by reason of the fact that the employer has obtained the worker's agreement as mentioned in paragraph (1).

(3)   Subject to paragraphs (4) and (5) and any agreement under regulation 23(b), the reference periods which apply in the case of a worker are—

    (a)   where a relevant agreement provides for the application of this regulation in relation to successive periods of 17 weeks, each such period, or

    (b)   in any other case, any period of 17 weeks in the course of his employment.

(4)   Where a worker has worked for his employer for less than 17 weeks, the reference period applicable in his case is the period that has elapsed since he started work for his employer.

(5)   Paragraphs (3) and (4) shall apply to a worker who is excluded from the scope of certain provisions of these Regulations by regulation 21 as if for each reference to 17 weeks there were substituted a reference to 26 weeks.

(6)   For the purposes of this regulation, a worker's average working time for each seven days during a reference period shall be determined according to the formula—

$$\frac{A + B}{C}$$

where—

A is the aggregate number of hours comprised in the worker's working time during the course of the reference period;

B is the aggregate number of hours comprised in his working time during the course of the period beginning immediately after the end of the reference period and ending when the number of days in that subsequent period on which he has worked equals the number of excluded days during the reference period; and

C is the number of weeks in the reference period.

(7)   In paragraph (6), 'excluded days' means days comprised in—

    (a)   any period of annual leave taken by the worker in exercise of his entitlement under regulation 13;

    (b)   any period of sick leave taken by the worker;

    (c)   any period of maternity, paternity, adoption or parental leave taken by the worker; and

    (d)   any period in respect of which the limit specified in paragraph (1) did not apply in relation to the worker by reason of the fact that the employer has obtained the worker's agreement as mentioned in paragraph (1).

5   **Agreement to exclude the maximum**

     (1) ...

     (2)   An agreement for the purposes of regulation 4—

         (a)   may either relate to a specified period or apply indefinitely; and

         (b)   subject to any provision in the agreement for a different period of notice, shall be terminable by the worker by giving not less than seven days' notice to his employer in writing.

     (3)   Where an agreement for the purposes of regulation 4 makes provision for the termination of the agreement after a period of notice, the notice period provided for shall not exceed three months.

     (4) ...

5A   **Maximum working time for young workers**

     (1)   A young worker's working time shall not exceed—

         (a)   eight hours a day, or

         (b)   40 hours a week.

     (2)   If, on any day, or, as the case may be, during any week, a young worker is employed by more than one employer, his working time shall be determined for the purpose of paragraph (1) by aggregating the number of hours worked by him for each employer.

     (3)   For the purposes of paragraphs (1) and (2), a week starts at midnight between Sunday and Monday.

     (4)   An employer shall take all reasonable steps, in keeping with the need to protect the health and safety of workers, to ensure that the limits specified in paragraph (1) are complied with in the case of each worker employed by him in relation to whom they apply.

6   **Length of night work**

     (1)   A night worker's normal hours of work in any reference period which is applicable in his case shall not exceed an average of eight hours for each 24 hours.

     (2)   An employer shall take all reasonable steps, in keeping with the need to protect the health and safety of workers, to ensure that the limit specified in paragraph (1) is complied with in the case of each night worker employed by him.

     (3)   The reference periods which apply in the case of a night worker are—

         (a)   where a relevant agreement provides for the application of this regulation in relation to successive periods of 17 weeks, each such period, or

         (b)   in any other case, any period of 17 weeks in the course of his employment.

     (4)   Where a worker has worked for his employer for less than 17 weeks, the reference period applicable in his case is the period that has elapsed since he started work for his employer.

     (5)   For the purposes of this regulation, a night worker's average normal hours of work for each 24 hours during a reference period shall be determined according to the formula—

$$\frac{A}{B-C}$$

where—

A is the number of hours during the reference period which are normal working hours for that worker;

B is the number of days during the reference period; and

C is the total number of hours during the reference period comprised in rest periods spent by the worker in pursuance of his entitlement under regulation 11, divided by 24.

     ...

     (7)   An employer shall ensure that no night worker employed by him whose work involves special hazards or heavy physical or mental strain works for more than eight hours in any 24-hour period during which the night worker performs night work.

     (8)   For the purposes of paragraph (7), the work of a night worker shall be regarded as involving special hazards or heavy physical or mental strain if—

         (a)   it is identified as such in—

    (i)   a collective agreement, or

    (ii)   a workforce agreement,

    which takes account of the specific effects and hazards of night work, or

  (b)   it is recognised in a risk assessment made by the employer under regulation 3 of the Management of Health and Safety at Work Regulations 1992 as involving a significant risk to the health or safety of workers employed by him.

6A   Night work by young workers

An employer shall ensure that no young worker employed by him works during the restricted period.

7   Health assessment and transfer of night workers to day work

(1) An employer—

  (a)   shall not assign an adult worker to work which is to be undertaken during periods such that the worker will become a night worker unless—

    (i)   the employer has ensured that the worker will have the opportunity of a free health assessment before he takes up the assignment; or

    (ii)   the worker had a health assessment before being assigned to work to be undertaken during such periods on an earlier occasion, and the employer has no reason to believe that that assessment is no longer valid, and

  (b)   shall ensure that each night worker employed by him has the opportunity of a free health assessment at regular intervals of whatever duration may be appropriate in his case.

(2) Subject to paragraph (4), an employer—

  (a)   shall not assign a young worker to work during the the restricted period unless—

    (i)   the employer has ensured that the young worker will have the opportunity of a free assessment of his health and capacities before he takes up the assignment; or

    (ii)   the young worker had an assessment of his health and capacities before being assigned to work during the restricted period on an earlier occasion, and the employer has no reason to believe that that assessment is no longer valid; and

  (b)   shall ensure that each young worker employed by him and assigned to work during the restricted period has the opportunity of a free assessment of his health and capacities at regular intervals of whatever duration may be appropriate in his case.

(3) For the purposes of paragraphs (1) and (2), an assessment is free if it is at no cost to the worker to whom it relates.

(4) The requirements in paragraph (2) do not apply in a case where the work a young worker is assigned to do is of an exceptional nature.

(5) No person shall disclose an assessment made for the purposes of this regulation to any person other than the worker to whom it relates, unless—

  (a)   the worker has given his consent in writing to the disclosure, or

  (b)   the disclosure is confined to a statement that the assessment shows the worker to be fit—

    (i)   in a case where paragraph (1)(a)(i) or (2)(a)(i) applies, to take up an assignment, or

    (ii)   in a case where paragraph (1)(b) or (2)(b) applies, to continue to undertake an assignment.

(6) Where—

  (a)   a registered medical practitioner has advised an employer that a worker employed by the employer is suffering from health problems which the practitioner considers to be connected with the fact that the worker performs night work, and

  (b)   it is possible for the employer to transfer the worker to work—

    (i)   to which the worker is suited, and

    (ii)   which is to be undertaken during periods such that the worker will cease to be a night worker,

the employer shall transfer the worker accordingly.

8   Pattern of work

Where the pattern according to which an employer organises work is such as to put the health and safety of a worker employed by him at risk, in particular because the work is monotonous or the work-rate is predetermined, the employer shall ensure that the worker is given adequate rest breaks.

9   Records

An employer shall—

(a)   keep records which are adequate to show whether the limits specified in regulations 4(1), 5A(1) and 6(1) and (7) and the requirements in regulations 6A and 7(1) and (2) are being complied with in the case of each worker employed by him in relation to whom they apply; and

(b)   retain such records for two years from the date on which they were made.

10   Daily rest

(1)   A worker is entitled to a rest period of not less than eleven consecutive hours in each 24-hour period during which he works for his employer.

(2)   Subject to paragraph (3), a young worker is entitled to a rest period of not less than twelve consecutive hours in each 24-hour period during which he works for his employer.

(3)   The minimum rest period provided for in paragraph (2) may be interrupted in the case of activities involving periods of work that are split up over the day or of short duration.

11   Weekly rest period

(1)   Subject to paragraph (2), a worker is entitled to an uninterrupted rest period of not less than 24 hours in each seven-day period during which he works for his employer.

(2)   If his employer so determines, a worker shall be entitled to either—

(a)   two uninterrupted rest periods each of not less than 24 hours in each 14-day period during which he works for his employer; or

(b)   one uninterrupted rest period of not less than 48 hours in each such 14-day period, in place of the entitlement provided for in paragraph (1).

(3)   Subject to paragraph (8), a young worker is entitled to a rest period of not less than 48 hours in each seven-day period during which he works for his employer.

(4)   For the purpose of paragraphs (1) to (3), a seven-day period or (as the case may be) 14-day period shall be taken to begin—

(a)   at such times on such days as may be provided for for the purposes of this regulation in a relevant agreement; or

(b)   where there are no provisions of a relevant agreement which apply, at the start of each week or (as the case may be) every other week.

(5)   In a case where, in accordance with paragraph (4), 14-day periods are to be taken to begin at the start of every other week, the first such period applicable in the case of a particular worker shall be taken to begin—

(a)   if the worker's employment began on or before the date on which these Regulations come into force, on 5 October 1998; or

(b)   if the worker's employment begins after the date on which these Regulations come into force, at the start of the week in which that employment begins.

(6)   For the purposes of paragraphs (4) and (5), a week starts at midnight between Sunday and Monday.

(7)   The minimum rest period to which a worker is entitled under paragraph (1) or (2) shall not include any part of a rest period to which the worker is entitled under regulation 10(1), except where this is justified by objective or technical reasons or reasons concerning the organisation of work.

(8)   The minimum rest period to which a young worker is entitled under paragraph (3)—

(a)   may be interrupted in the case of activities involving periods of work that are split up over the day or are of short duration; and

(b)   may be reduced where this is justified by technical or organisation reasons, but not to less than 36 consecutive hours.

12   Rest breaks

(1)   Where a worker's daily working time is more than six hours, he is entitled to a rest break.

(2)   The details of the rest break to which a worker is entitled under paragraph (1), including its duration and the terms on which it is granted, shall be in accordance with any provisions for the purposes of this regulation which are contained in a collective agreement or a workforce agreement.

(3)   Subject to the provisions of any applicable collective agreement or workforce agreement, the rest break provided for in paragraph (1) is an uninterrupted period of not less than 20 minutes, and the worker is entitled to spend it away from his workstation if he has one.

(4)   Where a young worker's daily working time is more than four and a half hours, he is entitled to a rest break of at least 30 minutes, which shall be consecutive if possible, and he is entitled to spend it away from his workstation if he has one.

(5)   If, on any day, a young worker is employed by more than one employer, his daily working time shall be determined for the purpose of paragraph (4) by aggregating the number of hours worked by him for each employer.

13   Entitlement to annual leave

(1)   Subject to paragraph (5), a worker is entitled to four weeks' annual leave in each leave year.

(2)   ...

(3)   A worker's leave year, for the purposes of this regulation, begins—

     (a)   on such date during the calendar year as may be provided for in a relevant agreement; or

     (b)   where there are no provisions of a relevant agreement which apply—

         (i)   if the worker's employment began on or before 1 October 1998, on that date and each subsequent anniversary of that date; or

         (ii)   if the worker's employment begins after 1 October 1998, on the date on which that employment begins and each subsequent anniversary of that date.

(4)   Paragraph (3) does not apply to a worker to whom Schedule 2 applies (workers employed in agriculture) except where, in the case of a worker partly employed in agriculture, a relevant agreement so provides.

(5)   Where the date on which a worker's employment begins is later than the date on which (by virtue of a relevant agreement) his first leave year begins, the leave to which he is entitled in that leave year is a proportion of the period applicable under paragraph (2) equal to the proportion of that leave year remaining on the date on which his employment begins.

(6), (7), (8) ...

(9)   Leave to which a worker is entitled under this regulation may be taken in instalments, but—

     (a)   it may only be taken in the leave year in respect of which it is due, and

     (b)   it may not be replaced by a payment in lieu except where the worker's employment is terminated.

13A   Entitlement to additional annual leave

(1)   Subject to regulation 26A and paragraphs (3) and (5), a worker is entitled in each leave year to a period of additional leave determined in accordance with paragraph (2).

(2)   The period of additional leave to which a worker is entitled under paragraph (1) is—

     (a)   in any leave year beginning on or after 1st October 2007 but before 1st April 2008, 0.8 weeks;

     (b)   in any leave year beginning before 1st October 2007, a proportion of 0.8 weeks equivalent to the proportion of the year beginning on 1st October 2007 which would have elapsed at the end of that leave year;

     (c)   in any leave year beginning on 1st April 2008, 0.8 weeks;

     (d)   in any leave year beginning after 1st April 2008 but before 1st April 2009, 0.8 weeks and a proportion of another 0.8 weeks equivalent to the proportion of the year beginning on 1st April 2009 which would have elapsed at the end of that leave year;

     (e)   in any leave year beginning on or after 1st April 2009, 1.6 weeks.

(3) The aggregate entitlement provided for in paragraph (2) and regulation 13(1) is subject to a maximum of 28 days.

(4) A worker's leave year begins for the purposes of this regulation on the same date as the worker's leave year begins for the purposes of regulation 13.

(5) Where the date on which a worker's employment begins is later than the date on which his first leave year begins, the additional leave to which he is entitled in that leave year is a proportion of the period applicable under paragraph (2) equal to the proportion of that leave year remaining on the date on which his employment begins.

(6) Leave to which a worker is entitled under this regulation may be taken in instalments, but it may not be replaced by a payment in lieu except where—

    (a) the worker's employment is terminated; or

    (b) the leave is an entitlement that arises under paragraph (2)(a), (b) or (c); or

    (c) the leave is an entitlement to 0.8 weeks that arises under paragraph (2)(d) in respect of that part of the leave year which would have elapsed before 1 April 2009.

(7) A relevant agreement may provide for any leave to which a worker is entitled under this regulation to be carried forward into the leave year immediately following the leave year in respect of which it is due.

(8) This regulation does not apply to workers to whom the Agricultural Wages (Scotland) Act 1949 applies (as that Act had effect on 1 July 1999).

14 Compensation related to entitlement to leave

(1) This regulation applies where—

    (a) a worker's employment is terminated during the course of his leave year, and

    (b) on the date on which the termination takes effect ('the termination date'), the proportion he has taken of the leave to which he is entitled in the leave year under regulation 13 and regulation 13A differs from the proportion of the leave year which has expired.

(2) Where the proportion of leave taken by the worker is less than the proportion of the leave year which has expired, his employer shall make him a payment in lieu of leave in accordance with paragraph (3).

(3) The payment due under paragraph (2) shall be—

    (a) such sum as may be provided for for the purposes of this regulation in a relevant agreement, or

    (b) where there are no provisions of a relevant agreement which apply, a sum equal to the amount that would be due to the worker under regulation 16 in respect of a period of leave determined according to the formula—

$$(A \times B) - C$$

where—

A is the period of leave to which the worker is entitled under regulation 13 and regulation 13A;
B is the proportion of the worker's leave year which expired before the termination date, and
C is the period of leave taken by the worker between the start of the leave year and the termination date.

(4) A relevant agreement may provide that, where the proportion of leave taken by the worker exceeds the proportion of the leave year which has expired, he shall compensate his employer, whether by a payment, by undertaking additional work or otherwise.

15 Dates on which leave is taken

(1) A worker may take leave to which he is entitled under regulation 13 and regulation 13A on such days as he may elect by giving notice to his employer in accordance with paragraph (3), subject to any requirement imposed on him by his employer under paragraph (2).

(2) A worker's employer may require the worker—

    (a) to take leave to which the worker is entitled under regulation 13 or regulation 13A; or

    (b) not to take such leave,

on particular days, by giving notice to the worker in accordance with paragraph (3).

(3) A notice under paragraph (1) or (2)—

(a)   may relate to all or part of the leave to which a worker is entitled in a leave year;

(b)   shall specify the days on which leave is or (as the case may be) is not to be taken and, where the leave on a particular day is to be in respect of only part of the day, its duration; and

(c)   shall be given to the employer or, as the case may be, the worker before the relevant date.

(4)   The relevant date, for the purposes of paragraph (3), is the date—

(a)   in the case of a notice under paragraph (1) or (2)(a), twice as many days in advance of the earliest day specified in the notice as the number of days or part-days to which the notice relates, and

(b)   in the case of a notice under paragraph (2)(b), as many days in advance of the earliest day so specified as the number of days or part-days to which the notice relates.

(5)   Any right or obligation under paragraphs (1) to (4) may be varied or excluded by a relevant agreement.

(6)   This regulation does not apply to a worker to whom Schedule 2 applies (workers employed in agriculture) except where, in the case of a worker partly employed in agriculture, a relevant agreement so provides.

15A   Leave during the first year of employment

(1)   During the first year of his employment, the amount of leave a worker may take at any time in exercise of his entitlement under regulation 13 or regulation 13A is limited to the amount which is deemed to have accrued in his case at that time under paragraph (2) or (2A), as modified under paragraph (3) in a case where that paragraph applies, less the amount of leave (if any) that he has already taken during that year.

(2)   For the purposes of paragraph (1), in the case of workers to whom the Agricultural Wages (Scotland) Act 1949 applies, leave is deemed to accrue over the course of the worker's first year of employment, at the rate of one-twelfth of the amount specified in regulation 13(1) on the first day of each month of that year.

(2A) Except where paragraph (2) applies, for the purposes of paragraph (1), leave is deemed to accrue over the course of the worker's first year of employment, at the rate of one-twelfth of the amount specified in regulation 13(1) and regulation 13A(2), subject to the limit contained in regulation 13A(3), on the first day of each month of that year.

(3)   Where the amount of leave that has accrued in a particular case includes a fraction of a day other than a half-day, the fraction shall be treated as a half-day if it is less than a half-day and as a whole day if it is more than a half-day.

(4)   This regulation does not apply to a worker whose employment began on or before 25th October 2001.

16   Payment in respect of periods of leave

(1)   A worker is entitled to be paid in respect of any period of annual leave to which he is entitled under regulation 13 and regulation 13A, at the rate of a week's pay in respect of each week of leave.

(2)   Sections 221 to 224 of the 1996 Act shall apply for the purpose of determining the amount of a week's pay for the purposes of this regulation, subject to the modifications set out in paragraph (3).

(3)   The provisions referred to in paragraph (2) shall apply—

(a)   as if references to the employee were references to the worker;

(b)   as if references to the employee's contract of employment were references to the worker's contract;

(c)   as if the calculation date were the first day of the period of leave in question; and

(d)   as if the references to sections 227 and 228 did not apply.

(4)   A right to payment under paragraph (1) does not affect any right of a worker to remuneration under his contract ('contractual remuneration').

(5)   Any contractual remuneration paid to a worker in respect of a period of leave goes towards discharging any liability of the employer to make payments under this regulation in respect of

that period; and, conversely, any payment of remuneration under this regulation in respect of a period goes towards discharging any liability of the employer to pay contractual remuneration in respect of that period.

17   Entitlements under other provisions

Where during any period a worker is entitled to a rest period, rest break or annual leave both under a provision of these Regulations and under a separate provision (including a provision of his contract), he may not exercise the two rights separately, but may, in taking a rest period, break or leave during that period, take advantage of whichever right is, in any particular respect, the more favourable.

PART III

EXCEPTIONS

18   Excluded sectors

(1)   These Regulations do not apply—

    (a)   to workers to whom the European Agreement on the organisation of working time of seafarers dated 30th September 1998 and put into effect by Council Directive 1999/63/EC of 21st June 1999 applies;

    (b)   to workers to whom the Fishing Vessels (Working Time: Sea-fishermen) Regulations 2004 apply; or

    (c)   to workers to whom the Merchant Shipping (Working Time: Inland Waterways) Regulations 2003 apply

(2)   Regulations 4(1) and (2), 6(1), (2) and (7), 7(1) and (6), 8, 10(1), 11(1) and (2), 12(1), 13, 13A and 16 do not apply—

    (a)   where characteristics peculiar to certain specific services such as the armed forces or the police, or to certain specific activities in the civil protection services, inevitably conflict with the provisions of these Regulations;

    (b)   to workers to whom the European Agreement on the organisation of working time of mobile staff in civil aviation concluded on 22nd March 2000 and implemented by Council Directive 2000/79/EC of 27th November 2000 applies; or

    (c)   to the activities of workers who are doctors in training.

(3)   Paragraph (2)(c) has effect only until 31st July 2004.

(4)   Regulations 4(1) and (2), 6(1), (2) and (7), 8, 10(1), 11(1) and (2) and 12(1) do not apply to workers to whom Directive 2002/15/EC of the European Parliament and of the Council on the organisation of the working time of persons performing mobile road transport activities, dated 11th March 2002 applies.

19   Domestic service

Regulations 4(1) and (2), 5A(1) and (4), 6(1), (2) and (7), 6A, 7(1), (2) and (6) and 8 do not apply in relation to a worker employed as a domestic servant in a private household.

20   Unmeasured working time

(1)   Regulations 4(1) and (2), 6(1), (2) and (7), 10(1), 11(1) and (2) and 12(1) do not apply in relation to a worker where, on account of the specific characteristics of the activity in which he is engaged, the duration of his working time is not measured or predetermined or can be determined by the worker himself, as may be the case for—

    (a)   managing executives or other persons with autonomous decision-taking powers;

    (b)   family workers; or

    (c)   workers officiating at religious ceremonies in churches and religious communities.

(2)   ...

21   Other special cases

Subject to regulation 24, regulations 6(1), (2) and (7), 10(1), 11(1) and (2) and 12(1) do not apply in relation to a worker—

    (a)   where the worker's activities are such that his place of work and place of residence are distant from one another, including cases where the worker is employed in offshore work, or his different places of work are distant from one another;

(b) where the worker is engaged in security and surveillance activities requiring a permanent presence in order to protect property and persons, as may be the case for security guards and caretakers or security firms;

(c) where the worker's activities involve the need for continuity of service or production, as may be the case in relation to—

    (i) services relating to the reception, treatment or care provided by hospitals or similar establishments (including the activities of doctors in training), residential institutions and prisons;

    (ii) work at docks or airports;

    (iii) press, radio, television, cinematographic production, postal and telecommunications services and civil protection services;

    (iv) gas, water and electricity production, transmission and distribution, household refuse collection and incineration;

    (v) industries in which work cannot be interrupted on technical grounds;

    (vi) research and development activities;

    (vii) agriculture;

    (viii) the carriage of passengers on regular urban transport services;

(d) where there is a foreseeable surge of activity, as may be the case in relation to—

    (i) agriculture;

    (ii) tourism; and

    (iii) postal services;

(e) where the worker's activities are affected by—

    (i) an occurrence due to unusual and unforeseeable circumstances, beyond the control of the worker's employer;

    (ii) exceptional events, the consequences of which could not have been avoided despite the exercise of all due care by the employer; or

    (iii) an accident or the imminent risk of an accident;

(f) where the worker works in railway transport and—

    (i) his activities are intermittent;

    (ii) he spends his working time on board trains; or

    (iii) his activities are linked to transport timetables and to ensuring the continuity and regularity of traffic

22 Shift workers

(1) Subject to regulation 24—

(a) regulation 10(1) does not apply in relation to a shift worker when he changes shift and cannot take a daily rest period between the end of one shift and the start of the next one;

(b) paragraphs (1) and (2) of regulation 11 do not apply in relation to a shift worker when he changes shift and cannot take a weekly rest period between the end of one shift and the start of the next one; and

(c) neither regulation 10(1) nor paragraphs (1) and (2) of regulation 11 apply to workers engaged in activities involving periods of work split up over the day, as may be the case for cleaning staff.

(2) For the purposes of this regulation—

'shift worker' means any worker whose work schedule is part of shift work; and

'shift work' means any method of organising work in shifts whereby workers succeed each other at the same workstations according to a certain pattern, including a rotating pattern, and which may be continuous or discontinuous, entailing the need for workers to work at different times over a given period of days or weeks.

23 Collective and workforce agreements

A collective agreement or a workforce agreement may—

(a) modify or exclude the application of regulations 6(1) to (3) and (7), 10(1), 11(1) and (2) and 12(1), and

(b)   for objective or technical reasons or reasons concerning the organisation of work, modify the application of regulation 4(3) and (4) by the substitution, for each reference to 17 weeks, of a different period, being a period not exceeding 52 weeks,

in relation to particular workers or groups of workers.

24   Compensatory rest

Where the application of any provision of these Regulations is excluded by regulation 21 or 22, or is modified or excluded by means of a collective agreement or a workforce agreement under regulation 23(a), and a worker is accordingly required by his employer to work during a period which would otherwise be a rest period or rest break—

(a)   his employer shall wherever possible allow him to take an equivalent period of compensatory rest, and

(b)   in exceptional cases in which it is not possible, for objective reasons, to grant such a period of rest, his employer shall afford him such protection as may be appropriate in order to safeguard the worker's health and safety.

24A   Mobile workers

(1)   Regulations 6(1), (2) and (7), 10(1), 11(1) and (2) and 12(1) do not apply to a mobile worker in relation to whom the application of those regulations is not excluded by any provision of regulation 18.

(2)   A mobile worker, to whom paragraph (1) applies, is entitled to adequate rest, except where the worker's activities are affected by any of the matters referred to in regulation 21(e).

(3)   For the purposes of this regulation, 'adequate rest' means that a worker has regular rest periods, the duration of which are expressed in units of time and which are sufficiently long and continuous to ensure that, as a result of fatigue or other irregular working patterns, he does not cause injury to himself, to fellow workers or to others and that he does not damage his health, either in the short term or in the longer term.

25   Workers in the armed forces

(1)   Regulation 9 does not apply in relation to a worker serving as a member of the armed forces.

(2)   Regulations 5A, 6A, 10(2) and 11(3) do not apply in relation to a young worker serving as a member of the armed forces.

(3)   In a case where a young worker is accordingly required to work during the restricted period or is not permitted the minimum rest period provided for in regulation 10(2) or 11(3) he shall be allowed an appropriate period of compensatory rest.

25A   Doctors in training

(1)   Paragraph (1) of regulation 4 is modified in its application to workers who are doctors in training as follows—

(a)   for the reference to 48 hours there is substituted a reference to 58 hours with effect from 1st August 2004 until 31st July 2007;

(b)   for the reference to 48 hours there is substituted a reference to 56 hours with effect from 1st August 2007 until 31st July 2009.

(2)   In the case of workers who are doctors in training, paragraphs (3)–(5) of regulation 4 shall not apply and paragraphs (3) and (4) of this regulation shall apply in their place.

(3)   Subject to paragraph (4), the reference period which applies in the case of a worker who is a doctor in training is, with effect from 1st August 2004—

(a)   where a relevant agreement provides for the application of this regulation in relation to successive periods of 26 weeks, each such period; and

(b)   in any other case, any period of 26 weeks in the course of his employment.

(4)   Where a doctor in training has worked for his employer for less than 26 weeks, the reference period applicable in his case is the period that has elapsed since he started work for his employer.

27   Young workers: *force majeure*

(1)   Regulations 5A, 6A, 10(2) and 12(4) do not apply in relation to a young worker where his employer requires him to undertake work which no adult worker is available to perform and which—

     (a)   is occasioned by either—
        (i)   an occurrence due to unusual and unforeseeable circumstances, beyond the employer's control, or
        (ii)   exceptional events, the consequences of which could not have been avoided despite the exercise of all due care by the employer;
     (b)   is of a temporary nature; and
     (c)   must be performed immediately.
(2) Where the application of regulation 5A, 6A, 10(2) or 12(4) is excluded by paragraph (1), and a young worker is accordingly required to work during a period which would otherwise be a rest period or rest break, his employer shall allow him to take an equivalent period of compensatory rest within the following three weeks.

27A   Other exceptions relating to young workers

(1) Regulation 5A does not apply in relation to a young worker where—
     (a)   the young worker's employer requires him to undertake work which is necessary either to maintain continuity of service or production or to respond to a surge in demand for a service or product;
     (b)   no adult worker is available to perform the work, and
     (c)   performing the work would not adversely affect the young worker's education or training.
(2) Regulation 6A does not apply in relation to a young worker employed—
     (a)   in a hospital or similar establishment, or
     (b)   in connection with cultural, artistic, sporting or advertising activities,
   in the circumstances referred to in paragraph (1).
(3) Regulation 6A does not apply, except in so far as it prohibits work between midnight and 4 a.m., in relation to a young worker employed in—
     (a)   agriculture;
     (b)   retail trading;
     (c)   postal or newspaper deliveries;
     (d)   a catering business;
     (e)   a hotel, public house, restaurant, bar or similar establishment, or
     (f)   a bakery,
   in the circumstances referred to in paragraph (1).
(4) Where the application of regulation 6A is excluded by paragraph (2) or (3), and a young worker is accordingly required to work during a period which would otherwise be a rest period or rest break—
     (a)   he shall be supervised by an adult worker where such supervision is necessary for the young worker's protection, and
     (b)   he shall be allowed an equivalent period of compensatory rest.

PART IV
MISCELLANEOUS

29   Offences

(1) An employer who fails to comply with any of the relevant requirements shall be guilty of an offence.
(2) The provisions of paragraph (3) shall apply where an inspector is exercising or has exercised any power conferred by Schedule 3.
(3) It is an offence for a person—
     (a)   to contravene any requirement imposed by the inspector under paragraph 2 of Schedule 3;
     (b)   to prevent or attempt to prevent any other person from appearing before the inspector or from answering any question to which the inspector may by virtue of paragraph 2(2)(e) of Schedule 3 require an answer;
     (c)   to contravene any requirement or prohibition imposed by an improvement notice or a prohibition notice (including any such notice as is modified on appeal);

(d)   intentionally to obstruct the inspector in the exercise or performance of his powers or duties;

(e)   to use or disclose any information in contravention of paragraph 8 of Schedule 3;

(f)   to make a statement which he knows to be false or recklessly to make a statement which is false, where the statement is made in purported compliance with a requirement to furnish any information imposed by or under these Regulations.

(4)   An employer guilty of an offence under paragraph (1) shall be liable—

(a)   on summary conviction, to a fine not exceeding the statutory maximum;

(b)   on conviction on indictment, to a fine.

(5)   A person guilty of an offence under paragraph (3) shall be liable to the penalty prescribed in relation to that provision by paragraphs (6), (7) or (8) as the case may be.

(6)   A person guilty of an offence under sub-paragraph (3)(a), (b) or (d) shall be liable on summary conviction to a fine not exceeding level 5 on the standard scale.

(7)   A person guilty of an offence under sub-paragraph (3)(c) shall be liable—

(a)   on summary conviction, to imprisonment for a term not exceeding three months, or a fine not exceeding the statutory maximum;

(b)   on conviction on indictment, to imprisonment for a term not exceeding two years, or a fine, or both.

(8)   A person guilty of an offence under any of the sub-paragraphs of paragraph (3) not falling within paragraphs (6) or (7) above, shall be liable—

(a)   on summary conviction, to a fine not exceeding the statutory maximum;

(b)   on conviction on indictment—

(i)   if the offence is under sub-paragraph (3)(e), to imprisonment for a term not exceeding two years or a fine or both;

(ii)   if the offence is not one to which the preceding sub-paragraph applies, to a fine.

(9)   The provisions set out in regulations 29A–29E below shall apply in relation to the offences provided for in paragraphs (1) and (3).

29A   Offences due to fault of other person

Where the commission by any person of an offence is due to the act or default of some other person, that other person shall be guilty of the offence, and a person may be charged with and convicted of the offence by virtue of this paragraph whether or not proceedings are taken against the first-mentioned person.

30   Remedies

(1)   A worker may present a complaint to an employment tribunal that his employer—

(a)   has refused to permit him to exercise any right he has under—

(i)   regulation 10(1) or (2), 11(1), (2) or (3), 12(1) or (4), 13 or 13A;

(ii)   regulation 24, in so far as it applies where regulation 10(1), 11(1) or (2) or 12(1) is modified or excluded;

(iii)   regulation 24A, in so far as it applies where regulation 10(1), 11(1) or (2) or 12(1) is excluded; or

(iv)   regulation 25(3), 27A(4)(b) or 27(2); or

(b)   has failed to pay him the whole or any part of any amount due to him under regulation 14(2) or 16(1).

(2)   An employment tribunal shall not consider a complaint under this regulation unless it is presented—

(a)   before the end of the period of three months (or, in a case to which regulation 38(2) applies, six months) beginning with the date on which it is alleged that the exercise of the right should have been permitted (or in the case of a rest period or leave extending over more than one day, the date on which it should have been permitted to begin) or, as the case may be, the payment should have been made;

(b)   within such further period as the tribunal considers reasonable in a case where it is satisfied that it was not reasonably practicable for the complaint to be presented before the end of that period of three or, as the case may be, six months.

(2A) Where the period within which a complaint must be presented in accordance with paragraph (2) is extended by regulation 15 of the Employment Act 2002 (Dispute Resolution) Regulations 2004, the period within which the complaint must be presented shall be the extended period rather than the period in paragraph (2).

(3) Where an employment tribunal finds a complaint under paragraph (1)(a) well-founded, the tribunal—

(a) shall make a declaration to that effect, and

(b) may make an award of compensation to be paid by the employer to the worker.

(4) The amount of the compensation shall be such as the tribunal considers just and equitable in all the circumstances having regard to—

(a) the employer's default in refusing to permit the worker to exercise his right, and

(b) any loss sustained by the worker which is attributable to the matters complained of.

(5) Where on a complaint under paragraph (1)(b) an employment tribunal finds that an employer has failed to pay a worker in accordance with regulation 14(2) or 16(1), it shall order the employer to pay to the worker the amount which it finds to be due to him.

35 Restrictions on contracting out

(1) Any provision in an agreement (whether a contract of employment or not) is void in so far as it purports—

(a) to exclude or limit the operation of any provision of these Regulations, save in so far as these Regulations provide for an agreement to have that effect, or

(b) to preclude a person from bringing proceedings under these Regulations before an employment tribunal.

(2) Paragraph (1) does not apply to—

(a) any agreement to refrain from instituting or continuing proceedings where a conciliation officer has taken action under section 18 of the Employment Tribunals Act 1996 (conciliation); or

(b) any agreement to refrain from instituting or continuing proceedings within section 18(1)(ff) of the Employment Tribunals Act 1996 (proceedings under these Regulations where conciliation is available), if the conditions regulating compromise agreements under these Regulations are satisfied in relation to the agreement.

(3) For the purposes of paragraph (2)(b) the conditions regulating compromise agreements under these Regulations are that—

(a) the agreement must be in writing,

(b) the agreement must relate to the particular complaint,

(c) the worker must have received advice from a relevant independent adviser as to the terms and effect of the proposed agreement and, in particular, its effect on his ability to pursue his rights before an employment tribunal,

(d) there must be in force, when the adviser gives the advice, a contract of insurance, or an indemnity provided for members of a profession or professional body, covering the risk of a claim by the worker in respect of loss arising in consequence of the advice,

(e) the agreement must identify the adviser, and

(f) the agreement must state that the conditions regulating compromise agreements under these Regulations are satisfied.

(4) A person is a relevant independent adviser for the purposes of paragraph (3)(c)—

(a) if he is a qualified lawyer,

(b) if he is an officer, official, employee or member of an independent trade union who has been certified in writing by the trade union as competent to give advice and as authorised to do so on behalf of the trade union, or

(c) if he works at an advice centre (whether as an employee or as a volunteer) and has been certified in writing by the centre as competent to give advice and as authorised to do so on behalf of the centre.

(5) But a person is not a relevant independent adviser for the purposes of paragraph (3)(c) in relation to the worker—

    (a)   if he is, is employed by or is acting in the matter for the employer or an associated employer,

    (b)   in the case of a person within paragraph (4)(b) or (c), if the trade union or advice centre is the employer or an associated employer, or

    (c)   in the case of a person within paragraph (4)(c), if the worker makes a payment for the advice received from him.

(6)   In paragraph (4)(a), 'qualified lawyer' means—

    (a)   as respects England and Wales, a barrister (whether in practice as such or employed to give legal advice), a solicitor who holds a practising certificate, or a person other than a barrister or solicitor who is an authorised advocate or authorised litigator (within the meaning of the Courts and Legal Services Act 1990); and

    (b)   as respects Scotland, an advocate (whether in practice as such or employed to give legal advice), or a solicitor who holds a practising certificate.

(6A) A person shall be treated as being a qualified lawyer within paragraph 6(a) if he is a Fellow of the Institute of Legal Executives employed by a solicitors' practice.

(7)   For the purposes of paragraph (5) any two employers shall be treated as associated if—

    (a)   one is a company of which the other (directly or indirectly) has control; or

    (b)   both are companies of which a third person (directly or indirectly) has control; and 'associated employer' shall be construed accordingly.

PART V
SPECIAL CLASSES OF PERSON

36   Agency workers not otherwise 'workers'

(1)   This regulation applies in any case where an individual ('the agency worker')—

    (a)   is supplied by a person ('the agent') to do work for another ('the principal') under a contract or other arrangements made between the agent and the principal; but

    (b)   is not, as respects that work, a worker, because of the absence of a worker's contract between the individual and the agent or the principal; and

    (c)   is not a party to a contract under which he undertakes to do the work for another party to the contract whose status is, by virtue of the contract, that of a client or customer of any profession or business undertaking carried on by the individual.

(2)   In a case where this regulation applies, the other provisions of these Regulations shall have effect as if there were a worker's contract for the doing of the work by the agency worker made between the agency worker and—

    (a)   whichever of the agent and the principal is responsible for paying the agency worker in respect of the work; or

    (b)   if neither the agent nor the principal is so responsible, whichever of them pays the agency worker in respect of the work,

and as if that person were the agency worker's employer.

37   Crown employment

(1)   Subject to paragraph (4) and regulation 38, these Regulations have effect in relation to Crown employment and persons in Crown employment as they have effect in relation to other employment and other workers.

(2)   In paragraph (1) 'Crown employment' means employment under or for the purposes of a government department or any officer or body exercising on behalf of the Crown functions conferred by a statutory provision.

(3)   For the purposes of the application of the provisions of these Regulations in relation to Crown employment in accordance with paragraph (1)—

    (a)   references to a worker shall be construed as references to a person in Crown employment; and

    (b)   references to a worker's contract shall be construed as references to the terms of employment of a person in Crown employment.

(4)   No act or omission by the Crown which is an offence under regulation 29 shall make the Crown criminally liable, but the High Court or, in Scotland, the Court of Session may, on the

application of a person appearing to the Court to have an interest, declare any such act or omission unlawful.

42 Non-employed trainees

For the purposes of these Regulations, a person receiving relevant training, otherwise than under a contract of employment, shall be regarded as a worker, and the person whose undertaking is providing the training shall be regarded as his employer.

SCHEDULE 1
WORKFORCE AGREEMENTS

1.   An agreement is a workforce agreement for the purposes of these Regulations if the following conditions are satisfied—

   (a)   the agreement is in writing;

   (b)   it has effect for a specified period not exceeding five years;

   (c)   it applies either—

      (i)   to all of the relevant members of the workforce, or

      (ii)   to all of the relevant members of the workforce who belong to a particular group;

   (d)   the agreement is signed—

      (i)   in the case of an agreement of the kind referred to in sub-paragraph (c)(i), by the representatives of the workforce, and in the case of an agreement of the kind referred to in sub-paragraph (c)(ii) by the representatives of the group to which the agreement applies (excluding, in either case, any representative not a relevant member of the workforce on the date on which the agreement was first made available for signature), or

      (ii)   if the employer employed 20 or fewer workers on the date referred to in sub-paragraph (d)(i), either by the appropriate representatives in accordance with that sub-paragraph or by the majority of the workers employed by him;

   (e)   before the agreement was made available for signature, the employer provided all the workers to whom it was intended to apply on the date on which it came into effect with copies of the text of the agreement and such guidance as those workers might reasonably require in order to understand it fully.

2.   For the purposes of this Schedule—

   'a particular group' is a group of the relevant members of a workforce who undertake a particular function, work at a particular workplace or belong to a particular department or unit within their employer's business;

   'relevant members of the workforce' are all of the workers employed by a particular employer, excluding any worker whose terms and conditions of employment are provided for, wholly or in part, in a collective agreement;

   'representatives of the workforce' are workers duly elected to represent the relevant members of the workforce, 'representatives of the group' are workers duly elected to represent the members of a particular group, and representatives are 'duly elected' if the election at which they were elected satisfied the requirements of paragraph 3 of this Schedule.

3.   The requirements concerning elections referred to in paragraph 2 are that—

   (a)   the number of representatives to be elected is determined by the employer;

   (b)   the candidates for election as representatives of the workforce are relevant members of the workforce, and the candidates for election as representatives of a group are members of the group;

   (c)   no worker who is eligible to be a candidate is unreasonably excluded from standing for election;

   (d)   all the relevant members of the workforce are entitled to vote for representatives of the workforce, and all the members of a particular group are entitled to vote for representatives of the group;

   (e)   the workers entitled to vote may vote for as many candidates as there are representatives to be elected;

   (f)   the election is conducted so as to secure that—

(i) so far as is reasonably practicable, those voting do so in secret, and
(ii) the votes given at the election are fairly and accurately counted.

MATERNITY AND PARENTAL LEAVE ETC. REGULATIONS 1999
(SI 1999 No. 3312)

PART I
GENERAL

2 **Interpretation**

(1) In these Regulations—

'the 1996 Act' means the Employment Rights Act 1996;

'additional adoption leave' means leave under section 75B of the 1996 Act;

'additional maternity leave' means leave under section 73 of the 1996 Act;

'business' includes a trade or profession and includes any activity carried on by a body of persons (whether corporate or unincorporated);

'child' means a person under the age of eighteen;

'childbirth' means the birth of a living child or the birth of a child whether living or dead after 24 weeks of pregnancy;

'collective agreement' means a collective agreement within the meaning of section 178 of the Trade Union and Labour Relations (Consolidation) Act 1992, the trade union parties to which are independent trade unions within the meaning of section 5 of that Act;

'contract of employment' means a contract of service or apprenticeship, whether express or implied, and (if it is express) whether oral or in writing;

'disability living allowance' means the disability living allowance provided for in Part III of the Social Security Contributions and Benefits Act 1992;

'employee' means an individual who has entered into or works under (or, where the employment has ceased, worked under) a contract of employment;

'employer' means the person by whom an employee is (or, where the employment has ceased, was) employed;

'expected week of childbirth' means the week, beginning with midnight between Saturday and Sunday, in which it is expected that childbirth will occur, and 'week of childbirth' means the week, beginning with midnight between Saturday and Sunday, in which childbirth occurs;

'job', in relation to an employee returning after … maternity leave or parental leave, means the nature of the work which she is employed to do in accordance with her contract and the capacity and place in which she is so employed;

'ordinary maternity leave' means leave under section 71 of the 1996 Act;

'parental leave' means leave under regulation 13(1);

'parental responsibility' has the meaning given by section 3 of the Children Act 1989, and 'parental responsibilities' has the meaning given by section 1(3) of the Children (Scotland) Act 1995;

'statutory leave' means leave provided for in Part 8 of the 1996 Act;

'statutory maternity leave' means ordinary maternity leave and additional maternity leave;

'statutory maternity leave period' means the period during which the employee is on statutory maternity leave;

'workforce agreement' means an agreement between an employer and his employees or their representatives in respect of which the conditions set out in Schedule 1 to these Regulations are satisfied.

(2) A reference in any provision of these Regulations to a period of continuous employment is to a period computed in accordance with Chapter I of Part XIV of the 1996 Act, as if that provision were a provision of that Act.

(3) For the purposes of these Regulations any two employers shall be treated as associated if—

(a) one is a company of which the other (directly or indirectly) has control; or

(b) both are companies of which a third person (directly or indirectly) has control;

and 'associated employer' shall be construed accordingly.

...

PART II
MATERNITY LEAVE

4   **Entitlement to ordinary maternity leave and to additional maternity leave**

(1) An employee is entitled to ordinary maternity leave and to additional maternity leave provided that she satisfies the following conditions—

    (a)   no later than the end of the fifteenth week before her expected week of childbirth, or, if that is not reasonably practicable, as soon as is reasonably practicable, she notifies her employer of—

       (i)   her pregnancy;

       (ii)   the expected week of childbirth, and

       (iii)   the date on which she intends her ordinary maternity leave period to start,

   and

    (b)   if requested to do so by her employer, she produces for his inspection a certificate from—

       (i)   a registered medical practitioner, or

       (ii)   a registered midwife,

    stating the expected week of childbirth.

(1A) An employee who has notified her employer under paragraph (1)(a)(iii) of the date on which she intends her ordinary maternity leave period to start may subsequently vary that date, provided that she notifies her employer of the variation at least—

    (a)   28 days before the date varied, or

    (b)   28 days before the new date,

whichever is the earlier, or, if that is not reasonably practicable, as soon as is reasonably practicable.

(2) Notification under paragraph (1)(a)(iii) or (1A)—

    (a)   shall be given in writing, if the employer so requests, and

    (b)   shall not specify a date earlier than the beginning of the eleventh week before the expected week of childbirth.

(3) Where, by virtue of regulation 6(1)(b), an employee's ordinary maternity leave period commences with the day which follows the first day after the beginning of the fourth week before the expected week of childbirth on which she is absent from work wholly or partly because of pregnancy—

    (a)   paragraph (1) does not require her to notify her employer of the date specified in that paragraph, but

    (b)   (whether or not she has notified him of that date) she is not entitled to ordinary maternity leave or to additional maternity leave unless she notifies him as soon as is reasonably practicable that she is absent from work wholly or partly because of pregnancy and of the date on which her absence on that account began

(4) Where, by virtue of regulation 6(2), an employee's ordinary maternity leave period commences on the day which follows the day on which childbirth occurs—

    (a)   paragraph (1) does not require her to notify her employer of the date specified in that paragraph, but

    (b)   (whether or not she has notified him of that date) she is not entitled to ordinary maternity leave or to additional maternity leave unless she notifies him as soon as is reasonably practicable after the birth that she has given birth and of the date on which the birth occurred.

(5) The notification provided for in paragraphs (3)(b) and (4)(b) shall be given in writing, if the employer so requests.

6   **Commencement of maternity leave periods**

(1) Subject to paragraph (2), an employee's ordinary maternity leave period commences with the earlier of—

(a)   the date which she notifies to her employer, in accordance with regulation 4, as the date on which she intends her ordinary maternity leave period to start, or, if by virtue of the provision for variation in that regulation she has notified more than one such date, the last date she notifies, and

(b)   the day which follows the first day after the beginning of the fourth week before the expected week of childbirth on which she is absent from work wholly or partly because of pregnancy.

(2)   Where the employee's ordinary maternity leave period has not commenced by virtue of paragraph (1) when childbirth occurs, her ordinary maternity leave period commences on the day which follows the day on which childbirth occurs.

(3)   An employee's additional maternity leave period commences on the day after the last day of her ordinary maternity leave period.

7   Duration of maternity leave periods

(1)   Subject to paragraphs (2) and (5), an employee's ordinary maternity leave period continues for the period of twenty six weeks from its commencement, or until the end of the compulsory maternity leave period provided for in regulation 8 if later.

(2)   Subject to paragraph (5), where any requirement imposed by or under any relevant statutory provision prohibits the employee from working for any period after the end of the period determined under paragraph (1) by reason of her having recently given birth, her ordinary maternity leave period continues until the end of that later period.

(3)   In paragraph (2), 'relevant statutory provision' means a provision of—

(a)   an enactment, or

(b)   an instrument under an enactment,

other than a provision for the time being specified in an order under section 66(2) of the 1996 Act.

(4)   Subject to paragraph (5), where an employee is entitled to additional maternity leave her additional maternity leave period continues until the end of the period of 26 weeks from the day on which it commenced.

(5)   Where the employee is dismissed after the commencement of an ordinary or additional maternity leave period but before the time when (apart from this paragraph) that period would end, the period ends at the time of the dismissal.

(6)   An employer who is notified under any provision of regulation 4 of the date on which, by virtue of any provision of regulation 6, an employee's ordinary maternity leave period will commence or has commenced shall notify the employee of the date on which her additional maternity leave period shall end.

(7)   The notification provided for in paragraph (6) shall be given to the employee—

(a)   where the employer is notified under regulation 4(1)(a)(iii), (3)(b) or (4)(b), within 28 days of the date on which he received the notification;

(b)   where the employer is notified under regulation 4(1A), within 28 days of the date on which the employee's ordinary maternity leave period commenced.

8   Compulsory maternity leave

The prohibition in section 72 of the 1996 Act, against permitting an employee who satisfies prescribed conditions to work during a particular period (referred to as a 'compulsory maternity leave period'), applies—

(a)   in relation to an employee who is entitled to ordinary maternity leave, and

(b)   in respect of the period of two weeks which commences with the day on which childbirth occurs.

9   Application of terms and conditions during ordinary maternity leave

(1)   An employee who takes ordinary maternity leave—

(a)   is entitled, during the period of leave, to the benefit of all of the terms and conditions of employment which would have applied if she had not been absent, and

(b)   is bound, during that period, by any obligations arising under those terms and conditions, subject only to the exception in section 71(4)(b) of the 1996 Act.

(2) In paragraph (1)(a), 'terms and conditions' has the meaning given by section 71(5) of the 1996 Act, and accordingly does not include terms and conditions about remuneration.

(3) For the purposes of section 71 of the 1996 Act, only sums payable to an employee by way of wages or salary are to be treated as remuneration.

10 Redundancy during maternity leave

(1) This regulation applies where, during an employee's ordinary or additional maternity leave period, it is not practicable by reason of redundancy for her employer to continue to employ her under her existing contract of employment.

(2) Where there is a suitable available vacancy, the employee is entitled to be offered (before the end of her employment under her existing contract) alternative employment with her employer or his successor, or an associated employer, under a new contract of employment which complies with paragraph (3) (and takes effect immediately on the ending of her employment under the previous contract).

(3) The new contract of employment must be such that—

    (a) the work to be done under it is of a kind which is both suitable in relation to the employee and appropriate for her to do in the circumstances, and

    (b) its provisions as to the capacity and place in which she is to be employed, and as to the other terms and conditions of her employment, are not substantially less favourable to her than if she had continued to be employed under the previous contract.

11 Requirement to notify intention to return during a maternity leave period

(1) An employee who intends to return to work earlier than the end of her additional maternity leave period shall give to her employer not less than 8 weeks' notice of the date on which she intends to return.

(2) If an employee attempts to return to work earlier than the end of her additional maternity leave period without complying with paragraph (1), her employer is entitled to postpone her return to a date such as will secure, subject to paragraph (3), that he has 8 weeks' notice of her return.

(2A) An employee who complies with her obligations in paragraph (1) or whose employer has postponed her return in the circumstances described in paragraph (2), and who then decides to return to work—

    (a) earlier than the original return date, must give her employer not less than 8 weeks' notice of the date on which she now intends to return;

    (b) later than the original return date, must give her employer not less than 8 weeks' notice ending with the original return date.

(2B) In paragraph (2A) the 'original return date' means the date which the employee notified to her employer as the date of her return to work under paragraph (1), or the date to which her return was postponed by her employer under paragraph (2).

(3) An employer is not entitled under paragraph (2) to postpone an employee's return to work to a date after the end of the relevant maternity leave period.

(4) If an employee whose return to work has been postponed under paragraph (2) has been notified that she is not to return to work before the date to which her return was postponed, the employer is under no contractual obligation to pay her remuneration until the date to which her return was postponed if she returns to work before that date.

(5) This regulation does not apply in a case where the employer did not notify the employee in accordance with regulation 7(6) and (7) of the date on which her additional maternity leave period would end.

12A Work during maternity leave period

(1) Subject to paragraph (5), an employee may carry out up to 10 days' work for her employer during her statutory maternity leave period without bringing her maternity leave to an end.

(2) For the purposes of this regulation, any work carried out on any day shall constitute a day's work.

(3) Subject to paragraph (4), for the purposes of this regulation, work means any work done under the contract of employment and may include training or any activity undertaken for the purposes of keeping in touch with the workplace.

(4)   Reasonable contact from time to time between an employee and her employer which either party is entitled to make during a maternity leave period (for example to discuss an employee's return to work) shall not bring that period to an end.

(5)   Paragraph (1) shall not apply in relation to any work carried out by the employee at any time from childbirth to the end of the period of two weeks which commences with the day on which childbirth occurs.

(6)   This regulation does not confer any right on an employer to require that any work be carried out during the statutory maternity leave period, nor any right on an employee to work during the statutory maternity leave period.

(7)   Any days' work carried out under this regulation shall not have the effect of extending the total duration of the statutory maternity leave period.

PART III

PARENTAL LEAVE

13   Entitlement to parental leave

(1)   An employee who—

    (a)   has been continuously employed for a period of not less than a year [or is to be treated as having been so employed by virtue of paragraph (1A)]; and

    (b)   has, or expects to have, responsibility for a child,

is entitled, in accordance with these Regulations, to be absent from work on parental leave for the purpose of caring for that child.

(1A) If, in a case where regulation 15(2) or (3) applies—

    (a)   the employee was employed, during the period between 15th December 1998 and 9th January 2002, by a person other than the person who was his employer on 9th January 2002, and

    (b)   the period of his employment by that person (or, if he was employed by more than one person during that period, any such person) was not less than a year,

then, for the purposes of paragraph (1), he shall be treated as having been continuously employed for a period of not less than a year.

(2)   An employee has responsibility for a child, for the purposes of paragraph (1), if—

    (a)   he has parental responsibility or, in Scotland, parental responsibilities for the child; or

    (b)   he has been registered as the child's father under any provision of section 10(1) or 10A(1) of the Births and Deaths Registration Act 1953 or of section 18(1) or (2) of the Registration of Births, Deaths and Marriages (Scotland) Act 1965.

(3)   …

14   Extent of entitlement

(1)   Except in the case referred to in paragraph (1A), an employee is entitled to thirteen weeks' leave in respect of any individual child.

(1A) An employee is entitled to eighteen weeks' leave in respect of a child who is entitled to a disability living allowance

(2)   Where the period for which an employee is normally required, under his contract of employment, to work in the course of a week does not vary, a week's leave for the employee is a period of absence from work which is equal in duration to the period for which he is normally required to work.

(3)   Where the period for which an employee is normally required, under his contract of employment, to work in the course of a week varies from week to week or over a longer period, or where he is normally required under his contract to work in some weeks but not in others a week's leave for the employee is a period of absence from work which is equal in duration to the period calculated by dividing the total of the periods for which he is normally required to work in a year by 52.

(4)   Where an employee takes leave in periods shorter than the period which constitutes, for him, a week's leave under whichever of paragraphs (2) and (3) is applicable in his case, he completes a week's leave when the aggregate of the periods of leave he has taken equals the period constituting a week's leave for him under the applicable paragraph.

15   When parental leave may be taken

(1)   Except in the cases referred to in paragraphs (2)–(4), an employee may not exercise any entitlement to parental leave in respect of a child after the date of the child's fifth birthday or, in the case of a child placed with the employee for adoption by him, on or after—

(a)   the fifth anniversary of the date on which the placement began, or

(b)   the date of the child's eighteenth birthday,

whichever is the earlier.

(2)   In the case of child—

(a)   born before 15th December 1999, whose fifth birthday was or is on or after that date, or

(b)   placed with the employee for adoption by him before 15th December 1999, the fifth anniversary of whose placement was or is on or after that date,

not being a case to which paragraph (3) or (4) applies, any entitlement to parental leave may not be exercised after 31st March 2005.

(3)   In the case of a child who is entitled to a disability living allowance, any entitlement to parental leave may not be exercised on or after the date of the child's eighteenth birthday.

(4)   In a case where—

(a)   the provisions set out in Schedule 2 apply, and

(b)   the employee was unable to take leave in respect of a child within the time permitted in the case of that child under paragraphs (1) or (2) because the employer postponed the period of leave under paragraph 6 of that Schedule,

the entitlement to leave is exercisable until the end of the period to which the leave was postponed

16   Default provisions in respect of parental leave

The provisions set out in Schedule 2 apply in relation to parental leave in the case of an employee whose contract of employment does not include a provision which—

(a)   confers an entitlement to absence from work for the purpose of caring for a child, and

(b)   incorporates or operates by reference to all or part of a collective agreement or workforce agreement.

PART IV
PROVISIONS APPLICABLE IN RELATION TO MORE THAN ONE KIND
OF ABSENCE

17   Application of terms and conditions during periods of leave

An employee who takes additional maternity leave or parental leave—

(a)   is entitled, during the period of leave, to the benefit of her employer's implied obligation to her of trust and confidence and any terms and conditions of her employment relating to—

(i)   notice of the termination of the employment contract by her employer;

(ii)   compensation in the event of redundancy, or

(iii)   disciplinary or grievance procedures;

(b)   is bound, during that period, by her implied obligation to her employer of good faith and any terms and conditions of her employment relating to—

(i)   notice of the termination of the employment contract by her;

(ii)   the disclosure of confidential information;

(iii)   the acceptance of gifts or other benefits, or

(iv)   the employee's participation in any other business.

18   Right to return after maternity or parental leave

(1)   An employee who returns to work after a period of ordinary maternity leave, or a period of parental leave of four weeks or less, which was—

(a)   an isolated period of leave, or

(b)   the last of two or more consecutive periods of statutory leave which did not include any period of additional maternity leave or additional adoption leave, or a period of parental leave of more than four weeks, is entitled to return to the job in which she was employed before her absence.

(2) An employee who returns to work after—

    (a) a period of additional maternity leave, or a period of parental leave of more than four weeks, whether or not preceded by another period of statutory leave, or

    (b) a period of ordinary maternity leave, or a period of parental leave of four weeks or less, not falling within the description in paragraph (1)(a) or (b) above,

is entitled to return from leave to the job in which she was employed before her absence or, if it is not reasonably practicable for the employer to permit her to return to that job, to another job which is both suitable for her and appropriate for her to do in the circumstances.

(3) The reference in paragraphs (1) and (2) to the job in which an employee was employed before her absence is a reference to the job in which she was employed—

    (a) if her return is from an isolated period of statutory leave, immediately before that period began;

    (b) if her return is from consecutive periods of statutory leave, immediately before the first such period.

(4) This regulation does not apply where regulation 10 applies.

18A Incidents of the right to return

(1) An employee's right to return under regulation 18(1) or (2) is a right to return—

    (a) with her seniority, pension rights and similar rights—

        (i) in a case where the employee is returning from additional maternity leave, or consecutive periods of statutory leave which included a period of additional maternity leave or additional adoption leave, as they would have been if the period or periods of her employment prior to her additional maternity leave or (as the case may be) additional adoption leave were continuous with the period of employment following it;

        (ii) in any other case, as they would have been if she had not been absent, and

    (b) on terms and conditions not less favourable than those which would have applied if she had not been absent.

(2) The provision in paragraph (1)(a)(i) concerning the treatment of periods of additional maternity leave or additional adoption leave is subject to the requirements of paragraphs 5 and 6 of Schedule 5 to the Social Security Act 1989 (equal treatment under pension schemes: maternity absence and family leave).

(3) The provisions in paragraph (1)(a)(ii) and (b) for an employee to be treated as if she had not been absent refer to her absence—

    (a) if her return is from an isolated period of statutory leave, since the beginning of that period;

    (b) if her return is from consecutive periods of statutory leave, since the beginning of the first such period.

19 Protection from detriment

(1) An employee is entitled under section 47C of the 1996 Act not to be subjected to any detriment by any act, or any deliberate failure to act, by her employer done for any of the reasons specified in paragraph (2).

(2) The reasons referred to in paragraph (1) are that the employee—

    (a) is pregnant;

    (b) has given birth to a child;

    (c) is the subject of a relevant requirement, or a relevant recommendation, as defined by section 66(2) of the 1996 Act;

    (d) took, sought to take or availed herself of the benefits of, ordinary maternity leave;

    (e) took or sought to take—

        (i) additional maternity leave;

        (ii) parental leave, or

        (iii) time off under section 57A of the 1996 Act;

(ee) failed to return after a period of ordinary or additional maternity leave in a case where—

    (i) the employer did not notify her, in accordance with regulation 7(6) and (7) or otherwise, of the date on which the period in question would end, and she reasonably believed that that period had not ended, or

    (ii) the employer gave her less than 28 days' notice of the date on which the period in question would end, and it was not reasonably practicable for her to return on that date;

(eee) undertook, considered undertaking or refused to undertake work in accordance with regulation 12A;

(f) declined to sign a workforce agreement for the purpose of these Regulations, or

(g) being—

    (i) a representative of members of the workforce for the purposes of Schedule 1, or

    (ii) a candidate in an election in which any person elected will, on being elected, become such a representative,

performed (or proposed to perform) any functions or activities as such a representative or candidate.

(3) For the purposes of paragraph (2)(d), a woman avails herself of the benefits of ordinary maternity leave if, during her ordinary maternity leave period, she avails herself of the benefit of any of the terms and conditions of her employment preserved by section 71 of the 1996 Act and regulation 9 during that period.

(4) Paragraph (1) does not apply in a case where the detriment in question amounts to dismissal within the meaning of Part X of the 1996 Act.

(5) Paragraph (2)(b) only applies where the act or failure to act takes place during the employee's ordinary or additional maternity leave period.

(6) For the purposes of paragraph (5)—

(a) where an act extends over a period, the reference to the date of the act is a reference to the last day of that period, and

(b) a failure to act is to be treated as done when it was decided on.

(7) For the purposes of paragraph (6), in the absence of evidence establishing the contrary an employer shall be taken to decide on a failure to act—

(a) when he does an act inconsistent with doing the failed act, or

(b) if he has done no such inconsistent act, when the period expires within which he might reasonably have been expected to do the failed act if it were to be done.

20 Unfair dismissal

(1) An employee who is dismissed is entitled under section 99 of the 1996 Act to be regarded for the purposes of Part X of that Act as unfairly dismissed if—

(a) the reason or principal reason for the dismissal is of a kind specified in paragraph (3), or

(b) the reason or principal reason for the dismissal is that the employee is redundant, and regulation 10 has not been complied with.

(2) An employee who is dismissed shall also be regarded for the purposes of Part X of the 1996 Act as unfairly dismissed if—

(a) the reason (or, if more than one, the principal reason) for the dismissal is that the employee was redundant;

(b) it is shown that the circumstances constituting the redundancy applied equally to one or more employees in the same undertaking who held positions similar to that held by the employee and who have not been dismissed by the employer, and

(c) it is shown that the reason (or, if more than one, the principal reason) for which the employee was selected for dismissal was a reason of a kind specified in paragraph (3).

(3) The kinds of reason referred to in paragraphs (1) and (2) are reasons connected with—

(a) the pregnancy of the employee;

(b) the fact that the employee has given birth to a child;

(c) the application of a relevant requirement, or a relevant recommendation, as defined by section 66(2) of the 1996 Act;

   (d)   the fact that she took, sought to take or availed herself of the benefits of, ordinary
         maternity leave;
   (e)   the fact that she took or sought to take—
         (i)   additional maternity leave;
         (ii)   parental leave, or
         (iii) time off under section 57A of the 1996 Act;
   (ee) the fact that she failed to return after a period of ordinary or additional maternity leave
         in a case where—
         (i)   the employer did not notify her, in accordance with regulation 7(6) and (7) or
                otherwise, of the date on which the period in question would end, and she
                reasonably believed that that period had not ended, or
         (ii)   the employer gave her less than 28 days' notice of the date on which the period in
                question would end, and it was not reasonably practicable for her to return on that
                date;
   (eee) the fact that she undertook, considered undertaking or refused to undertake work in
         accordance with regulation 12A;
   (f)   the fact that she declined to sign a workforce agreement for the purposes of these
         Regulations, or
   (g)   the fact that the employee, being—
         (i)   a representative of members of the workforce for the purposes of Schedule 1, or
         (ii)   a candidate in an election in which any person elected will, on being elected,
                become such a representative,
   performed (or proposed to perform) any functions or activities as such a representative or
   candidate.
(4) Paragraphs (1)(b) and (3)(b) only apply where the dismissal ends the employee's ordinary or
   additional maternity leave period.
(5) Paragraph (3) of regulation 19 applies for the purposes of paragraph (3)(d) as it applies for the
   purpose of paragraph (2)(d) of that regulation.
(6) ...
(7) Paragraph (1) does not apply in relation to an employee if—
   (a)   it is not reasonably practicable for a reason other than redundancy for the employer
         (who may be the same employer or a successor of his) to permit her to return to a job
         which is both suitable for her and appropriate for her to do in the circumstances;
   (b)   an associated employer offers her a job of that kind, and
   (c)   she accepts or unreasonably refuses that offer.
(8) Where on a complaint of unfair dismissal any question arises as to whether the operation of
   paragraph (1) is excluded by the provisions of paragraph (7), it is for the employer to show that
   the provisions in question were satisfied in relation to the complainant.

21   Contractual rights to maternity or parental leave
(1) This regulation applies where an employee is entitled to—
   (a)   ordinary maternity leave;
   (b)   additional maternity leave, or
   (c)   parental leave,
   (referred to in paragraph (2) as a 'statutory right') and also to a right which corresponds to that
   right and which arises under the employee's contract of employment or otherwise.
(2) In a case where this regulation applies—
   (a)   the employee may not exercise the statutory right and the corresponding right
         separately but may, in taking the leave for which the two rights provide, take advantage
         of whichever right is, in any particular respect, the more favourable, and
   (b)   the provisions of the 1996 Act and of these Regulations relating to the statutory right
         apply, subject to any modifications necessary to give effect to any more favourable
         contractual terms, to the exercise of the composite right described in sub-paragraph (a)
         as they apply to the exercise of the statutory right.

SCHEDULE 1
WORKFORCE AGREEMENTS

1.   An agreement is a workforce agreement for the purposes of these Regulations if the following conditions are satisfied—

   (a)   the agreement is in writing;

   (b)   it has effect for a specified period not exceeding five years;

   (c)   it applies either—

      (i)   to all of the relevant members of the workforce, or

      (ii)   to all of the relevant members of the workforce who belong to a particular group;

   (d)   the agreement is signed—

      (i)   in the case of an agreement of the kind referred to in sub-paragraph (c)(i), by the representatives of the workforce, and in the case of an agreement of the kind referred to in sub-paragraph (c)(ii), by the representatives of the group to which the agreement applies (excluding, in either case, any representative not a relevant member of the workforce on the date on which the agreement was first made available for signature), or

      (ii)   if the employer employed 20 or fewer employees on the date referred to in sub-paragraph (d)(i), either by the appropriate representatives in accordance with that sub-paragraph or by the majority of the employees employed by him; and

   (e)   before the agreement was made available for signature, the employer provided all the employees to whom it was intended to apply on the date on which it came into effect with copies of the text of the agreement and such guidance as those employees might reasonably require in order to understand it in full.

2.   For the purposes of this Schedule—

   'a particular group' is a group of the relevant members of a workforce who undertake a particular function, work at a particular workplace or belong to a particular department or unit within their employer's business;

   'relevant members of the workforce' are all of the employees employed by a particular employer, excluding any employee whose terms and conditions of employment are provided for, wholly or in part, in a collective agreement;

   'representatives of the workforce' are employees duly elected to represent the relevant members of the workforce, 'representatives of the group' are employees duly elected to represent the members of a particular group, and representatives are 'duly elected' if the election at which they were elected satisfied the requirements of paragraph 3 of this Schedule.

3.   The requirements concerning elections referred to in paragraph 2 are that—

   (a)   the number of representatives to be elected is determined by the employer;

   (b)   the candidates for election as representatives of the workforce are relevant members of the workforce, and the candidates for election as representatives of a group are members of the group;

   (c)   no employee who is eligible to be a candidate is unreasonably excluded from standing for election;

   (d)   all the relevant members of the workforce are entitled to vote for representatives of the workforce, and all the members of a particular group are entitled to vote for representatives of the group;

   (e)   the employees entitled to vote may vote for as many candidates as there are representatives to be elected, and

   (f)   the election is conducted so as to secure that—

      (i)   so far as is reasonably practicable, those voting do so in secret, and

      (ii)   the votes given at the election are fairly and accurately counted.

SCHEDULE 2
DEFAULT PROVISIONS IN RESPECT OF PARENTAL LEAVE

Conditions of entitlement

1.   An employee may not exercise any entitlement to parental leave unless—

     (a)   he has complied with any request made by his employer to produce for the employer's inspection evidence of his entitlement, of the kind described in paragraph 2;

     (b)   he has given his employer notice, in accordance with whichever of paragraphs 3 to 5 is applicable, of the period of leave he proposes to take, and

     (c)   in a case where paragraph 6 applies, his employer has not postponed the period of leave in accordance with that paragraph.

2.   The evidence to be produced for the purpose of paragraph 1(a) is such evidence as may reasonably be required of—

     (a)   the employee's responsibility or expected responsibility for the child in respect of whom the employee proposes to take parental leave;

     (b)   the child's date of birth or, in the case of a child who was placed with the employee for adoption, the date on which the placement began, and

     (c)   in a case where the employee's right to exercise an entitlement to parental leave under regulation 15, or to take a particular period of leave under paragraph 7, depends upon whether the child is entitled to a disability living allowance, the child's entitlement to that allowance.

Notice to be given to employer

3.   Except in a case where paragraph 4 or 5 applies, the notice required for the purpose of paragraph 1(b) is notice which—

     (a)   specifies the dates on which the period of leave is to begin and end, and

     (b)   is given to the employer at least 21 days before the date on which that period is to begin.

4.   Where the employee is the father of the child in respect of whom the leave is to be taken, and the period of leave is to begin on the date on which the child is born, the notice required for the purpose of paragraph 1(b) is notice which—

     (a)   specifies the expected week of childbirth and the duration of the period of leave, and

     (b)   is given to the employer at least 21 days before the beginning of the expected week of childbirth.

5.   Where the child in respect of whom the leave is to be taken is to be placed with the employee for adoption by him and the leave is to begin on the date of the placement, the notice required for the purpose of paragraph 1(b) is notice which—

     (a)   specifies the week in which the placement is expected to occur and the duration of the period of leave, and

     (b)   is given to the employer at least 21 days before the beginning of that week, or, if that is not reasonably practicable, as soon as is reasonably practicable.

Postponement of leave

6.   An employer may postpone a period of parental leave where—

     (a)   neither paragraph 4 nor paragraph 5 applies, and the employee has accordingly given the employer notice in accordance with paragraph 3;

     (b)   the employer considers that the operation of his business would be unduly disrupted if the employee took leave during the period identified in his notice;

     (c)   the employer agrees to permit the employee to take a period of leave—

        (i)   of the same duration as the period identified in the employee's notice, and

        (ii)   beginning on a date determined by the employer after consulting the employee, which is no later than six months after the commencement of that period;

     (d)   the employer gives the employee notice in writing of the postponement which—

      (i)   states the reason for it, and

      (ii)   specifies the dates on which the period of leave the employer agrees to permit the employee to take will begin and end, and

    (e)   that notice is given to the employee not more than seven days after the employee's notice was given to the employer.

Minimum periods of leave

7.   An employee may not take parental leave in a period other than the period which constitutes a week's leave for him under regulation 14 or a multiple of that period, except in a case where the child in respect of whom leave is taken is entitled to a disability living allowance.

Maximum annual leave allowance

8.   An employee may not take more than four weeks' leave in respect of any individual child during a particular year.

9.   For the purposes of paragraph 8, a year is the period of twelve months beginning—

    (a)   except where sub-paragraph (b) applies, on the date on which the employee first became entitled to take parental leave in respect of the child in question, or

    (b)   in a case where the employee's entitlement has been interrupted at the end of a period of continuous employment, on the date on which the employee most recently became entitled to take parental leave in respect of that child,

and each successive period of twelve months beginning on the anniversary of that date.

PART-TIME WORKERS (PREVENTION OF LESS FAVOURABLE TREATMENT) REGULATIONS 2000 (SI 2000 No. 1551)

PART I
GENERAL AND INTERPRETATION

1   Citation, commencement and interpretation

    (1)   These Regulations may be cited as the Part-time Workers (Prevention of Less Favourable Treatment) Regulations 2000 and shall come into force on 1 July 2000.

    (2)   In these Regulations—

    'the 1996 Act' means the Employment Rights Act 1996;

    'contract of employment' means a contract of service or of apprenticeship, whether express or implied, and (if it is express) whether oral or in writing;

    'employee' means an individual who has entered into or works under or (except where a provision of these Regulations otherwise requires) where the employment has ceased, worked under a contract of employment;

    'employer', in relation to any employee or worker, means the person by whom the employee or worker is or (except where a provision of these Regulations otherwise requires) where the employment has ceased, was employed;

    'pro rata principle' means that where a comparable full-time worker receives or is entitled to receive pay or any other benefit, a part-time worker is to receive or be entitled to receive not less than the proportion of that pay or other benefit that the number of his weekly hours bears to the number of weekly hours of the comparable full-time worker;

    'worker' means an individual who has entered into or works under or (except where a provision of these Regulations otherwise requires) where the employment has ceased, worked under—

    (a)   a contract of employment; or

    (b)   any other contract, whether express or implied and (if it is express) whether oral or in writing, whereby the individual undertakes to do or perform personally any work or services for another party to the contract whose status is not by virtue of the contract that of a client or customer of any profession or business undertaking carried on by the individual.

(3) In the definition of the pro rata principle and in regulations 3 and 4 'weekly hours' means the number of hours a worker is required to work under his contract of employment in a week in which he has no absences from work and does not work any overtime or, where the number of such hours varies according to a cycle, the average number of such hours.

2 Meaning of full-time worker, part-time worker and comparable full-time worker

(1) A worker is a full-time worker for the purpose of these Regulations if he is paid wholly or in part by reference to the time he works and, having regard to the custom and practice of the employer in relation to workers employed by the worker's employer under the same type of contract, is identifiable as a full-time worker.

(2) A worker is a part-time worker for the purpose of these Regulations if he is paid wholly or in part by reference to the time he works and, having regard to the custom and practice of the employer in relation to workers employed by the worker's employer under the same type of contract, is not identifiable as a full-time worker.

(3) For the purposes of paragraphs (1), (2) and (4), the following shall be regarded as being employed under different types of contract—

 (a) employees employed under a contract that is not a contract of apprenticeship;

 (b) employees employed under a contract of apprenticeship;

 (c) workers who are not employees;

 (d) any other description of worker that it is reasonable for the employer to treat differently from other workers on the ground that workers of that description have a different type of contract.

(4) A full-time worker is a comparable full-time worker in relation to a part-time worker if, at the time when the treatment that is alleged to be less favourable to the part-time worker takes place—

 (a) both workers are—

  (i) employed by the same employer under the same type of contract, and

  (ii) engaged in the same or broadly similar work having regard, where relevant, to whether they have a similar level of qualification, skills and experience; and

 (b) the full-time worker works or is based at the same establishment as the part-time worker or, where there is no full-time worker working or based at that establishment who satisfies the requirements of sub-paragraph (a), works or is based at a different establishment and satisfies those requirements.

3 Workers becoming part-time

(1) This regulation applies to a worker who—

 (a) was identifiable as a full-time worker in accordance with regulation 2(1); and

 (b) following a termination or variation of his contract, continues to work under a new or varied contract, whether of the same type or not, that requires him to work for a number of weekly hours that is lower than the number he was required to work immediately before the termination or variation.

(2) Notwithstanding regulation 2(4), regulation 5 shall apply to a worker to whom this regulation applies as if he were a part-time worker and as if there were a comparable full-time worker employed under the terms that applied to him immediately before the variation or termination.

(3) The fact that this regulation applies to a worker does not affect any right he may have under these Regulations by virtue of regulation 2(4).

4 Workers returning part-time after absence

(1) This regulation applies to a worker who—

 (a) was identifiable as a full-time worker in accordance with regulation 2(1) immediately before a period of absence (whether the absence followed a termination of the worker's contract or not);

 (b) returns to work for the same employer within a period of less than twelve months beginning with the day on which the period of absence started;

 (c) returns to the same job or to a job at the same level under a contract, whether it is a different contract or a varied contract and regardless of whether it is of the same type, under which he is required to work for a number of weekly hours that is lower than the number he was required to work immediately before the period of absence.

(2) Notwithstanding regulation 2(4), regulation 5 shall apply to a worker to whom this regulation applies ('the returning worker') as if he were a part-time worker and as if there were a comparable full-time worker employed under—

    (a)   the contract under which the returning worker was employed immediately before the period of absence; or

    (b)   where it is shown that, had the returning worker continued to work under the contract mentioned in sub-paragraph (a) a variation would have been made to its term during the period of absence, the contract mentioned in that sub-paragraph including that variation.

(3) The fact that this regulation applies to a worker does not affect any right he may have under these Regulations by virtue of regulation 2(4).

PART II

RIGHTS AND REMEDIES

5   Less favourable treatment of part-time workers

(1) A part-time worker has the right not to be treated by his employer less favourably than the employer treats a comparable full-time worker—

    (a)   as regards the terms of his contract; or

    (b)   by being subjected to any other detriment by any act, or deliberate failure to act, of his employer.

(2) The right conferred by paragraph (1) applies only if—

    (a)   the treatment is on the ground that the worker is a part-time worker, and

    (b)   the treatment is not justified on objective grounds.

(3) In determining whether a part-time worker has been treated less favourably than a comparable full-time worker the pro rata principle shall be applied unless it is inappropriate.

(4) A part-time worker paid at a lower rate for overtime worked by him in a period than a comparable full-time worker is or would be paid for overtime worked by him in the same period shall not, for that reason, be regarded as treated less favourably than the comparable full-time worker where, or to the extent that, the total number of hours worked by the part-time worker in the period, including overtime, does not exceed the number of hours the comparable full-time worker is required to work in the period, disregarding absences from work and overtime.

6   Right to receive a written statement of reasons for less favourable treatment

(1) If a worker who considers that his employer may have treated him in a manner which infringes a right conferred on him by regulation 5 requests in writing from his employer a written statement giving particulars of the reasons for the treatment, the worker is entitled to be provided with such a statement within twenty-one days of his request.

(2) A written statement under this regulation is admissible as evidence in any proceedings under these Regulations.

(3) If it appears to the tribunal in any proceedings under these Regulations—

    (a)   that the employer deliberately, and without reasonable excuse, omitted to provide a written statement, or

    (b)   that the written statement is evasive or equivocal,

it may draw any inference which it considers it just and equitable to draw, including an inference that the employer has infringed the right in question.

(4) This regulation does not apply where the treatment in question consists of the dismissal of an employee, and the employee is entitled to a written statement of reasons for his dismissal under section 92 of the 1996 Act.

7   Unfair dismissal and the right not to be subjected to detriment

(1) An employee who is dismissed shall be regarded as unfairly dismissed for the purposes of Part X of the 1996 Act if the reason (or, if more than one, the principal reason) for the dismissal is a reason specified in paragraph (3).

(2) A worker has the right not to be subjected to any detriment by any act, or any deliberate failure to act, by his employer done on a ground specified in paragraph (3).

(3) The reasons or, as the case may be, grounds are—

    (a) that the worker has—

        (i) brought proceedings against the employer under these Regulations;

        (ii) requested from his employer a written statement of reasons under regulation 6;

        (iii) given evidence or information in connection with such proceedings brought by any worker;

        (iv) otherwise done anything under these Regulations in relation to the employer or any other person;

        (v) alleged that the employer had infringed these Regulations; or

        (vi) refused (or proposed to refuse) to forgo a right conferred on him by these Regulations, or

    (b) that the employer believes or suspects that the worker has done or intends to do any of the things mentioned in sub-paragraph (a).

(4) Where the reason or principal reason for dismissal or, as the case may be, ground for subjection to any act or deliberate failure to act, is that mentioned in paragraph (3)(a)(v), or (b) so far as it relates thereto, neither paragraph (1) nor paragraph (2) applies if the allegation made by the worker is false and not made in good faith.

(5) Paragraph (2) does not apply where the detriment in question amounts to the dismissal of an employee within the meaning of Part X of the 1996 Act.

8   Complaints to employment tribunals etc.

(1) Subject to regulation 7(5), a worker may present a complaint to an employment tribunal that his employer has infringed a right conferred on him by regulation 5 or 7(2).

(2) Subject to paragraph (3), an employment tribunal shall not consider a complaint under this regulation unless it is presented before the end of the period of three months (or, in a case to which regulation 13 applies, six months) beginning with the date of the less favourable treatment or detriment to which the complaint relates or, where an act or failure to act is part of a series of similar acts or failures comprising the less favourable treatment or detriment, the last of them.

(3) A tribunal may consider any such complaint which is out of time if, in all the circumstances of the case, it considers that it is just and equitable to do so.

(4) For the purposes of calculating the date of the less favourable treatment or detriment under paragraph (2)—

    (a) where a term in a contract is less favourable, that treatment shall be treated, subject to paragraph (b), as taking place on each day of the period during which the term is less favourable;

    (b) where an application relies on regulation 3 or 4 the less favourable treatment shall be treated as occurring on, and only on, in the case of regulation 3, the first day on which the applicant worked under the new or varied contract and, in the case of regulation 4, the day on which the applicant returned; and

    (c) a deliberate failure to act contrary to regulation 5 or 7(2) shall be treated as done when it was decided on.

(5) In the absence of evidence establishing the contrary, a person shall be taken for the purposes of paragraph (4)(c) to decide not to act—

    (a) when he does an act inconsistent with doing the failed act; or

    (b) if he has done no such inconsistent act, when the period expires within which he might reasonably have been expected to have done the failed act if it was to be done.

(6) Where a worker presents a complaint under this regulation it is for the employer to identify the ground for the less favourable treatment or detriment.

(7) Where an employment tribunal finds that a complaint presented to it under this regulation is well founded, it shall take such of the following steps as it considers just and equitable—

    (a) making a declaration as to the rights of the complainant and the employer in relation to the matters to which the complaint relates;

(b)   ordering the employer to pay compensation to the complainant;

(c)   recommending that the employer take, within a specified period, action appearing to the tribunal to be reasonable, in all the circumstances of the case, for the purpose of obviating or reducing the adverse effect on the complainant of any matter to which the complaint relates.

(8) ...

(9) Where a tribunal orders compensation under paragraph (7)(b), the amount of the compensation awarded shall be such as the tribunal considers just and equitable in all the circumstances having regard to—

(a)   the infringement to which the complaint relates, and

(b)   any loss which is attributable to the infringement having regard, in the case of an infringement of the right conferred by regulation 5, to the pro rata principle except where it is inappropriate to do so.

(10) The loss shall be taken to include—

(a)   any expenses reasonably incurred by the complainant in consequence of the infringement, and

(b)   loss of any benefit which he might reasonably be expected to have had but for the infringement.

(11) Compensation in respect of treating a worker in a manner which infringes the right conferred on him by regulation 5 shall not include compensation for injury to feelings.

(12) In ascertaining the loss the tribunal shall apply the same rule concerning the duty of a person to mitigate his loss as applies to damages recoverable under the common law of England and Wales or (as the case may be) Scotland.

(13) Where the tribunal finds that the act, or failure to act, to which the complaint relates was to any extent caused or contributed to by action of the complainant, it shall reduce the amount of the compensation by such proportion as it considers just and equitable having regard to that finding.

(14) If the employer fails, without reasonable justification, to comply with a recommendation made by an employment tribunal under paragraph (7)(c) the tribunal may, if it thinks it just and equitable to do so—

(a)   increase the amount of compensation required to be paid to the complainant in respect of the complaint, where an order was made under paragraph (7)(b); or

(b)   make an order under paragraph (7)(b).

9   Restrictions on contracting out

Section 203 of the 1996 Act (restrictions on contracting out) shall apply in relation to these Regulations as if they were contained in that Act.

PART III
MISCELLANEOUS

11   Liability of employers and principals

(1) Anything done by a person in the course of his employment shall be treated for the purposes of these Regulations as also done by his employer, whether or not it was done with the employer's knowledge or approval.

(2) Anything done by a person as agent for the employer with the authority of the employer shall be treated for the purposes of these Regulations as also done by the employer.

(3) In proceedings under these Regulations against any person in respect of an act alleged to have been done by a worker of his, it shall be a defence for that person to prove that he took such steps as were reasonably practicable to prevent the worker from—

(a)   doing that act; or

(b)   doing, in the course of his employment, acts of that description.

TRADE UNION RECOGNITION (METHOD OF COLLECTIVE BARGAINING) ORDER 2000
(SI 2000 No. 1300)

2   Specification of method

The method specified for the purposes of paragraphs 31(3) and 63(2) of Schedule A1 to the Trade Union and Labour Relations (Consolidation) Act 1992 is the method set out under the heading 'the specified method' in the Schedule to this Order.

THE SCHEDULE
PREAMBLE

The method specified below ('the specified method') is one by which collective bargaining might be conducted in the particular, and possibly rare, circumstances discussed in the following paragraph. The specified method is not designed to be applied as a model for voluntary procedural agreements between employers and unions.

Because most voluntary agreements are not legally binding and are usually concluded in a climate of trust and co-operation, they do not need to be as prescriptive as the specified method. However, the Central Arbitration Committee ('CAC') must take the specified method into account when exercising its powers to impose a method of collective bargaining under paragraphs 31(3) and 63(2) of Schedule A1 to the Trade Union and Labour Relations (Consolidation) Act 1992. In exercising those powers the CAC may depart from the specified method to such extent as it thinks appropriate in the circumstances of individual cases.

Paragraph 31(3) provides for the CAC to impose a method of collective bargaining in cases where a union (or unions, where two or more unions act jointly) has been recognised by an employer by means of an award of the CAC under Part 1 of Schedule A1, but the employer and union(s) have been unable to agree a method of bargaining between themselves, or have failed to follow an agreed method. Paragraph 63(2) provides for the CAC to impose a bargaining method in cases where an employer and a union (or unions) have entered an agreement for recognition, as defined by paragraph 52 of Part II of Schedule A1, but cannot agree a method of bargaining, or have failed to follow the agreed method.

The bargaining method imposed by the CAC has effect as if it were a legally binding contract between the employer and the union(s). If one party believes the other is failing to respect the method, the first party may apply to the court for an order of specific performance, ordering the other party to comply with the method. Failure to comply with such an order could constitute contempt of court.

Once the CAC has imposed a bargaining method, the parties can vary it, including the fact that it is legally binding, by agreement provided that they do so in writing.

The fact that the CAC has imposed a method does not affect the rights of individual workers under either statute or their contracts of employment. For example, it does not prevent or limit the rights of individual workers to discuss, negotiate or agree with their employer terms of their contract of employment, which differ from the terms of any collective agreement into which the employer and the union may enter as a result of collective bargaining conducted by this method. Nor does the imposed method affect an individual's statutory entitlement to time off for trade union activities or duties.

In cases where the CAC imposes a bargaining method on the parties, the employer is separately obliged, in accordance with Section 70B of the Trade Union and Labour Relations (Consolidation) Act 1992 (as inserted by section 5 of the Employment Relations Act 1999), to consult union representatives periodically on his policy, actions and plans on training. The specified method does not discuss how such consultations should be organised.

The law confers certain entitlements on independent trade unions which are recognised for collective bargaining purposes. For example, employers must disclose, on request, certain types of information to the representatives of the recognised unions. The fact that the CAC has imposed a bargaining method does not affect these existing statutory entitlements.

THE SPECIFIED METHOD

The Parties

1. The method shall apply in each case to two parties, who are referred to here as the 'employer' and the 'union'. Unless the text specifies otherwise, the term 'union' should be read to mean 'unions' in cases where two or more unions are jointly recognised.

The Purpose

2. The purpose is to specify a method by which the employer and the union conduct collective bargaining concerning the pay, hours and holidays of the workers comprising the bargaining unit.

3. The employer shall not grant the right to negotiate pay, hours and holidays to any other union in respect of the workers covered by this method.

The Joint Negotiating Body

4. The employer and the union shall establish a Joint Negotiating Body (JNB) to discuss and negotiate the pay, hours and holidays of the workers comprising the bargaining unit. No other body or group shall undertake collective bargaining on the pay, hours and holidays of these workers, unless the employer and the union so agree.

JNB Membership

5. The membership of the JNB shall usually comprise three employer representatives (who together shall constitute the Employer Side of the JNB) and three union representatives (who together shall constitute the Union Side of the JNB). Each union recognised by the employer in respect of the bargaining unit shall be entitled to one seat at least. To meet this requirement, the Union Side may need to be larger than three and in this eventuality the employer shall be entitled to increase his representation on the JNB by the same number, if he wishes.

6. The employer shall select those individuals who comprise the Employer Side. The individuals must either be those who take the final decisions within the employer's organisation in respect of the pay, hours and holidays of the workers in the bargaining unit or who are expressly authorised by the employer to make recommendations directly to those who take such final decisions. Unless it would be unreasonable to do so, the employer shall select as a representative the most senior person responsible for employment relations in the bargaining unit.

7. The union shall select those individuals who comprise the Union Side in accordance with its own rules and procedures. The representatives must either be individuals employed by the employer or individuals employed by the union who are officials of the union within the meaning of sections 1 and 119 of the Trade Union and Labour Relations (Consolidation) Act 1992 ('the 1992 Act').

8. The JNB shall determine their own rules in respect of the attendance at JNB meetings of observers and substitutes who deputise for JNB members.

Officers

9. The Employer Side shall select one of its members to act as its Chairman and one to act as its Secretary. The Union Side shall select one of its members to act as its Chairman and one to act as its Secretary. The same person may perform the roles of Chairman and Secretary of a Side.

10. For the twelve months from the date of the JNB's first meeting, meetings of the JNB shall be chaired by the Chairman of the Employer Side. The Chairman of the Union Side shall chair the JNB's meetings for the following twelve months. The chairmanship of JNB meetings will alternate in the same way thereafter at intervals of twelve months. In the absence of the person who should chair JNB meetings, a JNB meeting shall be chaired by another member of that person's Side.

11. The Secretary of the Employer Side shall act as Secretary to the JNB. He shall circulate documentation and agendas in advance of JNB meetings, arrange suitable accommodation for meetings, notify members of meetings and draft the written record of JNB meetings. The Secretary of the Employer Side shall work closely with the Secretary of the Union Side in the discharge of these duties, disclosing full information about his performance of these tasks.

JNB Organisation

12.   Draft agendas shall be circulated at least three working days in advance of JNB meetings. The draft record of JNB meetings shall be circulated within ten working days of the holding of meetings for approval at the next JNB meeting. The record does not need to be a verbatim account, but should fully describe the conclusions reached and the actions to be taken.

13.   Subject to the timetable of meetings stipulated in paragraphs 15, 17, 20 and 28 below, the date, timing and location of meetings shall be arranged by the JNB's Secretary, in full consultation with the Secretary of the Union Side, to ensure maximum attendance at meetings. A meeting of the JNB shall be quorate if 50% or more of each Side's members (or, where applicable, their substitutes) are in attendance.

Bargaining Procedure

14.   The union's proposals for adjustments to pay, hours and holidays shall be dealt with on an annual basis, unless the two Sides agree a different bargaining period.

15.   The JNB shall conduct these negotiations for each bargaining round according to the following staged procedure.

Step 1 — The union shall set out in writing, and send to the employer, its proposals (the 'claim') to vary the pay, hours and holidays, specifying which aspects it wants to change. In its claim, the union shall set out the reasons for its proposals, together with the main supporting evidence at its disposal at the time. In cases where there is no established annual date when the employer reviews the pay, hours and holidays of all the workers in the bargaining unit, the union shall put forward its first claim within three months of this method being imposed (and by the same date in subsequent rounds). Where such a common review date is established, the union shall submit its first claim at least a month in advance of that date (and by the same date in subsequent rounds). In either case, the employer and the union may agree a different date by which the claim should be submitted each year. If the union fails to submit its claim by this date, then the procedure shall be ended for the bargaining round in question. Exceptionally, the union may submit a late claim without this penalty if its work on the claim was delayed while the Central Arbitration Committee considered a relevant complaint by the union of failure by the employer to disclose information for collective bargaining purposes.

Step 2 — Within ten working days of the Employer Side's receipt of the union's letter, a quorate meeting of the JNB shall be held to discuss the claim. At this meeting, the Union Side shall explain its claim and answer any reasonable questions arising to the best of its ability.

Step 3 —

(a)   Within fifteen working days immediately following the Step 2 meeting, the employer shall either accept the claim in full or write to the union responding to its claim. If the Employer Side requests it, a quorate meeting of the JNB shall be held within the fifteen day period to enable the employer to present this written response directly to the Union Side. In explaining the basis of his response, the employer shall set out in this written communication all relevant information in his possession. In particular, the written communication shall contain information costing each element of the claim and describing the business consequences, particularly any staffing implications, unless the employer is not required to disclose such information for any of the reasons specified in section 182(1) of the 1992 Act. The basis of these estimated costs and effects, including the main assumptions that the employer has used, shall be set out in the communication. In determining what information is disclosed as relevant, the employer shall be under no greater obligation that he is under the general duty imposed on him by sections 181 and 182 of the 1992 Act to disclose information for the purposes of collective bargaining.

(b)   If the response contains any counter-proposals, the written communication shall set out the reasons for making them, together with the supporting evidence. The letter shall provide information estimating the costs and staffing consequences of implementing each element of the counter proposals, unless the employer is not required to disclose such information for any of the reasons specified in section 182(1) of the 1992 Act.

Step 4 — Within ten working days of the Union Side's receipt of the employer's written communication, a further quorate meeting of the JNB shall be held to discuss the employer's response. At this meeting, the Employer Side shall explain its response and answer any reasonable questions arising to the best of its ability.

Step 5 — If no agreement is reached at the Step 4 meeting (or the last of such meetings if more than one is held at that stage in the procedure), another quorate meeting of the JNB shall be held within ten working days. The union may bring to this meeting a maximum of two other individuals employed by the union who are officials within the meaning of the sections 1 and 119 of the 1992 Act. The employer may bring to the meeting a maximum of two other individuals who are employees or officials of an employer's organisation to which the employer belongs. These additional persons shall be allowed to contribute to the meeting, as if they were JNB members.

Step 6 — If no agreement is reached at the Step 5 meeting (or the last of such meetings if more than one meeting is held at that stage in the procedure), within five working days the employer and the union shall consider, separately or jointly, consulting ACAS about the prospect of ACAS helping them to find a settlement of their differences through conciliation. In the event that both parties agree to invite ACAS to conciliate, both parties shall give such assistance to ACAS as is necessary to enable it to carry out the conciliation efficiently and effectively.

16. The parties shall set aside half a working day for each JNB meeting, unless the Employer Side Chairman and the Union Side Chairman agree a different length of time for the meeting. Unless it is essential to do otherwise, meetings shall be held during the normal working time of most union members of the JNB. Meetings may be adjourned, if both Sides agree. Additional meetings at any point in the procedure may be arranged, if both Sides agree. In addition, if the Employer Side requests it, a meeting of the JNB shall be held before the union has submitted its claim or before the employer is required to respond, enabling the Employer Side to explain the business context within which the employer shall assess the claim.

17. The employer shall not vary the contractual terms affecting the pay, hours or holidays of workers in the bargaining unit, unless he has first discussed his proposals with the union. Such proposals shall normally be made by the employer in the context of his consideration of the union's claim at Steps 3 or 4. If, however, the employer has not tabled his proposals during that process and he wishes to make proposals before the next bargaining round commences, he must write to the union setting out his proposals and the reasons for making them, together with the supporting evidence. The letter shall provide information estimating the costs and staffing consequences of implementing each element of the proposals, unless the employer is not required to disclose such information for any of the reasons specified in section 182(1) of the 1992 Act. A quorate meeting of the JNB shall be held within five working days of the Union Side's receipt of the letter. If there is a failure to resolve the issue at that meeting, then meetings shall be arranged, and steps shall be taken, in accordance with Steps 5 and 6 of the above procedure.

18. Paragraph 17 does not apply to terms in the contract of an individual worker where that worker has agreed that the terms may be altered only by direct negotiation between the worker and the employer.

Collective Agreements

19. Any agreements affecting the pay, hours and holidays of workers in the bargaining unit, which the employer and the union enter following negotiations, shall be set down in writing and signed by the Chairman of the Employer Side and by the Chairman of the Union Side or, in their absence, by another JNB member on their respective Sides.

20. If either the employer or union consider that there has been a failure to implement the agreement, then that party can request in writing a meeting of the JNB to discuss the alleged failure. A quorate meeting shall be held within five working days of the receipt of the request by the JNB Secretary. If there is a failure to resolve the issue at that meeting, then meetings shall be arranged, and steps shall be taken, in accordance with Steps 5 and 6 of the above procedure.

Facilities and Time Off

21. If they are employed by the employer, union members of the JNB:

— shall be given paid time off by the employer to attend JNB meetings;

— shall be given paid time off by the employer to attend a two hour pre-meeting of the Union Side before each JNB meeting; and shall be given paid time off by the employer to hold a day-long meeting to prepare the claim at Step 1 in the bargaining procedure.

The union members of the JNB shall schedule such meetings at times which minimise the effect on production and services. In arranging these meetings, the union members of the JNB shall provide the employer and their line management with as much notice as possible and give details of the purpose of the time off, the intended location of the meeting and the timing and duration of the time off. The employer shall provide adequate heating and lighting for these meetings, and ensure that they are held in private.

22.   If they are not employed by the employer, union members of the JNB or other union officials attending JNB meetings shall be given sufficient access to the employer's premises to allow them to attend Union Side pre-meetings, JNB meetings and meetings of the bargaining unit as specified in paragraph 23.

23.   The employer shall agree to the union's reasonable request to hold meetings with members of the bargaining unit on company premises to discuss the Step 1 claim, the employer's offer or revisions to either. The request shall be made at least three working days in advance of the proposed meeting. However, the employer is not required to provide such facilities, if the employer does not possess available premises which can be used for meetings on the scale suggested by the union. The employer shall provide adequate heating and lighting for meetings, and ensure that the meeting is held in private. Where such meetings are held in working time, the employer is under no obligation to pay individuals for the time off. Where meetings take place outside normal working hours, they should be arranged at a time which is otherwise convenient for the workers.

24.   Where resources permit, the employer shall make available to the Union Side of the JNB such typing, copying and word-processing facilities as it needs to conduct its business in private.

25.   Where resources permit, the employer shall set aside a room for the exclusive use of the Union Side of the JNB. The room shall possess a secure cabinet and a telephone.

26.   In respect of issues which are not otherwise specified in this method, the employer and the union shall have regard to the guidance issued in the ACAS Code of Practice on Time Off for Trade Union Duties and Activities and ensure that there is no unwarranted or unjustified failure to abide by it.

Disclosure of Information

27.   The employer and the union shall have regard to the ACAS Code of Practice on the Disclosure of Information to Trade Unions for Collective Bargaining Purposes and ensure that there is no unwarranted or unjustified failure to abide by it in relation to the bargaining arrangements specified by this method.

Revision of the Method

28.   The employer or the union may request in writing a meeting of the JNB to discuss revising any element of this method, including its status as a legally binding contract. A quorate meeting of the JNB shall be held within ten working days of the receipt of the request by the JNB Secretary. This meeting shall be held in accordance with the same arrangements for the holding of other JNB meetings.

General

29.   The employer and the union shall take all reasonable steps to ensure that this method to conduct collective bargaining is applied efficiently and effectively.

30.   The definition of a 'working day' used in this method is any day other than a Saturday or a Sunday, Christmas Day or Good Friday, or a day which is a bank holiday.

31.   All time limits mentioned in this method may be varied on any occasion, if both the employer and the union agree.

TELECOMMUNICATIONS (LAWFUL BUSINESS PRACTICE) (INTERCEPTION OF COMMUNICATIONS) REGULATIONS 2000
(SI 2000 No. 2699)

2 **Interpretation**

In these Regulations—

    (a)   references to a business include references to activities of a government department, of any public authority or of any person or office holder on whom functions are conferred by or under any enactment;

    (b)   a reference to a communication as relevant to a business is a reference to—

        (i)   a communication—

            (aa) by means of which a transaction is entered into in the course of that business, or

            (bb) which otherwise relates to that business, or

        (ii)   a communication which otherwise takes place in the course of the carrying on of that business;

    (c)   'regulatory or self-regulatory practices or procedures' means practices or procedures—

        (i)   compliance with which is required or recommended by, under or by virtue of—

            (aa) any provision of the law of a member state or other state within the European Economic Area, or

            (bb) any standard or code of practice published by or on behalf of a body established in a member state or other state within the European Economic Area which includes amongst its objectives the publication of standards or codes of practice for the conduct of business, or

        (ii)   which are otherwise applied for the purpose of ensuring compliance with anything so required or recommended;

    (d)   'system controller' means, in relation to a particular telecommunication system, a person with a right to control its operation or use.

3 **Lawful interception of a communication**

    (1)   For the purpose of section 1(5)(a) of the Act, conduct is authorised, subject to paragraphs (2) and (3) below, if it consists of interception of a communication, in the course of its transmission by means of a telecommunication system, which is effected by or with the express or implied consent of the system controller for the purpose of—

        (a)   monitoring or keeping a record of communications—

            (i)   in order to—

                (aa) establish the existence of facts, or

                (bb) ascertain compliance with regulatory or self-regulatory practices or procedures which are—

                    applicable to the system controller in the carrying on of his business or applicable to another person in the carrying on of his business where that person is supervised by the system controller in respect of those practices or procedures, or

                (cc) ascertain or demonstrate the standards which are achieved or ought to be achieved by persons using the system in the course of their duties, or

            (ii)   in the interests of national security, or

            (iii)   for the purpose of preventing or detecting crime, or

            (iv)   for the purpose of investigating or detecting the unauthorised use of that or any other telecommunication system, or

            (v)   where that is undertaken—

                (aa) in order to secure, or

                (bb) as an inherent part of,

the effective operation of the system (including any monitoring or keeping of a record which would be authorised by section 3(3) of the Act if the conditions in paragraphs (a) and (b) thereof were satisfied); or

(b)   monitoring communications for the purpose of determining whether they are communications relevant to the system controller's business which fall within regulation 2(b)(i) above; or

(c)   monitoring communications made to a confidential voice-telephony counselling or support service which is free of charge (other than the cost, if any, of making a telephone call) and operated in such a way that users may remain anonymous if they so choose.

(2)   Conduct is authorised by paragraph (1) of this regulation only if—

(a)   the interception in question is effected solely for the purpose of monitoring or (where appropriate) keeping a record of communications relevant to the system controller's business;

(b)   the telecommunication system in question is provided for use wholly or partly in connection with that business;

(c)   the system controller has made all reasonable efforts to inform every person who may use the telecommunication system in question that communications transmitted by means thereof may be intercepted; and

(d)   in a case falling within—

(i)   paragraph (1)(a)(ii) above, the person by or on whose behalf the interception is effected is a person specified in section 6(2)(a) to (i) of the Act;

(ii)   paragraph (1)(b) above, the communication is one which is intended to be received (whether or not it has been actually received) by a person using the telecommunication system in question.

(3)   Conduct falling within paragraph (1)(a)(i) above is authorised only to the extent that Article 5 of Directive 97/66/EC of the European Parliament and of the Council of 15 December 1997 concerning the processing of personal data and the protection of privacy in the telecommunications sector so permits.

FIXED-TERM EMPLOYEES (PREVENTION OF LESS FAVOURABLE TREATMENT) REGULATIONS 2002 (SI 2002 No. 2034)

PART 1

GENERAL AND INTERPRETATION

1   Citation, commencement and interpretation

(1)   These Regulations may be cited as the Fixed-term Employees (Prevention of Less Favourable Treatment) Regulations 2002 and shall come into force on 1st October 2002.

(2)   In these Regulations—

'the 1996 Act' means the Employment Rights Act 1996;

'collective agreement' means a collective agreement within the meaning of section 178 of the Trade Union and Labour Relations (Consolidation) Act 1992; the trade union parties to which are independent trade unions within the meaning of section 5 of that Act;

'employer', in relation to any employee, means the person by whom the employee is (or, where the employment has ceased, was) employed;

'fixed-term contract' means a contract of employment that, under its provisions determining how it will terminate in the normal course, will terminate—

(a)   on the expiry of a specific term,

(b)   on the completion of a particular task, or

    (c)   on the occurrence or non-occurrence of any other specific event other than the attainment by the employee of any normal and bona fide retiring age in the establishment for an employee holding the position held by him,

and any reference to 'fixed-term' shall be construed accordingly;

'fixed-term employee' means an employee who is employed under a fixed-term contract;

'permanent employee' means an employee who is not employed under a fixed-term contract, and any reference to 'permanent employment' shall be construed accordingly;

'pro rata principle' means that where a comparable permanent employee receives or is entitled to pay or any other benefit, a fixed-term employee is to receive or be entitled to such proportion of that pay or other benefit as is reasonable in the circumstances having regard to the length of his contract of employment and to the terms on which the pay or other benefit is offered;

'renewal' includes extension and references to renewing a contract shall be construed accordingly;

'workforce agreement' means an agreement between an employer and his employees or their representatives in respect of which the conditions set out in Schedule 1 to these Regulations are satisfied.

2   Comparable employees

(1)   For the purposes of these Regulations, an employee is a comparable permanent employee in relation to a fixed-term employee if, at the time when the treatment that is alleged to be less favourable to the fixed-term employee takes place,

    (a)   both employees are—

        (i)   employed by the same employer, and

        (ii)   engaged in the same or broadly similar work having regard, where relevant, to whether they have a similar level of qualification and skills; and

    (b)   the permanent employee works or is based at the same establishment as the fixed-term employee or, where there is no comparable permanent employee working or based at that establishment who satisfies the requirements of sub-paragraph (a), works or is based at a different establishment and satisfies those requirements.

(2)   For the purposes of paragraph (1), an employee is not a comparable permanent employee if his employment has ceased.

PART 2

RIGHTS AND REMEDIES

3   Less favourable treatment of fixed-term employees

(1)   A fixed-term employee has the right not to be treated by his employer less favourably than the employer treats a comparable permanent employee—

    (a)   as regards the terms of his contract; or

    (b)   by being subjected to any other detriment by any act, or deliberate failure to act, of his employer.

(2)   Subject to paragraphs (3) and (4), the right conferred by paragraph (1) includes in particular the right of the fixed-term employee in question not to be treated less favourably than the employer treats a comparable permanent employee in relation to—

    (a)   any period of service qualification relating to any particular condition of service,

    (b)   the opportunity to receive training, or

    (c)   the opportunity to secure any permanent position in the establishment.

(3)   The right conferred by paragraph (1) applies only if—

    (a)   the treatment is on the ground that the employee is a fixed-term employee, and

    (b)   the treatment is not justified on objective grounds.

(4)   Paragraph (3)(b) is subject to regulation 4.

(5)   In determining whether a fixed-term employee has been treated less favourably than a comparable permanent employee, the pro rata principle shall be applied unless it is inappropriate.

(6)   In order to ensure that an employee is able to exercise the right conferred by paragraph (1) as described in paragraph (2)(c) the employee has the right to be informed by his employer of available vacancies in the establishment.

(7)   For the purposes of paragraph (6) an employee is 'informed by his employer' only if the vacancy is contained in an advertisement which the employee has a reasonable opportunity of reading in the course of his employment or the employee is given reasonable notification of the vacancy in some other way.

4   Objective justification

(1)   Where a fixed-term employee is treated by his employer less favourably than the employer treats a comparable permanent employee as regards any term of his contract, the treatment in question shall be regarded for the purposes of regulation 3(3)(b) as justified on objective grounds if the terms of the fixed-term employee's contract of employment, taken as a whole, are at least as favourable as the terms of the comparable permanent employee's contract of employment.

(2)   Paragraph (1) is without prejudice to the generality of regulation 3(3)(b).

5   Right to receive a written statement of reasons for less favourable treatment

(1)   If an employee who considers that his employer may have treated him in a manner which infringes a right conferred on him by regulation 3 requests in writing from his employer a written statement giving particulars of the reasons for the treatment, the employee is entitled to be provided with such a statement within twenty-one days of his request.

(2)   A written statement under this regulation is admissible as evidence in any proceedings under these Regulations.

(3)   If it appears to the tribunal in any proceedings under these Regulations—
   (a)   that the employer deliberately, and without reasonable excuse, omitted to provide a written statement, or
   (b)   that the written statement is evasive or equivocal,
   it may draw any inference which it considers it just and equitable to draw, including an inference that the employer has infringed the right in question.

(4)   This regulation does not apply where the treatment in question consists of the dismissal of an employee, and the employee is entitled to a written statement of reasons for his dismissal under section 92 of the 1996 Act.

6   Unfair dismissal and the right not to be subjected to detriment

(1)   An employee who is dismissed shall be regarded as unfairly dismissed for the purposes of Part 10 of the 1996 Act if the reason (or, if more than one, the principal reason) for the dismissal is a reason specified in paragraph (3).

(2)   An employee has the right not to be subjected to any detriment by any act, or any deliberate failure to act, of his employer done on a ground specified in paragraph (3).

(3)   The reasons or, as the case may be, grounds are—
   (a)   that the employee—
      (i)   brought proceedings against the employer under these Regulations;
      (ii)   requested from his employer a written statement under regulation 5 or regulation 9;
      (iii)   gave evidence or information in connection with such proceedings brought by any employee;
      (iv)   otherwise did anything under these Regulations in relation to the employer or any other person;
      (v)   alleged that the employer had infringed these Regulations;
      (vi)   refused (or proposed to refuse) to forgo a right conferred on him by these Regulations;
      (vii)   declined to sign a workforce agreement for the purposes of these Regulations, or
      (viii) being—

        (aa)   a representative of members of the workforce for the purposes of Schedule 1, or

        (bb)   a candidate in an election in which any person elected will, on being elected,

        become such a representative,

      performed (or proposed to perform) any functions or activities as such a representative or candidate, or

   (b)   that the employer believes or suspects that the employee has done or intends to do any of the things mentioned in sub-paragraph (a).

(4)   Where the reason or principal reason for dismissal or, as the case may be, ground for subjection to any act or deliberate failure to act, is that mentioned in paragraph (3)(a)(v), or (b) so far as it relates thereto, neither paragraph (1) nor paragraph (2) applies if the allegation made by the employee is false and not made in good faith.

(5)   Paragraph (2) does not apply where the detriment in question amounts to dismissal within the meaning of Part 10 of the 1996 Act.

7   Complaints to employment tribunals etc.

(1)   An employee may present a complaint to an employment tribunal that his employer has infringed a right conferred on him by regulation 3, or (subject to regulation 6(5)), regulation 6(2).

(2)   Subject to paragraph (3), an employment tribunal shall not consider a complaint under this regulation unless it is presented before the end of the period of three months beginning—

   (a)   in the case of an alleged infringement of a right conferred by regulation 3(1) or 6(2), with the date of the less favourable treatment or detriment to which the complaint relates or, where an act or failure to act is part of a series of similar acts or failures comprising the less favourable treatment or detriment, the last of them;

   (b)   in the case of an alleged infringement of the right conferred by regulation 3(6), with the date, or if more than one the last date, on which other individuals, whether or not employees of the employer, were informed of the vacancy.

(3)   A tribunal may consider any such complaint which is out of time if, in all the circumstances of the case, it considers that it is just and equitable to do so.

(4)   For the purposes of calculating the date of the less favourable treatment or detriment under paragraph (2)(a)—

   (a)   where a term in a contract is less favourable, that treatment shall be treated, subject to paragraph (b), as taking place on each day of the period during which the term is less favourable;

   (b)   a deliberate failure to act contrary to regulation 3 or 6(2) shall be treated as done when it was decided on.

(5)   In the absence of evidence establishing the contrary, a person shall be taken for the purposes of paragraph (4)(b) to decide not to act—

   (a)   when he does an act inconsistent with doing the failed act; or

   (b)   if he has done no such inconsistent act, when the period expires within which he might reasonably have been expected to have done the failed act if it was to be done.

(6)   Where an employee presents a complaint under this regulation in relation to a right conferred on him by regulation 3 or 6(2) it is for the employer to identify the ground for the less favourable treatment or detriment.

(7)   Where an employment tribunal finds that a complaint presented to it under this regulation is well founded, it shall take such of the following steps as it considers just and equitable—

   (a)   making a declaration as to the rights of the complainant and the employer in relation to the matters to which the complaint relates;

   (b)   ordering the employer to pay compensation to the complainant;

   (c)   recommending that the employer take, within a specified period, action appearing to the tribunal to be reasonable, in all the circumstances of the case, for the purpose of obviating or reducing the adverse effect on the complainant of any matter to which the complaint relates.

(8) Where a tribunal orders compensation under paragraph (7)(b), the amount of the compensation awarded shall be such as the tribunal considers just and equitable in all the circumstances having regard to—

    (a)   the infringement to which the complaint relates, and

    (b)   any loss which is attributable to the infringement.

(9) The loss shall be taken to include—

    (a)   any expenses reasonably incurred by the complainant in consequence of the infringement, and

    (b)   loss of any benefit which he might reasonably be expected to have had but for the infringement.

(10) Compensation in respect of treating an employee is a manner which infringes the right conferred on him by regulation 3 shall not include compensation for injury to feelings.

(11) In ascertaining the loss the tribunal shall apply the same rule concerning the duty of a person to mitigate his loss as applies to damages recoverable under the common law of England and Wales or (as the case may be) the law of Scotland.

(12) Where the tribunal finds that the act, or failure to act, to which the complaint relates was to any extent caused or contributed to by action of the complainant, it shall reduce the amount of the compensation by such proportion as it considers just and equitable having regard to that finding.

(13) If the employer fails, without reasonable justification, to comply with a recommendation made by an employment tribunal under paragraph (7)(c) the tribunal may, if it thinks it just and equitable to do so—

    (a)   increase the amount of compensation required to be paid to the complainant in respect of the complaint, where an order was made under paragraph (7)(b); or

    (b)   make an order under paragraph (7)(b).

8   Successive fixed-term contracts

(1) This regulation applies where—

    (a)   an employee is employed under a contract purporting to be a fixed-term contract, and

    (b)   the contract mentioned in sub-paragraph (a) has previously been renewed, or the employee has previously been employed on a fixed-term contract before the start of the contract mentioned in sub-paragraph (a).

(2) Where this regulation applies then, with effect from the date specified in paragraph (3), the provision of the contract mentioned in paragraph (1)(a) that restricts the duration of the contract shall be of no effect, and the employee shall be a permanent employee, if—

    (a)   the employee has been continuously employed under the contract mentioned in paragraph 1 (a), or under that contract taken with a previous fixed-term contract, for a period of four years or more, and

    (b)   the employment of the employee under a fixed-term contract was not justified on objective grounds—

        (i)   where the contract mentioned in paragraph (1)(a) has been renewed, at the time when it was last renewed;

        (ii)   where that contract has not been renewed, at the time when it was entered into.

(3) The date referred to in paragraph (2) is whichever is the later of—

    (a)   the date on which the contract mentioned in paragraph (1)(a) was entered into or last renewed, and

    (b)   the date on which the employee acquired four years' continuous employment.

(4) For the purposes of this regulation Chapter 1 of Part 14 of the 1996 Act shall apply in determining whether an employee has been continuously employed, and any period of continuous employment falling before the 10th July 2002 shall be disregarded.

(5) A collective agreement or a workforce agreement may modify the application of paragraphs (1) to (3) of this regulation in relation to any employee or specified description of employees, by substituting for the provisions of paragraph (2) or paragraph (3), or for the provisions of both of those paragraphs, one or more different provisions which, in order to prevent abuse arising from the use of successive fixed-term contracts, specify one or more of the following—

(a)   the maximum total period for which the employee or employees of that description may be continuously employed on a fixed-term contract or on successive fixed-term contracts;

(b)   the maximum number of successive fixed-term contracts and renewals of such contracts under which the employee or employees of that description may be employed; or

(c)   objective grounds justifying the renewal of fixed-term contracts, or the engagement of the employee or employees of that description under successive fixed-term contracts,

and those provisions shall have effect in relation to that employee or an employee of that description as if they were contained in paragraphs (2) and (3).

9   Right to receive written statement of variation

(1)   If an employee who considers that, by virtue of regulation 8, he is a permanent employee requests in writing from his employer a written statement confirming that his contract is no longer fixed-term or that he is now a permanent employee, he is entitled to be provided, within twenty-one days of his request, with either—

(a)   such a statement, or

(b)   a statement giving reasons why his contract remains fixed-term.

(2)   If the reasons stated under paragraph (1)(b) include an assertion that there were objective grounds for the engagement of the employee under a fixed-term contract, or the renewal of such a contract, the statement shall include a statement of those grounds.

(3)   A written statement under this regulation is admissible as evidence in any proceedings before a court, an employment tribunal and the Commissioners of the Inland Revenue.

(4)   If it appears to the court or tribunal in any proceedings—

(a)   that the employer deliberately, and without reasonable excuse, omitted to provide a written statement, or

(b)   that the written statement is evasive or equivocal,

it may draw any inference which it considers it just and equitable to draw.

(5)   An employee who considers that, by virtue of regulation 8, he is a permanent employee may present an application to an employment tribunal for a declaration to that effect.

(6)   No application may be made under paragraph (5) unless—

(a)   the employee in question has previously requested a statement under paragraph (1) and the employer has either failed to provide a statement or given a statement of reasons under paragraph (1)(b), and

(b)   the employee is at the time the application is made employed by the employer.

PART 3

MISCELLANEOUS

10   Restrictions on contracting out

Section 203 of the 1996 Act (restrictions on contracting out) shall apply in relation to these Regulations as if they were contained in that Act.

12   Liability of employers and principals

(1)   Anything done by a person in the course of his employment shall be treated for the purposes of these Regulations as also done by his employer, whether or not it was done with the employer's knowledge or approval.

(2)   Anything done by a person as agent for the employer with the authority of the employer shall be treated for the purposes of these Regulations as also done by the employer.

(3)   In proceedings under these Regulations against any person in respect of an act alleged to have been done by an employee of his, it shall be a defence for that person to prove that he took such steps as were reasonably practicable to prevent the employee from—

(a)   doing that act, or

(b)   doing, in the course of his employment, acts of that description.

PART 5
EXCLUSIONS

18   Government training schemes etc.
(1) These Regulations shall not have effect in relation to a fixed-term employee who is employed on a scheme, designed to provide him with training or work experience for the purpose of assisting him to seek or obtain work, which is either—
    (a)   provided to him under arrangements made by the Government, or
    (b)   funded in whole or part by an Institution of the European Community.
(2) These Regulations shall not have effect in relation to a fixed-term employee whose employment consists in attending a period of work experience not exceeding one year that he is required to attend as part of a higher education course.
(3) For the purpose of paragraph (2) 'a higher education course' means—
    (a)   in England and Wales, a course of a description referred to in Schedule 6 to the Education Reform Act 1988;
    (b)   in Scotland, a course of a description falling within section 38 of the Further and Higher Education (Scotland) Act 1992; and
    (c)   in Northern Ireland, a course of a description referred to in Schedule 1 to the Further Education (Northern Ireland) Order 1997.

19   Agency workers
(1) These Regulations shall not have effect in relation to employment under a fixed-term contract where the employee is an agency worker.
(2) In this regulation 'agency worker' means any person who is supplied by an employment business to do work for another person under a contract or other arrangements made between the employment business and the other person.
(3) In this regulation 'employment business' means the business (whether or not carried on with a view to profit and whether or not carried on in conjunction with any other business) of supplying persons in the employment of the person carrying on the business, to act for, and under the control of, other persons in any capacity.

20   Apprentices
These Regulations shall not have effect in relation to employment under a fixed-term contract where the contract is a contract of apprenticeship.

SCHEDULE 1
WORKFORCE AGREEMENTS

1.   An agreement is a workforce agreement for the purposes of these Regulations if the following conditions are satisfied—
    (a)   the agreement is in writing;
    (b)   it has effect for a specified period not exceeding five years;
    (c)   it applies either—
        (i)   to all of the relevant members of the workforce, or
        (ii)   to all of the relevant members of the workforce who belong to a particular group;
    (d)   the agreement is signed—
        (i)   in the case of an agreement of the kind referred to in subparagraph (c)(i), by the representatives of the workforce, and in the case of an agreement of the kind referred to in sub-paragraph (c)(ii) by the representatives of the group to which the agreement applies (excluding, in either case, any representative not a relevant member of the workforce on the date on which the agreement was first made available for signature), or
        (ii)   if the employer employed 20 or fewer employees on the date referred to in sub-paragraph (d)(i), either by the appropriate representatives in accordance with that sub-paragraph or by the majority of the employees employed by him;
    (e)   before the agreement was made available for signature, the employer provided all the employees to whom it was intended to apply on the date on which it came into effect

with copies of the text of the agreement and such guidance as those employees might reasonably require in order to understand it fully.

2.   For the purposes of this Schedule—

'a particular group' is a group of the relevant members of a workforce who undertake a particular function, work at a particular workplace or belong to a particular department or unit within their employer's business;

'relevant members of the workforce' are all of the employees employed by a particular employer, excluding any employee whose terms and conditions of employment are provided for, wholly or in part, in a collective agreement;

'representatives of the workforce' are employees duly elected to represent the relevant members of the workforce, 'representatives of the group' are employees duly elected to represent the members of a particular group, and representatives are 'duly elected' if the election at which they were elected satisfied the requirements of paragraph 3 of this Schedule.

3.   The requirements concerning elections referred to in paragraph 2 are that—

(a)   the number of representatives to be elected is determined by the employer;

(b)   the candidates for election as representatives of the workforce are relevant members of the workforce, and the candidates for election as representatives of a group are members of that group;

(c)   no employee who is eligible to be a candidate is unreasonably excluded from standing for election;

(d)   all the relevant members of the workforce are entitled to vote for representatives of the workforce, and all the members of a particular group are entitled to vote for representatives of the group;

(e)   the employees entitled to vote may vote for as many candidates as there are representatives to be elected;

(f)   the election is conducted so as to secure that—

(i)   so far as is reasonably practicable, those voting do so in secret, and

(ii)   the votes given at the election are fairly and accurately counted.

FLEXIBLE WORKING (PROCEDURAL REQUIREMENTS) REGULATIONS 2002
(SI 2002 No. 3207)

2   Interpretation

(1)   In these Regulations—

'the 1996 Act' means the Employment Rights Act 1996;

'application' means an application under section 80F of the 1996 Act (statutory right to request a contract variation);

'contract of employment' means a contract of service or apprenticeship, whether express or implied, and (if it is express) whether oral or in writing;

'contract variation' means a change in the terms and conditions of a contract of employment of a kind specified in section 80F(1)(a) of the 1996 Act;

'electronic communication' means an electronic communication within the meaning of section 15(1) of the Electronic Communications Act 2000;

'employee' means an individual who has entered into or works under (or, where the employment has ceased, worked under) a contract of employment;

'employer' means the person by whom an employee is (or, where the employment has ceased, was) employed;

'worker' means an individual who has entered into or works under (or, where the employment has ceased, worked under)—

   (a)   a contract of employment, or

   (b)   any other contract, whether express or implied and (if it is express) whether oral or in writing, whereby the individual undertakes to do or perform personally any work or services for another party to the contract whose status is not by virtue of the contract that of a client or customer of any profession or business undertaking carried on by the individual.

'writing' includes writing delivered by means of electronic communication.

(2)   For the purposes of these Regulations, unless the contrary is proved, an application is taken as having been made on the day the application is received.

(3)   The reference in paragraph (2) to the day on which an application is received is a reference—

   (a)   in relation to an application transmitted by electronic communication, to the day on which it is transmitted,

   (b)   in relation to an application sent by post, to the day on which the application would be delivered in the ordinary course of post.

(4)   For the purpose of these Regulations, unless the contrary is proved, a notice is taken as being given—

   (a)   in relation to a notice transmitted by electronic communication, on the day on which it is transmitted,

   (b)   in relation to a notice sent by post, the day on which the notice would be delivered in the ordinary course of post.

3   The meeting to discuss an application with an employee

(1)   Subject to paragraph (2) and regulation 13, an employer to whom an application for a contract variation is made shall hold a meeting to discuss the application with the employee within 28 days after the date on which the application is made.

(2)   Paragraph (1) does not apply where the employer agrees to the application and notifies the employee accordingly in writing within the period referred to in that paragraph.

(3)   A notice under paragraph (2) shall specify—

   (a)   the contract variation agreed to, and

   (b)   the date from which the variation is to take effect.

4   Where a meeting is held to discuss an application the employer shall give the employee notice of his decision on the application within 14 days after the date of the meeting.

5   A notice under regulation 4 shall—

   (a)   be in writing,

   (b)   (i)   where the employees decision is to agree to the application, specify the contract variation agreed to and state the date on which the variation is to take effect,

       (ii)   where the decision is to refuse the application, state which of the grounds for refusal specified in section 80G(I)(b) of the 1996 Act are considered by the employer to apply, contain a sufficient explanation as to why those grounds apply in relation to the application, and set out the appeal procedure, and

   (c)   be dated.

6   Appeals

An employee is entitled to appeal against his employer's decision to refuse an application by giving notice in accordance with regulation 7 within 14 days after the date on which notice of a decision is given.

7   A notice of appeal under regulation 6 shall—

   (a)   be in writing,

   (b)   set out the grounds of appeal, and

   (c)   be dated.

8   (1)   Subject to paragraph (2), the employer shall hold a meeting with the employee to discuss the appeal within 14 days after the employee's notice under regulation 6 is given.

   (2)   Paragraph (1) does not apply where, within 14 days after the date on which notice under regulation 6 is given, the employer—

       (a)   upholds the appeal, and

     (b)   notifies the employee in writing of his decision, specifying the contract variation agreed to and stating the date from which the contract variation is to take effect.

9   Where a meeting is held to discuss the appeal, the employer shall notify the employee of his decision on the appeal within 14 days after the date of the meeting.

10   Notice under regulation 9 shall—

     (a)   be in writing,

     (b)   (i)   where the employer upholds the appeal, specify the contract variation agreed to and state the date from which the variation is to take effect, or

              (ii)   where the employer dismisses the appeal, state the grounds for the decision and contain a sufficient explanation as to why those grounds apply, and

     (c) be dated.

11   The time and place of a meeting under regulation 3(1) or 8(1) shall be convenient to the employer and the employee.

12   Extension of periods

(1)   An employer and an employee may agree to an extension of any of the periods referred to in regulations 3, 4, 6, 8, 9 and 13.

(2)   An agreement under paragraph (1) must be recorded in writing by the employer.

(3)   The employer's record referred to in paragraph (2) must—

     (a)   specify what period the extension relates to,

     (b)   specify the date on which the extension is to end,

     (c)   be dated, and

     (d)   be sent to the employee.

13   Where the individual who would ordinarily consider an application is absent from work on annual leave or on sick leave on the day on which the application is made, the period referred to in regulation 3(1) commences on the day the individual returns to work or 28 days after the application is made, whichever is the sooner.

14   Right to be accompanied

(1)   This regulation applies where—

     (a)   a meeting is held under regulation 3(1) or 8(1), and

     (b)   the employee reasonably requests to be accompanied at the meeting.

(2)   Where this regulation applies the employer must permit the employee to be accompanied at the meeting by a single companion who—

     (a)   is chosen by the employee and is within paragraph (3),

     (b)   is to be permitted to address the meeting (but not to answer questions on behalf of the employee), and

     (c)   is to be permitted to confer with the employee during the meeting.

(3)   A person comes within this paragraph if he is a worker employed by the same employer as the employee.

(4)   If—

     (a)   an employee has a right under this regulation to be accompanied at a meeting,

     (b)   his chosen companion will not be available at the time proposed for the meeting by the employer, and

     (c)   the employee proposes an alternative time which satisfies paragraph (5),

    the employer must postpone the meeting to the time proposed by the employee.

(5)   An alternative time must—

     (a)   be convenient for employer, employee and companion, and

     (b)   fall before the end of the period of seven days beginning with the first day after the day proposed by the employer.

(6)   An employer shall permit a worker to take time off during working hours for the purpose of accompanying an employee in accordance with a request under paragraph (1)(b).

(7)   Sections 168(3) and (4), 169 and 171 to 173 of the Trade Union and Labour Relations (Consolidation) Act 1992 (time off for carrying out trade union duties) shall apply in relation to paragraph (6) above as they apply in relation to section 168(1) of that Act.

15   **Complaint to employment tribunal**

(1)   An employee may present a complaint to an employment tribunal that his employer has failed, or threatened to fail, to comply with regulation 14(2) or (4).

(2)   A tribunal shall not consider a complaint under this regulation in relation to a failure or threat unless the complaint is presented—

     (a)   before the end of the period of three months beginning with the date of the failure or threat, or

     (b)   within such further period as the tribunal considers reasonable in a case where it is satisfied that it was not reasonably practicable for the complaint to be presented before the end of that period of three months.

(3)   Where a tribunal finds that a complaint under this regulation is well-founded it shall order the employer to pay compensation to the worker of an amount not exceeding two weeks' pay.

(4)   Chapter 2 of Part 14 of the 1996 Act (calculation of a week's pay) shall apply for the purposes of paragraph (3); and in applying that Chapter the calculation date shall be taken to be the date on which the relevant meeting took place (or was to have taken place).

(5)   The limit in section 227(1) of the Employment Rights Act 1996 (maximum amount of a week's pay) shall apply for the purposes of paragraph (3) above.

16   **Detriment and dismissal**

(1)   A person has the right not to be subjected to any detriment by any act, or any deliberate failure to act, by his employer done on the ground that he—

     (a)   exercised or sought to exercise the right under regulation 14(2) or (4), or

     (b)   accompanied or sought to accompany an employee pursuant to a request under that regulation.

(2)   Section 48 of the 1996 Act shall apply in relation to contraventions of paragraph (1) above as it applies in relation to contraventions of certain sections of that Act.

(3)   A person who is dismissed shall be regarded for the purposes of Part 10 of the 1996 Act as unfairly dismissed if the reason (or, if more than one, the principle reason) for the dismissal is that he—

     (a)   exercised or sought to exercise his right under regulation 14(2) or (4), or

     (b)   accompanied or sought to accompany an employee pursuant to a request under that regulation.

(4)   Sections 108 and 109 of the 1996 Act (qualifying period of employment and upper age limit) shall not apply in relation to paragraph (3) above.

(5)   Sections 128 to 132 of the 1996 Act (interim relief) shall apply in relation to dismissal for the reason specified in paragraph 3(a) or (b) above as they apply in relation to dismissal for a reason specified in section 128(1)(b) of that Act.

(6)   In the application of Chapter 2 of Part 10 of the 1996 Act in relation to paragraph (3) above, a reference to an employee shall be taken as a reference to a worker.

17   **Withdrawal of application by the employee**

(1)   An employer shall treat an application as withdrawn where the employee has—

     (a)   notified to him whether orally or in writing that he is withdrawing the application,

     (b)   without reasonable cause, failed to attend a meeting under regulation 3(1) or 8(1) more than once, or

     (c)   without reasonable cause, refused to provide the employer with information the employer requires in order to assess whether the contract variation should be agreed to.

(2)   An employer shall confirm the withdrawal of the application to the employee in writing unless the employee has provided him with written notice of the withdrawal under paragraph 1(a).

FLEXIBLE WORKING (ELIGIBILITY, COMPLAINTS AND REMEDIES) REGULATIONS 2002
(SI 2002 No. 3236)

2   Interpretation

(1)   In these Regulations—

'the 1996 Act' means the Employment Rights Act 1996;

'the Procedure Regulations' means the Flexible Working (Procedural Requirements) Regulations 2002;

'adopter', in relation to a child, means—

(a)   a person with whom an adoption agency has decided the child should be placed for adoption, or

(b)   a person who has given notice of his intention to apply for an adoption order as required by section 44 of the Adoption and Children Act 2002 or section 22 of the Adoption (Scotland) Act 1978;

'adoption agency' means an adoption agency within the meaning of section 2 of the Adoption and Children Act 2002, Article 3(3) of the Adoption (Northern Ireland) Order 1987 or section 1(4) of the Adoption (Scotland) Act 1978;

'application' means an application under section 80F of the 1996 Act (statutory right to request contract variation);

'contract of employment' means a contract of service or apprenticeship, whether express or implied, and (if it is express) whether oral or in writing;

'contract variation', means a change in the terms and conditions of a contract of employment of a kind specified in section 80F(I)(a) of the 1996 Act;

'disabled' means entitled to a disability living allowance within the meaning of section 71 of the Social Security Contributions and Benefits Act 1992;

'electronic communication' means an electronic communication within the meaning of section 15(1) of the Electronic Communications Act 2000;

'employee' means an individual who has entered into or works under (or, where the employment has ceased, worked under) a contract of employment;

'employer' means the person by whom an employee is (or, where the employment has ceased, was) employed;

'foster parent' means a foster parent within the meaning of regulation 2(1) of the Fostering Services Regulations 2002 or a foster carer within the meaning of regulation 2(1) of the Fostering of Children (Scotland) Regulations 1996;

'guardian' means a person appointed as a guardian under section 5 of the Children Act 1989 or section 7 or 11 of the Children (Scotland) Act 1995;

'partner' means the other member of a couple consisting of—

(a)   a man and a woman who are not married to each other but are living together as if they were husband and wife, or

(b)   two people of the same sex who are not civil partners of each other but are living together as if they were civil partners;

'private foster carer' means a person fostering a child privately within the meaning of section 66 of the Children Act 1989 or an individual other than a parent of the child who maintains the child as a foster child for the purposes of the Foster Children (Scotland) Act 1984, or otherwise looks after the child in circumstances in which that Act applies by virtue of section 17 of that Act;

'relative' means a mother, father, adopter, guardian, special guardian, parent-in-law, step-parent, son, step-son, son-in-law, daughter, step-daughter, daughter-in-law, brother, step-brother, brother-in-law, sister, step-sister, sister-in-law, uncle, aunt or grandparent, and includes adoptive relationships and relationships of the full blood or half blood or, in the case of an adopted person, such of those relationships as would exist but for the adoption;

'residence order' means a residence order as defined by section 8(1) of the Children Act 1989 or section 11(2)(c) of the Children (Scotland) Act 1995;

'special guardian', means a person appointed as a special guardian under section 14A of the Children Act 1989;

'writing' includes writing delivered by means of electronic communication.

(2)   A reference in any provision of these Regulations to a period of continuous employment is to a period computed in accordance with Chapter 1 of Part 14 of the 1996 Act, as if the provision were a provision of that Act.

(3)   ...

3   Entitlement to request a contract variation to care for a child

(1)   An employee is entitled to make an application to his employer for a contract variation to enable him, in accordance with section 80F(1)(b)(i) of the 1996 Act, to care for a child if he—

    (a)   has been continuously employed for a period of not less than 26 weeks;

    (b)   is either—

        (i)   the mother, father, adopter, guardian, special guardian or foster parent of the child or;

        (ii)   married to, the civil partner or the partner of the child's mother, father, adopter, guardian, special guardian or foster parent;

    (c)   has, or expects to have responsibility for the upbringing of the child.

(2)   ...

3A   Age of child

An application under regulation 3 must be made before the day on which the child concerned reaches the age of 6 or, if disabled, 18.

3B   Entitlement to request a contract variation to care for an adult

An employee is entitled to make an application to his employer for a contract variation to enable him, in accordance with section 80F(1)(b)(ii) of the 1996 Act, to care for a person aged 18 or over if the employee—

    (a)   has been continuously employed for a period of not less than 26 weeks;

    (b)   is or expects to be caring for a person in need of care who is either—

        (i)   married to or the partner or civil partner of the employee;

        (ii)   a relative of the employee; or

        (iii)   living at the same address as the employee.

4   Form of the application

An application shall—

    (a)   be made in writing,

    (b)   state whether a previous application has been made by the employee to the employer and, if so, when, and

    (c)   be dated.

5   Date when an application is taken as made

(1)   Unless the contrary is proved, an application is taken as having been made on the day the application is received.

(2)   The reference in paragraph (1) to the day on which an application is received is a reference—

    (a)   in relation to an application transmitted by electronic communication, to the day on which it is transmitted,

    (b)   in relation to an application sent by post, to the day on which the application would be delivered in the ordinary course of post.

6   Breaches of the Procedure Regulations by the employer entitling an employee to make a complaint to an employment tribunal

The breaches of the Procedure Regulations which entitle an employee to make a complaint to an employment tribunal under section 80H of the 1996 Act notwithstanding the fact that his application has not been disposed of by agreement or withdrawn are—

    (a)   failure to hold a meeting in accordance with regulation 3(1) or 8(1),

    (b)   failure to notify a decision in accordance with regulation 4 or 9.

7   Compensation

The maximum amount of compensation that an employment tribunal may award under section 80I of the 1996 Act where it finds a complaint by an employee under section 80H of the Act well-founded is 8 weeks' pay.

PATERNITY AND ADOPTION LEAVE REGULATIONS 2002
(SI 2002 No. 2788)

PART I

GENERAL

2   Interpretation

(1)   In these Regulations—

'the 1996 Act' means the Employment Rights Act 1996;

'additional adoption leave' means leave under section 75B of the 1996 Act;

'additional maternity leave' means leave under section 73 of the 1996 Act;

'adopter', in relation to a child, means a person who has been matched with the child for adoption, or, in a case where two people have been matched jointly, whichever of them has elected to be the child's adopter for the purposes of these Regulations;

'adoption agency' has the meaning given, in relation to England and Wales, by section 1(4) of the Adoption Act 1976 and, in relation to Scotland, by section 1(4) of the Adoption (Scotland) Act 1978;

'adoption leave' means ordinary or additional adoption leave;

'child' means a person who is, or when placed with an adopter for adoption was, under the age of 18;

'contract of employment' means a contract of service or apprenticeship, whether express or implied, and (if it is express) whether oral or in writing;

'employee' means an individual who has entered into or works under (or, where the employment has ceased, worked under) a contract of employment;

'employer' means the person by whom an employee is (or, where the employment has ceased, was) employed;

'expected week', in relation to the birth of a child, means the week, beginning with midnight between Saturday and Sunday, in which it is expected that the child will be born;

'ordinary adoption leave' means leave under section 75A of the 1996 Act;

'parental leave' means leave under regulation 13(1) of the Maternity and Parental Leave etc. Regulations 1999;

'partner', in relation to a child's mother or adopter, means a person (whether of a different sex or the same sex) who lives with the mother or adopter and the child in an enduring family relationship but is not a relative of the mother or adopter of a kind specified in paragraph (2);

'paternity leave' means leave under regulation 4 or regulation 8 of these Regulations;

'statutory adoption leave' means ordinary adoption leave and additional adoption leave;

'statutory adoption leave period' means the period during which the adopter is on statutory adoption leave;

'statutory leave' means leave provided for in Part 8 of the 1996 Act.

(2)   The relatives of a child's mother or adopter referred to in the definition of 'partner' in paragraph (1) are the mother's or adopter's parent, grandparent, sister, brother, aunt or uncle.

(3)   References to relationships in paragraph (2)—

(a)   are to relationships of the full blood or half blood or, in the case of an adopted person, such of those relationships as would exist but for the adoption, and

(b)   include the relationship of a child with his adoptive, or former adoptive, parents,

but do not include any other adoptive relationships.

(4)   For the purposes of these Regulations—

(a)   a person is matched with a child for adoption when an adoption agency decides that that person would be a suitable adoptive parent for the child, either individually or jointly with another person, and

(b)   a person is notified of having been matched with a child on the date on which he receives notification of the agency's decision, under regulation 11(2) of the Adoption Agencies Regulations 1983 or regulation 12(3) of the Adoption Agencies (Scotland) Regulations 1996;

(c)   a person elects to be a child's adopter, in a case where the child is matched with him and another person jointly, if he and that person agree, at the time at which they are matched, that he and not the other person will be the adopter.

(5)   A reference in any provision of these Regulations to a period of continuous employment is to a period computed in accordance with Chapter 1 of Part 14 of the 1996 Act, as if that provision were a provision of that Act.

(6)   For the purposes of these Regulations, any two employers shall be treated as associated if—

(a)   one is a company of which the other (directly or indirectly) has control; or

(b)   both are companies of which a third person (directly or indirectly) has control;

and 'associated employer' shall be construed accordingly.

3   Application

(1)   The provisions relating to paternity leave under regulation 4 below have effect only in relation to children—

(a)   born on or after 6th April 2003, or

(b)   whose expected week of birth begins on or after that date.

(2)   The provisions relating to paternity leave under regulation 8 and adoption leave under regulation 15 below have effect only in relation to children—

(a)   matched with a person who is notified of having been matched on or after 6th April 2003, or

(b)   placed for adoption on or after that date.

(3)   Regulation 28 (protection from detriment) has effect only in relation to an act or failure to act which takes place on or after 8th December 2002.

(4)   For the purposes of paragraph (3)—

(a)   where an act extends over a period, the reference to the date of the act is a reference to the last day of that period, and

(b)   a failure to act is to be treated as done when it was decided on.

(5)   For the purposes of paragraph (4), in the absence of evidence establishing the contrary an employer shall be taken to decide on a failure to act—

(a)   when he does an act inconsistent with doing the failed act, or

(b)   if he has done no such inconsistent act, when the period expires within which he might reasonably have been expected to do the failed act if it was to be done.

(6)   Regulation 29 (unfair dismissal) has effect only in relation to dismissals where the effective date of termination (within the meaning of section 97 of the 1996 Act) falls on or after 8th December 2002.

PART 2
PATERNITY LEAVE

4   Entitlement to paternity leave: birth

(1)   An employee is entitled to be absent from work for the purpose of caring for a child or supporting the child's mother if he—

(a)   satisfies the conditions specified in paragraph (2), and

(b)   has complied with the notice requirements in regulation 6 and, where applicable, the evidential requirements in that regulation.

(2)   The conditions referred to in paragraph (1) are that the employee—

(a)   has been continuously employed for a period of not less than 26 weeks ending with the week immediately preceding the 14th week before the expected week of the child's birth;

(b)   is either—

(i)   the father of the child or;

(ii)   married to or the partner of the child's mother, but not the child's father;

(c)   has, or expects to have—

       (i)   if he is the child's father, responsibility for the upbringing of the child;

       (ii)   if he is the mother's husband or partner but not the child's father, the main responsibility (apart from any responsibility of the mother) for the upbringing of the child.

(3)   An employee shall be treated as having satisfied the condition in paragraph (2)(a) on the date of the child's birth notwithstanding the fact that he has not then been continuously employed for a period of not less than 26 weeks, where—

    (a)   the date on which the child is born is earlier than the 14th week before the week in which its birth is expected, and

    (b)   the employee would have been continuously employed for such a period if his employment had continued until that 14th week.

(4)   An employee shall be treated as having satisfied the condition in paragraph (2)(b)(ii) if he would have satisfied it but for the fact that the child's mother has died.

(5)   An employee shall be treated as having satisfied the condition in paragraph (2)(c) if he would have satisfied it but for the fact that the child was stillborn after 24 weeks of pregnancy or has died.

(6)   An employee's entitlement to leave under this regulation shall not be affected by the birth, or expected birth, of more than one child as a result of the same pregnancy.

5   Options in respect of leave under regulation 4

(1)   An employee may choose to take either one week's leave or two consecutive weeks' leave in respect of a child under regulation 4.

(2)   The leave may only be taken during the period which begins with the date on which the child is born and ends—

    (a)   except in the case referred to in sub-paragraph (b), 56 days after that date;

    (b)   in a case where the child is born before the first day of the expected week of its birth, 56 days after that day.

(3)   Subject to paragraph (2) and, where applicable, paragraph (4), an employee may choose to begin his period of leave on—

    (a)   the date on which the child is born;

    (b)   the date falling such number of days after the date on which the child is born as the employee may specify in a notice under regulation 6, or

    (c)   a predetermined date, specified in a notice under that regulation, which is later than the first day of the expected week of the child's birth.

(4)   In a case where the leave is in respect of a child whose expected week of birth begins before 6th April 2003, an employee may choose to begin a period of leave only on a predetermined date, specified in a notice under regulation 6, which is at least 28 days after the date on which that notice is given.

6   Notice and evidential requirements for leave under regulation 4

(1)   An employee must give his employer notice of his intention to take leave in respect of a child under regulation 4, specifying—

    (a)   the expected week of the child's birth;

    (b)   the length of the period of leave that, in accordance with regulation 5(1), the employee has chosen to take, and

    (c)   the date on which, in accordance with regulation 5(3) or (4), the employee has chosen that his period of leave should begin.

(2)   The notice provided for in paragraph (1) must be given to the employer—

    (a)   in or before the 15th week before the expected week of the child's birth, or

    (b)   in a case where it was not reasonably practicable for the employee to give the notice in accordance with sub-paragraph (a), as soon as is reasonably practicable.

(3)   Where the employer requests it, an employee must also give his employer a declaration, signed by the employee, to the effect that the purpose of his absence from work will be that specified in regulation 4(1) and that he satisfies the conditions of entitlement in regulation 4(2)(b) and (c).

(4) An employee who has given notice under paragraph (1) may vary the date he has chosen as the date on which his period of leave will begin, subject to paragraph (5) and provided that he gives his employer notice of the variation—

    (a) where the variation is to provide for the employee's period of leave to begin on the date on which the child is born, at least 28 days before the first day of the expected week of the child's birth;

    (b) where the variation is to provide for the employee's period of leave to begin on a date that is a specified number of days (or a different specified number of days) after the date on which the child is born, at least 28 days before the date falling that number of days after the first day of the expected week of the child's birth;

    (c) where the variation is to provide for the employee's period of leave to begin on a predetermined date (or a different predetermined date), at least 28 days before that date,

or, if it is not reasonably practicable to give the notice at least 28 days before whichever day or date is relevant, as soon as is reasonably practicable.

(5) In a case where regulation 5(4) applies, an employee may only vary the date which he has chosen as the date on which his period of leave will begin by substituting a different predetermined date.

(6) In a case where—

    (a) the employee has chosen to begin his period of leave on a particular predetermined date, and

    (b) the child is not born on or before that date,

the employee must vary his choice of date, by substituting a later predetermined date or (except in a case where regulation 5(4) applies) exercising an alternative option under regulation 5(3), and give his employer notice of the variation as soon as is reasonably practicable.

(7) An employee must give his employer a further notice, as soon as is reasonably practicable after the child's birth, of the date on which the child was born.

(8) Notice under paragraph (1), (4), (6) or (7) shall be given in writing, if the employer so requests.

7   Commencement of leave under regulation 4

(1) Except in the case referred to in paragraph (2), an employee's period of paternity leave under regulation 4 begins on the date specified in his notice under regulation 6(1), or, where he has varied his choice of date under regulation 6(4) or (6), on the date specified in his notice under that provision (or the last such notice if he has varied his choice more than once).

(2) In a case where—

    (a) the employee has chosen to begin his period of leave on the date on which the child is born, and

    (b) he is at work on that date,

the employee's period of leave begins on the day after that date.

8   Entitlement to paternity leave: adoption

(1) An employee is entitled to be absent from work for the purpose of caring for a child or supporting the child's adopter if he—

    (a) satisfies the conditions specified in paragraph (2), and

    (b) has complied with the notice requirements in regulation 10 and, where applicable, the evidential requirements in that regulation.

(2) The conditions referred to in paragraph (1) are that the employee—

    (a) has been continuously employed for a period of not less than 26 weeks ending with the week in which the child's adopter is notified of having been matched with the child;

    (b) is either married to or the partner of the child's adopter, and

    (c) has, or expects to have, the main responsibility (apart from the responsibility of the adopter) for the upbringing of the child.

(3) In paragraph (2)(a), 'week' means the period of seven days beginning with Sunday.

(4) An employee shall be treated as having satisfied the condition in paragraph (2)(b) if he would have satisfied it but for the fact that the child's adopter died during the child's placement.

(5) An employee shall be treated as having satisfied the condition in paragraph (2)(c) if he would have satisfied it but for the fact that the child's placement with the adopter has ended.

(6) An employee's entitlement to leave under this regulation shall not be affected by the placement for adoption of more than one child as part of the same arrangement.

9 Options in respect of leave under regulation 8

(1) An employee may choose to take either one week's leave or two consecutive weeks' leave in respect of a child under regulation 8.

(2) The leave may only be taken during the period of 56 days beginning with the date on which the child is placed with the adopter.

(3) Subject to paragraph (2) and, where applicable, paragraph (4), an employee may choose to begin a period of leave under regulation 8 on—

    (a) the date on which the child is placed with the adopter;

    (b) the date falling such number of days after the date on which the child is placed with the adopter as the employee may specify in a notice under regulation 10, or

    (c) a predetermined date, specified in a notice under that regulation, which is later than the date on which the child is expected to be placed with the adopter.

(4) In a case where the adopter was notified of having been matched with the child before 6th April 2003, the employee may choose to begin a period of leave only on a predetermined date, specified in a notice under regulation 10, which is at least 28 days after the date on which that notice is given.

10 Notice and evidential requirements for leave under regulation 8

(1) An employee must give his employer notice of his intention to take leave in respect of a child under regulation 8, specifying—

    (a) the date on which the adopter was notified of having been matched with the child;

    (b) the date on which the child is expected to be placed with the adopter;

    (c) the length of the period of leave that, in accordance with regulation 9(1), the employee has chosen to take, and

    (d) the date on which, in accordance with regulation 9(3) or (4), the employee has chosen that his period of leave should begin.

(2) The notice provided for in paragraph (1) must be given to the employer—

    (a) no more than seven days after the date on which the adopter is notified of having been matched with the child, or

    (b) in a case where it was not reasonably practicable for the employee to give notice in accordance with sub-paragraph (a), as soon as is reasonably practicable.

(3) Where the employer requests it, an employee must also give his employer a declaration, signed by the employee, to the effect that the purpose of his absence from work will be that specified in regulation 8(1) and that he satisfies the conditions of entitlement in regulation 8(2)(b) and (c).

(4) An employee who has given notice under paragraph (1) may vary the date he has chosen as the date on which his period of leave will begin, subject to paragraph (5) and provided that he gives his employer notice of the variation—

    (a) where the variation is to provide for the employee's period of leave to begin on the date on which the child is placed with the adopter, at least 28 days before the date specified in the employee's notice under paragraph (1) as the date on which the child is expected to be placed with the adopter;

    (b) where the variation is to provide for the employee's period of leave to begin on a date that is a specified number of days (or a different specified number of days) after the date on which the child is placed with the adopter, at least 28 days before the date falling that number of days after the date specified in the employee's notice under paragraph (1) as the date on which the child is expected to be placed with the adopter;

    (c) where the variation is to provide for the employee's period of leave to begin on a predetermined date, at least 28 days before that date,

or, if it is not reasonably practicable to give the notice at least 28 days before whichever date is relevant, as soon as is reasonably practicable.

(5) In a case where regulation 9(4) applies, an employee may only vary the date which he has chosen as the date on which his period of leave will begin by substituting a different predetermined date.

(6) In a case where—

    (a) the employee has chosen to begin his period of leave on a particular predetermined date, and

    (b) the child is not placed with the adopter on or before that date,

the employee must vary his choice of date, by substituting a later predetermined date or (except in a case where regulation 9(4) applies) exercising an alternative option under regulation 9(3), and give his employer notice of the variation as soon as is reasonably practicable.

(7) An employee must give his employer a further notice, as soon as is reasonably practicable after the child's placement, of the date on which the child was placed.

(8) Notice under paragraph (1), (4), (6) or (7) shall be given in writing, if the employer so requests.

11   Commencement of leave under regulation 8

(1) Except in the case referred to in paragraph (2), an employee's period of paternity leave under regulation 8 begins on the date specified in his notice under regulation 10(1), or, where he has varied his choice of date under regulation 10(4) or (6), on the date specified in his notice under that provision (or the last such date if he has varied his choice more than once).

(2) In a case where—

    (a) the employee has chosen to begin his period of leave on the date on which the child is placed with the adopter, and

    (b) he is at work on that date,

the employee's period of leave begins on the day after that date.

12   Application of terms and conditions during paternity leave

(1) An employee who takes paternity leave—

    (a) is entitled, during the period of leave, to the benefit of all of the terms and conditions of employment which would have applied if he had not been absent, and

    (b) is bound, during that period, by any obligations arising under those terms and conditions, subject only to the exception in section 80C(1)(b) of the 1996 Act.

(2) In paragraph (1)(a), 'terms and conditions of employment' has the meaning given by section 80C(5) of the 1996 Act, and accordingly does not include terms and conditions about remuneration.

(3) For the purposes of section 80C of the 1996 Act, only sums payable to an employee by way of wages or salary are to be treated as remuneration.

13   Right to return after paternity leave

(1) An employee who returns to work after a period of paternity leave which was—

    (a) an isolated period of leave, or

    (b) the last of two or more consecutive periods of statutory leave, which did not include any period of additional maternity leave or additional adoption leave or a period of parental leave of more than four weeks,

is entitled to return from leave to the job in which he was employed before his absence.

(2) An employee who returns to work after a period of paternity leave not falling within the description in paragraph (1)(a) or (b) above is entitled to return from leave to the job in which he was employed before his absence, or, if it is not reasonably practicable for the employer to permit him to return to that job, to another job which is both suitable for him and appropriate for him to do in the circumstances.

(3) The reference in paragraphs (1) and (2) to the job in which an employee was employed before his absence is a reference to the job in which he was employed—

    (a) if his return is from an isolated period of paternity leave, immediately before that period began;

    (b) if his return is from consecutive periods of statutory leave, immediately before the first such period.

14   Incidents of the right to return after paternity leave

(1)   An employee's right to return under regulation 13 is a right to return—

    (a)   with his seniority, pension rights and similar rights—

        (i)   in a case where the employee is returning from consecutive periods of statutory leave which included a period of additional adoption leave or additional maternity leave, as they would have been if the period or periods of his employment prior to the additional adoption leave or (as the case may be) additional maternity leave were continuous with the period of employment following it;

        (ii)   in any other case, as they would have been if he had not been absent, and

    (b)   on terms and conditions not less favourable than those which would have applied if he had not been absent.

(2)   The provision in paragraph (1)(a)(i) concerning the treatment of periods of additional maternity leave or additional adoption leave is subject to the requirements of paragraphs 5, 5B and 6 of Schedule 5 to the Social Security Act 1989 (equal treatment under pension schemes: maternity absence, adoption leave and family leave).

(3)   The provisions in paragraph (1)(a)(ii) and (b) for an employee to be treated as if he had not been absent refer to his absence—

    (a)   if his return is from an isolated period of paternity leave, since the beginning of that period;

    (b)   if his return is from consecutive periods of statutory leave, since the beginning of the first such period.

PART III

ADOPTION LEAVE

15   Entitlement to ordinary adoption leave

(1)   An employee is entitled to ordinary adoption leave in respect of a child if he—

    (a)   satisfies the conditions specified in paragraph (2), and

    (b)   has complied with the notice requirements in regulation 17 and, where applicable, the evidential requirements in that regulation.

(2)   The conditions referred to in paragraph (1) are that the employee—

    (a)   is the child's adopter;

    (b)   has been continuously employed for a period of not less than 26 weeks ending with the week in which he was notified of having been matched with the child, and

    (c)   has notified the agency that he agrees that the child should be placed with him and on the date of placement.

(3)   In paragraph (2)(b), 'week' means the period of seven days beginning with Sunday.

(4)   An employee's entitlement to leave under this regulation shall not be affected by the placement for adoption of more than one child as part of the same arrangement.

16   Options in respect of ordinary adoption leave

(1)   Except in the case referred to in paragraph (2), an employee may choose to begin a period of ordinary adoption leave on—

    (a)   the date on which the child is placed with him for adoption, or

    (b)   a predetermined date, specified in a notice under regulation 17, which is no more than 14 days before the date on which the child is expected to be placed with the employee and no later than that date.

(2)   In a case where the employee was notified of having been matched with the child before 6th April 2003, the employee may choose to begin a period of leave only on a predetermined date, specified in a notice under regulation 17, which is after 6th April 2003 and at least 28 days after the date on which that notice is given.

17   Notice and evidential requirements for ordinary adoption leave

(1)   An employee must give his employer notice of his intention to take ordinary adoption leave in respect of a child, specifying—

    (a)   the date on which the child is expected to be placed with him for adoption, and

      (b)   the date on which, in accordance with regulation 16(1) or (2), the employee has chosen that his period of leave should begin.

  (2)   The notice provided for in paragraph (1) must be given to the employer—

      (a)   no more than seven days after the date on which the employee is notified of having been matched with the child for the purposes of adoption, or

      (b)   in a case where it was not reasonably practicable for the employee to give notice in accordance with sub-paragraph (a), as soon as is reasonably practicable.

  (3)   Where the employer requests it, an employee must also provide his employer with evidence, in the form of one or more documents issued by the adoption agency that matched the employee with the child, of—

      (a)   the name and address of the agency;

      (b)   ...

      (c)   the date on which the employee was notified that he had been matched with the child, and

      (d)   the date on which the agency expects to place the child with the employee.

  (4)   An employee who has given notice under paragraph (1) may vary the date he has chosen as the date on which his period of leave will begin, subject to paragraph (5) and provided that he gives his employer notice of the variation—

      (a)   where the variation is to provide for the employee's period of leave to begin on the date on which the child is placed with him for adoption, at least 28 days before the date specified in his notice under paragraph (1) as the date on which the child is expected to be placed with him;

      (b)   where the variation is to provide for the employee's period of leave to begin on a predetermined date (or a different predetermined date), at least 28 days before that date,

      or, if it is not reasonably practicable to give the notice 28 days before whichever date is relevant, as soon as is reasonably practicable.

  (5)   In a case where regulation 16(2) applies, an employee may only vary the date which he has chosen as the date on which his period of leave will begin by substituting a different predetermined date.

  (6)   Notice under paragraph (1) or (4) shall be given in writing, if the employer so requests.

  (7)   An employer who is given notice under paragraph (1) or (4) of the date on which an employee has chosen that his period of ordinary adoption leave should begin shall notify the employee, within 28 days of his receipt of the notice, of the date on which the period of additional adoption leave to which the employee will be entitled (if he satisfies the conditions in regulation 20(1)) after his period of ordinary adoption leave ends.

  (8)   The notification provided for in paragraph (7) shall be given to the employee—

      (a)   where the employer is given notice under paragraph (1), within 28 days of the date on which he received that notice;

      (b)   where the employer is given notice under paragraph (4), within 28 days of the date on which the employee's ordinary adoption leave period began.

18   Duration and commencement of ordinary adoption leave

  (1)   Subject to regulations 22 and 24, an employee's ordinary adoption leave period is a period of 26 weeks

  (2)   Except in the case referred to in paragraph (3), an employee's ordinary adoption leave period begins on the date specified in his notice under regulation 17(1), or, where he has varied his choice of date under regulation 17 (4), on the date specified in his notice under that provision (or the last such date if he has varied his choice more than once).

  (3)   In a case where—

      (a)   the employee has chosen to begin his period of leave on the date on which the child is placed with him, and

      (b)   he is at work on that date,

      the employee's period of leave begins on the day after that date.

19   Application of terms and conditions during ordinary adoption leave

(1)   An employee who takes ordinary adoption leave—

  (a)   is entitled, during the period of leave, to the benefit of all of the terms and conditions of employment which would have applied if he had not been absent, and

  (b)   is bound, during that period, by any obligations arising under those terms and conditions, subject only to the exception in section 75A(3)(b) of the 1996 Act.

(2)   In paragraph (1)(a), 'terms and conditions of employment' has the meaning given by section 75A(4) of the 1996 Act, and accordingly does not include terms and conditions about remuneration.

(3)   For the purposes of section 75A of the 1996 Act, only sums payable to an employee by way of wages or salary are to be treated as remuneration.

20   Additional adoption leave: entitlement, duration and commencement

(1)   An employee is entitled to additional adoption leave in respect of a child if—

  (a)   the child was placed with him for adoption,

  (b)   he took ordinary adoption leave in respect of the child, and

  (c)   his ordinary adoption leave period did not end prematurely under regulation 22(2)(a) or 24.

(2)   Subject to regulations 22 and 24, an employee's additional adoption leave period is a period of 26 weeks beginning on the day after the last day of his ordinary adoption leave period.

21   Application of terms and conditions during additional adoption leave

An employee who takes additional adoption leave—

  (a)   is entitled, during the period of leave, to the benefit of his employer's implied obligation to him of trust and confidence and of any terms and conditions of his employment relating to—

  (i)   notice of the termination of the employment contract by his employer;

  (ii)   compensation in the event of redundancy, or

  (iii)   disciplinary or grievance procedures; and

  (b)   is bound, during that period, by his implied obligation to his employer of good faith and of any terms and conditions of his employment relating to—

  (i)   notice of the termination of the employment contract by him,

  (ii)   the disclosure of confidential information;

  (iii)   the acceptance of gifts or other benefits, or

  (iv)   the employee's participation in any other business.

21A   Work during adoption leave period

(1)   An employee may carry out up to 10 days' work for his employer during his statutory adoption leave period without bringing his statutory adoption leave to an end.

(2)   For the purposes of this regulation, any work carried out on any day shall constitute a day's work.

(3)   Subject to paragraph (4), for the purposes of this regulation, work means any work done under the contract of employment and may include training or any activity undertaken for the purposes of keeping in touch with the workplace.

(4)   Reasonable contact from time to time between an employee and his employer which either party is entitled to make during an adoption leave period (for example to discuss an employee's return to work) shall not bring that period to an end.

(5)   This regulation does not confer any right on an employer to require that any work be carried out during the statutory adoption leave period, nor any right on an employee to work during the statutory adoption leave period.

(6)   Any days' work carried out under this regulation shall not have the effect of extending the total duration of the statutory adoption leave period.

22   Disrupted placement in the course of adoption leave

(1)   This regulation applies where—

    (a)   an employee has begun a period of adoption leave in respect of a child before the placement of the child with him, and the employee is subsequently notified that the placement will not be made, or

    (b)   during an employee's period of adoption leave in respect of a child placed with him—

        (i)   the child dies, or

        (ii)   the child is returned to the adoption agency under section 30(3) of the Adoption Act 1976 or section 30(3) of the Adoption (Scotland) Act 1978.

(2)   Subject to regulation 24, in a case where this regulation applies—

    (a)   except in the circumstances referred to in sub-paragraphs (b) and (c), the employee's adoption leave period ends eight weeks after the end of the relevant week specified in paragraph (3);

    (b)   where the employee is taking ordinary adoption leave and the period of 26 weeks provided for in regulation 18 ends within eight weeks of the end of the relevant week—

        (i)   the employee's ordinary adoption leave period ends on the expiry of the 26-week period;

        (ii)   the employee is entitled to additional adoption leave, and

        (iii)   the employee's additional adoption leave period ends eight weeks after the end of the relevant week;

    (c)   where the employee is taking additional adoption leave and the period of 26 weeks provided for in regulation 20 ends within eight weeks of the end of the relevant week, the employee's additional adoption leave period ends on the expiry of the 26-week period.

(3)   The relevant week referred to in paragraph (2) is—

    (a)   in a case falling within paragraph (1)(a), the week during which the person with whom the child was to be placed for adoption is notified that the placement will not be made;

    (b)   in a case falling within paragraph (1)(b)(i), the week during which the child dies;

    (c)   in a case falling within paragraph (1)(b)(ii), the week during which the child is returned.

(4)   In paragraph (3), 'week' means the period of seven days beginning with Sunday.

23   Redundancy during adoption leave

(1)   This regulation applies where, during an employee's ordinary or additional adoption leave period, it is not practicable by reason of redundancy for his employer to continue to employ him under his existing contract of employment.

(2)   Where there is a suitable available vacancy, the employee is entitled to be offered (before the end of his employment under his existing contract) alternative employment with his employer or his employer's successor, or an associated employer, under a new contract of employment which complies with paragraph (3) and takes effect immediately on the ending of his employment under the previous contract.

(3)   The new contract of employment must be such that—

    (a)   the work to be done under it is of a kind which is both suitable in relation to the employee and appropriate for him to do in the circumstances, and

    (b)   its provisions as to the capacity and place in which he is to be employed, and as to the other terms and conditions of his employment, are not substantially less favourable to him than if he had continued to be employed under the previous contract.

24   Dismissal during adoption leave

Where an employee is dismissed after an ordinary or additional adoption leave period has begun but before the time when (apart from this regulation) that period would end, the period ends at the time of the dismissal.

25   Requirement to notify intention to return during adoption leave period

(1)   An employee who intends to return to work earlier than the end of his additional adoption leave period must give his employer at least 8 weeks' notice of the date on which he intends to return.

(2)   If an employee attempts to return to work earlier than the end of his additional adoption leave period without complying with paragraph (1), his employer is entitled to postpone his return

to a date such as will secure, subject to paragraph (3), that he has at least 8 weeks' notice of the employee's return.

(2A) An employee who complies with his obligations in paragraph (1) or whose employer has postponed his return in the circumstances described in paragraph (2), and who then decides to return to work—

    (a)   earlier than the original return date, must give his employer not less than 8 weeks' notice of the date on which he now intends to return;

    (b)   later than the original return date, must give his employer not less than 8 weeks' notice ending with the original return date.

(2B) In paragraph (2A) the 'original return date' means the date which the employee notified to his employer as the date of his return to work under paragraph (1), or the date to which his return was postponed by his employer under paragraph (2).

(3)   An employer is not entitled under paragraph (2) to postpone an employee's return to work to a date after the end of the employee's additional adoption leave period.

(4)   If an employee whose return has been postponed under paragraph (2) has been notified that he is not to return to work before the date to which his return was postponed, the employer is under no contractual obligation to pay him remuneration until the date to which his return was postponed if he returns to work before that date.

(5)   This regulation does not apply in a case where the employer did not notify the employee in accordance with regulation 17(7) and (8) of the date on which the employee's additional adoption leave period would end.

(6)   In a case where an employee's adoption leave is curtailed because regulation 22 applies, the references in this regulation to the end of an employee's additional adoption leave period are references to the date on which that period would have ended had that regulation not applied, irrespective of whether it was the employee's ordinary adoption leave period or his additional adoption leave period that was curtailed.

26   Right to return after adoption leave

(1)   An employee who returns to work after a period of ordinary adoption leave which was—

    (a)   an isolated period of leave, or

    (b)   the last of two or more consecutive periods of statutory leave, which did not include any period of additional maternity leave or additional adoption leave or a period of parental leave of more than four weeks,

is entitled to return from leave to the job in which he was employed before his absence.

(2)   An employee who returns to work after—

    (a)   a period of additional adoption leave, whether or not preceded by another period of statutory leave, or

    (b)   a period of ordinary adoption leave not falling within the description in paragraph (1)(a) or (b) above,

is entitled to return from leave to the job in which he was employed before his absence, or, if it is not reasonably practicable for the employer to permit him to return to that job, to another job which is both suitable for him and appropriate for him to do in the circumstances.

(3)   The reference in paragraphs (1) and (2) to the job in which an employee was employed before his absence is a reference to the job in which he was employed—

    (a)   if his return is from an isolated period of adoption leave, immediately before that period began;

    (b)   if his return is from consecutive periods of statutory leave, immediately before the first such period.

(4)   This regulation does not apply where regulation 23 applies.

27   Incidents of the right to return from adoption leave

(1)   An employee's right to return under regulation 26 is to return—

    (a)   with his seniority, pension rights and similar rights—

        (i)   in a case where the employee is returning from additional adoption leave, or consecutive periods of statutory leave which included a period of additional adoption leave or additional maternity leave, as they would have been if the period or periods of his employment prior to his additional adoption leave or (as the case may be) additional maternity leave were continuous with the period of employment following it;

    (ii)   in any other case, as they would have been if he had not been absent, and

  (b)   on terms and conditions not less favourable than those which would have been applied to him if he had not been absent.

(2)   The provision in paragraph (1)(a)(i) concerning the treatment of periods of additional adoption leave or additional maternity leave is subject to the requirements of paragraphs 5, 5B and 6 of Schedule 5 to the Social Security Act 1989 (equal treatment under pension schemes: maternity absence, adoption leave and family leave).

(3)   The provisions in paragraph (1)(a)(ii) and (b) for an employee to be treated as if he had not been absent refer to his absence—

  (a)   if his return is from an isolated period of ordinary adoption leave, since the beginning of that period;

  (b)   if his return is from consecutive periods of statutory leave, since the beginning of the first such period.

PART 4
PROVISIONS APPLICABLE IN RELATION TO BOTH PATERNITY AND ADOPTION LEAVE

28   Protection from detriment

(1)   An employee is entitled under section 47C of the 1996 Act not to be subjected to any detriment by any act, or any deliberate failure to act, by his employer because—

  (a)   the employee took or sought to take paternity leave or ordinary or additional adoption leave;

  (b)   the employer believed that the employee was likely to take ordinary or additional adoption leave,

  (bb)   the employee undertook, considered undertaking or refused to undertake work in acordance with regulation 21A; or

  (c)   the employee failed to return after a period of additional adoption leave in a case where—

      (i)   the employer did not notify him, in accordance with regulation 17(7) and (8) or otherwise, of the date on which that period ended, and he reasonably believed that the period had not ended, or

      (ii)   the employer gave him less than 28 days' notice of the date on which the period would end, and it was not reasonably practicable for him to return on that date.

(2)   Paragraph (1) does not apply where the detriment in question amounts to dismissal within the meaning of Part 10 of the 1996 Act.

29   Unfair dismissal

(1)   An employee who is dismissed is entitled under section 99 of the 1996 Act to be regarded for the purpose of Part 10 of that Act as unfairly dismissed if—

  (a)   the reason or principal reason for the dismissal is of a kind specified in paragraph (3), or

  (b)   the reason or principal reason for the dismissal is that the employee is redundant, and regulation 23 has not been complied with.

(2)   An employee who is dismissed shall also be regarded for the purposes of Part 10 of the 1996 Act as unfairly dismissed if—

  (a)   the reason (or, if more than one, the principal reason) for the dismissal is that the employee was redundant;

  (b)   it is shown that the circumstances constituting the redundancy applied equally to one or more employees in the same undertaking who had positions similar to that held by the employee and who have not been dismissed by the employer, and

  (c)   it is shown that the reason (or, if more than one, the principal reason) for which the employee was selected for dismissal was a reason of a kind specified in paragraph (3).

(3) The kinds of reason referred to in paragraph (1) and (2) are reasons connected with the fact that—

(a) the employee took, or sought to take, paternity or adoption leave;

(b) the employer believed that the employee was likely to take ordinary or additional adoption leave,

(bb) the employee undertook, considered undertaking or refused to undertake work in accordance with regulation 21A; or

(c) the employee failed to return after a period of additional adoption leave in a case where—

(i) the employer did not notify him, in accordance with regulation 17(7) and (8) or otherwise, of the date on which that period would end, and he reasonably believed that the period had not ended, or

(ii) the employer gave him less than 28 days' notice of the date on which the period would end, and it was not reasonably practicable for him to return on that date.

(4) Paragraph (1) does not apply in relation to an employee who took adoption leave if—

(a) immediately before the end of his additional adoption leave period (or, if it ends by reason of dismissal, immediately before the dismissal) the number of employees employed by his employer, added to the number employed by any associated employer of his employer, did not exceed five, and

(b) it is not reasonably practicable for the employer (who may be the same employer or a successor of his) to permit the employee to return to a job which is both suitable for the employee and appropriate for him to do in the circumstances or for an associated employer to offer the employee a job of that kind.

(5) Paragraph (1) does not apply in relation to an employee if—

(a) it is not reasonably practicable for a reason other than redundancy for the employer (who may be the same employer or a successor of his) to permit the employee to return to a job which is both suitable for the employee and appropriate for him to do in the circumstances;

(b) an associated employer offers the employee a job of that kind, and

(c) the employee accepts or unreasonably refuses that offer.

(6) Where, on a complaint of unfair dismissal, any question arises as to whether the operation of paragraph (1) is excluded by the provisions of paragraph (4) or (5), it is for the employer to show that the provisions in question were satisfied in relation to the complainant.

30 Contractual rights to paternity or adoption leave

(1) This regulation applies where an employee is entitled to—

(a) paternity leave,

(b) ordinary adoption leave, or

(c) additional adoption leave,

(referred to in paragraph (2) as a 'statutory right') and also to a right which corresponds to that right and which arises under the employee's contract of employment or otherwise.

(2) In a case where this regulation applies—

(a) the employee may not exercise the statutory right and the corresponding right separately but may, in taking the leave for which the two rights provide, take advantage of whichever right is, in any particular respect, the more favourable, and

(b) the provisions of the 1996 Act and of these Regulations relating to the statutory right apply, subject to any modifications necessary to give effect to any more favourable contractual terms, to the exercise of the composite right described in sub-paragraph (a) as they apply to the exercise of the statutory right.

EMPLOYMENT EQUALITY (RELIGION OR BELIEF) REGULATIONS 2003
(SI 2003 No. 1660)

PART I

GENERAL

2   **Interpretation**

(1) In these Regulations—

    (a)   'religion' means any religion

    (b)   'belief' means any religious or philosophical belief,

    (c)   a reference to religion includes a reference to lack of religion, and

    (d)   a reference to belief includes a reference to lack of belief.

(2) In these Regulations, references to discrimination are to any discrimination falling within regulation 3 (discrimination on grounds of religion or belief) or 4 (discrimination by way of victimisation) and related expressions shall be construed accordingly, and references to harassment shall be construed in accordance with regulation 5 (harassment on grounds of religion or belief).

(3) In these Regulations—

'act' includes a deliberate omission;

'benefits' includes facilities and services;

'detriment' does not include harassment within the meaning of regulation 5;

references to 'employer', in their application to a person at any time seeking to employ another, include a person who has no employees at that time;

'employment' means employment under a contract of service or of apprenticeship or a contract personally to do any work. and related expressions shall be construed accordingly;

'Great Britain', except where the context otherwise requires in regulation 26 (protection of Sikhs from discrimination in connection with requirements as to wearing of safety helmets), includes such of the territorial waters of the United Kingdom as are adjacent to Great Britain;

'Minister of the Crown' includes the Treasury and the Defence Council;

'proprietor', in relation to a school in England and Wales, has the meaning given by section 579 of the Education Act 1996, and, in relation to a school in Scotland, means the governing body, trustees, or other person or body of persons responsible for the management of the school; and

'school', in England and Wales, has the meaning given by section 4 of the Education Act 1996; and, in Scotland, has the meaning given by section 135(1) of the Education (Scotland) Act 1980, and references to a school are to an institution in so far as it is engaged in the provision of education under those sections.

3   **Discrimination on grounds of religion or belief**

(1) For the purposes of these Regulations, a person ('A') discriminates against another person ('B') if—

    (a)   on grounds of the religion or belief of B or of any other person except A (whether or not it is also A's religion or belief) A treats B less favourably than he treats or would treat other persons; or

    (b)   A applies to B a provision, criterion or practice which he applies or would apply equally to persons not of the same religion or belief as B, but—

        (i)   which puts or would put persons of the same religion or belief as B at a particular disadvantage when compared with other persons,

        (ii)   which puts B at that disadvantage, and

        (iii)   which A cannot show to be a proportionate means of achieving a legitimate aim.

(2) ...

(3) A comparison of B's case with that of another person under paragraph (1) must be such that the relevant circumstances in the one case are the same, or not materially different, in the other.

4   Discrimination by way of victimisation

(1) For the purposes of these Regulations, a person ('A') discriminates against another person ('B') if he treats B less favourably than he treats or would treat other persons in the same circumstances, and does so by reason that B has—

   (a) brought proceedings against A or any other person under these Regulations;

   (b) given evidence or information in connection with proceedings brought by any person against A or any other person under these Regulations;

   (c) otherwise done anything under or by reference to these Regulations in relation to A or any other person; or

   (d) alleged that A or any other person has committed an act which (whether or not the allegation so states) would amount to a contravention of these Regulations,

   or by reason that A knows that B intends to do any of those things, or suspects that B has done or intends to do any of them.

(2) Paragraph (1) does not apply to treatment of B by reason of any allegation made by him, or evidence or information given by him, if the allegation, evidence or information was false and not made (or, as the case may be, given) in good faith.

5   Harassment on grounds of religion or belief

(1) For the purposes of these Regulations, a person ('A') subjects another person ('B') to harassment where, on grounds of religion or belief, A engages in unwanted conduct which has the purpose or effect of—

   (a) violating B's dignity; or

   (b) creating an intimidating, hostile, degrading, humiliating or offensive environment for B.

(2) Conduct shall be regarded as having the effect specified in paragraph (1)(a) or (b) only if, having regard to all the circumstances. including in particular the, perception of B, it should reasonably be considered as having that effect.

PART II

DISCRIMINATION IN EMPLOYMENT AND VOCATIONAL TRAINING

6   Applicants and employees

(1) It is unlawful for an employer, in relation to employment by him at an establishment in Great Britain, to discriminate against a person—

   (a) in the arrangements he makes for the purpose of determining to whom he should offer employment;

   (b) in the terms on which he offers that person employment; or

   (c) by refusing to offer, or deliberately not offering, him employment.

(2) It is unlawful for an employer, in relation to a person whom he employs at an establishment in Great Britain, to discriminate against that person—

   (a) in the terms of employment which he affords him;

   (b) the opportunities which he affords him for promotion, transfer, training, or receiving any other benefit;

   (c) by refusing to afford him, or deliberately not affording him, any such opportunity; or

   (d) by dismissing him, or subjecting him to any other detriment.

(3) It is unlawful for an employer, in relation to employment by him at an establishment in Great Britain, to subject to harassment a person whom he employs or who has applied to him for employment.

(4) Paragraph (2) does not apply to benefits of any description if the employer is concerned with the provision (for payment or not) of benefits of that description to the public, or to a section of the public which includes the employee in question, unless—

   (a) that provision differs in a material respect from the provision of the benefits by the employer to his employees; or

   (b) the provision of the benefits to the employee in question is regulated by his contract of employment; or

  (c) the benefits relate to training.

(5) In paragraph (2)(d) reference to the dismissal of a person from employment includes reference—

  (a) to the termination of that person's employment by the expiration of any period (including a period expiring by reference to an event or circumstance), not being a termination immediately after which the employment is renewed on the same terms; and

  (b) to the termination of that person's employment by any act of his (including the giving of notice) in circumstances such that he is entitled to terminate it without notice by reason of the conduct of the employer.

7 Exception for genuine occupational requirement

(1) In relation to discrimination falling within regulation 3 (discrimination on grounds of religion or belief)—

  (a) regulation 6(1)(a) or (c) does not apply to any employment;

  (b) regulation 6(2)(b) or (c) does not apply to promotion or transfer to, or training for, any employment; and

  (c) regulation 6(2)(d) does not apply to dismissal from any employment,

  where paragraph (2) or (3) applies.

(2) This paragraph applies where, having regard to the nature of the employment or the context in which it is carried out—

  (a) being of a particular religion or belief is a genuine and determining occupational requirement;

  (b) it is proportionate to apply that requirement in the particular case; and

  (c) either—

    (i) the person to whom that requirement is applied does not meet it, or

    (ii) the employer is not satisfied, and in all the circumstances it is reasonable for him not to be satisfied, that that person meets it,

  and this paragraph applies whether or not the employer has an ethos based on religion or belief.

(3) This paragraph applies where an employer has an ethos based on religion or belief and, having regard to that ethos and to the nature of the employment or the context in which it is carried out—

  (a) being of a particular religion or belief is a genuine occupational requirement for the job;

  (b) it is proportionate to apply that requirement in the particular case; and

  (c) either—

    (i) the person to whom that requirement is applied does not meet it, or

    (ii) the employer is not satisfied, and in all the circumstances it is reasonable for him not to be satisfied, that that person meets it.

8 Contract workers

(1) It is unlawful for a principal, in relation to contract work at an establishment in Great Britain, to discriminate against a contract worker—

  (a) in the terms on which he allows him to do that work;

  (b) by not allowing him to do it or continue to do it;

  (c) in the way he affords him access to any benefits or by refusing or deliberately not affording him access to them; or

  (d) by subjecting him to any other detriment.

(2) It is unlawful for a principal, in relation to contract work at an establishment in Great Britain, to subject a contract worker to harassment.

(3) A principal does not contravene paragraph (1)(b) by doing any act in relation to a contract worker where, if the work were to be done by a person taken into the principal's employment, that act would be lawful by virtue of regulation 7 (exception for genuine occupational requirement).

(4) Paragraph (1) does not apply to benefits of any description if the principal is concerned with the provision (for payment or not) of benefits of that description to the public, or to a section of the public to which the contract worker in question belongs, unless that provision differs in a material respect from the provision of the benefits by the principal to his contract workers.

(5) In this regulation—

'principal' means a person ('A') who makes work available for doing by individuals who are employed by another person who supplies them under a contract made with A;

'contract work' means work so made available; and

'contract worker' means any individual who is supplied to the principal under such a contract.

9   Meaning of employment and contract work at establishment in Great Britain

(1) For the purposes of this Part ('the relevant purposes'), employment is to be regarded as being at an establishment in Great Britain if the employee—

    (a)   does his work wholly or partly in Great Britain; or

    (b)   does his work wholly outside Great Britain and paragraph (2) applies.

(2) This paragraph applies if—

    (a)   the employer has a place of business at an establishment in Great Britain;

    (b)   the work is for the purposes of the business carried on at that establishment; and

    (c)   the employee is ordinarily resident in Great Britain—

        (i)   at the time when he applies for or is offered the employment, or

        (ii)   at any time during the course of the employment.

(3) The reference to 'employment' in paragraph (1) includes—

    (a)   employment on board a ship only if the ship is registered at a port of registry in Great Britain, and

    (b)   employment on an aircraft or hovercraft only if the aircraft or hovercraft is registered in the United Kingdom and operated by a person who has his principal place of business, or is ordinarily resident, in Great Britain.

(4) Subject to paragraph (5), for the purposes of determining if employment concerned with the exploration of the sea bed or sub-soil or the exploitation of their natural resources is outside Great Britain, this regulation has effect as if references to Great Britain included—

    (a)   any area designated under section 1(7) of the Continental Shelf Act 1964 except an area or part of an area in which the law of Northern Ireland applies, and

    (b)   in relation to employment concerned with the exploration or exploitation of the Frigg Gas Field, the part of the Norwegian sector of the Continental Shelf described in Schedule 1.

(5) Paragraph (4) shall not apply to employment which is concerned with the exploration or exploitation of the Frigg Gas Field unless the employer is—

    (a)   a company registered under the Companies Act 1985;

    (b)   an oversea company which has established a place of business within Great Britain from which it directs the exploration or exploitation in question; or

    (c)   any other person who has a place of business within Great Britain from which he directs the exploration or exploitation in question.

(6) In this regulation—

'the Frigg Gas Field' means the naturally occurring gas-bearing sand formations of the lower Eocene age located in the vicinity of the intersection of the line of latitude 59 degrees 53 minutes North and of the dividing line between the sectors of the Continental Shelf of the United Kingdom and the Kingdom of Norway and includes all other gas-bearing strata from which gas at the start of production is capable of flowing into the above-mentioned gas-bearing sand formations;

'oversea company' has the same meaning as in section 744 of the Companies Act 1985.

(7) This regulation applies in relation to contract work within the meaning of regulation 8 as it applies in relation to employment; and, in its application to contract work, references to 'employee', 'employer' and 'employment' are references to (respectively) 'contract worker', 'principal' and 'contract work' within the meaning of regulation 8.

PART III
OTHER UNLAWFUL ACTS

22 Liability of employers and principals

(1) Anything done by a person in the course of his employment shall be treated for the purposes of these Regulations as done by his employer as well as by him, whether or not it was done with the employer's knowledge or approval.

(2) Anything done by a person as agent for another person with the authority (whether express or implied, and whether precedent or subsequent) of that other person shall be treated for the purposes of these Regulations as done by that other person as well as by him.

(3) In proceedings brought under these Regulations against any person in respect of an act alleged to have been done by an employee of his it shall be a defence for that person to prove that he took such steps as were reasonably practicable to prevent the employee from doing that act, or from doing in the course of his employment acts of that description.

23 Aiding unlawful acts

(1) A person who knowingly aids another person to do an act made unlawful by these Regulations shall be treated for the purpose of these Regulations as himself doing an unlawful act of the like description.

(2) For the purposes of paragraph (1) an employee or agent for whose act the employer or principal is liable under regulation 22 (or would be so liable but for regulation 22(3)) shall be deemed to aid the doing of the act by the employer or principal.

(3) A person does not under this regulation knowingly aid another to do an unlawful act if—

(a) he acts in reliance on a statement made to him by that other person that, by reason of any provision of these Regulations, the act which he aids would not be unlawful; and

(b) it is reasonable for him to rely on the statement.

(4) A person who knowingly or recklessly makes a statement such as is referred to in paragraph (3)(a) which in a material respect is false or misleading commits an offence, and shall be liable on summary conviction to a fine not exceeding level 5 on the standard scale.

PART IV
GENERAL EXCEPTIONS FROM PARTS II AND III

24 Exception for national security

Nothing in Part II or III shall render unlawful an act done for the purpose of safeguarding national security, if the doing of the act was justified by that purpose.

25 Exceptions for positive action

(1) Nothing in Part II or III shall render unlawful any act done in or in connection with—

(a) affording persons of a particular religion or belief access to facilities for training which would help fit them for particular work; or

(b) encouraging persons of a particular religion or belief to take advantage of opportunities for doing particular work,

where it reasonably appears to the person doing the act that it prevents or compensates for disadvantages linked to religion or belief suffered by persons of that religion or belief doing that work or likely to take up that work.

(2) Nothing in Part II or III shall render unlawful any act done by a trade organisation within the meaning of regulation 15 in or in connection with—

(a) affording only members of the organisation who are of a particular religion or belief access to facilities for training which would help fit them for holding a post of any kind in the organisation; or

(b) encouraging only members of the organisation who are of a particular religion or belief to take advantage of opportunities for holding such posts in the organisation,

where it reasonably appears to the organisation that the act prevents or compensates for disadvantages linked to religion or belief suffered by those of that religion or belief holding such posts or likely to hold such posts.

(3) Nothing in Part II or III shall render unlawful any act done by a trade organisation within the meaning of regulation 15 in or in connection with encouraging only persons of a particular religion or belief to become members of the organisation where it reasonably appears to the organisation that the act prevents or compensates for disadvantages linked to religion or belief suffered by persons of that religion or belief who are, or are eligible to become, members.

28 Jurisdiction of employment tribunals

(1) A complaint by any person ('the complainant') that another person ('the respondent')—
   (a)   has committed against the complainant an act to which this regulation applies; or
   (b)   is by virtue of regulation 22 (liability of employers and principals) or 23 (aiding unlawful acts) to be treated as having committed against the complainant such an act,
   may be presented to an employment tribunal.

(2) This regulation applies to any act of discrimination or harassment which is unlawful by virtue of any provision of Part II other than—
   (a)   where the act is one in respect of which an appeal or proceedings in the nature of an appeal may be brought under any enactment, regulation 16 (qualifications bodies);
   (b)   regulation 20 (institutions of further and higher education); or
   (c)   where the act arises out of and is closely connected to a relationship between the complainant and the respondent which has come to an end but during the course of which an act of discrimination against, or harassment of, the complainant by the respondent would have been unlawful by virtue of regulation 20, regulation 21 (relationships which have come to an end).

(3) In paragraph (2)(c), reference to an act of discrimination or harassment which would have been unlawful includes, in the case of a relationship which has come to an end before the coming into force of these Regulations, reference to an act of discrimination or harassment which would, after the coming into force of these Regulations, have been unlawful.

(4) In this regulation, 'enactment' includes an enactment comprised in, or in an instrument made under, an Act of the Scottish Parliament.

29 Burden of proof: employment tribunals

(1) This regulation applies to any complaint presented under regulation 28 to an employment tribunal.

(2) Where, on the hearing of the complaint, the complainant proves facts from which the tribunal could, apart from this regulation, conclude in the absence of an adequate explanation that the respondent—
   (a)   has committed against the complainant an act to which regulation 28 applies; or
   (b)   is by virtue of regulation 22 (liability of employers and principals) or 23 (aiding unlawful acts) to be treated as having committed against the complainant such an act,
   the tribunal shall uphold the complaint unless the respondent proves that he did not commit, or as the case may be, is not to be treated as having committed, that act.

30 Remedies on complaints in employment tribunals

(1) Where an employment tribunal finds that a complaint presented to it under regulation 28 is well-founded, the tribunal shall make such of the following as it considers just and equitable—
   (a)   an order declaring the rights of the complainant and the respondent in relation to the act to which the complaint relates;
   (b)   an order requiring the respondent to pay to the complainant compensation of an amount corresponding to any damages he could have been ordered by a county court or by a sheriff court to pay to the complainant if the complaint had fallen to be dealt with under regulation 31 (jurisdiction of county and sheriff courts);
   (c)   a recommendation that the respondent take within a specified period action appearing to the tribunal to be practicable for the purpose of obviating or reducing the adverse effect on the complainant of any act of discrimination or harassment to which the complaint relates.

(2)   As respects an unlawful act of discrimination falling within regulation 3(1)(b), if the respondent proves that the provision, criterion or practice was not applied with the intention of treating the complainant unfavourably on grounds of religion or belief, an order may be made under paragraph (1)(b) only if the employment tribunal—

    (a)   makes such order under paragraph (1)(a) (if any) and such recommendation under paragraph (1)(c) (if any) as it would have made if it had no power to make an order under paragraph (1)(b); and

    (b)   where it makes an order under paragraph (1)(a) or a recommendation under paragraph (1)(c) or both) considers that it is just and equitable to make an order under paragraph (1)(b) as well.

(3)   If without reasonable justification the respondent to a complaint fails to comply with a recommendation made by an employment tribunal under paragraph (1)(c), then, if it thinks it just and equitable to do so—

    (a)   the tribunal may increase the amount of compensation required to be paid to the complainant in respect of the complaint by an order made under paragraph (1)(b); or

    (b)   if an order under paragraph (1)(b) was not made, the tribunal may make such an order.

(4)   Where an amount of compensation falls to be awarded under paragraph (1)(b), the tribunal may include in the award interest on that amount subject to, and in accordance with, the provisions of the Employment Tribunals (Interest on Awards in Discrimination Cases) Regulations 1996.

EMPLOYMENT EQUALITY (SEXUAL ORIENTATION) REGULATIONS 2003
(SI 2003 No. 1661)

PART I

GENERAL

2   **Interpretation**

(1)   In these Regulations, 'sexual orientation' means a sexual orientation towards—

    (a)   persons of the same sex;

    (b)   persons of the opposite sex; or

    (c)   persons of the same sex and of the opposite sex.

(2)   In these Regulations, references to discrimination are to any discrimination falling within regulation 3 (discrimination on grounds of sexual orientation) or 4 (discrimination by way of victimisation) and related expressions shall be construed accordingly, and references to harassment shall be construed in accordance with regulation 5 (harassment on grounds of sexual orientation).

(3)   In these Regulations—

'act' includes a deliberate omission;

'benefits' includes facilities and services;

'detriment' does not include harassment within the meaning of regulation 5;

references to 'employer', in their application to a person at any time seeking to employ another, include a person who has no employees at that time;

'employment' means employment under a contract of service or of apprenticeship or a contract personally to do any work, and related expressions shall be construed accordingly;

'Great Britain' includes such of the territorial waters of the United Kingdom as are adjacent to Great Britain;

'Minister of the Crown' includes the Treasury and the Defence Council;

'proprietor', in relation to a school in England and Wales, has the meaning given by section 579 of the Education Act 1996, and, in relation to a school in Scotland, means the governing body, trustees, or other person or body of persons responsible for the management of the school; and

'school', in England and Wales, has the meaning given by section 4 of the Education Act 1996, and, in Scotland, has the meaning given by section 135(1) of the Education (Scotland) Act

1980, and references to a school are to an institution in so far as it is engaged in the provision of education under those sections.

3   Discrimination on grounds of sexual orientation

(1) For the purposes of these Regulations, a person ('A') discriminates against another person ('B') if—

    (a) on grounds of sexual orientation, A treats B less favourably than he treats or would treat other persons; or

    (b) A applies to B a provision, criterion or practice which he applies or would apply equally to persons not of the same sexual orientation as B, but—

        (i) which puts or would put persons of the same sexual orientation as B at a particular disadvantage when compared with other persons,

        (ii) which puts B at that disadvantage, and

        (iii) which A cannot show to be a proportionate means of achieving a legitimate aim.

(2) A comparison of B's case with that of another person under paragraph (1) must be such that the relevant circumstances in the one case are the same, or not materially different, in the other.

(3) For the purposes of paragraph (2), in a comparison of B's case with that of another person the fact that one of the persons (whether or not B) is a civil partner while the other is married shall not be treated as a material difference between their respective circumstances.

4   Discrimination by way of victimisation

(1) For the purposes of these Regulations, a person ('A') discriminates against another person ('B') if he treats B less favourably than he treats or would treat other persons in the same circumstances, and does so by reason that B has—

    (a) brought proceedings against A or any other person under these Regulations;

    (b) given evidence or information in connection with proceedings brought by any person against A or any other person under these Regulations;

    (c) otherwise done anything under or by reference to these Regulations in relation to A or any other person; or

    (d) alleged that A or any other person has committed an act which (whether or not the allegation so states) would amount to a contravention of these Regulations,

or by reason that A knows that B intends to do any of those things, or suspects that B has done or intends to do any of them.

(2) Paragraph (1) does not apply to treatment of B by reason of any allegation made by him, or evidence or information given by him, if the allegation, evidence or information was false and not made (or, as the case may be, given) in good faith.

5   Harassment on grounds of sexual orientation

(1) For the purposes of these Regulations, a person ('A') subjects another person ('B') to harassment where, on grounds of sexual orientation, A engages in unwanted conduct which has the purpose or effect of—

    (a) violating B's dignity; or

    (b) creating an intimidating, hostile, degrading, humiliating or offensive environment for B.

(2) Conduct shall be regarded as having the effect specified in paragraph (1)(a) or (b) only if, having regard to all the circumstances, including in particular the perception of B, it should reasonably be considered as having that effect.

PART II
DISCRIMINATION IN EMPLOYMENT AND VOCATIONAL TRAINING

6   Applicants and employees

(1) It is unlawful for an employer, in relation to employment by him at an establishment in Great Britain, to discriminate against a person—

    (a) in the arrangements he manes for the purpose of determining to whom he should offer employment;

     (b)   in the terms on which he offers that person employment; or

     (c)   by refusing to offer, or deliberately not offering, him employment.

(2)   It is unlawful for an employer, in relation to a person whom he employs at an establishment in Great Britain, to discriminate against that person—

     (a)   in terms of employment which he affords him;

     (b)   in the opportunities which he affords him for promotion, a transfer, training, or receiving any other benefit;

     (c)   by refusing to afford him, or deliberately not affording him, any such opportunity; or

     (d)   by dismissing him, or subjecting him to any other detriment.

(3)   It is unlawful for an employer, in relation to employment by him at an establishment in Great Britain, to subject to harassment a person whom he employs or who has applied to him for employment.

(4)   Paragraph (2) does not apply to benefits of any description if the employer is concerned with the provision (for payment or not) of benefits of that description to the public, or to a section of the public which includes the employee in question, unless—

     (a)   that provision differs in a material respect from the provision of the benefits by the employer to his employees; or

     (b)   the provision of the benefits to the employee in question is regulated by his contract of employment; or

     (c)   the benefits relate to training.

(5)   In paragraph (2)(d) reference to the dismissal of a person from employment includes reference—

     (a)   to the termination of that person's employment by the expiration of any period (including a period expiring by reference to an event or circumstance), not being a termination immediately after which the employment is renewed on the same terms; and

     (b)   to the termination of that person's employment by any act of his (including the giving of notice) in circumstances such that he is entitled to terminate it without notice by reason of the conduct of the employer.

7   Exception for genuine occupational requirement etc.

(1)   In relation to discrimination falling within regulation 3 (discrimination on grounds of sexual orientation)—

     (a)   regulation 6(1)(a) or (c) does not apply to any employment;

     (b)   regulation 6(2)(b) or (c) does not apply to promotion or transfer to, or training for, any employment; and

     (c)   regulation 6(2)(d) does not apply to dismissal from any employment,

    where paragraph (2) or (3) applies.

(2)   This paragraph applies where, having regard to the nature of the employment or the context in which it is carried out—

     (a)   being of a particular sexual orientation is a genuine and determining occupational requirement;

     (b)   it is proportionate to apply that requirement in the particular case; and

     (c)   either—

         (i)   the person to whom that requirement is applied does not meet it, or

         (ii)   the employer is not satisfied, and in all the circumstances it is reasonable for him not to be satisfied, that that person meets it,

     and this paragraph applies whether or not the employment is for purposes of an organised religion.

(3)   This paragraph applies where—

     (a)   the employment is for purposes of an organised religion;

     (b)   the employer applies a requirement related to sexual orientation—

         (i)   so as to comply with the doctrines of the religion, or

         (ii)   because of the nature of the employment and the context in which it is carried out, so as to avoid conflicting with the strongly held religious convictions of a significant number of the religion's followers; and

(c)   either—
    (i)   the person to whom that requirement is applied does not meet it, or
    (ii)   the employer is not satisfied, and in all the circumstances it is reasonable for him not to be satisfied, that that person meets it.

8   Contract workers

(1)   It is unlawful for a principal, in relation to contract work at an establishment in Great Britain, to discriminate against a contract worker—
    (a)   in the terms on which he allows him to do that work;
    (b)   by not allowing him to do it or continue to do it;
    (c)   in the way he affords him access to any benefits or by refusing or deliberately not affording him access to them; or
    (d)   by subjecting him to any other detriment.

(2)   It is unlawful for a principal, in relation to contract work at an establishment in Great Britain, to subject a contract worker to harassment.

(3)   A principal does not contravene paragraph (1)(b) by doing any act in relation to a contract worker where, if the work were to be done by a person taken into the principal's employment, that act would be lawful by virtue of regulation 7 (exception for genuine occupational requirement etc).

(4)   Paragraph (1) does not apply to benefits of any description if the principal is concerned with the provision (for payment or not) of benefits of that description to the public, or to a section of the public to which the contract worker in question belongs, unless that provision differs in a material respect from the provision of the benefits by the principal to his contract workers.

(5)   In this regulation—
'principal' means a person ('A') who makes work available for doing by individuals who are employed by another person who supplies them under a contract made with A;
'contract work' means work so made available; and
'contract worker' means any individual who is supplied to the principal under such a contract.

9   Meaning of employment and contract work at establishment in Great Britain

(1)   For the purposes of this Part ('the relevant purposes'), employment is to be regarded as being at an establishment in Great Britain if the employee—
    (a)   does his work wholly or partly in Great Britain; or
    (b)   does his work wholly outside Great Britain and paragraph (2) applies.

(2)   This paragraph applies if—
    (a)   the employer has a place of business at an establishment in Great Britain;
    (b)   the work is for the purposes of the business carried on at that establishment; and
    (c)   the employee is ordinarily resident in Great Britain—
        (i)   at the time when he applies for or is offered the employment, or
        (ii)   at any time during the course of the employment.

(3)   The reference to 'employment' in paragraph (1) includes—
    (a)   employment on board a ship only if the ship is registered at a port of registry in Great Britain, and
    (b)   employment on an aircraft or hovercraft only if the aircraft or hovercraft is registered in the United Kingdom and operated by a person who has his principal place of business, or is ordinarily resident, in Great Britain.

(4)   Subject to paragraph (5), for the purposes of determining if employment concerned with the exploration of the sea bed or subsoil or the exploitation of their natural resources is outside Great Britain, this regulation has effect as if references to Great Britain included—
    (a)   any area designated under section 1(7) of the Continental Shelf Act 1964 an area or part of an area in which the law of Northern Ireland applies; and
    (b)   in relation to employment concerned with the exploration or exploitation of the Frigg Gas Field, the part of the Norwegian sector of the Continental Shelf described in Schedule 1.

(5)   Paragraph (4) shall not apply to employment which is concerned with the exploration or exploitation of the Frigg Gas Field unless the employer is—

   (a)   a company registered under the Companies Act 1985;

   (b)   an oversea company which has established a place of business within Great Britain from which it directs the exploration or exploitation in question; or

   (c)   any other person who has a place of business within Great Britain from which he directs the exploration or exploitation in question.

(6)   In this regulation—

   'the Frigg Gas Field' means the naturally occurring gas-bearing sand formations of the lower Eocene age located in the vicinity of the intersection of the line of latitude 59 degrees 53 minutes North and of the dividing line between the sectors of the Continental Shelf of the United Kingdom and the Kingdom of Norway and includes all other gas-bearing strata from which gas at the start of production is capable of flowing into the above-mentioned gas-bearing sand formations;

   'oversea company' has the same meaning as in section 744 of the Companies Act 1985.

(7)   This regulation applies in relation to contract work within the meaning of regulation 8 as it applies in relation to employment; and, in its application to contract work, references to 'employee', 'employer' and 'employment' and references to (respectively) 'contract worker', 'principal' and 'contract work' within the meaning of regulation 8.

PART III
OTHER UNLAWFUL ACTS

22   Liability of employers and principals

(1)   Anything done by a person in the course of his employment shall be treated for the purposes of these Regulations as done by his employer as well as by him, whether or not it was done with the employer's knowledge or approval.

(2)   Anything done by a person as agent for another person with the authority (whether express or implied, and whether precedent or subsequent) of that other person shall be treated for the purposes of these Regulations as done by that other person as well as by him.

(3)   In proceedings brought under these Regulations against any person in respect of an act alleged to have been done by an employee of his it shall be a defence for that person to prove that he took such steps as were reasonably practicable to prevent the employee from doing that act, or from doing in the course of his employment acts of that description.

23   Aiding unlawful acts

(1)   A person who knowingly aids another person to do an act made unlawful by these Regulations shall be treated for the purpose of these Regulations as himself doing an unlawful act of the like description.

(2)   For the purposes of paragraph (1) an employee or agent for whose act the employer or principal is liable under regulation 22 (or would be so liable but for regulation 22(3)) shall be deemed to aid the doing of the act by the employer or principal.

(3)   A person does not under this regulation knowingly aid another to do an unlawful act if—

   (a)   he acts in reliance on a statement made to him by that other person that, by reason of any provision of these Regulations, the act which he aids would not be unlawful; and

   (b)   it is reasonable for him to rely on the statement.

(4)   A person who knowingly or recklessly makes a statement such as is referred to in paragraph (3)(a) which in a material respect is false or misleading commits an offence, and shall be liable on summary conviction to a fine not exceeding level 5 on the standard scale.

PART IV
GENERAL EXCEPTIONS FROM PARTS II AND III

24   Exception for national security

Nothing in Part II or III shall render unlawful an act done for the purpose of safeguarding national security, if the doing of the act was justified by that purpose.

25   Exception for benefits dependent on a person's status

Nothing in Part II or III shall render unlawful—

    (a)   anything which prevents or restricts access to a benefit by reference to marital status where the right to the benefit accrued or the benefit is payable in respect of periods of service prior to the coming into force of the Civil Partnership Act 2004;

    (b)   the conferring of a benefit on married persons and civil partners to the exclusion of all other persons.

26   Exceptions for positive action

    (1)   Nothing in Part II or III shall render unlawful any act done in or in connection with—

        (a)   affording persons of a particular sexual orientation access to facilities for training which would help fit them for particular work; or

        (b)   encouraging persons of a particular sexual orientation to take advantage of opportunities for doing particular work,

    where it reasonably appears to the person doing the act that it prevents or compensates for disadvantages linked to sexual orientation suffered by persons of that sexual orientation doing that work or likely to take up that work.

    (2)   Nothing in Part II or III shall render unlawful any act done by a trade organisation within the meaning of regulation 15 in or in connection with—

        (a)   affording only members of the organisation who are of a particular sexual orientation access to facilities for training which would help fit them for holding a post of any kind in the organisation; or

        (b)   encouraging only members of the organisation who are of a particular sexual orientation to take advantage of opportunities for holding such posts in the organisation,

    where it reasonably appears to the organisation that the act prevents or compensates for disadvantages linked to sexual orientation suffered by those of that sexual orientation holding such posts or likely to hold such posts.

    (3)   Nothing in Part II or III shall render unlawful any act done by a trade organisation within the meaning of regulation 15 in or in connection with encouraging only persons of a particular sexual orientation to become members of the organisation where it reasonably appears to the organisation that the act prevents or compensates for disadvantages linked to sexual orientation suffered by persons of that sexual orientation who are, or are eligible to become, members.

PART V
ENFORCEMENT

28   Jurisdiction of employment tribunals

    (1)   A complaint by any person ('the complainant') that another person ('the respondent')—

        (a)   has committed against the complainant an act to which this regulation applies; or

        (b)   is by virtue of regulation 22 (liability of employers and principals) or 23 (aiding unlawful acts) to be treated as having committed against the complainant such an act,

    may be presented to an employment tribunal.

    (2)   This regulation applies to any act of discrimination or harassment which is unlawful by virtue of any provision of Part II other than—

        (a)   where the act is one in respect of which an appeal or proceedings in the nature of an appeal may be brought under any enactment, regulation 16 (qualifications bodies);

        (b)   regulation 20 (institutions of further and higher education); or

        (c)   where the act arises out of and is closely connected to a relationship between the complainant and the respondent which has come to an end but during the course of which an act of discrimination against, or harassment of, the complainant by the respondent would have been unlawful by virtue of regulation 20, regulation 21 (relationships which have come to an end).

    (3)   In paragraph (2)(c), reference to an act of discrimination or harassment which would have been unlawful includes, in the case of a relationship which has come to an end before the coming into force of these Regulations, reference to an act of discrimination or harassment which would, after the coming into force of these Regulations, have been unlawful.

(4)   In this regulation, 'enactment' includes an enactment comprised in, or in an instrument made under, an Act of the Scottish Parliament.

29   Burden of proof: employment tribunals

(1)   This regulation applies to any complaint presented under regulation 28 to an employment tribunal.

(2)   Where, on the hearing of the complaint, the complainant proves facts from which the tribunal could, apart from this regulation, conclude in the absence of an adequate explanation that the respondent—

    (a)   has committed against the complainant an act to which regulation 28 applies; or

    (b)   is by virtue of regulation 22 (liability of employers and principals) or 23 (aiding unlawful acts) to be treated as having committed against the complainant such an act,

the tribunal shall uphold the complaint unless the respondent proves that he did not commit, or as the case may be, is not to be treated as having committed, that act.

30   Remedies on complaints in employment tribunals

(1)   Where an employment tribunal finds that a complaint presented to it under regulation 28 is well-founded, the tribunal shall make such of the following as it considers just and equitable—

    (a)   an order declaring the rights of the complainant and the respondent in relation to the act to which the complaint relates;

    (b)   an order requiring the respondent to pay to the complainant compensation of an amount corresponding to any damages he could have been ordered by a county court or by a sheriff court to pay to the complainant if the complaint had fallen to be dealt with under regulation 31 Jurisdiction of county and sheriff courts);

    (c)   a recommendation that the respondent take within a specified period action appearing to the tribunal to be practicable for the purpose of obviating or reducing the adverse effect on the complainant of any act of discrimination or harassment to which the complaint relates.

(2)   As respects an unlawful act of discrimination falling within regulation 3(1)(b), if the respondent proves that the provision, criterion or practice was not applied with the intention of treating the complainant unfavourably on grounds of sexual orientation, an order may be made under paragraph (1)(b) only if the employment tribunal—

    (a)   makes such order under paragraph (1)(a) (if any) and such recommendation under paragraph (1)(c) (if any) as it would have made if it had no power to make an order under paragraph (1)(b); and

    (b)   (where it makes an order under paragraph (1)(a) or a recommendation under paragraph (1)(c) or both) considers that it is just and equitable to make an order under paragraph (1)(b) as well.

(3)   if without reasonable justification the respondent to a complaint fails to comply with a recommendation made by an employment tribunal under paragraph (1)(c), then, if it thinks it just and equitable to do so—

    (a)   the tribunal may increase the amount of compensation required to be paid to the complainant in respect of the complaint by an order made under paragraph (1)(b); or

    (b)   if an order under paragraph (1)(b) was not made, the tribunal may make such an order.

(4)   Where an amount of compensation falls to be awarded under paragraph (1)(b), the tribunal may include in the award interest on that amount subject to, and in accordance with, the provisions of the Employment Tribunals(Interest on Awards in Discrimination Cases) Regulations 1996.

EMPLOYMENT ACT 2002 (DISPUTE RESOLUTION) REGULATIONS 2004 (SI 2004 No. 752)

2   Interpretation

(1)   In these Regulations—

    'the 1992 Act' means the Trade Union and Labour Relations (Consolidation) Act 1992;

'the 1996 Act' means the Employment Rights Act 1996;

'the 1999 Act' means the Employment Relations Act 1999;

'the 2002 Act' means the Employment Act 2002;

'action' means any act or omission;

'applicable statutory procedure' means the statutory procedure that applies in relation to a particular case by virtue of these Regulations;

'collective agreement' has the meaning given to it by section 178(1) of the 1992 Act;

'dismissal and disciplinary procedures' means the statutory procedures set out in Part 1 of Schedule 2;

'dismissed' has the meaning given to it in section 95(1)(a) and (b) of the 1996 Act;

'employers' association' has the meaning given to it by section 122 of the 1992 Act;

'grievance' means a complaint by an employee about action which his employer has taken or is contemplating taking in relation to him;

'grievance procedures' means the statutory procedures set out in Part 2 of Schedule 2;

'independent trade union' has the meaning given to it by section 5 of the 1992 Act;

'modified dismissal procedure' means the procedure set out in Chapter 2 of Part 1 of Schedule 2;

'modified grievance procedure' means the procedure set out in Chapter 2 of Part 2 of Schedule 2;

'non-completion' of a statutory procedure includes non-commencement of such a procedure except where the term is used in relation to the non-completion of an identified requirement of a procedure or to circumstances where a procedure has already been commenced;

'party' means the employer or the employee;

'relevant disciplinary action' means action, short of dismissal, which the employer asserts to be based wholly or mainly on the employee's conduct or capability, other than suspension on full pay or the issuing of warnings (whether oral or written);

'standard dismissal and disciplinary procedure' means the procedure set out in Chapter 1 of Part 1 of Schedule 2;

'standard grievance procedure' means the procedure set out in Chapter 1 of Part 2 of Schedule 2; and a reference to a Schedule is a reference to a Schedule to the 2002 Act.

(2)   In determining whether a meeting or written communication fulfils a requirement of Schedule 2, it is irrelevant whether the meeting or communication deals with any other matter (including a different matter required to be dealt with in a meeting or communication intended to fulfil a requirement of Schedule 2).

3   Application of dismissal and disciplinary procedures

(1)   Subject to paragraph (2) and regulation 4, the standard dismissal and disciplinary procedure applies when an employer contemplates dismissing or taking relevant disciplinary action against an employee.

(2)   Subject to regulation 4, the modified dismissal procedure applies in relation to a dismissal where—

(a)   the employer dismissed the employee by reason of his conduct without notice,

(b)   the dismissal occurred at the time the employer became aware of the conduct or immediately thereafter,

(c)   the employer was entitled, in the circumstances, to dismiss the employee by reason of his conduct without notice or any payment in lieu of notice, and

(d)   it was reasonable for the employer, in the circumstances, to dismiss the employee before enquiring into the circumstances in which the conduct took place,

but neither of the dismissal and disciplinary procedures applies in relation to such a dismissal where the employee presents a complaint relating to the dismissal to an employment tribunal at a time when the employer has not complied with paragraph 4 of Schedule 2.

4   Dismissals to which the dismissal and disciplinary procedures do not apply

(1)   Neither of the dismissal and disciplinary procedures applies in relation to the dismissal of an employee where—

(a)   all the employees of a description or in a category to which the employee belongs are dismissed, provided that the employer offers to re-engage all the employees so dismissed either before or upon the termination of their contracts;

(b)   the dismissal is one of a number of dismissals in respect of which the duty in section 188 of the 1992 Act (duty of employer to consult representatives when proposing to dismiss as redundant a certain number of employees) applies;

(c)   at the time of the employee's dismissal he is taking part in—

   (i)   an unofficial strike or other unofficial industrial action, or

   (ii)   a strike or other industrial action (being neither unofficial industrial action nor protected industrial action), unless the circumstances of the dismissal are such that, by virtue of section 238(2) of the 1992 Act, an employment tribunal is entitled to determine whether the dismissal was fair or unfair;

(d)   the reason (or, if more than one, the principal reason) for the dismissal is that the employee took protected industrial action and the dismissal would be regarded, by virtue of section 238A(2) of the 1992 Act, as unfair for the purposes of Part 10 of the 1996 Act;

(e)   the employer's business suddenly ceases to function, because of an event unforeseen by the employer, with the result that it is impractical for him to employ any employees;

(f)   the reason (or, if more than one principal reason) for the dismissal is that the employee could not continue to work in the position which he held without contravention (either on his part or on that of his employer) of a duty or restriction imposed by or under any enactment;

(g)   the employee is one to whom a dismissal procedures agreement designated by an order under section 110 of the 1996 Act applies at the date of dismissal; or

(h)   the reason (or, if more than one, the principal reason) for the dismissal is retirement of the employee (to be determined in accordance with section 98ZA to 98ZF of the 1996 Act).

(2)   For the purposes of paragraph (1)—

'unofficial' shall be construed in accordance with subsections (2) to (4) of section 237 of the 1992 Act;

'strike' has the meaning given to it by section 246 of the 1992 Act;

'protected industrial action' shall be construed in accordance with section 238A(1) of the 1992 Act;

and an employer shall be regarded as offering to re-engage an employee if that employer, a successor of that employer or an associated employer of that employer offers to re-engage the employee, either in the job which he held immediately before the date of dismissal or in a different job which would be suitable in his case.

5   Circumstances in which parties are treated as complying with the dismissal and disciplinary procedures

(1)   Where—

(a)   either of the dismissal and disciplinary procedures is the applicable statutory procedure in relation to a dismissal,

(b)   the employee presents an application for interim relief to an employment tribunal pursuant to section 128 of the 1996 Act (interim relief pending determination of complaint) in relation to his dismissal, and

(c)   at the time the application is presented, the requirements of paragraphs 1 and 2 or, as the case may be, paragraph 4 of Schedule 2 have been complied with but the requirements of paragraph 3 or 5 of Schedule 2 have not,

the parties shall be treated as having complied with the requirements of paragraph 3 or 5 of Schedule 2.

(2)   Where either of the dismissal and disciplinary procedures is the applicable statutory procedure in relation to the dismissal of an employee or to relevant disciplinary action taken against an employee but—

(a)   at the time of the dismissal or the taking of the action an appropriate procedure exists,

(b)   the employee is entitled to appeal under that procedure against his dismissal or the relevant disciplinary action taken against him instead of appealing to his employer, and

    (c)   the employee has appealed under that procedure,

the parties shall be treated as having complied with the requirements of paragraph 3 or 5 of Schedule 2.

(3)   For the purposes of paragraph (2) a procedure is appropriate if it—

    (a)   gives the employee an effective right of appeal against dismissal or disciplinary action taken against him, and

    (b)   operates by virtue of a collective agreement made between two or more employers or an employers' association and one or more independent trade unions.

6 Application of the grievance procedures

(1)   The grievance procedures apply, in accordance with the paragraphs (2) to (7) of this regulation, in relation to any grievance about action by the employer that could form the basis of a complaint by an employee to an employment tribunal under a jurisdiction listed in Schedule 3 or 4, or could do so if the action took place.

(2)   Subject to paragraphs (3) to (7), the standard grievance procedure applies in relation to any such grievance.

(3)   Subject to paragraphs (4) to (7), the modified grievance procedure applies in relation to a grievance where—

    (a)   the employee has ceased to be employed by the employer;

    (b)   the employer—

        (i)   was unaware of the grievance before the employment ceased, or

        (ii)   was so aware but the standard grievance procedure was not commenced or was not completed before the last day of the employee's employment; and

    (c)   the parties have agreed in writing in relation to the grievance, whether before, on or after that day, but after the employer became aware of the grievance, that the modified procedure should apply.

(4)   Neither of the grievance procedures applies where—

    (a)   the employee has ceased to be employed by the employer;

    (b)   neither procedure has been commenced; and

    (c)   since the employee ceased to be employed it has ceased to be reasonably practicable for him to comply with paragraph 6 or 9 of Schedule 2.

(5)   Neither of the grievance procedures applies where the grievance is that the employer has dismissed or is contemplating dismissing the employee.

(6)   Neither of the grievance procedures applies where the grievance is that the employer has taken or is contemplating taking relevant disciplinary action against the employee unless one of the reasons for the grievance is a reason mentioned in regulation 7(1).

(7)   Neither of the grievance procedures applies where regulation 11(1) applies.

7 Circumstances in which parties are treated as complying with the grievance procedures

(1)   Where the grievance is that the employer has taken or is contemplating taking relevant disciplinary action against the employee and one of the reasons for the grievance is—

    (a)   that the relevant disciplinary action amounted to or, if it took place, would amount to unlawful discrimination, or

    (b)   that the grounds on which the employer took the action or is contemplating taking it were or are unrelated to the grounds on which he asserted that he took the action or is asserting that he is contemplating taking it,

the standard grievance procedure or, as the case may be, modified grievance procedure shall apply but the parties shall be treated as having complied with the applicable procedure if the employee complies with the requirement in paragraph (2).

(2)   The requirement is that the employee must set out the grievance in a written statement and send the statement or a copy of it to the employer—

    (a)   where either of the dismissal and disciplinary procedures is being followed, before the meeting referred to in paragraph 3 or 5 (appeals under the dismissal and disciplinary procedures) of Schedule 2, or

(b)   where neither of those procedures is being followed, before presenting any complaint arising out of the grievance to an employment tribunal.

(3) In paragraph (1)(a) 'unlawful discrimination' means an act or omission in respect of which a right of complaint lies to an employment tribunal under any of the following tribunal jurisdictions (specified in Schedules 3 and 4)—

section 2 of the Equal Pay Act 1970;

section 63 of the Sex Discrimination Act 1975;

section 54 of the Race Relations Act 1976;

section 17A of the Disability Discrimination Act 1995;

regulation 28 of the Employment Equality (Religion or Belief) Regulations 2003;

regulation 28 of the Employment Equality (Sexual Orientation) Regulations 2003;

regulation 36 of the Employment Equality (Age) Regulations 2006.

8   (1) Where—

(a)   the standard grievance procedure is the applicable statutory procedure,

(b)   the employee has ceased to be employed by the employer,

(c)   paragraph 6 of Schedule 2 has been complied with (whether before or after the end of his employment); and

(d)   since the end of his employment it has ceased to be reasonably practicable for the employee, or his employer, to comply with the requirements of paragraph 7 or 8 of Schedule 2,

the parties shall be treated, subject to paragraph (2), as having complied with such of those paragraphs of Schedule 2 as have not been complied with.

(2) In a case where paragraph (1) applies and the requirements of paragraphs 7(1) to (3) of Schedule 2 have been complied with but the requirement in paragraph 7(4) of Schedule 2 has not, the employer shall be treated as having failed to comply with paragraph 7(4) unless he informs the employee in writing of his decision as to his response to the grievance.

9   (1) Where either of the grievance procedures is the applicable statutory procedure, the parties shall be treated as having complied with the requirements of the procedure if a person who is an appropriate representative of the employee having the grievance has—

(a)   written to the employer setting out the grievance; and

(b)   specified in writing to the employer (whether in setting out the grievance or otherwise) the names of at least two employees, of whom one is the employee having the grievance, as being the employees on behalf of whom he is raising the grievance.

(2) For the purposes of paragraph (1), a person is an appropriate representative if, at the time he writes to the employer setting out the grievance, he is—

(a)   an official of an independent trade union recognised by the employer for the purposes of collective bargaining in respect of a description of employees that includes the employee having the grievance, or

(b)   an employee of the employer who is an employee representative elected or appointed by employees consisting of or including employees of the same description as the employee having the grievance and who, having regard to the purposes for which and method by which he was elected or appointed, has the authority to represent employees of that description under an established procedure for resolving grievances agreed between employee representatives and the employer.

(3) For the purposes of paragraph (2)(a) the terms 'official', 'recognised' and 'collective bargaining' have the meanings given to them by, respectively, sections 119, 178(3) and 178(1) of the 1992 Act.

10   Where either of the grievance procedures is the applicable statutory procedure but—

(a)   at the time the employee raises his grievance there is a procedure in operation, under a collective agreement made between two or more employers or an employers' association and one or more independent trade unions, that provides for employees of the employer to raise grievances about the behaviour of the employer and have them considered, and

(b)   the employee is entitled to raise his grievance under that procedure and does so,

the parties shall be treated as having complied with the applicable statutory procedure.

11   General circumstances in which the statutory procedures do not apply or are treated as being complied with

(1)   Where the circumstances specified in paragraph (3) apply and in consequence the employer or employee does not commence the procedure that would otherwise be the applicable statutory procedure (by complying with paragraph 1, 4, 6 or 9 of Schedule 2), the procedure does not apply.

(2)   Where the applicable statutory procedure has been commenced, but the circumstances specified in paragraph (3) apply and in consequence a party does not comply with a subsequent requirement of the procedure, the parties shall be treated as having complied with the procedure.

(3) The circumstances referred to in paragraphs (1) and (2) are that—

(a)   the party has reasonable grounds to believe that commencing the procedure or complying with the subsequent requirement would result in a significant threat to himself, his property, any other person or the property of any other person;

(b)   the party has been subjected to harassment and has reasonable grounds to believe that commencing the procedure or complying with the subsequent requirement would result in his being subjected to further harassment; or

(c)   it is not practicable for the party to commence the procedure or comply with the subsequent requirement within a reasonable period.

(4)   In paragraph (3)(b), 'harassment' means conduct which has the purpose or effect of—

(a)   violating the person's dignity, or

(b)   creating an intimidating, hostile, degrading, humiliating or offensive environment for him,

but conduct shall only be regarded as having that purpose or effect if, having regard to all the circumstances, including in particular the perception of the person who was the subject of the conduct, it should reasonably be considered as having that purpose or effect.

12   Failure to comply with the statutory procedures

(1)   If either party fails to comply with a requirement of an applicable statutory procedure, including a general requirement contained in Part 3 of Schedule 2, then, subject to paragraph (2), the non-completion of the procedure shall be attributable to that party and neither party shall be under any obligation to comply with any further requirement of the procedure.

(2)   Except as mentioned in paragraph (4), where the parties are to be treated as complying with the applicable statutory procedure, or any requirement of it, there is no failure to comply with the procedure or requirement.

(3)   Notwithstanding that if regulation 11(1) applies the procedure that would otherwise be the applicable statutory procedure does not apply, where that regulation applies because the circumstances in sub-paragraph (a) or (b) of regulation 11(3) apply and it was the behaviour of one of the parties that resulted in those circumstances applying, that party shall be treated as if—

(a)   the procedure had applied, and

(b)   there had been a failure to comply with a requirement of the procedure that was attributable to him.

(4)   In a case where regulation 11(2) applies in relation to a requirement of the applicable statutory procedure because the circumstances in sub-paragraph (a) or (b) of regulation 11(3) apply, and it was the behaviour of one of the parties that resulted in those circumstances applying, the fact that the requirement was not complied with shall be treated as being a failure, attributable to that party, to comply with a requirement of the procedure.

13   Failure to attend a meeting

(1)   Without prejudice to regulation 11(2) and (3)(c), if it is not reasonably practicable for—

(a)   the employee, or, if he is exercising his right under section 10 of the 1999 Act (right to be accompanied), his companion; or

(b)   the employer,

to attend a meeting organised in accordance with the applicable statutory procedure for a reason which was not foreseeable when the meeting was arranged, the employee or, as the case may be, employer shall not be treated as having failed to comply with that requirement of the procedure.

(2)   In the circumstances set out in paragraph (1), the employer shall continue to be under the duty in the applicable statutory procedure to invite the employee to attend a meeting and, where the employee is exercising his rights under section 10 of the 1999 Act and the employee proposes an alternative time under subsection (4) of that section, the employer shall be under a duty to invite the employee to attend a meeting at that time.

(3)   The duty to invite the employee to attend a meeting referred to in paragraph (2) shall cease if the employer has invited the employee to attend two meetings and paragraph (1) applied in relation to each of them.

(4)   Where the duty in paragraph (2) has ceased as a result of paragraph (3), the parties shall be treated as having complied with the applicable statutory procedure.

14   Questions to obtain information not to constitute statement of grievance

(1)   Where a person aggrieved questions a respondent under any of the provisions set out in paragraph (2), those questions shall not constitute a statement of grievance under paragraph 6 or 9 of Schedule 2.

(2)   The provisions referred to in paragraph (1) are—

section 7B of the Equal Pay Act 1970;

section 74 of the Sex Discrimination Act 1975;

section 65 of the Race Relations Act 1976;

section 56 of the Disability Discrimination Act 1995;

regulation 33 of the Employment Equality (Religion or Belief) Regulations 2003;

regulation 33 of the Employment Equality (Sexual Orientation) Regulations 2003;

regulation 41 of the Employment Equality (Age) Regulations 2006.

15   Extension of time limits

(1)   Where a complaint is presented to an employment tribunal under a jurisdiction listed in Schedule 3 or 4 and—

    (a)   either of the dismissal and disciplinary procedures is the applicable statutory procedure and the circumstances specified in paragraph (2) apply; or

    (b)   either of the grievance procedures is the applicable statutory procedure and the circumstances specified in paragraph (3) apply;

the normal time limit for presenting the complaint is extended for a period of three months beginning with the day after the day on which it would otherwise have expired.

(2)   The circumstances referred to in paragraph (1)(a) are that the employee presents a complaint to the tribunal after the expiry of the normal time limit for presenting the complaint but had reasonable grounds for believing, when that time limit expired, that a dismissal or disciplinary procedure, whether statutory or otherwise (including an appropriate procedure for the purposes of regulation 5(2)), was being followed in respect of matters that consisted of or included the substance of the tribunal complaint.

(3)   The circumstances referred to in paragraph (1)(b) are that the employee presents a complaint to the tribunal—

    (a)   within the normal time limit for presenting the complaint but in circumstances in which section 32(2) or (3) of the 2002 Act does not permit him to do so; or

    (b)   after the expiry of the normal time limit for presenting the complaint, having complied with paragraph 6 or 9 of Schedule 2 in relation to his grievance within that normal time limit.

(4)   For the purposes of paragraph (3) and section 32 of the 2002 Act the following acts shall be treated, in a case to which the specified regulation applies, as constituting compliance with paragraph 6 or 9 of Schedule 2—

    (a)   in a case to which regulation 7(1) applies, compliance by the employee with the requirement in regulation 7(2);

    (b)   in a case to which regulation 9(1) applies, compliance by the appropriate representative with the requirement in sub-paragraph (a) or (b) of that regulation, whichever is the later; and

    (c)   in a case to which regulation 10 applies, the raising of his grievance by the employee in accordance with the procedure referred to in that regulation.

(5)   In this regulation 'the normal time limit' means—

    (a)   subject to sub-paragraph (b), the period within which a complaint under the relevant jurisdiction must be presented if there is to be no need for the tribunal, in order to be entitled to consider it to—

       (i)   exercise any discretion, or

      (ii)   make any determination as to whether it is required to consider the complaint, that the tribunal would have to exercise or make in order to consider a complaint presented outside that period; and

    (b)   in relation to claims brought under the Equal Pay Act 1970, the period ending on the date on or before which proceedings must be instituted in accordance with section 2(4) of that Act.

16   National security

Where it would not be possible to comply with an applicable statutory procedure without disclosing information the disclosure of which would be contrary to the interests of national security, nothing in these Regulations requires either party to comply with that procedure.

TRANSFER OF UNDERTAKINGS (PROTECTION OF EMPLOYMENT) REGULATIONS 2006
(SI 2006 No. 246)

2   Interpretation

(1)   In these Regulations—

'assigned' means assigned other than on a temporary basis;

'collective agreement', 'collective bargaining' and 'trade union' have the same meanings respectively as in the 1992 Act;

'contract of employment' means any agreement between an employee and his employer determining the terms and conditions of his employment;

references to 'contractor' in regulation 3 shall include a subcontractor;

'employee' means any individual who works for another person whether under a contract of service or apprenticeship or otherwise but does not include anyone who provides services under a contract for services and references to a person's employer shall be construed accordingly;

'insolvency practitioners has the meaning given to the expression by Part XIII of the Insolvency Act 1986;

references to 'organised grouping of employees' shall include a single employee;

'recognised' has the meaning given to the expression by section 178 (3) of the 1992 Act;

'relevant transfer' means a transfer or a service provision change to which these Regulations apply in accordance with regulation 3 and 'transferor' and 'transferee' shall be construed accordingly and in the case of a service provision change falling within regulation 3(1)(b), 'the transferor' means the person who carried out the activities prior to the service provision change and 'the transferee' means the person who carries out the activities as a result of the service provision change;

'the 1992 Act' means the Trade Union and Labour Relations (Consolidation) Act 1992;

'the 1996 Act' means the Employment Rights Act 1996;

'the 1996 Tribunals Act' means the Employment Tribunals Act 1996

'the 1981 Regulations' means the Transfer of Undertakings (Protection of Employment) Regulations 1981

(2)   For the purposes of these Regulations the representative of a trade union recognised by an employer is an official or other person authorised to carry on collective bargaining with that employer by that trade union.

(3) In the application of these Regulations to Northern Ireland the Regulations shall have effect as set out in Schedule 1.

3   A relevant transfer

(1) These Regulations apply to—

    (a) a transfer of an undertaking, business or part of an undertaking or business situated immediately before the transfer in the United Kingdom to another person where there is a transfer of an economic entity which retains its identity;

    (b) a service provision change, that is a situation in which—

        (i) activities cease to be carried out by a person ('a client') on his own behalf and are carried out instead by another person on the client's behalf ('a contractor');

        (ii) activities cease to be carried out by a contractor on a client's behalf (whether or not those activities had previously been carried out by the client on his own behalf) and are carried out instead by another person ('a subsequent contractor') on the client's behalf, or

        (iii) activities cease to be carried out by a contractor or a subsequent contractor on a client's behalf (whether or not those activities had previously been carried out by the client on his own behalf) and are carried out instead by the client on his own behalf,

    and in which the conditions set out in paragraph (3) are satisfied.

(2) In this regulation 'economic entity' means an organised grouping of resources which has the objective of pursuing an economic activity, whether or not that activity is central or ancillary.

(3) The conditions referred to in paragraph (1)(b) are that—

    (a) immediately before the service provision change—

        (i) there is an organised grouping of employees situated in Great Britain which has as its principal purpose the carrying out of the activities concerned on behalf of the client;

        (ii) the client intends that the activities will, following the service provision change, be carried out by the transferee other than in connection with a single specific event or task of shortterm duration; and

    (b) the activities concerned do not consist wholly or mainly of the supply of goods for the client's use.

(4) Subject to paragraph (1), these Regulations apply to—

    (a) public and private undertakings engaged in economic activities whether or not they are operating for gain;

    (b) a transfer or service provision change howsoever effected notwithstanding—

        (i) that the transfer of an undertaking, business or part of an undertaking or business is governed or effected by the law of a country or territory outside the United Kingdom or that the service provision change is governed or effected by the law of a country or territory outside Great Britain;

        (ii) that the employment of persons employed in the undertaking, business or part transferred or, in the case of a service provision change, persons employed in the organised grouping of employees, is governed by any such law;

    (c) a transfer of an undertaking, business or part of an undertaking or business (which may also be a service provision change) where persons employed in the undertaking, business or part transferred ordinarily work outside the United Kingdom.

(5) An administrative reorganisation of public administrative authorities or the transfer of administrative functions between public administrative authorities is not a relevant transfer.

(6) A relevant transfer—

    (a) may be effected by a series of two or more transactions; and

    (b) may take place whether or not any property is transferred to the transferee by the transferor.

(7) Where, in consequence (whether directly or indirectly) of the transfer of an undertaking, business or part of an undertaking or business which was situated immediately before the

transfer in the United Kingdom, a ship within the meaning of the Merchant Shipping Act 1995 registered in the United Kingdom ceases to be so registered, these Regulations shall not affect the right conferred by section 29 of that Act (right of seamen to be discharged when ship ceases to be registered in the United Kingdom) on a seaman employed in the ship.

4   Effect of relevant transfer on contracts of employment

(1)   Except where objection is made under paragraph (7), a relevant transfer shall not operate so as to terminate the contract of employment of any person employed by the transferor and assigned to the organised grouping of resources or employees that is subject to the relevant transfer, which would otherwise be terminated by the transfer, but any such contract shall have effect after the transfer as if originally made between the person so employed and the transferee.

(2)   Without prejudice to paragraph (1), but subject to paragraph (6), and regulations 8 and 15(9), on the completion of a relevant transfer—

    (a)   all the transferor's rights, powers, duties and liabilities under or in connection with any such contract shall be transferred by virtue of this regulation to the transferee; and

    (b)   any act or omission before the transfer is completed, of or in relation to the transferor in respect of that contract or a person assigned to that organised grouping of resources or employees, shall be deemed to have been an act or omission of or in relation to the transferee.

(3)   Any reference in paragraph (1) to a person employed by the transferor and assigned to the organised grouping of resources or employees that is subject to a relevant transfer, is a reference to a person so employed immediately before the transfer, or who would have been so employed if he had not been dismissed in the circumstances described in regulation 7(1), including, where the transfer is effected by a series of two or more transactions, a person so employed and assigned or who would have been so employed and assigned immediately before any of those transactions.

(4)   Subject to regulation 9, in respect of a contract of employment that is, or will be, transferred by paragraph (1), any purported variation of the contract shall be void if the sole or principal reason for the variation is—

    (a)   the transfer itself; or

    (b)   a reason connected with the transfer that is not an economic, technical or organisational reason entailing changes in the workforce.

(5)   Paragraph (4) shall not prevent the employer and his employee, whose contract of employment is, or will be, transferred by paragraph (1), from agreeing a variation of that contract if the sole or principal reason for the variation is—

    (a)   a reason connected with the transfer that is an economic, technical or organisational reason entailing changes in the workforce; or

    (b)   a reason unconnected with the transfer.

(6)   Paragraph (2) shall not transfer or otherwise affect the liability of any person to be prosecuted for, convicted of and sentenced for any offence.

(7)   Paragraphs (1) and (2) shall not operate to transfer the contract of employment and the rights, powers, duties and liabilities under or in connection with it of an employee who informs the transferor or the transferee that he objects to becoming employed by the transferee.

(8)   Subject to paragraphs (9) and (11), where an employee so objects, the relevant transfer shall operate so as to terminate his contract of employment with the transferor but he shall not be treated, for any purpose, as having been dismissed by the transferor.

(9)   Subject to regulation 9, where a relevant transfer involves or would involve a substantial change in working conditions to the material detriment of a person whose contract of employment is or would be transferred under paragraph (1), such an employee may treat the contract of employment as having been terminated, and the employee shall be treated for any purpose as having been dismissed by the employer.

(10) No damages shall be payable by an employer as a result of a dismissal falling within paragraph (9) in respect of any failure by the employer to pay wages to an employee in respect of a notice period which the employee has failed to work.

(11) Paragraphs (1), (7), (8) and (9) are without prejudice to any right of an employee arising apart from these Regulations to terminate his contract of employment without notice in acceptance of a repudiatory breach of contract by his employer.

5   Effect of relevant transfer on collective agreements

Where at the time of a relevant transfer there exists a collective agreement made by or on behalf of the transferor with a trade union recognised by the transferor in respect of any employee whose contract of employment is preserved by regulation 4(1) above, then—

    (a)   without prejudice to sections 179 and 180 of the 1992 Act (collective agreements presumed to be unenforceable in specified circumstances) that agreement, in its application in relation to the employee, shall, after the transfer, have effect as if made by or on behalf of the transferee with that trade union, and accordingly anything done under or in connection with it, in its application in relation to the employee, by or in relation to the transferor before the transfer, shall, after the transfer, be deemed to have been done by or in relation to the transferee; and

    (b)   any order made in respect of that agreement, in its application in relation to the employee, shall, after the transfer, have effect as if the transferee were a party to the agreement.

6   Effect of relevant transfer on trade union recognition

(1)   This regulation applies where after a relevant transfer the transferred organised grouping of resources or employees maintains an identity distinct from the remainder of the transferee's undertaking.

(2)   Where before such a transfer an independent trade union is recognised to any extent by the transferor in respect of employees of any description who in consequence of the transfer become employees of the transferee, then, after the transfer—

    (a)   the trade union shall be deemed to have been recognised by the transferee to the same extent in respect of employees of that description so employed; and

    (b)   any agreement for recognition may be varied or rescinded accordingly.

7   Dismissal of employee because of relevant transfer

(1)   Where either before or after a relevant transfer, any employee of the transferor or transferee is dismissed, that employee shall be treated for the purposes of Part X of the 1996 Act (unfair dismissal) as unfairly dismissed if the sole or principal reason for his dismissal is—

    (a)   the transfer itself, or

    (b)   a reason connected with the transfer that is not an economic, technical or organisational reason entailing changes in the workforce.

(2)   This paragraph applies where the sole or principal reason for the dismissal is a reason connected with the transfer that is an economic, technical or organisational reason entailing changes in the workforce of either the transferor or the transferee before or after a relevant transfer.

(3)   Where paragraph (2) applies—

    (a)   paragraph (1) shall not apply;

    (b)   without prejudice to the application of section 98(4) of the 1996 Act (test of fair dismissal), the dismissal shall, for the purposes of sections 98(1) and 135 of that Act (reason for dismissal), be regarded as having been for redundancy where section 98(2)(c) of that Act applies, or otherwise for a substantial reason of a kind such as to justify the dismissal of an employee holding the position which that employee held.

(4)   The provisions of this regulation apply irrespective of whether the employee in question is assigned to the organised grouping of resources or employees that is, or will be, transferred.

(5)   Paragraph (1) shall not apply in relation to the dismissal of any employee which was required by reason of the application of section 5 of the Aliens Restriction (Amendment) Act 1919 to his employment.

(6)   Paragraph (1) shall not apply in relation to a dismissal of an employee if the application of section 94 of the 1996 Act to the dismissal of the employee is excluded by or under any provision of the 1996 Act, the 1996 Tribunals Act or the 1992 Act.

8   Insolvency

(1)   If at the time of a relevant transfer the transferor is subject to relevant insolvency proceedings paragraphs (2) to (6) apply.

(2)   In this regulation 'relevant employee' means an employee of the transferor—

(a)   whose contract of employment transfers to the transferee by virtue of the operation of these Regulations; or

(b)   whose employment with the transferor is terminated before the time of the relevant transfer in the circumstances described in regulation 7(1).

(3)   The relevant statutory scheme specified in paragraph (4)(b) (including that sub-paragraph as applied by paragraph 5 of Schedule 1) shall apply in the case of a relevant employee irrespective of the fact that the qualifying requirement that the employee's employment has been terminated is not met and for those purposes the date of the transfer shall be treated as the date of the termination and the transferor shall be treated as the employer.

(4)   In this regulation the 'relevant statutory schemes' are—

(a)   Chapter VI of Part XI of the 1996 Act;

(b)   Part XII of the 1996 Act.

(5)   Regulation 4 shall not operate to transfer liability for the sums payable to the relevant employee under the relevant statutory schemes.

(6)   In this regulation 'relevant insolvency proceedings' means insolvency proceedings which have been opened in relation to the transferor not with a view to the liquidation of the assets of the transferor and which are under the supervision of an insolvency practitioner.

(7)   Regulations 4 and 7 do not apply to any relevant transfer where the transferor is the subject of bankruptcy proceedings or any analogous insolvency proceedings which have been instituted with a view to the liquidation of the assets of the transferor and are under the supervision of an insolvency practitioner.

9   Variations of contract where transferors are subject to relevant insolvency proceedings

(1)   If at the time of a relevant transfer the transferor is subject to relevant insolvency proceedings these Regulations shall not prevent the transferor or transferee (or an insolvency practitioner) and appropriate representatives of assigned employees agreeing to permitted variations.

(2)   For the purposes of this regulation 'appropriate representatives' are—

(a)   if the employees are of a description in respect of which an independent trade union is recognised by their employer, representatives of the trade union; or

(b)   in any other case, whichever of the following employee representatives the employer chooses—

(i)   employee representatives appointed or elected by the assigned employees (whether they make the appointment or election alone or with others) otherwise than for the purposes of this regulation, who (having regard to the purposes for, and the method by which they were appointed or elected) have authority from those employees to agree permitted variations to contracts of employment on their behalf,

(ii)   employee representatives elected by assigned employees (whether they make the appointment or election alone or with others) for these particular purposes, in an election satisfying requirements identical to those contained in regulation 14 except those in regulation 14(1)(d).

(3)   An individual may be an appropriate representative for the purposes of both this regulation and regulation 13 provided that where the representative is not a trade union representative he is either elected by or has authority from assigned employees (within the meaning of this regulation) and affected employees (as described in regulation 13(1)).

...

(5)   Where assigned employees are represented by non-trade union representatives—

(a)   the agreement recording a permitted variation must be in writing and signed by each of the representatives who have made it or, where that is not reasonably practicable, by a duly authorised agent of that representative; and

    (b)   the employer must, before the agreement is made available for signature, provide all employees to whom it is intended to apply on the date on which it is to come into effect with copies of the text of the agreement and such guidance as those employees might reasonably require in order to understand it fully.

(6) A permitted variation shall take effect as a term or condition of the assigned employee's contract of employment in place, where relevant, of any term or condition which it varies.

(7) In this regulation—

'assigned employees' means those employees assigned to the organised grouping of resources or employees that is the subject of a relevant transfer;

'permitted variation' is a variation to the contract of employment of an assigned employee where—

    (a)   the sole or principal reason for it is the transfer itself or a reason connected with the transfer that is not an economic, technical or organisational reason entailing changes in the workforce; and

    (b)   it is designed to safeguard employment opportunities by ensuring the survival of the undertaking, business or part of the undertaking or business that is the subject of the relevant transfer;

'relevant insolvency proceedings' has the meaning given to the expression by regulation 8(6).

10   Pensions

(1) Regulations 4 and 5 shall not apply—

    (a)   to so much of a contract of employment or collective agreement as relates to an occupational pension scheme within the meaning of the Pension Schemes Act 1993; or

    (b)   to any rights, powers, duties or liabilities under or in connection with any such contract or subsisting by virtue of any such agreement and relating to such a scheme or otherwise arising in connection with that person's employment and relating to such a scheme.

(2) For the purposes of paragraphs (1) and (3), any provisions of an occupational pension scheme which do not relate to benefits for old age, invalidity or survivors shall not be treated as being part of the scheme.

(3) An employee whose contract of employment is transferred in the circumstances described in regulation 4(1) shall not be entitled to bring a claim against the transferor for—

    (a)   breach of contract; or

    (b)   constructive unfair dismissal under section 95(1)(c) of the 1996 Act,

arising out of a loss or reduction in his rights under an occupational pension scheme in consequence of the transfer, save insofar as the alleged breach of contract or dismissal (as the case may be) occurred prior to the date on which these Regulations took effect.

11   Notification of Employee Liability Information

(1) The transferor shall notify to the transferee the employee liability information of any person employed by him who is assigned to the organised grouping of resources or employees that is the subject of a relevant transfer —

    (a)   in writing; or

    (b)   by making it available to him in a readily accessible form.

(2) In this regulation and in regulation 12 'employee liability information' means—

    (a)   the identity and age of the employee;

    (b)   those particulars of employment that an employer is obliged to give to an employee pursuant to section 1 of the 1996 Act;

    (c)   information of any—

        (i)   disciplinary procedure taken against an employee;

        (ii) grievance procedure taken by an employee,

        within the previous two years, in circumstances where the Employment Act 2002 (Dispute Resolution) Regulations 2004 apply;

    (d)   information of any court or tribunal case, claim or action—

        (i)   brought by an employee against the transferor, within the previous two years;

> (ii)   that the transferor has reasonable grounds to believe that an employee may bring against the transferee, arising out of the employee's employment with the transferor; and
>
> (e)   information of any collective agreement which will have effect after the transfer, in its application in relation to the employee, pursuant to regulation 5(a).

(3)   Employee liability information shall contain information as at a specified date not more than fourteen days before the date on which the information is notified to the transferee.

(4)   The duty to provide employee liability information in paragraph (1) shall include a duty to provide employee liability information of any person who would have been employed by the transferor and assigned to the organised grouping of resources or employees that is the subject of a relevant transfer immediately before the transfer if he had not been dismissed in the circumstances described in regulation 7(1), including, where the transfer is effected by a series of two or more transactions, a person so employed and assigned or who would have been so employed and assigned immediately before any of those transactions.

(5)   Following notification of the employee liability information in accordance with this regulation, the transferor shall notify the transferee in writing of any change in the employee liability information.

(6)   A notification under this regulation shall be given not less than fourteen days before the relevant transfer or, if special circumstances make this not reasonably Practicable, as soon as reasonably Practicable thereafter.

(7)   A notification under this regulation may be given—

> (a)   in more than one instalment;
>
> (b)   indirectly, through a third party.

12   Remedy for failure to notify employee liability information

(1)   On or after a relevant transfer, the transferee may present a complaint to an employment tribunal that the transferor has failed to comply with any provision of regulation 11.

(2)   An employment tribunal shall not consider a complaint under this regulation unless it is presented—

> (a)   before the end of the period of three months beginning with the date of the relevant transfer;
>
> (b)   within such further period as the tribunal considers reasonable in a case where it is satisfied that it was not reasonably practicable for the complaint to be presented before the end of that period of three months.

(3)   Where an employment tribunal finds a complaint under paragraph (1) well-founded, the tribunal—

> (a)   shall make a declaration to that effect; and
>
> (b)   may make an award of compensation to be paid by the transferor to the transferee.

(4)   The amount of the compensation shall be such as the tribunal considers just and equitable in all the circumstances, subject to paragraph (5), having particular regard to—

> (a)   any loss sustained by the transferee which is attributable to the matters complained of; and
>
> (b)   the terms of any contract between the transferor and the transferee relating to the transfer under which the transferor may be liable to pay any sum to the transferee in respect of a failure to notify the transferee of employee liability information.

(5)   Subject to paragraph (6), the amount of compensation awarded under paragraph (3) shall be not less than £500 per employee in respect of whom the transferor has failed to comply with a provision of regulation 11, unless the tribunal considers it just and equitable, in all the circumstances, to award a lesser sum.

(6)   In ascertaining the loss referred to in paragraph (4)(a) the tribunal shall apply the same rule concerning the duty of a person to mitigate his loss as applies to any damages recoverable under the common law of England and Wales, Northern Ireland or Scotland, as applicable.

(7)   Section 18 of the 1996 Tribunals Act (conciliation) shall apply to the right conferred by this regulation and to proceedings under this regulation as it applies to the rights conferred by that Act and the employment tribunal proceedings mentioned in that Act.

13 Duty to inform and consult representatives

(1) In this regulation and regulations 14 and 15 references to affected employees, in relation to a relevant transfer, are to any employees of the transferor or the transferee (whether or not assigned to the organised grouping of resources or employees that is the subject of a relevant transfer) who may be affected by the transfer or may be affected by measures taken in connection with it; and references to the employer shall be construed accordingly.

(2) Long enough before a relevant transfer to enable the employer of any affected employees to consult the appropriate representatives of any affected employees, the employer shall inform those representatives of—

   (a) the fact that the transfer is to take place, the date or proposed date of the transfer and the reasons for it;

   (b) the legal, economic and social implications of the transfer for any affected employees;

   (c) the measures which he envisages he will, in connection with the transfer, take in relation to any affected employees or, if he envisages that no measures will be so taken, that fact; and

   (d) if the employer is the transferor, the measures, in connection with the transfer, which he envisages the transferee will take in relation to any affected employees who will become employees of the transferee after the transfer by virtue of regulation 4 or, if he envisages that no measures will be so taken, that fact.

(3) For the purposes of this regulation the appropriate representatives of any affected employees are—

   (a) if the employees are of a description in respect of which an independent trade union is recognised by their employer, representatives of the trade union; or

   (b) in any other case, whichever of the following employee representatives the employer chooses—

      (i)   employee representatives appointed or elected by the affected employees otherwise than for the purposes of this regulation, who (having regard to the purposes for, and the method by which they were appointed or elected) have authority from those employees to receive information and to be consulted about the transfer on their behalf,

      (ii) employee representatives elected by any affected employees, for the purposes of this regulation, in an election satisfying the requirements of regulation 14(1).

(4) The transferee shall give the transferor such information at such a time as will enable the transferor to perform the duty imposed on him by virtue of paragraph (2)(d).

(5) The information which is to be given to the appropriate representatives shall be given to each of them by being delivered to them, or sent by post to an address notified by them to the employer, or (in the case of representatives of a trade union) sent by post to the trade union at the address of its head or main office.

(6) An employer of an affected employee who envisages that he will take measures in relation to an affected employee, in connection with the relevant transfer, shall consult the appropriate representatives of that employee with a view to seeking their agreement to the intended measures.

(7) In the course of those consultations the employer shall—

   (a) consider any representations made by the appropriate representatives; and

   (b) reply to those representations and, if he rejects any of those representations, state his reasons.

(8) The employer shall allow the appropriate representatives access to any affected employees and shall afford to those representatives such accommodation and other facilities as may be appropriate.

(9) If in any case there are special circumstances which render it not reasonably practicable for an employer to perform a duty imposed on him by any of paragraphs (2) to (7), he shall take all such steps towards performing that duty as are reasonably practicable in the circumstances.

(10) Where—

    (a)   the employer has invited any of the affected employee to elect employee representatives; and

    (b)   the invitation was issued long enough before the time when the employer is required to give information under paragraph (2) to allow them to elect representatives by that time, the employer shall be treated as complying with the requirements of this regulation in relation to those employees if he complies with those requirements as soon as is reasonably practicable after the election of the representatives.

(11) If, after the employer has invited any affected employees to elect representatives, they fail to do so within a reasonable time, he shall give to any affected employees the information set out in paragraph (2).

(12) The duties imposed on an employer by this regulation shall apply irrespective of whether the decision resulting in the relevant transfer is taken by the employer or a person controlling the employer.

14   Election of employee representatives

(1)   The requirements for the election of employee representatives under regulation 13(3) are that—

    (a)   the employer shall make such arrangements as are reasonably practicable to ensure that the election is fair;

    (b)   the employer shall determine the number of representatives to be elected so that there are sufficient representatives to represent the interests of all affected employees having regard to the number and classes of those employees;

    (c)   the employer shall determine whether the affected employees should be represented either by representatives of all the affected employees or by representatives of particular classes of those employees;

    (d)   before the election the employer shall determine the term of office as employee representatives so that it is of sufficient length to enable information to be given and consultations under regulation 13 to be completed;

    (e)   the candidates for election as employee representatives are affected employees on the date of the election;

    (f)   no affected employee is unreasonably excluded from standing for election;

    (g)   all affected employees on the date of the election are entitled to vote for employee representatives;

    (h)   the employees entitled to vote may vote for as many candidates as there are representatives to be elected to represent them or, if there are to be representatives for particular classes of employees, may vote for as many candidates as there are representatives to be elected to represent their particular class of employee;

    (i)   the election is conducted so as to secure that—

        (i)   so far as is reasonably practicable, those voting do so in secret; and

        (ii)   the votes given at the election are accurately counted.

(2)   Where, after an election of employee representatives satisfying the requirements of paragraph (1) has been held, one of those elected ceases to act as an employee representative and as a result any affected employees are no longer represented, those employees shall elect another representative by an election satisfying the requirements of paragraph (1)(a), (e), (f) and (i).

15   Failure to inform or consult

(1)   Where an employer has failed to comply with a requirement of regulation 13 or regulation 14, a complaint may be presented to an employment tribunal on that ground—

    (a)   in the case of a failure relating to the election of employee representatives, by any of his employees who are affected employees;

    (b)   in the case of any other failure relating to employee representatives, by any of the employee representatives to whom the failure related;

    (c)   in the case of failure relating to representatives of a trade union, by the trade union; and

    (d)   in any other case, by any of his employees who are affected employees.

(2) If on a complaint under paragraph (1) a question arises whether or not it was reasonably practicable for an employer to perform a particular duty or as to what steps he took towards performing it, it shall be for him to show—

  (a) that there were special circumstances which rendered it not reasonably practicable for him to perform the duty; and

  (b) that he took all such steps towards its performance as were reasonably practicable in those circumstances.

(3) If on a complaint under paragraph (1) a question arises as to whether or not an employee representative was an appropriate representative for the purposes of regulation 13, it shall be for the employer to show that the employee representative had the necessary authority to represent the affected employees.

(4) On a complaint under paragraph (1)(a) it shall be for the employer to show that the requirements in regulation 14 have been satisfied.

(5) On a complaint against a transferor that he had failed to perform the duty imposed upon him by virtue of regulation 13(2)(d) or, so far as relating thereto, regulation 13(9), he may not show that it was not reasonably practicable for him to perform the duty in question for the reason that the transferee had failed to give him the requisite information at the requisite time in accordance with regulation 13(4) unless he gives the transferee notice of his intention to show that fact; and the giving of the notice shall make the transferee a party to the proceedings.

(6) In relation to any complaint under paragraph (1), a failure on the part of a person controlling (directly or indirectly) the employer to provide information to the employer shall not constitute special circumstances rendering it not reasonably practicable for the employer to comply with such a requirement.

(7) Where the tribunal finds a complaint against a transferee under paragraph (1) well-founded it shall make a declaration to that effect and may order the transferee to pay appropriate compensation to such descriptions of affected employees as may be specified in the award.

(8) Where the tribunal finds a complaint against a transferor under paragraph (1) well-founded it shall make a declaration to that effect and may—

  (a) order the transferor, subject to paragraph (9), to pay appropriate compensation to such descriptions of affected employees as may be specified in the award; or

  (b) if the complaint is that the transferor did not perform the duty mentioned in paragraph (5) and the transferor (after giving due notice) shows the facts so mentioned, order the transferee to pay appropriate compensation to such descriptions of affected employees as may be specified in the award.

(9) The transferee shall be jointly and severally liable with the transferor in respect of compensation payable under sub-paragraph (8)(a) or paragraph (11).

(10) An employee may present a complaint to an employment tribunal on the ground that he is an employee of a description to which an order under paragraph (7) or (8) relates and that—

  (a) in respect of an order under paragraph (7), the transferee has failed, wholly or in part, to pay him compensation in pursuance of the order;

  (b) in respect of an order under paragraph (8), the transferor or transferee, as applicable, has failed, wholly or in part, to pay him compensation in pursuance of the order.

(11) Where the tribunal finds a complaint under paragraph (10) wellfounded it shall order the transferor or transferee as applicable to pay the complainant the amount of compensation which it finds is due to him.

(12) An employment tribunal shall not consider a complaint under paragraph (1) or (10) unless it is presented to the tribunal before the end of the period of three months beginning with—

  (a) in respect of a complaint under paragraph (1), the date on which the relevant transfer is completed; or

  (b) in respect of a complaint under paragraph (10), the date of the tribunal's order under paragraph (7) or (8),

  or within such further period as the tribunal considers reasonable in a case where it is satisfied that it was not reasonably practicable for the complaint to be presented before the end of the period of three months.

16   Failure to inform or consult: supplemental

(1)   Section 205(1) of the 1996 Act (complaint to be sole remedy for breach of relevant rights) and section 18 of the 1996 Tribunals Act (conciliation) shall apply to the rights conferred by regulation 15 and to proceedings under this regulation as they apply to the rights conferred by those Acts and the employment tribunal proceedings mentioned in those Acts.

(2)   An appeal shall lie and shall lie only to the Employment Appeal Tribunal on a question of law arising from any decision of, or arising in any proceedings before, an employment tribunal under or by virtue of these Regulations; and section 11(1) of the Tribunals and Inquiries Act 1992 (appeals from certain tribunals to the High Court) shall not apply in relation to any such proceedings.

(3)   'Appropriate compensation' in regulation 15 means such sum not exceeding thirteen weeks' pay for the employee in question as the tribunal considers just and equitable having regard to the seriousness of the failure of the employer to comply with his duty.

(4)   Sections 220 to 228 of the 1996 Act shall apply for calculating the amount of a week's pay for any employee for the purposes of paragraph (3) and, for the purposes of that calculation, the calculation date shall be—

(a)   in the case of an employee who is dismissed by reason of redundancy (within the meaning of sections 13 9 and 15 5 of the 1996 Act) the date which is the calculation date for the purposes of any entitlement of his to a redundancy payment (within the meaning of those sections) or which would be that calculation date if he were so entitled;

(b)   in the case of an employee who is dismissed for any other reason, the effective date of termination (within the meaning of sections 95(1) and (2) and 97 of the 1996 Act) of his contract of employment;

(c)   in any other case, the date of the relevant transfer.

17   Employers' Liability Compulsory Insurance

(1)   Paragraph (2) applies where—

(a)   by virtue of section 3(1)(a) or (b) of the Employers' Liability (Compulsory Insurance) Act 1969 ('the 1969 Act'), the transferor is not required by that Act to effect any insurance; or

(b)   by virtue of section 3(1)(c) of the 1969 Act, the transferor is exempted from the requirement of that Act to effect insurance.

(2)   Where this paragraph applies, on completion of a relevant transfer the transferor and the transferee shall be jointly and severally liable in respect of any liability referred to in section 1(1) of the 1969 Act, in so far as such liability relates to the employee's employment with the transferor.

18   Restriction on contracting out

Section 203 of the 1996 Act (restrictions on contracting out) shall apply in relation to these Regulations as if they were contained in that Act, save for that section shall not apply in so far as these Regulations provide for an agreement (whether a contract of employment or not) to exclude or limit the operation of these Regulations.

21   Transitional provisions and savings

(1)   These Regulations shall apply in relation to—

(a)   a relevant transfer that takes place on or after 6 April 2006;

(b)   a transfer or service provision change, not falling within subparagraph (a), that takes place on or after 6 April 2006 and is regarded by virtue of any enactment as a relevant transfer.

(2)   The 1981 Regulations shall continue to apply in relation to—

(a)   a relevant transfer (within the meaning of the 1981 Regulations) that took place before 6 April 2006;

(b)   a transfer, not falling within sub-paragraph (a), that took place before 6 April 2006 and is regarded by virtue of any enactment as a relevant transfer (within the meaning of the 1981 Regulations).

(3) In respect of a relevant transfer that takes place on or after 6 April 2006, any action taken by a transferor or transferee to discharge a duty that applied to them under regulation 10 or 10A of the 1981 Regulations shall be deemed to satisfy the corresponding obligation imposed by regulations 13 and 14 of these Regulations, insofar as that action would have discharged those obligations had the action taken place on or after 6 April 2006.

(4) The duty on a transferor to provide a transferee with employee liability information shall not apply in the case of a relevant transfer that takes place on or before 19 April 2006.

EMPLOYMENT EQUALITY (AGE) REGULATIONS 2006
(SI 2006 No. 1031)

3   Discrimination on grounds of age

(1) For the purposes of these Regulations, a person ('A') discriminates against another person ('B') if—

   (a) on grounds of B's age, A treats B less favourably than he treats or would treat other persons, or

   (b) A applies to B a provision, criterion or practice which he applies or would apply equally to persons not of the same age group as B, but—

      (i) which puts or would put persons of the same age group as B at a particular disadvantage when compared with other persons, and

      (ii) which puts B at that disadvantage,

      and A cannot show the treatment or, as the case may be, provision, criterion or practice to be a proportionate means of achieving a legitimate aim.

(2) A comparison of B's case with that of another person under paragraph (1) must be such that the relevant circumstances in the one case are the same, or not materially different, in the other.

(3) In this regulation—

   (a) 'age group' means a group of persons defined by reference to age, whether by reference to a particular age or a range of ages; and

   (b) the reference in paragraph (1)(a) to B's age includes B's apparent age.

4   Discrimination by way of victimisation

(1) For the purposes of these Regulations, a person ('A') discriminates against another person ('B') if he treats B less favourably than he treats or would treat other persons in the same circumstances, and does so by reason that B has—

   (a) brought proceedings against A or any other person under or by virtue of these Regulations;

   (b) given evidence or information in connection with proceedings brought by any person against A or any other person under or by virtue of these Regulations;

   (c) otherwise done anything under or by reference to these Regulations in relation to A or any other person; or

   (d) alleged that A or any other person has committed an act which (whether or not the allegation so states) would amount to a contravention of these Regulations,

   or by reason that A knows that B intends to do any of those things, or suspects that B has done or intends to do any of them.

(2) Paragraph (1) does not apply to treatment of B by reason of any allegation made by him, or evidence or information given by him, if the allegation, evidence or information was false and not made (or, as the case may be, given) in good faith.

5   Instructions to discriminate

For the purposes of these Regulations, a person ('A') discriminates against another person ('B') if he treats B less favourably than he treats or would treat other persons in the same circumstances, and does so by reason that—

   (a) B has not carried out (in whole or in part) an instruction to do an act which is unlawful by virtue of these Regulations, or

    (b)   B, having been given an instruction to do such an act, complains to A or to any other person about that instruction.

6   Harassment on grounds of age

(1)   For the purposes of these Regulations, a person ('A') subjects another person ('B') to harassment where, on grounds of age, A engages in unwanted conduct which has the purpose or effect of—

    (a)   violating B's dignity; or

    (b)   creating an intimidating, hostile, degrading, humiliating or offensive environment for B.

(2)   Conduct shall be regarded as having the effect specified in paragraph (1)(a) or (b) only if, having regard to all the circumstances, including in particular the perception of B, it should reasonably be considered as having that effect.

PART 2

DISCRIMINATION IN EMPLOYMENT AND VOCATIONAL TRAINING

7   Applicants and employees

(1)   It is unlawful for an employer, in relation to employment by him at an establishment in Great Britain, to discriminate against a person—

    (a)   in the arrangements he makes for the purpose of determining to whom he should offer employment;

    (b)   in the terms on which he offers that person employment; or

    (c)   by refusing to offer, or deliberately not offering, him employment.

(2)   It is unlawful for an employer, in relation to a person whom he employs at an establishment in Great Britain, to discriminate against that person—

    (a)   in the terms of employment which he affords him;

    (b)   in the opportunities which he affords him for promotion, a transfer, training, or receiving any other benefit;

    (c)   by refusing to afford him, or deliberately not affording him, any such opportunity; or

    (d)   by dismissing him, or subjecting him to any other detriment.

(3)   It is unlawful for an employer, in relation to employment by him at an establishment in Great Britain, to subject to harassment a person whom he employs or who has applied to him for employment.

(4)   Subject to paragraph (5), paragraph (1)(a) and (c) does not apply in relation to a person—

    (a)   whose age is greater than the employer's normal retirement age or, if the employer does not have a normal retirement age, the age of 65; or

    (b)   who would, within a period of six months from the date of his application to the employer, reach the employer's normal retirement age or, if the employer does not have a normal retirement age, the age of 65.

(5)   Paragraph (4) only applies to a person to whom, if he was recruited by the employer, regulation 30 (exception for retirement) could apply.

(6)   Paragraph (2) does not apply to benefits of any description if the employer is concerned with the provision (for payment or not) of benefits of that description to the public, or to a section of the public which includes the employee in question, unless—

    (a)   that provision differs in a material respect from the provision of the benefits by the employer to his employees; or

    (b)   the provision of the benefits to the employee in question is regulated by his contract of employment; or

    (c)   the benefits relate to training.

(7)   In paragraph (2)(d) reference to the dismissal of a person from employment includes reference—

    (a)   to the termination of that person's employment by the expiration of any period (including a period expiring by reference to an event or circumstance), not being a termination immediately after which the employment is renewed on the same terms; and

    (b)   to the termination of that person's employment by any act of his (including the giving of notice) in circumstances such that he is entitled to terminate it without notice by reason of the conduct of the employer.

(8) In paragraph (4) 'normal retirement age' is an age of 65 or more which meets the requirements of section 98ZH of the 1996 Act.

8 Exception for genuine occupational requirement etc

(1) In relation to discrimination falling within regulation 3 (discrimination on grounds of age)—

    (a)   regulation 7(1)(a) or (c) does not apply to any employment;

    (b)   regulation 7(2)(b) or (c) does not apply to promotion or transfer to, or training for, any employment; and

    (c)   regulation 7(2)(d) does not apply to dismissal from any employment,

where paragraph (2) applies.

(2) This paragraph applies where, having regard to the nature of the employment or the context in which it is carried out—

    (a)   possessing a characteristic related to age is a genuine and determining occupational requirement;

    (b)   it is proportionate to apply that requirement in the particular case; and

    (c)   either—

        (i)   the person to whom that requirement is applied does not meet it, or

        (ii) the employer is not satisfied, and in all the circumstances it is reasonable for him not to be satisfied, that that person meets it.

9 Contract workers

(1) It is unlawful for a principal, in relation to contract work at an establishment in Great Britain, to discriminate against a contract worker—

    (a)   in the terms on which he allows him to do that work;

    (b)   by not allowing him to do it or continue to do it;

    (c)   in the way he affords him access to any benefits or by refusing or deliberately not affording him access to them; or

    (d)   by subjecting him to any other detriment.

(2) It is unlawful for a principal, in relation to contract work at an establishment in Great Britain, to subject a contract worker to harassment.

(3) A principal does not contravene paragraph (1)(b) by doing any act in relation to a contract worker where, if the work were to be done by a person taken into the principal's employment, that act would be lawful by virtue of regulation 8 (exception for genuine occupational requirement etc).

(4) Paragraph (1) does not apply to benefits of any description if the principal is concerned with the provision (for payment or not) of benefits of that description to the public, or to a section of the public to which the contract worker in question belongs, unless that provision differs in a material respect from the provision of the benefits by the principal to his contract workers.

(5) In this regulation—

'principal' means a person ('A') who makes work available for doing by individuals who are employed by another person who supplies them under a contract made with A;

'contract work' means work so made available; and

'contract worker' means any individual who is supplied to the principal under such a contract.

PART 3

OTHER UNLAWFUL ACTS

25 Liability of employers and principals

(1) Anything done by a person in the course of his employment shall be treated for the purposes of these Regulations as done by his employer as well as by him, whether or not it was done with the employer's knowledge or approval.

(2) Anything done by a person as agent for another person with the authority (whether express or implied, and whether precedent or subsequent) of that other person shall be treated for the purposes of these Regulations as done by that other person as well as by him.

(3) In proceedings brought under these Regulations against any person in respect of an act alleged to have been done by an employee of his it shall be a defence for that person to prove that he took such steps as were reasonably practicable to prevent the employee from doing that act, or from doing in the course of his employment acts of that description.

26 Aiding unlawful acts

(1) A person who knowingly aids another person to do an act made unlawful by these Regulations shall be treated for the purpose of these Regulations as himself doing an unlawful act of the like description.

(2) For the purposes of paragraph (1) an employee or agent for whose act the employer or principal is liable under regulation 25 (or would be so liable but for regulation 25(3)) shall be deemed to aid the doing of the act by the employer or principal.

(3) A person does not under this regulation knowingly aid another to do an unlawful act if—

    (a) he acts in reliance on a statement made to him by that other person that, by reason of any provision of these Regulations, the act which he aids would not be unlawful; and

    (b) it is reasonable for him to rely on the statement.

(4) A person who knowingly or recklessly makes a statement such as is referred to in paragraph (3)(a) which in a material respect is false or misleading commits an offence, and shall be liable on summary conviction to a fine not exceeding level 5 on the standard scale.

PART 4

GENERAL EXCEPTIONS FROM PARTS 2 AND 3

27 Exception for statutory authority

(1) Nothing in Part 2 or 3 shall render unlawful any act done in order to comply with a requirement of any statutory provision.

(2) In this regulation 'statutory provision' means any provision (whenever enacted) of—

    (a) an Act or an Act of the Scottish Parliament;

    (aa) a measure or Act of the National Assembly of Wales;

    (b) an instrument made by a Minister of the Crown under an Act;

    (c) an instrument made under an Act or an Act of the Scottish Parliament by the Scottish Ministers or a member of the Scottish Executive;

    (d) an instrument made after the end of the initial period under an Act, or under a Measure or Act of the National Assembly for Wales, by the Welsh Ministers, the First Minister for Wales or the Counsel General to the Welsh Assembly Government.

(3) In paragraph (2)(d) 'the initial period' has the same meaning as in the Government of Wales Act 2006 (see section 161(6) of that Act).

28 Exception for national security

Nothing in Part 2 or 3 shall render unlawful an act done for the purpose of safeguarding national security, if the doing of the act was justified by that purpose.

29 Exceptions for positive action

(1) Nothing in Part 2 or 3 shall render unlawful any act done in or in connection with—

    (a) affording persons of a particular age or age group access to facilities for training which would help fit them for particular work; or

    (b) encouraging persons of a particular age or age group to take advantage of opportunities for doing particular work;

where it reasonably appears to the person doing the act that it prevents or compensates for disadvantages linked to age suffered by persons of that age or age group doing that work or likely to take up that work.

(2) Nothing in Part 2 or 3 shall render unlawful any act done by a trade organisation within the meaning of regulation 18 in or in connection with—

    (a)   affording only members of the organisation who are of a particular age or age group access to facilities for training which would help fit them for holding a post of any kind in the organisation; or

    (b)   encouraging only members of the organisation who are of a particular age or age group to take advantage of opportunities for holding such posts in the organisation,

where it reasonably appears to the organisation that the act prevents or compensates for disadvantages linked to age suffered by those of that age or age group holding such posts or likely to hold such posts.

(3)   Nothing in Part 2 or 3 shall render unlawful any act done by a trade organisation within the meaning of regulation 18 in or in connection with encouraging only persons of a particular age or age group to become members of the organisation where it reasonably appears to the organisation that the act prevents or compensates for disadvantages linked to age suffered by persons of that age or age group who are, or are eligible to become, members.

30   Exception for retirement

(1)   This regulation applies in relation to an employee within the meaning of section 230(1) of the 1996 Act, a person in Crown employment, a relevant member of the House of Commons staff, and a relevant member of the House of Lords staff.

(2)   Nothing in Part 2 or 3 shall render unlawful the dismissal of a person to whom this regulation applies at or over the age of 65 where the reason for the dismissal is retirement.

(3)   For the purposes of this regulation, whether or not the reason for a dismissal is retirement shall be determined in accordance with sections 98ZA to 98ZF of the 1996 Act.

31   Exception for the national minimum wage

(1)   Nothing in Part 2 or 3 shall render it unlawful for a relevant person ('A') to be remunerated in respect of his work at a rate which is lower than the rate at which another such person ('B') is remunerated for his work where—

    (a)   the hourly rate of the national minimum wage for a person of A's age is lower than that for a person of B's age, and

    (b)   the rate at which A is remunerated is below the single hourly rate for the national minimum wage prescribed by the Secretary of State under section 1(3) of the National Minimum Wage Act 1998.

(2)   Nothing in Part 2 or 3 shall render it unlawful for an apprentice who is not a relevant person to be remunerated in respect of his work at a rate which is lower than the rate at which an apprentice who is a relevant person is remunerated for his work.

(3)   In this regulation—

'apprentice' means a person who is employed under a contract of apprenticeship or, in accordance with regulation 12(3) of the National Minimum Wage Regulations 1999, is to be treated as employed under such a contract;

'relevant person' means a person who qualifies for the national minimum wage (whether at the single hourly rate for the national minimum wage prescribed by the Secretary of State under section 1(3) of the National Minimum Wage Act 1998 or at a different rate).

32   Exception for provision of certain benefits based on length of service

(1)   Subject to paragraph (2), nothing in Part 2 or 3 shall render it unlawful for a person ('A'), in relation to the award of any benefit by him, to put a worker ('B') at a disadvantage when compared with another worker ('C'), if and to the extent that the disadvantage suffered by B is because B's length of service is less than that of C.

(2)   Where B's length of service exceeds 5 years, it must reasonably appear to A that the way in which he uses the criterion of length of service, in relation to the award in respect of which B is put at a disadvantage, fulfils a business need of his undertaking (for example, by encouraging the loyalty or motivation, or rewarding the experience, of some or all of his workers).

(3)   In calculating a worker's length of service for these purposes, A shall calculate—

    (a)   the length of time the worker has been working for him doing work which he reasonably considers to be at or above a particular level (assessed by reference to the demands made on the worker, for example, in terms of effort, skills and decision making); or

(b)   the length of time the worker has been working for him in total;
and on each occasion on which he decides to use the criterion of length of service in relation to the award of a benefit to workers, it is for him to decide which of these definitions to use to calculate their lengths of service.

(4)   For the purposes of paragraph (3), in calculating the length of time a worker has been working for him—

(a)   A shall calculate the length of time in terms of the number of weeks during the whole or part of which the worker was working for him;

(b)   A may discount any period during which the worker was absent from work (including any period of absence which at the time it occurred was thought by A or the worker to be permanent) unless in all the circumstances (including the way in which other workers' absences occurring in similar circumstances are treated by A in calculating their lengths of service) it would not be reasonable for him to do so;

(c)   A may discount any period of time during which the worker was present at work ('the relevant period') where—

(i)   the relevant period preceded a period during which the worker was absent from work, and

(ii)   in all the circumstances (including the length of the worker's absence, the reason for his absence, the effect his absence has had on his ability to discharge the duties of his work, and the way in which other workers are treated by A in similar circumstances) it is reasonable for A to discount the relevant period.

(5)   For the purposes of paragraph (3)(b), a worker shall be treated as having worked for A during any period during which he worked for another if—

(a)   that period is treated as a period of employment with A for the purposes of the 1996 Act by virtue of the operation of section 218 of that Act;

(b)   were the worker to be made redundant by A, that period and the period he has worked for A would amount to 'relevant service' within the meaning of section 155 of that Act; or

(c)   in any case to which sub-paragraph (a) or (b) does not apply, that period is treated as a period of employment with A by or under an enactment pursuant to which his employment was transferred to A.

(6)   In paragraph (5)—

(a)   the reference to being made redundant is a reference to being dismissed by reason of redundancy for the purposes of the 1996 Act;

(b)   the reference to section 155 of that Act is a reference to that section as modified by the Redundancy Payments (Continuity of Employment in Local Government, etc.) (Modification) Order 1999.

(7)   In this regulation—
'benefit' does not include any benefit awarded to a worker by virtue of his ceasing to work for A;
'enactment' includes an enactment comprised in, or in an instrument made under, an Act of the Scottish Parliament; and
'year' means a year of 12 calendar months.

33   Exception for provision of enhanced redundancy payments to employees

(1)   Nothing in Part 2 or 3 shall render it unlawful for an employer—

(a)   to give a qualifying employee an enhanced redundancy payment which is less in amount than the enhanced redundancy payment which he gives to another such employee if both amounts are calculated in the same way;

(b)   to give enhanced redundancy payments only to those who are qualifying employees by virtue of sub-paragraph (a) or (c)(i) of the definition of qualifying employee below.

(2)   In this regulation—
'the appropriate amount', 'a redundancy payment' and 'a week's pay' have the same meaning as they have in section 162 of the 1996 Act;

'enhanced redundancy payment' means a payment of an amount calculated in accordance with paragraph (3) or (4);

'qualifying employee' means—

(a)   an employee who is entitled to a redundancy payment by virtue of section 135 of the 1996 Act;

(b)   an employee who would have been so entitled but for the operation of section 155 of that Act;

(c)   an employee who agrees to the termination of his employment in circumstances where, had he been dismissed—

  (i)   he would have been a qualifying employee by virtue of sub-paragraph (a) of this definition; or

  (ii)   he would have been a qualifying employee by virtue of sub-paragraph (b).

(3)   For an amount to be calculated in accordance with this paragraph it must be calculated in accordance with section 162(1) to (3) of the 1996 Act.

(4)   For an amount to be calculated in accordance with this paragraph—

(a)   it must be calculated as in paragraph (3);

(b)   however, in making that calculation, the employer may do one or both of the following things—

  (i)   he may treat a week's pay as not being subject to a maximum amount or as being subject to a maximum amount above the amount laid down in section 227 of the 1996 Act;

  (ii)   he may multiply the appropriate amount allowed for each year of employment by a figure of more than one;

(c)   having made the calculation as in paragraph (3) (whether or not in making that calculation he has done anything mentioned in sub-paragraph (b)) the employer may increase the amount thus calculated by multiplying it by a figure of more than one.

(5)   For the purposes of paragraphs (3) and (4), the reference to 'the relevant date' in section 162(1)(a) of the 1996 Act is to be read, in the case of a qualifying employee who agrees to the termination of his employment, as a reference to the date on which that termination takes effect.

34   Exception for provision of life assurance cover to retired workers

(1)   Where a person ('A') arranges for workers to be provided with life assurance cover after their early retirement on grounds of ill health, nothing in Part 2 or 3 shall render it unlawful—

(a)   where a normal retirement age applied in relation to any such workers at the time they took early retirement, for A to arrange for such cover to cease when such workers reach that age;

(b)   in relation to any other workers, for A to arrange for such cover to cease when the workers reach the age of 65.

(2)   In this regulation, 'normal retirement age', in relation to a worker who has taken early retirement, means the age at which workers in A's undertaking who held the same kind of position as the worker held at the time of his retirement were normally required to retire.

PART 5
ENFORCEMENT

35   Restriction of proceedings for breach of Regulations

(1)   Except as provided by these Regulations no proceedings, whether civil or criminal, shall lie against any person in respect of an act by reason that the act is unlawful by virtue of a provision of these Regulations.

(2)   Paragraph (1) does not prevent the making of an application for judicial review or the investigation or determination of any matter in accordance with Part 10 (investigations: the Pensions Ombudsman) of the Pension Schemes Act 1993 by the Pensions Ombudsman.

36   Jurisdiction of employment tribunals

(1)   A complaint by any person ('the complainant') that another person ('the respondent')—

(a)   has committed against the complainant an act to which this regulation applies; or

(b)   is by virtue of regulation 25 (liability of employers and principals) or 26 (aiding unlawful acts) to be treated as having committed against the complainant such an act;

may be presented to an employment tribunal.

(2)   This regulation applies to any act of discrimination or harassment which is unlawful by virtue of any provision of Part 2 other than—

(a)   where the act is one in respect of which an appeal or proceedings in the nature of an appeal may be brought under any enactment, regulation 19 (qualifications bodies);

(b)   regulation 23 (institutions of further and higher education); or

(c)   where the act arises out of and is closely connected to a relationship between the complainant and the respondent which has come to an end but during the course of which an act of discrimination against, or harassment of, the complainant by the respondent would have been unlawful by virtue of regulation 23, regulation 24 (relationships which have come to an end).

(3)   In paragraph (2)(c), reference to an act of discrimination or harassment which would have been unlawful includes, in the case of a relationship which has come to an end before the date on which the act of discrimination or harassment became unlawful by virtue of these Regulations, reference to an act of discrimination or harassment which would, after that date, have been unlawful.

(4)   In this regulation, 'enactment' includes an enactment comprised in, or in an instrument made under, an Act of the Scottish Parliament.

37   Burden of proof: employment tribunals

(1)   This regulation applies to any complaint presented under regulation 36 to an employment tribunal.

(2)   Where, on the hearing of the complaint, the complainant proves facts from which the tribunal could, apart from this regulation, conclude in the absence of an adequate explanation that the respondent—

(a)   has committed against the complainant an act to which regulation 36 applies; or

(b)   is by virtue of regulation 25 (liability of employers and principals) or 26 (aiding unlawful acts) to be treated as having committed against the complainant such an act,

the tribunal shall uphold the complaint unless the respondent proves that he did not commit, or as the case may be, is not to be treated as having committed, that act.

38   Remedies on complaints in employment tribunals

(1)   Where an employment tribunal finds that a complaint presented to it under regulation 36 is well-founded, the tribunal shall make such of the following as it considers just and equitable—

(a)   an order declaring the rights of the complainant and the respondent in relation to the act to which the complaint relates;

(b)   an order requiring the respondent to pay to the complainant compensation of an amount corresponding to any damages he could have been ordered by a county court or by a sheriff court to pay to the complainant if the complaint had fallen to be dealt with under regulation 39 (jurisdiction of county and sheriff courts);

(c)   a recommendation that the respondent take within a specified period action appearing to the tribunal to be practicable for the purpose of obviating or reducing the adverse effect on the complainant of any act of discrimination or harassment to which the complaint relates.

(2)   As respects an unlawful act of discrimination falling within regulation 3(1)(b) (discrimination on the grounds of age), if the respondent proves that the provision, criterion or practice was not applied with the intention of treating the complainant unfavourably on grounds of age, an order may be made under paragraph (1)(b) only if the employment tribunal—

(a)   makes such order under paragraph (1)(a) (if any) and such recommendation under paragraph (1)(c) (if any) as it would have made if it had no power to make an order under paragraph (1)(b); and

     (b)   (where it makes an order under paragraph (1)(a) or a recommendation under paragraph (1)(c) or both) considers that it is just and equitable to make an order under paragraph (1)(b) as well.

(3) If without reasonable justification the respondent to a complaint fails to comply with a recommendation made by an employment tribunal under paragraph (1)(c), then, if it thinks it just and equitable to do so—

     (a)   the tribunal may increase the amount of compensation required to be paid to the complainant in respect of the complaint by an order made under paragraph (1)(b); or

     (b)   if an order under paragraph (1)(b) was not made, the tribunal may make such an order.

(4) Where an amount of compensation falls to be awarded under paragraph (1)(b), the tribunal may include in the award interest on that amount subject to, and in accordance with, the provisions of the Employment Tribunals (Interest on Awards in Discrimination Cases) Regulations 1996.

(5) This regulation has effect subject to paragraph 6 of Schedule 2 (pension schemes).

39   Jurisdiction of county and sheriff courts

(1) A claim by any person ('the claimant') that another person ('the respondent')—

     (a)   has committed against the claimant an act to which this regulation applies; or

     (b)   is by virtue of regulation 25 (liability of employers and principals) or 26 (aiding unlawful acts) to be treated as having committed against the claimant such an act,

may be made the subject of civil proceedings in like manner as any other claim in tort or (in Scotland) in reparation for breach of statutory duty.

(2) Proceedings brought under paragraph (1) shall—

     (a)   in England and Wales, be brought only in a county court; and

     (b)   in Scotland, be brought only in a sheriff court.

(3) For the avoidance of doubt it is hereby declared that damages in respect of an unlawful act to which this regulation applies may include compensation for injury to feelings whether or not they include compensation under any other head.

(4) This regulation applies to any act of discrimination or harassment which is unlawful by virtue of—

     (a)   regulation 23 (institutions of further and higher education); or

     (b)   where the act arises out of and is closely connected to a relationship between the claimant and the respondent which has come to an end but during the course of which an act of discrimination against, or harassment of, the claimant by the respondent would have been unlawful by virtue of regulation 23, regulation 24 (relationships which have come to an end).

(5) In paragraph (4)(b), reference to an act of discrimination or harassment which would have been unlawful includes, in the case of a relationship which has come to an end before the date on which the act of discrimination or harassment became unlawful by virtue of these Regulations, reference to an act of discrimination or harassment which would, after that date, have been unlawful.

40   Burden of proof: county and sheriff courts

(1) This regulation applies to any claim brought under regulation 39 in a county court in England and Wales or a sheriff court in Scotland.

(2) Where, on the hearing of the claim, the claimant proves facts from which the court could, apart from this regulation, conclude in the absence of an adequate explanation that the respondent—

     (a)   has committed against the claimant an act to which regulation 39 applies; or

     (b)   is by virtue of regulation 25 (liability of employers and principals) or 26 (aiding unlawful acts) to be treated as having committed against the claimant such an act,

the court shall uphold the claim unless the respondent proves that he did not commit, or as the case may be, is not to be treated as having committed, that act.

ACAS — DISCIPLINARY AND GRIEVANCE PROCEDURES
CODE OF PRACTICE 1

SECTION 1
DISCIPLINARY RULES AND PROCEDURE

WHY HAVE DISCIPLINARY RULES AND PROCEDURES?

1.   Disciplinary rules and procedures help to promote orderly employment relations as well as fairness and consistency in the treatment of individuals. Disciplinary procedures are also a legal requirement in certain circumstances (see paragraph 6).

2.   Disciplinary rules tell employees what behaviour employers expect from them. If an employee breaks specific rules about behaviour, this is often called misconduct. Employers use disciplinary procedures and actions to deal with situations where employees allegedly break disciplinary rules. Disciplinary procedures may also be used where employees don't meet their employer's expectations in the way they do their job. These cases, often known as unsatisfactory performance (or capability), may require different treatment from misconduct, and disciplinary procedures should allow for this.

3.   Guidance an how to draw up disciplinary rules and procedures is contained in paragraphs 52–62.

4.   When dealing with disciplinary cases, employers need to be aware both of the law on unfair dismissal and the statutory minimum procedure contained in the Employment Act 2002 for dismissing or taking disciplinary action against an employee. Employers must also be careful not to discriminate on the grounds of gender, race (including colour, nationality and ethnic or national origins), disability, age, sexual orientation or religion.

The law on unfair dismissal

5.   The law on unfair dismissal requires employers to act reasonably when dealing with disciplinary issues. What is classed as reasonable behaviour will depend on the circumstances of each case, and is ultimately a matter for employment tribunals to decide. However, the core principles employers should work to are set out in the box overleaf. Drawing up and referring to a procedure can help employers deal with disciplinary issues in a fair and consistent manner.

Care principles of reasonable behaviour

- Use procedures primarily to help and encourabe employees to improve rather than just as a way of imposing a punishment.
- Inform the employee of the complaint against them, and provide the with an opportunity to state their case before decisions are reached.
- Allow employees to be accompanied at disciplinary meetings.
- Make sure that disciplinary action is not taken until the facts of the case have been established and that the action is reasonable in the circumstances.
- Never dismiss an employee for a first disciplinary offence, unless it is a case of gross misconduct.
- Give the employee a written explanation for any disciplinary action taken and make sure they know what improvement is expected.
- Give the employee an opportunity to appeal.
- Deal with issues as thoroughly and promptly as possible.
- Act consistently.

The statutory minimum procedure

6.   Employers are also required to follow a specific statutory minimum procedure if they are contemplating dismissing an employee or imposing some other disciplinary penalty that is not suspension on full pay or a warning. Guidance on this statutory procedure is provided in paragraphs 26–32. If an employee is dismissed without the employer following this statutory procedure, and makes a claim to an employment tribunal, providing they have the necessary qualifying service and providing they are not prevented from claiming unfair dismissal by virtue of their age, the dismissal will automatically be ruled unfair. The statutory procedure is a minimum requirement and even

where the relevant procedure is followed the dismissal may still be unfair if the employer has not acted reasonably in all the circumstances.

What about small businesses?

7. In small organisations it may not be practicable to adopt all the detailed good practice guidance set out in this Code. Employment tribunals will take account of an employer's size and administrative resources when deciding if it acted reasonably. However, all organisations regardless of size must follow the minimum statutory dismissal and disciplinary procedures,

DEALING WITH DISCIPLINARY ISSUES IN THE WORKPLACE

8. When a potential disciplinary matter arises, the employer should make necessary investigations to establish the facts promptly before memories of events fade. It is important to keep a written record for later reference. Having established the facts, the employer should decide whether to drop the matter, deal with it informally or arrange for it to be handled formally. Where an investigatory meeting is held solely to establish the facts of a case, it should be made clear to the employee involved that it is not a disciplinary meeting.

9. In certain cases, for example in cases involving gross misconduct, where relationships have broken down or there are risks to an employer's property or responsibilities to other parties, consideration should be given to a brief period of suspension with full pay whilst unhindered investigation is conducted. Such a suspension should only be imposed after careful consideration and should be reviewed to ensure it is not unnecessarily protracted. It should be made clear that the suspension is not considered a disciplinary action.

10. When dealing with disciplinary issues in the workplace employers should bear in mind that they are required under the Disability Discrimination Act 1995 to make reasonable adjustments to cater for employees who have a disability, for example providing for wheelchair access if necessary.

Informal action

11. Cases of minor misconduct or unsatisfactory performance are usually best dealt with informally. A quiet word is often all that is required to improve an employee's conduct or performance. The informal approach may be particularly helpful in small firms, where problems can be dealt with quickly and confidentially. There will, however, be situations where matters are more serious or where an informal approach has been tried but is not working.

12. If informal action does not bring about an improvement, or the misconduct or unsatisfactory performance is considered to be too serious to be classed as minor, employers should provide employees with a clear signal of their dissatisfaction by taking formal action.

Formal action

Inform the employee of the problem

13. The first step in any formal process is to let the employee know in writing what it is they are alleged to have done wrong. The letter or note should contain enough information for the individual to be able to understand both what it is they are alleged to have done wrong and the reasons why this is not acceptable. If the employee has difficulty reading, or if English is not their first language, the employer should explain the content of the letter or note to them orally. The letter or note should also invite the individual to a meeting at which the problem can be discussed, and it should inform the individual of their right to be accompanied at the meeting (see section 3). The employee should be given copies of any documents that will be produced at the meeting.

Hold a meeting to discuss the problem

14. Where possible, the timing and location of the meeting should be agreed with the employee. The length of time between the written notification and the meeting should be long enough to allow the employee to prepare but not so long that memories fade. The employer should hold the meeting in a private location and ensure there will be no interruptions.

15. At the meeting, the employer should explain the complaint against the employee and go through the evidence that has been gathered. The employee should be allowed to set out their case and answer any allegations that have been made. The employee should also be allowed to ask questions, present

evidence, call witnesses and be given an opportunity to raise points about any information provided by witnesses.

16. An employee who cannot attend a meeting should inform the employer in advance whenever possible. If the employee fails to attend through circumstances outside their control and unforeseeable at the time the meeting was arranged (eg illness) the employer should arrange another meeting. A decision may be taken in the employee's absence if they fail to attend the re-arranged meeting without good reason. If an employee's companion cannot attend on a proposed date, the employee can suggest another date so long as it is reasonable and is not more than five working days after the date originally proposed by the employer. This five day time limit may be extended by mutual agreement.

Decide on outcome and action

17. Following the meeting the employer must decide whether disciplinary action is justified or not. Where it is decided that no action is justified the employee should be informed. Where it is decided that disciplinary action is justified the employer will need to consider what form this should take, Before making any decision the employer should take account of the employee's disciplinary and general record, length of service, actions taken in any previous similar case, the explanations given by the employee and — most important of all whether the intended disciplinary action is reasonable under the circumstances.

18. Examples of actions the employer might choose to take are set out in paragraphs 19–25, It is normally good practice to give employees at least one chance to improve their conduct or performance before they are issued with a final written warning. However, if an employee's misconduct or unsatisfactory performance — or its continuance — is sufficiently serious, for example because it is having, or is likely to have, a serious harmful effect on the organisation, it may be appropriate to move directly to a final written warning. In cases of gross misconduct, the employer may decide to dismiss even though the employee has not previously received a warning for misconduct. (Further guidance on dealing with gross misconduct is set out at paragraphs 35–36.)

First formal action — unsatisfactory performance

19. Following the meeting, an employee who is found to be performing unsatisfactorily should be given a written note setting out:
   • the performance problem;
   • the improvement that is required;
   • the timescale for achieving this improvement;
   • a review date; and
   • any support the employer will provide to assist the employee.

20. The employee should be informed that the note represents the first stage of a formal procedure and that failure to improve could lead to a final written warning and, ultimately, dismissal. A copy of the note should be kept and used as the basis for monitoring and reviewing performance over a specified period (eg six months).

First formal action — misconduct

21. Where, following a disciplinary meeting, an employee is found guilty of misconduct, the usual first step would be to give them a written warning setting out the nature of the misconduct and the change in behaviour required.

22. The employee should be informed that the warning is part of the formal disciplinary process and what the consequences will be of a failure to change behaviour. The consequences could be a final written warning and ultimately, dismissal. The employee should also be informed that they may appeal against the decision. A record of the warning should be kept, but it should be disregarded for disciplinary purposes after a specified period (eg six months).

23. Guidance on dealing with cases of gross misconduct is provided in paragraphs 35–36.

Final written warning

24. Where there is a failure to improve or change behaviour in the timescale set at the first formal stage, or where the offence is sufficiently serious, the employee should normally be issued with a final

written warning — but only after they have been given a chance to present their case at a meeting. The final written warning should give details of, and grounds for, the complaint. It should warn the employee that failure to improve or modify behaviour may lead to dismissal or to some other penalty, and refer to the right of appeal. The final written warning should normally be disregarded for disciplinary purposes after a specified period (for example 12 months).

Dismissal or other penalty

25.   If the employee's conduct or performance still fails to improve, the final stage in the disciplinary process might be dismissal or (if the employee's contract allows it or it is mutually agreed) some other penalty such as demotion, disciplinary transfer, or loss of seniority/pay. A decision to dismiss should only be taken by a manager who has the authority to do so. The employee should be informed as soon as possible of the reasons for the dismissal, the date on which the employment contract will terminate, the appropriate period of notice and their right of appeal.

26.   It is important for employers to bear in mind that before they dismiss an employee or impose a sanction such as demotion, loss of seniority or loss of pay, they must as a minimum have followed the statutory dismissal and disciplinary procedures. The standard statutory procedure to be used in almost all cases requires the employer to:

Step 1
Write to the employee notifying them of the allegations against them and the basis of the allegations and invite them to a meeting to discuss the matter.
Step 2
Hold a meeting to discuss the allegations — at which the employee has the right to be accompanied — and notify the employee of the decision.
Step 3
If the employee wishes to appeal, hold an appeal meeting at which the employee has the right to be accompanied — and inform the employee of the final decision.

27.   More detail on the statutory standard procedure is set out at Annex A. There is a modified two-step procedure for use in special circumstances involving gross misconduct and details of this are set out at Annex B. Guidance on the modified procedure is contained in paragraph 36. There are a number of situations in which it is not necessary for employers to use the statutory procedures or where they will have been deemed to be completed and these are described in Annex E.

28.   If the employer fails to follow this statutory procedure (where it applies), and an employee who is qualified to do so makes a claim for unfair dismissal, the employment tribunal will automatically find the dismissal unfair. The tribunal will normally increase the compensation awarded by 10 per cent, or, where it feels it is just and equitable to do so, up to 50 per cent. Equally, if the employment tribunal finds that an employee has been dismissed unfairly but has failed to follow the procedure (for instance they have failed to attend the disciplinary meeting without good cause), compensation will be reduced by, normally, 10 per cent, or, if the tribunal considers it just and equitable to do so, up to 50 per cent,

29.   If the tribunal considers there are exceptional circumstances, compensation may be adjusted (up or down) by less than 10 per cent or not at all.

30.   Employers and employees will normally be expected to go through the statutory dismissal and disciplinary procedure unless they have reasonable grounds to believe that by doing so they might be exposed to a significant threat, such as violent, abusive or intimidating behaviour, or they will be harassed. There will always be a certain amount of stress and anxiety for both parties when dealing with any disciplinary case, but this exemption will only apply where the employer or employee reasonably believes that they would come to some serious physical or mental harm; their property or some third party is threatened or the other party has harassed them and this may continue.

31.   Equally, the statutory procedure does not need to be followed if circumstances beyond the control of either party prevent one or more steps being followed within a reasonable period. This will sometimes be the case where there is a long-term illness or a long period of absence abroad but, in the case of employers, wherever possible they should consider appointing another manager to deal with the procedure.

32.   Where an employee fails to attend a meeting held as part of the statutory discipline procedure without good reason the statutory procedure comes to an end. In those circumstances the employee's compensation may be reduced if they bring a successful complaint before an employment tribunal. If the ernployee does have a good reason for non-attendance, the employer must re-arrange the meeting. If the employee does not attend the second meeting for good reason the employer need not arrange a third meeting but there will be no adjustment of compensation.

WHAT IF A GRIEVANCE IS RAISED DURING A DISCIPLINARY CASE?

33.   In the course of a disciplinary process, an employee might raise a grievance that is related to the case. If this happens, the employer should consider suspending the disciplinary procedure for a short period while the grievance is dealt with. Depending on the nature of the grievance, the employer may need to consider bringing in another manager to deal with the disciplinary process. In small organisations this may not be possible, and the existing manager should deal with the case as impartially as possible.

34.   Where the action taken or contemplated by the employer is dismissal the statutory grievance procedure does not apply. Where the action taken or contemplated is paid suspension or a warning the statutory grievance procedure and not the dismissal and disciplinary procedure applies to any grievance. However, where the employer takes, or is contemplating other action short of dismissal and asserts that the reason for the action is conduct or capability related, the statutory grievance procedure does not apply unless the grievance is that the action amounts, or would amount, to unlawful discrimination, or that the true reason for the action is not the reason given by the employer. In those cases the employee must have raised a written grievance in accordance with the statutory grievance procedure before presenting any complaint to an employment tribunal about the issue raised by the grievance. However, if the written grievance is raised before any disciplinary appeal meeting, the rest of the grievance procedure does not have to be followed, although the employer may use the appeal meeting to discuss the grievance.

DEALING WITH GROSS MISCONDUCT

35.   If an employer considers an employee guilty of gross misconduct, and thus potentially liable for summary dismissal, it is still important to establish the facts before taking any action. A short period of suspension with full pay may be helpful or necessary, although it should only be imposed after careful consideration and should be kept under review, It should be made clear to the employee that the suspension is not a disciplinary action and does not involve any prejudgement.

36.   It is a core principle of reasonable behaviour that employers should give employees the opportunity of putting their case at a disciplinary meeting before deciding whether to take action, This principle applies as much to cases of gross misconduct as it does to ordinary cases of misconduct or unsatisfactory performance. There may however be some very limited cases where despite the fact that an employer has dismissed an employee immediately without a meeting an employment tribunal will, very exceptionally, find the dismissal to be fair, To allow for these cases there is a statutory modified procedure under which the employer is required to write to the employee after the dismissal setting out the reasons for the dismissal and to hold an appeal meeting, if the employee wants one. The statutory procedure that must be followed by employers in such cases is set out in Annex B. If an employer fails to follow this procedure and the case goes to tribunal, the dismissal will be found to be automatically unfair.

DEALING WITH ABSENCE FROM WORK

37.   When dealing with absence from work, it is important to determine the reasons why the employee has not been at work. If there is no acceptable reason, the matter should be treated as a conduct issue and dealt with as a disciplinary matter.

38.   If the absence is due to genuine (including medically certified) illness, the issue becomes one of capability, and the employer should take a sympathetic and considerate approach. When thinking about how to handle these cases, it is helpful to consider:

    •   how soon the employee's health and attendance will improve;

- whether alternative work is available;
- the effect of the absence on the organisation;
- how similar situations have been handled in the past; and
- whether the illness is a result of disability in which case the provisions of the Disability Discrimination Act 1995 will apply.

39.   The impact of long-term absences will nearly always be greater on small organisations, and they may be entitled to act at an earlier stage than large organisations.

40.   In cases of extended sick leave both statutory and contractual issues will need to be addressed and specialist advice may be necessary.

DEALING WITH SPECIAL SITUATIONS

If the full procedure is not immediately available

41.   Special arrangements might be required for handling disciplinary matters among nightshirt employees, employees in isolated locations or depots, or others who may be difficult to reach, Nevertheless the appropriate statutory procedure must be followed where it applies.

Trade union representatives

42.   Disciplinary action against a trade union representative can lead to a serious dispute if it is seen as an attack on the union's functions. Normal standards apply but, if disciplinary action is considered, the case should be discussed, after obtaining the employee's agreement, with a senior trade union representative or permanent union official.

Criminal charges or convictions not related to employment

43.   If an employee is charged with, or convicted of, a criminal offence not related to work, this is not in itself reason for disciplinary action. The employer should establish the facts of the case and consider whether the matter is serious enough to warrant starting the disciplinary procedure. The main consideration should be whether the offence, or alleged offence, is one that makes the employee unsuitable for their type of work. Similarly, an employee should not be dismissed solely because they are absent from work as a result of being remanded in custody.

APPEALS

44.   Employees who have had disciplinary action taken against them should be given the opportunity to appeal. It is useful to set a time limit for asking for an appeal — five working days is usually enough.

45.   An employee may choose to appeal for example because:
- they think a finding or penalty is unfair;
- new evidence comes to light; or
- they think the disciplinary procedure was not used correctly.

It should be noted that the appeal stage is part of the statutory procedure and if the employee pursues an employment tribunal claim the tribunal may reduce any award of compensation if the employee did not exercise the right of appeal.

46.   As far as is reasonably practicable a more senior manager not involved with the case should hear the appeal. In small organisations, even if a more senior manager is not available, another manager should hear the appeal, if possible. If that is not an option, the person overseeing the case should act as impartially as possible. Records and notes of the original disciplinary meeting should be made available to the person hearing the appeal.

47.   The employers should contact the employee with appeal arrangements as soon as possible, and inform them of their statutory right to be accompanied at the appeal meeting.

48.   The manager must inform the employee about the appeal decision, and the reasons for it, as soon as possible. They should also confirm the decision in writing. If the decision is the final stage of the organisation's appeals procedure, the manager should make this clear to the employee.

KEEPING RECORDS

49.   It is important, and in the interests of both employers and employees, to keep written records during the disciplinary process. Records should include:

- the complaint against the employee;
- the employee's defence;
- findings made and actions taken;
- the reason for actions taken;
- whether an appeal was lodged;
- the outcome of the appeal;
- any grievances raised during the disciplinary procedure; and
- subsequent developments.

50. Records should be treated as confidential and be kept no longer than necessary in accordance with the Data Protection Act 1 998. This Act gives individuals the right to request and have access to certain personal data.

51. Copies of meeting records should be given to the employee including copies of any formal minutes that may have been taken, In certain circumstances (for example to protect a witness) the employer might withhold some information.

DRAWING UP DISCIPLINARY RULES AND PROCEDURES

52. Management is responsible for maintaining and setting standards of performance in an organisation and for ensuring that disciplinary rules and procedures are in place. Employers are legally required to have disciplinary procedures. It is good practice to involve employees (and, where appropriate, their representatives) when making or changing rules and procedures, so that everyone affected by them understands them.

Rules

53. When making rules, the aim should be to specify those that are necessary for ensuring a safe and efficient workplace and for maintaining good employment relations.

54. It is unlikely that any set of rules will cover all possible disciplinary issues, but rules normally cover:
- bad behaviour, such as fighting or drunkenness;
- unsatisfactory work performance;
- harassment or victimisation;
- misuse of company facilities (for example ernail and internet);
- poor timekeeping:
- unauthorised absences; and
- repeated or serious failure to follow instructions.

55. Rules should be specific, clear and recorded in writing. They also need to be readily available to employees, for instance on a noticeboard or, in larger organisations, in a staff handbook or on the intranet. Management should do all they can to ensure that every employee knows and understands the rules, including those employees whose first language is not English or who have trouble reading. This is often best done as part of an induction process.

56. Employers should inform employees of the likely consequences of breaking disciplinary rules. In particular, they should list examples of acts of gross misconduct that may warrant summary dismissal.

57. Acts which constitute gross misconduct are those resulting in a serious breach of contractual terms and are best decided by organisations in the light of their own particular circumstances. However, examples of gross misconduct might include:
- theft or fraud;
- physical violence or bullying;
- deliberate and serious damage to property:
- serious misuse of an organisation's property or name;
- deliberately accessing internet sites containing pornographic, offensive or obscene material;
- serious insubordination;
- unlawful discrimination or harassment;
- bringing the organisation into serious disrepute;
- serious incapability at work brought on by alcohol or illegal drugs;
- causing loss, damage or injury through serious negligence;

- a serious breach of health and safety rules; and
- a serious breach of confidence.

Procedures

58.   Disciplinary procedures should not be seen primarily as a means of imposing sanctions but rather as a way of encouraging improvement amongst employees whose conduct or performance is unsatisfactory. Some organisations may prefer to have separate procedures for dealing with issues of conduct and capability. Large organisations may also have separate procedures to deal with other issues such as harassment and bullying.

59.   When drawing up and applying procedures employers should always bear in mind the requirements of natural justice. This means that employees should be given the opportunity of a meeting with someone who has not been involved in the matter. They should be informed of the allegations against them, together with the supporting evidence, in advance of the meeting. Employees should be given the opportunity to challenge the allegations before decisions are reached and should be provided with a right of appeal.

60.   Good disciplinary procedures should:
- be put in writing;
- say to whom they apply;
- be non-discriminatory;
- allow for matters to be dealt without undue delay;
- allow for information to be kept confidential;
- tell employees what disciplinary action might be taken;
- say what levels of management have the authority to take disciplinary action;
- require employees to be informed of the complaints against them and supporting evidence, before a meeting;
- give employees a chance to have their say before management reaches a decision;
- provide employees with the right to be accompanied;
- provide that no employee is dismissed for a first breach of discipline, except in cases of gross misconduct;
- require management to investigate fully before any disciplinary action is taken;
- ensure that employees are given an explanation for any sanction; and
- allow employees to appeal against a decision.

61.   It is important to ensure that everyone in an organisation understands the disciplinary procedures including the statutory requirements. In small firms this is best done by making sure all employees have access to a copy of the procedures, for instance on a noticeboard, and by taking a few moments to run through the procedures with the employee. In large organisations formal training for those who use and operate the procedures may be appropriate.

FURTHER ACTION

62.   It is sensible to keep rules and procedures under review to make sure they are always relevant and effective, New or additional rules should only be introduced after reasonable notice has been given to all employees and any employee representatives have been consulted.

SECTION 2
GRIEVANCE PROCEDURES

WHY HAVE GRIEVANCE PROCEDURES?

63.   Grievances are concerns, problems or complaints that employees raise with their employers.

64.   Grievance procedures are used by employers to deal with employees' grievances,

65.   Grievance procedures allow employers to deal with grievances fairly, consistently and speedily. Employers must have procedures available to employees so that their grievances can be properly considered.

66.   Guidance on drawing up grievance procedures is set out in paragraphs 90–95,

DEALING WITH GRIEVANCES IN THE WORKPLACE

67.   Employees should aim to resolve most grievances informally with their line manager. This has advantages for all workplaces, particularly where there might be a close personal relationship between a manager and an employee. It also allows for problems to be resolved quickly.

68.   If a grievance cannot be settled informally, the employee should raise it formally with management. There is a statutory grievance procedure that employees must invoke if they wish subsequently to use the grievance as the basis of certain applications to an employment tribunal.

69.   Under the standard statutory procedure, employees must:

Step 1
Inform the employer of their grievance in writing.
Step 2
Be invited by the employer to a meeting to discuss the grievance where the right to be accompanied will apply and be notified in writing of the decision. The employee must take all reasonable steps to attend the meeting.
Step 3
Be given the right to an appeal meeting if they feel the grievance has not been satisfactorily resolved and be notified of the final decision.

More detail on the standard statutory procedure is set out in Annex C.

70.   There are certain occasions when it is not necessary to follow the statutory procedure for example, if the employee is raising a concern in compliance with the Public Interest Disclosure Act or a grievance is raised on behalf of at least two employees by an appropriate representative such as an official of an independent trade union. A full list of exemptions is set out in Annex E.

71.   It is important that employers and employees follow the statutory grievance procedure where it applies. The employee should (subject to the exemptions described in Annex E) at least have raised the grievance in writing and waited 26 days before presenting any tribunal claim relating to the matter. A premature claim will be automatically rejected by the tribunal although (subject to special time limit rules) it may be presented again once the written grievance has been raised. Furthermore if a grievance comes before an employment tribunal and either party has failed to follow the procedure then the tribunal will normally adjust any award by 10 per cent or, where it feels it just and equitable to do so, by up to 50 per cent, depending on which party has failed to follow the procedure. in exceptional cases compensation can be adjusted by less than 10 per cent or not at all.

72.   Wherever possible a grievance should be dealt with before an employee leaves employment. A statutory grievance procedure ('the modified grievance procedure' described in Annex D), however, applies where an employee has already left employment, the standard procedure has not been commenced or completed before the employee left employment and both parties agree in writing that it should be used instead of the standard statutory procedure. Under the modified procedure the employee should write to the employer setting out the grievance as soon as possible after leaving employment and the employer must write back setting out its response.

RAISING A GRIEVANCE

73.   Employees should normally raise a grievance with their line manager unless someone else is specified in the organisation's procedure. If the complaint is against the person with whom the grievance would normally be raised the employee can approach that person's manager or another manager in the organisation. In small businesses where this is not possible, the line manager should hear the grievance and deal with it as impartially as possible.

74.   Managers should deal with all grievances raised, whether or not the grievance is presented in writing. However, employees need to be aware that if the statutory procedure applies, they will not subsequently be able to take the case to an employment tribunal unless they have first raised a grievance in writing and waited a further 28 days before presenting the tribunal claim.

75.   Setting out a grievance in writing is not easy — especially for those employees whose first language is not English or who have difficulty expressing themselves on paper. In these circumstances the employee should be encouraged to seek help for example from a work colleague, a trade union or other employee representative. Under the Disability Discrimination Act 1995 employers are

required to make reasonable adjustments which may include assisting employees to formulate a written grievance if they are unable to do so themselves because of a disability.

76.   In circumstances where a grievance may apply to more than one person and where a trade union is recognised it may be appropriate for the problem to be resolved through collective agreements between the trade union(s) and the employer.

GRIEVANCE MEETINGS

77.   On receiving a formal grievance, a manager should invite the employee to a meeting as soon as possible and inform them that they have the right to be accompanied. It is good practice to agree a time and place for the meeting with the employee. Small organisations might not have private meeting rooms, but it is important that the meeting is not interrupted and that the employee feels their grievance is being treated confidentially. If an employee's companion cannot attend on a proposed date, the employee can suggest another date so long as it is reasonable and is not more than five working days after the date originally proposed by the employer. This five day time limit may be extended by mutual agreement.

78.   The employee should be allowed to explain their complaint and say how they think it should be settled. If the employer reaches a point in the meeting where they are not sure how to deal with the grievance or feel that further investigation is necessary the meeting should be adjourned to get advice or make further investigation. This might be particularly useful in small organisations that lack experience of dealing with formal grievances. The employer should give the grievance careful consideration before responding.

79.   Employers and employees will normally be expected to go through the statutory grievance procedures unless they have reasonable grounds to believe that by doing so they might be exposed to a significant threat, such as violent, abusive or intimidating behaviour, or they will be harassed. There will always be a certain amount of stress and anxiety for both parties when dealing with grievance cases, but this exemption will only apply where the employer or employee reasonably believes that they would come to some serious physical or mental harm; their property or some third party is threatened or the other party has harassed them and this may continue.

80.   Equally, the statutory procedure does not need to be followed if circumstances beyond the control of either party prevent one or more steps being followed within a reasonable period. This will sometimes be the case where there is a long-term illness or a long period of absence abroad but wherever possible the employer should consider appointing another manager to deal with the procedure.

81.   The employer should respond in writing to the employee's grievance within a reasonable time and should let the employee know that they can appeal against the employer's decision if they are not satisfied with it. What is considered reasonable will vary from organisation to organisation, but five working days is normally long enough. If it is not possible to respond within five working days the employee should be given an explanation for the delay and told when a response can be expected.

APPEALS

82.   If an employee informs the employer that they are unhappy with the decision after a grievance meeting, the employer should arrange an appeal. It should be noted that the appeal stage is part of the statutory procedure and if the employee pursues an employment tribunal claim the tribunal may reduce any award of compensation if the employee did not exercise the right of appeal. As far as is reasonably practicable the appeal should be with a more senior manager than the one who dealt with the original grievance. In small organisations, even if there is no more senior manager available, another manager should, if possible, hear the appeal. If that is not an option, the person overseeing the case should act as impartially as possible. At the same time as inviting the employee to attend the appeal, the employer should remind them of their right to be accompanied at the appeal meeting.

83.   As with the first meeting, the employer should write to the employee with a decision on their grievance as soon as possible. They should also tell the employee if the appeal meeting is the final stage of the grievance procedure.

84.   In large organisations it is good practice to allow a further appeal to a higher level of management, such as a director. However, in smaller firms the first appeal will usually mark the end of the grievance procedure.

SPECIAL CONSIDERATIONS

85.   Complaints about discrimination, bullying and harassment in the workplace are sensitive issues, and large organisations often have separate grievance procedures for dealing with these. It is important that these procedures meet the statutory minimum requirements.

86.   Organisations may also wish to consider whether they need a whistleblowing procedure in the light of the Public Interest Disclosure Act 1998. This Act provides protection to employees who raise concerns about certain kinds of wrongdoing in accordance with its procedures.

KEEPING RECORDS

87.   It is important, and in the interests of both employer and employee, to keep written records during the grievance process. Records should include:
- the nature of the grievance raised;
- a copy of the written grievance;
- the employer's response;
- action taken;
- reasons for action taken;
- whether there was an appeal and, if so, the outcome; and
- subsequent developments.

88.   Records should be treated as confidential and kept in accordance with the Data Protection Act 1998, which gives individuals the right to request and have access to certain personal data.

89.   Copies of meeting records should be given to the employee including any formal minutes that may have been taken. In certain circumstances (for example to protect a witness) the employer might withhold some information.

DRAWING UP GRIEVANCE PROCEDURES

90.   When employers draw up grievance procedures, it pays to involve everybody they will affect, including managers, employees and, where appropriate, their representatives.

91.   Grievance procedures should make it easy for employees to raise issues with management and should:
- be simple and put in writing;
- enable an employee's line manager to deal informally with a grievance, if possible;
- keep proceedings confidential; and
- allow the employee to have a companion at meetings.

92.   Issues that may cause grievances include:
- terms and conditions of employment;
- health and safety:
- work relations;
- bullying and harassment;
- new working practices;
- working environment;
- organisational change; and
- equal opportunities.

93.   Where separate procedures exist for dealing with grievances on particular issues (for example, harassment and bullying) these should be used instead of the normal grievance procedure.

94.   It's important to ensure that everyone in the organisation understands the grievance procedures including the statutory requirements and that, if necessary, supervisors, managers and employee representatives are trained in their use. Employees must be given a copy of the procedures or have ready access to them, for instance on a noticeboard. Large organisations can include them with disciplinary procedures as part of an induction process.

95.   Take the time to explain the detail of grievance procedures to employees. This is particularly useful for people who do not speak English very well or who have difficulty with reading.

SECTION 3
A WORKER'S RIGHT TO BE COMPENSATED

WHAT IS THE RIGHT TO BE ACCOMPANIED?

96.   Workers have a statutory right to be accompanied by a fellow worker or trade union official where they are required or invited by their employer to attend certain disciplinary or grievance hearings. They must make a reasonable request to their employer to be accompanied. Further guidance on what is a reasonable request and who can accompany a worker appears at paragraphs 103–109.

WHAT IS A DISCIPLINARY HEARING?

97.   For the purposes of this right, disciplinary hearings are defined as meetings that could result in:
  • a formal warning being issued to a worker (ie a warning that will be placed on the worker's record);
  • the taking of some other disciplinary action (such as suspension without pay, demotion or dismissal) or other action; or
  • the confirmation of a warning or some other disciplinary action (such as an appeal hearing).

98.   The right to be accompanied will also apply to any disciplinary meetings held as part of the statutory dismissal and disciplinary procedures. This includes any meetings held after an employee has left employment.

99.   Informal discussions or counselling sessions do not attract the right to be accompanied unless they could result in formal warnings or other actions. Meetings to investigate an issue are not disciplinary hearings. If it becomes clear during the course of such a meeting that disciplinary action is called for, the meeting should be ended and a formal hearing arranged at which the worker will have the right to be accompanied.

WHAT IS THE GRIEVANCE HEARING?

100.   For the purposes of this right, a grievance hearing is a meeting at which an employer deals with a complaint about a duty owed by them to a worker, whether the duty arises from statute or common law (for example contractual commitments).

101.   For instance, an individual's request for a pay rise is unlikely to fall within the definition, unless a right to an increase is specifically provided for in the contract or the request raises an issue about equal pay. Equally, most employers will be under no legal duty to provide their workers with car parking facilities, and a grievance about such facilities would carry no right to be accompanied at a hearing by a companion. However, if a worker were disabled and needed a car to get to and from work, they probably would be entitled to a companion at a grievance hearing, as an issue might arise as to whether the employer was meeting its obligations under the Disability Discrimination Act 1995.

102.   The right to be accompanied will also apply to any meetings held as part of the statutory grievance procedures. This includes any meetings after the employee has left employment.

WHAT IS A REASONABLE REQUEST?

103.   Whether a request for a companion is reasonable will depend on the circumstances of the individual case and, ultimately, it is a matter for the courts and tribunals to decide. However, when workers are choosing a companion, they should bear in mind that it would not be reasonable to insist on being accompanied by a colleague whose presence would prejudice the hearing or who might have a conflict of interest. Nor would it be reasonable for a worker to ask to be accompanied by a colleague from a geographically remote location when someone suitably qualified was available on site. The request to be accompanied does not have to be in writing.

THE COMPANION

104.   The companion may be:
  • a fellow worker (ie another of the employer's workers);
  • an official employed by a trade union, or a lay trade union official, as long as they have been reasonably certified in writing by their union as having experience of, or having received

training in, acting as a worker's companion at disciplinary or grievance hearings. Certification may take the form of a card or letter.

105.   Some workers may, however, have additional contractual rights to be accompanied by persons other than those listed above (for instance a partner, spouse or legal representative). If workers are disabled, employers should consider whether it might be reasonable to allow them to be accompanied because of their disability.

106.   Workers may ask an official from any trade union to accompany them at a disciplinary or grievance hearing, regardless of whether the union is recognised or not. However, where a union is recognised in a workplace, it is good practice for workers to ask an official from that union to accompany them.

107.   Fellow workers or trade union officials do not have to accept a request to accompany a worker, and they should not be pressurised to do so.

108.   Trade unions should ensure that their officials are trained in the role of acting as a worker's companion. Even when a trade union official has experience of acting in the role, there may still be a need for periodic refresher training,

109.   A worker who has agreed to accompany a colleague employed by the same employer is entitled to take a reasonable amount of paid time off to fulfil that responsibility. This should cover the hearing and it is also good practice to allow time for the companion to familiarise themselves with the case and confer with the worker before and after the hearing. A lay trade union official is permitted to take a reasonable amount of paid time off to accompany a worker at a hearing, as long as the worker is employed by the same employer. In cases where a lay official agrees to accompany a worker employed by another organisation, time off is a matter for agreement by the parties concerned.

APPLYING THE RIGHT

110.   Where possible, the employer should allow a companion to have a say in the date and time of a hearing. If the companion cannot attend on a proposed date, the worker can suggest an alternative time and date so long as it is reasonable and it is not more than five working days after the original date.

111,   In the same way that employers should cater for a worker's disability at a disciplinary or grievance hearing, they should also cater for a companion's disability, for example providing for wheelchair access if necessary.

112.   Before the hearing takes place, the worker should tell the employer who they have chosen as a companion. In certain circumstances (for instance when the companion is an official of a non-recognised trade union) it can be helpful for the companion and employer to make contact before the hearing,

113.   The companion should be allowed to address the hearing in order to:
   • put the worker's case
   • sum up the worker's case
   • respond on the worker's behalf to any view expressed at the hearing.

114.   The companion can also confer with the worker during the hearing. It is good practice to allow the companion to participate as fully as possible in the hearing, including asking witnesses questions. The companion has no right to answer questions on the worker's behalf, or to address the hearing if the worker does not wish it, or to prevent the employer from explaining their case.

115.   Workers whose employers fail to comply with a reasonable request to be accompanied may present a complaint to an employment tribunal. Workers may also complain to a tribunal if employers fail to re-arrange a hearing to a reasonable date proposed by the worker when a companion cannot attend on the date originally proposed. The tribunal may order compensation of up to two weeks' pay. This could be increased if, in addition, the tribunal finds that the worker has been unfairly dismissed.

116.   Employers should be careful not to disadvantage workers for using their right to be accompanied or for being companions, as this is against the law and could lead to a claim to an employment tribunal.

SECTION 4
ANNEXES

ANNEX A:
STANDARD STATUTORY DISMISSAL AND DISCIPLINARY PROCEDURE

(This is a summary of the statutory procedure which is set out in full in Schedule 2 to the Employment Act 2002.)

This procedure applies to disciplinary action short of disrnissal (excluding oral and written warnings and suspension on full pay) based on either conduct or capability. It also applies to dismissals (except for constructive dismissals) including dismissals on the basis of conduct, capability, expiry of a fixed-term contract, redundancy and retirement. However, it does not apply in certain kinds of excepted cases that are described in Annex E.

Step 1: Statement of grounds for action and invitation to meeting

- The employer must set out in writing the employee's alleged conduct or characteristics, or other circumstances, which lead them to contemplate dismissing or taking disciplinary action against the employee.
- The employer must send the statement or a copy of it to the employee and invite the employee to attend a meeting to discuss the matter.

Step 2: The meeting

- The meeting must take place before action is taken, except in the case where the disciplinary action consists of suspension.
- The meeting must not take place unless:
    - (i)   the employer has informed the employee what the basis was for including in the statement under Step 1 the ground or grounds given in it; and
    - (ii)   the employee has had a reasonable opportunity to consider their response to that information.
- The employee must take all reasonable steps to attend the meeting.
- After the meeting, the employer must inform the employee of their decision and notify them of the right to appeal against the decision if they are not satisfied with it.
- Employees have the right to be accompanied at the meeting (see section 3).

Step 3: Appeal

- If the employee wishes to appeal, they must inform the employer.
- If the employee informs the employer of their wish to appeal, the employer must invite them to attend a further meeting.
- The employee must take all reasonable steps to attend the meeting.
- The appeal meeting need not take place before the dismissal or disciplinary action takes effect.
- Where reasonably practicable, the appeal should be dealt with by a more senior manager than attended the first meeting (unless the most senior manager attended that meeting).
- After the appeal meeting, the employer must inform the employee of their final decision.
- Employees have the right to be accompanied at the appeal meeting (see section 3).

ANNEX B:
MODIFIED STATUTORY DISMISSAL AND DISCIPLINARY PROCEDURE

(This is a summary of the statutory procedure which is set out in full in Schedule 2 to the Employment Act 2002.)

Step 1: Statement of grounds for action

- The employer must set out in writing:
    - (i)   the employee's alleged misconduct which has led to the dismissal;
    - (ii)   the reasons for thinking at the time of the dismissal that the employee was guilty of the alleged misconduct; and
    - (iii) the employee's right of appeal against dismissal,
- The employer must send the statement or a copy of it to the employee.

Step 2: Appeal

- If the employee does wish to appeal, they must inform the employer.
- If the employee informs the employer of their wish to appeal, the employer must invite them to attend a meeting.
- The employee must take all reasonable steps to attend the meeting.
- After the appeal meeting, the employer must inform the employee of their final decision.
- Where reasonably practicable the appeal should be dealt with by a more senior manager not involved in the earlier decision to dismiss,
- Employees have the right to be accompanied at the appeal meeting (see section 3).

ANNEX C:
STANDARD STATUTORY GRIEVANCE PROCEDURE

(This is a summary of the statutory procedure which is set out in full in Schedule 2 to the Employment Act 2002.)

Step 1: Statement of grievance

The employee must set out the grievance in writing and send the statement or a copy of it to the employer.

Step 2: Meeting

- The employer must invite the employee to attend a meeting to discuss the grievance.
- The meeting must not take place unless:
  - (i)   the employee has informed the employer what the basis for the grievance was when they made the statement under Step 1; and
  - (ii) the employer has had a reasonable opportunity to consider their response to that information.
- The employee must take all reasonable steps to attend the meeting.
- After the meeting, the employer must inform the employee of their decision as to their response to the grievance and notify them of the right of appeal against the decision if they are not satisfied with it.
- Employees have the right to be accompanied at the meeting (see section 3).

Step 3: Appeal

- If the employee does wish to appeal, they must inform the employer.
- If the employee informs the employer of their wish to appeal, the employer must invite them to attend a further meeting.
- The employee must take all reasonable steps to attend the meeting.
- After the appeal meeting, the employer must inform the employee of their final decision.
- Where reasonably practicable, the appeal should be dealt with by a more senior manager than attended the first meeting (unless the most senior manager attended that meeting).
- Employees have the right to be accompanied at the appeal meeting (see section 3).

ANNEX D;
MODIFIED STATUTORY GRIEVANCE PROCEDURE

(This is a summary of the statutory procedure which is set out in full in Schedule 2 to the Employment Act 2002.)

Step 1: Statement of grievance

- The employee must set out in writing:
  - (i)   the grievance; and
  - (ii) the basis for it.
- The employee must send the statement or a copy of it to the employer.

Step 2: Response

The employer must set out their response in writing and send the statement or a copy of it to the employee.

ANNEX E:
STATUTORY PROCEDURES: EXEMPTIONS AND DEEMED COMPLIANCE

The Employment Act 2002 (Dispute Resolution) Regulations 2004 contain detailed provisions about the application of the Statutory Dispute Resolution Procedures. This Annex summarises the particular provisions of the 2004 Regulations which describe:

(a)   certain situations in which the statutory procedures will not apply at all; and

(b)   other situations in which a party who has not completed the applicable procedure will nevertheless be treated as though they had done so.

Where a statutory procedure applies and one of the conditions for extending time limits contained in the 2004 Regulations has been met, then the normal time limit for presenting an employment tribunal claim will be extended by three months. The guidance notes accompanying tribunal application forms describe those conditions. However, in cases where the procedures do not apply at all, there can be no such extension.

(a)   Situations in which the Statutory Procedures do not apply at all

The Disciplinary and Dismissal Procedures do not apply where:

- factors beyond the control of either party make it impracticable to carry out or complete the procedure for the foreseeable future; or
- the employee is dismissed in circumstances covered by the modified dismissal procedure and presents a tribunal complaint before the employer has taken step 1; or
- all of the employees of the same description or category are dismissed and offered re-engagement either before or upon termination of their contract; or
- the dismissal is one of a group of redundancies covered by the duty of collective consultation of worker representatives under the Trade Union and Labour Relations (Consolidation) Act 1992; or
- the employee is dismissed while taking part in unofficial industrial action, or other industrial action which is not 'protected action' under the 1992 Act, unless the employment tribunal has jurisdiction to hear a claim of unfair dismissal; or
- the employee is unfairly dismissed for taking part in industrial action which is 'protected action' under the 1992 Act; or
- the employer's business suddenly and unexpectedly ceases to function and it becomes impractical to employ any employees; or
- the employee cannot continue in the particular position without contravening a statutory requirement: or
- the employee is one to whom a dismissal procedure agreement designated under section 110 of the Employment Relations Act 1996 applies.

The Grievance Procedures do not apply where:

- the employee is no longer employed, and it is no longer practicable for the employee to take step 1 of the procedure; or
- the employee wishes to complain about an actual or threatened dismissal; or
- the employee raises a concern as a 'protected disclosure' in compliance with the public interest disclosure provisions of the 1996 Act;
- the employee wishes to complain about (actual or threatened) action short of dismissal to which the standard disciplinary procedure applies, unless the grievance is that this involves unlawful discrimination (including under the Equal Pay Act) or is not genuinely on grounds of capability or conduct.

In addition, neither party need comply with an applicable statutory procedure where to do so would be contrary to the interests of national security.

(b)   Situations in which the Statutory Procedures have not been completed but are treated as having been complied with

The Disciplinary and Dismissal Procedures are treated as having been complied with where all stages of the procedure have been completed, other than the right of appeal, and:

- the employee then applies to the employment tribunal for interim relief; or
- a collective agreement provides for a right of appeal, which the employee exercises.

The Grievance Procedures are treated as having been complied with where:
- the employee is complaining that action short of dismissal to which the standard disciplinary procedure applies is not genuinely on grounds of conduct or capability, or involves unlawful discrimination, and the employee has raised that complaint as a written grievance before any appeal hearing under a statutory procedure or, if none is being followed, before presenting a tribunal complaint; or
- the employment has ended and the employee has raised a written grievance, but it has become not reasonably practical to have a meeting or an appeal. However, the employer must still give the employee a written answer to the grievance; or
- an official of a recognised independent union or other appropriate representative has raised the grievance on behalf of two or more named employees. Employees sharing the grievance may choose one of their number to act as a representative; or
- the employee pursues the grievance using a procedure available under an industry-level collective agreement.

(c) Other Special Circumstances in which the Statutory Procedures need not be begun or completed

Procedures need not be begun or completed in addition, neither the employer nor employee need begin a procedure (which will then be treated as not applying), or comply with a particular requirement of it (but will still be deemed to have complied) if the reason for not beginning or not complying is:
- the reasonable belief that doing so would result in a significant threat to themselves, any other person, or their or any other persons' property;
- because they have been subjected to harassment and reasonably believe that doing so would result in further harassment; or
- because it is not practicable to do so within a reasonable period.

INDEX